World Politics and the Challenges for International Security

Nika Chitadze
International Black Sea University, Georgia

A volume in the Advances in Digital Crime,
Forensics, and Cyber Terrorism (ADCFCT) Book
Series

Published in the United States of America by
IGI Global
Information Science Reference (an imprint of IGI Global)
701 E. Chocolate Avenue
Hershey PA, USA 17033
Tel: 717-533-8845
Fax: 717-533-8661
E-mail: cust@igi-global.com
Web site: http://www.igi-global.com

Copyright © 2022 by IGI Global. All rights reserved. No part of this publication may be reproduced, stored or distributed in any form or by any means, electronic or mechanical, including photocopying, without written permission from the publisher. Product or company names used in this set are for identification purposes only. Inclusion of the names of the products or companies does not indicate a claim of ownership by IGI Global of the trademark or registered trademark.

Library of Congress Cataloging-in-Publication Data

Names: Chitadze, Nika, 1969- editor.
Title: World politics and the challenges for international security / Nika Chitadze, editor.
Description: Hershey, PA : Information Science Reference, 2022. | Includes bibliographical references and index. | Summary: "The purpose of the book is to introduce the people who are interested in World politics - scientists, researchers, representatives of civil society, public sector, students etc. with the main characters of the modern political structure of the world, global problems related to International Security and ways for their resolution"-- Provided by publisher.
Identifiers: LCCN 2021047631 (print) | LCCN 2021047632 (ebook) | ISBN 9781799895862 (hardcover) | ISBN 9781799895879 (paperback) | ISBN 9781799895886 (ebook)
Subjects: LCSH: Security, International. | World politics--21st century.
Classification: LCC JZ5588 .W668 2022 (print) | LCC JZ5588 (ebook) | DDC 355.033--dc23/eng/20211105
LC record available at https://lccn.loc.gov/2021047631
LC ebook record available at https://lccn.loc.gov/2021047632

This book is published in the IGI Global book series Advances in Digital Crime, Forensics, and Cyber Terrorism (ADCF-CT) (ISSN: 2327-0381; eISSN: 2327-0373)

British Cataloguing in Publication Data
A Cataloguing in Publication record for this book is available from the British Library.

All work contributed to this book is new, previously-unpublished material. The views expressed in this book are those of the authors, but not necessarily of the publisher.

For electronic access to this publication, please contact: eresources@igi-global.com.

Advances in Digital Crime, Forensics, and Cyber Terrorism (ADCFCT) Book Series

Bryan Christiansen
Global Research Society, LLC, USA
Agnieszka Piekarz
Independent Researcher, Poland

ISSN:2327-0381
EISSN:2327-0373

Mission

The digital revolution has allowed for greater global connectivity and has improved the way we share and present information. With this new ease of communication and access also come many new challenges and threats as cyber crime and digital perpetrators are constantly developing new ways to attack systems and gain access to private information.

The **Advances in Digital Crime, Forensics, and Cyber Terrorism (ADCFCT) Book Series** seeks to publish the latest research in diverse fields pertaining to crime, warfare, terrorism and forensics in the digital sphere. By advancing research available in these fields, the **ADCFCT** aims to present researchers, academicians, and students with the most current available knowledge and assist security and law enforcement professionals with a better understanding of the current tools, applications, and methodologies being implemented and discussed in the field.

Coverage

- Data Protection
- Crime Scene Imaging
- Vulnerability
- Mobile Device Forensics
- Hacking
- Encryption
- Database Forensics
- Malicious Codes
- Information Warfare
- Criminology

IGI Global is currently accepting manuscripts for publication within this series. To submit a proposal for a volume in this series, please contact our Acquisition Editors at Acquisitions@igi-global.com or visit: http://www.igi-global.com/publish/.

The Advances in Digital Crime, Forensics, and Cyber Terrorism (ADCFCT) Book Series (ISSN 2327-0381) is published by IGI Global, 701 E. Chocolate Avenue, Hershey, PA 17033-1240, USA, www.igi-global.com. This series is composed of titles available for purchase individually; each title is edited to be contextually exclusive from any other title within the series. For pricing and ordering information please visit http://www.igi-global.com/book-series/advances-digital-crime-forensics-cyber/73676. Postmaster: Send all address changes to above address. Copyright © 2022 IGI Global. All rights, including translation in other languages reserved by the publisher. No part of this series may be reproduced or used in any form or by any means – graphics, electronic, or mechanical, including photocopying, recording, taping, or information and retrieval systems – without written permission from the publisher, except for non commercial, educational use, including classroom teaching purposes. The views expressed in this series are those of the authors, but not necessarily of IGI Global.

Titles in this Series

For a list of additional titles in this series, please visit: www.igi-global.com/book-series/advances-digital-crime-forensics-cyber/73676

Technologies to Advance Automation in Forensic Science and Criminal Investgation
Chung-Hao Chen (Old Dominion University, USA) Wen-Chao Yang (National Central Police University, Taiwan) and Lijian Chen (Henan University, China)
Information Science Reference • © 2022 • 289pp • H/C (ISBN: 9781799883869) • US $225.00

Intelligence and Law Enforcement in the 21st Century
Eugene de Silva (Virginia Research Institute, USA) and Asanga Abeyagoonesekera (Parliament of Sri Lanka, Sri Lanka)
Information Science Reference • © 2021 • 253pp • H/C (ISBN: 9781799879046) • US $225.00

Social Engineering and Information Warfare Operations Emerging Research and Opportunities
Rhonda L. Johnson (Upper Iowa University, USA)
Information Science Reference • © 2021 • 150pp • H/C (ISBN: 9781799842705) • US $145.00

Evaluating Emerging Threats and New Research Opportunities in Digital Crime and Forensics
Rhonda Johnson (Upper Iowa University, USA)
Information Science Reference • © 2021 • 350pp • H/C (ISBN: 9781799822288) • US $195.00

Confluence of AI, Machine, and Deep Learning in Cyber Forensics
Sanjay Misra (Covenant University, Nigeria) Chamundeswari Arumugam (Sri Sivasubramaniya Nadar College of Engineering, India) Suresh Jaganathan (Sri Sivasubramaniya Nadar College of Engineering, India) and Saraswathi S. (Sri Sivasubramaniya Nadar College of Engineering, India)
Information Science Reference • © 2021 • 248pp • H/C (ISBN: 9781799849001) • US $225.00

Cyber Security Auditing, Assurance, and Awareness Through CSAM and CATRAM
Regner Sabillon (Universitat Oberta de Catalunya, Spain)
Information Science Reference • © 2021 • 260pp • H/C (ISBN: 9781799841623) • US $195.00

Critical Concepts, Standards, and Techniques in Cyber Forensics
Mohammad Shahid Husain (Ministry of Higher Education, Oman) and Mohammad Zunnun Khan (Integral University, India)
Information Science Reference • © 2020 • 292pp • H/C (ISBN: 9781799815587) • US $225.00

701 East Chocolate Avenue, Hershey, PA 17033, USA
Tel: 717-533-8845 x100 • Fax: 717-533-8661
E-Mail: cust@igi-global.com • www.igi-global.com

Table of Contents

Preface xii

Acknowledgment xvii

Chapter 1
The States as the Main Actors of the World Politics 1
    Irakli Kervalishvili, Georgian Technical University, Georgia

Chapter 2
Global Security and Political Problems of the 21st Century 24
    Nika Chitadze, International Black Sea University, Georgia

Chapter 3
Recent Trends in Global Security: Challenges and Opportunities 96
    Kannadhasan S., Cheran College of Engineering, India
    Nagarajan R., Gnanamani College of Technology, India
    Shanmuganantham M., Tamilnadu Government Polytechnic College, India

Chapter 4
Conflicts in the Modern World and Their Impact on International Security 108
    Ketevan Chakhava, International Black Sea University, Georgia

Chapter 5
Climate Change as a Common Enemy: A New Threat to International Peace and Security 132
    Nima Norouzi, Bournemouth University, UK

Chapter 6
Negative Effects of Corruption on the Global Level 145
    Irakli Kervalishvili, Georgian Technical University, Georgia

Chapter 7
Terrorist Psychology and Its Impact on International Security 165
    Ketevan Chakhava, International Black Sea University, Georgia

Chapter 8
Main Characters of Globalization in the 21st Century 186
  Irakli Kervalishvili, Georgian Technical University, Georgia

Chapter 9
Psychological Factors During the Foreign Policy Decision-Making Process 207
  Natalia Beruashvili, International Black Sea University, Georgia

Chapter 10
The Branding of Political Leaders: Hamid Karzai as a Political Brand and His Matrix of Brand
Awareness and Positive Image 219
  Kakhaber Djakeli, International Black Sea University, Georgia

Chapter 11
The Interplay Between Territorial Control and Violent Non-State Actors (VNSAs): A Theoretical
Perspective on the Middle East and Africa 231
  Muhammed Karakuş, Adıyaman University, Turkey

Chapter 12
Benefits and Risks of Digital Diplomacy: Is Traditional Diplomacy in Decline? 261
  Diana Khomeriki, International Black Sea University, Georgia

Chapter 13
The Economic Component of World Politics and the Main Global Social and Economic Problems 282
  Nika Chitadze, International Black Sea University, Georgia

Chapter 14
Food and Nutrition Security: A Global Perspective 350
  Asim K. Karmakar, Netaji Subhas Open University, India
  Sebak Kumar Jana, Vidyasagar University, India

Chapter 15
Information-Cyberspace Operations in Real-World Politics 365
  Mari Malvenishvili, Cyber Security Studies and Education Center, Georgia

Compilation of References 390

About the Contributors 419

Index 421

Detailed Table of Contents

Preface xii

Acknowledgment xvii

Chapter 1
The States as the Main Actors of the World Politics 1
    Irakli Kervalishvili, Georgian Technical University, Georgia

The main purpose of the research is analysis of the states as main participants of world politics. In this regard, there are presented dates about the number of the states, their classification according to the socio-economic development (based on the GDP per capita and index of development), forms of governance (republican – presidential, semi-presidential, parliamentary; Monarchies – absolute and constitutional), administrative-territorial division (unitary and federal states), size of the territories, number of populations, geographical location, etc. Thus, it can be assumed that based on the geographic, political, socio-economic, legal, etc. factors, states differ from each other, which determines the differences in their foreign policy and national security priorities.

Chapter 2
Global Security and Political Problems of the 21st Century 24
    Nika Chitadze, International Black Sea University, Georgia

The purpose of this research is consideration and analysis of the main security and political problems of the world, which are connected with the arms race and arms control; problems of the proliferation the weapons of mass destruction; protection of human rights; failed states; the nuclear potential of the different countries; existence of the nuclear-weapons-free zones in the different regions of the world; problems related to the reduction of the conventional arms, arms supplies, arms trade, problems of organized crime, international terrorism in the framework of which there are discussed the different types of terrorism, the methods that are used by terrorist organizations for the implementation their activities, problems related to the enlargement of democracy and violation of the fundamental principles of human rights, etc.

Chapter 3
Recent Trends in Global Security: Challenges and Opportunities 96
    Kannadhasan S., Cheran College of Engineering, India
    Nagarajan R., Gnanamani College of Technology, India
    Shanmuganantham M., Tamilnadu Government Polytechnic College, India

With the emergence of the digital economy and an ever-increasing percentage of consumers conducting their business mostly from online or mobile devices, electronic shopping, or e-commerce, is fast being recognized as the way to go global at the click of a button. As a consequence, any modern company's ability to create a viable e-commerce model is becoming extremely significant. To secure themselves and their clients, an organization must overcome current security issues to ensure that the highest levels of e-commerce security are maintained. Failure to follow stringent ecommerce security procedures will result in the destruction of data, the compromise of transaction documents, and the leak of the customer's financial information. This will lead to legal and financial repercussions, as well as a negative image for the company. Cloud networking, web computing, e-commerce, net banking, and other cutting-edge technology also need a high degree of protection. Since these instruments hold personal information regarding a human, their security has become a top priority.

Chapter 4
Conflicts in the Modern World and Their Impact on International Security 108
    Ketevan Chakhava, International Black Sea University, Georgia

The central problem of the theory of international relations is the problem of international conflicts. And this is quite justified, if we bear in mind the goal that has been objectively facing all of humanity in recent decades – this is survival, the prevention of a global thermonuclear catastrophe. Since any armed clash is only an extreme expression of a political conflict, its highest stage, insofar as the study of the causes of conflicts and methods of their settlement, especially at those stages when it is still relatively easy to carry out, has not only theoretical but also great practical importance. An international conflict is a direct or indirect clash of interests of two or more parties (states, groups of states, peoples, political movements) based on the contradictions of an objective or subjective nature between them. By their origin, these contradictions and the problems they generate in relations between states can be territorial, national, religious, economic, military-strategic, scientific and technical, etc.

Chapter 5
Climate Change as a Common Enemy: A New Threat to International Peace and Security.............. 132
    Nima Norouzi, Bournemouth University, UK

New paradigm and military and hardware variables and political, economic, socio-cultural, and environmental components are considered factors that can act as a threat to the international security. Climate change is one of the most important and complex international challenges in the age of globalization. These small changes in global warming could pose a potential risk to global climate change. Our lives today depend on climate change. In the international arena, the effects of these threats are gradually observed in the relations between the countries. The Darfur War, for example, can be considered the first conflict in the field of climate change. In addition to social tensions, these threats will lead to political unrest and violent conflicts. This issue is recognized as a threat to international peace and security beyond the international agendas in the framework of the UN Framework Convention and the Secretary-General's follow-up and United Nation Bureau of Climate Change.

Chapter 6
Negative Effects of Corruption on the Global Level 145
    Irakli Kervalishvili, Georgian Technical University, Georgia

Corruption is a form of dishonesty or criminal offense undertaken by a person or organization entrusted with a position of authority to acquire illicit benefit or abuse power for one's private gain. Corruption may include many activities including bribery and embezzlement, though it may also involve practices that are legal in many countries. Political corruption occurs when an officeholder or other governmental employee acts in an official capacity for personal gain. Corruption is most commonplace in kleptocracies, oligarchies, narco-states, and mafia states. Corruption can occur on different scales. Corruption ranges from small favors between a small number of people (petty corruption) to corruption that affects the government on a large scale (grand corruption) and corruption that is so prevalent that it is part of the everyday structure of society, including corruption as one of the symptoms of organized crime.

Chapter 7
Terrorist Psychology and Its Impact on International Security 165
    Ketevan Chakhava, International Black Sea University, Georgia

Terrorism is a policy based on the systematic use of terror. Despite the legal force of the term "terrorism," its definition up to the present time remains ambiguous. But experts agree that the best definition of terrorism is the achievement of political, ideological, economic, and religious goals by violent means. Synonyms of the word "terror" are the words "violence" and "intimidation." This term became widespread in various countries after the "Age of Terror" during the Great French Revolution. During the discussion about terrorism, one of the main directions of this phenomenon represents terrorist psychology. Thus, in the chapter, the main attention is paid to the psychological aspects of terrorism, including the determination of the main types of terrorism and the psychological characteristics of the terrorists and terrorist groups.

Chapter 8
Main Characters of Globalization in the 21st Century 186
    Irakli Kervalishvili, Georgian Technical University, Georgia

The aim of this chapter is analysis of the main aspects of globalization, which are interrelated to the political, economic, information, cultural, etc. aspects of the global processes, and discussion about main characters of globalization, main approaches to the globalization problems, manifestations of globalization, development of new technologies, leading factors of the globalization process, ambiguity and non-equality of the globalization processes, and in general, about the main positive and negative sides of globalization.

Chapter 9
Psychological Factors During the Foreign Policy Decision-Making Process 207
    Natalia Beruashvili, International Black Sea University, Georgia

The problem of foreign policy decision-making has attracted attention since the 1950s. The study of this problem begins within the modernist direction. This is the direction that sought to apply the theoretical and methodological approaches of the natural and social sciences to the analysis of international relations. Political psychology has a special place in the given sciences. Since politics, including foreign policy, is the work of human beings, it is very important to analyze the motives by which they are guided.

Chapter 10
The Branding of Political Leaders: Hamid Karzai as a Political Brand and His Matrix of Brand Awareness and Positive Image 219
    Kakhaber Djakeli, International Black Sea University, Georgia

This chapter explores the success secrets of political figures, described by the matrix of brand awareness and a positive image. The leaders became famous in the political scene, geniuses, or felt the time and changed themselves according to the time. Can we explore their secrets of success? According to the hypothesis of the research, all is learnable, and the answer is, yes, we can. According to the theory of the matrix of brand awareness and a positive image, we can guess what should be done to become stronger politicians and when to start new performance in the market of politics.

Chapter 11
The Interplay Between Territorial Control and Violent Non-State Actors (VNSAs): A Theoretical Perspective on the Middle East and Africa 231
    Muhammed Karakuş, Adıyaman University, Turkey

The conundrum of the violent non-state actors (VNSAs) became the center of gravity in global politico-military settings especially after the disappearance of "patron-proxy" relationships. The threat to the authority of the central administration in internationally recognized boundaries by both deploying an assortment of tactics and more sophisticated structural stand points strengthened their competence. On the other side, social, economic, religious, environmental, and demographic conditions of the current century also contributed minacious divaricated frondeurs to sprout up. This chapter examines the interplay between territorial control and VNSA. There are empirical case studies related to the position of the VNSAs in the relevant literature, but little is known about the interplay between them that leads to governance functions and even foreign policy. The intention is to substantiate how these actors created legitimacy that ended up in almost all state activities although they are not recognized internationally.

Chapter 12
Benefits and Risks of Digital Diplomacy: Is Traditional Diplomacy in Decline? 261
    Diana Khomeriki, International Black Sea University, Georgia

Diplomacy is a key tool for conducting foreign policy, and it has experienced changes throughout the past centuries. Information and communication technologies (ICTs) and social media platforms began playing a highly important role in achieving diplomatic objectives leading to the emergence of the term "digital diplomacy." Being one of the main trends in contemporary diplomatic communication, especially during the COVID-19 pandemic, taking a closer look at digital diplomacy is worthwhile. This chapter analyzes the main characteristics of digital diplomacy as well as its opportunities and challenges, compares digital and traditional diplomacy, and aims to determine whether traditional diplomacy is in decline. The author argues that traditional diplomacy is not antiquated; traditional and digital diplomacy complement each other. Diplomats will need to function in a hybrid regime, both in offline and online environments. Utilizing digital diplomacy will improve the effectiveness of traditional diplomacy contributing to more multifaceted, comprehensive, and results-oriented foreign policy.

Chapter 13
The Economic Component of World Politics and the Main Global Social and Economic Problems 282
    Nika Chitadze, International Black Sea University, Georgia

The purpose of this research is consideration and analysis of the main social and economic problems of the world, which are connected with the existence of the gap between "Global North" and "Global South" and problems of the consumption of mineral resources, including energy and water resources, unemployment, illiteracy, health issues, food supply, demography, etc. We are watching the world become one. Countries and regions are interconnected by a thousand threads that make them interdependent. The world economy today is undergoing a process of globalization – the increasing interdependence of the economies of various countries of the world due to the growth in the movement of goods and services and the intensive exchange of goods, information, technologies, and labor migration.

Chapter 14
Food and Nutrition Security: A Global Perspective 350
    Asim K. Karmakar, Netaji Subhas Open University, India
    Sebak Kumar Jana, Vidyasagar University, India

Food and proper nutrition are crucial inputs into performance and well-being. Many development programmes, projects, and policies therefore include food and nutrition security objectives. Food and nutrition are crucial inputs for the performance of the economy. But the irony is that the present food system is going to be captured by multinational actors with their shrewd politics so that the livelihoods of the most people of the globe are at stake. Amidst this, the rise of a few powerful titans, both economically and politically, is a fearful phenomenon. Such circumstances are not only dangerous for consumers everywhere but also disastrous for poor populations vulnerable to food price fluctuations. Annoyed with the world food system dominated by MNCs, the concept of food sovereignty like La Via Campesina's food sovereignty movement has come to the fore as a protest against the corporate control of the food system. The major objective of the study is to assess food and nutrition security and its link with food politics in a global perspective.

Chapter 15
Information-Cyberspace Operations in Real-World Politics... 365
    Mari Malvenishvili, Cyber Security Studies and Education Center, Georgia

The chapter explores the concept of information and cyber operations. It identifies the role of cyberspace operations in modern military conflicts and addresses Western and Russian strategic approaches of using cyberspace as an emerging platform of modern warfighting. Since the end of the 19th century, the world entered the information age in which distribution of power is mostly dependent on the amount of information a state owns and knowledge of tools and tricks to use it. Information superiority is a power element and vulnerability at the same time. With the technological revolution, creation, distribution, and usage of information was simplified, but securing of created and distributed information became more difficult. Information itself can be used in different ways, starting from simple communication to military operations. Considering the fact that 'military power alone is insufficient to achieve sustainable political objectives', information operations and employment of information capabilities has been included at all stages of modern military operations.

Compilation of References 390

About the Contributors 419

Index 421

Preface

World politics is a new scientific discipline, which has been established only in the second half of the 20th century, but which gained rapid distribution in many countries. The focus of its attention is political processes, which are going on in the modern world, but with the perspectives of their further development. In this regard, world politics (in comparison for example from history) is oriented on the present and future periods and by this means has the closest ties with the political practice. One more significance of world politics relates to the fact that it cannot be understood without the knowledge of the relative fields – history, economics, law, social sciences, psychology, etc.

The events of the last 20-30 years, which were held in the world arena, have forced us to observe with the new approaches on such meanings and political processes, as national interests, conflicts and wars, terrorism, national sovereignty, foreign policy, and taking into consideration the process of globalization, into agenda of the world politics the topics related to the global threats and challenges, which concerns each country in the world have been included.

Furthermore, in world politics, new spheres of research have appeared, including topics, related to the education, development of new technologies, the environment, psychology, etc.

At the end of the 20th and the beginning of the 21st centuries, the formation of world politics as a scientific and educational discipline is connected with the exploration of the existing and again formulating political system of the world, its structures, institutes, and processes. More clearly have been determined the subjective spheres of other disciplines, including classical international relations, security studies. It is not by accident that the development had the neoclassical, or how it is sometimes called, neo-traditional realism form, which focuses its attention directly on the analysis of interstate relations and foreign policy of the different countries, the problems of disarmament and arms race. Those topics are not excluded from the agenda in the modern period too.

At the same time, World Politics is the discipline in the field of interest of which are modern political realities and tendencies for the future development of the world. It creates some difficulties for its study. Every day there are new facts about the development of the events in the world, some of them do not coincide with the previous imaginations and motivate us to rethink those or other regularities. Thus, in many relations, the key moments in the development of the world political processes were such events, as the disintegration of the USSR and the ending of the cold war. The serious challenges for international security became the terrorist acts in the USA on September 11 of 2001 and the other states, first of all, several European states (Great Britain, France, Spain). Also, at the focus of the international community were the processes, which were held in Afghanistan since 2001, Iraq since 2003, and Syria since 2011, occupation by Russian territories of Georgia in 2008 and Ukraine in 2014, the confrontation between USA and Iran in 2020, spreading of COVID 19, etc. It is possible that some events have not (or have

Preface

not now) such enough influence on the tendencies of world development, but can be important from the factorial point of view. For world politics as a scientific discipline, all those factors mean one: It can never be written finally, especially if we take into account the appearance of new threats and challenges for our planet.

If we are talking about the tendencies of the development of the global processes, in this case now, although somehow carefully (because military-political and economic thematic is dominated) declares about itself "the human factor". Humans with their problems, possibilities, knowledge, and skills are gradually coming to the front line of the research of world politics.

Writing books is always a difficult task. Do it under the conditions, when the science is young, and when this science is involved in the study the problems of the present and tendencies, which can declare about themselves only in the future, is more complex by the double-time.

Mass media sources every day spread information about events in the different regions of the world. And, most probably, there is no person, who by different levels of interest does not observe the news. On the information line, there are the meetings and negotiations, terrorist acts, conflicts and cooperation, wars, big financial and trade deals. How to understand and analyze all those factors? Which do regularities act in the world political arena?

At first sight, all news can be divided into those, which concern the internal policy and those, which belong to the foreign one. It is worth mentioning, that on such principle was constructed the headlines on the television and radio stations in many countries within the 20th century. Is such division considering the modern realities? The answer most probably can be negative. In the modern world, internal and external events are interconnected with each other by closest ties, which finds its reflection, in how the broadcasts are presented. Let`s bring one example which was broadcast by the leading US TV programs on January 8, 2020. Within the same day, there were discussed future Presidential elections in the United States, attack of Iran by the ballistic missiles to the US military bases, which are deployed in Iraq, increasing of international oil prices by 5%, air catastrophe of Ukrainian plane at the air space of Iran, escalation of the confrontation at the Armenian-Azerbaijan border, forest fires in Australia, activation of the rebel movement in Libya, etc. The first, which is in the focus of the interests, is the absence of a clear division on the events inside of the country and abroad. In this regard it should be mentioned, that the news is presented by the level of importance and by those fields, which are considered within that news: concretely political, politico-economic, environmental, military, humanitarian, security, etc. Approximately the same methodologies were presented in the news within the whole first decade of the 21st century. All this, having been taken together, has a direct attitude to World Politics.

The purpose of the book is to introduce the people who are interested in world politics, scientists, researchers, representatives of civil society and mass-media means, public sector, students, etc. with the main characters of the modern political structure of the world and presenting those global threats and challenges, which have economic, security, military, environmental, information, etc. character and also approaches for their resolution.

The book includes 15 chapters. Where the main aspects related to World Politics and main challenges for International Security are described and analyzed. Particularly:

Taking into consideration, that the states are the main actors in the framework of World Politics and International Relations, the first chapter, "The States as Main Actors of the World Politics," analyzed such important aspects, a number of the states in the World, classification of the states according to the socio-economic development – based on the GDP per capita and index of development; forms of governance (republican – presidential, semi-presidential, parliamentary; Monarchies – absolute and constitutional); administrative-territorial division (unitary and federal states); the size of the territories; the number of populations; geographical location; foreign-policy orientation, etc.

The main purpose of the second chapter, "Global Security and Political Problems of the 21st Century," is consideration and analysis of the main security and political problems of the world, which are connected with the arms race and arms control, problems of the proliferation of the weapons of mass destruction, the existence of failed states, the nuclear potential of the different countries, the existence of the free zones from the nuclear weapons in the different regions of the world, problems – related to the reduction of the conventional arms, arms supplies, and arms trade, problems of organized crime, international terrorism – in the framework of which there are discussed the different types of terrorism, the methods, which are used by terrorist organizations for the implementation their activities, problems related to the enlargement of democracy and violation of the fundamental principles of human rights, etc.

The third chapter, "Recent Trends in Global Security: Challenges and Opportunities," takes into consideration the emergence of the Digital Economy and an ever-increasing percentage of consumers conducting their business mostly from online or mobile devices, electronic shopping, or e-commerce, any modern company's potential to establish a viable E-Commerce model is becoming extremely important for the providing security of the company and its consumers. All the above-mentioned aspects are in detail reviewed and analyzed in this part of the book.

The fourth chapter, "Conflicts in the Modern World and Their Impact on International Security," presents an important analysis of the number of the conflicts on the global level, Features of the conflict at the end of the 20th - Beginning of the 21st century, reasons for the conflicts emergence, Regional and local conflicts in the modern world political map, Forms and methods of influencing the conflict with the aim of its prevention and peaceful settlement based on the principles of conflict prevention, peacekeeping, peacemaking, and peacebuilding mechanisms, etc.

The fifth chapter, "Climate Change as a Common Enemy: A New Threat to International Peace and Security," is focused on environmental problems. As it is known, Climate change is one of the most important and complex international challenges in the age of globalization. These small changes in global warming, air and water pollution, soil degradation, ozone *depletion, etc.* could cause a potential risk to the global environment. Thus, consideration of different aspects related to climate change gives an important significance to the chapter.

As to the topic "Negative Effects of Corruption on the Global Level," which is considered in the sixth chapter of the book, the main attention is paid to the financial volume of corruption on the global level, different methods and types of corruption, furthermore, in the research, it is presented the "Corruption Perception Index", which gives for the reader an opportunity to determine and understand the level of corruption in the various countries of our planet.

In the comparative, different styles are analyzed different aspects of terrorism in the seventh chapter, "Terrorist Psychology and Its Impact on International Security," where together with observing the types of terrorism, main characters of International terrorism, etc., the attention is paid to psychological approaches of Terrorism. In this regard, it should be pointed out, that according to many scholars, the motivation of a person to join a terrorist organization has socio-economic parameters. Particularly, poverty, lack of education, unemployment, lack of life prospects, also the need for a personality for self-realization, self-respect, desire for power, etc. are the main motivating factors for joining a terrorist organization or committing terrorist acts individually.

Chapter 8, "Main Characters of Globalization in the 21st Century," analyzed the main aspects of globalization, which are interrelated to the political, economic, information, cultural, etc. aspects of the

Preface

global processes, also are being discussed main characteristics of Globalization, main Approaches to the globalization problems, manifestations of globalization, development of new technologies as a leading factor of the globalization process, main positive and negative sides of globalization.

The role of psychology in world politics is once more reviewed in the ninth chapter, "Psychological Factors During the Foreign Policy Decision-Making Process," where together with the consideration of various directions of psychology, there are analyzed the behavior of politicians, particularly political leaders in the framework of the foreign policy decision-making process. It should be underlined, that Political psychology has a special place during reviewing various themes within this chapter. Thus, since politics, including foreign policy, is the work of human beings, it is very important to analyze the motives by which they are guided.

In the tenth chapter, "The Branding of Political Leaders: Hamid Karzai as a Political Brand and His Matrix of Brand Awareness and Positive Image," some political marketing aspects, based on using PR technologies on the International level are being discussed and considered. Separately is presented the policy of former President of Afghanistan Hamid Karzai.

In the eleventh chapter, "The Interplay Between Territorial Control and the Violent Non-State Actors (VNSAs): A Theoretical Perspective on the Middle East and Africa," the author observed different theoretical and practical aspects related to the weakness of the states and situation in such important geopolitical regions of the world as the Middle East and African continent.

Most probably, the special attention deserves the twelfth chapter of the book, "Benefits and Risks of Digital Diplomacy: Is Traditional Diplomacy in Decline?" It is interrelated with the fact, that the influence of digital technology in diplomacy and world politics, in general, is gradually increasing. Particularly, this chapter analyzes the main characteristics of digital diplomacy as well as its opportunities and challenges, compares digital and traditional diplomacy, and aims to determine whether traditional diplomacy is in decline. The author argues that traditional diplomacy is not antiquated and traditional and digital diplomacy complements each other. Diplomats will need to function in a hybrid regime, both in offline and online environments.

In the case of the thirteenth chapter with the title "Economic Component of the World Politics and Main Global Social and Economic Problems," there are being discussed such important problems of the socio-economic character as North-South gap, life expectancy, problems of poverty, illiteracy, health protection, unemployment, water, and energy resources consumption, etc.

As it is known, food and proper nutrition are crucial inputs into performance and well-being on the global level. Thus, many development programs, projects, and policies, therefore, include food and nutrition security objectives. Food and nutrition are crucial inputs for the well-performing of the world economy. Taking into account this factor, the major objectives of Chapter 14, "Food and Nutrition Security: A Global Perspective," are to assess food and nutrition security and their link with food politics from a global perspective.

The fifteenth chapter, "Information-Cyberspace Operations in Real-World Politics," explores the concept of information and cyber operations. It identifies the role of cyberspace operations in the modern world and addresses strategic approaches of using cyberspace as an emerging platform of modern warfighting. Since the end of the twentieth century, the world entered the information age in which, distribution of power is mostly dependent on the amount of information a state owns and knowledge of tools and tricks how to use it. Information superiority is a powerful element and vulnerability at the same time. Because 'military power alone is insufficient to achieve sustainable political objectives', information operations and employment of information capabilities, have been included at all stages of modern military operations.

In general, many meanings and approaches, which were worked out in the various countries and which become there as primary (for example, level of analysis, international political economy, theory of hegemonic stability theory, etc.), do not always be the same in the sciences of the other countries. Even in the modern epoch of the rapid development of communicational and information technologies, it is needed time for its introduction with the readers in many different countries.

For a second, the novelty of the research subject causes the introduction of new meanings, but it is clear that to do it should be very careful. It can be considered that one of such categories represents the understanding - *a political system of the world*, which means the approach to politics from the holistic positions, does not divide it into the internal and external ones. The world political system permits analysis of the political institutes and processes of the global level; to show how this level determines the functioning of lower political levels – regional, national and local.

Third, world politics is especially a dynamically developing discipline. It requires attention to the daily facts and events and permanent interest in the news. Due to it, even the most ideal handbook cannot be the only book during the study process. Scientific articles, monographs, and news of the information agencies permit permanently to match new events with those interpretations, which existed before. We can only approach to finding the mystery, to do our prognosis on the future and see how they justify themselves. But, political development permanently and by accelerated speed goes forward, presenting before us more and more new scientific and practical questions. Here is the great attractive power of world politics and its study.

Taking into consideration the above-mentioned factors, it should be pointed out that the novelty of the book and its contribution to the development of the academic disciplines World Politics and International Relations is connected with the fact, that in the book "World Politics and the Challenges for International Security" for the first time have been presented the combination of the topics, related to the modern development of the world (for example topics on globalization, role, and place of the states, etc.) and different, particularly - political, military, security, information, socio-economic, environmental, etc. threats and challenges before the international security and ways for those problems resolution.

Acknowledgment

In the framework of the working over the book *World Politics and the the Challenges for International Security*, I would like to express my special gratitude to Ms. Katelyn McLoughlin - Assistant Development Editor - Book Development of IGI Global for her assistance and attention within the different stages in the framework of the book preparation Process.

At the same time, I would like to dedicate a special thanks to each author of the chapter – citizens of the different countries and representatives of the different nationalities, who took to the Heart the global problems of our planet and implemented very important research in favor of development academic discipline – World Politics. So, without the contributions of such experienced scholars as *D. Khomeriki, S.Kannadhasan, M. Malvenishvili, R. Nagarajan, M. Shanmuganantham, N. Norouzi, K. Chakhava, N. Beruashvili, K. Djakeli, M. Karakuş, A. K. Karmakar, I. Kervalishvili, S. K. Jana,* it would be impossible the publishing of the book.

I am too much thankful to my native – International Black Sea University and its Administration, Academic and Administrative personnel for establishing for me an excellent scientific environment and great atmosphere during working over the book.

Chapter 1
The States as the Main Actors of the World Politics

Irakli Kervalishvili
Georgian Technical University, Georgia

ABSTRACT

The main purpose of the research is analysis of the states as main participants of world politics. In this regard, there are presented dates about the number of the states, their classification according to the socio-economic development (based on the GDP per capita and index of development), forms of governance (republican – presidential, semi-presidential, parliamentary; Monarchies – absolute and constitutional), administrative-territorial division (unitary and federal states), size of the territories, number of populations, geographical location, etc. Thus, it can be assumed that based on the geographic, political, socio-economic, legal, etc. factors, states differ from each other, which determines the differences in their foreign policy and national security priorities.

INTRODUCTION

During the founding of the Westphalian system, the state became the main actor - the creator of the system and, in fact, the only element of the new world order. It is clear that in the earlier historic periods states function, however, along with the signing of the Peace of Westphalia, the state, or rather the nation-state, acquires new characteristics - national sovereignty and its involvement in the system of relations with other, the same nation-states. On this basis, social and political practice is constructed: according to international law, all states are independent and are equal to each other and before the international law. At the same time, many political scientists joke, based on the famous phrase of George Orwell: "All animals are equal, but some animals are more" equal "than others" (Orwell, 1949).

Most of the states that exist in the modern world were founded in the twentieth century. The most intense process of state formation took place in the 1960s, as a result of the collapse of the colonial system. At the end of the twentieth century, newly independent states arose as a result of the collapse of the former socialist countries (USSR, Yugoslavia, Czechoslovakia).

DOI: 10.4018/978-1-7998-9586-2.ch001

Copyright © 2022, IGI Global. Copying or distributing in print or electronic forms without written permission of IGI Global is prohibited.

Figure 1. Political map of world with country flags
Source: https://www.123rf.com/photo_23540827_political-map-of-world-with-country-flags.html

After the ending of the "Cold War", more than 20 countries appeared on the political map of the world. Today, many national entities in the world intend to obtain the status of a state - so it seems that this process is not complete (Chitadze, 2017).

It is interesting!

During the foundation of the United Nations in 1945, their members were 51 states, in 1991, (before the disintegration of the USSR) – 166, in 2000, their number gained 189 and in 2021, there are already 193 plenipotentiary members of the United Nations. In general, the number of states has been increased three times from the beginning of the XX Century (United Nations, 2021)

Role of the States on the International arena

Nation-states are very heterogeneous and differ from each other in many ways, including political influence, military power, economic potential, size of the territory, geographic location, type of government, etc.

During the Cold War, it was acceptable to point about superpowers (USA and USSR), Big states (France, Canada, etc.), Small countries (Morocco, Liechtenstein).

After the end of the Cold War, this type of classification lost its significance, and economic factors, on the contrary, turned out to be politically formative, and therefore one of the leading ones. In the first decade of the 21st century, the World Bank identified three main categories of states in terms of GDP per capita for one year:

- Countries with Law income;
- Countries with Medium income - this group is very often divided into two subgroups;
- Countries with high income.

Approximately 40% of states with a population of more than 55% of the total population of our planet are included in the first category, while the percentage of states with a high level of income does not prevail 15% (Maksakovski, 2009). Most economically rich countries are members of the International Organization - Organization for Economic Cooperation and Development - OECD, the so-called "wealth club". High-income countries, in most cases, use economic methods to determine the directions of political development. The grouping of states by socio-economic development will be analyzed in more detail in the following subsections.

Some states, even though they are independent, are very weak. For them, this factor is characterized by the collapse of political institutions, the legal system, the existence of internal conflicts between various ethnic groups and societies, ethnic nationalism, etc. There are examples such as Somalia, Afghanistan, Rwanda, etc. In the literature, such states are called failed states (Stewart, 2007). Being weak, they pose a threat to stability for others, being real or potential sources of conflict, terrorism, drug distribution, etc. There are illegal arms formations on their territories etc.

Over the last decades, there has been intense discussion of topics related to what to do with these states. What is the effectiveness of influencing them from the outside to facilitate state-building in these countries, for example, organizing elections, formatting the government, creating other institutions of power, etc?

This is another group of countries that the United States is usually referred to as the so-called rogue states. When discussing this terminology itself, as well as which states belong to this group, based on the position of the US administration, the problem is related to the fact that the modern world is seriously considering the possibilities to fight against certain dictatorships. One of the main threats for the international community from those countries is the problem of obtaining weapons of mass destruction, nuclear technologies, etc. It is clear that there are mechanisms and procedures, especially within the framework of the UN, which make it possible to exert pressure on such states, but at the same time, the danger of their actions being uncontrollable by the international community remains (Blum, 2006).

There are many changes within economically developed states. Many authors draw attention to the fact that the modern state is not capable of acting alone effectively to solve such global problems as environmental protection, socio-economic development, and other areas. Together with states, other international actors should be involved in solving these problems, among which, first of all, should be pointed out about international intergovernmental and non-governmental organizations, various types of social movements, etc. In the modern period, they play a more significant role in resolving these problems in the international arena, influencing the international environment, limiting and controlling the actions of states, especially in the field of defense and security.

In this regard, in the early 90s, several authors started talking about the loss of some of their power by states, the limitation of the meaning of sovereignty, and even the disappearance of the state as such in the form in which we are used to seeing it. ... This point of view was expressed by L.D. Howell (1998). And, although such positions are not completely new (Marxists wrote about the death of the state), an opposite point of view was formulated to contradict this concept. According to these views, the state continues to retain its form, because state borders exist; the number of states becomes not less but more; states expanded their functions in the economic and social spheres; The possibilities of influencing one's citizens using electronic means have been expanded; The states themselves are actively creating international institutions and regimes. In other words, nothing comparatively happens regarding the change in the functions of the state. This position was defended by representatives of different realistic trends.

Subsequently, the extreme points of view softened. The existence of the changes began to be recognized by the majority, but, at the same time, the illusions associated with a change in the possibility of replacing the state with some "supranational" - an international organization or a "global government" remained. This position is used even by those researchers, who work within the framework of the neo-liberal concept and especially emphasize the increased multiplicity of the number of participants in the relationship in the international arena. Thus, Y. Ferguson and R. Mansbach write that a sovereign state continues to exist, despite all the challenges they face as a result of how the political structure can mobilize material and human resources. Since the founding of the Westphalian model of the world, the state has promoted the development of trade, collected taxes, and ensured the safety of its citizens (Ferguson, Mansbach, 2007). According to scholars, due to its effectiveness, this form of political organization has spread from Europe to other continents, including the existing norms of political organization.

At the same time, there are ongoing discussions related to what is happening with the state, by what parameters it is changing, and how serious it is. First of all, the problem of state sovereignty is discussed in a practical and theoretical context. In the modern world, states are increasingly forced to take into account, on the one hand, the positions of international organizations and institutions (as a result, there is a restriction of sovereignty "from above"), and on the other, from their side - internal regions, mega polices and municipalities within the state, which today are actively involved in the process within the international arena, developing trade, cultural and other relations (limiting sovereignty "from below"). In addition, states are forced to take into account the needs and interests of other participants in political processes - transnational corporations, non-governmental organizations, etc.

In this regard, it should be noted that the capabilities of the state in modern conditions are limited "in all spheres of its activity":

- in ensuring national security in the traditional sense of this terminology;
- in creating conditions for economic security and sustainable development of the economy;
- In maintaining internal order, which is undermined by terrorism, crime, corruption, illegal migration, etc.
- in ensuring civil rights and human freedoms;
- In protecting the environment in favor of environmental safety.

This list can be continued to include other areas that have traditionally been "under the control" of the state, including healthcare, education, etc.

The American researcher S. D. Krasner suggested discussing not only the change in sovereignty but also the change in Westphalian sovereignty (or sovereignty in its classical sense), that is, political organizations based on a problem that external actors cannot influence domestic politics (Krasner, 2009). But these processes did not begin today. The famous English diplomat and scientist H. Nicholson, while analyzing the consequences of the First World War, wrote that during this period "the content of the understanding of sovereignty (the understanding of sovereign power) has changed" (Lebedeva, 2007).

Discussion of Westphalian sovereignty in the modern world does not mean its disappearance as such but means the actual transfer of some of the functions that previously belonged to the state and other actors. At the same time, the state received additional opportunities that were not available before. For example, using modern technologies (plastic cards, cell phones, etc.), the State can relatively easily control the movement of citizens.

Along with the change in the content of sovereignty, differences appear in the norms and principles of international law - one of the components that should stabilize world development. In practice, these norms and principles contrast more clearly with each other. For example, the right of a nation for self-determination on the one hand and respect for territorial integrity on the other; the principles of non-interference in internal affairs and the provision of humanitarian assistance; protection of human rights and military intervention in the conflict to ensure peace (UN Charter, Chapter VII), as well as the problem of the nature of this intervention (the presence of UN sanctions, the possibility of using the Air Force or the Marine Corps), such actions as the fight against armed formations, ensuring the transportation of humanitarian supplies, "forcing peace", etc. The clearest examples of the existence of such and other contradictions are military intervention in internal conflicts in the late 20th and early 21st centuries, the NATO operation in Kosovo, the US intervention in Iraq, and Russia's military aggression against Georgia in 2008 and against Ukraine in 2014

The change in national sovereignty had serious consequences not only from a legal but also from a psychological point of view - the problem of the state and national identity arose. The Romanian researcher M. Malitsa noted that the peace signed in Europe after the Thirty Years' War, which laid the foundation for the system of nation-states, brought something new into life, namely, a sense of belonging to a concrete state (Chitadze, 2016). In the era of the undivided rule of the nation-state, the identification factor was largely based on the understanding of belonging to a particular state (Club of Rome Publications). At the end of the twentieth century. there was an erosion of state identity. The English researcher S. Strange pointed out that the state is no longer capable of demanding more loyalty of citizens to itself; in the place of the state citizens' feelings, their attitude towards the family, company, etc. have appeared (Strange, 1991). Her point of view is shared by the French researchers A. Dickhoff and C. Jaffrelot; there are also discussions about the reduction of citizens' ties with their state (Dieckhoff, Jaffrelot, 2006).

The weakening of national-state identity is very often accompanied by the formation of another identity - often of a religious or national character. As a result, xenophobia appears, some fascist organizations and movements are created, and the next steps are open conflicts on ethnic grounds. It is no coincidence that many of the conflicts that arose in the 1990s were called identity conflicts. In the most striking form, the conflict of identity, where the basis of identity is belonging to a particular civilization, is described in the hypothetical scenarios of S. Huntington (Huntington, 1993).

In other cases, the identity is "blurred", a new identity appears, which at the psychological level leads people to uncertainty and doubts. American writer A. Frank writes in this regard that "our mental and even our body is more and more based on a divided self-identification. In our soul, there is a struggle between various aspects of loyalty: to the family, ethnic group, nations, church, transnational corporations, to a specific organization, most likely to institutions that are based on the general ideals of humanism. "(Lebedeva, 2007).

However, this multi-identity has its positive aspects. That due to the choice of self-identification, the same person is simultaneously in several "intersecting" communities, which sometimes are not in conflict situations with each other. In any case, there is no open conflict. Ultimately, multiple identities can lead us to a higher level of identification that includes all these communities, to some kind of global or cosmopolitan self-identification.

However, in the modern period, cosmopolitan identity, that is, a sense of belonging to humanity as a whole, does not spread. According to a sociological survey by L. Heilmann and P. Esther in the United States, the largest percentage of people in the US, who felt they were "citizens of our planet" in the first decade of the 21st century was only 15.4% (Lebedeva, 2007).

Faced with the problem of "erosion" of state identity, weakening of state sovereignty in some areas, the authorities intend to somehow resist this process, trying to respond to the challenges and find new methods and opportunities to preserve their powers, because, from the point of view of any state, the disappearance of national borders, loss of national sovereignty is very undesirable. In such conditions, demands arose to resist the loss of sovereignty by establishing a dictatorship. As a result, it is possible to create corrupt regimes and quasi-states, which, using the legal guarantees obtained through the principle of sovereignty, try by all means to support the authorities, sometimes creating sources of terrorism and instability.

Thus, at the beginning of the 21st century, the state remained the main form of organization of political society, the main actor in the world arena. But at the same time, they change and develop, adapt to new conditions, and attract these realities to themselves. It does not disappear, but only changes the meaning of "national-state sovereignty." These processes are proceeding in a complex manner. As a result, the world collides on the one hand with different state and quasi-state formations, which for one reason or another are included from the negative side in international relations, on the other hand, the state as such collides earlier. New challenges, which are because in modern conditions state`s functions are changing, countries are forced to be in interconnection with other transnational actors, including non-state entities in the international arena.

Classification and Typology of Countries Based on Some Geographic Factors

Many political scientists and international relations specialists wrote in their works that, for all its originality - natural, economic, cultural, and political - the country is the main object of research in international relations and world politics, and political geography. However, with so many countries in the world, there is a need for some classification (grouping) and typology of the states according to geographic principles. The difference between the two of these terms is that the classification is usually based on different quantitative indicators, while the typology is based on more significant qualitative characteristics.

Classification of the countries, often based on the size of the territory, the population, and geographic and geopolitical location.

According to the size of the territory, the countries of the world are divided into very large (giant countries), large, medium, small, and very small (micro-states) formations. Undoubtedly, every geographer and political scientist should have information about the top ten largest countries in the world. Those countries together occupy 55% of the territory of the ground part of the world and it is difficult to expect any changes - no significant changes are foreseen in the future (Goldstein, Pevehouse. 2010-2011).

The largest country in the world - Russia is located in both Europe and Asia. The table below shows that three Asian countries, two North American and two South American, and one in Africa and one in Oceania are among the largest.

The concept of "large country" has its regional specifics. To be more specific, for Europe a large country is a state with an area of more than 500 km2 (France, Spain, Ukraine), while in Africa, for example, the area is more than 1 million km2 (Sudan, Algeria, Libya, Ethiopia, etc.) (Goldstein, J. Pevehouse, S. 2010-2011).

Such regional differences also exist for the medium and small states. As far as microstates are concerned, this concept is again more or less identical for different regions.

The States as the Main Actors of the World Politics

Table 1. Ten biggest countries by territory

Country	Area, Million Km²	Share of the area in the World %
Russia	17,1	12,7
Canada	10,0	7,4
China	9,6	7,2
USA	9,6	7,2
Brazil	8,5	6,4
Australia	7,7	5,7
India	3,3	2,5
Argentina	2,8	2,1
Kazakhstan	2,7	2,0
Algeria	2,3	1,9

Source: https://www.listofcountriesoftheworld.com/area-land.html

Classic examples of microstates are Andorra, Liechtenstein, San Marino, Monaco, and the Vatican in Western Europe. The largest of them - Andorra has an area of 468 km2, and the smallest Vatican - only 0.44 km2. Microstates, mainly islands, are also common in other regions of the world - for example, in the Caribbean (Grenada, Barbados, Antigua and Barbuda, Saint Kitts and Nevis), Oceania (Nauru, Tuvalu, Marshall Islands), and the Indian Ocean (Maldives and Seychelles). They are all smaller in area than Andorra (United Nations. 2005).

By the number of population, the same gradation of countries is possible. Obviously, unlike the area, this figure is much more dynamic and may need constant updating. First of all, this applies to the most densely populated countries, which together account for about 3/5 of the world's population. They can also be called - attributed to giant countries.

As you might expect, the list of ten countries in terms of population is dominated by Asian states. North America is represented by the United States and Mexico, while South America, Africa, Europe,

Table 2. Ten biggest countries according to the number of populations

Country	Population, million people (April, 2020)
1. China	1,439,323,776
2. India	1,380,004,385
3. USA	331,002,651
4. Indonesia	273,523,615
5. Pakistan	220,892,340
6. Brazil	212,559,417
7. Nigeria	206, 139, 589
8. Bangladesh	164,689,383
9. Russia	145,934,462
10. Mexico	128,932,753

Sources: Worldometer. https://www.worldometers.info/world-population/population-by-country/

and Asia are represented by Brazil, Nigeria, and Russia, respectively. If you add Japan, Ethiopia, the Philippines, and Egypt to this list, it will cover all countries with a population of over 100 million. In most of the countries presented on this table, the number of people continues to grow rapidly. To be more specific, in India the annual population growth at the beginning of the 21st century was 15 million people (which is comparable to the total population of Kazakhstan), while in China, Pakistan, the United States, and Nigeria - 8 million, 3.5 million and 3 million people, respectively (Maksakovsky, 2009). Roughly the same situation is observed in the second decade of the 21st century. On the other hand, the population of Japan has approximately stabilized, but the country has moved from 10th to 11th place, and only Russia remains a country with a constantly shrinking population. Therefore, back in 1998, Pakistan overtook it in the top ten, moving up to the seventh place, and in 2005 this Asian country eventually ousted Russia to ninth place, and Brazil - to sixth. Due to the rapid population growth of Bangladesh, this small country was ranked 8th (Worldometer, 2020).

Populations from 50 to 100 million people are registered only in the following countries: Germany, France, Great Britain, Italy and Turkey in Europe, Vietnam, Thailand, Myanmar and Iran in Asia, the Democratic Republic of the Congo in Africa. At the beginning of the second decade of the 21st century, 53 countries had populations ranging from 10 to 50 million, most of whom lived in Africa, followed by Asia, Europe, and Latin America. The population of most of the countries of the world (60) ranges from 1 to 10 million people, with Africa and Europe occupying the leading positions. More than 40 countries have less than one million inhabitants (United Nations Department of Economic and Social Affairs, 2013).

Among them are the countries of the world with the smallest population. To be more specific, the two microstates are Tuvalu, with a population of 11,000, Nauru (13,000), Palau (20,000) in Oceania, San Marino (28,000), and Liechtenstein (33,000) in Europe. The Vatican is no exception, with a population of less than 1,000 (UN Department of Economic and Social Affairs. 2013).

Countries According to Geographic and Geopolitical Positions

Depending on the importance of geographic and geopolitical position, political geographers usually distinguish between coastal and landlocked countries. The number of Landlocked countries - 42, from them 15 are located in Africa, 15 in Europe, 10 in Asia (not counting the outlets to the inland Caspian and Aral Seas), and 2 in Latin America. As you know, the lack of access to the oceans should be considered as a very unfavorable feature of the geographical position, which negatively affects socio-economic development. The countries of tropical Africa are the most striking examples of this.

Landlocked countries can also be divided into islands (e.g. Iceland, Ireland, Sri Lanka, Madagascar, Cuba, New Zealand, etc.), peninsulas (e.g. Spain, Portugal, Italy, Turkey, Saudi Arabia, Vietnam), and the countries of the archipelago. By the way, there are not so few archipelagic countries on the political map of the world as it might seem at first glance - there are quite a lot of archipelagic countries on the political map of the world. For example, Japan, the Philippines, and Indonesia, located on more than 4,000, 7,000, and 17,500 islands, respectively, are striking examples of such countries (Chitadze, 2017). However, the archipelagic states in Oceania should not be overlooked here. The number of islands there may be small, but they occupy vast expanses of water within the official boundaries. For example, the population of the Republic of Kiribati is about 100 thousand people on five million square kilometers! (Maksakovsky, 2009).

The number of neighboring countries directly bordering on each specific one affects the geographical, or rather the political and geographical position. Accordingly, Russia and China (bordering with 14

Table 3. Countries of the world, which have no exit to the Sea

Regions	Countries
Europe	Andorra, Armenia, Austria, Azerbaijan, Check Republic, Belorussia, Hungary, Lichtenstein, Luxemburg, Macedonia, Moldova, San-Marino, Slovakia, Switzerland, Vatican.
Asia	Afghanistan, Bhutan, Laos, Mongolia, Nepal, Kazakhstan, Kyrgyzstan, Tajikistan, Turkmenistan, Uzbekistan.
Africa	Botswana, Burkina-Faso, Burundi, Central African Republic, Chad, Ethiopia, Zambia, Zimbabwe, Lesotho, Malawi, Mali, Niger, Ruanda, Swaziland, Uganda.
Latin America	Bolivia, Paraguay

http://www.worldmapsonline.com/classic_colors_world_political_map_wall_mural.htm

countries) share the first and second places, followed by Brazil (10), Germany, Sudan and the Democratic Republic of the Congo (9), France, Austria, Turkey, Tanzania (8) (Davitashvili, Elizbarashvili, 2012). As for the countries with the longest borders, the land borders of Russia and China exceed 20 thousand kilometers, while Brazil, India, the United States, and the Democratic Republic of the Congo have 10 thousand kilometers (Chitadze, 2017).

COUNTRIES ACCORDING TO SOCIO-ECONOMIC DEVELOPMENT

The question of country typology from a socio-economic point of view is much more complex. Although usually the basis for adopting such a typology is determined by the political orientation and the level of their socio-economic development, the specific types and subtypes proposed by international organizations and individual scientists can vary quite significantly. Speaking about international organizations, the UN, the World Bank and the International Monetary Fund (IMF) should be mentioned first of all.

As discussed above, despite the discrepancies, the three main types of groupings of the states in the modern world from an economic point of view can be considered the most appropriate method of dividing countries. Until the early 90s of the twentieth century, these three types of countries were: 1) capitalist countries of the "first world", 2) communist countries of the "second world", 3) developing countries, countries of the "third world" (A. Heywood. 2007).

After the collapse of the world communist system, political scientists, economists, geographers, etc. presented the new typology of the countries, with all countries divided into 1) economically developed, 2) developing countries, 3) countries with economies in transition. (However, a binomial typology has also been adopted, e.g. developed - developing countries).

These three types are discussed in more detail below.

About 60 states in the modern world that have reached a higher level of socio-economic development, especially compared to developing countries, belong to the type of economically developed countries, as the name suggests (Chitadze, 2017).

Recently, however, a somewhat narrower interpretation of this important concept related to - economically developed countries has appeared. International organizations include more than 40 countries and territories around the world in this category, including 35, 7, 2, 2, and 1 in Europe, Asia, America,

Australia and Oceania, and Africa, respectively (Chitadze, 2017). All these countries have a highly developed market economy with a predominance of services and production, as well as significant scientific and technological potential, and are characterized by a high level of quality and standard of living of the population under, of course, a democratic political regime. ... They produce most of the world's industrial and agricultural products and various services.

Nevertheless, such countries differ quite noticeably in their internal heterogeneity, which makes it possible to distinguish four subtypes.

First, the main countries with developed market economies - the United States, Japan, Germany, France, Great Britain, Italy, and Canada, which make up the "big seven" leading countries in the world from a political and economic point of view. These seven countries account for about half of the gross national product (GNP) and industrial production, agricultural production (Chitadze, 2017). Their place in world politics cannot be quantified.

Secondly, small Western European countries, such as Austria, Belgium, Denmark, the Netherlands, Norway, Switzerland, Sweden, which have also reached a very high level of socio-economic development and are much more specialized in the international geographical division of labor and, therefore, are very active participants in it. The role of these countries in world politics is also very noticeable. In this regard, it is also worth mentioning that several UN offices and specialized agencies are located in Vienna and Geneva, while Brussels is the capital of NATO and the European Union.

Third, non-European countries such as Australia, New Zealand, South Africa, and Israel. The first three of these countries are former resettlement colonies (dominions) of Great Britain, which did not pass through the stages of feudalism, and today have a kind of political and economic development. To a large extent, Israel can also be called a country of resettlement. In fact, from a typological point of view, Canada also belongs to the former colony of settlers. However, it must be admitted that his current rating as a member of the G7 is much higher.

Fourth, it is a subtype of countries and territories representing innovative highly industrialized countries and territories. We are talking about the Republic of Korea, Singapore, Hong Kong, and Taiwan, which in the mid-90s were classified as economically developed countries by the International Monetary Fund. Cyprus was added to this list at the beginning of the 21st century.

About 150 countries and territories belonging to the type of developing countries, which together occupy more than half of the Earth's land area and where more than four-fifths of the world's population is concentrated (Chitadze, 2017). They form a vast belt on the political map of the world, stretching to Asia, Africa, Latin America, and Oceania to the north and even more to the south of the equator. Some of these countries (Iraq, Thailand, Ethiopia, Egypt, most Latin American countries) gained political independence even before World War II. However, among the developing countries, the so-called newly liberated countries predominate.

This type of state is characterized by a slowdown in economic growth, an economy based on agriculture and raw materials, and dependence on international assistance.

Therefore, it would be more correct to call these countries economically underdeveloped. However, instead of this "offensive" term, the UN initially chose the more optimistic term - developing countries. While this is not entirely true: some countries of this type are developing rapidly, many remain underdeveloped for decades.

Developing countries are inherently more heterogeneous than economically highly developed countries. There are also several subtypes.

The first of them forms the so-called core countries - China, India, Brazil, and Mexico, which have very important natural, human and economic potential and in many ways serve as the leading countries of the developing world. For example, four of these countries produce more industrial products than all other developing countries.

The second subtype includes those developing countries of the upper tier, which have also reached a sufficiently high level of socio-economic development. As a rule, these are countries that gained political independence a long time ago and, thus, have significant experience in self-development. Argentina, Venezuela, Uruguay, Chile are examples of such states.

New industrial economies (NIS) belong to the third subtype. These are primarily Asian countries, which made such a leap in their development in the 80s and 90s that they began to be called "tigers" and "dragons". To the greatest extent, this concerns the previously mentioned Republic of Korea, Singapore, Hong Kong, and Taiwan, which, as already noted, were transferred to the group of economically developed countries. Today we can talk about the "second wave" of Asian NIS - Malaysia, Thailand, Indonesia, and the Philippines. Some other countries are sometimes also referred to as this subtype.

Oil-exporting countries form a fourth subtype, which, thanks to oil exports and the constant flow of petrodollars, are far richer than any other country in the developing world. The leading countries of the Persian Gulf are Saudi Arabia, Kuwait, the United Arab Emirates (UAE), Qatar, Bahrain. But this subtype also includes Libya and Brunei.

Classical underdeveloped countries that are still lagging in their socio-economic development belong to the fifth subtype. So, this includes many developing countries. Sri Lanka in Asia, Ghana, Guinea, Zimbabwe in Africa, Bolivia, Guyana, Honduras in Latin America are examples (Sullivan, Sheffrin 2003).

The sixth subtype of the country deserves special attention. According to UN terminology, these are the least developed countries, the list of which is updated annually according to three main factors: low income, backward agriculture, and a high level of illiteracy among the adult population. Now there are about 50 such countries on the UN list. Most of them are in Africa (34) and Asia (9) (Chitadze, 2017). The list of the least developed countries is contained in various manuals. Sometimes these countries are referred to as countries of the "fourth world" and, according to many scientists, these countries "lag forever."

The third type of country, as already noted, refers to countries with economies in transition. Many post-socialist countries are included, that is, several countries that were formerly part of the Soviet Union, and the former socialist countries of Central and Eastern Europe. Some of them in the late 1980s and early 1990s began the transition from an old, largely authoritarian political system to a democratic one, based on civil society, a multiparty system, and respect for human rights. No fewer revolutionary changes have taken place in the economic sphere, where the transition from the old command system and central planning to a market economy has already taken place.

China, Vietnam, North Korea, and Cuba must belong to a special subtype of countries that, following their constitutions and the programs of the ruling parties, continue to follow the communist path of development.

The economic level, which is measured by gross domestic product (GDP) per capita, serves as the main indicator based on which the typology of countries is determined. It is calculated using either the official exchange rate or purchasing power parity (PPP), and the second method is often used in international statistics. In most industrialized countries, GDP per capita is more than $ 20 thousand, or even $ 40-50 thousand (or more). Some countries with economies in transition, as well as some key developing ones, newly industrialized and oil-exporting countries are in the range of 5-10 thousand and 10-20 thousand

US dollars (OECD tax database for 2013). Most developing countries fall into the group, where GDP per capita is between $ 1,000 to $ 5,000, and many least developed countries fall into the group, where GDP per capita is under $ 1,000. It turns out that Burundi, Somalia, Sierra Leone, Malawi, where GDP per capita and GDP - even by PPP is about $ 600, are by 100 times inferior to Luxembourg! It should be borne in mind that the calculation of the official exchange rate for countries with economies in transition and developing countries is much less favorable: in this case, the PPP of Burundi compared to Luxembourg is more than 500 times less! (OECD Tax Database 2017).

It is important to note that the UN and other international organizations are looking for a new, more universal indicator to determine the level of socio-economic development of the modern world. As a result, their typology can now use the so-called Human Development Index (HDI). This index is calculated based on the following three components: 1) average life expectancy; 2) education; 3) the real value of the average income of the population. Based on these criteria, UN experts divide all countries into three groups (Human Development Concept. UNDP. 2012).

The first group includes countries with a high HDI exceeding 0.800 (Maximum evaluation is 1.000 score). In the first decade of the 21st century, there were 55 such countries, with Norway, Sweden, Australia, Canada, and the Netherlands (0.942-0.956) topping the list. 86 countries belonged to the second group of medium - HDI (from 0.500 to 0.800) and 36 countries - to the third group with a low HDI (less than 0.500), most of them belong to the least developed countries. At the same time, two of them - Niger and Sierra Leone - have HDI below 0.300. (Human Development Report 2014).

Completing the description of the modern political map of the world, we can take into account the following two other categories of territorial formations. The first unites self-proclaimed territories, which in most cases exist, but are not legally recognized or have been recognized by several states, and not by the international community.

In Europe, there are some foreign breakaway territories (e.g., Kosovo) that have been de facto separated from Serbia. In Asia, these are the Turkish Republic of Northern Cyprus, Azad Kashmir ("Free Kashmir"), and, in fact, Taiwan, where the Republic of China was proclaimed in 1949, but communist China (and the international community) considers Taiwan to be its province. In Africa, it is the Sahara Arab Democratic Republic (SADR). All these self-proclaimed territories, together with the occupied ones (for example Abkhazia and Tskhinvali region, illegally occupied by Russia, are two historical regions of Georgia) represents a source of international tension.

Non-self-governing territories belong to the second group on the political map. There is some variation here, but the remaining colonies, which do not have political or economic independence, still make up the bulk of these territories. The UN list of dependent territories includes 16 such territories, which are still under the control of Great Britain, France, the United States, Australia, Denmark, the Netherlands, and New Zealand. But their share in the area of the globe is only 0.2%, while the share of its population is 0.00016%. These figures can serve as yet another confirmation of the conclusion about the complete disintegration of the colonial system (15th session of the UN General Assembly).

FORMS OF POLITICAL REGIMES IN THE WORLD

When studying the political map of the world, undoubtedly, the question of the forms of governance of the states should be included. In turn, this issue includes three components - forms of political regimes, forms of government, and forms of administrative-territorial structure. Let's take a look at these components.

The States as the Main Actors of the World Politics

To begin with, according to the specifics of the political regime, all countries of the world can be divided into democratic and anti-democratic. In the West, there are non-governmental organizations that determine the "democracy index" of countries based mainly on the nature of legislative elections and the rule of law. The results of these calculations are easy to predict: Western countries usually get the highest score (10 points), and the lowest rate is the countries of Southwest Asia and North Africa. Nevertheless, the total number of states consistently supporting the adoption of the 1948 Universal Declaration of Human Rights is constantly increasing (Weiss, Forsythe, Coate. 1997). According to authoritative Western sources, if after the First World War democratic regimes were established in almost 30 countries, then during the Second World War only 12 democratic states remained. In the 1960s, there were 37 of them (Rondeli, 2003). In the mid-70s of the twentieth century, less than 1/3 of all countries in the world were included in the list of democratic states, while in 2019 the number of free and partially free countries was about 90 and 60, respectively (Freedom House in the World. 2019).

As for the number of non-free countries with authoritarian political regimes on the political map of the world, there are about 45 states (Freedom House in the World. 2019). It can be argued that among these modes, two varieties also appear. By an authoritarian regime, we mean a complete or partial absence of democratic freedoms, limited activities of political parties and public organizations, persecution of the opposition, the absence of a clear separation of the legislative, executive, and judicial powers (Mkurnalidze, Khamkhadze, 2000). In the modern world, authoritarian regimes are mainly located in Asia, Africa, and the Middle East (in Latin America authoritarian regimes existed during the "cold war" period, wherein some cases they had the character of a military dictatorship). Until 2011, an example of such a country was Libya, which was officially called the Jamahiriya, that is, when in 1969 under the mass support, revolutionary dictatorship under the leadership of Muammar Gaddafi was established, while many governmental institutions were abolished. On the one hand, the emergence of such political regimes can be explained by internal factors - the legacy of feudalism and colonialism, socio-economic backwardness, low cultural level, tribalism (from the Latin Tribus - tribe), i. e. manifestations of clashes between tribes, while, with, on the other hand, external factors should be considered, and above all also the confrontation between the two world systems that existed until the 90s.

When it comes to a totalitarian regime, it implies a special form of authoritarianism, in which the state establishes complete control over the public life of the state as a whole and concerning each citizen. It destroys constitutional norms and rights and takes tough measures against opposition and dissidents.

Political scientists have identified two types of totalitarianism - right and left. Examples of the first of these are the fascist regimes in Germany, Italy, Spain under General Franco, based on the ideology of National Socialism. The second type is based on the ideology of Marxism-Leninism, which took place in the Soviet Union under Stalin, China under Mao Zedong, in North Korea under Kim Il Sung (Mkurnalidze, Khamkhadze, 2000). In the second half of the 70s. In the twentieth century, a totalitarian regime that led to genocide, thus, to the extermination of its people, was established by the Khmer Rouge led by Paul Teng in Cambodia, and Saddam Hussein's regime in Iraq, which lasted until 2003, was too totalitarian.

CLASSIFICATION OF THE STATES BY THE FORMS OF GOVERNANCE

Let's start with a description of the forms of governance of the states, which, in principle, are the only two main types - republican and monarchical.

The republican form of government originated in antiquity but has become extremely popular in our time. It is important to note that during the collapse of the colonial system, the vast majority of the newly independent countries adopted a republican form of government. The republics were proclaimed in such countries of the millennial monarchy as Egypt, Ethiopia, Iran, Afghanistan, Tunisia, Libya, etc. As a result, in 1990 there were already 127 republics in the world, and after the collapse of the Soviet Union, Yugoslavia and Czechoslovakia, the total number approached 150. This means that the republican form of government has 4/5 of all independent states of the modern world (Chitadze, 2017).

In a republican system, legislative power is usually vested in parliament, which is elected by the entire population, and executive power is under government control. The system distinguishes between presidential, semi-presidential, and parliamentary republics.

In presidential republics, the president, who is the head of state, and in many cases the head of government, has high powers. There are more than 100 such republics. Most of them are in Africa - 45 (for example Egypt, Algeria, Nigeria, Zimbabwe, South Africa) and Latin America - 22 (for example, Mexico, Brazil, Venezuela, Argentina) (Maksakovsky, 2009). There are significantly fewer presidential republics in Asia (for example, Syria, Iran, Pakistan, Indonesia, the Philippines). The United States can be seen as the most prominent example of a typical presidential republic, where the president is the head of state and government (A. Heywood. 2007).

In Europe, there are several countries with a semi-presidential system of government (for example, France, Poland, Ukraine, Croatia). In this case, along with the institution of the president with high power, there is also the institution of the prime minister, which coordinates the work of the government (A. Heywood. 2007).

A parliamentary republic is based on the formal principle of the supremacy of parliament, to which the executive (government) power is accountable. The role of the president in these republics is much less, and the prime minister is the main political figure. Parliamentary republics are most typical for Europe (for example, Germany, Italy, Austria, Estonia, Latvia), but they also exist in Asia (for example, India, Israel) (A. Heywood. 2007).

As mentioned above, the monarchical system of government arose in the era of the ancient world, but it became more widespread in the Middle Ages and in modern times. The number of monarchies remains stable; there are only 30 of them (Neidze, 2004).

The facts of the formation of new monarchies in our time are very rare. In recent decades, only two have been observed. First, in Spain, where the monarchy was overthrown in 1931 and restored in 1975 after the death of the head of the Spanish government (caudillo) Franco (Raymond Carr. 1982). Secondly, in Cambodia, where, after a 23-year exile, Norodom Sihanouk again became king in 1993 (UN, 2005). The power of the monarch is usually exercised based on heredity, but in Malaysia and the United Arab Emirates, the monarch is elected every five years from among the local sheiks and sultans.

As it is shown from the table, most of the monarchies are in Asia (14) and Europe (12), only 3 in Africa and 1 in Oceania and, secondly, there are monarchies such as empires, kingdoms, duchies, principalities, sultanates, emirates. But more often they are divided into constitutional or limited and absolute monarchies.

Most currently existing monarchies belong to constitutional (limited) monarchies, where the real legislative and executive power belongs to the parliament and government, respectively, while the monarch, according to many experts, "rules but does not rule." "The system of monarchy is preserved as a specific type of government and is sometimes based on millennial traditions, often reminiscent of the former

The States as the Main Actors of the World Politics

Table 4. Countries in the world with a monarchical form of government

Countries	Forms of Governance	Countries	Forms of Governance
Europe			
Andorra	Principality	Lichtenstein	Principality
Belgium	Kingdom	Luxemburg	Great Principality
Vatican	Theocratic Monarchy	Monaco	Principality
Denmark	Kingdom	Netherlands	Kingdom
Spain	Kingdom	Norway	Kingdom
United Kingdom	Kingdom	Sweden	Kingdom
Asia			
Bahrain	Emirate	United Arab Emirates	Emirate
Brunei	Sultanate	Saudi Arabia	Kingdom
Bhutan	Kingdom	Thailand	Kingdom
Jordan	Kingdom	Japan	Empire
Cambodia	Kingdom	Nepal	Kingdom
Qatar	Emirate	Malaysia	Sultanate
Kuwait	Emirate		
Africa		**Oceania**	
Lesotho	Kingdom	Tonga	Kingdom
Morocco	Kingdom		
Swaziland	Kingdom		

Source: http://m.ranker.com/list/countries-ruled-by-monarchy/reference

greatness of the "crown." All monarchies in Europe and Africa and most Asian monarchies belong to the constitution. Britain is considered a classic example of such a form of monarchy.

Queen Elizabeth II of Britain has "ruled but not ruled" since 1952. Citizens of this country very often come across monarchical symbols. The country is governed by "Her Majesty's Government" and laws are promulgated "in the name of the Queen." Banknotes are printed by the Royal Mint and the Royal Mail delivers letters. The first toast at dinner parties usually goes to the queen, the English anthem begins with the sentence "God save the queen," and her silhouette is depicted on any postage stamp. The British Queen has considerable political power. She convenes and dissolves parliament, appoints and dismisses the prime minister, approves laws passed by parliament, awards honors and awards, and announces pardons (Dyer, Clare. 2003). However, in all these cases, he is guided by the advice and decisions of parliament and government. In addition, Queen Elizabeth II is one of the richest people in the country.

Given the political realities, many monarchs do not know how to "marry for love." In principle, this is true, because dynastic marriages in Europe are usually based on mutual consent, not love.

However, there are exceptions. For example, King Edward VIII, who ascended the British throne in 1936 after the death of George V, married for love to an American actress, who was twice divorced before. But after that, due to the crisis of the palace, he had to abdicate in favor of his younger brother. So, George VI - the father of Elizabeth II became king of Great Britain. It turns out that if this incident hadn't happened, Elizabeth would not have been queen, and the whole post-war history of England could have been different.

Japan is another example of how a monarch "is monarch but does not rule" in a constitutional monarchy, where, according to the constitution, the monarch (emperor) is a symbol of the state and the unity of the nation, the guarantor of people's freedoms. But he does not participate directly in the political life of the country, and his role is largely limited to the implementation of protocol functions.

Interestingly, in Japan, several systems of chronology are considered, and one of them is recorded during the reign of the next emperor. So, a special chronology was established for the reign of Emperor Hirohito, which lasted from 1926 to 1989 and from 1989 is the countdown to the reign of his son Emperor Akihito. This era was called "Heisei", which can be translated as "the establishment of universal peace on earth and in heaven."

In addition, the literature related to the constitutional monarchies contains materials about Great Britain, Sweden, Denmark, Norway, Spain, Japan and their comparison with the presidential republics in Latin America and Africa, especially at the level of democracy. It turns out that the level of democracy in constitutional monarchies is often much higher. Therefore, it can be considered a big mistake to consider that, in comparison with the monarchical form of government, the Republican one is always progressive.

However, along with most democratic constitutional monarchies, there are several absolute monarchies on the political map of the world that cannot be considered as countries with democratic political regimes. All these monarchies (Saudi Arabia, Oman, UAE, Qatar), except for Brunei, are located on the Arabian Peninsula. In Saudi Arabia, the head of state (king) exercises legislative and executive power. He is the Prime Minister, Commander-in-Chief of the Armed Forces, and Chief Justice. State structures are mainly formed from members of the royal family, which in total numbers are several thousand people. In Oman, all legislative and executive power also belongs to the Sultan as the head of state. The Sultan is the prime minister, minister of defense, foreign affairs, finance, and the supreme commander of the armed forces. There is no Constitution in this country. The United Arab Emirates consists of seven emirates, each of which is an absolute monarchy. In Qatar, too, all power belongs to the local emir.

A kind of absolute monarchy is theocratic monarchy (from the Greek. Teos - God and Kratos - power). In such a monarchy, the head of state is also a religious leader. The Kingdom of Saudi Arabia and the Sultanate of Brunei also belong to theocratic monarchies, and in Iran, despite the presidency, the head of state is the spiritual leader - the Ayatollah. The Vatican is undoubtedly a classic example of a theocratic monarchy. It is a city-state in which the highest legislative, executive and judicial power is in the hands of the Pope, who is elected by the College of Cardinals for the rest of his life. From 1997 to 2005, this post was held by the 264th Pope John Paul II. After his death, Pope Boniface XVI became a pontiff, that is, the head of the Roman Catholic Church, who later resigned from his post. Today Pope Francis is the head of state of the Vatican. He was born Jorge Mario Bergoglio in Buenos Aires, Argentina, who was elected to office on March 13, 2013.

In conclusion of the description of the forms of government, it is worth mentioning once again the Commonwealth, led by Great Britain. Most of its members have one of two traditional forms of government - a republic or a monarchy. However, 16 of these countries (e.g., Canada, Australia, New Zealand, many small island states in the Caribbean) are neither republics nor monarchies, but simply recognize the head of state, Queen Elizabeth II (Commonwealth Secretariat. 2008).

Figure 2. Border of the states of the continental part of U.S. A. Borders of the states: by the rivers; by the mountain ranges; along with the meridians and parallels.
Source: https://www.50states.com/us.htm

COUNTRIES BY ADMINISTRATIVE-TERRITORIAL DIVISION

Now let's consider the forms of the administrative-territorial structure of the countries of the world. Such a structure, which is expressed primarily in the grids of administrative-territorial Division (ATD), can be formed under the influence of several factors or approaches, the main of which is historical and ethnocultural. The countries of Western Europe serve as an example of a historical approach, where historical regions and provinces form the basis of ADT, which in the Middle Ages and the modern period of history were independent states, such as Saxony, Thuringia, Bavaria, Baden-Württemberg in Germany or Lombardy, Tuscany, Piedmont in Italy. The ethnocultural approach is mainly common in multinational countries. For example, in India, state boundaries have focused on ethnic boundaries. This principle was widely used in the formation of ADT in the former USSR. In practice, the historical and ethnocultural approaches often coincide, combining, in turn, with natural boundaries (river, mountain, etc.).

Parallels and meridians also marked administrative boundaries. The United States serves as an example of this kind of ATD.

The countries of the world differ greatly from each other in the degree of detail in their ADTs. In France (22 districts and 96 departments, including 4 overseas), Russia (86 subjects of the federation, including 21 republics), ADTs are very partial. USA (50 states), Spain (50 provinces), Japan (47 prefectures), India (28 states and 7 union territories), Germany after unification - 16 federal states, Austria - 8 states, Australia - 6 states and 2 territories (Chitadze, 2017) - countries with an average level of ADT detail. Some countries have recently launched policies to reduce their ADTs (e.g., India), while others, on the contrary, have begun to expand (e.g., Russia).

Thus, we can distinguish two main forms of the administrative-territorial division of the world - unitary and federal.

A unitary state (from Lat. Unitas - unity) is a form of administrative-territorial division, in which the country has one constitution, there is a common legislative, executive, and judicial branch and its constituent administrative units do not use any significant local governments. Most of the countries of the world are unitary states. This applies to Europe, where Great Britain, France, Italy, Sweden, Poland serve as examples of such states. In Asia, 33 independent states out of 38 have a unitary administrative-territorial structure (Chitadze, 2017). Unitary states also predominate in Africa and Latin America.

A federal state (from the Latin Federatio - union, association) is a form of administrative-territorial structure in which, along with federal authorities and laws, there are more or less self-governing administrative units - republics, states, provinces, lands, cantons, territories, federal districts, which have their own legislative and executive bodies of power, although they are "in the second-order" in comparison with federal institutions. In the United States, each state has its legislature (legislature) and executive (governor) bodies, the structure, and competence of which are determined by the constitution of that particular state. The legislation in different states can also vary quite a lot. In most federal states, the parliament consists of two chambers, one of which provides a representation of republics, states, provinces, etc. For example, in the United States it is the Senate, in Germany - the Bundesrat, in India - the Parliament, in Russia - the Federation Council.

The total number of federal states on the modern political map of the world is small - there are only 24 of them (Chitadze, 2017). Moreover, this number is relatively stable. However, there are also examples of new federal states: Belgium became a federation in 1993 and Ethiopia in 1998.

This table clearly shows how the federal states are distributed across the major regions of the world. It can also be noted that the federal structure is reflected in the official names of many of these countries.

Some representatives of political geography are working on the issue of developing a typology of federal states. For example, it is proposed to distinguish Western European, North American, Latin American, Afro-Asian, Nigerian, and island types of federations. But we will not consider them in detail. We can confine ourselves to the statement that the federal form of ATD is characteristic primarily of multinational or, at least, bi-national states. Examples of this are Russia, Switzerland, Belgium, India, Nigeria, Canada. Nevertheless, in most of the currently existing federations, there are countries with a more or less homogeneous national (ethnic) composition of the population. Consequently, the emergence of these federations reflects the historical and geographical features of their development, and not national and ethnic factors.

In addition, one of the types of the federation is a confederation, whose members retain formal sovereignty and the right to withdraw from this voluntary association. There are several such confederations in the world today. But at the beginning of the 21st century, the official name of a confederation was preserved only in Switzerland (De-facto this country is Federation). By the way, the first three cantons of the country united into a confederation long ago, in particular, in 1291 (Fleiner, Töpperwien. 2009).

It is also worth noting that in federal states with a complex national and ethnic composition, everyday conflict situations are more common, which are reflected on the political map of the world.

COUNTRIES ACCORDING TO FOREIGN POLICY COURSE

Many countries in the modern world are united in various military, political or economic organizations. At present, there are three major military-political unions on a global scale. One of them is NATO (North Atlantic Treaty Organization), which was created in 1949 to defend itself from the Soviet Union and today unites 30 states from North America (2 states) and Europe and is responsible for ensuring security in the Euro-Atlantic space. The second organization is the CIS Collective Security Treaty Organization, which was established in 1992 by the initiative of Russia and includes several post-Soviet republics.

The States as the Main Actors of the World Politics

Table 5. Countries of the world with a federal administrative-territorial division

Countries by the Region
Europe
Austria
Belgium
Bosnia and Herzegovina
Federal Republic of Germany
Russian Federation
Switzerland
Asia
India
Malaysia
Myanmar
United Arab Emirates
Islamic Republic of Pakistan
Africa
Federal Islamic Republic of Camorra Islands
Nigeria
Federal Democratic Republic Ethiopia
South African Republic
Latin America
Argentina
Brazil
Venezuela
Mexico
Federation of Sent-Kits and Nevis
Australia and Oceania
Australian Union
Federal States of Micronesia

Source: https://www.answers.com/Q/List_of_federal_countries_in_the_world

The Third Military Union - ANZUS was formed in September 1951 in San Francisco by the initiative of the United States, comprising the three countries - The United States, Australia, and New Zealand. The main purpose of this military bloc is to ensure collective defense security in the Pacific basin. It is noteworthy that in 1978 the organization expanded its area ofoperation to the Indian Ocean basin.

In the post-World War II period, there were also several other military organizations in the world, such as ANZUK (Australia, Great Britain, Malaysia, New Zealand, and Singapore), SEATO - Southeast Asia Treaty Organization (Australia, Great Britain, New Zealand, Pakistan, USA, Thailand, Philippines, and France), based on the Manila Declaration in 1954, and the SENTO - Central Treaty Organization (UK, Iraq, Iran, Pakistan, and Turkey, with the US as observer status), based on the 1959 Baghdad Pact.

As for the communist camp states, in 1955, by the initiative of the USSR, the Warsaw Pact was established, which included several Central and Eastern European states along with the Soviet Empire.

All the countries that are united in this or that military-political alliance are called bloc states.

Regarding the neutral states, traditionally, there have been two forms of neutrality: permanent and eventual. In addition to renouncing military blocs and actions in the event of permanent neutrality, there should also be no troops or military bases of warring countries on the territory of the country. The country takes the position of eventual neutrality during a certain military-political situation. For example, during the First or Second World Wars, several states declared neutrality and therefore did not engage in either war. The most "experienced" countries in terms of neutrality are Sweden (since 1814), Switzerland (since 1815), and San Marino (since 1862). Finland, Austria, Ireland became neutral countries after World War II and Moldova and Turkmenistan after the collapse of the Soviet Union.

Most of the countries in the world are called United in the non-aligned movement. The main priority of their foreign policy is non-participation and non-alignment in the military blocs. Unlike neutral countries, they believe that a military solution to a foreign problem is permissible. The Non-Aligned Movement was founded in 1961 in Belgrade. The "Group-77" - Union of Non-Aligned Countries was also established. At present, about 150 countries around the world are united in the non-aligned movement.

DEPENDENT AND NEUTRAL TERRITORIES ON THE WORLD POLITICAL MAP

As for the so-called Depending territories, their number is about 30. The island of Greenland is the largest area depending on the size of the area, with an area of more than 2 million square kilometers and belongs to Denmark. The Faroe Islands belong to the same country. Territories in different regions of the world are also owned by the USA (e.g., Puerto Rico, Eastern Samoa, etc.), Great Britain (e.g., Bermuda, St. Helena Island), France (e.g., New Caledonia, Reunion), as well as the Netherlands, Australia, New Zealand, etc. As it was already mentioned, dependent territories account for only 0.2% of the world area and 0.00016% of the world population.

It is also noteworthy that the international community has defined the legal status of Antarctica - it is an international territory that does not belong to any state. Unlike the Arctic, it is a continent whose geographical center is the South Pole, which includes the South Polar Area, surrounding islands, shelf ice, as well as parts of the Atlantic, India, and Pacific Oceans.

The international legal regime of Antarctica was established by an international treaty signed on December 1, 1959, in Washington, DC, which entered into force in 1961. According to the agreement, the use of these territories for military purposes (deployment of military bases, testing of military weapons, and conducting military maneuvers) is prohibited in the region. Its ecological pollution is also prohibited. The agreement allows for the conducting of scientific research in Antarctica for peaceful purposes and the development of scientific cooperation between the states on the continent (Aleksidze, 2004).

CONCLUSION

Nation-states are traditionally the object of political research, which deals with topics related to the political systems of states, political changes, political culture, and political ideology. For more than 350 years, the nation-state has undergone significant changes: it has complicated its political organization, expanded its sphere of responsibility and activity.

Its fact, which state system exists and how the state functions, largely determine its behavior in foreign policy, relations with other states. Almost all scientists agree with this thesis. The problem is how long this connection will last.

REFERENCES

Aleksidze, L. (2004). *Dictionary of International Law*. Tbilisi State University.

Basic facts about the United Nations. (2005). UN Department of Public Information.

Blum, W. (2006). *Rogue state: A guide to the world's only superpower*. Zed Books.

Chitadze, N. (2017). *World Geography. Political, economic and demographic dimensions*. Scholar Press.

Commonwealth Network. (2008). *Commonwealth Secretariat*. Retrieved from: https://www.commonwealthofnations.org/commonwealth/commonwealth-secretariat/

Countries of the world ordered by land area. (2021). Retrieved from: https://www.listofcountriesoftheworld.com/area-land.html

Davitashvili, Z., & Elizbarashvili, N. (2012). *Global Geography*. Tbilisi State University.

Dieckhoff, A., & Jaffrelot, C. (2006). *Revisiting nationalism: Theories and processes*. Palgrave Macmillan.

Ferguson, Y., & Mansbach, R. (2007). *A World of Polities Essays on Global Politics*. Routledge.

Fleiner, T. (2009). *Current Situation with Federalism*. Dialnet.

Freedom House. (2020). *Freedom House in the World 2019*. https://freedomhouse.org/report/freedom-world/2019/scores

Goldstein, J., & Pavehouse, J. (n.d.). *International Relations: 2010-2011*. Longman Publishing Group.

Heywood, A. (2007). *Politics*. Palgrave Foundations.

Howell, L. (1998). *International Business in the 21st Century* (Vol. 3). Praeger Perspectives.

Huntington, S. (1993). Clashes of Civilizations. *Foreign Affairs*, 72(3), 22. doi:10.2307/20045621

Krasner. (2009). Power, the State, and Sovereignty. In *Essays on International Relations*. Routledge.

Lebedeva. (2007). *World Politics*. Aspects Press.

Maksakovski, V. (2009). *World Social and Economic Geography*. Aspect Press.

Mkurnalidze, K. (2000). *Political Science*. Georgian Technical University.

Neidze, V. (2004). *World Social and Economic Geography*. Institute of Geography.

Number of Federal Countries in the World. (2021). Retrieved from: https://www.answers.com/Q/List_of_federal_countries_in_the_world

OECD. (2014). *OECD tax database for 2013*. Retrieved from: https://www.oecd.org/ctp/tax-policy/tax-database/

Orwell, G. (1949). *Nineteen Eighty-Four.* Secker & Warburg.

Ranker. (2021). *Around the World.* Retrieved from: http://m.ranker.com/list/countries-ruled-by-monarchy/reference

RF. (2021). *Political map of world with country flags.* Retrieved from: https://www.123rf.com/photo_23540827_political-map-of-world-with-country-flags.html

Rondeli. (2003). *International Relations*. Neckeri.

States.com. (2021). *Map of the United States of America.* https://www.50states.com/us.htm

Stewart, P. (2007). 'Failed' States and Global Security: Empirical Questions and Policy Dilemmas. *International Studies Review.*

Strange, S. (1991). *Big Business and the State1*. Department of Political Science at the European University Institute in Florence. doi:10.1177/03058298910200021501

Sullivan, A., & Sheffrin, M. S. (2003). *Economics: Principles in Action.* Pearson Prentice Hall.

UNDP. (2015). *Human Development Report 2014*. Retrieved from: http://hdr.undp.org/en/content/human-development-report-2014?utm_source=EN&utm_medium=GSR&utm_content=US_UNDP_PaidSearch_Brand_English&utm_campaign=CENTRAL&c_src=CENTRAL&c_src2=GSR&gclid=Cj0KCQjw4eaJBhDMARIsANhrQACsgGtmnDMR7DRy6qsvCHvDt8pnOHJFySJDMEWK_zaIGK-bW9LrUosQaAto-EALw_wcB

United Nations. (1960). *General Assembly, 15th session: 885th plenary meeting, Tuesday, 4 October 1960, New York*. Retrieved from: https://digitallibrary.un.org/record/740836?ln=en

United Nations. (2021). *About Us*. Retrieved from: https://www.un.org/en/about-us

United Nations Department of Economic and Social Affairs. (2013). *Report on World Social Situation 2013: Inequality Matters*. Retrieved from: https://www.un.org/en/development/desa/publications/world-social-situation-2013.html

Weiss, F. C. (1997). The United Nations and Changing World Politics. Westview Press.

Wordometers. (2021). *World Population by Country*. Retrieved from: https://www.worldometers.info/world-population/population-by-country/

World Maps Online. (2021). *Classic Colors World Political Map Wall Mural - Peel & Stick Removable Wallpaper*. Retrieved from: http://www.worldmapsonline.com/classic_colors_world_political_map_wall_mural.htm

The States as the Main Actors of the World Politics

KEY TERMS AND DEFINITIONS

Alliances: Coalitions that form when two or more states combine their military capabilities and promise to coordinate their policies to increase mutual security.

Armed Aggression: Combat between the military forces of two or more states or groups.

Balance of Power: The theory that peace and stability are most likely to be maintained when military power is distributed to prevent a single superpower hegemon or bloc from controlling the world.

Bilateral Agreements: Exchange between two states, such as arms control agreements, negotiated cooperatively to set ceilings on military force levels.

Collective Security: A security regime agreed to by the great powers that set rules for keeping peace, guided by the principle that an act of aggression by any state will be met by a collective response from the rest.

Democratic Peace: The theory that although democratic states sometimes wage wars against non-democratic states, they do not fight one another.

Ethnic Groups: People whose identity is primarily defined by their sense of sharing a common ancestral nationality, language, cultural heritage, and kinship.

Ethnic Nationalism: Devotion to a cultural, ethnic or linguistic community.

Failed States: Countries whose governments have so mismanaged policy that their citizens in rebellion, threaten revolution to divide the country into separate independent states.

Great Powers: The most powerful countries, military, and economically in the global system.

Group of 77 (G-77): The coalition of Third World countries that sponsored the 1963 Joint Declaration of Developing Countries calling for reform to allow greater equality in North-South trade.

Long Peace: Long-lasting periods of peace between any of the military strongest great powers.

Nation: A collectively whose people see themselves as members of the same group because they share the same ethnicity, culture, or language.

National Interest: The goals that states pursue to maximize what they perceive to be selfishly best for their country.

National Security: A country's psychological freedom from fears that the state will be unable to resist threats to its survival and national values emanating from abroad or at home.

Neutrality: The legal doctrine that provides rights for the state to remain nonaligned with adversaries waging war against each other.

Non-Aligned Movement (NAM): A group of more than one hundred newly independent mostly less developed states that joined together as a group of neutrals to avoid entanglement with the superpowers competing alliances in the Cold War and to advance the Global South primary interest in economic cooperation and growth.

Non-Aligned States: Countries that do not form alliances with opposed great-powers and practice neutrality on issues that divide great powers.

Small Powers: Countries with limited political military economic capabilities and influence.

Third World: A Cold War term to describe the less-developed countries of Africa, Asia, The Caribbean and Latin America.

Chapter 2
Global Security and Political Problems of the 21st Century

Nika Chitadze
International Black Sea University, Georgia

ABSTRACT

The purpose of this research is consideration and analysis of the main security and political problems of the world, which are connected with the arms race and arms control; problems of the proliferation the weapons of mass destruction; protection of human rights; failed states; the nuclear potential of the different countries; existence of the nuclear-weapons-free zones in the different regions of the world; problems related to the reduction of the conventional arms, arms supplies, arms trade, problems of organized crime, international terrorism in the framework of which there are discussed the different types of terrorism, the methods that are used by terrorist organizations for the implementation their activities, problems related to the enlargement of democracy and violation of the fundamental principles of human rights, etc.

INTRODUCTION – THE NATURE AND TYPOLOGY OF THE GLOBAL PROBLEMS

At the beginning of the XXI century, one of the most important topics for world politics represents the resolution of global problems. The term itself "global problems" in the scientific and political literature has appeared in the 60th of the XX Century. For the first time the discussions about global problems of humanity have started within the non-governmental organization "Club of Rome" (Club of Rome, 2021).

This influential organization unites the representatives of the political, finance, the cultural, scientific elite of the World.

During the discussions at the events of the "Club of Rome," it was pointed out that global problems represent such issues, for the resolving of which is dependent on the future and in some cases the existence of whole humanity.

From its turn, those topics, there were and still are the different positions and points of views among the scientists and political and civil activists – to concretely for which problems should be given global, regional or local importance. The part of the world intellectual elite in the modern world considering that

DOI: 10.4018/978-1-7998-9586-2.ch002

there are in general three or four problems of the global level, but according to others, that the number of global problems prevails a few dozen.

In the current stage is accepted the dividing of the problems with global character into three groups.

To the first group, there are those global problems, which exist as a result of a confrontation between society and nature, particularly: ecological, energetic, problems of the exhausting of natural resources, food problems.

To the second group, there are belonged the contradictions – which are the result of the society development: demographic issues, the problems related to the fighting against epidemic and pandemic spreading, the socio-economic problems of the countries from the "third world" – related to misery, unemployment, the existence of internal and international conflicts, problems of the weapons of mass destruction, international terrorism, international organized crime, illegal trade of drugs, etc.

To the third group are the problems which have emerged on the base of the first and second group of problems, particularly, it is a problem of searching for alternative sources of energy, exploitation of the cosmic space, consumption of the resources of the world ocean, etc.

The whole list of the demographic problems is not limited only to the above-mentioned categories. Their number can be even more. From one side, together with the global ecological problems very often are pointed out the problem of global climate change. On the other side, it is being discussed about the dilemma related to the exhausting the global energy and natural resources, because the issue of energy problems is connected with the fact, that in the modern period the humanity consumes such energy, as oil, coal, natural gas, which represent the Exhaustive resources.

All global problems are interconnected with each other: very often one problem emerges from the other one etc. For example, the demographic problem, which is reflected in the rapid growth of the world population, strengthens the problem of the population`s food supply. Within the last fifty years, within the scientific circles and world political elite, at the first line, the different actual global problems were presented. "Club of Rome", one of the main tasks considered was increasing the public awareness of the international society toward the global problems.

Based on the above-mentioned facts, it should be pointed out, that one of the most important global problems are related to the security and political problems

MAIN ASPECTS RELATED TO DEFENSE AND SECURITY ISSUES

Security Problems are classical in the Westphalian political system of the world. The state from the moment of the emergence cared for maintaining sovereignty, i. e. the national security was understood initially first of all as prevention of external aggression. In modern conditions, this concept also includes the questions connected with the danger of internal destabilization. Due to the growth of interdependence of the world the problem receives further development within regional security and international security.

All three terms characterize state and Interstate relations. They are more often used in realistic and neo-realistic concepts.

At the same time as a starting point served situation according to which the power of the state necessary for the realization of national interests and influence on the international situation was defined first of all based on its military force, or, by analogy with computer terminology, on a base of "hard power", but not based on culture, the strength of the authority on the world scene and some type of "soft power".

As a result, the problem of military strengths was central in international relations from both, practical and the research point of view.

The situation changed at the end of the XX century. Experts in the field of economy and finance and also environment were some of the first who have paid attention to nonmilitary threats to security. The first group has started talking about an economic component of safety, the second that ecological disruption by pollution poses a huge threat to mankind on the national and global level. However, a controversy was caused by the fact, in which cases the ecological problems are caused by human activity and when the objective reasons. Also, how this problem can be resolved.

A Revolution in the field of new technologies became another factor that has influenced reconsideration of security concerns. As a result, non-state actors were capable of playing a huge role in the field of safety which they didn't have earlier. This has brought to the understanding that it isn't enough to build concepts of security, to be based on the fact that the threat can proceed only from other states or groups of states. With special evidence, it was shown by events of September 11, 2001, when the planes skyjacked by terrorists crashed into buildings of the World Trade Center in New York and the Pentagon in Washington, explosions of the train in Madrid and London, etc. Even though the defeat targets have remained the same, as well as were assumed by strategic doctrines of the leading states: the large cities, the central ministries, departments - the source of threats was extremely amorphous and uncertain.

At the end of the XX century many researchers including adhering to realistic views, for whom the emphasis on military aspects and interstate relations is characterized, have begun to speak about such factors in ensuring national security as education, development of the modern technologies, growth of economic power, drug trafficking, AIDS, etc. Within neo-realism one of the most important works within such direction represented research of B. Buzan "People, states, fear" which appeared in 1983, and where the limitations of the traditional understanding of security are shown (Buzan, 1983). Except for this author, the so-called "broad" definition of security concerns including not only military aspects, is connected with the names of several European researchers, in particular U. Beck (Beck, 1998). Along with the work of B. Buzan, in the same year in the journal "International Security," the article of the American researcher R. Ullman was published. The author wrote that the emphasis on military security problems leads to the fact that other threats are overlooked, including the threats, which are coming from the inside of the state (Ullman, 1983).

In the modern period, the discussions concerning a ratio of military-political factors, from one hand, and social and economic, ecological, information, and technological from another continue. Supporters of a "wide" approach to security problems point to the amplifying role of economic and other factors. Their opponent's object: in this case a security problem "is blurring" by many other aspects which exist in international relations and world politics.

One more important question in the theoretical plan - a ratio of regional, international and global security. The last term sometimes is used to emphasize that a security concern has not only internal but interstate measurement. There also is no unambiguous decision.

In this regard, the problems about the ways of the harmonization of the national interests of the states – the content of the concept of regional, international and global security cannot be limited only by taking into account the national interests of the states. The coincidence of the national interests of the group of the states causes different types of regional and international unions, which are guided by the determined views (concepts) about the ways of the harmonization and protecting their group interests as a balance between each other, also in the relations with the third countries.

In connection with it, all those questions of International and regional security, are closely connected with the problems of International Organizations. Under modern conditions among the institutes, which are engaged in providing international security, first of all, should be pointed out about the United Nations. The significant role in security issues also plays several regional institutions, especially in Europe, where they have rather accurate functions and responsibilities. First of all, OSCE, NATO. The main problems which are intensively discussed now, reforming of the UN, that to make its activity in the field of providing security and peacemaking, peacekeeping, and peacebuilding more effective and also to fix the place and role of NATO in the European structures related to defense and security, taking into account the fact that this organization has been formed in the years of the Cold War with definite purposes and tasks.

THE ARMS RACE AND ARMS CONTROL

The problem of the arms race and disarmament especially existed in the years of the Cold War. During this period expenses of the states on arms have reached a record point (the peak is considered 1985). Releasing the important funds on defense is going on today at quite a high level even though after the ending of the cold war, the comparative share to GDP of the leading European countries has been decreased.

The military power of the states is defined not only by the facts, how much the state spends on the military needs but also by the fact, what type of weapon is possessed by the concrete country. The Character and quantity of arms were the decisive factors in the world arena during the cold war period. The sides were constantly increasing military power, which led to the arms race.

It is Interesting!

According to several estimates, the share of the budget, which was going for the military needs during the cold war, was for the USA from about 5 to 10%, and for the USSR was reaching 20%.

In 1999, the Military expenditures in the whole world were about 745 billion USD (Kegley, Wittkopf, 2011).

Within the first decade of the XXI Century, World military spending was about 1 trillion every year (Joshua S. Goldstein. Jon C. Pevehouse. 2007).

About the second decade of the XXI Century, World military expenditure is estimated to have been $1 822 billion in 2018, accounting for 2.1 percent of world gross domestic product (GDP) or $239 per person. Total expenditure grew for the second consecutive year and exceeded $1.8 trillion for the first time; it was 2.6 percent higher than in 2017 and 5.4 percent higher than in 2009 (SIPRI, 2019).

With the advent of nuclear weapons in 1945 and its use by the United States of America against Japan in August 1945, the new – nuclear era in the history of humanity has come. Nuclear weapon becomes one of the leading, if not the first factors in international relations. There are two types of nuclear weapons: Atomic (A-bomb), which is based on nuclear fission, and thermonuclear, or hydrogen (H-bomb), with thermonuclear synthesis as a base. The first type is simpler and less expensive, but at the same time has less potential.

Nuclear weapons are the *Weapon of Mass Destruction* (WMD), with the purpose of the large-scale defeat of the enemy and do not act selectively – only against Armed Forces, but cover the civil population too. In comparison with the other types of weapons, it possesses the most destructive power and long-term consequences. Due to those factors, special attention is paid to nuclear weapons.

Figure 1.
Source: https://www.icanw.org/ican_releases_2019_nuclear_weapons_spending_research

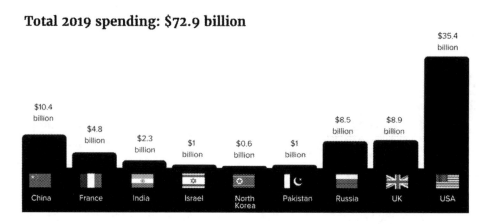

"Official" members of the "nuclear club", or the states, which own nuclear weapons (Nuclear Weapon State, NWS), are all five permanent members of the UN Security Council – United Kingdom, China, USA, France, Russian Federation. Concretely to those states, which till January 1, 1967, produced and exploded nuclear weapons or other nuclear devices, according to article IX.3 of them which was signed in 1968, the status of the nuclear power was fixed (Aleksidze, 2012). The biggest nuclear potential is the USA and Russian Federation.

Besides the above-mentioned countries, several other states also possess nuclear weapons. India, for example, in 1974 carried out nuclear tests and in 1998 the nuclear testaments were implemented by India and Pakistan. It is assumed that India possesses a few dozen warheads, and Pakistan more than ten (Lebedeva, 2007).

In 1980th, the nuclear test was carried out by the South African Republic, which later abolished its nuclear program and destroyed not only devices but also capacities for its production. According to many specialists' estimations, nuclear weapons are owned by Israel. North Korea in 1994 agreed to freeze its nuclear program instead of humanitarian aid, but there are no absolute dates on this issue. There are some concerns about the nuclear program of Iran, at the same time, during the last years this country has been under special attention from the international community (Goldstein, 2011).

Some countries, by having resources - necessary for the acquisition of nuclear weapons, have voluntarily refused this purpose. After the collapse of the USSR in 1991, several former Soviet republics became owners of nuclear weapons. However, all of them later voluntarily refused it. The only post-soviet republic which possesses nuclear weapons is Russian Federation.

A new report has found nuclear-armed states spent a record $73 billion on nuclear weapons in 2019, a $7.1 billion increase from 2018 expenditures (ICAN, 2019).

Chemical and bacteriological weapons as well as nuclear, being weapons of mass destruction, also causes concern in the modern world. A chemical weapon is calculated for the use of the different toxic substances during the fighting against enemy Binary weapon assumes to use the low-toxic reagents which at interaction with each other during military operations form a highly poisoning toxic agent. The bacteriological weapon is based on the using bacteria, viruses, and products of their life activity.

In comparison with nuclear technologies, the production of chemical and bacteriological weapons is rather cheap and accessible. Due to it, these types of weapons have received the name of "weapon for the poor". At the same time, it has a considerable striking effect. The special alarm concerning the possibility of their use is determined by the existence of the politically unstable countries, with the authoritative forms of government and also the terrorist organizations.

In the history of military operations, chemical weapons were seldom used. For the first time, it has occurred during World War I in April of 1915, when yperite has been used (US National Library of Medicine, 2021). Concern about the possibility of the use of chemical weapons has caused the result, that in 1925 during the conducting of multilateral negotiations by 37 states, in Geneva in 1925, "Protocol for the Prohibition of the Use in War of Asphyxiating, Poisonous or Other Gases, and of Bacteriological Methods of Warfare" was signed. As to 2019, to this protocol, there are joined more than 100 states (UN, 2021). During World War 2, Germany and the USSR possessed chemical weapons but did not use them. In 1980th this type of weapon was used by Iraq against Iran (Fassihi, 2002).

The protocol of 1925 provided non-use of chemical weapons but didn't raise the questions of its production and storage. The problem is that it is quite difficult to detect because a similar process is possible also for peace purposes. However, there were many cases, when this or another country was accused of the production of chemical weapons. The USA had similar suspicions, for example, in the 1990s concerning Libya, Sudan, or Iraq.

In January 1993 after several years of negotiations in Paris, the Chemical Weapons Convention (CWC) related to the prohibition of production, accumulation, and use of chemical weapons and their destruction was signed. At the beginning of 2019, the participants of this convention were more than 145 states, but among those states, there are not Libya and North Korea (CWC, 2020). The convention provides the ban on the production of chemical weapons and also strict sanctions concerning those countries, who violate these agreements, including the states, which are not members of the Convention.

Bacteriological weapons have several similar characteristics with chemical ones related to production, use, and control. However, in comparison to chemical weapons, this type of weapon was not used in droves, except in the case of it being used by Japan in several villages of China during World War 2. In 1972 the Convention on the prohibition of the development, production, and accumulation of stocks of bacteriological (biological) and weapon and their destruction was signed (Aleksidze, 2012). The official name of the convention is the Biological and Toxin Weapons Convention, BWC. To this convention, as of the beginning of 2019 more than 140 states have been signed (UNODA, 2021).

The weapons of mass destruction demand delivery systems. Their existence defines the military-political position of the state, not to a lesser extent, than the fact of possession of nuclear weapons and technologies of its production. Delivery systems are subdivided into two types: Strategic and Tactical.

The strategic delivery systems aiming to strike the opponent in its territory assume the overcoming of enough huge distances (for example, between Russia and the USA). The main among them are ballistic missiles. They differ by the distance which they can overcome, the accuracy of hit, and what type of charge they own. Ballistic missiles can be stationary or to be on mobile platforms. In the latter case, they become less vulnerable to the opponent.

The greatest range of action has intercontinental ballistic missiles (ICBMs). This type of weapon is mostly owned by the USA and Russian Federation. Significantly a smaller number of ICBMs have other nuclear countries. Medium-range missiles are in the arms of France, Great Britain, and China. Russia and the USA have them also. Their range of action is from 1000 to 5500 km. Deployment on the European continent of medium-range missiles by the last two countries was limited by the agreement, which was

Table 1. World nuclear forces

It is Important!
World Nuclear Forces, 2018 Deployed Warheads Other Total Country Warheads Warheads Inventory
USA 1 750 4 435 6 185 Russia 1 600 4 900 6 500 UK 120 80 200 France 280 20 300 China – 290 290 India – 130–140 130–140 Pakistan – 150–160 150–160 Israel – 80–90 80–90 North Korea – (20–30) (20–30) Total 3 750 10 115 13 865

Source: SIPRI (2019)

signed in 1987. Rockets of smaller range, short-range ballistic missiles with the range from 500 to 1000 km have, as a rule, the bigger accuracy of hit (NATO, 2006). They can be used also for the delivery of usual warheads as it was, in particular, during the war in the Persian Gulf.

As delivery systems also, cruise missiles can be used. They represent the small pilotless shells equipped with their propulsion system. Cruise missiles possess the high-precision system of targeting for the defeat of the purpose and can bear as a nuclear charge (such cruise missiles possess Russia and the USA) also usual.

Except for rockets, the strategic delivery systems of weapons, first of all nuclear, are represented by the bombers and submarines (equipped with rockets and nuclear torpedoes too). These three types can make a so-called strategic triad, therefore at negotiations on disarmament and arms limitation, they usually are considered complex.

Tactical nuclear weapons have the purpose to be used concretely in the theatre of conducting military operations. It is delivered using nuclear warheads for tactical missiles, artillery charges, fighting surface ships, multi-purpose submarines, aviation, nuclear min.

When developing nuclear strategy originally American experts were based on the fact that the opponent had to be destroyed. In this regard, among the military and political analysts the term "mutually assured destruction, MAD" has appeared. It has characterized a hypothetical situation, which can be emerged as a result of nuclear opposition and assumed extermination of the opponent in case of nuclear attack.

Later, when it became clear the senseless idea of "mutual destruction", and it especially was shown during the Cuban Crisis, American military strategy became oriented on the principle of adequate retaliation. Its meaning is that the reply must correspond to the damage caused.

During the years of the Cold War, the doctrine of nuclear deterrence, which was also logically connected with the developed nuclear strategies, has appeared. This was based on the fact that the possibility of using nuclear weapons keeps the enemy from aggression.

This doctrine is based on a principle, that participants of the international relations try to behave exclusively rationally to avoid destructive consequences of the use of nuclear weapons and according to it, the state has to be sure that such threat, not just of a word, the nuclear weapon can be used in case of aggression.

This doctrine had also opponents. Their argumentation was based on the fact that first, the logic itself of the gradual development of the conflict can lead to the nuclear collision as a result. Secondly, random error is also possible, which will be interpreted by the opposite side as a nuclear attack that will cause a fatal result.

There were developments in the field of nuclear defense. Thus, the US was involved in the development of the Strategic Defense Initiative, SDI, so-called "Star Wars. It gained development in the 1980- the years when the US President was R. Reagan and the essence consisted in attempts of the creation of a defensive shield for the USA in case of the nuclear threat. However, on the practical level, this idea hasn't been realized.

One of the most important issues in a military-political sphere is the problem of the non-proliferation of weapons of mass destruction, first of all, nuclear and also means of its delivery. Usually, there is distinguished so-called horizontal proliferation of weapons, when it is increasing the number of the countries which have this type of weapons and vertical proliferation, which means capacity building. However, when it is mentioned about the non-proliferation of nuclear weapons, first of all, experts mean concretely the horizontal option.

There are various approaches to a non-proliferation problem. The authors, who are focused on the realistic tradition of research in the field of international relations, in general, have a calmer attitude to this issue, by not seeing any special danger in proliferation, as they believe that the states will behave rationally and not apply for the use of nuclear weapons. In this regard, it is important the point of view of K. Waltz, who recognizes that the expansion of "nuclear club" will even help to preserve the peace, as here the deterrence factor restraining the military confrontation of the parties plays the decisive role (Waltz, 1979).

The opposite position is taken by researchers and analysts, who share different theoretical views. The problem of non-proliferation is extremely important for them as in the proliferation of weapons of mass destruction they see one of the main threats to international peace. At the same time, they not without justification emphasize that the states, and first of all their leaders, cannot always behave rationally. Besides, in modern conditions, there is a danger of falling into the hands of terrorist groups, weapons of mass destruction, and also the danger of technogenic accidents connected with the storage of this weapon, a human mistake, etc.

The states having nuclear weapons are also quite sensitive to the questions of its non-proliferation. They try to limit a circle of the participants, who have nuclear technologies and appropriate technologies. However, this problem also has another part. The matter is that technologies that can be used for the production of a nuclear weapon, are closely intertwined with the technologies which are used in the field of nuclear energy, which is produced for peaceful purposes.

The existence of delivery systems of nuclear weapons is more difficult to control than possession of nuclear weapons. At the beginning of the XXI Century, the intermediate and shorter-range missiles were developed by Iraq, Iran, Israel, Saudi Arabia, India, Pakistan, North Korea, and also, perhaps, Brazil and Argentina.

During the Cold War, the country saved up a huge arsenal of weapons. As a result, questions of disarmament and arms control remain and today represent one of the key points in world politics. Arms control is understood as efforts of two or more countries on the regulation of the relations in this area.

The Cuban (Caribbean) crisis of 1962, when the threat of the nuclear missile conflict became obvious, was a significant impulse for negotiating disarmament. Soon after the crisis, in August 1963, in Moscow representatives of the USSR, USA, and Great Britain signed the agreement on the prohibition of nuclear weapons testaments in the atmosphere, space, and underwater. This agreement became known as the Limited Test Ban Treaty. It has termless character and has been open for signing (more than 100 states have joined it subsequently) (Aleksidze, 2004).

In 1968 was signed an agreement on the non-proliferation of nuclear weapons, which became known as the Non-Proliferation Treaty, NPT. Those agreements received the continuation on March 5, 1970. Later, 187 countries joined the treaty (Aleksidze, 2004).

Distinguish two categories of member countries of the agreement about non-proliferation of nuclear weapons - those who were possessing this type of weapon for January 1, 1967 (Great Britain, China, USSR, USA, France) and those who had not those types of weapons. The non-nuclear countries took the responsibility not to purchase nuclear weapons and completely followed normative provisions of the International Atomic Energy Agency, IAEA which is engaged in monitoring the development and distribution of nuclear technologies. In 1993 North Korea left the IAEA. However, as it was noted, later this country has held negotiations and has undertaken the responsibility to freeze the nuclear programs in exchange for rendering economic aid. In September 2002 North Korea declared again about its aspiration to continue the nuclear program (Goldstein, 2011).

In general, it is being discussed the issue of nuclear non-proliferation. Under this regime it can be understood the totality of international agreements and organizations with participation as nuclear, also non-nuclear states, and also internal legislation of the member states, the purpose of which is the prevention the gaining of nuclear status by those countries, which had not it before 1967.

Several important arrangements in the field of disarmament and arms control were reached in the 1970s. Among them, first of all, it is necessary to mention the agreement on the limitation of the systems of anti-missile defense – Antiballistic Missile Treaty, ABM, which was signed in 1972. It limits the capabilities of each of the parties - USA and USSR/Russia - to use anti-missile defense for reflection of nuclear attack. At the beginning of the 2000th, the USA started to plan the creation of the national missile defense system and the withdrawal from the Missile Defense Treaty of 1972 (UN, 2005). The argument was based that the agreement of the thirty-year prescription doesn't reply to modern realities. In the XXI century, according to official American statements, the threat proceeded not from Russia, but from the terrorist organizations that was especially accurately shown by the events of September 11, 2001. Besides, it was supposed, though wasn't advertised, that the new system would become an incentive to develop new technologies in the USA.

The American side, together with European partners, have tried several times to assure the Russian side that this type of defense shield was not directed against Russia. In 2001, during several meetings of the president of Russia and the USA, agreements on carrying out consultations in the field of national missile defense were reached. Nevertheless, positions remained various. And at the end of 2001, the USA officially notified Russia about withdrawal from the treaty of 1972, and in June 2002 left it (Chitadze, 2019). The consequent years, after the military aggression of Russia against Georgia and Ukraine, proved the necessity of the creation of a new system of anti-missile defense by the American side in Europe, which should be positively reflected on European Security.

Other important documents during the period of the cold war in the field of arms limitation were Strategic Arms Limitations Treaties, Salt-1, and Salt – 2, which were signed accordingly in 1972 and 1979 which have gained further development in the Treaties of 1990th and the first decade of the 21-st century. Particularly, Strategic Arms Limitation Treaties – START 1 and START 2, which were signed in 1991 and 2010. According to the agreement, the USA and Russia had to limit their strategic arsenals by approximately 30%. It is interesting to point out that the START2 agreement was signed in 1993, which was ratified by Russia 8 years later. It offered the reduction of the remaining armaments for 50%, in accordance to which the USA would possess 3000 nuclear warheads, USA- 3500. However, it was not ratified by the American side. Thus, a new agreement was signed in 2010 and later ratified by the legislative bodies of both countries (Chitadze, 2019).

One of the most important USA-USSR agreements in the field of defense and security was The Intermediate-Range Nuclear Forces Treaty (INF Treaty, formally Treaty Between the United States of America and the Union of Soviet Socialist Republics on the Elimination of Their Intermediate-Range and Shorter-Range Missiles is an Arms Control Treaty between the United States and the Soviet Union (and its successor state, the Russian Federation). U.S. President Ronald Reagan and Soviet General Secretary Mikhail Gorbachev signed the treaty on 8 December 1987. The United States Senate approved the treaty on 27 May 1988, and Reagan and Gorbachev changed the ratified documents on 1 June 1988 (Chitadze, 2019).

The INF Treaty eliminated all of the two nations' land-based ballistic missiles, cruise missiles, and missile launchers with ranges of 500–1,000 kilometers (310–620 mi) (short medium-range) and 1,000–5,500 km (620–3,420 mi) (intermediate-range). The treaty did not apply to air- or sea-launched missiles (Garthoff, 1994).

During the "Cold War" in the 1970s and 1980s, there was going on a dangerous race in Europe between the USSR and the US for nuclear weapon production. The Soviet Union began to deploy SS-20s and SS-18s medium and small range intercontinental ballistic missiles in Hungary, Czechoslovakia, and the German Democratic Republic, which threatened the Western European countries of NATO. The Alliance responded by deploying ballistic missiles and ground-based cruise missiles of medium-range "Pershing 2" in Britain, Italy, and Germany (Kramer, 2019).

Around 250 small and mid-range missile complexes were installed in Europe by both sides and in case of the starting the nuclear war, the whole European continent could be destroyed. By the way, small-range ballistic missiles were located by both sides accordingly on the territories of Turkey and Georgia (Resonance, 2019).

"According to the agreement, the Soviet side removed from the operative duty and destroyed the following type of missiles, including mobile: P-10 (SS-20), P-12 (SS-4 for NATO classification), P-14 (SS-5), cruise missiles PK-55, short-range missiles - OTP-22 (SS-12), OTP-23 (SS-23). On the other hand, the American side has destroyed the average interstellar rockets "Persing 2", ground-based winged missiles "VGM" (Tomahawk), and a small rangeland bases "Pershing-1a" (they were deployed in Western Europe, mainly in Italy, Great Britain and Germany) and "Pursing-2b" missiles (Resonance, 2019).

Within the 36 months after signing the treaty, both sides have destroyed 898 already deployed and 700 non-deployed medium interstellar missiles, and a small range of 1096 missiles. 56% of these missiles were coming on the part of the Soviet Union. Thus, withdrawal from the treaty by both sides can transfer Europe to a more dangerous region.

By May 1991, the nations had eliminated 2,692 missiles, followed by 10 years of on-site verification inspections (SIPRI, 2007).

President Donald Trump announced on 20 October 2018 that the US was withdrawing from the treaty, accusing Russia of non-compliance with the conditions of the agreement. The U.S. formally suspended the treaty on 1 February 2019, and Russia did so the following day in response to the U.S. withdrawal.

An important element in the field of control over the nuclear threats during the "Cold War" period represented the creation of *a Nuclear-weapon-free-zone, NWFZ*.

A **nuclear-weapons-free zone** (**NWFZ**) is defined by the United Nations as an agreement which a group of states has freely established by treaty or convention that bans the use, development, or deployment of nuclear weapons in a given area, that has mechanisms of verification and control to enforce its obligations, and that is recognized as such by the General Assembly of the United Nations. NWFZs have a similar purpose but are distinct from, the Treaty on the Non-Proliferation of Nuclear Weapons to which most countries including five nuclear weapons states are a party. Another term, nuclear-free zone, often means an area that has banned both nuclear power and nuclear weapons, and sometimes nuclear waste and nuclear propulsion, and usually does not mean an UN-acknowledged international treaty (Arms Control Association, 2021).

Today five zones are covering continental or subcontinental groups of countries (including their territorial waters and airspace), and three govern Antarctica, the seabed, and outer space which are not part of any state. The Antarctic, seabed, and space zones preceded all but one of the zones on national territories. Most of the Earth's oceans above the seabed are not covered by NWFZs since freedom of the seas restricts restrictions in international waters. The UN has also recognized one additional country, Mongolia, as having nuclear-weapon-free status.

NWFZs do not cover international waters (where there is freedom of the seas) or the transit of nuclear missiles through space (as opposed to the deployment of nuclear weapons in space).

As of 15 July 2009 when the African NWFZ came into force, the six land zones cover 56% of the Earth's land area of 149 million square kilometers and 60% of the 195 states on Earth, up from 34% and 30% of the previous year; however, only 39% of the world's population lives in NWFZs, while the nine nuclear weapons states have 28% of the world's land area and 46% of the world population (Arms Control Association, 2021).

The Antarctic, Latin American, and South Pacific zones are defined by lines of latitude and longitude, except for the northwestern boundary of the South Pacific zone which follows the limit of Australian territorial waters, and these three zones form a contiguous area, though treaty provisions do not apply to international waters within that area. In contrast, the Southeast Asian zone is defined as the territories of its members including their Exclusive Economic Zones, and the African zone is also defined as the countries and territories considered part of Africa by the OAU (now the African Union) which include islands close to Africa and Madagascar. An AU member, Mauritius, claims the British Indian Ocean Territory where Diego Garcia is currently a US military base.

In general, as a result of the diplomatic efforts and activities of the different International Organizations, there have been agreements about four non-nuclear zones – in Antarctica, Latino America, South Pacific, Latino America, South-East Asia, and Africa. Particularly:

The **Antarctic Treaty** and related agreements, collectively known as the **Antarctic Treaty System** (**ATS**), regulate international relations concerning Antarctica, Earth's only continent without a native human population. For the treaty system, Antarctica is defined as all of the land and ice shelves south of 60°S latitude. The treaty entered into force in 1961 and currently has 54 parties. The treaty sets aside Antarctica as a scientific preserve, establishes freedom of scientific investigation, and bans military activity on the continent. The treaty was the first arms control agreement established during the Cold War. Since September 2004, the Antarctic Treaty Secretariat headquarters has been located in Buenos Aires, Argentina.

The main treaty was opened for signature on December 1, 1959, and officially entered into force on June 23, 1961. The original signatories were the 12 countries active in Antarctica during the International Geophysical Year (IGY) of 1957–58. The twelve countries that had significant interests in Antarctica at the time were: Argentina, Australia, Belgium, Chile, France, Japan, New Zealand, Norway, South Africa, the Soviet Union, the United Kingdom, and the United States. These countries had established over 55 Antarctic stations for the IGY. The treaty was a diplomatic expression of the operational and scientific cooperation that had been achieved "on the ice" (Secretariat of the Antarctic Treaty, 1959).

The **Treaty of Tlatelolco, which** is the conventional name given to the **Treaty for the Prohibition of Nuclear Weapons in Latin America and the Caribbean**. It is embodied in the **OPANAL** (Spanish: *Organismo para la Proscripción de las Armas Nucleares en la América Latina y el Caribe*, English: the Agency for the Prohibition of Nuclear Weapons in Latin America and the Caribbean). Signed in 1967, it was the first treaty of its kind covering a populated area of the world, but now around 40% of the world's population live in a Nuclear-weapon-free zone (Arms Control Association, 2021).

The second agreement concerned the Southern part of the Pacific Ocean – Rarotonga Treaty – The **Treaty of Rarotonga** is the common name for the **South Pacific Nuclear Free Zone Treaty**, which formalizes a Nuclear-Weapon-Free Zone in the South Pacific. The treaty bans the use, testing, and possession of nuclear weapons within the borders of the zone.

It was signed by the South Pacific nations of Australia, the Cook Islands, Fiji, Kiribati, Nauru, New Zealand, Niue, Papua New Guinea, the Solomon Islands, Tonga, Tuvalu, Vanuatu, and Western Samoa on the island of Rarotonga (where the capital of the Cook Islands is located) on 6 August 1985, came into force on 11 December 1986 with the 8th ratification and has since been ratified by all of those states (UN, 2005).

The **Southeast Asian Nuclear-Weapon-Free Zone Treaty (SEANWFZ)** or the **Bangkok Treaty** of 1995, is a nuclear weapons moratorium treaty between 10 Southeast Asian member-states under the auspices of the ASEAN: Brunei, Cambodia, Indonesia, Laos, Malaysia, Myanmar, Philippines, Singapore, Thailand, and Vietnam. It was opened for signature at the treaty conference in Bangkok, Thailand, on 15 December 1995 and it entered into force on March 28, 1997, and obliges its members not to develop, manufacture, or otherwise acquire, possess, or have control over nuclear weapons.

The Zone is the area comprising the territories of the states and their respective continental shelves and Exclusive Economic Zones (EEZ); "Territory" means the land territory, internal waters, territorial sea, archipelagic waters, the seabed and the subsoil thereof, and the airspace above them.

The treaty includes a protocol under which the five nuclear-weapon states recognized by the Treaty on the Non-Proliferation of Nuclear Weapons (NPT), namely China, the United States, France, Russia and the United Kingdom (who are also the five permanent members of the United Nations Security Council) undertake to respect the Treaty and do not contribute to a violation of it by State parties. None of the nuclear-weapon states have signed this protocol (UNODA, 2021).

Concerning Africa, The **African Nuclear Weapon Free Zone Treaty**, also known as the **Treaty of Pelindaba** (named after South Africa's main Nuclear Research Centre, run by The South African Nuclear Energy Corporation and was the location where South Africa's atomic bombs of the 1970s were developed, constructed and subsequently stored) established a Nuclear-Weapon-Free Zone in Africa. The treaty was signed in 1996 and came into effect with the 28th ratification on 15 July 2009. The Treaty prohibits the research, development, manufacture, stockpiling, acquisition, testing, possession, control, or stationing of nuclear explosive devices in the territory of parties to the Treaty and the dumping of radioactive wastes in the African zone by Treaty parties. The Treaty also prohibits any attack against nuclear installations in the zone by Treaty parties and requires them to maintain the highest standards of physical protection of nuclear material, facilities, and equipment, which are to be used exclusively for peaceful purposes. The Treaty requires all parties to apply full-scope International Atomic Energy

Agency safeguards to all their peaceful nuclear activities. A mechanism to verify compliance, including the establishment of the African Commission on Nuclear Energy, has been established by the Treaty. Its office will be in South Africa. The Treaty affirms the right of each party to decide for itself whether to allow visits by foreign ships and aircraft to its ports and airfields, explicitly upholds the freedom of navigation on the high seas, and does not affect rights to passage through territorial waters guaranteed by international law (Arms Control Association, 2021).

There are also other regions, in which it is possible the appearance of the non-nuclear zones, particularly the Korean peninsula, Central Asia, etc.

In 1996, by the initiative of the developing countries, by 129 votes against three (Great Britain, USA, France) and by 38 states who abstained, the resolution of UN 51/45 about declaration the southern hemisphere as a zone – free from the nuclear weapon (UN Security Council Report, 2000).

At the same time, the Conference on Disarmament (CD) began its substantive negotiations on a comprehensive nuclear-test-ban treaty in January 1994 within the framework of an Ad Hoc Committee established for that purpose. Although the CD had long been involved with the issue of a test ban, only in 1982 did it establish a subsidiary body on the item. Disagreement over a mandate for that body blocked tangible progress for years.

After more than two years of intensive negotiations, the Chairman of the Ad Hoc Committee, Ambassador Jaap Ramaker of the Netherlands, presented a final draft treaty to the CD in June 1996. An overwhelming majority of Member States of the CD expressed their readiness to support the draft treaty. India, for its part, stated that it could not go along with a consensus on the draft text and its transmittal to the United Nations General Assembly. The main reasons for such a decision, as India pointed out, were related to its strong misgivings about the provision for the entry-into-force of the treaty, which is considered unprecedented in multilateral practice and running contrary to customary international law, and the failure of the treaty to include a commitment by the nuclear-weapon States to eliminate nuclear weapons within a time-bound framework.

As a result, Australia, on 22 August 1996, requested that the General Assembly resume the consideration of agenda item 65, entitled "Comprehensive Nuclear-Test-Ban Treaty" as provided for in resolution 50/65 of 12 December 1995. For that purpose, it also submitted the draft CTBT, identical to that negotiated in the CD, for adoption by the General Assembly. On 10 September, the General Assembly by resolution (A/RES/50/245) adopted the Comprehensive Nuclear-Test-Ban Treaty and requested the Secretary-General of the United Nations, in his capacity as Depositary of the Treaty, to open it for signature at the earliest possible date. The Treaty was opened for signature in September 1996 (UN, 2005).

On 29 May 2009, the Secretary-General launched "Securing our Common Future: An Agenda for Disarmament." The agenda highlights the norm against testing nuclear weapons of a measure that serves both disarmament and non-proliferation objectives (Chitadze, 2016). In that context, the Secretary-General appealed to all remaining States whose ratifications are required for the Comprehensive Nuclear-Test-Ban Treaty (CTBT) to enter into force to commit to signing the Treaty at an early date if they have not already done so and to accelerate the completion of their ratification processes.

Conventional arms also are at the center of attention of politicians and the public. They are widely used in modern conflicts. For example, they were used by Iraq in the Persian Gulf in the early 1990th of the XX Century for the occupation of Kuwait and missile attacks against Israel. Conventional arms were used in the former Yugoslavia and other regional conflicts during the 1990th and the beginning of the 2000th years.

Based on the above-mentioned problems, The original **Treaty on Conventional Armed Forces in Europe** (**CFE**) was negotiated and concluded during the last years of the Cold War, particularly in 1990, and established comprehensive limits on key categories of conventional military equipment in Europe (from the Atlantic to the Urals) and mandated the destruction of excess weaponry. The treaty proposed equal limits for the two "groups of states-parties", the North Atlantic Treaty Organization (NATO) and the Warsaw Pact (UN, 2005). In 2007, Russia "suspended" its participation in the treaty, and on 10 March 2015, citing NATO's *de facto* breach of the Treaty, Russia formally announced it was "completely" halting its participation in it as of the next day (Chitadze, 2016).

CFE and Troop Ceilings

The CFE Treaty set equal ceilings for each bloc (NATO and the Warsaw Treaty Organization), from the Atlantic to the Urals, on key armaments essential for conducting surprise attacks and initiating large-scale offensive operations. Collectively, the treaty participants agreed that neither side could have more than:

· 20,000 tanks;
· 20,000 artillery pieces;
· 30,000 armored combat vehicles (ACVs);
· 6,800 combat aircraft; and
· 2,000 attack helicopters.

To further limit the readiness of armed forces, the treaty set equal ceilings on equipment that could be deployed with active units. Other ground equipment had to be placed in designated permanent storage sites. The limits for equipment each side could have inactive units were:

· 16,500 tanks;
· 17,000 artillery pieces; and
· 27,300 armored combat vehicles (ACVs);

The treaty further limited the proportion of armaments that could be held by any one country in Europe to about one-third of the total for all countries in Europe - the "sufficiency" rule.

All sea-based Naval forces were excluded from CFE Treaty accountability (US Department of State, 1992).

A serious Political problem, especially because of the existence of the internal conflicts, is the use of antipersonnel mines which are installed to establish control over the concrete territory. Minefields in Afghanistan, Bosnia, Angola, and other conflicts have resulted in a large number of victims among civilians, and their number continues to increase also after the end of the conflict. So, according to J. According to Goldstein's data, about 25 thousand people annually are victims of those mines, a third of which are children (Goldstein, 2011). In the late nineties, several non-governmental organizations supported the idea of the prohibition of antipersonnel mines, for which the organizer of this campaign J. Williams was granted the Nobel prize award in 1997 (The Nobel Peace Prize, 1997). Within the same year, more than one hundred states have signed the agreement on the prohibition of the use of antipersonnel mines.

On the way of arms control and disarmament, there are many barriers. First of all, it is necessary to consider that violations of arrangements by any country are possible. For this reason, much attention is

Figure 2. Heads of state sign treaty on conventional armed forces in Europe
Source: https://www.osce.org/node/58665

paid to various procedures of inspection, for example, on-site inspection. Often agreements provide such an opportunity. However, not all questions are possible to be resolved: the states delay the carrying out the inspections, object on the personal list of the inspection team, as it was, in particular, with inspections of the UN in Iraq in the 1990s. Besides, if the countries for which those procedures are organized - actually refuse to cooperate, then similar inspections are ineffective. Other ways of observation consist of the use of national technical means, NTM – spacecraft, seismic stations, etc. But with their help not all objects can be detected: for example, it is difficult to define how many charges are carried by one rocket.

The serious problem represents the constant improvement of armament with the introduction of new scientific and technological developments. As a result, negotiations and the agreements concluded on their results practically are always late about the real situation. For example, the emergence of rockets with the divided warheads – multiple independently targetable reentry vehicles, MIRVs, has sharply increased the possibility of striking blows on different objects at the same quantity of rockets.

There Exist many internal political barriers on the way of disarmament. Several analysts, in particular, recognize that disarmament doesn't lead to tension reduction at all. From these positions, they act at the political institutes of their states, and it influences the adoption of political decisions. The representatives of the military-industrial complex, military-industrial complex who are economically interested in an increase in military orders. And still in general, despite difficulties, the process of disarmament and arms control has a forward focus.

ARMS SUPPLIES AND ARMS TRADE

The volume of the arms trade in the modern world is very impressive. So, by official American estimations, if their cumulative sale in the world was estimated in 1964 with an approximate sum of 4 billion US dollars, then in 1987 it has already consisted of 82,4 billion. And now, despite the end of the Cold

Figure 3. Arms sales in 2017
Source: SIPRI, 2018

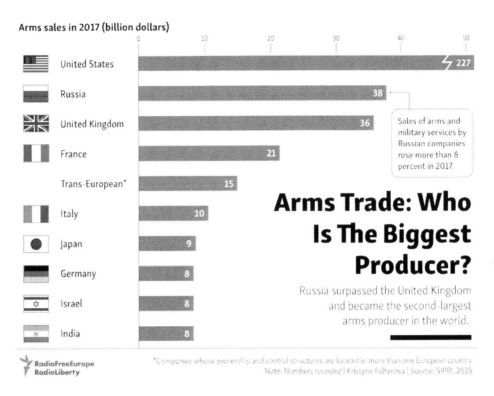

War, traffic in arms hasn't stopped. Its main deliveries go to developing countries. Exactly there the most unstable political and economic situation is often observed.

The total amount from deliveries of arms to the period from 1991 to 1998, according to R. Grimmett, has exceeded 250 billion dollars, and three-quarters of those arms were acquired by developing countries. The leading role of the arms market is taken by the Middle East. As it is mentioned by R. Wittkopf and Ch. W. Kegley, if in 1967 deliveries of arms to the Middle East made 11% of a total number of deliveries, then during the period from 1991 to 1994 this figure had increased to 77%. However, with the appearance of the new "hot places," the situation has changed. In 2019, the volume of arms sales in the world reached US$ 361 Billion (SIPRI, 2019).

From 1995 till 1998, according to R. Grimmett, the world structure of armament had the following structure: USA – 28,3%; main western European states – 31,2%; Russia – 18,4%; China – 3,6%; all other states – 18,5% (Lebedeva, 2007).

About the second decade of the 21-st century, the volume of international transfers of major arms grew by 7.8 percent between 2009–13 and 2014–18, reaching its highest level since the end of the cold war. This growth is a continuation of the steady upward trend that began in the early 2000s. The five largest suppliers in 2014–18 were the United States, Russia, France, Germany, and China, and they accounted for 75 percent of the total global volume of exports (SIPRI, 2019).

The USA and the USSR were the main exporters of arms during the Cold War. Their share was coming from 50 to 75% of all armament markets. After the end of the Cold War, the USA began to dominate obviously. So, by official American sources, they possessed more than 40% of the export of arms. Even though through the late nineties - the beginning of the 2000th years Russia became more active in deliveries of arms the USA continues to be the leader in this market. As for 2018, the share of the USA was about 60% of the total arms sales in the world (SIPRI, 2019).

Income from the sale of weapons goes on the further development of the military-industrial complex. However, the motive of these deliveries is not only economic but also political goals abroad can serve as a fact, that was especially characterized for the eras of the Cold War. For example, by estimations, which gives M. Klara, the USA in the 1980s supplied with weapons 59 countries, the USSR - 42. As for 2020, the USA was exporting military weapons to 60 countries of the world (Statista, 2020).

Deliveries and traffic with arms cause vigilance as it is obvious that, along with positive economic and political reasons for weapon suppliers, it is characterized also by a set of negative moments. So, increasing the number of weapons in a concrete region can lead to escalation of the conflict, especially in case of instability of the mode which receives it. By estimates of several researchers, in particular to M. Klara, L. Lyumpa, A. Hashim (And. Hashim), and some others, exists a direct correlation between traffic in arms and armed conflicts. It is in many respects caused by the fact that the purchase of weapons by one of the conflicting parties involves similar actions by the other side in the conflict. And sometimes weapons are purchased by both parties from the same state supplier.

It is necessary to mention also trade in the production of dual purposes, i.e., that which can be used by both sides in the conflict for peace and military purposes (for example, several chemical compounds).

Recently the increasing alarm is caused by uncontrollable arms supplies to the states which conflict with the neighbors and also the insurgent movements and various terrorist organizations. By different estimations, more than 10% of all trade is coming on illegal operations in the framework of the arms market.

PART 2. PROBLEMS OF ORGANIZED CRIME

At the end of the XX century, security concern goes more and more beyond interstate cooperation and disarmament issues. With the development of the globalization process, organized crime sharply became a more actual topic. According to several estimates, since the 1980s the number of criminal acts, having been carried out within organized crime, has increased by 5% annually (Chitadze, 2020).

Members of organized criminal groups gain huge income. By estimates, which were presented in 1999 the total amount of so-called dirty money in the world was from 500 to 1500 billion dollars per year, which was equal to 5% of the world GDP during this period (Lebedeva, 2007). In 2009 it was estimated to generate $870 billion - an amount equal to 1.5 percent of global GDP for this period (UNODC, 2010). As of 2016, Transnational Crime was a $1.6 trillion to $2.2 trillion Annual "Business" (Global Financial Integrity, 2017).

One of the fields of activity of organized crime is caused by the fact that several goods are not taxed. The illegal transfer of these goods from one country to another brings considerable revenue to the members of the groups of organized crime. Other areas of organized crime are connected with illegal arms supplies, illegal activity in the conflict zones, including recruitment of mercenaries, etc. Processes of privatization in the countries of Central and Eastern Europe have also drawn attention.

This problem already holds a specific place because of the scale but has received an additional boost in connection with globalization and the openness of borders generated by it. Considerable streams of drugs go via post-soviet space from Asia, the USA faces the same problem from Colombia and some other

Figure 4. Typical activities of organized crime
Source: https://www.crimemuseum.org/crime-library/organized-crime/typical-activities-of-organized-crime/

countries in Latin America. In general drug trafficking within the second decade of the XXI Century, by different estimates, has increased tens of times, giving more than 500% of profit (Chitadze, 2016).

Fighting against drug distribution has become one of the global problems of the contemporary period. At the same time, their main production is arranged in countries with badly developed economies and a set of internal conflicts, with the military and quasi-military regime. The chief suppliers of opium poppy on the market today are Afghanistan and Burma today. By the estimates given by J. Goldstein, the production of opium from 1998 to 1999 has increased in Afghanistan twice and has made three-quarters of the world's production. More and more synthetic drugs which don't demand vegetable raw materials are widely adopted (Goldstein, 2011).

APPROACHES FOR DETERMINATIONS OF ORGANIZED CRIME

Approaches to the determination of organized criminality are an extremely complex phenomenon, given which there are many different approaches to the fixation of its basic meaningful elements in the normative and doctrinal determinations.

Historically, in the USA, the first attempts to determine the concept of "organized criminality", as they indicated by D.L.Herbertand, X.Tritt, were made in the 1950-1960th years, "when the committees of Congress began to reveal the proofs of the existence of secret criminal society or cartel by the name of „the Mafia" or "the goat of nostra" (FBA, 2021).

During the Oyster Bay conferences, in 1965 and 1966, which were dedicated to the issue of the fighting with an organized crime the following definition was formulated: "Organized crime is the product of a self-perpetuating criminal conspiracy to wring exorbitant profits from our society by any means - fair and foul, legal and illegal. Despite personnel changes, the conspiratorial entity continues" (Oyster Bay Conferences, 1965/66).

The US Law of 1968 Omnibus Crime Control and Safe Streets Act gives the other definition:

"Organized crime' means the unlawful activities of the members of a highly organized, disciplined association engaged in supplying illegal goods and services, including but not limited to gambling, prostitution, loan sharking, narcotics, labor racketeering, and other unlawful activities of members of such organizations" (National Institute of Justice, 2011).

In general, organized crime — this is the form of criminality, which is characterized by the steady criminal activity, achieved by the criminal organizations (organized groups and criminal associations), which have the hierarchical structure, material, and financial base, and connections with the state structures, based on the corruption mechanisms. The first main reasons for the development of organized crime can belong to the following processes: the inosculation of leaders and active participants in the organized criminal formations with the representatives of the legislative, executive, and judicial branches of the authority, business, commerce, mass media, and culture; the incapacity of the state to protect several basic constitutional rights and interests of citizens and society; the cultivation of the ideas of market and private property without the proper legal guarantee; the unjustified delay of the adoption of the basic laws, which ensure normal passage to the market, first of all, related to the fighting with organized crime and corruption; Impoverishment and the legal nihilism of the majority of the population of the country; the lobbying of the interests of separate groups by responsible officials for mercenary purposes. The conditions of criminality - this is the totality of the phenomena, which by themselves cannot create the criminality, but they serve as the circumstances, which facilitate its appearance and existence.

ORGANIZED CRIMINAL FORMATIONS

The organized criminal formations differ from each other, they have both geographical and national specific character and they are distinguished according to the degree of globalization: they can act within the limits of one city, country and even exceed the borders of individual states, becoming transnational. It should be mentioned, that under the common name "organized criminal formations" in the literature are united two types of collective criminal subjects:

- Criminal organization—all forms of the associations of the persons, directly directed toward to the committing of a crime, conducting the criminal activity: the organized criminal groups, gangs, Illegal Armed Formations and so forth;
- Criminal community (association)—forming, which unites the first type of organizations, which organizes, coordinates, and guides their activity, ensures the interests of the criminal association; also it can fulfill the functions of "criminal trade union", ensuring the social protection of its members. As a rule, such associations are not directly involved in criminal activities, turning these functions to smaller organizations, which are under their influence.

PREVALENCE OF THE ORGANIZED CRIMINALITY

The scale of the activity of organized criminality is extremely high and damage from it is enormous. In the report of national reconnaissance Intelligence Council of USA "Global trend of development of humanity until 2015" is mentioned: "Accessible to us data show, that they early incomes from the organized criminal activity comprise: 100-300 billion of dollars from the trade-in narcotics; 10-12 billion of dollars from the flood of toxic and other dangerous withdrawals; 9 billion of dollars from the embezzlements of vehicles in the USA and Europe; 7 billion of dollars from the displacement through the boundaries of illegal migrants; about Billions of dollars from the violation of rights to intellectual property by the illegal copying of video films, computer programs, and other goods" (Intelligence Council of USA, 2015). Harm from corruption is approximately 500 billion dollars, which is about 1% of the world GNP. This damage is the consequence of retarding economic growth, a decrease in foreign investments, and a reduction in profits. For example, according to the data of the European Bank for Reconstruction and the Developments, firms, which carry out business in Russia, spend from 4 to 8 percent of their annual earnings on bribes (Dolgovaya, 2005).

TRANSNATIONAL CRIMINAL ORGANIZATIONS

The organized criminality sufficiently frequently established international contacts; however, during the centuries these connections were irregular and usually short-term till the middle of XX. Their bloom began only after the internationalization of the economy and the propagation of trade by the illegal goods (narcotics, weapons, etc.) that led to significant income growth from the trans-border criminal operations.

Following basic transnational criminal organizations can be listed:

- Italian Mafia, which is the union of several criminal organizations: "Ndrangheta" from Calabria. In the article "Move over, Cosa Nostra", published by *The Guardian*, on 8 June 2006, within this period this group included approximately 100 families, totaling between 4,000 and 5,000 members in Reggio Calabria. Other estimates mention 6,000-7,000 men; worldwide there might be some 10,000 members. In the FBI report under the name "Italian Organized Crime", there are the following dates about other criminal groups in Italy: "*Kamorra*" from Naples Consists of 111 families and totals more than 6 700 members. "*Nuova* Sacra Corona Unita" from Puglia consists of about 50 clans with approximately 2,000 members and finally the Mafia "Cosa *Nostra*" of *Sicily* 25,000 members total, with 250,000 affiliates worldwide. There are more than 3,000 members and affiliates in the U.S., scattered mostly throughout the major cities in the Northeast, the Midwest, California, and the South. Their largest presence centers around New York, southern New Jersey, and Philadelphia (Chitadze, 2015).

The basic source of income for the Italian Mafia is the trade of narcotics; however, it is occupied by other illegal operations too. Particularly: Smuggling of weapons, alcohol, tobacco, taking hostages, and so forth. In the '90s of the XX century, the influence of the Italian Mafia because of the matched efforts of the law-enforcement agencies of Italy was somewhat reduced, however, it continues to preserve one of the leading places in the list of the criminal organizations in the World.

Figure 5. Al Capone and his mafia members
Source: https://www.pinterest.com/drigol/italian-mafia/

In the article of the journal LE MONDE: "Atlas der Globalisierung - Die Welt von morgen": Kriminalitätohne Grenzen is pointed out about number and activities of the Chinese, Japanese, Columbian and Nigerian criminal groups, particularly:

- Chinese "triads" mostly operate in the territory of Hong Kong and Taiwan; there are about 50 different organizations, which relate to this group, whose number counts according to the different estimations from 160 to 300 thousand people. Despite the rigid hierarchical structure, the components of triads, which directly accomplish the criminal operations, are part of the flexible net system, capable of changing their structure, being adjusted slightly under the ambient conditions. Triads are occupied by extortion, drug trafficking, prostitution, gambling, are the important suppliers of heroin in the USA.
- Japanese"*yakudza*" also known as **gokudō,** are members of transnational organized crime syndicates originating in Japan. The Japanese police, and media by request of the police, call them **bōryokudan** ("violent groups"), while the yakuza call themselves "**ninkyōdantai**" ("chivalrous organizations"). It also consists of several self-contained organizations, from which the largest is Yamaguchi -Gumi, which counts more than 26000 members, then comes Inagava-kay (8600 members) and Sumiesi-kay (more than 7000 members). These organizations conduct fights between themselves; however, it is also implemented as a matched activity for the involvement in corruption of the government officials and criminalization of the economy. Besides, the interference in the internal economic processes (by yakudza is controlled the film industry, entertainment industry, professional sport, lottery, the financial sphere, and the sphere of the real estate),

Figure 6. Neo-paramilitary group "Los Urabeños" has taken the majority stake in Colombia's drug trafficking business
Source: https://colombiareports.com/how-the-urabenos-beat-los-rastrojos/

it achieves the smuggling of sea products and stealing the motor transport, narcotics (including methamphetamine) and weapon (Le Monde, 2007).

- Colombian drug cartels are occupied practically exclusively by the drug trafficking business, being basic suppliers on the World Market of cocaine (to 80%). The two most known cartels existed in the cities of Medellín and Cali. The Medellin cartel was founded by the families of Pablo Eskobar and Ochao, and Cali`s - by the families of Santacruz and Rodriguez Orikhuella. The leading level of the cartels is built according to a rigid hierarchical diagram, and various cells are separated at the lower level, each of which is occupied by the specific form of criminal activity and it is not informed about the other operations of the cartel. At the end of the 1990's years, the operation of the Colombian police and law-enforcement agencies of other countries led to a significant decrease in the volume of the operations which were carried out by cartels; however, the liberated places have been taken by the smaller criminal organizations.

- Nigerian criminal organizations appeared at the beginning of the 1980's years as a result of the crisis of the economy of Nigeria, connected with a drop in the prices of oil. These criminal organizations specialize in drug trafficking, and also in the knavish operations including the use of new financial instruments and extortion. As a rule, the majority of operations are small, but this is compensated by their large number (Chitadze, 2016).

Criminal Organizations in Europe

In the report of the European Union about the situation in the sphere of organized criminality in 2004 (European Union Organized Crime Report 2004) and the subsequent years ((European Organized Crime Threat Assessment (OCTA) 2007)) are listed the basic international criminal organizations, which act in the territory of Europe. To this number most dangerous of them are referred Albanian (occupying by trade in narcotics and by people, and also being approached the establishment of control of the criminal markets, including by forced methods) and Russian (economic crimes, extortion, illegal immigration).

Furthermore, it is indicated the action of other ethnic groups: Turkish (trade in narcotics and weapon, money laundering, racket), Nigerian (trade in narcotics and by people, swindle), Moroccan (trade by narcotics and smuggling), Colombian (trade-in cocaine), Chinese (illegal migration), Vietnamese (smuggling, illegal migration, other criminal services).

According to the article, presented by the journal LE MONDE: "Atlas der Globalisierung - Die Welt von morgen": Kriminalitätohne Grenzen, one of the most dangerous criminal activities in Europe, fulfills Russian Mafia. It includes about 160 000 members and 12 000 groups.

Based on the research, prepared by Chris Matthews under the name: "The biggest organized crime groups in the world" on the first place was located the Russian Organized Criminal Organization "Solntsevskaya Bratva" (Solntsevo is the district in Moscow), the revenue of which was estimated $8,5 billion in 2014 (Matthews, 2014).

THE INTERNATIONAL EXPERIENCE OF FIGHTING AGAINST THE TRANSNATIONAL ORGANIZED CRIME

Understanding with the International community of the seriousness of threats, which emanate from narcotics trafficking, Money laundering, corruption, and other crimes began only in the XX century as the result of the understanding of the increasing of the scales of these challenges, which emerge beyond the framework of individual state and in connection with their negative influence on sociopolitical, economic spheres, National Security and person. The leading role in the legal regulation of the efforts of states and the International Community for the combating transnational organized crime belongs to the UN; in the recent decades, when it became obvious, that the ability of states to separately resist the spreading of international criminality does not correspond to the scales of crimes, under the aegis of the UN many universal documents on the resistance to Transnational Organized Crime (TOC) were adopted, and the work of the world community in this direction acquire sever more system nature. The first international experience of the fighting with the criminal challenges of the international nature was connected with the signing of intergovernmental agreements, including against the slave trade (Viennese convention of 1815), the propagation of pornography (Parisian convention of 1910), forgery of monetary terms (convention of 1929).

At the beginning of the XX century, the international nature of several crimes did not make it possible to carry them exclusively to the scope of one state, and an appropriate situation was emerging, when international collaboration in this field became necessary. In 1927, in Warsaw took place the first International Conference on the unification of the criminal legislation, where the number of crimes of international nature was related to piracy, slave trade, narcotics trafficking, trade of pornography materials, the forgery of monetary terms. A number of the legal norms in the sphere of combating international criminality, which was reflected in the international-legal documents were worked out, particularly: The international convention about the fight with the acts of nuclear terrorism (2005), Convention of the UN against the transnational organized criminality (2000), convention of the United Nations against corruption (2003), convention of the UN in the fight against the illegal circulation of narcotic drugs and psychotropic substances (1988), *Convention* of the *Council* of *Europe* about *washing up*, *revealing*, *withdrawal* and *confiscation* of *incomes* from *criminal activity* (1990) (Chitadze, 2016).

In the framework of the Council of Europe were adopted 9 conventions in the field of a fight with the international criminality. Among them –the European convention about compensation to the victims of crimes (1998), protocol to the convention about cyber terrorism (2003), and others. Furthermore, as a rule, many international agreements contain positions about the collaboration in the fight with one or another form of international criminality.

About the European Union, it is important to discuss the EU's 'solidarity clause', Article 222 of the Lisbon Treaty (TFEU), which means the mutual assistance and common fighting of the EU member states against terrorism, including the terrorism prevention by EU member states (Parkes, 2015).

The UN since the beginning of its existence was involved with the problems of warning and suppression of the crimes: under the aegis of the UN adopted several international conventions, the General Assembly of UN regularly considers resolutions with the recommendations regarding the combating of separate types of crimes of international nature. Since 1955, every five years the congress of the UN for warning of criminality and rotation with the lawbreakers is organized. XI Congress of the UN on warning of criminality and criminal justice took place in Bangkok in April 2005. Based on the results, the Bangkok declaration "Synergies and Responses:

Strategic Alliances in Crime Prevention and Criminal Justice" was adopted (UN Congress on Crime Prevention, 2005).

At the beginning of the 1990s, within the framework of the UN was undertaken several major steps, directed toward an increase the effectiveness of the coordination of member states in the fight with the TOC. In 1990, the General Assembly of the UN approved the model standard agreements (in the spheres of criminal justice, extradition, etc.) and the program of the UN in the field of warning of criminality and criminal justice was adopted in 1991. The basic purpose of the program—organize assistance to member nations in a matter of warning crimes and criminal justice.

A Ministerial conference on the fight with transnational organized criminality took place in Naples in November 1994. In the work conference were the representatives of 142 countries; Based on the results, the General Assembly of the UN adopted the Global Action Plan against Transnational organized crime. In 1997, at the sixth session of the commission for warning of crime and criminal justice, a working group was created on the performance of the Naples Declaration (Chitadze, 2016). The working over the determination of the organized crime became a central question in the framework of the working group: as the compromise version was designated the key elements, which characterize the phenomenon of the organized crime—the presence of organization, a constant nature, division of labor inside the group, violence, and deference, the hierarchy, tendency toward obtaining the profit, influence on the society, media means and political structures. In 1998, for developing the text of convention-related the resistance to transnational crime, the commission created the intergovernmental committee of ad hoc, which was opened for the participation of all states, including the states, which were not the members of the UN (Chitadze, 2016). In the operation of the committee, important role-played individual states, which focused attention on the problems, which they directly encountered as most closely. In particular, Austria and Italy raised a question about the illegal migration, Argentina—to trade by children, Japan and Canada offered the inclusion in the text of the future convention a new tool on the fight with the illegal production and trade of firearms.

The signing in 2000 of the convention of the United Nations against transnational organized crime and also three protocols to it became a watershed in the fight with a transnational crime within the framework of the UN. The convention of the UN against transnational organized crime adapts concerning the crimes of transnational nature, perfected with the participation of the organized criminal group.

Organized crime is understood through characteristics of the organized criminal groups, the seriousness of the violence accomplished by them (UN, 2000). The convention defines the organized criminal group as "the structurally designed group in the composition of three or more persons, that exists during the specific period and acting in concord to commit of one or several serious crime or crimes, acknowledged as the same following the present convention, to obtain, directly or indirectly, financial or another material benefit" (article.2).

So, fighting against organized crime is a much more complex problem, than fighting with the different types of individual criminality. Effective fighting with organized crime is impossible without the measures, directed toward the sanitation of society as a whole, called to give the legal alternative" to the social services" of the criminal society: the state must ensure to population the availability for the necessary goods and services, employment of the population, normal functioning of ideological and educational institutes, availability of the lawful means of the resolution the social conflicts.

Which of the enumerated measures will prove to be more effective—it depends on the model, on which is built the activity of the organized criminality under the specific social conditions.

The specialist on organized crime issues, Jay Albanese, in his report "The Use of Models in the Study of Organized Crime" presented at the 2003 conference of the European Consortium for Political Research (ECPR), (Marburg, Germany, 19 September 2003), separated three types of these models:

- Traditional model of the large-scale criminal conspiracy, controlled by a small group of leaders. In that case, the most effective will be the measures, directed toward the neutralization of the leaders via their arrest or by another method, which will lead to the collapse of the Arrangement.
- Model of the local organized ethnic groups. In this case, since no centralized organization exists, the neutralization of leaders will not give the desired result, since they will be replaced by new ones. In this case, the basic directions of the fight can become the measures of financial, social, and other control, and also other steps, directed toward the removal of financial flows from the shady ("black") sector of the economy.
- The model of enterprise, according to which organized crime is characterized by the informal decentralized structure and appears under the specified social and economic conditions, when the legal mechanisms of the guarantee of the needs of the population are ineffective. To deal with this type it is necessary to, first of all, eliminate the reasons, which created the results of crime, stabilizing and after making transparent social and economic processes.

Furthermore, the law-enforcement agencies could reach significant results in the fighting with organized crime, were necessary the special normative-legal and material and technical base of their activity, allowing taking the necessary measures for the prevention of commission of a crime as the organized groups, to disorganize their activity, not to allow members of the organized criminal associations the fallen in the field of the sight of the organs of the protection of law to leave from the criminal responsibility.

PART 3. PROBLEMS OF TERRORISM IN THE MODERN WORLD

The general point of view on terrorism as a rare and relatively remote threat was challenged by the tragic events of September 11, 2001. The terrible incidents, visited on the World Trade Center, the Pentagon, and the crash victims in Pennsylvania forced the International Community to confront a grim new reality:

Terrorist Organizations had an appropriate resource for executing catastrophic attacks almost in each region of the World, even without an arsenal of sophisticated weapons.

9/11 became the first turning point for the whole world to focus on the issues of national as well international security.

As for the most recent developments show terrorism is assumed to be the most significant "enemy" of the 21-st century.

The US State Department listed 44 terrorist organizations in 2008 (Joshua S. Goldstein. Jon C. Pevehouse. 2010).

Today`s Boko Haram, Tamil Tigers, Al-Qaeda, Hezbollah play very significant roles even in deciding the scope of the foreign policy of leading superpowers.

It is necessary to add, about the existence of states on the World political map, that fund and supports different terrorist groups and illegal armed formations in the different regions of the World. United Nations, by Resolution 39/159 "Inadmissibility of the policy of State terrorism and any actions by States aimed at undermining the socio-political system in other sovereign States", condemns any actions of state-terrorism (UN, 1984).

In general, Terrorism represents one of the most serious problems which not only has become aggravated at the end of the 20th and the beginning of the 21st century but also has appeared, in fact, among the main threats to security especially in its new forms, which have several new directions. It is caused, first of all, by the level of technological development and possibilities to impact the world, therefore large-scale terrorist attacks can be conducted by small groups of people or even by one person. Secondly, in the modern world, the potential range of terrorist organizations (national and cultural symbols, government buildings, places of big congestion of people, etc.) and also types of weapons which can be used are various. The third, modern terrorists, or, by U. Lakyyuer's definition, terrorists of an era of postmodernism, together with other criminal structures, look for allies in public institutions that lead to corruption. The considerable sums are spent on bribery of officials and also the intelligence agencies, which are designed to prevent illegal activity.

Terrorism by itself is not a new phenomenon. It has been known since Ancient Greece and Ancient Rome. In the 19th century, terrorism is connected with anarchical and also some nationalist organizations. By estimates of a number of authors, for example, R. Kidder, terrorism becomes a really international problem since 1960th years. In the 1970-1980th years, the world faced a surge in terrorist operations in Europe (Lebedeva, 2007).

Despite the centuries-old existence of a terrorism phenomenon, in the theoretical plan, this problem is quite difficult to give in to definition. The matter is that the same actions are considered at the same time by the different parties as terrorism from one side and freedom fighting from the other side. For this reason, the attempts to define terrorism within the UN (and various criteria were offered by the USA, Great Britain, other countries) in general have not been crowned with success.

However, the fact that, first, it is politically motivated violent acts or their threat is undoubtedly important in terrorism definition, secondly, they are directed against civilians, and not just directly concerning the power. Concerning them, terrorist attacks for the purpose of realization of these or those political goals are conducted. Terrorism is substantially focused on the achievement of a psychological effect. Therefore, terrorists are, as a rule, interested in that their acts have found as much as possible extended coverage in mass media. The psychological effect has multiple focuses, including drawing attention to the organization and its purposes, demonstration of opportunities, population or its certain groups, etc.

Figure 7. Most brutal terrorist attacks. New York, USA, September 11, 2001.
Source: https://zeenews.india.com/world/9/11-attacks-new-york-marks-19th-anniversary-of-the-dreadful-terror-attack-2308932.html

Another important feature when determining terrorism is in what is carried out by the non-state actors. Therefore, any armed actions, let unjustified and illegal (for example, capture by Iraq of Kuwait in the early nineties), don't get under terrorism definitions. At the same time, the state can give anyway, support to the terrorist organizations (including financial or in the form of granting the territory for the terrorist bases, refusal of delivering terrorists to the other states, approvals of their actions, etc.). In this regard, there has appeared a term "State Terrorism". The USA, for example, calls even the states which, according to them, get to this category. However, the state in such cases practically never takes the responsibility for recognition in the assistance to terrorism, and to prove the state`s participation in the terrorist act is quite difficult.

The period of the beginning of the 21st century when the political structure of the world is in process of cardinal changes represents itself the convenient base for terrorism development. In modern conditions of globalization terrorists often act out of national borders. Therefore, it is being discussed about international terrorism, or transnational terrorism (that is more precise), which means the use of the territory or involvement of the citizens in terrorist actions in more than one country. And despite the fact that it is quite difficult to outline borders between internal and international terrorism as practically all rather large terrorist organizations have links outside national borders, nevertheless feature of the first is the fact that the challenge is thrown down not to the concrete state or group of the states, but to the model of development of the world. Construction of transnational terrorist structures to the network principle and finding the structural division in many states of the world strongly complicates the fight against this threat.

Terrorist actions not seldom are included in an arsenal of the means of fighting by various ethnic, religious, and other groups, factually being as a form of the political struggle and favorable business. Among the different terrorist group's good connections, including military and commercial are established.

Some interact with the criminal structures, in particular, which are connected with the drug business. Incomes from the sale of drugs quite often go for the financing of acts of terrorism.

Special concern is caused by a possibility of access by the terrorist organizations to the modern types of weapons and weapons of mass destruction. So, in March 1995, the Japanese religious sect Aum Shinrikyo has conducted a terrorist attack with the use of nervously-paralytic gas in the subway, as a result of which 10 people have been killed and about 5000 have been forced to ask for medical care. However, one of the biggest shocks was the actions of terrorists on September 11, 2001, when in the USA several planes, which were captured by terrorists have were directed to the buildings of the World Trade Center in New York and also to the Pentagon. One more plane has been crashed with passengers, but in this case, at least it was succeeded to avoid the much bigger victims. Results of the attack were comparable with the destructive effect during the missile attack.

This act of terrorism has raised many security issues differently. Earlier many estimates have been brought out of the calculation of the time of flight of ballistic missiles. Now, this indicator is insufficient. The second moment is connected with the definition of a source of aggression. If before in strategic concepts one or several states' main threats were coming from the foreign states, then today to the list of potential attackers are included, terrorist groups. The international terrorists, on the one hand, have bases, as a rule, in various countries, with another directly and openly isn't connected with government institutions (if to exclude a possibility of creation of corruption). As it was noted, terrorists act as independent actors on the world scene. At last, threats are extremely certain: poisoning of water of the megalopolis or the gas attack in the subway can be done by civilian airliners, tomorrow. At last, the last major moment connected with lessons on September 11, 2001, and the governments of certain countries (even such powerful as the USA) and the international community, in general, were not ready to adequate answer. The tragic events in Beslan on September 1, 2004, connected with the taking of hostages in the school, have once again confirmed new parameters of modern threats: surprise (several minutes are absent even for preparation for reflection of the attacks), plurality, and heterogeneity of terrorist acts and also means of attack.

The USA, for example, even the states which, according to them, get to this category. However, the state in such cases practically never takes the responsibility for recognition in the assistance to terrorism, and to prove the state`s participation in the terrorist act is quite difficult.

Another sphere of modern terrorism - cyberterrorism, including information attacks, is connected with a possibility of destabilization of work of computer systems and networks. Considering the role of such systems in the modern world, it is easy to imagine the consequences of the large failures in the work of transport, communication, power supply, governmental and municipal structures - so-called "Critical infrastructures" of modern society. The feature of cyberterrorism consists of the fact, that the threat of information terrorism is realized quite well by different international actors. According to one of the computer magazines (information Week), viruses and actions of hackers cost large businesses about 1,6 billion dollars in 2000. In May of the same year in Paris, the meeting at the level of computer terrorism experts has taken place. They expressed opinions that the threat of cyberterrorism constitutes a danger for mankind, comparable with nuclear, chemical, bacteriological wars.

All this also induces the states to coordinate the actions in the fight against terrorism. A number of the international agreements, in particular, on providing safe civil avia transportation and shipping (The international conventions 1963, 1970, 1988) have been adopted, for example; on the fight against taking of hostages (1979); to the protection of nuclear materials (1980). International terrorism has received condemnation in 1985 on the UN General Assembly where the relevant Resolution has been adopted

(Aleksidze, 2005). The question of the fight against terrorism was repeatedly raised at meetings of heads of states, including members of the G7.

Special divisions in the fight against terrorism exist in many countries. Coordination of national efforts is on the practical level carried out by different international institutes, including Interpol.

INTERNATIONAL TERRORISM - THE MAIN THREAT TO THE WORLD COMMUNITY IN THE XXI CENTURY

Definition and History of the Notion and its Evolution through the Centuries

Terrorism is not a new phenomenon and even though it has been used since the beginning of recorded history, it can be relatively hard to make the exact definition of terrorism. Terrorism has been analyzed variously as both a tactic and strategy; a crime and a "liberation movement". Obviously, it very much depends on whose position and opinion are being represented. Terrorism has often been an effective tactic for the weaker side in a conflict. As an asymmetric form of the conflict, it confers coercive power with many of the advantages of military force at a fraction of the cost. Taking into account the secretive nature and small size of the terrorist organizations, those groups do not offer to their opponents any clear structure. Because of this, preemption is being considered to be so significant. In some cases, terrorism has been a means to continue a conflict without the adversary realizing the nature of the threat, mistaking terrorism for criminal activity. Taking into consideration these characteristics, terrorism has become increasingly common among those pursuing extreme purposes throughout our planet. But despite its popularity, terrorism can be a nebulous concept.

Even in the case of the U.S. Government, state agencies responsible for different functions in the ongoing combating terrorism activities, use various definitions. With regard to the free online dictionary, terrorism is defined as "The unlawful use or threatened use of force or violence by a person or an organized group against people or property with the intention of intimidating or coercing societies or governments, often for ideological or political reasons" (Free Dictionary, 2020).

Discussing this definition, there are three main factors - violence, fear, and intimidation and each element produces terror in its victims. The FBI uses this type of determination: "Terrorism is the unlawful use of force and violence against persons or property to intimidate or coerce a government, the civilian population, or any segment thereof, in furtherance of political or social objectives." (Atrain Education, 2021) The U.S. Department of State, based on the title 22 of the U.S. Code, Section 2656f(d), defines "terrorism" to be "premeditated politically-motivated violence perpetrated against non-combatant targets by sub-national groups or clandestine agents, usually intended to influence an audience" (US Department of State, 2007).

Besides the determination from the United States Government`s side, there are greater variations in what features of terrorism are emphasized in definitions. One of the leading experts on Combating Terrorism issues, Prof. Alex Schmid presented his definition, which is the following: "An anxiety-inspiring method of repeated violent action, employed by (semi-) clandestine individual, group or state actors, for idiosyncratic, criminal or political reasons, whereby - in contrast to assassination - the direct targets of violence are not the main targets"(NATO, 2007) The most recently distributed academic determination is added to the above-mentioned definition. Two more sentences include 77 words in general; containing such verbose concepts as "message generators" and "violence" based communication processes."

Less specific and considerably less verbose, the British Government definition of 1974 is"…the use of violence for political ends, and includes any use of violence for the purpose of putting the public, or any section of the public, in fear (Cambridge, 2017)."

In general, Terrorism is a criminal act that influences an audience beyond the immediate victim. The strategy of terrorists is to commit acts of violence that draw the attention of the local population, the government, and the world to their cause. During the planning of the terrorist attack, the main purpose of terrorists is to obtain the greatest publicity, choosing targets that symbolize what they oppose. The effectiveness of the terrorist act lies not in the act itself, but in the public's or government's reaction to the act. For example, in 1972, during the Olympic Games in Munich, 11 members of the Israeli delegation were killed by the Black September Organization. The Israelis were the immediate victims, but the real target was the estimated 1 billion people watching the televised event.

The organization – „Black September" used the high visibility of the Olympic games to publicize its views on the problems of the Palestinian refugees. Besides, in October 1983, terrorists from the Middle East Region committed a terrorist act at the Marine Battalion Landing Team Headquarters at Beirut International Airport. Their immediate victims were the 241 U.S. military personnel who were killed and over 100 others who were wounded. The direct target of those terrorists was the American people and the government. This one act of violence influenced the United States' decision to withdraw the Marines from Beirut and was therefore considered a successful result for the terrorists. There are three targets of terrorism: the terrorists, the victims, and the general public. The phrase "one man's terrorist is another man's freedom fighter" is a view terrorists themselves would accept. Terrorists do not consider themselves criminals. They are sure that they are legitimate combatants, fighting for the protection of their ideas by any possible means. A victim of a terrorist act and the majority of society sees the terrorist as evil with no regard for human life. The general public's view is the most unstable. The terrorists do their best to create the image of "Robin Hood" with the hope to find additional supporters among the members of society. This sympathetic view of terrorism has become an integral part of their psychological warfare and needs to be countered vigorously.

SEVERAL HISTORIC ASPECTS OF TERRORIST ACTIVITIES

Terrorism and terrorist groups have the deep roots since the ancient period. The first known organization that exhibited aspects of a modern terrorist organization was the Zealots of Judea. Known to the Romans as Sicarii, or dagger-men, they committed an underground campaign of murdering Roman occupation forces, as well as any Jews, whom they considered to be allies of Romans and who were serving to the Roman authorities. The motive of those groups was an uncompromising belief that they could not remain faithful to the dictates of Judaism while living under pressure from the Roman Empire. Eventually, the Zealot rebel movement became open and they were finally besieged and were forced to commit mass suicide at the fortification of Masada (Hoffman, 1988).

Several centuries later, the Assassins were the next group, whose activities were interrelated with the modern standards of terrorism. A breakaway faction of Shia Islam called the Nizari Ismailis worked out the tactic of the assassination of enemy leaders because the cult's limited manpower prevented open combat. The head of this group, Hassam-I Sabbah, based the cult in the mountains of Northern Iran. Their tactic of sending a lone assassin to successfully kill a key enemy leader at the certain sacrifice of

Figure 8. 2019 global terrorism index
Source: https://impakter.com/global-terrorism-in-continuous-downfall/

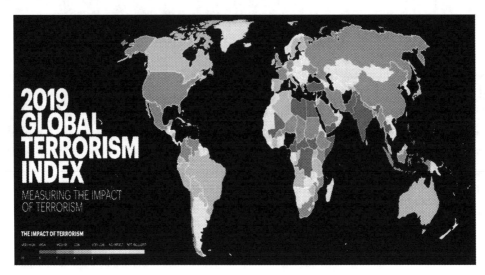

his own life (the killers waited next to their victims to be killed or captured) inspired fearful awe in their enemies (Hoffman, 1988).

Despite the fact that Zealots and the Assassins were involved in terrorist activities a long time ago, they are relevant nowadays: First as forerunners of modern terrorists in aspects of motivation, organization, targeting, and goals. Secondly, although both were ultimate failures, the fact that they are remembered hundreds of years later demonstrates the deep psychological impact they caused.

From the period of the Assassin's (late 13th century) activities to the beginning of the 18th Century, terror and barbarism were widely used in warfare and conflict, but key ingredients for terrorism were lacking. After the ending of the 30-year war and the signing of the Treaty of Westphalia in 1648, when the modern nation-states were founded, the sort of central authority and cohesive society that terrorism attempts to influence barely existed. Communications were inadequate and controlled, and the causes that could inspire terrorism (religious schism, insurrection, ethnic strife) movements typically led to open military operations. By the time kingdoms and principalities became nations, they had an appropriate resource to enforce their power and prevent such activities, as terrorism.

The Revolution in France provided the first uses of the meaning "Terrorist" and "Terrorism". Using this terminology - "terrorism" began in 1795 in reference to the Reign of Terror initiated by the Revolutionary government of France against supporters of the monarchy. The representatives of the Committee of Public Safety and the National Convention that enforced the policies of "The Terror" were referred to as 'Terrorists" (Palmer, 2014). The Revolutionary processes in France within the period 1789-1793 created the precedent for the other states in oppressing their populations in the future. It also inspired a reaction by royalists and other opponents of the Revolution who was involved in the implementation of terrorist tactics such as assassination and intimidation in resistance to the Revolutionary agents. The Parisian mobs played a decisive role at key points before, during, and after the Revolution. Such extra-radical activities as murder prominent officials and aristocrats in gruesome spectacles started long before the invention of the first time guillotine.

At the end of the 19th century, the development of the political theories, which were based on the principles of radicalism and improvements in the technology of producing the weapons, spurred the formation of small groups of revolutionaries who were involved in the effective attack of the state institutions. Anarchists espousing belief in the "propaganda of the deed" produced some striking successes, killing heads of the states from Russia, France, Spain, Italy, and the United States. However, their weak organizational structure and ignorance of the cooperation with the other social groups and movements in political efforts rendered anarchists ineffective as a political ideology and movement. In contrast, Communism's role as an ideological basis, based on the radical theory of Marxism, found the convenient way for political terrorism. At the beginning of the XX Century, it was just activating and finally became much more influential in the first half of the last century.

Another tendency in the late 19th century, when many territories of our planet were under the colonial rules of the leading powers, was the increasing wave of nationalism in the different regions of the world, in which the nation (the identity of a people) and the political state were combined. As nations started to protect their national identities - language, religion, cultural heritage, etc. people that had been conquered or colonized could, like the Jews at the times of the Zealots, opt for assimilation or struggle. One of the most known ethnic and religious conflicts in Europe from this time is still not finally resolved - the multi-century struggle of Irish nationalism which is combined with the protection of the principles of Catholicism in Northern Ireland. The anti-colonial type of Nationalism, like communism, became a much greater ideological force in the 20th century.

The terrorist group from this period that is represented as a model of many directions of the terrorist activities was the Russian Narodnya Volya (Peoples Will). Taking into account the strategy and tactics of this group, it should be mentioned that it differed in some ways from modern terrorists, especially in that they would sometimes call off attacks that might endanger individuals other than their intended target. Other than this quirk, it can be noticed many of the traits of terrorism here for the first time; clandestine, cellular organization; impatience and inability for the task of organizing the constituents they claim to represent; and a tendency to increase the level of violence as pressures on the group mount.

The first half of the 20th century was characterized by the two events that influenced the nature of the conflict to the present day. The effects of two World Wars inflamed passions and hopes of nationalists throughout the world, and severely damaged the legitimacy of the international order and governments. The activation of the nationalism movement became more intensified during the early 20th century throughout the world. It transferred to an especially powerful force in the subject peoples of various colonial empires. Although dissent and resistance were common in many colonial possessions, and sometimes resulted in open warfare, national identities became a focal point for these actions (Goldstein, Pevehouse. 2010).

Gradually, as peoples and nations became closely connected with the concepts of race and ethnicity, international political developments began to support such approaches. Members of ethnic groups whose territories had been occupied by the other states or had ceased to exist as independent nations considered the new opportunities to realize their nationalist ambitions. Several of these ethnic and religious groups chose terror as a method to conduct their struggle and make their situation known to the international community, they hoped would be sympathetic. In Europe, both the Irish and the Basks separatist groups were involved in the terrorist campaigns as part of their ongoing struggle for independence but had to initiate bloody uprisings to further their cause. Both were partially successful.

Further development of Terrorism is interrelated with the Cold War period. The bipolar international system of the Cold War changed the perception of conflicts in the world. Relatively, minor confrontations took on significance as arenas where the superpowers could compete without risking escalation to full nuclear war. Warfare between the East and the West, between two economic and political systems, and between two ideologies took place on the peripheries and was limited in scope to prevent escalation. During the immediate postwar period, terrorism was more of a tactical choice by leaders of nationalist insurgencies and revolutions. National-Liberation movements for independence from colonial rule occurred throughout the world and many employed terrorisms as a supporting tactic. In several cases, terrorism was used within the framework of larger movements and coordinated with political, social, and military actions. Even when terrorism came to dominate the other aspects of a nationalist struggle, such as the Palestinian campaign against Israel, it was (and is) combined with other activities (Chitadze, 2011).

TERRORIST ACTIONS OR THE THREAT OF SUCH TYPES OF ACTIVITIES HAVE BEEN IN EXISTENCE FOR MILLENNIA.

Despite the fact, that the history of the terrorism movement prevails over the history of the modern nation-state, the implementation of the terrorist acts by the different groups or even by some state institutions and those that contest their power remains hardly researched. From one side, the term - terror itself is more or less clear, when it is associated with acts and actors in the real world it becomes confused. Party it is determined by the fact – using terror strategies and tactics by organizers at all levels in the social and political environment. Who is the person, who uses an appropriate military and another kind of equipment for the explosion of the various civil and military objects, a criminal? Or a member of any revolutionary movement? (UN, 2008).

Is it possible, that some people to be compared to the French revolutionary governments who used the term terrorism by justification the systematic state terror against this part of the population of France in the 1790s, which was considered as opposition to the new government by killing tens of thousands? Are either they the same as revolutionary terrorist groups such as the Baader-Meinhof Gang of West Germany or the Weather Underground in the United States?

So, it can be noticed that distinction of size and political legitimacy of the actors using terror raise questions as to which action can be considered a terrorist act and which not. The concept related to moral equivalency is very often used as an argument to broaden and blur the definition of terrorism as well. This approach argues that the outcome of an action is what matters, not the intent. Collateral or unintended damage to civilians from an attack by illegal paramilitary forces on a legitimate military target is the same as a terrorist bomb directed deliberately at the civilian target with the purpose of creating that damage. Simply put, a car bomb on a city street and a jet fighter dropping a bomb on a tank are both acts of violence that produce death and terror. Therefore (at the extreme end of this argument) any illegal activities with the use of weapons are simply terrorism with its different interpretation. This is the reasoning behind the famous phrase "One man's terrorist is another man's freedom fighter" (UN, 2008). It is also a legacy of legitimizing the use of terror by successful revolutionary movements after the fact.

The very flexibility and adaptability of terror during the long period of time have contributed to the confusion. Those seeking to disrupt, reorder or destroy the status quo have continuously sought new and creative ways to achieve their goals. Some changes in the strategy and tactics and development of techniques by terrorists have been significant, but even more significant is the increase in the number of causes and social contexts where terrorist acts are committed. During the past 20 years, terrorists have implemented extremely violent acts for alleged political or religious reasons. Political ideology, on which terrorists are based, ranges from the extreme left to the extreme right. For example, the leftist groups can be represented by such terrorist organizations as Marxists and Leninists who propose a revolution of workers led by the revolutionary elite. On the contrary, right-wing-oriented groups are based on the typical belief in a merging of state and business leadership. Nationalism is the devotion to the interests or culture of a group of people or a nation. Typically, nationalists share a common ethnic background and desire to establish an independent state. Religious extremists often ignore the power of secular authorities and consider legal systems that are not based on their religious beliefs as illegitimate. They often reject all types of modernization efforts, which they view as corrupting influences on traditional culture. Special interest groups include people on the radical fringe of many legitimate causes; e.g., groups of the people, who commit terrorist acts to uphold antiabortion views, animal rights, radical environmentalism. These people strongly believe that violence is morally justifiable to achieve their purposes.

TERRORIST INCIDENTS AND TECHNIQUES-TERRORIST GROUPS AND TERRORIST BEHAVIOR

These are the most common terrorist incidents include:

Bombings

It is already proved, that improvised explosive devices are not expensive and easy to produce. Modern devices have smaller shapes and are harder to detect. Those devices include very destructive capabilities; for example, on August 7, 1998, two American diplomatic representations, in Africa, particularly in Kenya and Tanzania were under the bomb attack terrorist acts claimed the lives of over 200 people, including 12 innocent American citizens, and injured over 5,000 civilians (US Department of State, 2018). Terrorists can also use materials that are readily available to the average consumer to construct a bomb.

Kidnappings and Hostage-Takings

One of the main policies of the terrorist groups represents kidnapping and hostage-taking. Terrorists implement this type of action for the establishment of a bargaining position and to elicit publicity (Davitashvili, Elizbarashvili, 2012). Kidnapping is one of the most difficult acts for a terrorist organization to fulfill, but, if in case of the successful implementation of the operation, terrorists obtain an opportunity to attract more financial resources, which later they can use for the releasing of the jailed comrades, and publicity for an extended period. Hostage-taking involves the seizure of a facility or location and the taking of hostages. Unlike a kidnapping, hostage-taking provokes a confrontation with authorities. It determines the positions of the governments of the various countries related to choosing the concrete strategy - either to make dramatic decisions or to conduct negotiations with terrorists and listen to their position. It is overt and designed to attract and hold media attention. The terrorists' intended target is the audience affected by the hostage's confinement, not the hostage.

The legal definition of kidnapping is the taking away of a person by force, threat, or deceit, with intent to detain that person against his will. Kidnapping can be implemented with the request for ransom (economic reasons) or for political or other purposes, for example requiring the releasing of the members of the terrorist group from the prison or changing the official policy of the government related

Figure 9. Rescue workers evacuating the bodies of victims of a terrorist train bombing near Atocha Station, Madrid, March 11, 2004
Source: https://www.britannica.com/topic/terrorism

to the internal and external policy of the country. In history, under common law, kidnapping was only a misdemeanor, but in different parts of the world as in most states of the United States, the practice is now punishable by death or life imprisonment (TRAC, 2013).

Armed Attacks and Assassinations

Armed attacks include raids and ambushes. Assassinations are the killing of a selected victim, usually by the use of special explosive equipment or small arms. Drive-by shootings are a common technique employed by unsophisticated or loosely organized terrorist groups. From the historic point of view, it can be assumed, that terrorists have murdered specific persons for psychological effect (Chitadze, 2014).

Arsons and Fire Bombings

Incendiary devices are cheap and easy to hide. Arson and fire-bombings are easily conducted by terrorist organizations, that may not be as well-organized, equipped, or trained as a major terrorist group. An arson or firebombing against a utility, hotel, government building, or industrial center portrays an image that the ruling government is incapable of maintaining order (Chitadze, 2014).

Hijackings and Skyjackings

Hijacking is the seizure by using the force of a surface vehicle, passengers, who are inside, and/or its cargo. Skyjacking represents the occupation of an aircraft, which creates a mobile, hostage barricade situation. It provides terrorists with hostages from many nations and draws heavy media attention. Skyjacking also provides mobility for the terrorists to relocate the aircraft to a country that supports their cause and provides them with a human shield, making retaliation to be complicated (Chitadze, 2014).

Other Types of Terrorist Incidents

In addition to the above-mentioned types of terrorist acts and acts of violence, there are also numerous other methods of violence that can exist under the framework of terrorism. Terrorist organizations conduct violence against their own people also by implementing robberies and extortion when they need additional financial resources for the continuation of their activities and when they don't have other sources of funding.

Cyber-terrorism is a new type of terrorism activity that is ever-increasing taking into account that humanity relies on computer networks to obtain a different kinds of important information and provide connectivity to today's modern and fast-paced world. Cyber-terrorism gives an opportunity to the terrorist groups to fulfill their operations with little or almost no risk to themselves. It also provides terrorists a resource to disrupt or destroy networks and computer systems. The main purpose is the interruption of the functioning of the leading governmental institutions or business companies. This type of terrorism isn't as high profile as other types of terrorist attacks, but its impact is just as destructive (Canetti, 2017). Historically, terrorist actions by using **nuclear, biological, and chemical (NBC) weapons** are not held very often. Taking into account the extremely high number of victims that NBC weapons produce, they are also considered as weapons of mass destruction (WMD). However, most of the countries are involved in arms races with neighboring countries because they view the development of WMD as a key deterrent of attack by hostile neighbors. The increased development of WMD also raises the chance for terrorist groups to obtain access to WMD. Some experts consider the issue that in the future terrorists will have more opportunities to purchase the WMD, because some states with a high level of corruption and un-stability may fail to protect their stockpiles of WMD from accidental losses, illicit sales, or outright theft or seizure. Determined terrorist groups can also gain access to WMD through covert independent research efforts or by hiring technically skilled professionals to construct the WMD (Goldstein, Pevehouse. 2010).

TYPES AND FORMS OF TERRORISM

The main types of terrorism include:

Political terrorism in the broadest sense encompasses all forms of terrorism aimed at changing the social order. In a narrow sense, political terrorism refers to the issue, aimed at making (or preventing) a decision related to the arrangement of the state.

Social terrorism is formed on the basis of internal socio-political confrontation and is mainly presented in two forms: left-wing and right-wing terrorism. Left-wing terrorism is based on any left-wing ideological doctrine (Marxism, Leninism, Trotskyism, Maoism, anarchism, etc.), while right-wing terrorism is based on trans nationalist, conservative values and is directed against the left.

Nationalist terrorism operates on ethnic grounds. It singles out separatist terrorism carried out by nationalist-political groups of ethnic minorities with the aim of achieving independence or broad autonomy; Repressive nationalist terrorism perpetrated by the nationalist groups of the dominant nation against ethnic minorities

Worldview terrorism is formed on the basis of contradictory contradictions with prevailing values and norms. The most common form of such terrorism is religious terrorism, which in turn is divided into fundamentalist and sectarian terrorism. The types of worldview terrorism are ecological terrorism, feminist terrorism, and others.

Criminal terrorism is a conditional concept because any terror is a crime. But in a narrow sense, criminal terrorism refers to terrorism that is not related to political, social, nationalist, or worldview goals and is used by ordinary criminals, criminals, to achieve their criminal goals. Therefore, many think that such an act is a common criminal offense and does not fit the classical definition of terrorism.

The main forms of carrying out terrorist acts are sabotage, kidnapping, assault and murder, robbery (expropriation); Hijacking (seizure of vehicles and taking hostages).

A new form of terrorism is cyber terrorism, or hacking of computer networks, which can cause great damage to a country's defense and security system (Davitashvili, Elizbarashvili, 2012).

STATE TERRORISM

Definition

As it was mentioned, there is neither an academic nor an international legal consensus regarding the proper definition of the word "terrorism" (Williamson, 2009). Some scholars believe the actions of governments can be labeled "terrorism" (Nairn, 2005). Using the term 'terrorism' to mean violent action used with the predominant intention of causing terror, Paul James and Jonathan Friedman distinguish between state terrorism against non-combatants and state terrorism against combatants, including 'shock and awe' tactics:

Shock and Awe" as a subcategory of "rapid dominance" is the name given to massive intervention designed to strike terror into the minds of the enemy. It is a form of state terrorism. The concept was however developed long before the Second Gulf War by Harlan Ullman as chair of a forum of retired military personnel (James, 2006).

However, others, including governments, international organizations, private institutions, and scholars, believe the term is applicable only to the actions of violent non-state actors. Historically, the term terrorism was used to refer to actions taken by governments against their own citizens whereas now it is more often perceived as targeting of non-combatants as part of a strategy directed against governments (Williamson, 2009).

Historian Henry Commager wrote that "Even when definitions of terrorism allow for state terrorism, state actions in this area tend to be seen through the prism of war or national self-defense, not terror"(Hor, 2005). While states may accuse other states of state-sponsored terrorism when they support insurgencies, individuals who accuse their governments of terrorism are seen as radicals, because actions by legitimate governments are not generally seen as illegitimate. Academic writing tends to follow the definitions accepted by states. Most states use the term "terrorism" for non-state actors only (Schmid, 2011).

The Encyclopedia Britannica Online defines terrorism generally as "the systematic use of violence to create a general climate of fear in a population and thereby to bring about a particular political objective", and states that "terrorism is not legally defined in all jurisdictions." The encyclopedia adds that "establishment terrorism, often called state or state-sponsored terrorism, is employed by governments—or more often by factions within governments—against that government's citizens, against factions within the government, or against foreign governments or groups" (Britannica, 2020).

While the most common modern usage of the word terrorism refers to civilian-victimizing political violence by insurgents or conspirators (Purkitt, 1984), several scholars make a broader interpretation of the nature of terrorism that encompasses the concepts of state terrorism and state-sponsored terrorism. Michael Stohl argues, "The use of terror tactics is common in international relations and the state has been and remains a more likely employer of terrorism within the international system than insurgents. Stohl clarifies, however, that "not all acts of state violence are terrorism. It is important to understand that in terrorism the violence threatened or perpetrated, has purposes broader than simple physical harm to a victim. The audience of the act or threat of violence is more important than the immediate victim" (Stohl, 1988).

Scholar Gus Martin describes state terrorism as terrorism "committed by governments and quasi-governmental agencies and personnel against perceived threats", which can be directed against both domestic and foreign targets (Martin, 2006). Noam Chomsky defines state terrorism as "terrorism practiced by states (or governments) and their agents and allies"(Chomsky, 2002).

Stohl and George A. Lopez have designated three categories of state terrorism, based on the openness/secrecy with which the alleged terrorist acts are performed, and whether states directly perform the acts, support them, or acquiesce in them (Stohl & Lopez, 1988).

History of the State Terrorism

Aristotle wrote critically of terror employed by tyrants against their subjects (The Claremont Institute, 2001). The earliest use of the word terrorism identified by the Oxford English Dictionary is a 1795 reference to tyrannical state behavior, the "reign of terrorism" in France (Oxford Dictionary, 2002). In that same year, Edmund Burke decried the "thousands of those hell-hounds called terrorists" who he believed threatened Europe (Laqueur, 2007). During the Reign of Terror, the Jacobin government and other factions of the French Revolution used the apparatus of the state to kill and intimidate political opponents, and the Oxford English Dictionary includes as one definition of terrorism "Government by intimidation carried out by the party in power in France between 1789–1794" (Teichman). The original general meaning of terrorism was terrorism by the state, as reflected in the 1798 supplement of the Dictionnaire of the Académie française, which described terrorism as *a system, regime de la terreur* (Laquer, 2007). Myra Williamson wrote:

"The meaning of "terrorism" has undergone a transformation. During the Reign of Terror, a regime or system of terrorism was used as an instrument of governance, wielded by a recently established revolutionary *state* against the enemies of the people. Now the term "terrorism" is commonly used to describe terrorist acts committed by *non-state or subnational entities* against a state" (Williamson, 2009).

Later examples of state terrorism include the police state measures employed by the Soviet Union beginning in the 1930s, and by Germany's Nazi regime in the 1930s and 1940s (Primoratz, 2007). According to Igor Primoratz, "Both (the Nazis and the Soviets) sought to impose total political control on society. Such a radical aim could be pursued only by a similarly radical method: by terrorism directed by extremely powerful political police at an atomized and defenseless population. Its success was due largely to its arbitrary character—to the unpredictability of its choice of victims. In both countries, the regime first suppressed all opposition; when it no longer had any opposition to speak of, political police took to persecuting 'potential' and 'objective opponents'. In the Soviet Union, it was eventually unleashed on victims chosen at random." (Primoratz, 2007).

Military actions primarily directed against non-combatant targets have also been referred to as state terrorism. For example, the bombing of Guernica has been called an act of terrorism (Goodin, 2006). Other examples of state terrorism may include the World War II bombings of Pearl Harbor, London, Dresden, Chongqing, and Hiroshima (Stohl, 1984).

In the modern period, state terrorism can be considered the military operation of Russia in Chechnya during the two wars on the territory of this North Caucasian Republic at the end of the XX century and the beginning of the XXI Century. As a result of those wars, more than 200 thousand people, first of all, a peaceful population, have been killed by Russian militaries (Modebadze, 2016).

The second example of state terrorism is supported by Kremlin separatist and terrorist movements on the territories of Georgia and Ukraine. For example, at the beginning of the 90th of the 20th Century, Russia supplied military equipment and financed the activities of the so-called " Confederation of Mountain Peoples of the Caucasus ". This group included the terrorist formations from the North Caucasus, who themselves supported the separatist movements in Abkhazia and the former South Ossetian Autonomous District on the territory of Georgia. Those illegal formations committed ethnic cleansing against the Georgian population of Abkhazia. As a result, more than 300 thousand ethnic Georgians and representatives of other nationalities were forced to be exiled from their native places (Chitadze, 2016).

Later, after the occupation of Crimea, Russia supported illegal armed formations in the eastern part of Ukraine.

9/11 Events and a New Determination of Terrorism

September 11, 2001, a date when the most brutal in the history of terrorism attack was made on the twin-towers - World Trade Center in New York. As a result of this action, almost 3000 individuals died at the WTC complex. United States Authorities attributed responsibility for the attack to Osama bin Laden and the Al Qaeda organization.

The American nation and the whole International community were mobilized; combating terrorism and crippling Al Qaeda and other terrorist groups, together with those regimes, which were supporting terrorism became top national and international priorities. Preemptive use of Armed Forces against foreign terrorist organizations and infrastructure gained increasing acceptance in Administration policy circles. A full-scale campaign was launched, using all aspects of national and international resources, to go after Al Qaeda and its affiliates and support structures. The anti-terrorism campaign included rallying the international community, especially law enforcement and intelligence units with the purpose of destroying Al Qaeda cells and financial networks.

As a result, the Taliban, which supported terrorism on the territory of Afghanistan, was removed from power with the support of US and British forces of the "Northern Alliance" (paramilitary group, which was opposing the Taliban in the Northern part of Afghanistan), all known Al Qaeda training sites were destroyed, and a number of Taliban and Al Qaeda leaders were killed. Since then, according to

President Bush in his address to the nation on May 1, 2003, nearly half of the known Al Qaeda leadership has been captured or killed. As it is known, later, top Al Qaeda leaders Osama bin Laden and Ayman al Zawahiri also were eliminated.

In the post-9/11 world, threats are defined more by the fault lines within societies than by the territorial boundaries between them. From terrorism to global disease or environmental degradation, the challenges have become transnational rather than international. That is the defining quality of world politics in the twenty-first century. Terrorism became a large-scale threat to all.

During the making an analysis on International Terrorism issues, it can be listed several aspects, based on which the research is conducted. Those issues can be the analytical approach of terrorism, its international character, the stages of its evolution and development, the tactics and strategies used by terrorist groups, and the new dimensional character of international terrorism.

Through the definition seems to be clear, terrorism still proves to be the notion hardly identifiable. What the International society possesses right now are the constant threat and tools to confront the evil of terrorism. Terror has its biases from a very ancient period of history. It is considered a way of conduct in the constant war epoch as a constituent part of the rebellion of non-compliance. It is still hard to believe that in the modern world when the process of democratic enlargement is going on, the existence of terrorism creates constant awareness of counter actions and war against the war. The historical line witnesses are even more strengthening of the position and the terrorist ideologies. The eternal evil in humankind always finds the reason to kill and even has the approval.

The suppressed minority takes the flour in the new dimension of terrorism which emerged in the second half of the 20th century. Nowadays, terrorist organizations are better equipped and significantly developed from psychological and financial points of view. The strengthening of the "Al-Qaeda", "Hamas" etc., and other leading terrorist organizations and the foundation of the new training centers for potential terrorists took place during the 80s and 90s of the last century. The global threat that comes from those countries, which were or are involved in the state-sponsored terrorism activities, posed the rest world astonished.

The tactic and equipment usage by terrorists of the modern era cannot be compared to that of the early centuries. Because of vast financial support, such terrorist groups as the Taliban and al Qaeda established their self-destructive roots in the development of terrorism worldwide. All the tactics and the training results can be seen in the planning of terrorist attacks. So, as the evil became sophisticatedly highly dangerous it is the task of each state to confront it.

The world was stunned and put aside when the time brought the tragedy of 11 September of 2001. The terrorists went too far and dug their death graves. Now the war to be declared and the elimination of terrorism in the world is a moral obligation of each human wishing a peaceful world without terrorism. The terrorist groups were weakened and a good number of their leaders have been destroyed. Terrorism possesses the everlasting dilemma of every society in the world. The world is fighting to heal its torn and suffered organism from cancer plaguing it. The human sufferings are of human invention and the further future of the planet is of our creation. The only message is to do the best to make the world a bit better than it was yesterday, a decade earlier, a century and millennia ago.

Figure 10. ISIS Fighters shown in propaganda video produced by the group
Source: https://upfront.scholastic.com/issues/2017-18/100917/are-we-winning-the-war-against-isis.html

"THE ISLAMIC STATE" AND THE IRAQI REBEL MOVEMENT

Within the second decade of the XXI Century, the main threat within the terrorist activities was the "Islamic State" or ISIS. Its activity represented the new form of terrorism, when this terrorist group, which controlled huge territories, even oil fields of Iraq and Syria, established de facto state formation of the Islamic Caliphate. In August 2014, the Syrian Observatory for Human Rights claimed that the number of fighters in the group had increased to 50,000 in Syria and 30,000 in Iraq, while the CIA estimated in September 2014 that in both countries it had between 20,000 and 31,500 fighters (Janus, 2015).

Thus, the principal actor in the crisis beginning in June 2014 was the Sunni radical movement, the so-called Islamic State of Iraq and al-Sham. Approximately a month after the commencement of the crisis, the organization announced the establishment of a caliphate subsequently concisely referring to itself as "the Islamic State" and, has named its leader, Abu Bakr al-Baghdadi, Caliph Ibrahim. On July 5, a video recording emerged, where the latter calls upon Muslims in all countries to declare subservience to the newly elected Caliph and combat infidels and traitors to strengthen and expand the Caliphate. The battle should especially intensify during the holy month of Ramadan, which began on June 28. The aforementioned organization has already been described as the most influential, well-organized, well-funded, and well-armed in the region. It has been noted that the organization is distinguished by its brutal methods of fighting and treatment of opponents. The organization was founded in 2003, when, after the replacement of Saddam Hussein's regime, an insurgent movement began against the Americans and the Shiite government. Initially, the group was called Tawhid and Jihad (Jama'at al-Tawhid Wal-Jihad), headed by the Jordanian Abu Musab al-Zarqawi, who soon became "enemy number one" for the US. In 2004, the organization associated itself with al-Qaeda and became known as Al-Qaeda in Iraq (AQI). In 2006, after the death of al-Zarqawi, the organization was renamed the "Islamic State of Iraq", with Abu Omar al-Baghdadi as its new leader. Following al-Baghdadi's death in 2010, Abu Bakr al-Baghdadi, referred to as the Caliph by the members of the organization, was named the leader of the group. During his leadership, the organization declared its international claims, even though its reputation was initially based on its Iraqi origins unlike its predecessors, who, due to their so-called 'foreignness', we're unable to attain a similar degree of trust among the insurgents, which was also reflected on the authority of the organization. In 2011, the organization became involved in the Syrian conflict as it took part in the establishment of the Syrian radical group, the Al-Nusra Front. The leader of the Front, Abu Mohammad al-Jawlani was sent to Syria by al-Baghdadi himself. At a later stage, there was an altercation between them. Al-Nusra remained affiliated to al-Qaeda, while al-Baghdadi's group openly opposed Ayman al-Zawahiri, al-Qaeda's leader.

Later, Al-Nusra Front was under a fair amount of persecution, and the situation on insurgent territory in Syria was controlled by the Iraqi group. As mentioned above, the group was rather well-armed. Moreover, in late July 2014, the organization conducted a so-called military parade in the Syrian city of Ar-Raqqah, where it deployed its heavy machinery, which it had acquired as a result of fighting against government forces. As is well known, upon taking control over Mosul and Tikrit, the Iraqi state troops abandoned military equipment and weaponry. Iraq's government has already confirmed that the group had control over the former Iraqi chemical weapons base, where thousands of warheads loaded with the Sarin nerve agent were being prepared for destruction. Even though, given the condition of the substances and weapons, the US and Iraqi specialists ruled out the possibility that the chemical weapons would be employed. According to specialists, the "Islamic State" had a financial system superior to all similar organizations. They had imposed taxes on areas controlled by them. They controlled oil extraction plants in Iraq and Syria. A portion of their income was constituted by ransom received from kidnappings. According to some experts view, upon capturing Mosul, the organization managed to obtain approximately half a billion US dollars from banks in the city. There was also talk of donations from the Sunni states of the Persian Gulf, although, according to experts, this amount was no more than 5% of the organization's income. By unofficial reports, their assets exceeded USD 2 billion. In a relatively short period, they managed to occupy a fairly large territory in Iraq and Syria. Their control was so commanding that al Baghdadi did not shy away from holding worship services at the mosque. All of a sudden, he has become a public figure. His address did not resemble the customary speeches of insurgent leaders issued from clandestine locations; on the contrary, he addressed Muslims from a particular place, the Grand Mosque of Mosul, which was significant to underscore his stature as Caliph, rather than simply a combatant leader. He was a political and religious leader, who was also able to conduct worship services. The proclamation of the Caliphate also signified a certain opposition with all other radical and non-radical Islamic unions. Al-Baghdadi called on all Muslims to obey him as Caliph, and also, as a politician should encourage them to criticize him. To broadcast its activities, the organization effectively utilized social media (Chitadze, 2016).

PART 4. DEMOCRATIZATION OF THE WORLD

The Concept of Democratization and Democratic "Wave"

Various authors indicate democratization as a tendency of modern world development. At the same time, the concept itself in political science is mainly used in two meanings. The democratization, firstly, is understood as the indication of raising the number of democratic states; secondly, strengthening and developing democratic institutions and processes in different countries. The latter has special value for states that are in the process of transition to building a democratic state i.e., democratic transition. G. O'Donnel and Ph. Schmitter distinguishes the following steps in democratic transition: Liberalization, democratization, and consolidation (Schmitter, 2017).

And yet, in world politics, in contrast to political science, the notion of "democratization" is more often used in the first sense, as an increase in the number of democratic states. A more understanding of the democratization of the modern world is possible – as an expansion of the circle of participants in international cooperation. However, this approach is not yet well established in world politics.

There are different views and procedures for assessing which countries can be considered democratic. Disputes are often caused related to the states who are in the transition period, in which several signs of democratic development are present, while some other signs are not evident. However, in the most general form, according to the data of American researcher D. Caldwell, in 1941 approximately 25% of the states could be considered as democratic, and in 1996 their number already reached 40%, and in the second decade of the XXI Century – about 50%. If we take into account countries that are in the process of democratic transition, then this figure, according to the American institute Freedom House, which analyses democratic development in the world, can reach about 75% in the third and fourth decade of the XXI century (Freedom House, 2019).

American researcher and editor-in-chief of Foreign Affairs, F. Zakaria, was writing that at the beginning of the 21-st century, 118 countries were democratic (Zakaria, 2003). In any case, no matter what specific figures will be taken as a basis, almost all authors agree with the fact that the number of democratic countries in the world is increasing. In this case, however, many researchers have several doubts, which will be discussed later.

The emergence of democratic states in the world was not linear. S. Huntington published in the "Journal of Democracy" an article called "Democracy's Third Wave", as well as a book "The Third Wave: Democratization in the Late of Twentieth Century", distinguishing periods in world history, associated with the development of democratization processes (Waves of Democratization), and peculiar democratic backsliding (Huntington, 1991). Some authors, such as R. Dix, pushing away from some specific events, indicate slightly different dates for the development of waves of democratization than S. Huntington. Or the events of late 1989 – early 1991 in Eastern Europe are distinguished in another fourth separate wave of democratization, for example by Ph. Schmitter (Schmitter, 1991). Nevertheless, in general, if we do not take into account the differences in approaches of various researchers, we can distinguish the following waves, or stages, of democratization.

The first wave of democratization is the longest, it lasted for a century and dates back to S. Huntington 1820-1920. During this "wave" more than 20 democratic states were formed (29 – according to S. Huntington and 21 – according to R. Dix) (Chitadze, 2016). These countries were characterized by parliamentary and party systems with wide voting rights. The first "wave" was followed by a "backsliding" from the main road of democratic development, which lasted from the second half of the 1920s through the first half of the 1940s. and is associated with the advent of fascism in several countries around the world (Huntington, 1991).

The second "wave" (mid-1940 – early 1960s) was caused by the defeat of fascism in the Second World War and the collapse of the colonial system after it comes, according to S. Huntington, a new regressive wave, during which several military and authoritarian regimes were formed (including in 1967 in Greece and 1973 – in Chile). In general, the second backsliding lasts from the early 1960s through the early 1970s (Huntington, 1991).

Finally, a new, third "wave" begins in the first half of the 1970s. democratic processes grip the Wester Europe (Greece – 1974, Portugal – 1975, Spain – 1977); Latin America (Dominican Republic – 1975, Honduras – 1982, Brazil – 1985, Peru – 1988, Chile – 1990 and others); Asia (Turkey – 1988, Philippines – 1986, South Korea – 1988); Eastern Europe (Hungary – 1989, Czechoslovakia – 1989, Poland

– 1989, Bulgaria – 1989 Baltic states in 1991, etc.); Africa (In South Africa the first general elections were held in 1994) (Chitadze, 2016).

What causes the democratization processes? Different authors give different answers to the question about the cases contributing to this. Political scientists usually consider two groups of factors, variables:

· Structural (independent variables) – the level of economic and social development, social–class processes, dominant values in society, etc.
· Procedural (dependent variables) – accepted decisions, personal characteristics of politicians, etc.

A detailed analysis of these two groups of factors is conducted by the researcher A. Y. Melville. Modified in the "funnel of causality" model, which was proposed by American author D. Campbell and his colleagues to analyze the behavior of the voter, he used it to study transition problems. At the same time in the very process of democratic transition A., Y. Melville highlighted the phases of the establishment and consolidation of democracy (Chitadze, 2016). Further, in the study of factors influencing the institution of democracy, he proposes "a gradual transition from predominantly structural to predominantly procedural analysis", and while studying the second phase - from micro to macro factors.

In political science, the external environment, the trends of world development are usually considered as one of the structural variables of the democratization process: how much does it contribute (or not) to this process? However, in the modern world, with an ever-closer interweaving of foreign and domestic policy, the international environment can act as a structural and procedural variable. And the latter seems to be more and more significant. Decision-making (which is a procedural variable) by the world community about this or that country can lead to the development of democratic processes in them. The UN has repeatedly adopted resolutions regarding the apartheid regime in South Africa, as well as the decision on sanctions, which was the factor influencing the country's refusal from the policy of apartheid and the holding of democratic elections in 1994.

The end of the twentieth century, which coincided with the third "wave" of democratization, which by several states, and by the degree of their involvement in democratic processes, is, perhaps, particularly turbulent, brought with its other trend of world development – globalization and integration of the world. All these processes strengthen each other. Following democratic principles and traditions for the big number of participants is a vital example. Staying out of the world "democratic club" in the modern globalizing world means to be a kind of an outcast. This encourages more and more new associations to be guided by democratic values.

To deny the democratic path of development, state leaders are deliberately going, opposing their country to the rest of the world. In this context, one can view the process of democratic transformation at the end of the twentieth century precisely as a tendency of the political development of the world, in the implementation of which the non - endogenous (internal) factors are becoming more important (level of social-economic development, political processes in society, etc.) and exogenous regarding this state, i.e. international environment. Exactly this encourages democratic transformation.

The democratization of the late twentieth century gave the foundation to F. Fukuyama to talk about the end of history. In the sense that the historical development of humanity has made its choice in favor of democracy enlargement. His article has been criticized a lot. Objections were made by such statements as the forecast about the ending of the conflicts in the world in connection with the ending of ideological confrontation between East and West, linearity and uniformity of historical development, etc. however, the thesis about the processes of democratization as a common tendency, perhaps, was least contested.

Figure 11. Democracy index, 2019
Source: https://blog.pressreader.com/public-libraries-have-an-important-role-in-sustaining-democracy

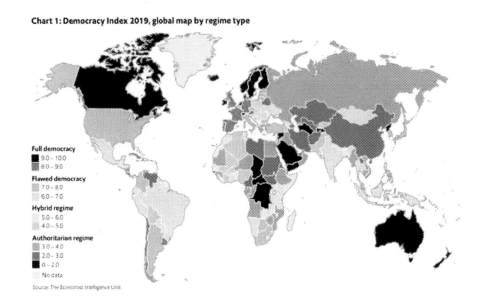

Indeed, if at the beginning of the twentieth century, a relatively small number of states could be considered as democratic, they not always take responsibility for the electoral and other rights (in several countries the rights of women and national minorities, also people without property were limited) in the start of the twenty-first century these problems turned out to be if not solve, solvable (Fukuyama, 1989).

However, it should be emphasized that democratization is not an unambiguous process. With particular clarity, this appeared as a result of the last "wave" of democratization, when illiberal democracies, hybrid regimes, and imitation of democracies were formed. Their essence lies in the fact that democratic institutions and processes in various states are used as an external form, sometimes used as a way to cover the undemocratic mechanisms for the realization of power. Perhaps, the term "illiberal democracies" has received the greatest distribution due to the work of F. Zakaria, published in 1997, in "Foreign Policy" journal. F. Zakaria pushes away the statement of R. Holbrooke, who in 1996, offered to imagine the example, that during free democratic elections in the country the candidate who openly confesses racist, fascists or separatists' views and opposes a peaceful solution of the conflict, particularly in Yugoslavia is elected by population (Holbrooke, 1998). This leader democratically comes to power, but he professes undemocratic views and pursues a corresponding policy. F. Zakaria breaks this logic of reasoning and draws attention to the fact that the emergence of the so-called illiberal democracies is possible i.e., those who took only external attributes of democratic transformation. In addition, the number of these kinds of countries, as he wrote, had been increasing. In 1990 they were 22% of the total number of democratic states, and in 1997 – already 35% (Zakaria, 1997).

THEORY OF THE DEMOCRATIC PEACE

The special interest in world politics as a scientific discipline is the analysis of the interaction of democratic states, which is reflected in the theory of the democratic world, which was mentioned when considering the theories of international relations. The origins of this theory go back to the thesis of Immanuel Kant about "perpetual peace." The philosopher put forward the hypothesis that democratic states will behave differently than non-democratic states in the international arena. Focusing on better moral principles, these countries will establish peace with each other (Kant, 1795). The idea of I. Kant was developed in the twentieth century, has emerged as a theory of a democratic world. First, several authors engaged in studying the problems of the world drew attention to the fact that developed democracies are not at war with each other, confirming this based on statistical analysis. But immediately began to raise objections. In general, they boiled down to the following provisions.

1. The history of the interaction of democracies is too small to draw general conclusions based on statistical data.
2. There is no clear definition of which states can be called developed democratic, and it is not always clear what does it mean, "they do not fight with each other."

Discussing within the framework of these two main arguments, opponents of the theory of a democratic world cite historical examples, which, in their opinion, contradict the thesis that "democracies do not fight each other." For example, during the Second World War, Great Britain declared war on Finland, although there was no armed action. Is it possible to consider this fact of declaring war as its actual conduct? There is no answer to this question.

Germany, during the outbreak of the First World War, is often referred to as another historical example of hostilities between democracies. The question here is how far Germany can be viewed as a democratic state if we take into account such features of its government as the de facto independent role of the Kaiser in decision-making. There are other examples too.

In all cases, supporters and opponents of the theory of democratic peace put forward their arguments and counterarguments. In general, at least as a general pattern with possible exceptions, the theory of the democratic world justifies itself. Therefore, discussions are of greater interest not as to whether this is the case and what the exceptions maybe, but why developed democracies do not enter into war with each other.

In general, the analysis of the theory of the democratic world can be presented in full detail by giving a comparative analysis of two main concepts - M. Doyle and B. Russet. The first, based on the ideas of I. Kant, argues that in foreign policy, developed democracies rely on the same principles as in internal ones (Doyle, 1983). Governments of democratic countries, including when entering a war, must justify themselves in front of their citizens. The presence of common principles and values among democratic countries forms their "peaceful union" and at the same time aggressive behavior towards autocracies. B. Russet offers a different explanation of the phenomenon of a democratic world. It comes from the cultural and structural features of democratic states and argues that citizens in democratic countries see themselves as free people who are accustomed to respecting the rights of others (Russet, 1998). The openness of borders, the free exchange of information in democratic states reinforce this perception. These cultural characteristics, which are absorbed by man since childhood, limit the manifestation of aggression against other humans. In addition, people in democratic countries are used to resolving conflicts peacefully - through negotiations, agreements, judicial procedures.

The second factor explaining the phenomenon of a democratic world, according to B. Russet, is the principle of decision-making in democratic countries, including the beginning of the war. War-oriented leaders must conduct these decisions through appropriate legitimate procedures. In the event of a conflict, democratic countries are forced to spend more on making decisions about the start of hostilities. As a result, a "cooling" period arises, allowing to pay off the first emotional reactions and look for a rational way out of the conflict.

In principle, both concepts do not contradict each other. Rather, the latter is only a more developed approach. Nevertheless, many questions remain. For example, why is the aggression of democratic countries towards non-democratic states possible? Is there always a response, or defensive, reaction? If so, what is perceived as a threat? Why did democratic countries wage imperialist wars? If these were not mature democracies, then where is the maturity criterion?

MAIN ASPECTS OF THE PROVIDING THE PROTECTION OF HUMAN RIGHTS AND PROMOTION OF DEMOCRACY ON THE GLOBAL LEVEL. PESSIMISTIC AND OPTIMISTIC SCENARIOS AND WAYS FOR THE RESOLUTION OF THE PROBLEM.

Main principles of Human Rights and Democracy

Human rights represent the moral and legal principles or norms, which determine the concrete standards of human action and are regularly recognized as legal rights in internal municipal and international law (Nickel, Pogge, Smith, Wenar, 2013). They are commonly understood as inalienable fundamental rights "to which a person is inherently entitled simply because she or he is a human being," and which are "inherent in all human beings" (Weston, 2014) regardless of their nation, location, language, religion, ethnic origin or any other status (The United Nations, Office of the High Commissioner of Human Rights, 2014). They are applicable everywhere and at every time in the sense of being universal, and they are egalitarian in the sense of being the same for everyone. They are regarded as requiring empathy and the rule of law Bass (book reviewer), Samuel Moyn, 2010) and imposing an obligation on persons to respect the human rights of others, and it is generally considered that they should not be taken away except as a result of due process based on specific circumstances; for example, human rights may include freedom from unlawful imprisonment, torture, and execution (Merriam-Webster dictionary, 2010).

The concept of human rights has been highly influential within international public law, also within the International Intergovernmental and non-governmental organizations. The policy of the countries and different governmental or non-governmental institutions form the public policy on the global level. The idea of human rights suggests that "if the public discourse of peacetime global society can be said to have a common moral language, it is that of human rights" (Beitz 2009).

Many principles and concepts were formulated by the human rights movement after the Second World War. Within the UN, in 1946 the Human Rights Commission was established, which implemented huge work for the adoption of the *Universal Declaration of Human Rights* in Paris by the United Nations General Assembly in 1948. It was followed by the adoption of new International conventions, particularly, the "International Covenant on Economic, Social and Cultural Rights" and "the International Covenant

Figure 12. UN adopts a universal declaration on human rights
Source: https://www.theguardian.com/law/from-the-archive-blog/2018/nov/28/un-adopts-universal-declaration-human-rights-paris-1948

on Civil and Political Rights" were adopted by UN General Assembly in 1966, "The Convention on the Prevention and Punishment of the Crime of Genocide" (1948), "The Convention Relating to the Status of Refugees" (1951), "The International Convention on the Elimination of all Forms of Racial Discrimination" (1966), "The Convention on the Elimination of all forms of discrimination against Women" (1979), "The Convention against Torture and Other Inhuman or Degrading Treatment or Punishment" (1984, "The Convention on the Rights of the Child" (1989), etc. (UN, 2005).

Democracy: Demokrátiya (other - Greek. δημοκρατία —"government by the people", from δῆμος —"people" and κράτος — "authority") — represents the political regime, main principles of which includes the method of collective decision, which is implemented with the equal action of participants on the final result of the concrete process

(Hyland, 1995) or on its essential stages (Christiano, 2006).

Although this method applies to any public structure, the state today is the most important institution, since it possesses large authority. In this case, the determination of democracy usually narrows to one of the following signs:

· The election of leaders by the people as a result of the free and fair elections (Huntington, 2003);
· People is a singularly legitimate source of power;
· Society achieves self-governance for the satisfaction the common interests (Aristotle)

Public governance requires the guarantee of several rights for each member of society. With democracy are connected several values: legality, political and social equality, freedom, right to self-determination, human rights, and others.

Since the ideal democracy is not easily attainable and is the subject of different interpretations, there were proposed sets of practical models. Until the XVIII century, the most known model was direct democracy, where the citizens achieved their right by the adoption of the political decisions directly, due to the reaching of the consensus or with the assistance of the procedures of the subordination of the minority to the majority. In a representative democracy, the citizens achieve the same right through the elected by the deputies and other officials by delegation to them the part of their rights. At the same time, the elected leaders make decisions by taking into account the preferences of their voters (Shumpeter, 1995).

One of the basic purposes of democracy is the limitation of arbitrariness and abuses of power. This purpose frequently could not be reached in those countries, where human rights and other democratic values were not universally recognized or they did not have effective protection from the legal system's side. Today, in many countries democracy is identified with liberal democracy, where, in the framework of the fair, periodic and general election, the candidates, for the attraction of the voter's votes, are involved in the free competition, which also includes the supremacy of law, separation of the branches of powers and constitutional limitations of the rule of the majority via the guarantees of the specific person or group freedoms.

On the other side, prominent economists, and also such representatives of the Western political elite as the former President of the USA Barack Obama, the Executive Director of the IMF (International Monetary Fund) Christine Lagarde, and another assert, that the realization of the right of the adoption of political decisions, the influence of citizens on the policy of the country will be impossible without the guarantee of social rights, equality of opportunities and with the presence of low level of social and economic inequality.

Several authoritarian regimes had the external signs of democratic administration; however, in those states, the power was possessed only by one party and the conducted policy did not depend on the preferences of voters. During the last quarter of the XX Century, the World was characterized by the tendency of democracy enlargement.

To the number of comparatively new problems related to the development of the democratic institutions are belonged separatism, terrorism, the migration of population, increasing political and social inequality. The international organizations, such as the UN, OSCE, and European Union, assume that the control over the internal affairs of the state, including questions of democracy and observance of human rights, parts must be in the sphere of the influence of the international community.

ENLARGEMENT OF DEMOCRACY IN THE MODERN TIMES

After the ending of the "Cold War" and disintegration of the communist system, the convenient base for the enlargement of democracy and promotion of peaceful co-existence among the states has been created. While discussing the democratization of the World, it should be pointed out that it is a comparatively new process, which was characterized for the second of the XX and beginning of the XXI Century. For example, if after World War I, democratic regimes were established in almost 30 countries, during period World War II, only 12 Democratic states have been remained (Rondeli, 2003) In the 60s of previous century, the number of liberal countries was 37, in the mid of 70s of the twentieth century, to the list of democratic states were belonged less than 1/3 of all countries in the world. After the collapse of the USSR and the failure of the communist ideology, the new wave of democratization has started. As a result, in 2012 the number of Free countries in the World was 90, and 83 in 2020 (Freedom House, 2020) In the modern world, the wealth is concentrated in the democratic states. As it is known, in the countries with a strong market economy, as a result of the socio-economic development, the middle class is becoming much stronger, the level of education is increasing and the population expresses its interest in peace when it will be possible to continue the enlargement of the business, trade and accordingly, attraction of more profit. Due to it, the society in the democratic states considers the importance of peace and international cooperation. At the same time, in the democratic state, the process of decision-making does not promote the introduction of the chauvinistic or imperialistic policy and dominance of the militaristic ideas in the foreign policy. It especially concerns the relations among the democratic states and those relations are based on each other's respect and deeper economic and cultural cooperation. Even more, democratic states create a so-called "zone of peace", which is gradually enlarging. However, there are many obstacles in the way of the enlargement of democracy and providing the protection of human rights in the World. In this regard, it should be mentioned about the following negative factors

MAIN OBSTACLES, RELATED TO THE DEMOCRACY ENLARGEMENT

However, there are many obstacles in the way of the enlargement of democracy and providing the protection of human rights in the World. In this regard should be mentioned about the following negative factors:

Absence of Democracy in Most of the Countries of the World: Despite the increasing number of democratic states in the World after the ending of the cold war, according to the Freedom House Report in 2020: "Democracy and pluralism are under assault. Dictators are toiling to stamp out the last vestiges of domestic dissent and spread their harmful influence to new corners of the world. At the same time, many freely elected leaders are dramatically narrowing their concerns to a blinkered interpretation of the national interest. As a result of these and other trends, Freedom House found that 2019 was the 14th consecutive year of decline in global freedom. The gap between setbacks and gains widened compared with 2018, as individuals in 64 countries experienced deterioration in their political rights and civil liberties while those in just 37 experienced improvements".

Thus, according to the above-mentioned report, there were only 63 partly Free and 64 non-free countries and territories with authoritarian political regimes.

For example, if we take into consideration the most populated part of the World, Asia - where the population in 2021 prevails to 4 Billion 670 Million people (Worldometer, 2021), there are only 3 free countries and one territory (Taiwan), accordingly, it can be assumed, that more than 4 billion people in Asia live in the counties with authoritarian and semi-authoritarian regimes. About Africa, there are only 5 free countries among those 54 states, which are located on the political map of this continent.

Problems of Education Related to Democracy and Human Rights: It can be assumed that one of the main reasons for the weaknesses of the democratic institutions represents the educational factors. First of all, there is a lack of information in the Societies of the different countries regarding knowledge by citizens of their own civil, political, economic, social, and cultural rights. In this regard it is necessary to point out the following issues:

* *Lack of information about main principles of Human Rights Protection and models of Democracy in International society, particularly among the Scientific circles, representatives of the governmental agencies, students, NGO-s, representatives of the different regions, etc.*

In this case, the following factors are worthy of mentioning:

* Even though today practically in all countries of the World many educational Institutions – Schools, Universities, Colleges, Institutes are registered, there is a lack of Institutes, where discipline-Human Rights Law/Democracy or other directly related to Human rights protection subject is taught. The subjects related to Human Rights are not taught at the Faculties of Political Sciences and law even in the leading Universities of many countries.
* There are no reference literature-for example books about Human Rights Law and Models of Democracy in official state languages of many countries, and if we take into consideration the fact, that according to the data for 2012, approximately no more than 1,5 Billion people speaks the first International language - English (native language for about 400 Million people and second language for about 1,1 Billion) (N. Elizbarashvili, Z. Davitashvili, N. Beruchashvili. 2012) and in most of the schools and Institutes lectures are given in native languages, it is very difficult for many school pupils and students to study Human Rights and democracy issues (for example various International conventions on Human Rights issues) and Democracy in official languages of the different states;
* *Shortage of materials about Human rights and Democratic standards can also be observed in central and local governmental agencies. Besides, if we take into consideration the fact, that in most of the regions of the world majority of the population does not speak English on which the Information about Human Rights legislation-first of all International Conventions and Principles of Democracy can be obtained and more than 50% of the world population has no access to the internet (for example the number of internet users worldwide was 3.17 billion in 2015 (Chitadze, 2017), it is clear that majority of the population in the World has no or limited information about main principles of democracy;*
* -There are a deficit of qualified NGO-s in the different regions of our planet specialized in Human Rights and Democracy studies issues;
* There are a lack of analytical journals on Human Rights protection issues;
* -Limited information about models of democracy and legislation in the sphere of human rights protection is presented by television and other mass-media means in many countries;
* -Only a limited number of journalists are familiar with the Human rights and Democracy issues. Thus, there are few qualified opinions on this matter in the mass media of many countries.

PART 5. ROLE OF HYBRID WAR IN WORLD POLITICS

Nowadays, hybrid war and its role in world politics is a very important and actual issue. In this subchapter, there will be a discussion of what hybrid war means in general, how it was formed and used throughout the time, its effectiveness, hybrid warfare as a new type of global competition, also hybrid war as an old concept, which acquired new techniques during the time.

Definition of Hybrid War

While talking about the role of hybrid war in world politics, it is significant to understand what hybrid war means in general. Hybrid War is a military strategy that employs political warfare and blends conventional warfare, irregular warfare, and cyber warfare with other influencing methods, such as fake news, violation of the conducting diplomatic methods, and foreign electoral intervention (Deep, 2015). By combining kinetic operations with subversive efforts, the aggressor intends to avoid attribution or retribution. Hybrid warfare can be used to describe the flexible and complex dynamics of the battlespace requiring a highly adaptable and resilient response. There are a variety of terms used to refer to the hybrid war concept: hybrid war, hybrid threats, hybrid influencing or hybrid adversary (as well as non-linear war, non-traditional war, or special war). It should be mentioned that there is no universally accepted definition of hybrid warfare which leads to some debate whether the term is useful at all. Some argue that the term is too abstract and only the latest term to refer to irregular methods to counter a conventionally superior force. The abstractness of the term means that it is often used as a catch-all term for all non-linear threats.

History

Nowadays, hybrid warfare has its definition, but it is interesting to know the history of the development of hybrid warfare as a military strategy. The combination of conventional and irregular methods is not new and has been used throughout history. Some historians find the origins of the concept in the campaigns waged in ancient Hispania by the Lusitanian leader Viriathus or the renegade general Sertorius against the forces of the Roman Republic in the 2nd and 3rd centuries B.C. respectively. Elements of hybrid warfare are also seen in the concept of la petite guerre, a sort of reconnaissance in force practiced by troops with light armaments in European armies during the 17th and 18th centuries. A few examples of this type of combat are found in the American Revolution (a combination of Washington's Continental Army with militia forces) and Napoleonic Wars (British regulars cooperated with Spanish guerrillas). One can also find examples of hybrid warfare in smaller conflicts during the nineteenth century. For instance, between 1837 and 1840 Rafael Carrera, a Conservative peasant rebel leader in Guatemala, waged a successful military campaign against the Liberals and the Federal government of Central America utilizing a strategy that combined classical guerrilla tactics with conventional operations. Carrera's hybrid approach to warfare gave him the edge over his numerically superior and better-armed enemies.

It is worth noting that the end of the Cold War caused the creation of a new kind of system of hybrid war. The end of the Cold War created a unipolar system with a preponderant American military power, and though this has tempered traditional conflicts, regional conflicts and threats that leverage the weaknesses of the conventional military structure are becoming more frequent.

At the same time, the sophistication and lethality of non-state actors increased. These actors are well armed with technologically advanced weapons that are now available at low prices. Similarly, commercial technologies such as cell phones and digital networks are adapted to the battlefield. Another new element is the ability of non-state actors to persist within the modern system.

The Vietnam War saw hybrid warfare tactics on both sides, with the US using the CIA to support civil war parties in Laos and the Cambodian Civil War as well as ethnic groups inside Vietnam for their cause, while the USSR supported the Viet Cong militia (Greg, 2008).

Figure 13. Hybrid warfare and the concept of interfaces
Source: https://www.maanpuolustus-lehti.fi/the-hybrid-face-of-warfare-in-the-21st-century/

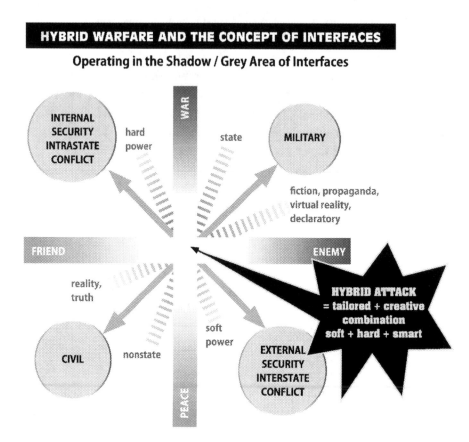

Effectiveness

Traditional militaries find it hard to respond to hybrid warfare. Collective defense security organizations such as NATO might find it hard to agree on the source of the conflict making the response difficult. To discuss the issue, "What Is Hybrid Warfare?" It should be compared to the notion of hybrid warfare to the Russian concept of "non-linear" warfare. It defines non-linear warfare as the deployment of "conventional and irregular military forces in conjunction with psychological, economic, political, and cyber assaults" (Chitadze, 2020). This approach partially attributes this difficulty to the "rigid" or static military taxonomy used by NATO to define the concept of warfare. Also, to counter a hybrid threat, hard power is often insufficient. Often the conflict evolves under the radar and even a "rapid" response turns out to be too late. Overwhelming force is an insufficient deterrent. Many traditional militaries lack the flexibility to shift tactics, priorities, and objectives constantly.

Figure 14. Elements of hybrid war
Source: https://www.researchgate.net/figure/Elements-of-hybrid-war_fig2_311517571

Hybrid Warfare – New Face of Global Competition

Hybrid Warfare can be perceived as the new face of global competition. It is alternatively called "grey zone" conflict and is in the news almost daily. Yet the main focus to date of "hybrid warfare" — which uses non-military means to achieve warlike ends — has predominantly been on tactical methods such as cyber-attacks, fake news campaigns, and espionage. But understanding hybrid warfare's strategic context equips political and business leaders better to address it. In simplest terms, hybrid warfare uses capabilities not normally associated with war to coerce or subvert. Such techniques are intended to delay the recognition that an attack is underway, paralyze decision-making through confusion and discourage the victim from responding forcefully due to the absence of "legitimate" military targets. China, Russia (and to lesser degrees Iran and North Korea) is involved in the processes inside of democratic states and hoping to re-make the international political, economic, and trade systems through a coordinated hybrid effort that is taking place largely outside the traditional military or diplomatic spheres.

Hybrid War: Old Concept, New Techniques

Another very important point, which should be discussed is that hybrid war is old as a concept but acquired with new techniques in the modern world. While how state and non-state actors conduct hybrid war today have changed, the fundamental principle of utilizing a combination of conventional and irregular methods to achieve a political objective is consistent with older forms of conflict. This blending has historic examples in the American Revolution with George Washington's Continental Army and robust militia forces; the Napoleonic Wars where British regulars challenged French control of major Spanish cities, while Spanish guerrillas attacked their lines of communication; and the Arab Revolt where the British Army combined conventional operations in Palestine with irregular forces under British operational control. However, despite having its roots in history, modern hybrid war has the potential to transform the strategic calculations of potential belligerents due to the rise of non-state actors, information technology, and the proliferation of advanced weapons systems (Deep, 2015).

The unipolar system that has persisted since the fall of the Soviet Union has given rise to an international system in which unconventional challenges to the idea of traditional state-on-state war are increasingly prevalent. The preponderance of American military power has tempered conflicts in Southeast Asia, the Indian subcontinent, and the South China Sea, but has given rise to a method of war that attempts to leverage the weaknesses of the conventional military structure. Where wars traditionally have regular and irregular components in different areas of operation, modern hybrid war tends to combine these aspects. Modern hybrid war practitioners apply "conventional capabilities, irregular tactics and formations, and terrorist acts including indiscriminate violence, coercion, and criminal activity" simultaneously. Under this model, war takes place in a variety of operating environments, has synchronous effects across multiple battlefields, and is marked by asymmetric tactics and techniques. These tactics are difficult to defeat for militaries that lack the flexibility to shift mindsets constantly, especially since the interconnected nature of modern society is such that hybrid war takes place on three distinct battlefields: the conventional battlefield, the indigenous population of the conflict zone, and the international community.

Major Powers have historically sponsored irregular fighters and non-state actors in the execution of broader military campaigns, and modern examples such as Iranian support to Hezbollah and other Shia militant groups are continuations of these policies. The Israel-Hezbollah War of 2006 showed that although the concept of hybrid war in this fashion is not a novelty, some of the sophistication and lethality of non-state actors, along with their ability to persist within the modern state system, is a new occurrence.

Hybrid organizations such as Hezbollah are well armed and equipped due to the availability of technologically advanced weapon systems at low prices and pre-existing commercial technologies such as cell phones and digital networks. During the Israel-Hezbollah War of 2006, decentralized cells composed of guerrillas and regular troops armed with precision-guided missiles, short and medium-range rockets, armed unmanned aerial vehicles, and advanced improvised explosive devices executed an irregular urban campaign against a conventional Israeli opponent. With Iranian Quds Force operatives as mentors and suppliers of advanced systems, Hezbollah cells downed Israeli helicopters, damaged Merkava IV tanks, communicated with encrypted cell phones, and monitored Israeli troops' movements with night vision and thermal imaging devices. Hezbollah leveraged information technology as fighters immediately uploaded and distributed battlefield pictures and videos in near real-time, dominating the battle of perception throughout the operation. The Israeli military did not lose the war in 2006 on the conventional battlefield, but did little to alter the strategic environment in Southern Lebanon and lost the information campaign as the overwhelming perception within the international community was of Israeli military defeat from Hezbollah.

Apart from the increased effectiveness of non-state actors within hybrid war, the symbiotic relationship between sponsor and client is another variable that differentiates modern hybrid war from traditional forms of conflict. The Syrian Civil War and strengthening of the Islamic State (ISIS) presents a complex strategic challenge for Iran and Hezbollah as modern hybrid war practitioners. Iran cannot afford to lose its link with its non-state proxy in Lebanon as its means to implement the foreign policy goals. At the same time, Hezbollah cannot afford to lose that same link to its principal supporter, otherwise, it forfeits its ability to remain relevant as a pseudo-state in Lebanon. Therefore, while Iran has been supplying advisors, weapons, and equipment to Shia groups in Syria, it also compelled Hezbollah to send 2,000 fighters into the conflict zone as it simultaneously orchestrates a modern hybrid war in Syria.

The Israel-Hezbollah War and the Syrian Civil War also show how modern hybrid war increasingly focuses on non-state entities within the state system. Just as Clausewitz assumed that the belligerents in war are hierarchically organized states, the dominant force within traditional hybrid war examples has been the state.

However, non-state and sub-state actors are the focal points in modern hybrid wars as proxies for state sponsors at certain times, but also executing their independent policies. It was the policy of Hassan Nasrullah, rather than Iran, of kidnapping Israeli troops that led Israel to war with a non-state actor. Furthermore, the spread of IS to Iraq was initially a non-state executing a hybrid war against a conventional Iraqi military. However, this has transformed to the state of Iraq executing its version of hybrid war utilizing non-state, sub-state, and international actors to counter ISIS advances (Deep, 2015).

A modern hybrid war that simultaneously combines conventional, irregular, and terrorist components is a complex challenge that requires an adaptable and versatile military to overcome. The United States has increasingly focused on counterinsurgency doctrine in the wake of its wars in Iraq and Afghanistan. However, insurgency alone is not the singular challenge against which the United States must structure its military. Clausewitz stated, "Every age has its kind of war, its limiting conditions, and its peculiar preconceptions." (Clausewitz, 1989) It is important that the United States, and other global powers, do not focus on insurgency as the war of the post-Cold War era. On the contrary, the commander of a military fighting a hybrid war will need to leverage a wide range of capabilities including conventional high-intensity conflict units, decentralized special operations forces, and sophisticated information operations and technology platforms. The concept of hybrid war is not new, but its means are increasingly sophisticated and deadly and require a response in kind.

Russian Activities in the 2010s as an Example of Hybrid War

The Russian government's widely used in conflicts such as in Syria and in Ukraine the private military contractors such as those of the Wagner Group was in 2018 singled out by experts as a key part of Russia's strategy of hybrid warfare to advance her interests while obfuscating her involvement and role.

In respect of Russia, Jānis Bērziņš, director of the Center for Security and Strategic Research, has widely published arguing that using the term Hybrid to characterize the Russian strategy is misleading since the Russian has their definitions and concepts. Accordingly, to him, "the word "hybrid" is catchy since it can represent a mix of anything. However, its basic framework differs from the one developed by the Russians due to the former being a military concept and the result of American military thought. Moreover, the concept of New Generation Warfare includes conventional operations. In other words, Hybrid Warfare might be part of New Generation Warfare but cannot define it. Michael Kofman, a senior research scientist at CNA and a fellow at the Wilson Center's Kennan Institute, noted that the West's frequent references to hybrid warfare were in effect "an unintelligible Western reaction, after decades of wars of choice against paltry adversaries, to confrontation with another power that is capable across the full spectrum of conflict" (Kofman, 2016).

To conclude, it can be said that Hybrid warfare involves the synchronized use of military and non-military means against specific vulnerabilities to create effects against its opponent. Its instruments can be ratcheted up and down simultaneously, using different tools against different targets, across the whole of society. In this respect, hybrid warfare expands the battlefield. Moreover, it increases the possibility of a hybrid warfare actor inflicting significant damage on its opponent before that opponent can respond to, or possibly even detect, a hybrid warfare attack. This strong and fluid element of ambiguity within hybrid warfare adds a new dimension to how coercion, aggression, conflict, and war are to be understood. In this respect, new geostrategic contexts, new applications of technologies, and new organizational forms suggest the likelihood that this form of warfare will persist and continue to evolve into the future. The Analytical Framework model developed here provides a practical guide for understanding and countering this hybrid warfare threat at the national and multinational levels.

FAKE NEWS AND BATTLING MISINFORMATION IN THE MODERN WORLD AS A PART OF HYBRID WAR

The use of information is regarded as a foundation stone in an era of the information society. The impact of particular information may be crucial for society in a historic perspective, as it also concerns political life, economy, education, and level of democracy. Nowadays it is extremely difficult to reveal truthful and objective news in a huge ocean of facts, opinions, descriptions, calculations, etc. where false information is distributed via technology and people's trust. Hence, the pressing issues of fake news, which a priori possess detrimental components, and their identities are as ever as today. The talks on fake news' importance were exacerbated during the 2016 presidential elections in the US, thus acquiring security and strategic significance for modern states. Nevertheless, humankind managed to conduct methods that facilitate fake news detection processes like "automatic deception detection". Methods, described in this sub-chapter, involve the use of linguistics and information technology aimed to prevent the spread of fake news through systematic scientific mechanisms based on automatic detection of untruthfulness (Tufekci, 2016).

So, this part of the book will be addressed toward the issues relating to the history and essence of such terms as "fake news" as well as "weapons", created to combat this phenomenon. Importantly, it is worth saying that it is necessary to understand what stands behind the title of "fake news". Therefore, the description of the history of emergence, further occurrences throughout the ages, and proper definition of fake news are indispensable while investigating the ontological component of the paper's core matter.

Historical Background

According to several sources, the history of fake news started with the spread of anti-Semitic blood libels in XV century Italy, noting the simultaneous character of the emergence of both news and fake news: "Fake news took off at the same time that news began to circulate widely after Johannes Gutenberg invented the printing press in 1439. "Real" news was hard to verify in that era. There were plenty of news sources—from official publications by political and religious authorities to eyewitness accounts from sailors and merchants—but no concept of journalistic ethics or objectivity. Readers in search of facts had to pay close attention." So, people did not have enough resources and technologies to efficiently distinguish truthful information from lies. Even historical progress, entailing the age of Enlightenment with its inherent rationalism was powerless facing the constant flow of fake news: "For example, in the years preceding the French Revolution, a cascade of pamphlets appeared in Paris exposing for the first time the details of the near-bankrupt government's spectacular budget deficit. Each came from a separate political camp, and each contradicted the other with different numbers, blaming the deficit on different finance ministers" (Soll, 2016). Fortunately, after-war period the American press emphasized the importance of source reputability. However, it was not until the advent of the information society, in which, with the help of the Net, the size of information increased astronomically. Newsfeeds are not required to publish objective verified information, which gives certain people a huge arena for information manipulation in most sophisticated manners, that have not been known before the invention of the Internet.

Classification

Wardle in 2017 studied the phenomenon of fake news and dissemination mechanisms and eventually elaborated classification of fake news, which shows seven types, each possessing its specific features, different means and objectives: satire or parody ("no intention to cause harm but has potential to fool"), false connection ("when headlines, visuals or captions don't support the content"), misleading content ("misleading use of information to frame an issue or an individual"),

False context ("when genuine content is shared with false contextual information") impostor content ("when genuine sources are impersonated" with false, made-up sources), manipulated content ("when genuine information or imagery is manipulated to deceive", as with a "doctored" photo), fabricated content ("new content is 100% false, designed to deceive and do harm")".

Technology

Two variables guarantee an enabling environment for effective distribution for fake news: technology and trust. Firstly, the Internet and especially social media are regarded as decent channels for false information circulation and distribution (Warwick & Lewis, 2017). Various social network feeds, and wikis are robust tools through which fake news can be spread. For example, Facebook became a huge platform for posting news in lots of countries and a source of receiving them (Kalsnes, 2018). Moreover, Facebook was involved in debatable 2016 presidential elections, entailing accusations against Zuckerberg, who eventually admitted that Facebook has to face bigger responsibilities than a regular tech company: "Facebook works directly with candidates, campaigns, and political parties via our political outreach teams to provide information on potential online risks and ways our users can stay safe on our platform and others. Additionally, our peers are making similar efforts to increase community resources around security" (Weedon, Nuland & Stamos, 2017).

Elements of Trust

Secondly, if people are unable to differentiate between what is verified or false, whether one can trust the news or not, it makes people confused about the state of affairs, particularly during an election when voters need reliable information to make unimportant political decisions. But low trust in information and news media can also make it more likely for people to spread fake news and disinformation. As argued by some researchers, the declining trust in mainstream media could be both a cause and consequence of fake news gaining more traction (Kalsnes, 2018). Besides, social networks lack transparency, which is demonstrated in the creation of special algorithms based on tracking of users' preferences: "Importantly, the provision of information through opaque technologies disrupts the layer of organizational credibility and reputational trust established in the process of professional reporting. This lack of transparency is also problematic in the sense that information literacy, defined as the ability to "recognize when information is needed and have the ability to locate, evaluate, and use [it]" (American Library Association,

2000) is less useful when the mechanisms used to "locate" and "evaluate" the information (e.g., topical search results) are not fully known" (Albright, 2017).

Figure 15. Warning fake news
Source: https://www.idginsiderpro.com/article/3528792/only-ai-can-us-from-a-world-of-fakes-a-world-ai-is-also-creating.html

METHODS FOR FINDING FAKE NEWS: LINGUISTIC APPROACHES

Most liars use their language strategically to avoid being caught. Despite the attempt to control what they are saying, language "leakage" occurs with certain verbal aspects that are hard to monitor such as frequencies and patterns of pronoun, conjunction, and negative emotion word usage. The goal in the linguistic approach is to look for such instances of leakage or, so-called "predictive deception cues" found in the content of a message (Conroy, Rubin & Chen, 2015). Analysis of word use is often not enough in predicting deception. Deeper language structures (syntax) have been analyzed to predict instances of deception. "Deep syntax analysis is implemented through Probability Context-Free Grammars (PCFG). Sentences are transformed to a set of rewrite rules (a parse tree) to describe syntax structure, for example, noun and verb phrases, which are in turn rewritten by their syntactic constituent parts" (Feng, Banerjee & Choi, 2012) Sentiment classification by Pang & Lee (2013) is based on the fundamental presumption that deceivers use unintended emotional contact, judgment, or effective state appraisal (Hancock, Woodworth, & Porter, 2011). Similarly, syntactic patterns can be used by associating learned patterns in argumentation style groups to differentiate feelings from fact-based arguments.

Network Approaches

Innovative and varied, using network properties and behavior are the ways to complement content-based approaches that rely on deceptive language and leakage cues to predict deception. As real-time content on current events is increasingly proliferated through micro-blogging applications such as Twitter, deception analysis tools are all the more important (Conroy, Rubin & Chen, 2015). Technology can be used as a systematic mechanism against fake news by at least reducing the capacity of the spread of detrimental information: "In connection with crises or emergencies, such as shootings or riots, we always see a lot of false information on social media. This means there is a lot of noise disturbing those trying to help. Here, the technology can filter rumors and false information, so that organizations better prioritize aid" (Arildsen, 2019). Using information networks can be a major step towards automated methods of computational fact-checking. False "factual statements" can be a form of deception for certain data as they can be collected and tested alongside findable statements about the known world. This approach leverages an existing body of collective human knowledge to assess the truth of new statements. The method depends on querying existing knowledge networks, or publicly available structured data, such as the Google Relation Extraction Corpus (GREC). The principle of trust is central to the verification of identity on social media. The abundance of news through mass media such as micro-blogs in the form of current events encourages ways to determine the difference between false and legitimate content. The use of metadata and telltale behavior of questionable sources are outside the

Fake News - Study of Content

Centering resonance analysis, a network-based text analysis method, describes the output of broad text sets by defining the most important words in the network that connect other words. Combining opinion and behavior research has shown the argument that emotion-focused comments by singleton users have a significant impact on the online ranking (Wu, Greene, Smyth & Cunningham, 2010), and that this is an example of "shilling" or posting fake reviews to falsely skew a rating.

To sum up, it can be argued that the world society must give timely responses to the problem of fake news since false information can be very dangerous for society and even the state's security. The manipulation of news can cause serious damage to the resilience of statehood, democracy, and level of education. And modern linguistic and network battling methods, in their turn, are aimed to filter information through detecting potential lies in mass media.

CONCLUSION

The global security problem in the modern world is revealed in two ways: in the aspect of the security of the world community and the aspect of the personal security of a person.

The problem of the security of the world community includes the issues of preserving and maintaining peace, the international policy of preventing the escalation of conflicts and the growth of local wars, the reduction of weapons of mass destruction and conventional weapons, the prohibition of certain types of weapons and the complete elimination of their stocks, etc.

The problem of human security in the modern global world includes the provision of such conditions as:

- Personal freedom;
- Observance and protection of her rights and freedoms;
- The possibility of human participation in public policy and local self-government processes;
- State and international guarantees of peace, access to life support resources (including work, health care, and education services);
- Environment favorable for life and reproduction.

The problematic nature of the international, national, public and personal security for people in the modern global world creates risks and threats of various scales and nature.

At the global level, these are:

· International political tension and the state of the "cold war" between geopolitical antagonists;
· The arms race and the failure to fully comply with decisions on international programs to reduce strategic stockpiles of arms;
· Interethnic, religious, and intercultural conflicts;
· International terrorism;
· Activity of illegitimate political regimes;
· A gap in the levels of socio-economic development of regions and countries of the world as a destabilizing factor.

At the personal level, a person's safety in the modern global world is threatened by:

· Factors of socio-economic instability;
· Intrastate interethnic, religious, and intercultural conflicts;
· Crime (primarily organized crime);
· Corruption in all spheres of public life;
· Violations of human rights and restrictions on her democratic and personal freedoms;
· Inaccessibility of vital resources and funds;
· Unsatisfactory social and environmental conditions of life.
· International peace and security activities within the existing practice include:
· international agreements and programs on arms reduction;
· arms production control and trade restrictions programs;
· armed intervention of international peacekeeping forces in interstate conflicts;
· diplomatic mediation in negotiations between warring parties;
· a ban on the sale of weapons, as well as an embargo on the export or import of countries participating in conflicts;
· provision of humanitarian and financial assistance on certain conditions.
· Activities to protect and ensure the safety of the human person generally include:
· law enforcement activities of the state;
· human rights activities of civil society institutions;
· activities in the field of health care and disease prevention;
· functioning of systems of social and political socialization and participation.

In different societies and cultures, these institutions and mechanisms operate in different volumes and with different indicators of effectiveness.

Over the past few years, the problem of global security has again taken a priority place among other global problems, because of the large-scale and acute manifestation of its signs (geopolitical tension between nuclear powers; local armed conflicts and civil wars; the activity of terrorists and illegal armed groups; the emergence and illegal functioning illegitimate political regimes; non-compliance with international agreements in the field of weapons of mass destruction and conventional weapons, etc.). Proposals for solving the problem of global security are again more relevant today than ever.

REFERENCES

A Train Education. (2021). *What Terrorism Is, and Is Not*. https://www.atrainceu.com/content/1-what-terrorism-and-not https://www.atrainceu.com/content/1-what-terrorism-and-not

Albright, J. (2017). *Welcome to the Era of Fake News*. Columbia University Press. doi:10.17645/mac.v5i2.977

Aleksidze, L. (2012a). *Dictionary of International Law*. Logo Press.

Aleksidze, L. (2012b). *UN 1984. State-sponsored terrorism*. Logo Press.

Arms Control Association. (2021a). *African Nuclear-Weapons-Free Zone Treaty*. Retrieved from: https://www.armscontrol.org/treaties/african-nuclear-weapons-free-zone-treaty

Arms Control Association. (2021b). *Treaties and agreement*. Retrieved from: https://www.armscontrol.org/treaties

Banerjee, Ferg, & Choi. (2012). *Fake news Syntactic Stylometry for Deception Detection*. Retrieved from: https://www.researchgate.net/publication/233844582_Syntactic_Stylometry_for_Deception_Detection

Basic Facts about the United Nations. (2005). UN Department of Public Affairs.

Beck, U. (1998). *World Risk Society*. Polity Press.

Beck, U. (1998). *World Risk Society*. Polity Press.

Beitz. (2009). *Human Rights*. Author.

Bull, H. (1979). *Theory of International Politics*. Cambridge University Press.

Buzan, B. (1991). People, States & Fear: The National Security Problem in International Relations. Academic Press.

Canetti, D., Gross, M., Waismel-Manor, I., Levanon, A., & Cohen, H. (2017). How Cyberattacks Terrorize: Cortisol and Personal Insecurity Jump in the Wake of Cyberattacks. *Cyberpsychology, Behavior, and Social Networking*, 20(2), 72–77. doi:10.1089/cyber.2016.0338

Chitadze, N. (2015). *Global Dimensions of the organized Crime and Ways of the Preventing Threats at the International Level. Connections. The Quarterly Journal Connections. Partnership for Peace Consortium of Defense Academics and Security Studies Institutes.*

Chitadze, N. (2016). *Political Science.* International Black Sea University.

Chitadze, N. (2019). *Is New Cold War Started? Possible Military Confrontation between USA and Russia on the Examples of Comparing the Military Potentials of Two Powers and Withdrawal from Intermediate-Range Nuclear Forces Treaty by Both Countries.* Journal in Humanities, 8(1).

Chochua, D. (2015). *Caliphate reloaded: Why the isil is not unique.* Retrieved from: https://www.gfsis.org/files/library/opinion-papers/38-expert-opinion-eng.pdf

Chomsky, N. (2002). What Anthropologists Should Know about the Concept of Terrorism. *Anthropology Today, 18*(2).

Christiano, T. (2006). A Democratic Theory of Territory and Some Puzzles about Global Democracy. *Journal of Social Philosophy, 37.*

Club of Rome. (2021). *History.* https://www.cluboframe.org/about-us/history/

Conroy, Rubin, & Chen. (2015). *Deception detection for news: Three types of fakes.* Retrieved from: https://asistdl.onlinelibrary.wiley.com/doi/full/10.1002/pra2.2015.145052010083

Crime Museum. (2021). *Typical Activities of Organized Crime.* Retrieved from: https://www.crimemuseum.org/crime-library/organized-crime/typical-activities-of-organized-crime/

Cunnigham, W., & Greene, S. (2010). Distortion as a Validation Criterion in the Identification of Suspicious Reviews. *Conference: 1st Workshop on Social Media Analytics.*

Davitashvili, E. (2012). *Global Geography.* Tbilisi State University.

Deep, A. (2015). Hybrid War: Old Concept, New Techniques. *Small War Journal.*

Defining Terrorism. One Size Fits All? (2017). *Cambridge University Press.* Retrieved from: https://www.cambridge.org/core/journals/international-and-comparative-law-quarterly/article/defining-terrorism-one-size-fits-all/0E707CD33E7F656573C777BE23C27168

Dolgovaya, A. (2005). Criminology (3rd ed.). Norma.

Doyle, M. (1983). *Kant, Liberal Legacies, and Foreign Affairs. In Immanuel Kant.* Routledge.

Elgan, M. (2020). *Only AI can save us from a world of fakes (a world AI is also creating).* Retrieved from: https://www.idginsiderpro.com/article/3528792/only-ai-can-us-from-a-world-of-fakes-a-world-ai-is-also-creating.html

Fassihi, F. (2002, Oct. 27). In Iran, grim reminders of Saddam's arsenal. *New Jersey Star-Ledger.*

FBA. (2021). *Transnational Organized Crime.* Retrieved from: https://www.fbi.gov/investigate/organized-crime

Fitzgerald, G. (2008). *Chemical Warfare and Medical Response During World War I*. Retrieved from: https://www.ncbi.nlm.nih.gov/pmc/articles/PMC2376985/

Freedom House. (2020). *Freedom in the World*. Retrieved from: https://freedomhouse.org/report/freedom-world

Fukuyama. (1989). End of the History? *The National Interest*.

Garthoff, R. (1994). The Great Transition: American-Soviet Relations and the End of the Cold War. Brookings Institution Press.

Global Financial Integrity. (2017). *Transnational Crime and the Developing World*. Retrieved from: https://www.gfintegrity.org/wp-content/uploads/2017/03/Transnational_Crime-final.pdf

Goldstein, J., & Pevehouse, C. (2007). *International relations. International Relations. Update* (8th ed.). Pearson Longman.

Goldstein, J., & Pevehouse, C. (2011). *International relations. International Relations: 2010-2011 Update* (9th ed.). Pearson Longman.

Gooding, R. (2006). *What's wrong with terrorism?* SAGE Journals.

Hancock, Woodworth, & Porter. (2011). *Hungry like the wolf: A word-pattern analysis of the language of psychopaths*. ResearchGate.net.

Hoffman, B. (1988). *Inside Terrorism*. Columbia University Press.

Hor, M. Y. M. (2005). *Global anti-terrorism law and policy*. Cambridge University Press.

Huntington. (1993). The Third Wave: Democratization in the Late of Twentieth Century. *Journal of Democracy*.

Hyland, J. (1995). *Democratic Theory: The Philosophical Foundations*. Manchester University Press.

ICAN. (2019). *Nuclear-armed states set record $73bn spending on nukes as pandemic spreads: New report*. Retrieved from: https://www.icanw.org/ican_releases_2019_nuclear_weapons_spending_research

James, P., & Friedman, J. (2006). *Globalizing War and Intervention* (Vol. 3). Sage Publications.

Kalsnes, B. (2018). *Fake news*. Retrieved from: https://oxfordre.com/communication/view/10.1093/acrefore/9780190228613.001.0001/acrefore-9780190228613-e-809

Kant. (1995). *Perpetual Peace: A Philosophical Sketch*. Retrieved from: https://www.mtholyoke.edu/acad/intrel/kant/kant1.htm

Kegley, C., & Wittkopf, E. (2011). *World Politics: Trend and Transformation* (8th ed.). Wadsworth Publishing.

Kofman, M. (2016). *Russian Hybrid Warfare and other dark arts*. Retrieved from: https://warontherocks.com/2016/03/russian-hybrid-warfare-and-other-dark-arts/

Kramer, A., & Specia, M. (2019). What Is the I.N.F. Treaty and Why Does It Matter? *The New York Times*.

Laqueur, W. (2007). *History of Terrorism*. Transaction Publishers, Emerald Group Publishing Limited.

Lebedeva. (2007). *World Politics*. Aspect Press.

Mansfield, H. (2001). *Those Hell-Hounds Called Terrorists*. The Claremont Institute.

Modebadze. (2016). *Two Wars in Chechnya*. Universal Press.

Nairn, T., & James, P. (2005). *Global Matrix: Nationalism, Globalism and State-Terrorism*. Pluto Press.

National Institute of Justice. (2011). *The Evolution of Transnational Organized Crime*. Retrieved from: https://nij.ojp.gov/topics/articles/evolution-transnational-organized-crime

NATO Handbook, . (2007). *NATO Public Diplomacy Division*.

OPCV. (2021). *Chemical Weapon Convention*. Retrieved from: https://www.opcw.org/chemical-weapons-convention

Oyster Bay Conferences. (1966). *Definitions of Organized Crime*. Retrieved from: http://www.organized-crime.de/OCDEF1.htm

Palmer, R. (2014). The French Directory Between Extremes. In *The Age of the Democratic Revolution: A Political History of Europe and America, 1760–1800*. Princeton University Press.

Pressreader. (2019). *Public libraries have an important role in sustaining democracy*. Retrieved from: https://blog.pressreader.com/public-libraries-have-an-important-role-in-sustaining-democracy

Primoratz, I. (2007). *Terrorism*. Stanford Encyclopedia of Philosophy.

Purkitt, H. (1984). *Dealing with Terrorism*. Conflict in World Society.

Rondeli, A. (2003). *International Relations*. Edition House "Neckeri".

Schmid, A. (2011). *Routledge Handbook of Terrorism Research*. Routledge. doi:10.4324/9780203828731

Schmid, J. (2019). *The Hybrid Face of Warfare in the 21st Century*. Retrieved from: https://www.maanpuolustus-lehti.fi/the-hybrid-face-of-warfare-in-the-21st-century/

Secretariat of the Antarctic Treaty. (1959). Retrieved from: https://www.ats.aq/e/antarctictreaty.html#:~:text=The%20Antarctic-,Treaty,to%20by%20many%20other%20nations

SIPRI. (2019a). *Trends in World Military Expenditure, 2019*. Retrieved from: https://www.sipri.org/publications/2020/sipri-fact-sheets/trends-world-military-expenditure-2019

SIPRI. (2019b). *World Nuclear Forces*. Retrieved from: https://www.sipri.org/yearbook/2019/06#:~:text=At%20the%20start%20of%202019,were%20deployed%20with%20operational%20forces

Soll. (2016). Fake News. *Politico Magazine*. Retrieved from: https://www.politico.com/magazine/story/2016/12/fake-news-history-long-violent-214535/

Stockholm International Peace Research Institute. (2007). *SIPRI Yearbook 2007: Armaments, Disarmament, and International Security*. Oxford University Press.

Stohl, M. (1984). *The Superpowers and International Terror*. Paper presented at the Annual Meeting of the International Studies Association, Atlanta, GA.

Stohl, M. (1988). *National Interests and State Terrorism, The Politics of Terrorism*. Marcel Dekker.

The Nobel Prize. (1997). *The Nobel Peace Prize, 1997*. Retrieved from: https://www.nobelprize.org/prizes/peace/1997/summary/

Tome, L. (2015). *The "Islamic state": trajectory and reach a year after its self-proclamation as a "caliphate"*. Retrieved from: https://www.redalyc.org/pdf/4135/413541154008.pdf

Ullman, R. (1983). *Redefining Security. International Security*. The MIT Press. Retrieved from: https://muse.jhu.edu/article/446023/summary

UN Reform, . (2005). *United Nations. March 21, 2005. Freedom from Fear backs the definition of terrorism–an issue so divisive agreement on it has long eluded the world community – as any action*. United Nations.

UN Security Council. (2000). *UN 51/45 about declaration the southern hemisphere as a zone – free from the nuclear weapon*. UN Security Council Report.

United National Office for Disarmament Affairs. (2021). *1925 Geneva Protocol. Protocol for the Prohibition of the Use in War of Asphyxiating, Poisonous or Other Gases, and of Bacteriological Methods of Warfare*. Retrieved from: https://www.un.org/disarmament/wmd/bio/1925-geneva-protocol/

UNODA. (2021). *Biological Weapons Convention*. United Nations Office for Disarmament Affairs.

U.S. arms exports in 2020, by country (in TIV expressed in million constant 1990 U.S. dollars). (n.d.). https://www.statista.com/statistics/248552/us-arms-exports-by-country/

US Department of State. (1992). *Treaty on Conventional Armed Forces in Europe (CFE)*. https://2001-2009.state.gov/t/vci/cca/cfe/index.htm

US Department of State. (2007). *Office of Coordinator for Counterterrorism*. Retrieved from: https://2001-2009.state.gov/s/ct/info/c16718.htm

US Department of State. (2018). *Remembering the 1998 Embassy Bombings*. Retrieved from: https://www.state.gov/remembering-the-1998-embassy-bombings-2/

US National Intelligence Council. (2015). *Global Trends 2015. Dialogue about future with non-governmental experts*. Author.

US National library of Medicine. (2021). *Chemical Warfare and Medical Response During World War I*. National Institutes of Health.

Warwick & Lewis. (2017). *Media Manipulation and Disinformation Online*. https://datasociety.net/library/media-manipulation-and-disinfo-online/

Weedon, Nuland, & Stamos. (2017). *Information Operations and Facebook*. Retrieved from: https://i2.res.24o.it/pdf2010/Editrice/ILSOLE24ORE/ILSOLE24ORE/Online/_Oggetti_Embedded/Documenti/2017/04/28/facebook-and-information-operations-v1.pdf

Williamson, M. (2009). *Terrorism, war and international law: the legality of the use of force against Afghanistan in 2001*. Ashgate Publishing.

Worldometer. (2021). *World Population*. Retrieved from: https://www.worldometers.info/world-population/#:~:text=7.9%20Billion%20(2021),Nations%20estimates%20elaborated%20by%20Worldometer

Zakaria, F. (2015). *Is Democracy Safe in the World?* https://www.youtube.com/watch?v=eIeRJmNS3rkForeignpolicy

KEY TERMS AND DEFINITIONS

Actor: An individual, group, state, or organization that plays a major role in world politics.

Agency: The capacity of actors to harness the power to achieve objectives.

Alliances: Coalitions form when two or more states combine their military capabilities and promise to coordinate their policies to increase mutual security.

Anarchy: A condition in which the units in the global system are subjected to few if any overarching institutions to regulate their conduct.

Antipersonnel Landmines (APLs): Weapons buried below the surface of the soil that explodes on contact with any person-soldier or citizen-stepping on them.

Armed Aggression: Combat between the military forces of two or more states or groups.

Arms Control: Multilateral or bilateral agreements to contain arms races by setting limits on the number and types of weapons states are permitted.

Arms Race: The buildup of weapons and armed forces by two or more states that threaten each other, with the competition driven by the conviction that gaining a lead is necessary for security.

Asymmetric Warfare: Armed conflict between belligerents of vastly unequal military strength, in which the weaker side is often a nonstate actor that relies on unconventional tactics.

Balance of Power: The theory that peace and stability are most likely to be maintained when military power is distributed to prevent a single superpower hegemon or bloc from controlling the world.

Bandwagoning: The tendency for weak states to seek an alliance with the strongest power, irrespective of that power's ideology or type of government, to increase their security.

Bilateral: Interactions between two transnational actors, such as treaties they have accepted to govern their future relationship.

Bilateral Agreements: Exchange between two states, such as arms control agreements, negotiated cooperatively to set ceilings on military force levels.

Bush Doctrine: The unilateral policies of the George W. Bush administration proclaiming that the United States will make decisions only to meet America's perceived national interests, not to concede to other countries' complaints or to gain their acceptance.

Civil Wars: Wars between opposing groups within the same country or by rebels against the government.

Clash of Civilizations: Political scientist Samuel Huntington's controversial thesis that in the twenty-first century the globe's major civilizations will conflict with one another, leading to anarchy and warfare similar to that resulting from conflicts between states over the past five hundred years.

Coercive Diplomacy: The use of threats or limited armed force to persuade an adversary to alter its foreign and/or domestic policies.

Cold War: The 42-year (1949-1991) rivalry between the United States and the Soviet Union, as well as their competing coalitions, which sought to contain each other's expansion and win worldwide predominance.

Collective Security: A security regime agreed to by the great powers that set rules for keeping the peace, guided by the principle that an act of aggression by any state will be met by a collective response from the rest.

Conciliation: A conflict-resolution procedure in which a third party assists both parties in a dispute but does not propose a solution.

Conflict: Discord, often arising in international relations over perceived incompatibilities of interest.

Consequentialism: An approach to evaluating moral choices based on the results of the action taken.

Coup d'etat: A sudden, forcible takeover of government by a small group within that country, typically carried out by violent or illegal means intending to install their leadership in power.

Crimes Against Humanity: A category of activities, made illegal at the Nuremberg war crime trials, condemning states that abuse human rights.

Crisis: A situation in which the threat of escalation to warfare is high and the time available for making decisions and reaching compromised solutions in negotiation is compressed.

Cyberspace: A metaphor used to describe the global electronic web of people, ideas, and interactions on the Internet, which is unencumbered by the borders of the geopolitical world.

Democratic Peace: The theory that although democratic states sometimes wage wars against non-democratic states, they do not fight one another.

Détente: In general, a strategy of seeking to relax tensions between adversaries to reduce the possibility of war.

Diplomacy: Communication and negotiation between global actors that is not dependent upon the use of force and seeks a cooperative solution.

Disarmament: Agreements to reduce or destroy weapons or other means of attack.

Diversionary Theory of War: The hypothesis that leaders sometimes initiate conflict abroad as a way of increasing national public attention away from controversial domestic issues and internal problems.

Doctrines: The guidelines that a great power or an alliance embraces as a strategy to specify the conditions under which it will use military power and armed force for political purposes abroad.

Ethnic Cleansing: The extermination of an ethnic minority group by a state.

Ethnic Groups: People whose identity is primarily defined by their sense of sharing a common ancestral nationality, language, cultural heritage, and kinship.

Ethnic Nationalism: Devotion to a cultural, ethnic, or linguistic community.

Failed States: Countries whose governments have so mismanaged policy that their citizens in rebellion, threaten revolution to divide the country into separate independent states.

Fascism: A far-right ideology that promotes extreme nationalism and the establishment of an authoritarian society built around a single party with dictatorial leadership.

Genocide: The attempt to eliminate in whole or in part, an ethnic, racial religious, or national minority group.

Geopolitics: The relationship between geography and politics and their consequences for states' national interests and relative power.

Global North: A term used to refer to the world`s wealthy, industrialized countries located primarily in the Northern hemisphere.

Global South: A term now often used instead of the Third World to designate the less developed countries located primarily in the Southern Hemisphere.

Good Offices: The provision by a third party to offer a place for negotiation among disputants but does not serve as a mediator in the actual negotiations.

Great Powers: The most powerful countries, military, and economically in the global system.

Group of 77 (G-77): The coalition of Third World countries that sponsored the 1963 Joint Declaration of Developing Countries calling for reform to allow greater equality in North-South trade.

Hard Power: The ability to exercise international influence utilizing a country's military capabilities.

Hegemon: A preponderant state capable of dominating the conduct of international political and economic relations.

Hegemonic Stability Theory: A body of theory that maintains that the establishment of hegemony for the global dominance by a single great power is a necessary condition for global order in commercial transactions and international military security.

Hegemony: The ability of one state to lead in world politics by promoting its worldview and ruling over arrangements governing international economics and politics.

High Politics: Geostrategic issues of national and international security that pertain to matters of war and peace.

Horizontal Nuclear Proliferation: An increase in the number of states that possess nuclear weapons.

Humanitarian Intervention: The use of peacekeeping troops by foreign states or international organizations to protect endangered people from gross violations of their human rights and mass murder.

Imperialism: The policy of expanding state power through the conquest and or military domination of foreign territory.

Info War-Tactics: Attacks on an adversary's telecommunications and computer networks to penetrate and degrade an enemy whose defense capabilities depend heavily on these technological systems.

Information Warfare: Attacks on an adversary's telecommunications and computer networks to degrade the technological systems vital to its defense and economic well-being.

Intergovernmental Organizations (IGOs): Institutions created and joined by state governments that give them authority to make collective decisions to manage particular problems on the global agenda.

Intermediate-Range Nuclear Forces (INF) Treaty: The U.S-Russian agreement to eliminate an entire class of nuclear weapons by removing all intermediate and short-range ground-based missiles and launchers with ranges between 300 and 3.500 miles from Europe.

International Aggression: Killing others that are not members of one's species.

International Court of Justice (ICJ): The primary court established by the United Nations for resolving legal disputes between states and providing advisory opinions to international agencies and the UN General Assembly.

International Criminal Court (ICC): A court established by the UN for indicting and administering justice to people committing war crimes.

International Criminal Tribunals: Special tribunals established by the UN prosecute those responsible for wartime atrocities and genocide bring justice to victims and deter such crimes.

International Terrorism: The threat or use of violence as a tactic of terrorism against targets in other countries.

Irredentism: A movement by an ethnic-national group to recover control of lost territory by force so that the new state boundaries will no longer divide the group.

Jus ad Bellum: A component of just a war doctrine that establishes criteria under which a just war may be initiated.

Jus in Bello: A component of just war doctrine that sets limits on the acceptable use of force.

Just War Doctrine: The moral criteria identifying when a war may be undertaken and how it should be fought once it begins.

Just War Theory: The theoretical criteria under which it is morally permissible or just for a state to go to war and the methods by which a just war might be fought.

Kellogg-Briand Pact: A multilateral treaty negotiated in 1928 that outlawed war as a method for settling interstate conflicts.

Long Cycle Theory: A theory that focuses on the rise and fall of the leading global power as the central political process of the modern world system.

Long Peace: Long-lasting periods of peace between any of the military strongest great powers.

Massive Retaliation: The Eisenhower administration`s policy doctrine for containing Soviet Communism By pledging to respond to any act of aggression with the most destructive capabilities available including nuclear weapons.

Mediation: A conflict-solution procedure in which a third party proposes a nonbinding solution to the disputants.

Militant Religious Movements: Politically active organizations whose members are fanatically devoted to the global promotion of their religious beliefs.

Military Intervention: Over or covert use of force by one or more countries to affect the target counties government and policies.

Military Necessity: The legal principle that violation of the rules of warfare may be excused for defensive purposes during periods of extreme emergency.

Military-Industrial Complex: A combination of defense establishments, contractors who supply arms for them, and government agencies that benefit from high military spending which act as a lobbying coalition to pressure governments to appropriate large expenditures for military preparedness.

Multilateral Agreements: Cooperative compacts among many states to ensure that a concerted policy is implemented toward alleviating a common problem such as levels of future weapons capabilities.

Multilateralism: Cooperative approaches to managing shared problems through collective and coordinated actions.

Nation: A collective whose people see themselves as members of the same group because they share the same ethnicity, culture, or language.

National Interest: The goals that states pursue to maximize what they perceive to be selfishly best for their country.

National Security: A country's psychological freedom from fears that the state will be unable to resist threats to its survival and national values emanating from abroad or at home.

Negotiation: Diplomatic dialogue and discussion between two or more parties to resolve through give-and-take bargaining perceived differences of interests and the conflict they cause.

Neocolonialism (Neo-Imperialism): The economic rather than military domination of foreign countries.

Neutrality: The legal doctrine that provides rights for the state to remain nonaligned with adversaries waging war against each other.

Non-Aligned Movement (NAM): A group of more than one hundred newly independent mostly less developed states that joined together as a group of neutrals to avoid entanglement with the superpowers competing alliances in the Cold War and to advance the Global South primary interest in economic cooperation and growth.

Non-Aligned States: Countries that do not form alliances with opposed great powers and practice neutrality on issues that divide great powers.

Nonalignment: A foreign policy posture that rejects participating in military alliances with the rival blocs for fear that formal alignment will entangle the state in an unnecessary involvement in the war.

Noncombatant Immunity: The legal principle that military force should not be used against innocent civilians.

Nonlethal Weapons: The wide array of soft kill low- intensify methods of incapacitating an enemy's people, vehicles, communications system, or entire cities without killing either combatants or non - combatants.

Nonproliferation Regime: Rules to contain arms races so that weapons or technology do not spread to states that do not have them.

North Atlantic Treaty Organization: A military alliance created in 1949 to deter a Soviet attack on Western Europe that since has expanded and redefined its missions to emphasize not only the maintenance of peace but also the promotion of democracy.

Pacifism: The liberal idealist school of ethical thought that recognizes no conditions that justify the taking of another human's life even when authorized by a head of state.

Peace Enforcement: The application of military force to warring parties or the threat of it normally according to international authorization to compel compliance with resolutions or with sanctions designed to maintain or restore peace and order.

Peace Operations: A general category encompassing both peacekeeping and peace enforcement operations undertaken to establish and maintain peace between disputants.

Peaceful Coexistence: Soviet leader Nikita Khrushchev`s 1956 doctrine that war between capitalist and communist states is not inevitable and that inter-block competition could be peaceful.

Peacebuilding: Post-conflict actions predominantly diplomatic and economic that strengthen and rebuild governmental infrastructure and institutions to avoid renewed recourse to armed conflict.

Peacemaking: The process of democracy mediation negotiation or other forms of peaceful settlement that arranges an end to a dispute and resolves the issues that led to conflict.

Polarity: The degree to which military and economic capabilities are concentrated in the global system that determines the number of centers of power or poles.

Polarization: The formation of competition coalitions or blocs composed of allies that align with one of the major competing poles of centers of power.

Policy Agenda: The changing list of problems or issues to which governments pay special attention at any given moment.

Policy Networks: Leaders and organized interests (such as lobbies) that form temporary alliances to influence a particular foreign policy decision.

Politics: To Harold Lasswell the study of who gets what when and how.

Preemptive War: A quick first strike attack that seeks to defeat an adversary before it can organize an initial attack or a retaliatory response.

Preventive Diplomacy: Diplomatic actions taken in advance of a predictable crisis to prevent or limit violence.

Proliferation: The spread of weapon capabilities from a few too many states in a chain reaction so that an increasing number of states gain the ability to launch an attack on other states with devastating weapons.

Rapprochement: Diplomacy is a policy seeking to reestablish normal cordial relations between enemies.

Realism: A paradigm based on the premise that world politics is essentially and unchangeably a struggle among self-interest states for power and position under anarchy, with each competing state pursuing its national interest.

Realpolitik: The theoretical outlook prescribing that countries should increase their power and wealth to compete with and domestic other countries.

Retorsion: Retaliatory acts (such as economic sanctions) against a target's behavior that is regarded as objectionable but legal such as trade restrictions to punish the target with the measures that are legal under international law.

Sanctions: Punitive actions by one global actor against another to retaliate for its previous objectionable behavior.

Second-Strike Capability: A state's capacity to retaliate after absorbing an adversary's first-strike attack with weapons of mass destruction.

Security Regime: Norms and rules for interaction agreed to by a set of states to increase security.

Small Powers: Countries with limited political military economic capabilities and influence.

Smart Bombs: Precision-guided military technology that enables a bomb to search for its target and detonate at the precise time it can do the most damage.

Terrorism: Premeditated violence perpetrated against non-combat targets by subnational or transnational groups or clandestine agents usually intended to influence an audience.

Third World: A Cold War term to describe the less-developed countries of Africa, Asia, The Caribbean, and Latin America.

Uni-Multipolar: A global system where there is a single dominant power but the settlement of key international issues always requires action by the dominant power in combination with that of other great powers.

Unilateralism: An approach that relies on self-help independent strategies in foreign policy.

Unipolarity: A condition in which the global system has a single dominant power or hegemon capable of prevailing over all other states.

Vertical Nuclear Proliferation: The expansion of the capabilities of existing nuclear powers to inflict increasing destruction with their nuclear weapons.

World Politics: The study of how global actors' activities entail the exercise of influence to achieve and defend their goals and ideas and how it affects the world at large.

World-System Theory: A body of theory that treats the capitalistic world economy originating in the sixteenth century as an interconnected unit of analysis encompassing the entire globe.

Xenophobia: The suspicious dislike disrespect, and disregard for members of a foreign nationality ethnic, or linguistic group.

Yalta Conference: The 1945 summit meeting of the Allied victors to resolve postwar territorial issues and to establish voting procedures in the UN to collectively manage world order.

Zero-Sum: An exchange in a purely conflictual relationship in which what is gained by one competitor is lost by another.

Chapter 3
Recent Trends in Global Security:
Challenges and Opportunities

Kannadhasan S.
https://orcid.org/0000-0001-6443-9993
Cheran College of Engineering, India

Nagarajan R.
Gnanamani College of Technology, India

Shanmuganantham M.
Tamilnadu Government Polytechnic College, India

ABSTRACT

With the emergence of the digital economy and an ever-increasing percentage of consumers conducting their business mostly from online or mobile devices, electronic shopping, or e-commerce, is fast being recognized as the way to go global at the click of a button. As a consequence, any modern company's ability to create a viable e-commerce model is becoming extremely significant. To secure themselves and their clients, an organization must overcome current security issues to ensure that the highest levels of e-commerce security are maintained. Failure to follow stringent ecommerce security procedures will result in the destruction of data, the compromise of transaction documents, and the leak of the customer's financial information. This will lead to legal and financial repercussions, as well as a negative image for the company. Cloud networking, web computing, e-commerce, net banking, and other cutting-edge technology also need a high degree of protection. Since these instruments hold personal information regarding a human, their security has become a top priority.

INTRODUCTION

One of the most important problems faced by e-commerce is the flow of expertise from business to

DOI: 10.4018/978-1-7998-9586-2.ch003

business, inside the same business, and from business to consumers. When dealing with various parties and exchanging with them, companies are confronted with a growing number of different data types, connectivity needs, and process specifications. As a result, security concerns and threats must be addressed first, rather than secondarily, and must be treated seriously. Businesses must be able to respond to the demands of their partners in a prompt, reliable, and secure manner or risk losing out on a strong and global sector. In order to gain and sustain consumer loyalty and confidence in this new type of economy, they must conform to security standards and disciplines. (Barskar & Deen, 2010; Evdokimov et al., 2011; Minerva et al., 2015; Vermesan & Friess, 2014; Yazdanifard & Al-Huda Edres, 2011).

Protection guidelines for applications and networks can be read and applied by the workers in charge of e-commerce sites. Client-side Trojan horse programs, on the other hand, represent the greatest threat to e-commerce since they will bypass or subvert the bulk of the authentication and authorization protocols used in an e-commerce transaction. The most convenient way to operate these applications on a remote computer is through email attachments. As E-commerce advances at a rapid rate, people's attention is attracted to security issues. One of the most critical facets of E-commerce development is transaction security. The security problems of Ecommerce operations necessitated a solution approach based on two factors: technology and framework, in order to improve the environment for E-commerce development and promote further progress. Travel and tourism have often necessitated heightened security and privacy.

However, it is undeniable that in the last two decades, protection and security considerations have become much more relevant in the tourism industry. The world has changed dramatically in the past two decades. Security has deteriorated dramatically as a result of violent attacks, local conflicts, environmental hazards, epidemics, and pandemics that we have seen. These incidents had a detrimental effect on the travel and tourism industries, which could not be avoided. Furthermore, some of these incidents demonstrated the tourism industry's weakness on both a national and regional scale. As a result, analysis and review of the relationship between security concerns and tourism is needed, as is the establishment of a modern, up-to-date description of the term security and protection in tourism. The tourism industry has realized the importance of researching protection and security issues. Tourism and hospitality science and education could discuss emerging issues of health and safety in tourism in order to educate future tourism practitioners by incorporating latest study results into university curricula. This may be achieved by either introducing additional subjects (such as risk assessment in tourism) or supplementing the quality of existing subjects with new security and safety skills (e.g. marketing, Consumer Relations, Tourism Destination Management). Is it ridiculous to believe that in the future, Safety Sells in Tourism could become a popular mantra in the travel and tourism industry. The Internet has rapidly become the primary commerce and networking medium for virtually every industry, large or small. (Ladan, 2010; Moftah, 2012; Rane & Meshram, 2012; Stergiou et al., 2018; Yoon et al., 2015).

E-commerce is rapidly being recognized as the way to go global at the click of a button as a result of the Emerging Economy's emergence. In addition, the Internet has made it easy to link to a large network of people and businesses at a low cost. This convergence of low-cost hardware and ubiquitous Internet connectivity lays the groundwork for a dramatic shift in how everybody does business. E-commerce refers to the buying and selling of products and services over the Internet. E-commerce allows for the integration of external and internal systems as well as the reduction of transaction costs, resulting in the expansion of retail networks and an increase in revenue and earnings. E-commerce can be used in a wide spectrum of sectors. The two main industries where it is used are business-to-business (B2B) and business-to-consumer (B2C) (Al Hinai & Singh, 2017; Banerjee et al., 2018; Mahdavinejad et al., 2018; Saarikko et al., 2017; Sudeendra et al., 2017).

E-COMMERCE

E-commerce has not been able to hit its maximum potential due to a spike in media alerts regarding protection and privacy violations such as identity theft and financial fraud, as well as increased concern among online shoppers about the risks of conducting purchases online. Many consumers fail to conduct online purchases due to a sense of confidence or concern about the security of their personal details. E-commerce provides great opportunities for the banking sector, but it also introduces additional challenges and vulnerabilities, such as security threats. As a result, information protection is a critical management and technological necessity for all safe and profitable internet payment processing activities. Nonetheless, due to constant technological and market shift, defining it is a difficult task that necessitates an organized match of algorithm and strategic solutions. The impact of security, privacy, and confidence on customers, as well as attitudes, is critical in the adoption of e-commerce. Furthermore, critical data may be stored in parallel with data flowing from external ecommerce purchases, allowing for robust and accurate alignment into operational processes.

Consumers must clearly reveal a vast volume of confidential personal details to the seller during an online sale, putting themselves at considerable risk. Understanding customer confidence is critical to e-continued commerce's development. The new advancements in Internet and Web Technology have had a major impact on almost all aspects of industry and trade. It entails more than just moving existing company activities to a different platform. Redefining market strategies, evolving organizational culture, and establishing dependable customer support are all part of the equation. It must also confront and solve a wide range of obstacles. E-commerce is a relatively modern medium of marketing that is expected to expand rapidly in the coming years. It can be described as conducting business over the Internet or exchanging products and services. The development and success of e-commerce has been fueled by rapid advancements in mobile computing, networking technology, e-payment systems, and other emerging technologies. New security threats and challenges, on the other hand, are the key roadblocks to e-commerce development. While any e-commerce framework may use a variety of defense techniques to greatly minimize the likelihood of assault and breach, new attack strategies and weaknesses are only discovered and exploited after an attacker has discovered and exploited them. Furthermore, as technological expertise grows and becomes more widely available on the internet, offenders become more sophisticated and professional in the kinds of attacks they may carry out. The exponential growth in e-commerce has coincided with a spike in the amount and types of security attacks and threats. These attacks target a variety of weaknesses, including loopholes in third-party components used by websites, such as shopping cart applications, as well as SQL injection, cross-site scripting, knowledge leakage, session capture, message manipulation, buffer overflows, and others, as described in the previous parts. Securing an e-Commerce infrastructure is a complex process in which new threats emerge every day.

As a result, careful preparation is required to remain safe from potential new security threats while maintaining consumer confidence in the system. To summarize, e-commerce is increasingly expanding, and a variety of innovations have converged to aid in the spread of e-commerce programs. However, in terms of the protection vulnerabilities that these devices would avoid, they face a difficult future. With technologies evolving at such a fast pace, no e-commerce system will ever claim to be completely safe. Security concerns are critical to any system's sustainability, and as a result, they must be continually assessed and addressed. Furthermore, protection concerns and interventions must be prioritized rather than afterthoughts, and they must be treated seriously. Companies should adopt protection guidelines and disciplines to achieve and maintain customer interest and loyalty in this emerging form of economy if they choose to look forward to the bright and exciting future of e-commerce with optimism. Employees who operate on e-commerce devices can read and obey the guidelines for securing apps and networks. Consumer education on protection issues is still in its infancy, but it can prove to be a critical component of the e-commerce security ecosystem.

CYBER SECURITY

Protecting privacy is one of the most daunting challenges in today's world. The first thing that comes to mind when we think about cyber security is "cyber threats," which are on the increase at an unprecedented pace. Various governments and businesses are taking a variety of steps to combat cybercrime. After different initiatives, data protection remains a major issue for many people. This paper reflects on the problems that data protection faces in the modern era. It also covers the most recent developments of network protection tactics, ethics, and patterns that are altering the face of cyber security. With the click of a button, today's man will send and receive info, whether it's an e-mail, an audio or video file, but has he ever noticed how safely his data is shared or transmitted to the other party without any information being leaked? The answer is cyber security. The Internet is the fastest-growing infrastructure in today's world. In today's technological landscape, several new technologies are changing the face of mankind. However, as a result of these latest technologies, we are unable to secure our sensitive information as well as we would want, and cybercrime is on the increase. Since more than 70% of all commercial transactions are now conducted electronically, this area necessitated a high level of protection to ensure transparent and efficient transactions. As a result, data defense has been a hot topic. The reach of cyber protection extends beyond protecting knowledge in the IT sector to include a variety of other areas such as cyber space.

To avoid being a victim of these crimes, one should always use a safer browser, particularly during important transactions. Both independent, medium, and big businesses are gradually embracing cloud technology these days. Under other terms, the world is gradually approaching the clouds. Since traffic will bypass conventional points of inspection, this new development poses a significant challenge for cyber security. In order to avoid the loss of valuable knowledge, policy controls for web apps and cloud servers would need to change as the amount of applications accessible in the cloud increases. Despite the fact that cloud providers are building their own models, security concerns continue to be raised. While the cloud offers many advantages, it is important to remember that when the cloud grows, so do the security challenges. APT (Advanced Persistent Threat) is a modern kind of cybercrime software. For years, network protection features like site filtering and intrusion prevention systems (IPS) have been critical in detecting such targeted attacks (mostly after the initial compromise). In order to detect threats, network defense must integrate with other security services as perpetrators get increasingly daring and use more ambiguous techniques.

We can now communicate with everyone in every part of the planet. However, stability is a major problem for these cell networks. Firewalls and other protection mechanisms are getting more porous as users utilize more gadgets such as laptops, computers, PCs, and other devices, many of which need additional security measures in addition to those provided by the apps. We must still keep the stability of these cell networks in mind. Furthermore, since cell networks are so vulnerable to cybercrime, extra caution must be exercised in the event of a security breach. IPv6 is a modern Internet protocol that would replace IPv4 (the previous version), which has served as the foundation of our networks and the Internet in general. It's not just a matter of porting IPv4 capability to IPv6. Though IPv6 is a complete substitute for IPv4 in terms of increasing the number of valid IP addresses, there are several fundamental modifications to the protocol that must be included in security policy. As a result, it is still preferable to upgrade to IPv6 as soon as possible to reduce the chance of cybercrime. Encryption is the method of encoding messages (or information) in such a way that it cannot be interpreted by eavesdroppers or hackers. An encryption scheme converts a letter or knowledge into unreadable cipher text by encrypting it using an encryption algorithm. This is typically accomplished by the use of an encryption key, which determines the message's encoding method. In the most basic stage, encryption safeguards data protection and honesty. However, more encryption means more electronic protection issues. Encryption is often used to encrypt data in transit, such as data sent via networks (e.g., the Internet, e-commerce), cell phones, wireless microphones, and wireless intercoms, among other things. As a result, by encrypting the file, one may determine whether or not information has been leaked.

Companies must develop innovative strategies to secure sensitive details as we grow more interactive in an increasingly linked environment. Social networking has a significant impact on internet protection which can play a significant role in personal cyber attacks. The use of social media by employees is on the rise, as is the possibility of an assault. Since most of us use social media or social networking platforms on a daily basis, it has become a major forum for cyber criminals to access private information and steal sensitive data. Companies must ensure that they are just as able to detect risks, react in real time, and prevent some sort of compromise in an environment where we are quick to offer up our personal details. Since these social networking sites draw people quickly, hackers use them as traps to obtain the knowledge and data they need. As a result, people must take adequate precautions, especially while engaging with social media, to avoid losing their data. The desire of people to exchange insights with a global audience is at the forefront of the social networking dilemma that companies face. In addition to allowing someone to disseminate economically confidential details, social networking often allows anyone to disseminate fake information, which may be almost as harmful.

Despite the fact that social networking may be used for cybercrime, these businesses cannot afford to avoid doing it because it is an integral part of their public relations strategy. Instead, they need solutions that can alert them to the danger so that they can react before any significant harm is done. Companies, on the other hand, should consider this and recognize the value of analyzing data, especially in social conversations, and providing adequate security strategies to avoid risks. Certain laws and technologies must be used to manage social networking. The benefits of information and communication technology, especially the Internet, have become an inextricable part of daily life. Are we, as people, countries, or the international community, adequately informed of and equipped for the challenges posed by cyberspace, or for the denial of access to that dimension of connectivity, trade, and even warfare.

Specifically, considering its increasing user base, the Internet remains unregulated or unregulated. It is exactly the environment in which hostile activity in cyberspace may be planned and carried out. There are security challenges in cyberspace that pose a modern-day security danger and threat. The advancement and deployment of knowledge and communication technologies has ushered in a modern era of conflict. Cyber warfare poses a unique threat to foreign security. In the twenty-first century, cyber defense would have a major impact on foreign affairs. This paper provides an outline of the definitions and values of cyber challenges that concern international protection and security. Terror and cyber engineering have no boundaries. Since such attacks may be carried out from everywhere in a very short time using current knowledge and messaging networks, action in cyberspace necessitates the dismissal of traditional ideas about time and space. Globalization dynamics also had an effect not only on humanity's successes, but also on the emergence of modern challenges to society. Terrorism and national security challenges have evolved as a result of the globalization transition and the Internet information movement. Intelligence and expertise are now the primary sources of strategic benefit, rather than military force or geographic position. For successful cyber threat prevention, international collaboration and information sharing are needed.

VARIOUS SECTOR OF GLOBAL SECURITY

The Internet plays a vital position in our everyday lives. It is a one-of-a-kind and interconnected mechanism that enables computers all over the world to interact using a set of communication protocols. Previously, the Internet was confined to browsing set websites and encouraging users to interact with one another through e-mail. A plethora of modern Internet technologies have appeared at this period. Intelligent computers, which can contact different information remotely at any moment, are becoming an extremely significant part of our daily lives. Since the number of linked smart devices increases growing every day, the Internet of Things (IoT) is the best solution for controlling and monitoring them. The "Internet of Stuff" is a phrase that defines the mechanism of connecting multiple artifacts to the Internet. Using an intelligent terminal, physical components may communicate with each other without the need for human interaction. The philosophical framework is used to express the meaning of the Internet of Things. The gradual translation of human existence into intelligence relies heavily on the evolution of Internet content. IoT technology is used in many smart systems, including smart houses, hospital monitoring, road preparation, building management, and smart cities. The Internet of Things (IoT) is the vital future of the Internet world. As a consequence, protection features like encryption and authentication are important for digital technology to enjoy the advantages of the Internet of Things. In addition, the Internet of Things is a great forum for economic growth and a better life. It does, however, pose significant security risks, especially if these devices are compromised or become vulnerable to cyber-attacks. As a consequence, a thorough and fast IoT implementation necessitates the use of sufficient security and authentication techniques.

One of the primary motives for this analysis is to monitor the spread and growth of IoT applications in different fields, considering the fact that IoT implementation will contribute to a slew of security problems and issues. The aim of this paper is to define the basic security specifications, risks, and shortcomings that affect the implementation of IoT technology. In this study, IoT architectures were classified into five layers. The most critical aspects of the IoT security guidelines that must be followed have been addressed. Furthermore, vulnerability flaws correlated with IoT devices, as well as general IoT security problems, have been investigated. This paper has paved the way for potential research in this area. We believe that this study is essential and that it will assist researchers in the creation of IoT defenses. For future research, a number of possible security issues, such as glitches, risks, and practical approaches to resolve IoT security threats, must be considered. Cyber-attacks on cellular data networks are very popular. Wireless networking networks are widely utilized in the military, manufacturing, clinics, retail, and transportation. These networks could be wired, cellular, or ad hoc in nature. Wireless sensor networks, actuator networks, and vehicular networks have received a lot of attention in the society and business. In recent years, the Internet of Things (IoT) has gained a lot of scholarly attention. The Internet of Things (IoT) is thought to be the future of the internet. In the future, the Internet of Things will play a vital role in changing our habits, beliefs, and business models. The use of IoT in different applications is expected to skyrocket in the coming years. The Internet of Things (IoT) helps billions of machines, consumers, and services to exchange knowledge and connect with one another. IoT networks are susceptible to a number of security risks as a consequence of the increased usage of IoT devices. Efficient security and privacy protocols, among other aspects, are essential in IoT networks for maintaining secrecy, authentication, access control, and integrity. This paper explores the security and privacy challenges that exist in IoT networks in depth.

In recent years, the Internet of Things (IoT) has attracted a lot of attention. In 1999, Kevin Ashton was the first to propose the Internet of Things concept. Thanks to rapid advancements in mobile networking, Wireless Sensor Networks (WSN), Radio Frequency Identification (RFID), and cloud computing, communication between IoT devices has become more simple than ever before. The Internet of Things (IoT) has the power to connect with one another. The Internet of Things also includes smart phones, mobile computers, PDAs, notebooks, ipads, and other hand-held mobile devices (IoT). IoT devices depend on low-cost sensors and wireless connectivity networks to communicate with one another and relay useful data to the centralized computer. Until being shipped to the targeted users, data from IoT devices is consolidated and processed in a single location. Our daily routines are being constantly based on a fictitious parallel world, thanks to rapid advancements in connectivity and internet technology. In the network's virtual universe, people will function, shop, speak, and keep pets and plants, but people must live in the real world. As a consequence, replacing all human activities with fully digital life is exceedingly challenging. There is a fictitious space bounding limit that restricts the internet's future development for better services. The Internet of Things has succeeded in bringing the fictional and real worlds together on a single network. One of the key aims of IoT is to build a digital environment and self-aware independent goods, such as smart life, smart stuff, smart health, and smart cities. With a growing abundance of devices connected to the internet, the adoption rate of IoT devices is now quite large. In the future, the Internet of Things would radically change our lives and economic systems. People and devices would be able to communicate at any time, from any place, from any machine, under optimal circumstances, through any network, and with any operation. The Internet of Things' main goal is to provide a better future world for humanity. Unfortunately, the majority of these devices and applications aren't set up to handle security and privacy risks, leading to a slew of security and privacy issues in IoT networks, including confidentiality, authentication, data confidentiality, access control, and confidentiality. Every day, hackers and intruders pose a danger to IoT computers.

An authorized person will trace the current location and progress of a vehicle in an intelligent IoT transportation scheme. The authorised consumer may even forecast its future location and traffic. The phrase "Internet of Things" was historically used to refer to the usage of RFID to identify special objects. According to the researchers, the Internet of Things (IoT) is now synonymous with sensors, GPS networks, mobile computers, and actuators. Data privacy and identification authentication are crucial for the adoption and services of new IoT technologies. Since the Internet of Things requires anything to be linked, tracked, and monitored, valuable information and personal information can be collected automatically. Because of the large number of assaults on IoT, privacy protection is a bigger issue in the IoT environment than it is in traditional networks. In healthcare environments, IoT instruments are more often used for patient monitoring and assessment. To monitor a patient's medical condition, personal medical devices (PMDs) are often inserted in the patient's body or attach to the patient's body externally. Personal Mobile Devices (PMDs) are lightweight electronic devices that are gaining in popularity. In the Smart House, the Internet of Things (IoT) Internet Protocol (IP) addresses make it simple for digital devices to communicate with one another, and IoT smart home networks are growing in popularity.

Both mobile home systems are related to the internet in the smart home environment. Malware attacks become more likely as the amount of sensors in the smart home increases. Since smart home devices are operated independently, malicious attacks are less possible. Smart home devices can now be activated through the internet at any time and from anywhere. As a consequence, malicious attempts on these networks are more likely. The four elements of a smart home are the service portal, mobile equipment, home gateway, and home network. In a smart home, several devices are linked, and information is intelligently transmitted through a home network. As a consequence, a home gateway has been developed to handle data transfer between smart devices linked to the internet. To deliver different utilities to the home network, the utility portal allows use of service provider networks.

A more comprehensive and secure policy is needed in the fight against cybercrime. Given that technical technologies alone cannot prevent any crime, it is critical that law enforcement agencies be provided with the resources they need to investigate and prosecute cybercrime effectively. Many countries and jurisdictions are already enacting stringent electronic security legislation in order to avoid the destruction of sensitive data. Every citizen must be educated on cyber protection in order to protect themselves from the growing number of cyber crimes. Attacks on web apps to steal data or spread malicious code are also a concern. Malicious code is distributed by cyber criminals via legal web servers that have been hacked. However, data-stealing threats, many of which garner public coverage, are still a significant concern. We must now place a stronger focus on the security of web servers and web apps. The most serious thing in IoT is reliability. In IoT implementations, industrial, company, consumer, or personal data can be used. The data in this program must be held confidential and safe from hacking and tampering. For example, IoT apps may save the results of a patient's health or shopping store. The Internet of Things increases device networking, but scalability, affordability, and reaction time remain issues. Security is a concern when data is securely exchanged over the internet. The most pressing IoT protection concerns are outlined below. The Internet of Things is susceptible to a range of attacks, both active and passive, that can effectively interrupt its functioning and make its services useless. In a passive assault, the intruder merely senses the node or extracts the information without attacking physically. Active attacks, on the other side, cause the effects to be physically disrupted. Internal attacks and external attacks are the two types of active attacks. Computers would be unable to communicate intelligently as a consequence of such vulnerable assaults. As a consequence, security measures must be implemented to prevent ransom ware assaults on machines.

The easiest platform for these computer criminals to steal data is via web servers. The use of new technology and networking mediums, as well as information transfer from business to industry, are both examples of this enterprise to customers, and within the organization, also created new protection problems. This paper describes the various technological and philosophical elements of e-commerce in general, as well as the various forms of protection threats that e-commerce companies face in particular.

Both machines and people are joined together in the Internet of Things to provide resources at any time and in any place. Most internet-connected devices ignore reliable security controls, leaving them vulnerable to a variety of privacy and security issues, including confidentiality, honesty, and authenticity. Any IoT security requirements must be fulfilled in order to secure the network against malicious assaults. Here are a few of the most significant characteristics of a secure network. If the system fails when transmitting data, it should be able to recover. In a multiuser setting, for example, a server must be intelligent and efficient enough to protect the network from intruders and eavesdroppers. When it goes down, it will immediately come back up without warning users. The data and relevant information must be verified. An authentication protocol allows only authenticated devices to send data. Only those who have been issued approval have access to the scheme. To ensure that different users have access to just the necessary sections of the database or resources, the server administrator must control the users' usernames and passwords, as well as their access rights. The records and knowledge should be held secure. Personal information can only be accessed by licensed individuals in order to preserve the rights of customers. It means that no other customer or unauthorized individual from the framework has access to the client's personal information. As a consequence of the Internet of Things age, our lives have changed. While the Internet of Things has a lot of benefits, it is susceptible to a number of security risks in our daily lives. Data loss and operation interruption account for the plurality of security threats. Security risks in IoT have a significant impact on physical security. The Internet of Things (IoT) is made up of a number of different devices and networks, each with its own collection of credentials and protection specifications. Since a lot of confidential data is shared between various types of devices, the user's privacy is also quite important. As a consequence, a secure infrastructure is needed to protect sensitive information. Furthermore, there are a number of devices that connect through different networks for IoT services. It means that there are multiple customer privacy and network layer security issues. A variety of approaches may be used to learn about a user's privacy.

Smart home services may remain susceptible to cyber-attacks since the bulk of service providers do not accept security standards at an early stage. In a smart house, eavesdropping, Distributed Denial of Service (DDoS) attacks, and information leakage are all possible security threats. Unauthorized access to smart home networks is an issue. Security is one of the key aims of a smart house. As a consequence, a number of sensors are used for a variety of uses, including fire prevention, kid monitoring, and housebreaking. If these devices are compromised, intruders would be able to monitor the home and access classified information. To combat this danger, data encryption between the gateway and the sensors is necessary, or user authentication may be used to recognize unwelcome guests. Attackers could obtain entry to the smart home network and send mass messages to smart devices using protocols including Clear To Send (CTS) and Request To Send (RTS) (RTS). They'll often use malicious code to harass a certain user in order to execute DoS attacks on other connected smart home gadgets. Smart devices are unable to perform their tasks adequately as a result of the draining of resources incurred by such assaults. To combat this threat, it's crucial to use authentication to avoid and monitor unauthorized access. The attacker can gather packets by changing the gateway's routing table as smart home devices connect with the application portal, as seen in An attacker can be able to get through the forged credential through the usage of SSL (secure socket layer). As a consequence, the attacker could misrepresent the data's contents or jeopardize data confidentiality. To secure the smart home network from this attack, an SSL technique with a proper authentication protocol should be used. It's also important to keep unauthorized devices away from your smart home network. The Internet of Things (IoT) is a futuristic term in which internet-connected physical items communicate with one another and describe themselves to other devices. The Internet of Things includes, among other things, smart objects, laptops, iPads, and autonomous machines. RFID, Quick Response (QR) codes, and wireless devices are used for such devices to connect with different computers. The Internet of Things aided human-to-human, human-to-physical-object, and physical-object-to-physical-object relationships.

Table.1. Number of papers published in global security

Year	Number of Papers Published		
	Web of Science	Scopus	Google Scholar
2010	56	80	50
2011	80	90	60
2012	92	88	70
2013	102	120	50
2014	105	140	80
2015	100	180	90
2016	88	198	150
2017	58	220	180
2018	80	250	200
2019	100	225	210
2020	50	200	250

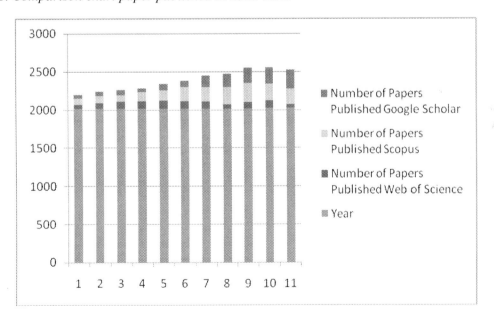

Figure 1. Comparison chart paper published in 2010-2020

CONCLUSION

The main aim of this paper was to highlight major IoT security issues, with a focus on security risks and countermeasures. Owing to a lack of security measures, IoT devices often become weak targets, and the users are unaware that they have been breached. This article discusses security principles such as confidentiality, honesty, and authentication. In this survey, 12 distinct forms of attacks are addressed, including low-level attacks, medium-level attacks, high-level attacks, and extremely high-level attacks, as well as their nature/behavior and proposed countermeasures. Installing security protocols in IoT devices and communication networks is important, considering the significance of safety in IoT systems. To protect against intruders or security attacks, it is also recommended not to use default passwords for devices and to read the security specs for devices before using them for the first time. Disabling non-operational roles may help to reduce the possibility of security breaches. It's also crucial to study the different security protocols used in IoT applications and networks.

REFERENCES

Al Hinai & Singh. (2017). *Internet of Things: Architecture, Security challenges and Solutions.* IEEE.

Banerjee, Lee, & Choo. (2018). Block chain future for internet of things security: A position paper. *Digital Communications and Networks, 4*, 149–160.

Barskar, R., & Deen, A. J. (2010). The algorithm analysis of e-commerce security issues for online payment transaction system in banking technology. IJCSIS, 8(1).

Evdokimov, S., Fabian, B., Günther, O., Ivantysynova, L., & Ziekow, H. (2011). RFID and the internet of things: Technology, applications, and security challenges. Foundations and Trends® in Technology. *Information and Operations Management, 4*(2), 105–185. doi:10.1561/0200000020

Ladan, M. (2010). E-commerce technologies and challenges. Journal of Communication and Computer, 7.

Mahdavinejad, Rezvan, Barekatain, Adibi, Barnaghi, & Sheth. (2018). Machine learning for internet of things data analysis: A survey. *Digital Communications and Networks, 4*, 161–175.

Minerva, R., Biru, A., & Rotondi, D. (2015). Towards a definition of the Internet of Things (IoT). *IEEE Internet Initiative, 1*, 1–86.

Moftah, A. A. A. (2012). Challenges of security, protection and trust on e-commerce: A case of online purchasing in Libya. Academic Press.

Rane, P. B., & Meshram, B. B. (2012). *Transaction security for ecommerce application.* IJECSE.

Saarikko, T., Westergren, U. H., & Blomquist, T. (2017). The Internet of Things: Are you ready for what's coming? *Business Horizons, 60*(5), 667–676. doi:10.1016/j.bushor.2017.05.010

Stergiou, C., Psannis, K. E., Kimb, B.-G., & Gupta, B. (2018). Secure integration of IoT and Cloud Computing. *Future Generation Computer Systems, 78*, 964–975. doi:10.1016/j.future.2016.11.031

Sudeendra, Sahoo, Mahapatra, Swain, & Mahapatra. (2017). Security Enhancements to System on Chip Devices for IoT Perception Layer. *IEEE International Symposium on Nanoelectronic and Information Systems.*

Vermesan, O., & Friess, P. (Eds.). (2014). Internet of things-from research and innovation to market deployment (Vol. 29). River Publishers.

Yazdanifard, R., & Al-Huda Edres, N. (2011). Security and privacy issues as a potential risk for further ecommerce development. *Proc. International Conference on Information Communication and Management*, 16.

Yoon, S., Park, H., & Yoo, H. S. (2015). *Security issues on smarthome in iot environment. In Computer Science and its Applications.* Springer.

Chapter 4
Conflicts in the Modern World and Their Impact on International Security

Ketevan Chakhava
International Black Sea University, Georgia

ABSTRACT

The central problem of the theory of international relations is the problem of international conflicts. And this is quite justified, if we bear in mind the goal that has been objectively facing all of humanity in recent decades – this is survival, the prevention of a global thermonuclear catastrophe. Since any armed clash is only an extreme expression of a political conflict, its highest stage, insofar as the study of the causes of conflicts and methods of their settlement, especially at those stages when it is still relatively easy to carry out, has not only theoretical but also great practical importance. An international conflict is a direct or indirect clash of interests of two or more parties (states, groups of states, peoples, political movements) based on the contradictions of an objective or subjective nature between them. By their origin, these contradictions and the problems they generate in relations between states can be territorial, national, religious, economic, military-strategic, scientific and technical, etc.

INTRODUCTION

International conflict can be viewed as a relatively independent phenomenon in the system of international relations. The subjects of an international conflict can be states, interstate associations, international organizations, including the UN, organizationally formed socio-political forces within the state or in the international arena. In the course of a conflict, the degree and even the nature of the parties' interest in the conflict can change, the place of the conflict in the hierarchy of goals of each of the participants can change, the number of participants can expand or decrease, and some direct or indirect parties can be replaced by others.

The study of the development of an international conflict makes it possible to establish many of its significant historical and cause-and-effect aspects for analysis, and the study of its system and structure

DOI: 10.4018/978-1-7998-9586-2.ch004

reveals mainly the structural and functional aspects of the conflict. These aspects of international conflicts cannot be perceived in isolation from each other. Analysis of the successively changing phases of the development of the conflict allows us to consider it as a single process with different, but interrelated sides.

The phases of development of an international conflict are not arbitrary, abstract periods in which a given conflict develops, they are real, determined by historical and social reasons. These reasons are manifested in specific signs related to changes in the internal characteristics of the states parties to the conflict, general political and specific interests, goals, means, external alliances and obligations of the parties to the conflict, the scale and intensity of the development of the conflict itself, the involvement of new participants with their inherent and applied in a given conflict using struggle, alliances, and obligations, the international context in which the conflict develops.

FEATURES OF CONFLICT AT THE END OF THE XX - BEGINNING OF THE XXI CENTURY

It is no exaggeration to say that conflicts are as old as the world. They were before the signing of the Westphalian peace treaty - the time taken for the birth point of the system of national States. Conflict situations and disputes will not disappear in the future, because, according to the aphoristic statement of one of the researchers R. Lee, a society without conflicts is a dead society (Chitadze, 2016). Moreover, many authors, particularly L. Coser, emphasizes that the contradictions that underline conflicts, have several positive functions: attract attention to the problem, be forced to seek the ways out of the situation, warn of stagnation - and thereby contribute to global development (Coser, 1957). Indeed, Conflicts are unlikely to be avoided at all.

It is another matter in what form they should be resolved - through dialogue and search for mutually acceptable solutions or armed confrontation. Speaking about the conflicts of the late XX-early XXI century, we should focus on two important issues that are not only theoretical but also practical. Whether the changing nature of conflicts? How can armed forms of conflict be prevented and regulated under modern conditions? The answers to these questions are directly related to the definition of the character of the modern political system and the possibility of its impact. Immediately after the end of the cold war, there were feelings that the world was on the threshold of a conflict-free era of existence. In academic circles, this position was most clearly expressed By F. Fukuyama, when he declared the end of history (Fukuyama, 1989). This position was sufficiently strongly supported by the official community, including the United States, despite the fact, the Republican party was in power at the beginning of the 1990s, as it is known, this party was less likely, compared to Democrats, to share the neo-liberal views.

Despite the fact, that after the end of the confrontation between the two systems and the ending of the "cold war", the number of conflicts has somehow decreased. For example, through negotiations became possible to find a solution to conflicts in Southeast Asia (Cambodia), in Africa (Namibia, Angola), Latin America (Nicaragua, El Salvador), etc. Nevertheless, regional and local conflicts at the beginning of the XXI century continue to threaten international security and democratization. In addition, many of them can generate a kind of terrorist wave and spread them sometimes far beyond the conflict zones. Shortly we can assume, that without understanding the nature of the conflict, it is impossible to fully understand how the protection of the fundamental principles of human rights on the global level should be provided.

About the issue - about the number of conflicts, in this case, if we trust the most authoritative data of the special institute for the study of conflict, which is located in Heidelberg (Germany), in 2013 the total number of conflicts in the different Regions of the World reached 414! (Heidelberg Institute, 2014).

According to the statistical data of the same institute for 2020, there were observed a total of 359 conflicts worldwide. About 60 percent, 220, were fought violently, while 139 were on a non-violent level. Compared to 2019, the overall number of full-scale wars increased from 15 to 21. The number of limited wars decreased from 23 to 19 (Heidelberg Institute, 2021).

Two World Wars, about 200 wars, local armed conflicts, terror, armed fighting for power, all those types of conflicts, killed within the previous Century about 300 million people (A. Antsupov. A. Shipolov. 2008).

As a result of the conflicts, it was violated the human rights of more than 20 million people, when at the beginning of the XXI Century, some 5,8 million people were displaced within their own countries and 14,8 million people had become refugees by fleering across international borders (United Nations. 2004). As the year 2020 dawned, according to the latest report of the UN High Commissioner on Refugees, "some 79.5 million people had been forced from their homes due to persecution, conflict, and human rights violations." That number includes 29.6 million refugees, 4.2 million asylum seekers, as well as 45.7 million internally displaced people (IDPs) (UNHCR, 2021).

So, President J. Bush, speaking of the conflict in the Persian Gulf, said, that "he interrupted a brief moment of hope, and anyway the international society is witnessing the birth of a new world free of terror " (Nye, 1992). Events in the world began to develop in such a way that the number of local and regional conflicts with violence in the world immediately after the end of the cold war has been increased. This is evidenced by the data of the Stockholm International Peace Research Institute (SIPRI), one of the leading international centers for conflict analysis. According to the Center, most conflicts were either in the developing countries or in the territory of the former USSR or former Yugoslavia (SIPRI, 2016). Only on the post-Soviet space, according to the estimates of the author V. N. Lysenko, in the 1990s, there were about 170 conflict zones, in 30 of which the conflicts were inactive form and 10 has become possible to the use of force (Lebedeva, 2007). In connection with the development of conflicts immediately after the end of the cold war and their appearance on the territory of Europe, which was a relatively safe continent after the Second world war, several researchers began to put forward various theories related to the growth of conflict potential in the world politics. One of the most striking representatives of this direction was S. Huntington with his hypothesis about the clash of civilizations (Huntington, 1993). However, in the second half of the 1990s, the number of conflicts, as well as conflict zones in the world, according to SIPRI, began to decrease. Thus, in 1995 there were 30 major armed conflicts in 25 countries, in 1999 - 27 in the 25 points of the globe, while in 1989 there were 36 in 32 zones (SIPRI, 2016).

It should be noted that the data on conflicts may differ depending on the source since there are no clear criteria for what should be the "level of violence" (the number of killed and injured in the conflict, its duration, the nature of relations between the conflicting parties, etc.) to be considered as a conflict, not an incident, criminal disassembly or terrorist acts. For example, Swedish researchers M. Sollenberg and P. Wallensteen define a major armed conflict as "a prolonged confrontation between the armed forces of two or more countries, or one government and at least one organized armed group, resulting in military action to the death of at least 1000 people, the authors call the figure of 100 and even 500 dead (Wallensteen, Sollenberg, 2001).

In general, if we talk about the general trend in the development of conflicts on the planet, most researchers agree that after a certain period, the number of conflicts in the late 1980s and early 1990s began to decrease, and in the mid-1990s it continues to fluctuate by about one level. Nevertheless, modern conflicts pose a very serious threat to humanity due to their possible expansion in the context of globalization, the development of environmental disasters (for example, just remember the arson of oil fields in the Persian Gulf during the occupation of Kuwait by Iraq), serious humanitarian consequences associated with a large number refugees among the civilian population, etc. The emergence of armed conflict in Europe at the end of the 20th century - a region where two world wars erupted and where the density is extremely high population and where many chemical and other products are concentrated, the destruction of which during military operations can lead to man-made disasters.

What are the causes of modern conflicts? Various factors contributed to their development. Thus, the problems associated with the proliferation of weapons, their uncontrolled use, and the complex relations between industrial and commodity countries, while increasing their interdependence, have made themselves felt. To this should be added the development of urbanization and migration to the cities and many States, in particular Africa, were unprepared to those processes, the growth of nationalism and fundamentalism as a sharpness for the development of globalization processes. It turned out to be significant that during the cold war the global confrontation between the East and the West to some extent "removed" the conflicts to a lower level. These conflicts have often been used by the superpowers during their military and political confrontation, although they have tried to keep them under control, realizing that otherwise regional conflicts could be escalated into a global war. Therefore, in the most dangerous cases, the leaders of the bipolar world, despite the fierce confrontation between themselves, coordinated actions to reduce tension to avoid a direct collision. Several times during the cold war such a danger, for example, arose during the development of the Arab-Israeli conflict. Then each of the superpowers exerted influence on "their" ally to reduce the intensity of conflict relations. After the collapse of the bipolar structure, regional and local conflicts largely "lived by their lives". And yet, among the large number of factors affecting the development of conflicts in recent years, it is particularly necessary to highlight the restructuring of the world political system, its "departure" from the Westphalian model that prevailed for a long time. This process of transformation is associated with the nodal points in world political development. Under the new conditions, conflicts have acquired a qualitatively different character. First of all, the "classical" interstate conflicts, which were typical for the heyday of the state-centrist political model of the world, practically disappeared from the world arena. Thus, according to the researchers M. Sollenberg and P. Wallenstein, among the 94 conflicts that existed in the world during the period 1989-1994, only four could be considered as interstate (Sollenberg, Wallenstein, 2001).

In 1999, according to another author of the SIPRI Yearbook, T. B. Seybolt, only 2 conflicts among 27 were interstate (Seybolt, 2008). About the SIPRI report for 2019, "Active armed conflicts occurred in at least 32 states in 2019: 2 in the Americas, 7 in Asia and Oceania, 1 in Europe, 7 in the Middle East and North Africa and 15 in sub-Saharan Africa. As in preceding years, most took place within a single country (intrastate), between government forces and one or more armed non-state group(s). Three were major armed conflicts (with more than 10 000 conflict-related deaths in the year): Afghanistan, Yemen, and Syria. Fifteen were high-intensity armed conflicts (with 1000–9999 conflict-related deaths): Mexico, Nigeria, Somalia, the Democratic Republic of the Congo (DRC), Iraq, Burkina Faso, Libya, Mali, South Sudan, the Philippines, India, Myanmar, Cameroon, Pakistan, and Egypt. The others were low-intensity armed conflicts (with 25–999 conflict-related deaths). The only one-armed conflict was fought between states (border clashes between India and Pakistan), and two were fought between state forces and armed groups that aspired to statehood (between Israel and Palestinian groups and between

Turkey and Kurdish groups). All three major armed conflicts and most of the high-intensity armed conflicts were internationalized"(SIPRI, 2020).

In General, according to some sources, the number of interstate conflicts has been declining for quite a long period. However, a caveat should be made here: it is being discussed about "classic" interstate conflicts when both sides recognize each other's status as a state. This is also recognized by other States and leading international organizations. In several contemporary conflicts aimed for the separation of the territorial entity and the proclamation of a new state, one of the parties, declaring its independence, insists on the interstate nature of the conflict, although it is not recognized as a state by the international community. Three groups can be distinguished among them: conflicts between Central authorities and ethnic/religious groups (groups); between different ethnic or religious groups; between state/States and nongovernmental structure. Internal conflicts of the 1990s were called "identity conflicts" because they were connected with the problem of self-identification. At the end of XX century - beginning of XXI century identification is based primarily not on the state basis, and on the other, mainly ethnic and religious factors. By the opinion of the American author J.L. Rasmussen, two-thirds of the conflicts in 1993 could be defined as "conflicts of identity" (Yaacov, 2004). At the same time, according to the famous American politician S. Talbott, less than 10% of the countries of the modern world are ethnically homogeneous. This means that the emergence of the problems in more than 90% of States can be expected only on an ethnic basis (Der Spiegel, 2008). Of course, the expressed opinion is an exaggeration, but the problem of national self-determination, national identification remains one of the most significant. Another significant parameter of identification is the religious factor or, more broadly, what S. Huntington called civilizational. It includes, in addition to religion, historical aspects, cultural traditions, etc.

In General, the changing the function of the state, its inability in some cases to guarantee security and at the same time the identification of an individual, to the extent that it was previously in the heyday of the state - centrist model of the world, entails an increase the uncertainty, the development of protracted conflicts that are fading, then erupt again. At the same time, the internal conflicts involve not so much the interests of the parties but the values (religious, ethnic). For them, it is impossible to reach a compromise.

The intrastate nature of contemporary conflicts is often accompanied by a process involving at the same time several actors (different movements, formations, etc.). And each of the participants often comes up with their requirements. This makes conflict management extremely difficult, as it involves the agreement of several individuals and movements. The greater the area of convergence of interests, the greater the possibilities for finding a mutually acceptable solution. As the number of sides increases, this area narrows. However, this does not mean that there is less interest in reaching an agreement. For example, the presence of a global threat can lead to differences of interest becoming insignificant.

In addition to the "internal" participants, the conflict situation is affected by many external actors - state and non-state. The latter include, for example, organizations engaged in humanitarian assistance for the searching the missing persons in the conflict, as well as business, the media, and others. The impact of these actors on the conflict often adds an element of unpredictability to its development. Because of its diversity, it acquires the character of a "multi-headed Hydra" and, as a consequence, leads to an even greater weakening of state control. In this regard, several researchers, in particular A. Minc, R. Kaplan, K. Booth, R. Harvey, began to compare the end of the XX century with medieval fragmentation, talking about the "new middle ages", the coming "chaos" (Chitadze, 2016). According to such ideas, the usual interstate contradictions are added today also due to differences in culture, values, General degradation of behavior. States are too weak to cope with all these problems.

The decrease in conflict management is determined by other processes too, which are going on the level of the state, in which the conflict emerges. Regular forces, which are trained for the military actions during interstate conflicts, are not good prepared from the military and psychological point of view (first of all due to the conducting military operations on own territory) for the solution of internal conflicts by force. In this case, the army is very often demoralized. In its turn, the general weakening of the state leads to the deterioration of the financing the regular forces, which from itself includes the danger of losing the state control over the processes, which are going on in the state, as a result of which, the conflict region becomes somehow the "model of behavior".

It is important to mention, that under the conditions of the internal – especially protracted conflict, it is often is weakening not only control over the situation from the center`s side but also from the periphery too. Leaders of the different types of movements often are not able to support during a long time the discipline among their supporters, and field commanders go out of control, by acting the independent actions and operations. The Armed Forces are divided into several groups, which often have a conflict with each other. Forces, which are involved in the internal conflicts, are often disposed of by the extreme way, which is accompanied "to go to the end by all means" for the getting the purposes through the not necessary victims. The extreme form of extremism and fanatism leads to the using of terrorist means, taking the hostages. Those phenomena are more often and often be accompanied the different concrete conflicts.

Modern conflicts acquire a certain political and geographical orientation. They arise in the regions that are more likely to be developing or in the process of transition from authoritarian regimes of state management. Even in economically developed Europe, conflicts broke out in countries that were less developed. Generally speaking, modern armed conflicts are concentrated primarily in Africa and Asia and in the post-soviet space.

The emergence of large numbers of refugees is another factor complicating the situation in the conflict area. So, in connection with the conflict in Rwanda in 1994, this country has left about 2 million people seemed in Tanzania, Zaire, Burundi (UN, 2005). None of these countries were able to cope with the flow of refugees and provide them with the Essentials.

The change like conflicts from interstate to internal does not mean that their international significance is diminished. On the contrary, as a result of the processes of globalization and the problems, inherent in the conflicts of the late twentieth and early twenty-first centuries, the emergence of a large number of refugees in other countries, as well as the involvement of many States and international organizations in their settlement, or on the contrary by the involvement in the internal affairs of the independent states to encourage the tensions, (examples are Russian policy in Georgia and Ukraine) intrastate conflicts are becoming increasingly international.

One of the most important questions in the analysis of conflicts: why are some of them regulated by peaceful means, while others develop into an armed confrontation? In practical terms, the answer is extremely important. However, methodologically, the discovery of the factors in the escalation of conflict into armed form is far to be simple. Anyway, the researchers, who try to answer this question, usually consider two groups of factors:

- Structural factors, or, as they are often called in conflict studies, independent variables (structure of the society, the level of economic development, etc.);
- Procedural factors, or dependent variables (politics, which is carried out as by the conflict participants, as by the third side; the personal characteristics of the political activists, etc.).

Structural factors are often referred to as objective and procedural factors are subjective. Here there is a clear analogy in political science with others, in particular with the analysis of the problems of democratization.

There are usually several phases in the conflict. American researchers D. Pruitt and J. Rubin compare the life cycle of the conflict with the development of the plot in a play of three actions (Pruitt, Rubin, 2003). In the first, the essence of the conflict is determined; in the second, it reaches its maximum, and then the stalemate or denouement; finally, in the third act, there is a decline in conflict relations. Preliminary studies suggest the reason to suppose, that in the first phase of the conflict structural factors "set" a certain " threshold", which is critical in the development of conflict relations. The presence of this group of factors is necessary both for the development of the conflict in General and for the implementation of its armed form. At the same time, the more structural factors are expressed and more of them are "involved", the more likely the development of armed conflict (from here in the literature on conflict studies very often the armed forms of the conflict development is associated with its escalation) and everything is already becoming a possible field of activity of politicians (procedural factors). In other words, structural factors determine the potential for armed conflict development. It is highly doubtful that the conflict, and even more the armed one, arose "from scratch" without objective reasons.

In the second (culmination) phase, a special role is played by predominantly procedural factors, such as the orientation of political leaders on unilateral (conflictual) or joint (negotiation) with the opposite side of the action for overcoming the conflict. The influence of these factors (i. e. political solutions related to the negotiations or further development of the conflict) is quite clearly manifested, for example, when comparing the culmination points of the conflict situations in Chechnya and Tatarstan in the Russian Federation, where the actions of political leaders in 1994 led to the armed development of the conflict in the first case, and in the second - a peaceful way of its settlement.

Thus, in a fairly generalized form, it can be mentioned, that when studying the process of formation of a conflict situation, first of all, structural factors should be analyzed, and when identifying the form of its resolution - procedural.

REGIONAL AND LOCAL CONFLICTS IN THE MODERN WORLD POLITICAL MAP

In the era of the bipolar world and the "cold war", numerous regional and local conflicts served as one of the main sources of instability in the world, which the communist and capitalist systems tried to use according to their interests. These conflicts led to enormous damage to the economy, social and political development of many countries' deaths of millions of people, especially, in the developing countries. The establishment of a special section of Political Science - Conflict Studies enabled studying such conflicts and the direction of the geography of conflicts appeared in the system of political geography.

After the end of the confrontation between the two systems and the ending of the "cold war", the number of conflicts has somehow decreased. For example, through negotiations, it became possible to find a solution to conflicts in Southeast Asia (Cambodia), Africa (Namibia, Angola), and Latin America (Nicaragua, El Salvador). Nevertheless, regional and local conflicts at the beginning of the XXI century continue to threaten international security. In addition, many of them can generate a kind of terrorist wave and spread them sometimes far beyond the conflict zones. Therefore, it can be assumed that without understanding the nature of the conflict it is impossible to fully understand the modern political map of the world. Therefore, we consistently consider several related issues.

All conflicts can be divided into regional and local.

Regional conflicts, which in the modern world are quite a lot, of course, represent the greatest threat to international security. Not being able to consider all of them, we restrict ourselves by the few examples of such conflicts. You've probably already thought about the Middle East region – The Middle East region admittedly, plays the role of the "powder keg" throughout the postwar period, which is ready at any moment to undermine the entire system of international security. It is a sensitive nerve center of the planet, where historically a very complex interweaving of cultures and religions got formed and it serves not only the interests of the countries in the region but also many other countries in Europe, Asia, and America.

At the heart of this regional conflict is the Israeli- Palestinian (and wider - the Israeli- Arab) one, which has been in progress for more than half a century, remaining throughout this time perhaps the most complex one attracting the world's attention. (Mayers, David. 1998) More than one generation of Israelis and Arabs has grown in an atmosphere of mutual hatred and incessant sharp confrontations, including six wars between Israel and its Arab neighbors, which lasted for several years of the intifada (Arabic - rebel). Some substantial changes for the better situation came only in the early 90s when the Palestinian Autonomy was founded on the part of the State of Israel. But many controversial issues remain so that a sovereign Palestinian state does not exist on the political map of the world (Gachechiladze. 2008). This conflict got even more complicated at the beginning of 2006 after the victory at the parliamentary elections in the Palestinian autonomy by the radical Islamist group Hamas.

Besides this basic conflict in this region, there were others, such as the one between Iraq and Iran, leading to a bloody long war between them in the 80s between Iraq and Kuwait causing Iraq's aggression against Kuwait in 1990. In the remaining part of Asia, there are several regional conflicts. A long-term conflict in Afghanistan, the stand-off between India and Pakistan in Kashmir, and the conflicts related to the political reconstruction of the former Yugoslavia in Europe can also be included.

As to the local conflicts, i.e., relatively smaller-scale ones, they are the majority in the modern world. The fact that very often it is difficult to make a clear distinction between regional and local conflicts also needs to be taken into account.

The third question is the political status of the conflicts which can be subdivided into external (international) and internal (domestic).

The Israeli - Arab conflict, the conflict between India and Pakistan in Kashmir, conflicts in Afghanistan and Iraq, former Yugoslavia can serve as obvious examples of the major international conflicts. But the conflicts on ethnic grounds, for example, in Belgium or Canada, can be attributed to several domestic ones. At the beginning of the XXI Century, 71 were interstate and 178 intrastate conflicts (Maksakovsky. 2009).

Question four - to categorize the nature of the conflict. This approach, usually determine the violent (armed) and non-violent conflict. Admittedly, the first of them poses the greatest threat and international organizations monitor them carefully (Robert J. Art. Robert Jervis. 2005).

Armed (violence) conflicts, i.e., the actual "hot spots" of our planet are worth noting. The large-scale armed conflicts are officially considered to be the ones in which the loss exceeds one thousand persons. For example, during the conflicts in Afghanistan and Rwanda, there were millions of victims and hundreds of thousands of people were killed during the civil war in Bosnia and Herzegovina (1992-1996). In Africa, already in the post-colonial period, 35 armed conflicts were fixed, which killed a total of about 10 million people (Kegley, Blanton. 2010-2011).

Figure 1. The state of Israel and the Palestinian autonomy
Source: https://news.antiwar.com/2012/04/23/israeli-policies-making-two-state-solution-impossible-says-palestinian-leader

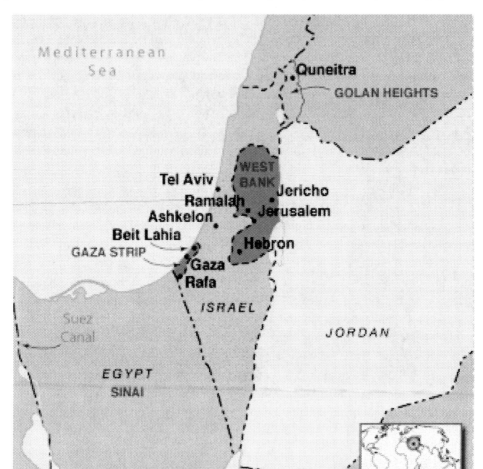

According to the Institute in Heidelberg, in 2013 the world had 45 highly violated conflicts, which were divided into two categories. The first one mainly includes domestic wars whereas outbreaks of serious crises of violently conflicting parties, or at least the threat of its use, constitute the second category, including, one international (between India and Pakistan), and another domestic. The majority of 45 armed conflicts took place in Africa and Asia, including, the Middle East (Heidelberg Institute for International Conflict Research, Germany. 2013).

The United Nations plays a crucial role in the prevention and peaceful settlement of armed conflict. Its main goal is to maintain peace on our planet. UN operations include peacekeeping and diplomatic measures and the direct intervention of peacekeeping forces of the organization in the events of military conflicts. During the existence of the UN, such "peace enforcement" action was carried out in several countries. However, experience in the 90s showed that the mere presence of the "blue helmets" in the conflict zone is not enough to stop the hostilities. Nevertheless, from 1948 till April 2004, overall, the UN has established 56 operations out of which 43 have been set up since 1988. As of April 2004, there were 14 active peacekeeping operations (United Nations, 2004) (in the Sudan and Rwanda, Israel and

Figure 2. World`s worst conflict zones
Source: https://newseu.cgtn.com/news/2021-08-24/War-and-want-How-conflict-drives-poverty-12ZzEMTXETS/index.html

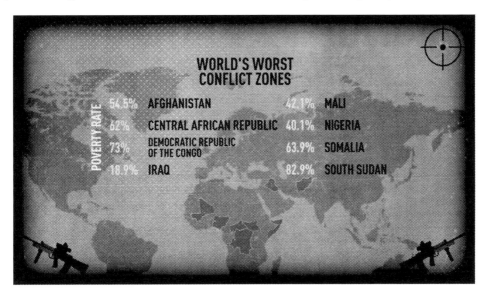

Palestine, India and Pakistan, Cyprus, Sierra Leone, etc.). At the same time, military-police forces have been reduced. At present, 90% of them are composed of soldiers and officers from such states as India, Pakistan, Bangladesh, Nepal rather than Western countries. At the same time, the UN Security Council approved the concept of active peacekeeping actions, even allowing peacekeepers to use heavy military equipment. The most ambitious and hardest of such operations have been recently carried out by them against the rebels in DR of Congo.

It should be taken into consideration that NATO and European Union were engaged in the post-cold war period in peacemaking and peacekeeping operations. Direct involvement of NATO in the armed conflicts in former Yugoslavia in (1992-1995 - Bosnia, 1999 - Kosovo) can be considered as an example of such actions (NATO Handbook. 2006). Two leading countries of the organization (USA and UK) have overthrown the ruling of the Afghan movement "Taliban" in 2001-2002. But undoubtedly, the biggest U.S. and U.K. military action was held in 2003 in Iraq to overthrow the dictatorial regime of Saddam Hussein.

Additionally, the Organization for Security and Cooperation in Europe (OSCE) also has several missions to the areas of European and non-European conflicts with military operations taking place in a relatively recent past. The same applies to the EU, which at present is involved in the peacekeeping operations in Bosnia, Macedonia, Georgia, etc.

The fact that non-violent conflicts are in majority in our world is to some extent misleading. Indeed, many of these conflicts used to be "hot spots" and scenes of civil wars and terrorism. That is why they are sometimes called hidden or smoldering conflicts that are dangerous because here the flames of war can kindle again at any time of the accidental spark.

Self-proclaimed but unrecognized territories (quasi-) already discussed briefly serve as notable examples of this kind. According to some estimates, the total number exceeds 120, and even 160, but these figures are yet highly exaggerated. The formation of such states is often associated with military conflicts, civil wars, and occupations, which then reached a temporary, but not a final political settlement (Maksakovsky. 2009).

The fifth question concerns the causes of conflict. Essentially, it is a matter of their typology, which from the standpoint of social and economic geography, perhaps is the most interesting. Reference literature gives different opinions about this issue. However, considering it from the standpoint of the most generalized positions three main causes of the conflict emerge territorial disputes, all sorts of internal political differences, and the ethnoreligious nature of conflicts.

Conflicts related to territorial disputes exist in all parts of the world. In Europe, the Rock of Gibraltar - the only remaining region of the colonial possessions serves as an excellent example of this because of a long-lasting dispute between the UK and Spain. In Asia, there are more than 30 such disputes. There are long-standing territorial disputes between Israel and Palestine, Turkey and Greece (over Cyprus and the Aegean islands), Iraq and Kuwait, Iran, Saudi Arabia with several neighboring countries, India and Pakistan over Kashmir, China, India, Vietnam, DPRK, and Japan over several islands in South-East Asia, Russia, and Japan because of the Northern Territories (Southern Kuril Islands), etc.

Africa is famous for its territorial disputes as well. In the colonial era, metropolises conducted the so-called bordering of their colonies without regard to ethnic boundaries. It is estimated that on the present political map of Africa 44% of the entire length of the state border runs along with the meridians and parallels and 30% - on a geometrically correct line (Political Map of Africa. 2013). This applies, especially, to West Africa, where in XIX century Fulani people were divided between 12 British and French colonies. But territorial disputes have often led to military conflicts prevailing in North Africa (e.g., between Morocco and Western Sahara, Mauritania), East Africa (e.g., between Somalia, Ethiopia, and Eritrea), and South Africa (e.g., between Namibia and South Africa).

In Latin America, there are about 20 territorial disputes (Domínguez. 2003) that have repeatedly led to military action. It is enough to recall the conflicts between the UK with Argentina over the disputed Falkland Islands, which Argentina tried to annex in 1982. Territorial disputes are also reported in Australia and Oceania.

Let`s now turn to internal political conflicts, which mostly are associated with an acute confrontation between political parties and groups, which causes disruptions not only in the political but also in the economic and social spheres of life. On the political map of the modern world, there are the countries with similar political instability and armed conflict fraught can be attributed primarily to many African countries, such as Algeria, where local Islamists are fighting with the secular state, Liberia, Ivory Coast, Central African Republic, DR Congo, Somalia, Uganda. The political map of Asia in this group of countries torn by internal contradictions includes Afghanistan, Nepal, Laos, and Latin America - Colombia, Guatemala.

At the same time, many conflicts in the modern world political map take place on the ethnoreligious ground. They are based, as a rule, on militant nationalism, which finds expression in the increasing trend towards creating the sovereignty of the large and small ethnic communities to create their independent states, the growing intolerance towards minorities. These centrifugal tendencies can be expressed using the concept of separatism (from Lat. Separatus - separate), meaning the desire for isolation, separation, i.e., obtaining by a part of the country full political independence or at least autonomy. It would be much more advisable to regard such conflicts as separatist ones based on national–religious grounds (Joseph. S. Nye. Jr. 2007).

Nowadays separatism has a great destabilizing effect on the entire world's geopolitical order. This is not surprising. The book "The Geographic Picture of the World" refers to a map of main sources of separatism, which are only 53 and which together occupy an area of 12.7 million km2 with a population of 220 million people (V. Maksakovsky. 2009). Some scientists connect those conflicts with the so-called "geopolitical fault" or "buffer zones" that are characteristic of the borderland between the world's ethnic and cultural civilizations.

When specific countries are concerned, it is obvious that primarily multinational states, which amount to 60 worldwide, and the states with a more or less significant number of national minorities, serve as centers of militant nationalism, separatism, and, accordingly, ethnoreligious conflicts. (V. Maksakovsky. 2009). Conflicts in these countries are mostly complex, contradictory, and of long-term nature based on territorial disputes and historically accumulating grievances related to national oppression, continuous mutual alienation, and hostility (Robert J. Art. Robert Jervis. 2005).

At the first glance, it may seem odd, but separatist conflicts in the national and religious divisions exist in the many Western States with economically advanced and democratic regimes. Europe serves as an excellent example of this, which, for many decades, despite all efforts, has failed to achieve the complete elimination of conflict in Northern Ireland (Ulster), where the confrontation between Catholics and Protestants remained at least until mid-2005. A similar tendency occurs in the Basque Country where extreme nationalists and separatists are fighting for an independent Basque state – the territory between Spain and France and Belgium where Flemish and Walloons are arguing over the disputed territory.

Separatist conflicts on the national-religious grounds caused by the decay in the former Yugoslavia undoubtedly occupy a special place in this region. Two of them serve as main ones. First, the conflict in Bosnia and Herzegovina, whose population are Serbs, Croats, and Muslims and who did not want to live in one state and after the bloody war finally the Muslim - Croat Federation and the Republika Srpska were proclaimed, which created the two subjects of federation within one State – Bosnia and Herzegovina. By the UN mandate, stabilization forces – consisting of 32 thousand people with a core of NATO troops - were deployed in this country (NATO Handbook. 2006). Second, the autonomous province of Kosovo and Metohija in the south of Serbia where 90% of the population are Muslim Albanians. When Yugoslavia began to disintegrate, Albanians of Kosovo proclaimed the establishment of the independent Republic of Kosovo, which led to a civil war between the separatist forces and central government of Serbia and then the establishment of the control on the breakaway republic by NATO peacekeeping force - KFOR. (NATO Handbook. 2006).

It can be said that in Bosnia and Kosovo the "old peace" is established. Another striking example of this kind of conflict in the West is a Canadian province with a predominantly French-speaking Quebec population. This is also a long-standing conflict in which the most radical forces are in favor of the separation of the French-speaking Quebec from federal Canada.

Developing countries serve as the main arena of conflicts with their often particularly complex ethnic and religious composition. This primarily relates to Asia and Africa.

In Asia, such conflicts are common to all four of its sub-regions. In Southwest Asia, this is the conflict over Kurdistan, which is divided by political borders between Turkey, Iraq, Syria, and Iran, around Cyprus, around Afghanistan. In South Asia - a whole series of conflicts in the most multi-ethnic country in the world - India. The conflict between India and Pakistan over Kashmir has been discussed in connection with territorial disputes but it is an equally separatist conflict too based on ethnic-religious confrontation with old Hindus and Muslims. Another "conflict" state of India – Punjab, settled by Sikhs is also worth noting.

Cultural, religious and then political isolation of the Sikh community from Hinduism began in the first half of the twentieth century. When in the middle of the century, independent states of India and

Figure 3. Autonomous province of Kosovo and Metohija
Source: http://mapsontheweb.zoom-maps.com/post/114574543300/occupation-zones-in-kosovo

Pakistan were founded and Punjab became part of India but at the same time, the idea of a sovereign state Khalistan was put forward which could become a kind of buffer between India and Pakistan. Even though this plan could not be implemented, Sikh separatists continue to insist on it making discord in their relationship with the state. It needs to be stated in this connection that in 1984 two Sikh bodyguards killed the Indian Prime Minister Indira Gandhi (Heywood. 1998).

Armed separatist conflicts based on ethnoreligious factors are characteristic to many other parts of India as well as Sri Lanka. The Countries of Southeast Asia, Cambodia, Indonesia, Myanmar, and the Philippines belong to the same list whereas, from East Asia, it is China (Xinjiang Uygur Autonomous Region, Tibet).

There is no one sub-region on the political map of Africa where such conflicts would not occur.

In North Africa, Sudan has already become a dangerous source of such conflicts, which is based on the contradiction between the Nilotic peoples of the south of the country professing Christianity and the peoples of northern Sudan, who accepted Islam. In West Africa, distinguished by a special ethnic diversity, conflicts on the ethnoreligious basis are common to many countries, especially, Nigeria, with a similarly highly unstable political situation. Eritrea, Ethiopia, Somalia, Uganda, Kenya, Rwanda, and Burundi belong to the list from East Africa, in Central Africa, these are DR Congo, Angola, and in the Southern part of Africa - South Africa. But the ethnic conflict in Rwanda undoubtedly deserves strong emphasis. It began in 1994 and led to the genocide, which is comparable to the actions of Nazi Germany in the occupied countries or the "Khmer Rouge" in Cambodia.

The former Belgian colony of Rwanda gained independence in 1962. However, this did not lead to the reconciliation between the warring ethnic groups - Tutsi pastoralists and Hutu farmers. Although Tutsis include only 15% of the population, they took practically all leadership positions in the government. This long-running feud escalated into civil war, at the end of which in 1994the Tutsis killed 500 thousand Hutu and forced more than 2 million people to flee from the country the entire civilized world was shaken by the violence which was accompanied by conflict (United Nations. 2004).

As a result, we can say that it is Africa, where the name "continent of the conflicts" is firmly established. As for the most radical solutions to this complex problem, we did not have time to put forward proposals to reshape the political map of Africa inherited from the colonial era by creating possible mono-ethnic states on the continent. In practice, it is quite impossible to implement. Ethnographers have calculated that in this case, the number of states on the continent would have to increase to 200-300! (V. Maksakovsky. 2009).

In conclusion, we can add that most of the conflicts in the post-soviet space, which, as we have already mentioned, are also categorized on a separatist ethnic basis. In most cases, Abkhazia and Tskhinvali District (Georgia), Transdniestria (Moldova), Karabakh (Azerbaijan) existed and still do so because of the illegal involvement of Russia in those conflicts. As for Russia itself, North Caucasus has been and remains the main area of such conflicts. In 2020 the world was a witness of the new war on the post-soviet space between Azerbaijan and Armenia when Azerbaijan managed to restore control on the almost whole territory of the country, but Russia was again involved at the last stage of the conflict as "peacekeeper".

Hopefully, now we have the basic approaches to such a complex problem as regional and local conflicts on the modern world political map.

FORMS AND METHODS OF INFLUENCING THE CONFLICT WITH THE AIM OF ITS PREVENTION AND PEACEFUL SETTLEMENT

Modern approaches to resolving conflicts largely stem from their features. At present, science and social practice, in principle, have sufficiently developed technologies for this.

Great importance to the procedures and methods of conflict resolution attaches to the UN. The Art. 33 of Chapter VI of the United Nations Charter states: "Parties involved in any dispute, the continuation of which could threaten the maintenance of international peace and security, should, first of all, try to resolve the dispute through negotiation, examination, mediation, conciliation, arbitration, judicial proceedings, recourse to regional authorities or agreements or other means of their choice. " For active activities related to peacekeeping, the UN was noted in 1988 by Nobel Prize (UN, 2005).

In the early 1990s, UN activity in the area of resolving and preventing open forms of conflict was intensified and the number of its peacekeeping missions was increased. Boutros Ghali, being the UN Secretary-General, proposed an expanded "Agenda for Peace", which details various procedures for the peaceful settlement and prevention of the conflicts. As a whole, in the second half of the 1990s, as well as in the early 2000s, the UN paid great attention to peacekeeping problems. For the activities in this area, the UN and its Secretary-General Kofi Annan were awarded the Nobel Peace Prize in 2001 (UN, 2005).

Since conflicts pose a serious threat to regional security, their settlement also lies in the focus of attention of many regional intergovernmental organizations, including the OSCE, AU, Leagues of the Arabic States, and others. Non-governmental organizations are also involved in resolving these issues, for example, "Doctors without Borders" (Médecins Sans Frontières), "International Red Cross". Nevertheless, the fact remains that the contemporary political conflicts - especially internal ones, with their ethnic and religious component, are extremely difficult to influence. They affect the deep value and emotional structures of the participants, therefore, as a rule, they require a long time for reconciliation.

Conflict resolution and prevention activities, depending on the situation, the nature of the threats, and the stage of development, include the main focus of activities - from mediation and monitoring the implementation of the agreement to military operations. Many of these technologies were developed and introduced into the practical field at the end of the 20th century. In general, the influence to the conflict for its peaceful end is affected by:

- Preventive diplomacy
- Peacekeeping
- Peacemaking
- Peacebuilding

Preventive diplomacy is used to prevent the conflict from entering an armed phase. It includes activities related to the "restoration of trust" between the conflicting parties: the work of civilian observers to ascertain the facts of violation of peace, the exchange of information, etc.

Preventive diplomacy began to develop particularly intensively after outbreaks of conflict in the the late 1980s and early 1990s, most of all in Europe, when voices were increasingly voiced in favor of the fact that early warning and conflict prevention are most perspectives. This topic was especially pronounced in the program "Agenda for the World". The idea of conflict prevention found active support from politicians.

However, a specific policy regarding conflict situations in many ways remains reactive, i.e. mostly the actions are adopted after the fact when this or other event was held - only in response to it. There are several reasons for this.

First, there are problems associated with the Search for indicators for which we can judge potential conflict areas. Even though the UN monitoring program for potentially hazardous areas have been deployed and is being implemented, there are no clear criteria by which to predict when and where it will arise, and in what form the next conflict will manifest itself.

Secondly, problems are justifying the need for intervention, making appropriate decisions about what kind of actions will be taken, obtaining the necessary permits for impacts, and finally, financing of the adopting actions. When discussing all these issues, purely psychological factors play an essential role, in particular, the need to prevent a threat that does not yet exist.

Figure 4. The mixed record of UN peacekeeping in South Sudan
Source: https://odihpn.org/magazine/the-mixed-record-of-un-peacekeeping-in-south-sudan/

Peacekeeping involves ceasefire measures. This maybe the deployment of missions of military observers, peacekeeping forces, the creation of buffer zones, as well as zones free from flights, etc. Peacekeeping forces can be called "emergency", "temporary", "protective", "separation forces" to have different mandates defining acceptable means of achieving the goal.

Peacekeeping activities for peace protection are oriented not on the peaceful solution of the problem, but only at reducing the severity of the conflict. It provides the separation between the conflict parties and the limitation of contacts between them. As a result, the military actions of the participants become difficult. However, during the underline the analogies with medicine, then peacekeeping efforts are more focused on alleviating the symptoms of the disease than on its treatment.

There are several other issues and limitations. Thus, peacekeeping forces cannot be brought in without the permission of the state, on whose territory they should be sent, and the host state, in its turn, may perceive this as interference in its internal affairs.

Another question is what should be the composition of the forces being introduced for their actions to be perceived as neutral, rather than supporting one or another side in the conflict. The activity of the forces being introduced is limited by their mandates. As a rule, they have no right to pursue the attacker. As a result, peacekeepers themselves often become a kind of target.

Peacemaking involves procedures, related to the organization of the negotiation process and the implementation of mediation efforts by a third party to find mutually acceptable solutions. Here it is important that, unlike peacekeeping, peacemaking activities should be directed not only at reducing the level of the confrontation between the parties but also to solve the problem peacefully, which would satisfy the conflicting parties.

The result of peacemaking activities is not always the resolution of contradictions. The parties are sometimes forced to sign agreements, knowing that the continuation of the conflict at this stage becomes impossible. In this case, one or the other side may not strive to implement them. In this case, guarantees of the implementation of agreements are often required. The third - party involved in the mediation often becomes such a guarantee. For example, within the agreements signed between Israel and Egypt in 1979, the role of mediator was taken by the United States.

Another problem related to using the measures to influence the conflict in the framework of peacemaking is that all negotiating means are focused on the rational behavior of the conflicting parties. In real conditions, the participants in the conflict are inclined to be unpredictable, even irrational actions, up to "suicidal steps" and emotional reactions.

Finally, the problem exists in the fact that actions to preserve peace are aimed at working with the leaders of the conflicting parties. The level of mass consciousness and behavior is not affected here. Therefore, after reaching agreements, outbreaks of violence often occur (UN, 2005).

Peacebuilding means the active involvement of a third party in a post-conflict settlement. This may be an activity aimed at preparing elections, managing territories until full restoration of peaceful life, transfer of power to local authorities, etc. In the framework of peacebuilding, measures are also being taken to reconcile the conflicting parties. The great importance has economic development, the development of the projects involving the cooperation of former adversaries (as was in the case, for example, after the end of the Second World War in western Europe). In addition, peacebuilding includes educational work, which is also aimed at reconciling the participants, the formation of tolerant behavior.

In addition to these concepts, in the literature related to the conflicts, one can often encounter others, including such as "peacekeeping operations" or "peace support operations" or missions. In principle, all terms are close to each other, although they do not always coincide. For example, the concept of "peacekeeping operations" is mainly used in NATO documentation (NATO, 2006).

In connection with the intensive development of the practice of influencing the conflicts by the end of the 20th century, the term "peacekeeping operations of the second generation" has been appeared. It suggests a wider range of third-party participation in the conflict and using various means, including the use of naval forces and aviation. At the same time, military operations began to be carried out without the consent of the state in which the conflict arose, as was in the case for example, in the former Yugoslavia. This practice has been called "peace enforcement" and is rather ambiguously perceived by various states, politicians, movements, etc.

Other terminologies have also been established in the scientific literature, particularly: *conflict prevention* of the open-armed forms of conflict, accompanied by violent actions - wars, riots, massive disorders, etc. *conflict management*, is aimed at reducing the level of hostility in the relations of the parties, which implies mediation and negotiations procedures: *conflict resolution*, is focused on eliminating their causes, the formation of a new level of interrelations between participants.

Two groups of concepts, having been distributed in the scientific research and practice of conflict resolution and prevention, are two close areas, which M. Lund called the "C-series" and the "P-series", respectively, by which the scientific terminology begins with the concept of "conflict ", but in practice, usually with the "peace" (Lund, 2002). In recent years, both fields have been increasingly influencing each other. As a result, there is often confusion in terms of terminology.

The practice of conflict resolution at the end of the XX century created also the problem, which is connected with the *humanitarian influence* on the conflict situation. In the framework of modern conflicts suffers first of all civilian population (from 80 till 90%), including the lacking of food, medicines, warm clothes, housing, etc. (Chitadze, 2016). In this regard, it is often existing the question of the emergence of a *humanitarian catastrophe* and the necessity for *humanitarian aid*.

At the same time, the humanitarian impact on the conflict situation became in some cases to be implemented without the consent of the state in which the conflict arose, which has created a legal problem.

The essence of the discussions is to review does it represent the interference in the internal affairs of the state? If the answer is positive, then there are other questions. How to deal with human rights? What to do if, in a conflict situation, the state violates the rights of the civilian population conducts ethnic cleansing, and by this way creates problems not only within its own country but also for its neighbors because of the flood of refugees rushing towards them? In the framework of existing standards, those problems are solved in an extremely difficult way.

Important in the practice of conflict resolution of 1990-2000 and the beginning of the XXI century has become the fact, that many participants are simultaneously connected to this process. In traditional diplomacy, the conflict's resolution is involved states and intergovernmental organizations — the so-called first line of diplomacy – *Track-I Diplomacy*, or *official diplomacy*.

In addition, non-governmental organizations and individuals (for example, former political activists, famous writers, scientists) also, take part in resolving the conflicts. This practice of *unofficial diplomacy* has gained the name of "*second direction of diplomacy*" - *Track-II Diplomacy* (Chitadze, 2016).

Such multiple impacts correspond to the current realities of varicosity of the conflicts, the multiplicity, and heterogeneity of their participants, as well as the general trend associated with the activation of non-state actors. It is known that different structures of the conflict require different involvement, and through many channels: unofficial participants are often more effectively affected by unofficial ones, and official agents, as a rule, are influenced by official mediators.

The activities of the non – governmental organizations under the conditions of the conflict can be extremely various. It includes the delivery of humanitarian aid concretely to those people, who especially suffered as a result of the conflict, collection of information about the real situation in the conflict zone, and mediation in the establishment contacts (both: officials and non-officials) to decrease the tensions between conflict participants and introduction of the educational programs, the main purpose of which is the change the orientation of the people – from the conflict behavior toward finding the agreement. Another activity of the non-governmental organizations is directly connected with the restoration of the different types of infrastructure, which has been damaged as a result of the military operations, particularly – the restoration of the communication means and providing the population in the conflict or within the post-conflict stage with food, water, etc.

Nongovernmental organizations mostly are oriented on making the influence on the mass level, which is very important for internal conflicts. They usually establish good and close relations with the various target groups of the local population. At the same time, NGO-s themselves on the level of mass understanding are considered in many cases as more neutral and independent mediators in comparison with governmental structures.

Working with the masses, nongovernmental organizations possess rather detailed information from the conflict places. For the official mediators, due to the smaller number of their representatives and other reasons are more difficult to collect such type of information.

However, activities in the framework of the second direction of diplomacy have a list of limitations. Sometimes the advantages, which are possessed by unofficial mediators, turn to weakness.

Thus, to work with the concrete people in the determined region and gain from their information, the representatives of the non-official diplomacy often cannot see the real picture as a whole. Even more, the information is not always checked by them out, and in some cases, some information is damaged.

Another limitation of the second direction of diplomacy represents the fact, that its representatives are not always well-prepared from the professional point of view. The nongovernmental organizations often go and are involved those people, who really want to help the people but they do not always have enough knowledge and skills. For example, the realization of the functions, which are connected with the psychological rehabilitation of the people in the conflict zones, requires special preparation in the field of psychology. One NGO-s pays the necessary attention to the professional preparation of their staff, who are based on the principle of Hippocrates "Do not damage!", when others ignore it, which creates difficulties during the involvement of such organizations, and individuals toward the conflict resolution process.

Causes several difficulties also the multiplicity of participants in this process. One of the main problems is coherence. Otherwise, activity may even cause an increase of hostile relations or give reason to new conflicts. The fact is that third parties act in conflict on the basic principles and norms that do not always coincide and sometimes contradict each other. This entails the development of conflicts, which is especially characterized by the non-state actors. For example, former Vice-President of the world's largest non-governmental organizations "world vision" A.S. Natsios gives an example of the spread of humanitarian assistance during the conflict (Rwanda 1994) in neighboring villages by various non-governmental organizations. In one humanitarian aid was provided for everyone while in a nearby village, another non-governmental organization delivered humanitarian aid only under the condition of participation in a project to be focused on reducing tensions. As a result, there was a conflict between the residents of these villages (Natsios, 2012).

A special issue is a relationship of non-governmental organizations with official structures. These contacts are not always easy to establish. Official authorities often try to limit the activities of non-governmental organizations in a conflict zone, considering it, if the NGO is international, as interference in internal affairs. The question of whether non-governmental organizations should be able to remain neutral in a conflict is far from to be a simple one. With this problem are faced even such famous and large organizations, as the International Red Cross.

In particular, in the 1960s, the French activist of the organization R. Bernard Kushner, the founder of the "doctors without borders" movement, spoke out against the principle of the neutrality of non-governmental organizations in a conflict situation (Chitadze, 2016). His arguments boiled down to the fact that under conditions of an accomplished genocide, humanist-oriented organizations cannot be neutral.

However, the abandonment of the principle of neutrality by all non-governmental organizations can generally block access to humanitarian aid through non-governmental channels for those, against whom the genocide was committed since the official authorities simply will not allow its delivery.

Another problem is the interactions of governmental and non-governmental structures to resolve the conflict.

Such contacts are necessary. And in this regard, the increasing popularity acquires a new direction of practice, which receives theoretical understanding as Multi-Truck diplomacy.

This meaning itself proposes the cooperation by the representatives of the official diplomacy with those, who are involved in the presented activity in the framework of the second direction of diplomacy. Multidirectional diplomacy represents itself not only the merger of two directions, but only joining to them the business structures, private persons, research and educational centers, religious activists, local activists, lawyers, philanthropic organizations, representatives of the mass-media means, and also dividing the functions among them.

CONCLUSION

The emergence and development of an international conflicts are associated not only with the objective contradictions arising in relations between states but also with such subjective factors as the foreign policy of the states themselves.

The conflict is provoked, "prepared", and resolved precisely by the deliberate purposeful the foreign policy of states, but such a subjective factor as the personal characteristics and qualities of politicians involved in decision-making cannot be ignored.

Sometimes personal relationships between leaders can have a significant impact on interstate relations, including the development of conflict situations.

Political science and practice of international relations know different types and types of international conflicts. However, there is no single typology of international conflicts recognized by all researchers. The most common classification of international conflicts is their division into symmetric and asymmetric. Symmetrical conflicts include those that are characterized by approximately equal strength of the parties involved. Asymmetric conflicts are conflicts with a sharp difference in the potential of the conflicting parties.

REFERENCES

Antiwar. (2012). *Israeli Policies Making Two-State Solution Impossible, Says Palestinian Leader.* Retrieved from: https://news.antiwar.com/2012/04/23/israeli-policies-making-two-state-solution-impossible-says-palestinian-leader/

Antsupov, A. S. (2008). *Conflict studies* (3rd ed.). Aspect Press.

Art, R., & Jervis, R. (2005). *International Politics.* Pearson.

Bar-Siman. (2004). *From Conflict Resolution to Reconciliation.* Oxford University Press.

Basic Facts about the United Nations. (2005). UN Department of Public Information.

CGTN. (2021). *World's Worst Conflict Zones.* Retrieved from: https://newseu.cgtn.com/news/2021-08-24/War-and-want-How-conflict-drives-poverty-12ZzEMTXETS/index.html

Chitadze. (2016). *Political Sciences.* International Black Sea University.

Coser. (1957). Social Conflict and the Theory of Social Change. *The British Journal of Sociology, 8*(3).

Der Spiegel. (2008). *Spiegel interview with Strobe Talbott.* Author.

Fukuyama. (1989). The end of the history? *National Interests.*

Gachechiladze, R. (2008). *Near East.* Tbilisi State University.

Heidelberg Institute for International Conflict Research. (2014). *Conflict Barometer 2013.* Retrieved from: https://hiik.de/de/downloads/data/downloads_2013/ConflictBarometer2013

Heidelberg Institute for International Conflict Research. (2021). *Conflict Barometer 2020.* Retrieved from: https://hiik.de/?lang=en

Heywood, A. (1998). *Political Ideologies.* Macmillan. doi:10.1007/978-1-349-26409-4

Info Migrants. (2021). *UNHCR: Numbers of displaced people in world passes 80 million.* Retrieved from: https://www.infomigrants.net/en/post/29030/unhcr-numbers-of-displaced-people-in-world-passes-80-million

Kegley, B. (2010-2011). *Trend and Transformation.* Academic Press.

Maksakovsky, V. (2005). *World Social and Economic Geography.* Academic Press.

NATO Handbook, . (2006). *NATO Public Diplomacy Division.*

Nye, J. (2007). *Public Diplomacy and Soft Power.* JSTOR Collection.

Occupation zones in Kosovo. (2000). Retrieved from: https://mapsontheweb.zoom-maps.com/post/114574543300/kfor-occupation-zones-via-reddit

Political Map of Africa. (2013). Retrieved from: https://www.pinterest.com/pin/96757091973420425/

Pruitt, G., & Rubin, Z. (1986). *Summary of "Social Conflict: Escalation, Stalemate and Settlement".* Retrieved from https://www.beyondintractability.org/bksum/pruitt-social

SIPRI. (2016). *Conflict, peace and security.* https://www.sipri.org/research/conflict-peace-and-security

Wallerstein, I. (2001). Democracy, Capitalism, and Transformation. Oxford University Press.

Wells, M. (2017). *The mixed record of UN peacekeeping in South Sudan.* Retrieved from: https://odihpn.org/magazine/the-mixed-record-of-un-peacekeeping-in-south-sudan/

KEY TERMS AND DEFINITIONS

Alliances: Coalitions that form when two or more states combine their military capabilities and promise to coordinate their policies to increase mutual security.

Armed Aggression: Combat between the military forces of two or more states or groups.

Arms Control: Multilateral or bilateral agreements to contain arms races by setting limits on the number and types of weapons states are permitted.

Arms Race: The buildup of weapons and armed forces by two or more states that threaten each other, with the competition driven by the conviction that gaining a lead is necessary for security.

Bandwagoning: The tendency for weak states to seek alliance with the strongest power, irrespective of that power's ideology or type of government, in order to increase their security.

Civil Wars: Wars between opposing groups within the same country or by rebels against the government.

Cold War: The 42-year (1949-1991) rivalry between the United States and the Soviet Union, as well as their competing coalitions, which sought to contain each other's expansion and win worldwide predominance.

Conciliation: A conflict-resolution procedure in which a third party assists both parties to a dispute but does not propose a solution.

Conflict: Discord, often arising in international relations over perceived incompatibilities of interest.

Coup d'etat: A sudden, forcible takeover of government by a small group within that country, typically carried out by violent or illegal means with the goal of installing their own leadership in power.

Covert Operations: Secret activities undertaken by a state outside its borders through clandestine means to achieve specific political or military goals with respect to another state.

Crimes Against Humanity: A category of activities, made illegal at the Nuremberg war crime trials, condemning states that abuse human rights.

Crisis: A situation in which the threat of escalation to warfare is high and the time available for making decisions and reaching compromised solutions in negotiation is compressed.

Decolonization: The achievement of sovereign independence by countries that were once colonies of the great powers.

Détente: In general, a strategy of seeking to relax tensions between adversaries to reduce the possibility of war.

Disarmament: Agreements to reduce or destroy weapons or other means of attack.

Diversionary Theory of War: The hypothesis that leaders sometimes initiate conflict abroad as a way of increasing national public attention away from controversial domestic issues and internal problems.

Ethnic Cleansing: The extermination of an ethnic minority group by a state.

Ethnic Groups: People whose identity is primarily defined by their sense of sharing a common ancestral nationality, language, cultural heritage, and kinship.

Ethnic Nationalism: Devotion to a cultural, ethnic, or linguistic community.

Ethnicity: Perceptions of likeness among members of a particular racial grouping leading them to prejudicially view other nationality groups as outsiders.

Failed States: Countries whose governments have so mismanaged policy that their citizens in rebellion, threaten revolution to divide the country into separate independent states.

Genocide: The attempt to eliminate in whole or in part, an ethnic, racial religious or national minority group.

Hard Power: The ability to exercise international influence by means of a country's military capabilities.

Humanitarian Intervention: The use of peacekeeping troops by foreign states or international organizations to protect endangered people from gross violations of their human rights and from mass murder.

Imperialism: The policy of expanding state power through the conquest and or military domination of foreign territory.

International Aggression: killing others that are not members of one's own species.

International Court of Justice (ICJ): The primary court established by the United Nations for resolving legal disputes between states and providing advisory opinions to international agencies and the UN General Assembly.

International Criminal Court (ICC): A court established by the UN for indicting and administering justice to people committing war crimes.

International Criminal Tribunals: Special tribunals established by the UN prosecute those responsible for war time atrocities and genocide bring justice to victims and deter such crimes.

Intraspecific Aggression: Killing members of one`s species.

Irredentism: A movement by an ethnic national group to recover control of lost territory by force so that the new state boundaries will no longer divide the group.

Jus in Bello: A component of just war doctrine that sets limits on the acceptable use of force.

Just War Doctrine: The moral criteria identifying when a war may be undertaken and how it should be fought once it begins.

Just War Theory: The theoretical criteria under which it is morally permissible or just for a state to go to war and the methods by which a just war might be fought.

Mediation: A conflict-solution procedure in which a third party proposes a nonbinding solution to the disputants.

Military Intervention: Over or covert use of force by one or more countries in order to affect the target counties government and policies.

Military-Industrial Complex: A combination of defense establishments, contractors who supply arms for them and government agencies that benefit from high military spending which act as a lobbying coalition to pressure governments to appropriate large expenditures for military preparedness.

Nation: A collectively whose people see themselves as members of the same group because they share the same ethnicity, culture, or language.

National Character: The collective characteristics ascribed to the people within a state.

National Interest: The goals that states pursue to maximize what they perceive to be selfishly best for their country.

National Security: A country's psychological freedom from fears that the state will be unable to resist threats to its survival and national values emanating from abroad or at home.

Nationalism: A mindset glorifying a particular state and the nationality group living in it which sees the states interest as a supreme value.

Neocolonialism (Neo Imperialism): The economic rather than military domination of foreign countries.

Negotiation: Diplomatic dialogue and discussion between two or more parties with the goal of resolving through give- and-take bargaining perceived differences of interests and the conflict they cause.

Neutrality: The legal doctrine that provides rights for the state to remain nonaligned with adversaries waging war against each other.

Non-Aligned States: Countries that do not form alliances with opposed great-powers and practice neutrality on issues that divide great powers.

Nonlethal Weapons: The wide array of soft kill low- intensify method of incapacitating an enemy's people, vehicles, communications system, or entire cities without killing either combatants or non-combatants.

Nonproliferation Regime: Rules to contain arms races so that weapons or technology do not spread to states that do not have them.

Pacifism: The liberal idealist school of ethical thought that recognizes no conditions that justify the taking of another human's life even when authorized by a head of state.

Peace Building: Post-conflict actions predominantly diplomatic and economic that strengthen and rebuild governmental infrastructure and institutions in order to avoid renewed recourse to armed conflict.

Peace Enforcement: The application of military force to warring parties or the threat of it normally pursuant to international authorization to compel compliance with resolutions or with sanctions designed to maintain or restore peace and order.

Peace Operations: A general category encompassing both peacekeeping and peace enforcement operations undertaken to establish and maintain peace between disputants.

Peaceful Coexistence: Soviet leader Nikita Khrushchev's 1956 doctrine that war between capitalist and communist states is not inevitable and that inter - bloc competition could be peaceful.

Peacemaking: The process of democracy mediation negotiation or other forms of peaceful settlement that arranges an end to a dispute and resolves the issues that led to conflict.

Preemptive War: A quick first strike attack that seeks to defeat an adversary before it can organize an initial attack or a retaliatory response.

Realism: A paradigm based on the premise that world politics is essentially and unchangeably a struggle among self-interest states for power and position under anarchy, with each competing state pursuing its own national interest.

Refugees: People who flee for safety to another country because of a well-founded fear of political persecution, environmental degradation, or famine.

Xenophobia: The suspicious dislike disrespect, and disregard for members of a foreign nationality ethnic or linguistic group.

Zero-Sum: An exchange in a purely conflictual relationship in which what is gained by one competitor is lost by another.

Chapter 5
Climate Change as a Common Enemy:
A New Threat to International Peace and Security

Nima Norouzi
https://orcid.org/0000-0002-2546-4288
Bournemouth University, UK

ABSTRACT

New paradigm and military and hardware variables and political, economic, socio-cultural, and environmental components are considered factors that can act as a threat to the international security. Climate change is one of the most important and complex international challenges in the age of globalization. These small changes in global warming could pose a potential risk to global climate change. Our lives today depend on climate change. In the international arena, the effects of these threats are gradually observed in the relations between the countries. The Darfur War, for example, can be considered the first conflict in the field of climate change. In addition to social tensions, these threats will lead to political unrest and violent conflicts. This issue is recognized as a threat to international peace and security beyond the international agendas in the framework of the UN Framework Convention and the Secretary-General's follow-up and United Nation Bureau of Climate Change.

INTRODUCTION

The rupture of the ozone layer and the greenhouse problem, one of the most important concerns of governments in the modern era, is a threat that endangers human health in Korea in the same and comprehensive way. This issue can no longer be raised in the form of the previous two periods. The study of security in this regard is equally proposed for all nations. This will result in global warming, including rainforests, acid rain, and toxic waste from the air, sea, and soil. The 11992 World Summit with the United Nations in Rio de Janeiro, Brazil, with the participation of 178 countries, endorsed this(Björnsdóttir, 2013).

DOI: 10.4018/978-1-7998-9586-2.ch005

The summit warned that the environment is a macro-policy in line with the international economy, national security. The summit helped shift the focus from unilateral security to multilateral security, meaning that unilateral and uncoordinated actions by countries are relatively useless, meaning that each country needs the cooperation of others to protect its environment. Two important aspects of environmental security are: 1) Changing natural human habitat, including global warming, ozone depletion, and the destruction of equatorial rainforests. 2) Pollution, including acid rain, toxic waste, and other air, sea, and soil pollution forms. The purpose of security here is to preserve the earth's physical environment and prevent situations that endanger the survival and quality of human life(Conway, 2010).

Both aspects of environmental security are closely related. Security problems in terms of pollution are more immediate for governments and their leaders, although in developed countries the issue of pollution is a high priority, the countries of the world are still at risk of another type of pollution.

Human life requires relatively constant climatic conditions. Humans upset the earth's energy balance by consuming energy from fossil fuels and over-producing greenhouse gases. Today, most aspects and areas of human life are affected by the increase of greenhouse gases. This increase has caused the earth's temperature to rise over the past century, and we expect to have an increase of 2 to 11.5 Fahrenheit over the next 100 years(Conca et al., 2017).

These small changes in the earth's temperature could pose a potential risk to global climate change. Our lives today depend on climate change. In the international arena, it can be seen that over time, the effects of these threats on relations between countries can be seen as an example of the Darfur War, which can be considered as the first conflict in the field of climate change. In addition to social tensions, these threats will lead to political unrest and violent conflict. The combination of this increase in temperature and the changes that have taken place in the international climate is called climate change. Therefore, climate change is defined as a change in a place's climatic conditions and characteristics in the long run (Conca et al., 2016). Of course, international climate change regimes have different views on the definition of climate change; On hand; according to Article 2, paragraph 1, of the United Nations Framework Convention on Climate Change, "Climate change" is a change that directly or indirectly as a result of human activities, leads to changes in global atmospheric composition. These changes are different from natural changes in climate that are observed in similar periods. Used when it results from natural change or human activity (Edenhofer et al., 2011). From this point of view, climate change has recently emerged as a combined result. Reaching an agreement through ambitious action to tackle climate change is critical to human progress in the 21st century. Several steps have been taken in this regard worldwide; In a way, the largest international body, the United Nations and the Security Council, as its security pillar, has also put this issue on its agenda as a threat to international peace and security. The emergence of these works and the increasing importance of the subject raises many questions in mind: can we reduce the risks of these changes? Despite a scientific consensus among scientists, is this consensus specific to climate change among world politicians? Do the strategies and actions taken by the United Nations fit the current needs of human societies? What is the main challenge of the UN and the international community in terms of climate change? Can the Security Council take key steps to reduce climate change in the future? If, outside the United Nations, states do not take basic measures; Can the UN and the Security Council force states to comply with global climate change standards?

But the present Chapter seeks to answer the key question: What has the United Nations, as the International Peace and Security Agency, done so far in dealing with these threats? In answer to the above question, we can say that we can hope for the solution to this problem, considering the actions taken by the United Nations, including the Secretary-General. But how fruitful these works have been questionable, and the need for more effective action is felt.

CLIMATE CHANGE IMPACTS

Greenhouse Gas Impact on Global Warming

Greenhouse gases include water vapor, carbon dioxide, ozone, troposphere, methane, nitrogen oxides, and industrial gases (halocarbons), which are present in the earth's atmosphere except for industrial gases and are naturally the result interaction. They create less than one percent of the earth's atmosphere. This amount of gas naturally maintains the earth's temperature under favorable conditions to create a greenhouse effect. As a result of increasing greenhouse gas emissions and increasing the concentration of these gases in the earth's atmosphere over the past 100 years, the sea level has increased by 10 to 20 centimeters (Dodds & Sherman, 2009). This increase is due to the warming of the planet earth. The earth's average temperature has warmed by 1.4 degrees Fahrenheit over the past century and is expected to reach 2 to 11.5 degrees Fahrenheit in the next 100 years.

The earth has also experienced a temperature increase of 0.74°C since 1900 due to an increase in greenhouse gases, although 70% of this increase occurred during the years 1970 to 2004. This increase will continue on a large scale for decades to come. According to the International Board of Climate Change studies, by 2100, the average global temperature will reach from 1.1 °C to 6.6 °C.

(Gupta, 2009). In the meantime, human activities have released large amounts of carbon monoxide and greenhouse gases into the atmosphere over the past century. These measures have been taken through fossil fuels for energy supply, deforestation, change of industrial and agricultural practices.

These small changes in global temperature can pose a potential risk to global climate change. Evidence shows. Climate changes accompany temperature changes. Oceans and glaciers have undergone many changes. The oceans are getting hotter and more acidic, glaciers are melting, and water levels are rising. Other effects include warmer seawater, more evaporation, and changes in the marine food network. Rising sea levels lead to unforeseen events such as severe hurricanes, submerging many coastal settlements, especially in island countries. Devastating floods and hurricanes, severe droughts, heavy rains, mass migration, and huge social and economic damage are other phenomena that global warming could challenge human society in the future.

Social Effects of Climate Change at the International Level

Climate change has been recognized internationally as one of the most important and complex challenges of the 21st century. Most aspects and areas of human life have been affected by these changes. Biodiversity, agriculture, drinking water resources, industry, health, and many other aspects of civilized human life have been affected by this factor. The increase in greenhouse gas emissions and the impact of climate change at the international level have raised fundamental questions. Of course, in recent years, the understanding of these changes has improved globally. Degradation of nature and increasing pressures on the environment have led to an increase in the formation of relevant conventions and agreements in climate change. But successive droughts, floods, and hot air, which can be expected to intensify with climate change, have displaced millions and reduced food supplies(Hagen, 2016).

Changes in rainfall, humidity, and temperature changes have led to biodiversity, ecosystems and personal hygiene, and lifestyles.

Other effects of climate change include rising sea levels and global warming, floods, and possible drowning in low-lying coastal areas, putting countries in the South Pacific and coastal areas of Asia at risk.

With these changes and the loss of landmass, the forced migration of refugees of climate change will occur, and the Security Council considers this migration a threat to international peace and security and considers this issue a prelude to ethnic and civil wars. Climate change is also reducing water resources and reducing rainfall, affecting agricultural production and creating food poverty. The UN Environment Program in Sudan's environmental assessment blames climate change and environmental degradation for some of the conflicts in Darfur. These changes have led to drought and desertification, which has also led to conflicts. These threats are increasing day by day and endangering international peace and security, which is the danger of water war (Sicurelli, 2016).

Another effect is political destabilization, which is likely to result in climate change in neighboring countries. Especially the negative effects of what we have seen and will happen in the future. These impacts have been described in urban areas of developing or less developed countries with the highest population concentrations and high risks. Climate change is also addressed concerning human rights and the rights of nations and is the basis for the threat of access to drinking water, access to adequate housing, and the basis for the sovereignty of UN member states (Tayebi & Zarabi, 2018). Among these, climate change, which is a serious global threat, is of great importance, referred to as "soft threat" (Gupta, 2009), and has transboundary and trans-regional effects, for example, in the Horn of Africa. It is obvious.

Transcontinental influences are also on the rise; for example, these changes have increased migration from Africa to Europe. Coastal cities are often directly vulnerable to environmental events and pressures, with economic and political consequences at the national level. Although the destructive effects are immediate, the damage will become apparent over time. Indigenous peoples' dependence on natural resources will increase their poverty. Although attention has recently shifted to cities, analysis shows that we have little information on systems in the process of warming, identifying high-risk areas, recognizing the link between climate change and urban poverty, and formulating and approving action plans.

The effects of climate change are not the same in all parts of the world. The world's poorest countries play the least role in greenhouse gas emissions and are paradoxically most affected by this phenomenon. That is why special funds have been allocated to help developing countries respond to the effects of this phenomenon. In such a phenomenon, structurally and economically weaker countries have a high degree of vulnerability(Kendall, 2012).

Evolution of International Debates on Climate Change

Many actions have been taken internationally on climate change in various circles, which we will briefly mention as: at the first Geneva Conference on Climate Change in 1979, it was pointed out as an absolute urgency at the international level that it wanted to anticipate climate change in most states. At the same time, the World Climate Program, in cooperation with the World Meteorological Organization and the Environment Program of the United Nations, and the International Council of Scientific Unions, was launched. Several intergovernmental conferences on climate change also followed. In 1988, the 46-nation Climate Change Conference was held in Toronto, with the need to develop a convention framework to protect the climate. In 1988, the World Meteorological Organization and the United Nations Environment Program established the International Climate Change Board to assess the totality and speed of change, its effects, and coping strategies. In 1990, the Second World Climate Conference and the International Atomic Energy Agency requested a treaty on climate change. Subsequently, the General Assembly's negotiations on a framework convention began. At the Ground Summit in Rio de Janeiro in 1992, the United Nations Framework Convention on Climate Change was signed for ratification at the same time as the United Nations Convention on Biological Diversity and the United Nations Convention to Combat Desertification. The United Nations Framework Convention on Climate Change was implemented in 1994, and its Secretariat was established to support the Convention. The Kyoto Protocol was formally adopted in December 1997 and implemented in 2005. Industrialized countries and those with a market economy (192 countries) are committed to reducing emissions by 2.5 percent during the years 2008-2012 (known as the first period)(Kelsen, 2000).

In 2001, the Morocco Agreement, together with the details of the implementation of the Protocol, was adopted by the members of the conference, which included the adjustment of new financial instruments and programs and the establishment of a technology transfer framework.2007 Bali roadmap was set. In 2010, the Cancun Agreements and the 2011 Durban Agreement were adopted. The 2012 amendment includes two: 1. New commitments were adopted for the annex members to the Kyoto Protocol to agree on commitments during the commitment period from 2013 to the end of 2020; 2. Members must report a revised list of greenhouse gases in the second commitment period; 3. Amendments were made to several articles of the Protocol relating to the first Commitment Period and those which need to be updated for the Second Commitment Period. The Warsaw Pact in 2013 and the Lima Summit in Peru in 2014. In 2015, the Paris Agreement was reached to achieve the Sustainable Development Goals as a roadmap to reduce greenhouse gas emissions and create flexibility for climate change(Norouzi & Ataei, 2021).

Intergovernmental Panel on Climate Change

The Climate Change Mission was established in 1988 by the United Nations Meteorological Agency and the United Nations Environment Program. Its main purpose was to study scientific, technical, social, and economic information related to climate change due to human activity, the potential effects of climate change, and options for mitigation and adaptation. The board has submitted four evaluation reports, guidelines for the developed method for the national greenhouse gas inventory, special reports, and technical articles. The board has three working groups and a special executive force(Norouzi & Ataei, 2021):

- The first working group that studies the science of climate change.
- The second working group examines the adaptation, effects, and adaptation to climate change.
- The third working group examines the reduction of greenhouse gases.

The Special Task Force (TFI) checks the national greenhouse gas inventory.
The Executive Task Force was formed in 1998 by the Climate Change Board for its fourteenth meeting to oversee the GHG inventory program. This program has been carried out since 1991 by the first working group of the delegation, which worked closely with the Organization for Economic Cooperation and Development and the International Energy Agency. The objectives of this special force are to develop and improve the internationally agreed method and software for calculating and reporting the emissions of national greenhouses and eliminating them. Encourage the widespread use of this method by States Parties to the UN Security Council and the signatories of the United Nations Framework Convention on Climate Change in 2007 and implement the UN Joint Action Plan. Gore was awarded the former Vice

Climate Change as a Common Enemy

President of the United States. In this regard, the head of the UN Environment Program stated that the award shows that climate change is very important for international peace and security. He went on to say in a statement that the Nobel Peace Prize Committee today made it clear that combating climate change is a fundamental policy for peace and security in the twenty-first century (Pachauri et al., 2014).

UNITED NATIONS ACTIONS

Evolution of the Concept of International Peace and Security

In the past, international security was often defined as military security. Still, after the conclusion of the Peace and Reconciliation Treaty in 1648 and the formation of the nation-state system, the concept of national security was introduced in international relations. Bring the arena to life. This issue is now defined in political, military, economic, and social dimensions.

Due to the limited nature of the concept of peace, the concept of international security was also limited in the past and did not go far beyond the borders of states, and was based on states' national security. Therefore, the independence and national sovereignty of governments were considered the most important element of international security. From this point of view, governments were considered both the main source of threat and responsible for establishing security, and the provision of international security was also dependent on the provision of national security. But with the onset of globalization, international security gradually lost its Westphalian connotation. They were also considered the source of many threats to non-state actors and other factors and individuals. The threats also extended from the military to other political, economic, social, and environmental dimensions. Population growth, uncontrolled migration, poverty development, environmental degradation, and global warming are among the threat factors in the contemporary world. In this context, Buzan examines security threats in five dimensions(Saul, 2009):

A) Political threats; According to him, political threats at the domestic level are related to issues such as lack of democracy and instability of governments. At the international level, the anarchist structure of the international system is considered to be threatening.

B) economic threats; He believes that poverty and the development of orthodoxy are the most important challenges of the economy, which in many cases exacerbates the mismanagement of their domestic political order.

) social threats; He says social and cultural threats are often rooted in economic factors. Problems such as illegal immigration, illiteracy, drugs, and organized crime are challenges that can lead to insecurity and the threat of peace.

D) military threats; Military threats have long been considered a threat to international peace and security. Today, the production and proliferation of weapons of mass destruction and land disputes between countries have added to these threats.

R) Environmental threats: According to him, global warming, piercing of the layer of climate change, the gradual decline of forests, especially rainforests, drought and shortage of fresh water, coal, and alumina, alumina. Many of them are threats that may not be the cause of military threats soon.

Many countries have put these changes on their security agenda and given them a special place in their foreign policy. In the text of the United States National Security Strategy in 2015, climate change, among other things, is introduced as one of the new security threats. The High-Level Commission on Threats, Challenges, and Changes, set up by the UN Secretary-General to redefine the concept of international peace and security, also identified environmental erosion and analysis as a potential threat to international security (Sicurelli, 2016). In the Board Report, climate change was identified as one of the greatest environmental challenges currently facing the international community. As we have mentioned, peace is not the same as non-military confrontation, but climate change and other new factors are seen as a threat to international peace and security. In this view, even interference in the internal affairs of governments is not only not illegal but is considered a precondition for international peace and security. Based on such an interpretation of international peace and security, the Security Council has identified climate change as a threat to international peace and security. In addition, the Security Council has considered the destruction of the environment, terrorism, and even AIDS as new threats to international peace and security (Sindico, 2007; Norouzi et al., 2021). In the international arena, it can be seen that the effects of these threats on relations between countries are gradually being seen. For example, the Darfur war can be considered as the first conflict in the field of climate change, which was started by the late UN Secretary-General Ban Ki-moon as: "The root of this drought war is the lack of arable land and water (Saul, 2009)".

Security Council and its Authority to Address Climate Change

In carrying out its principal function under Article 24 (1) of the Charter, the Security Council expressly respects international peace and security maintenance. The special powers conferred on the Security Council by Chapters 6, 7, 8, and 12 for the performance of the said tasks. The Security Council acts as a mediator within the framework of Chapter Seven. The drafters of the Charter deliberately did not define peace violations and threats of peace as aggression and provided the Security Council with the determination of each of these situations. The practice of the Security Council also confirms that it considers itself a competent body in determining and identifying threats to peace, breaches of peace and acts of aggression and considers it it'sright. But in recent years, the Security Council has adopted a broader interpretation of international peace and security, raising the question of the extent of the Security Council's powers. Is this council bound to determine the threat in compliance with the rules and regulations of international law, or how is there no restriction on the violation of the peace and the threat to peace? However, according to one view, the Security Council has no restrictions on the performance of its duties under Chapter VII, and the recognition of the Security Council is not bound by international law (Schachter, 1951).

However, efforts to coordinate peaceful international cooperation between governments are not new. The tools available to the Security Council are appropriate to improve the effectiveness of climate crisis intervention. The recent approach of establishing UN agreements, such as the Kyoto Protocol, is ineffective in achieving meaningful change and international desirability. The conflict between members of the Security Council will force other countries to comply with UN agreements.

Representatives of 55 countries attended the first Security Council meeting on climate change on international peace and security on 17 April 2007. The first achievement of these negotiations was the holding of this meeting itself because the main purpose of the UK in raising this issue in the Security Council was to increase the awareness of the world's countries on this issue. Some have been very cautious in this regard and have explicitly stated that the only reason they agree with the Security Council's proposal is that these discussions are not expected to have a direct result or action. These considerations have led some countries to consider climate change, not within the competence of the Security Council, and to hold other UN bodies responsible for it(Tayebi & Zarabi, 2018).

Countries that fundamentally agreed to address the security implications of climate change on the Security Council agenda saw it as part of a conflict prevention policy that is itself a tool for maintaining international peace and security. Among this group were European countries, small island countries, and some developing countries that were somehow victims of climate change, such as Bangladesh. These countries had a relatively broad interpretation of the concept of international peace and security. However, there is a range of different approaches within this group. Some countries, such as the United Kingdom, have argued that the main reason for raising this issue in the Security Council, as noted, is to increase global attention and awareness of the issue of climate change.

The second approach among the countries of this group was based on the principle of prevention. Germany and France, for example, believed that climate change was part of conflict prevention policy and should therefore be considered in the broader sense of preventive diplomacy. Thus, while broadly understanding the concept of international security, the country called for a holistic approach by the international community. The issue of climate change is directly related to other security issues such as poverty, water scarcity, or pervasive diseases.

However, the approach of the small island countries, which are more vulnerable to climate change than others, was that this issue has obvious security dimensions, and the Security Council should not only put it on its agenda but also Take appropriate measures in this regard as soon as possible (Norouzi, 2020).

Finally, the role played by the Security Council in this area was more of an advisory role than an active one, given the council's focus on prevention and how it deals with civilian threats. It is justifiable. During this period, climate change was considered the primary factor in conflicts or their accelerating or intensifying factor. Accordingly, the international community must do everything in its power to prevent civilian threats such as AIDS or climate change, which may lead to active conflict and a security threat in the traditional sense.

Role of the Secretary-General of the United Nations

The issue of climate change is of great interest to the Secretary-General of the United Nations, Mr. Ban Kimon. He called this issue "the problem of our time." At a rally in New York, he recently, in a crowd of more than 100,000 people, constantly called for a message to the world. "Now is the time to act," he told Euronews, referring to the importance of urgent international attention to climate change. If we do not act now, we will have to pay more. This is our world, and our planet is burning. For the sake of prosperity and success, we must adapt the planet to the environment for future generations socially and economically. This is our world and the world of future generations. We must have moral and political responsibility "(Euronews, 2014). Under his leadership, several climate conferences have been held to address emissions reductions, financial and technology issues, and compatibility.

The first members' conference was held in Bali, Indonesia, in 2007, Cancun 2010, and Durban in 2011. He has also organized conferences such as Sustainable Energy for All 2012 and the World Challenge Without Climate Control, and the UN Sustainable Development Conference (Rio 20) in 2012(Norouzi, 2021).

The Secretary-General also visited Antarctica and Chilean Patagonia in 2007 on climate change and other parts of the world. The official website of the United Nations, influenced by the instructions of the Secretary-General on Climate Change, has made the responsibility of each human being known and calls for action through social sites and the Internet to raise public awareness of the necessary measures to be taken.

Paris Conference 2015

Climate change is a global emergency that goes beyond national borders. It is an issue that requires international cooperation and coordinated solutions at all levels. To tackle climate change and its negative impacts, world leaders at the UN Climate Change Conference (COP21) in Paris reached a breakthrough on 12 December 2015: the historic Paris Agreement. The Agreement sets long-term goals to guide all nations as substantially reduce global greenhouse gas emissions to limit the global temperature increase in this century to 2 degrees Celsius while pursuing efforts to limit the increase even further to 1.5 degrees; review countries' commitments every five years; provide financing to developing countries to mitigate climate change, strengthen resilience and enhance abilities to adapt to climate impacts. The Agreement is a legally binding international treaty. It entered into force on 4 November 2016. Today, 191 Parties (190 countries plus the European Union) have joined the Paris Agreement. The Agreement includes commitments from all countries to reduce their emissions and work together to adapt to the impacts of climate change and calls on countries to strengthen their commitments over time. The Agreement provides a pathway for developed nations to assist developing nations in their climate mitigation and adaptation efforts while creating a framework for the transparent monitoring and reporting of countries' climate goals. The Paris Agreement provides a durable framework guiding the global effort for decades to come. It marks the beginning of a shift towards a net-zero emissions world. Implementation of the Agreement is also essential for the achievement of the Sustainable Development Goals. The Paris Agreement works on a five-year cycle of increasingly ambitious climate action carried out by countries. Each country is expected to submit an updated national climate action plan every five years - known as Nationally Determined Contribution, or NDC. In their NDCs, countries communicate actions to reduce their greenhouse gas emissions to reach the Paris Agreement's goals. Countries also communicate in the NDC's actions to build resilience to adapt to the impacts of rising temperatures. To better frame the efforts towards the long-term goal, the Paris Agreement invites countries to formulate and submit long-term strategies. Unlike NDCs, they are not mandatory. The operational details for the practical implementation of the Paris Agreement were agreed on at the UN Climate Change Conference (COP24) in Katowice, Poland, in December 2018, in what is colloquially called the Paris Rulebook, with a few unresolved issues(Sicurelli, 2016).

Future and Prospects of Climate Change Prevention Measures

On 28 September 2012, the Presidents of St. Kitts and Nice announced that Pure Energy would be the also world's absolute power Emotions are reflected in the Sustainable Energy Session for the General Assembly's initiatives (Norouzi & Movahedian, 2021). To prevent the adverse effects of climate change from progressing, a basic global policy must be adopted and implemented quickly. For example, the International Climate Change Regime must ensure that greenhouse gas emissions, one of the main causes of these changes, are reduced by half by the middle of the 21st century to what is seen today. A change in the power structure must accompany this international policy in the world political order. An official note from the German government in 2011 outlined how the Security Council would deal with the assumption of new responsibilities related to the climate change crisis. The blueprint outlined several scenarios for dealing with the problems: These scenarios were: dealing with the effects of rising temperatures and rising sea levels, how to deal with displaced persons affected by the change, how to prevent conflicts in parts of Asia and the east; It will be obvious to identify new problems that the council has to face (S/2011/408). Other commentators have reflected these feelings; By making proposals such as proper planning, disaster preparedness, developing a public understanding of the particular dangers to nations, and understanding the international community as a whole. The Security Council should consider facilitating the creation of international agreements committing governments to reduce greenhouse gas emissions. Several other proposals have been made to the UN General Assembly in this regard. Another tool of the United Nations in dealing with this issue is the International Court of Justice, which can be a solution to this issue by exercising jurisdiction, and Chapter 7 of the Charter can also be a guarantee for the implementation of votes (Kendall, 2012). The UN Convention on Climate Change, as one of the most important instruments of international law, calls for the broad cooperation of countries and international assistance. However, in dealing with climate change, it is better not to make a military choice because war is inherently harmful; As the Rio Declaration acknowledges, war is inherently destructive and endangers peace, development, and environmental protection (Sindico, 2007). Therefore, military action to combat climate change is contrary to the principles of protection of international climate change treaties. Article 42 of the Charter can not be a good solution to combat this change because the absence of war and military conflict between countries guarantees peace and security. It is international, and the only restriction that the Security Council must adhere to is the scope of Article 39 of the Charter.

CONCLUSION

There is a strong consensus in scientific circles that climate change is taking place and that human activities play a key role in this process. According to the Fifth Interim Board's evaluation report, this role accounts for approximately 95%. While there is no difference of opinion among scientists as to the role of the human factor, international debate seeks to determine how the climate responds to rising greenhouse gas emissions over time and in different parts of the world. Will. If climate change is recognized internationally as a threat to international security, it can give hope to the integration of actions through the establishment and cooperation mechanisms to deal with its destructive effects. Otherwise, climate change will deepen conflicts and conflicts in the field of international relations and will lead to the beginning of international conflicts over the distribution of water resources, land and migration management, or the issue of compensation to the minorities that will be the main culprits of change in trends and countries affected by its destructive effects.

The formation of international circles and regimes indicates an increase in public awareness and alarm bells of the effects of climate change worldwide and is gradually recognized by the international community. However, in addition to the Conference of the Parties to the Framework Convention on Climate Change, held annually, similar measures have been taken at the United Nations to bring about normalization and awareness-raising. The severity of the consequences of climate change has been raised on the Security Council agenda since 2007 as a threat to international peace and security. It seems that while the Security Council is discussing climate change and issues related to climate stability and security, the focus of future diplomats should be on the UN Framework Convention on Climate Change and the Kyoto Protocol.

Contrary to the fact that the countries participating in the Climate Change Negotiations of the Security Council have a consensus on the occurrence of climate change as a threat to international peace and security, but disagree on how to deal with the dangers of such changes. These differences are due to the views of these countries. Some see the issue as part of a conflict prevention policy, and others believe in the principle of climate change prevention. But the third group, which will receive the most impact in the future and understand the security of the issue, believes in immediate action in this regard. But in practice, these steps have always faced obstacles. For example, the United Nations Framework Convention on Climate Change and the Kyoto Protocol, a platform for global action in this area, is largely hampered by US opposition to the mandatory emission reductions set out in Annex I to the Kyoto Protocol have been exposed. The Security Council should facilitate the creation of international agreements that commit governments to reduce greenhouse gas emissions. In this regard, it can benefit from the tools of the Climate Change Framework Convention and even the International Court of Justice.

ACKNOWLEDGMENT

This research received no specific grant from any funding agency in the public, commercial, or not-for-profit sectors.

REFERENCES

Björnsdóttir, A. L. (2013). *The UN Security Council and Climate Change: Rising Seas Levels, Shrinking Resources, and the 'Green Helmets'* (Master's thesis).

Conca, K., Thwaites, J., & Lee, G. (2016). Bully Pulpit or Bull in a China Shop? Climate change and the UN Security Council. *Annu. Meet. Acad. Counc. United Nations Syst, 1*.

Conca, K., Thwaites, J., & Lee, G. (2017). Climate change and the UN Security Council: Bully pulpit or bull in a china shop? *Global Environmental Politics, 17*(2), 1–20. doi:10.1162/GLEP_a_00398

Conway, D. (2010). The United Nations Security Council and climate change: Challenges and opportunities. *Climate Law, 1*(3), 375–407. doi:10.1163/CL-2010-018

Dodds, F., & Sherman, R. (2009). *Climate Change and Energy Insecurity: The Challenge for Peace, Security and Development*. Routledge. doi:10.4324/9781849774406

Edenhofer, O., Pichs-Madruga, R., Sokona, Y., Seyboth, K., Kadner, S., Zwickel, T., & Matschoss, P. (Eds.). (2011). *Renewable energy sources and climate change mitigation: Special report of the intergovernmental panel on climate change*. Cambridge University Press. doi:10.1017/CBO9781139151153

Gupta, S. (2009). Environmental law and policy: Climate change as a threat to international peace and security. *Perspectives on Global Issues, 4*(1), 7–17.

Hagen, J. J. (2016). Queering women, peace and security. *International Affairs, 92*(2), 313–332. doi:10.1111/1468-2346.12551

Kelsen, H. (2000). *The law of the United Nations: a critical analysis of its fundamental problems: with supplement* (Vol. 11). The Lawbook Exchange, Ltd.

Kendall, R. (2012). Climate change as a security threat to the Pacific Islands. *New Zealand Journal of Environmental Law*, *16*, 83–116.

Norouzi, N. (2021). Post-COVID-19 and globalization of oil and natural gas trade: Challenges, opportunities, lessons, regulations, and strategies. *International Journal of Energy Research*, *45*(10), 14338–14356. doi:10.1002/er.6762 PMID:34219899

Norouzi, N., & Ataei, E. (2021). Covid-19 Crisis and Environmental law: Opportunities and challenges. *Hasanuddin Law Review*, *7*(1), 46–60. doi:10.20956/halrev.v7i1.2772

Norouzi, N., Khanmohammadi, H. U., & Ataei, E. (2021). The Law in the Face of the COVID-19 Pandemic: Early Lessons from Uruguay. *Hasanuddin Law Review*, *7*(2), 75–88. doi:10.20956/halrev.v7i2.2827

Norouzi, N., & Movahedian, H. (2021). Right to Education in Mother Language: In the Light of Judicial and Legal Structures. In Handbook of Research on Novel Practices and Current Successes in Achieving the Sustainable Development Goals (pp. 223-241). IGI Global.

Pachauri, R. K., Allen, M. R., Barros, V. R., Broome, J., Cramer, W., Christ, R., & van Ypserle, J. P. (2014). *Climate change 2014: synthesis report. Contribution of Working Groups I, II and III to the fifth assessment report of the Intergovernmental Panel on Climate Change*. IPCC.

Saul, B. (2009). Climate Change, Conflict and Security: International Law Challenges. *NZ Armed FL Rev.*, *9*, 1.

Schachter, O. (1951). *The Law of the United Nations*. Academic Press.

Sicurelli, D. (2016). *The European Union's Africa policies: norms, interests and impact*. Routledge. doi:10.4324/9781315239828

Sindico, F. (2007). Climate change: A security (council) issue. *Carbon & Climate L. Rev.*, *29*.

Tayebi, S., & Zarabi, M. (2018). Environmental Diplomacy and Climate Change; Constructive strategic approach to reducer. *Human & Environment*, *16*(4), 159–170.

ADDITIONAL READING

Gupta, S. (2009). Environmental law and policy: Climate change as a threat to international peace and security. *Perspectives on Global Issues*, *4*(1), 7–17.

Hagen, J. J. (2016). Queering women, peace and security. *International Affairs*, *92*(2), 313–332. doi:10.1111/1468-2346.12551

Kendall, R. (2012). Climate change as a security threat to the Pacific Islands. *New Zealand Journal of Environmental Law*, *16*, 83–116.

Saul, B. (2009). Climate Change, Conflict and Security: International Law Challenges. *NZ Armed FL Rev.*, *9*, 1.

Sicurelli, D. (2016). *The European Union's Africa policies: norms, interests and impact.* Routledge. doi:10.4324/9781315239828

Tayebi, S., & Zarabi, M. (2018). Environmental Diplomacy and Climate Change; Constructive strategic approach to reducer. *Human & Environment, 16*(4), 159–170.

KEY TERMS AND DEFINITIONS

Environmental Law: Environmental law is a collective term encompassing aspects of the law that protect the environment. A related but distinct set of regulatory regimes, now strongly influenced by environmental legal principles, focuses on managing specific natural resources, such as forests, minerals, or fisheries. Other areas, such as environmental impact assessment, may not fit neatly into either category but are nonetheless important components of environmental law. Previous research found that when environmental law reflects moral values for betterment, legal adoption is more likely to be successful, usually in well-developed regions. In less-developed states, changes in moral values are necessary for successful legal implementation when environmental law differs from moral values.

Polluter Pays Principle: The polluter pays principle stands for the idea that "the environmental costs of economic activities, including the cost of preventing potential harm, should be internalized rather than imposed upon society at large." All issues related to responsibility for cost for environmental remediation and compliance with pollution control regulations involve this principle.

Precautionary Principle: One of the most commonly encountered and controversial principles of environmental law, the Rio Declaration formulated the precautionary principle as follows, to protect the environment, States shall widely apply the precautionary approach according to their capabilities. Where there are threats of serious or irreversible damage, lack of full scientific certainty shall not be used as a reason for postponing cost-effective measures to prevent environmental degradation. The principle may play a role in any debate over the need for environmental regulation.

Prevention: The concept of prevention can perhaps better be considered an overarching aim that gives rise to a multitude of legal mechanisms, including prior assessment of environmental harm, licensing, or authorization that set out the conditions for operation and the consequences for violation of the conditions, as well as the adoption of strategies and policies. Emission limits and other product or process standards, the use of best available techniques, and similar techniques can all be seen as applications of the concept of prevention.

Transboundary Responsibility: Defined in the international law context as an obligation to protect one's environment. UNEP considers transboundary responsibility at the international level to prevent damage to neighboring environments at the international level as a potential limitation on the rights of the sovereign state. Laws that limit externalities imposed upon human health and the environment may be assessed against this principle.

Chapter 6
Negative Effects of Corruption on the Global Level

Irakli Kervalishvili
Georgian Technical University, Georgia

ABSTRACT

Corruption is a form of dishonesty or criminal offense undertaken by a person or organization entrusted with a position of authority to acquire illicit benefit or abuse power for one's private gain. Corruption may include many activities including bribery and embezzlement, though it may also involve practices that are legal in many countries. Political corruption occurs when an officeholder or other governmental employee acts in an official capacity for personal gain. Corruption is most commonplace in kleptocracies, oligarchies, narco-states, and mafia states. Corruption can occur on different scales. Corruption ranges from small favors between a small number of people (petty corruption) to corruption that affects the government on a large scale (grand corruption) and corruption that is so prevalent that it is part of the everyday structure of society, including corruption as one of the symptoms of organized crime.

INTRODUCTION: WHAT DOES CORRUPTION MEAN?

Corruption is a form of dishonesty or a criminal offense committed by a person or organization in power to obtain an illegal gain or abuse of power for personal gain. Corruption can include many activities, including bribery and theft, although it can also include activities that are legal in many countries (World Bank, 2015). Political corruption occurs when an official or other civil servant acts in an official capacity for personal interest. Corruption is most prevalent in kleptocracies, oligarchies, drug states, and mafia states (Longdom, 2020).

Corruption can be of different dimensions, from small favors between a small number of people (petty corruption) (Elliott, 2020) to corruption that affects the government on a large scale (large corruption) and corruption that is so pervasive that it is part of the daily fabric of society, including corruption as one of the symptoms of organized crime. Corruption and crime are endemic sociological phenomena that regularly occur in almost all countries on a global scale to varying degrees and proportions. Each country allocates internal resources to control and regulate corruption and crime. Anti-corruption strate-

DOI: 10.4018/978-1-7998-9586-2.ch006

gies are often summarized under the general term "anti-corruption". In addition, global initiatives such as the United Nations Sustainable Development Goals also aim to substantially reduce corruption in all forms (Doss, 2020).

DEFINITION AND SCOPE

Stephen D. Morris, professor of politics, wrote that political corruption is the illegal use of government power for personal profit (Morris, 1991). Economist Yang the Elder has defined corruption as an act of (a) secretly providing (b) a good or service to a third party (c) so that he or she can influence certain actions that (d) benefit a corrupt, third party. or both (e) in which the corrupt agent has power (Senior, 2006). World Bank economist Daniel Kaufmann has expanded the concept to include "legal corruption," in which power is abused within the law, as those in power often can legislate to protect themselves. Corruption in infrastructure leads to increased construction costs and time, reduced quality, and reduced benefits (Locatelli, 2017).

Corruption can be of different dimensions. Corruption ranges from small services between a small number of people (petty corruption) (Elliott, 1997) to corruption that affects the government on a large scale (large corruption) and corruption that is so pervasive that it is part of the day-to-day structure. society, including corruption as one of the symptoms of organized crime.

Several indicators and tools have been developed to more accurately measure various forms of corruption (Hamilton, 2017).

Petty Corruption

Petty corruption occurs on a smaller scale and occurs at the end of public service delivery when public officials meet with the public. For example, in many small locations such as registration offices, police stations, government licensing commissions, and many other private and public sectors (Mishler, 2020).

Corruption may include many activities including bribery and embezzlement

Great Corruption

Great corruption is defined as corruption that occurs at the highest levels of government and requires significant disruption of the political, legal, and economic systems. Such corruption is commonly found in countries with authoritarian governments, but also in countries where corruption is not adequately controlled (UN Office on Drugs and Crime, 2020). State system in many countries is divided into legislative, executive, and judicial branches of government in an attempt to provide independent services that are less prone to serious corruption due to their independence from each other (James, 2015).

Systemic Corruption

Systemic corruption (or endemic corruption) is corruption that primarily arises from a weakness in an organization or process. This can be compared to individual officials or agents who are corrupt in the system (U4 Anti-Corruption Resource Center, 2011).

Figure 1.
Source: https://www.gettyimages.com/photos/corruption?phrase=corruption&sort=mostpopular

Factors contributing to systemic corruption include conflicting incentives, discretionary powers; monopolistic powers; lack of transparency; low salary; and a culture of impunity (Andrade, 2001). Specific corrupt practices include "bribery, extortion, and waste" in a system where "corruption becomes the rule, not the exception" (Znoj, 2009). Scientists distinguish between centralized and decentralized systemic corruption, depending on what level of corruption in the state or government takes place; in countries such as post-Soviet states, both types are found (Legvord, 2009). Some scholars argue that Western governments have a negative responsibility to protect underdeveloped governments from systematic corruption (Merle, 2013).

Corruption has been a major problem in China, where society is highly dependent on personal relationships. Towards the end of the 20th century, this, combined with a renewed lust for wealth, led to an escalation of corruption. Historian Keith Schoppa says bribery was only one of the tools of Chinese corruption, which also included "embezzlement, nepotism, smuggling, extortion, nepotism, kickbacks, deception, fraud, squandering public money, illegal business transactions, stock, and real estate manipulation. fraud. "Given the repeated anti-corruption campaigns, it was prudent to move as much fraudulent money as possible abroad (Schoppa, 2020).

Causes

According to R. Klitgaard, corruption will take place if the corrupt benefit is greater than the fine multiplied by the probability of being caught and prosecuted (Klitgaard, 1989):

Corruption benefit> Fine × Probability of being caught and prosecuted

Klitgaard also came up with a metaphorical formula to illustrate how the size of corruption depends on three variables: monopoly (M) over the supply of a good or service, discretion (D) enjoyed by sup-

Figure 2.
Source: https://www.corruptionwatch.org.za/can-put-end-corruption/

pliers, and supplier accountability and transparency (A). others. The amount of corruption (C) can be expressed as (Klitgaard, 2000)

C = M + D - A.

Since a high degree of monopoly and discretion, combined with a low degree of transparency, does not automatically lead to corruption, a fourth variable, "morality" or "honesty", has been introduced by others. The moral dimension has an internal component and refers to the "problem of mentality", while the external component refers to circumstances such as poverty, inadequate remuneration, inappropriate working conditions, and unworkable or overly complex procedures that demoralize people and allow them to seek "alternative" solutions (Stefan, 2012). Therefore, the corrected Klitgaard equation has the form

Corruption rate = Monopoly + Discretion - Transparency - Morality

According to a 2017 study, the following factors were identified as causes of corruption: (Dimant, 2017)

DIFFERENT TYPES OF CORRUPTION

The greed of money, desires.

- Higher levels of market and political monopolization
- Low levels of democracy, weak civil participation, and low political transparency
- Higher levels of bureaucracy and inefficient administrative structures
- Low press freedom
- Low economic freedom

- Large ethnic divisions and high levels of in-group favoritism
- Gender inequality
- Poverty
- Political instability
- Weak property rights
- Contagion from corrupt neighboring countries
- Low levels of education
- Lack of commitment to society
- Extravagant family?

It was noted that when comparing the most corrupt countries with the least corrupt, the first group includes countries with huge socio-economic inequalities, and the second - countries with a high degree of social and economic justice.

IN DIFFERENT SECTORS

Corruption can occur in many sectors, be it public or private industry or even NGOs (especially in the public sector). However, only in democratically controlled institutions is the public (owner) interested in developing internal mechanisms to combat active or passive corruption, while in the private sector, as well as in NGOs, there is no public control. Thus, the profits of the owners, "investors" or sponsors are critical.

Government / public Sector

Government corruption includes corruption in the political process and government bodies such as the police, as well as corruption in the allocation of public funds for contracts, grants, and recruiting. A recent World Bank study shows that who makes political decisions (elected officials or bureaucrats) can be critical in determining the level of corruption due to the incentives faced by various politicians (Hamilton, 2013).

Inside the Political System

Political corruption is the abuse of government power, office, or resources by elected government officials for personal gain through extortion, extortion, or offering bribes. It can also take the form of officials retaining their positions by buying votes through laws that use taxpayer money (SOS, 2013). Evidence suggests that corruption can have political consequences: citizens who ask for bribes are less likely to identify with their country or region (Hamilton, 2014).

The political act of bribery (American English) is a well-known and now global form of political corruption, which is the dishonest and illegal use of power by a politician for personal gain, in which funds earmarked for public projects are deliberately misdirected to maximize revenue. benefits for the illegal private interests of corrupt individuals and their friends. In some cases, government agencies are "re-profiled" or diverted from their official mandate for other, often corrupt purposes (Chipkin, 2018). See also State Capture.

The golden toilet suitcase in Kaunas has become a major Lithuanian scandal. In 2009, Kaunas Municipality (headed by Mayor Andrius Kupčinskas) ordered the conversion of a transport container into an outdoor toilet for 500,000 litai (about 150,000 euros). It also required LTL 5,000 (EUR 1,500) as monthly maintenance costs (Auksinis, 2017). At the same time when Kaunas "Golden Toilet" was built, Kėdainiai Tennis Club acquired a very similar but more perfect solution for 4,500 euros (Auksionis, 2017). Due to the overpriced street toilet, it was nicknamed the "Golden Toilet". Despite the investment, the Golden Toilet remained closed due to a malfunction for many years and was the subject of a lengthy anti-corruption investigation against those who created it, with the local municipality even considering demolishing the building at some point. The group of civil servants involved in the purchase of the toilet was sentenced to various prison terms for recklessness, malfeasance, abuse of power, and falsification of documents in a 2012 trial, but they were cleared of corruption charges and compensated, which increased the total cost of construction and subsequent associated financial losses up to 352,000 euros.

Various sources cite the Spanish People's Party - Partido Popular - as the most corrupt party in Europe, with an annual corruption of around 45 billion euros (Plus de 45 billion euros in a year of corruption, 2017).

On July 7, 2020, the Global Think Tank of the Carnegie Endowment for International Peace released a report claiming the Emirati city of Dubai is a contributor to global corruption, crime, and illicit financial flows. It said that global corrupt and criminal actors operate either through Dubai or out of it. The city has also been called a trade money-laundering haven as it provides space for free trade zones with minimal regulatory laws and customs compliance (Carnegie Endowment for International Peace, 2020).

In the Police

Police corruption is a specific form of police misconduct aimed at obtaining a financial gain, personal gain, promotion for a police officer or officers in exchange for refusing to conduct or selectively conduct an investigation or arrest or aspects of the thinnest blue line when strength members conspire in lies to protect others from responsibility. One common form of police corruption is soliciting or accepting bribes in exchange for refusing to report organized drug trafficking or prostitution or other illegal activities.

Another example is police officers who disregard the police code of conduct to obtain convictions of suspects, for example, through abuse of surveillance, forced confessions, and/or falsified evidence. Less commonly, police officers may knowingly and systematically engage in organized crime. Most major cities have police departments to investigate suspicions of corruption or police misconduct. Similar structures include the British Independent Police Complaints Commission.

In the Judicial System

Corruption in the judiciary is understood as the misconduct of judges related to corruption by receiving or giving bribes, improper sentencing of convicted criminals, bias in considering and deciding on arguments, and other similar misconduct. Corruption in the judiciary can also be carried out by prosecutors and defenders. An example of prosecutorial misconduct would be a politician or crime boss bribing a prosecutor to investigate and bring charges against an opposing politician or rival crime boss to harm competition (Drugwarfacts, 2020). An example of lawyer misconduct would be a lawyer's refusal to represent a client for political or professional reasons.

Corruption of the judiciary in government is widespread in many transitions and developing countries, as the budget is almost entirely controlled by the executive branch. The latter undermines the separation of powers as it creates a critical financial dependence on the judiciary. The correct distribution of national wealth, including government spending on the judiciary, depends on constitutional economics.

It is important to distinguish between two methods of corruption in the judiciary: public (through budget planning and various privileges) and private (Barenboim, 2009). Corruption in the judiciary is difficult to eradicate, even in developed countries (Pahis, 2009). Corruption in the judiciary also involves the incumbent government using the judicial branch of government to suppress opposition parties to the detriment of the state.

In the Army

Corruption in the armed forces refers to the abuse of power by members of the armed forces for promotion or personal gain by a soldier or soldiers. One form of military corruption in the United States Armed Forces is a military soldier who is promoted or treated by officers better than their counterparts because of their race, sexual orientation, ethnicity, gender, religion, social class, or personal relationships with high-ranking officers, despite their merits. In addition to this, there have also been many incidents of sexual assault by officers in the US military, and in many cases, there have been reports that many attacks were covered up and victims were silenced by officers of the same rank or rank. higher rank. Another example of military corruption is a military officer or officers who use the power of their position to commit illegal acts, such as collecting logistical items such as food, medicine, fuel, body armor, or weapons to sell on the local black market. There have also been cases of military officials providing equipment and combat support to criminal syndicates, private military companies, and terrorist groups without the approval of their superiors. As a result, many countries have military police forces to ensure that the military abides by the laws and behavior of their countries, but sometimes the military police themselves have levels of corruption (UNODC, 2020).

In Healthcare

Corruption, the abuse of entrusted power for personal gain, according to Transparency International, is systemic in the health sector (Transparency International, 2019). The characteristics of health care systems, with their concentrated supply of services, the high discretionary power of their members in control of supply, and low accountability to others, are the exact set of variables described by Klitgaard on which corruption depends (Klitgaard, 2000).

Corruption in the health sector is more dangerous than in any other sector because it affects health conditions and is deadly. This is widespread, and yet little has been published on the topic in medical journals, and as of 2019, there is no data on what can reduce corruption in the health sector (Garcia, 2019). Corruption occurs in the private and public health sectors and can manifest itself as theft, waste, nepotism, bribery, even extortion, or undue influence (Transparency International Health Initiative, 2019). and occurs anywhere in the sector, be it service delivery, procurement, construction, or recruitment. In 2019, Transparency International described the 6 most common ways of corruption in services as follows: absenteeism, informal payments from patients, embezzlement, overpricing of services and service costs, favoritism, and data manipulation (billing for goods and services that never were sent. or done) (Transparency International Health Initiative, 2019).

In the Education System

Corruption in education is a worldwide phenomenon. Corruption in admission to universities is traditionally considered one of the most corrupt areas of the educational sector (Osipyan, 2013). Recent attempts in some countries, such as Russia and Ukraine, to curb corruption in admission by abolishing university entrance exams and introducing standardized computerized tests have largely failed (Osipian, 2015). Vouchers for applicants were never received. The cost of corruption is that it impedes sustainable economic growth.

Widespread corruption in educational institutions leads to the formation of stable corrupt hierarchies (Osipyan, 2015). While higher education in Russia is characterized by widespread bribery, corruption in the US and UK is characterized by a significant number of cases of fraud. The United States is characterized by gray areas and institutional corruption in the higher education sector. Authoritarian regimes, including those in the former Soviet republics, encourage educational corruption and control universities, especially during election campaigns. This is typical, in particular, of the regimes of Russia, Ukraine, and Central Asia. The general public is well aware of the high level of corruption in colleges and universities, including through the media.

Doctoral studies are no exception: there are dissertations and doctoral degrees on sale, including for politicians. The Russian parliament is notorious for its "highly educated" deputies. The high level of corruption is a result of the fact that universities cannot break away from their Stalinist past, bureaucratization, and the apparent lack of university autonomy. Both quantitative and qualitative methodologies are used to study corruption in education, but this topic remains largely overlooked by academics. In many societies and international organizations, corruption in education remains taboo. In some countries, such as some Eastern European countries, some Balkan countries, and some Asian countries, corruption is common in universities. This can include bribes to circumvent bureaucratic procedures and bribing teachers to obtain grades. Willingness to engage in corruption, such as accepting bribes in exchange for grades, is reduced if people perceive such behavior as highly undesirable, that is, a violation of social norms, and if they fear sanctions in terms of the severity and likelihood of sanctions (Osipian, 2015).

In Religion

The history of religion includes many examples where religious leaders drew attention to the corruption in religious practices and institutions of their time. The Jewish prophets Isaiah and Amos scold the rabbinical establishment of Ancient Judea for not meeting the ideals of the Torah. In the New Testament, Jesus accuses the rabbis of his day of hypocritically following only the ceremonial parts of the Torah and neglecting the more important elements of justice, mercy, and faithfulness. Corruption was one of the major issues during the investment controversy. In 1517, Martin Luther accused the Catholic Church of widespread corruption, including the sale of indulgences.

In 2015, Princeton University professor Kevin M. Cruz advanced the thesis that business leaders in the 1930s and 1940s collaborated with clerics, including James W. Fyfield, Jr., to develop and promote a new hermeneutic approach to Holy Scripture, which would not focus on social issues. Gospel and emphasis on topics such as individual salvation, closer to free enterprise (Kevin, 2015).

Business leaders, of course, have worked for a long time to "sell" themselves through the appropriation of religion. In organizations such as Spiritual Mobilization, Prayer Breakfast Groups, and the Freedom

Foundation, they linked capitalism and Christianity while at the same time likening the welfare state to godless paganism (Kevin, 2015).

In Philosophy

The 19th-century German philosopher Arthur Schopenhauer recognized that scientists, including philosophers, are subject to the same sources of corruption as the society in which they live. He distinguished the corrupt "university" philosophers, whose "the real concern is to earn an honest livelihood with honor and ... enjoy a certain prestige in the eyes of the public," from genuine philosophers whose only motive is to discover and testify about truth (Schopenhauer, 1974).

To be a philosopher, that is, a lover of wisdom (for wisdom is nothing but the truth), it is not enough for a person to love truth, since this is compatible with his interests, with the will of a person. his superiors, with the dogmas of the church or with the prejudices and tastes of his contemporaries; as long as he is content with this position, he is only φίλαυτος (loving himself) and not φιλόσοφος (lover of wisdom). For this honorary title is well and wisely conceived precisely because it says that you need to love the truth sincerely and with all your heart, which means, unconditionally and unconditionally, above all, and, if necessary, despite everything else. The reason for this is that it was previously said that the intellect has become free, and in this state, it does not even know or understand any other interest than an interest in truth (Schopenhauer, 1974).

WEAPONS FOR MONEY

Weapons for money can be supplied by either a government-approved arms dealer, a firm or the government itself to another party that it considers only a good business partner and not a political relative or ally, making them no better than conventional arms merchants. Arms smugglers who are already in the arms trade can work for them locally or with delivery. Money is often laundered and records are often destroyed. This often violates UN law, national or international law (Lin, 2016). Payment can also occur in strange or indirect ways, such as weapons paid for in post-war oil contracts, post-war hotel ownership, conflict diamonds, corporate shares, or long-term post-war promises of super-future contracts between the parties involved. etc...

Angolagat as an example of the illegal arms trade (Mitterrand-Pasqua case) - The Mitterrand-Pasqua case, also known informally as Angolagat, was an international political scandal involving the secret and illegal sale and supply of weapons from Central European countries to the Angolan government by the French government in 1990 - the years This led to arrests and lawsuits in the 2000s related to the illegal sale of arms to Angola, despite the UN embargo, with business interests in France and elsewhere, and the illegal acquisition of a share of Angolan oil revenues. Subsequently, the scandal was associated with several prominent figures in French politics (Transparency International).

42 people, including Jean-Christophe Mitterrand, Jacques Attali, Charles Pasqua, and Jean-Charles Marchiani, Pierre Falcone, Arkady Gaidamak, Paul-Loup Sulitzer, a deputy from the Union of Popular Movements Georges Fenech, Philippe Curroy, son of François Mitterrand (former President of France) and the former Minister of the Interior of France have been indicted, charged, charged or convicted of the illegal arms trade, tax fraud, embezzlement, money laundering and other crimes (Reuters, 2009).

Methods

In systemic corruption and large-scale corruption, several corruption methods are used simultaneously for similar purposes.

Corrupt Practices

Bribery involves the misuse of gifts and favors in exchange for personal gain. It is also known as kickbacks or, in the Middle East, as baksheesh. This is a common form of corruption. The types of services provided are varied and may include money, gifts, promotions, sexual favors, company promotions, entertainment, work, and political gain. The personal gain provided can be anything from actively giving preferential treatment to ignoring indiscretion or crime (Wang, 2013). Sometimes bribery can be part of the systemic use of corruption for other purposes, for example, to further commit corruption. Bribery can make officials more vulnerable to blackmail or extortion.

Embezzlement, Theft, and Fraud

Embezzlement and theft are associated with the fact that someone with access to funds or assets illegally takes control of them. Fraud involves the use of deception to persuade the owner of funds or assets to transfer them to an unauthorized party.

Examples include diverting company funds to "shadow companies" (and then into the pockets of corrupt employees), withdrawing money from foreign aid, fraud, electoral fraud, and other corrupt activities.

Graft

A political act of bribery is when funds earmarked for government projects are deliberately misdirected to maximize the benefit to the private interests of corrupt individuals.

Extortion and Blackmail

While bribery is the use of positive incentives for corrupt purposes, extortion and blackmail is centered around the use of threats. This can be the threat of physical violence or false imprisonment, as well as the exposure of personal secrets or previous crimes.

This includes behavior such as threatening the influencer to go to the media if they do not receive urgent medical attention (at the expense of other patients), threatening a public official with their secrets if they do not vote in a certain way, or demanding money in exchange for the preservation of secrecy. Another example would be a police officer who was threatened by his superiors to lose their job if they continued to investigate a high-ranking official.

Influence Trading

Influence trading is the illegal practice of using one's influence in government or contacts with persons in positions of authority to obtain services or preferential treatment, usually for a fee.

Networks

Networking (both business and personal) can be an effective way for job seekers to gain a competitive edge over others in the job market. The idea is to develop personal relationships with potential employers, selection committee members, and others in the hope that these personal attachments will influence future hiring decisions. This form of networking has been described as an attempt to distort the formal recruitment process, whereby all candidates are given an equal opportunity to demonstrate their merits to the recruiter. The networker is accused of seeking a non-meritocratic advantage over other candidates; an advantage based on personal sympathy rather than any objective assessment of which candidate is most suitable for the position (Dobos, 2015).

Abuse of Discretion

Abuse of margin of appreciation means abuse of one's authority and decision-making power. Examples include a judge unlawfully dismissing a criminal case or a customs official using his discretion to bring a prohibited substance through a port.

Favoritism, Nepotism, and Clientelism

Favoritism, nepotism, and clientelism involve giving preference not to the perpetrator of corruption, but to someone related to him, such as a friend, family member, or member of an association. Examples might include hiring or promoting a family member or employee for a position to which they are not eligible, who belongs to the same political party as you, regardless of merit (Santa Clara, 2017).

Some states do not prohibit these forms of corruption.

LINK TO ECONOMIC GROWTH

Corruption is strongly negatively associated with the share of private investment and, therefore, reduces the rate of economic growth.

Corruption reduces the return on productive activities. If the return on production falls faster than the return on corruption and rent-seeking activities, resources will eventually flow from productive activity to corruption. This will lead to a reduction in productive resources, such as human capital, in corrupt countries.

Corruption creates opportunities for increasing inequality, reduces the return on productive activities, and therefore makes rent-seeking and corruption more attractive. This opportunity for increased inequality not only creates psychological frustration among the disadvantaged but also reduces productivity growth, investment, and employment opportunities (Journal of Comparative Economics, 2001).

PREVENTION

According to the revised Klitgaard equation (Stephan, 2012), limited monopoly and regulatory discretion by individuals and a high degree of transparency through independent oversight by non-governmental organizations (NGOs) and the media, as well as public access to reliable information, can reduce the problem. ... Dyankov and other researchers independently examined the role of information in the fight against corruption, using data from both developing and developed countries (Rohini, 2012). Public disclosure of the financial information of civil servants is associated with improved institutional accountability and the elimination of misconduct such as vote-buying. The effect is especially noticeable when disclosures concern sources of income, liabilities, and the level of assets of politicians, and not just the level of income. Any external aspects that could reduce morality must be eliminated. In addition, the country must establish a culture of ethical behavior in the community, and the government must set a good example for enhancing domestic morality.

In 1969, Christian anarchist Dorothy Day argued that God would permit economic abuses such as corruption. She wrote: "Fortunately, the Papal States were cut off from the Church in the last century, but there is still the problem of papal investment." It always pleases me to think that if we have goodwill and we still cannot find a remedy for the economic abuse of our time in our family, our ward, and the mighty church as a whole, God will take matters into his own hands. and they do this work for us (Catholic Worker, 1969).

INCREASED PARTICIPATION OF CIVIL SOCIETY

Building bottom-up mechanisms, encouraging citizen participation, and promoting the values of honesty, accountability and transparency are essential components of the fight against corruption. As of 2012, the implementation of Advocacy and Legal Advice Centers (ALACs) in Europe has led to a significant increase in the number of received and documented complaints from citizens about corrupt practices, as well as to the development of good governance strategies by involving citizens wishing to fight corruption (SIOR, 2012).

ANTI-CORRUPTION PROGRAMS

The Foreign Corruption Act (FCPA, USA 1977) was the first paradigmatic law for many Western countries, that is, the industrialized countries of the OECD. There, for the first time, the old principal-agent approach was carried back, where it was mainly about the victim (society, private or public) and the passive corrupt member (individual), while the active corrupt part was not in the spotlight. prosecution. It is unprecedented that the law of an industrial country explicitly condemned active corruption, especially in international business transactions, which at the time ran counter to the anti-corruption activities of the World Bank and its subsidiary Transparency International.

Back in 1989, the OECD established an ad hoc working group to study "... the concepts underlying the crime of corruption and the exercise of national jurisdiction over crimes committed in whole or in part abroad." (IMF, 2020) Building on the FCPA concept, the Working Group introduced the then-OECD Anti-Bribery Recommendation in 1994 as a precursor to the OECD Convention on Combating Bribery of Foreign Public Officials in International Business Transactions (OECD, 2020), which was signed in 1997 by all member states and finally entered into force in 1999. However, due to ongoing latent corruption in international transactions, the OECD has since developed several country monitoring tools (OECD, 2020) to facilitate and evaluate related national anti-corruption activities abroad. One study

Figure 3. Corruption perception index 2019
Source: https://www.caribbeannewsglobal.com/us-hits-new-low-in-global-corruption-index/

shows that after the enhanced scrutiny of multinational companies under the convention in 2010, firms from signatory countries have become less likely to bribery (Jensen, 2017).

In 2013, a document prepared by the Economic Information and Private Sector Support Services and Applied Knowledge Services document discusses some of the existing anti-corruption practices. They found (Forgues-Puccio, 2013):

- Theories underlying the fight against corruption move from the agent-principal approach to the collective action problem. Chief agent theories seem unsuitable for dealing with systemic corruption.
- The role of multilateral institutions has been critical in the fight against corruption. The UNCAC is a one-stop guide for countries around the world. Both Transparency International and the World Bank help national governments diagnose and develop anti-corruption policies.
- The use of anti-corruption agencies has increased in recent years following the signing of the UN Convention against Corruption. They did not find convincing evidence of the scale of their contribution or a better way to structure them.
- Traditionally, anti-corruption policies have been based on good practices and common sense. In recent years, attempts have been made to provide a more systematic assessment of the effectiveness of anti-corruption policies. They found that this literature is still in its infancy.
- Anti-corruption policies that can be generally recommended to developing countries may not be appropriate for post-conflict countries. Anti-corruption policies in fragile states must be carefully adapted.
- Anti-corruption policies can improve the business environment. There is evidence that reducing corruption can make it easier to do business and improve firm productivity. Rwanda has made

tremendous progress over the past decade in improving governance and the business environment, creating a role model for post-conflict countries (Forgues-Puccio, 2013).

· Corruption in popular culture

Legal Corruption

Although corruption is often considered illegal, the concept of legal corruption has been described by Daniel Kaufmann and Pedro Vicente (Kaufmann, 2011). These can be called corrupt processes, but protected by a legal (that is, specifically permitted or at least not prohibited by law) structure (Kaufmann, 2011).

Examples: In 1994, the German Parliamentary Finance Commission in Bonn presented a comparative study of "legal corruption" in industrialized OECD countries. They reported that in most industrialized countries, foreign corruption is legal and that their foreign corruption practices range from simple to government subsidies. (tax deduction), to the extreme, as in Germany, where foreign corruption was encouraged while domestic corruption was prosecuted. The German Parliamentary Finance Commission rejected an opposition parliamentary proposal that aimed to curb German foreign corruption based on the US Foreign Corrupt Practices Act (FCPA of 1977), thereby fostering the development of national export corporations. In 1997, its members signed the relevant OECD Anti-Bribery Convention (OECD, 2020). Only in 1999, after the entry into force of the OECD Anti-Bribery Convention, did Germany abolish the legalization of foreign corruption (Income Tax Act 1999).

FOREIGN CORRUPT PRACTICES OF INDUSTRIALIZED COUNTRIES OECD 1994 STUDY

Corruption abroad in industrialized OECD countries, 1994 (study by the Parliamentary Finance Commission, Bonn).

Belgium: Bribes are generally deductible as a business expense if the recipient's name and address are disclosed. Under the following conditions, kickbacks in connection with export abroad are allowed for deduction even without confirmation of the recipient:

- Payments must be necessary to survive in the face of foreign competition.
- They should be common to the industry.
- An application must be submitted to the Treasury every year.
- Payments must be adequate
- The payer must pay in a lump sum to the tax office, which is established by the Minister of Finance (at least 20% of the amount paid).

In the absence of the necessary conditions, companies subject to corporate tax that give bribes without confirmation of the recipient are subject to a special tax of 200%. However, this special tax can be reduced along with the amount of the bribe as operating expenses.

Denmark: Bribes are deducted where there is a clear operational context and its adequacy.

France: Almost all operating expenses can be deducted. However, personnel costs should be commensurate with the work performed and should not be excessive about the operational value. This also applies to payments to foreign parties. Here the beneficiary must indicate the name and address if the total amount of payments to the beneficiary does not exceed 500 FF. If the recipient is not disclosed, the payments are considered "occult" and are associated with the following disadvantages:

- The deduction of business expenses (from the bribe amount) is excluded.
- Corporations and other legal entities are subject to a tax penalty of 100% for "occult fees" and 75% for voluntary declarations by mail.
- A general fine of up to CHF 200 may be imposed per case.

Japan: In Japan, bribes are deducted as business expenses that are justified by the activities of (the company) if the name and address of the recipient are indicated. This also applies to payments to foreigners. In case of refusal to indicate the name, the declared expenses are not recognized as operating expenses.

Canada: There is no general rule on the deduction or inability to withhold kickbacks and bribes. Consequently, there is a rule that the costs necessary to generate income (contract) are deductible. Payments to civil servants and local justice authorities, officials and employees, as well as to persons collecting fees, entrance fees, etc. to persuade the recipient to violate his official duties cannot be reduced, since business expenses as well as illegal payments following the Criminal Code.

Luxembourg: Bribes justified by (company) activities are deducted as business expenses. However, the tax authorities may require the payer to provide the name of the recipient. Otherwise, expenses are not recognized as operating expenses.

Netherlands: All expenses directly or closely related to the business are deductible. This also applies to costs outside the scope of actual business transactions if, for good reason, management considers them to be beneficial to the transaction. Good merchant customs are important. Neither the law nor the administration has the authority to determine which costs are not operationally justifiable and therefore not deductible. For the deduction of business expenses, it is not necessary to indicate the recipient. It is enough to explain to the satisfaction of the tax authorities that payments are made in the interests of the transaction.

Austria: Bribes justified by (company) activities are deducted as business expenses. However, the tax authority may require the payer to identify the exact recipient of the withholding payments. If a name is denied, for example, for reasons of business ethics, the reported expense is not considered an operating expense. This principle also applies to payments to foreigners.

Switzerland: Bribes are not taxed if the transaction is initiated and the recipient is specified.

USA: (approximate summary: "normally operating expenses are deducted unless they are illegal under the FCPA")

UK: Kickbacks and bribes are deducted if they were paid for production purposes. The tax authority may request the name and address of the recipient. "

"Specific" legal corruption: exclusively against foreign countries

Referring to the recommendation of the aforementioned study of the Parliamentary Finance Commission, the then Kohl administration (1991-1994) decided to maintain the legality of corruption against officials exclusively in foreign transactions and confirmed the possibility of full deduction of bribes, thus co-financing the specific practice of nationalist corruption (§4 Abs. 5 Nr. 10 EStG, valid until March 19, 1999) contrary to the OECD recommendation 1994 (OECD, 2020). The relevant law was not amended until the entry into force of the OECD Convention also in Germany (1999) (OECD, 2020). However, according to a study by the Parliamentary Finance Commission, in 1994, corruption practices in most countries were not nationalist and were much more restricted by relevant laws than in Germany (Parliamentary Finance Commission study, 1994).

In particular, not disclosing the name of the recipient of a bribe on tax returns was a powerful tool of legal corruption in the 1990s for German corporations, allowing them to block foreign legal jurisdictions that intended to fight corruption in their countries. Consequently, they uncontrollably created a strong network of clientelism throughout Europe (eg SIEMENS) (HRRS, 2008) along with the formation of a single European market in the coming European Union and Eurozone. Moreover, to further exacerbate active corruption, prosecutions for tax evasion have been severely limited during this decade. German tax authorities have been instructed to refuse to disclose the names of recipients of tax bribes to German prosecutions (Transparency International, 2020). As a result, German corporations have systematically increased the size of the informal economy from 1980 to the present to 350 billion euros per year (see chart on the right), continuously fueling their reserves of black money (Statista, 2015).

CONCLUSION

In general, corruption involves the conduct of public officials, be they political officials or civil servants, by which they improperly and illegally enrich or enrich their relatives through the abuse of their public office.

It should be noted that the existence of corruption reduces the degree of trust in society, weakens democracy, hinders economic development, deepens inequality, significantly increases poverty and social inequality. Corruption can be eliminated and its negative consequences can be avoided only if the schemes and systems through which corruption operates are considered.

Corruption can take various forms and include actions such as public officials asking for a certain amount of money or benefits in exchange for their services; State political officials who abuse the power in their hands, misappropriate state budget funds, employ them through their influence, occupy various state positions, family members and relatives, and influence the results of state tenders. Corruption in itself also includes bribing public officials by corporations to make the desired deal.

Corruption and corrupt practices can take place in any field, be it business, government, the judiciary, the media, civil society, the healthcare system, or infrastructure and sports. However, corruption can be related to anyone in the field, be it a politician, a public servant, a businessman, or a public figure. In most cases, corruption is carried out secretly, with the help of representatives of such spheres as bankers, lawyers, financial managers, mainly through the creation of opaque financial schemes.

It should be noted that in most cases, states do not directly criminalize corruption, but are held accountable for certain acts through which corrupt acts are committed, such as bribery, misappropriation, fraud, extortion, etc.

REFERENCES

Alcazar & Raul. (2001). *Diagnosis corruption*. Academic Press.

Alt, J. (2015). *Political and Judicial Checks on Corruption: Evidence from American State Governments*. Projects at Harvard.

Angolagate: les principaux acteurs de l'affaire. (2007). *Le Figaro*.

Barenboim, P. (2009). *Defining the rules. Issue 90*. The European Lawyer.

Bilefsky, D. (2013). On the Crony Safari, a Tour of a City's Corruption. *The New York Times*.

Blavatskyy, P. (2020). Obesity of politicians and corruption in post-Soviet countries. *Economics of Transition and Institutional Change*.

Cameron, R. (2014, June 2). *Corruption redefined as tourism in Czech Republic*. BBC News.

Carney, G. F. A. S. (2016). Czech Republic Has Its Answer to the Beverly Hills Star Tour. *Wall Street Journal*.

Chipkin, I., & Swilling, M. (2018). Shadow State: The Politics of State Capture. Wits University Press.

Dimant, E., & Tosato, G. (2017). Causes and Effects of Corruption: What Has Past Decade's Empirical Research Taught Us? A Survey. *Journal of Economic Surveys*.

Dobos, N. (2015). Networking, Corruption, and Subversion. *Journal of Business Ethics*.

Doss, E. (2020). *Sustainable Development Goal 16*. United Nations and the Rule of Law.

Dubai's Role in Facilitating Corruption and Global Illicit Financial Flows. (2020). Carnegie Endowment for International Peace.

Economia UOL. (2017). *Commercial dollar: quotation and charts*. Author.

Eddiegilman. (2016). Petrobras. *Fortune*.

Elliott, K. A. (1997). *Corruption as an international policy problem: overview and recommendations*. Institute for International Economics.

Fitz-Gibbon, A. (2000). *In the World but Not of the World: Christian Social Thinking at the End of the Twentieth Century*. Academic Press.

Fonseca, P. (2016). *Former Odebrecht CEO sentenced in Brazil kickback case*. Reuters.

Forgues-Puccio, G.F. (2013). *Existing practices on anti-corruption, Economic and private sector professional evidence and applied knowledge services helpdesk request*. Academic Press.

García, P. J. (2019). Corruption in global health: The open secret. *Lancet, 394*(10214), 2119–2124. doi:10.1016/S0140-6736(19)32527-9 PMID:31785827

Graeff, P., Sattler, S., Mehlkop, G., & Sauer, C. (2014). Incentives and Inhibitors of Abusing Academic Positions: Analysing University Students' Decisions about Bribing Academic Staff. *European Sociological Review, 30*(2), 230–241. doi:10.1093/esr/jct036

Hamilton, A. (2013). *Small is beautiful, at least in high-income democracies: the distribution of policy-making responsibility, electoral accountability, and incentives for rent extraction*. World Bank. doi:10.1596/1813-9450-6305

Hamilton, A., & Hudson. (2014). *Bribery and Identity: Evidence from Sudan*. Bath Economic Research Papers, No 21/14.

Heyneman, S. P., Anderson, K. H., & Nuraliyeva, N. (2008). The cost of corruption in higher education. *Comparative Education Review*, 52(1), 1–25. doi:10.1086/524367

Index of Economic Freedom. (2008). The Heritage Foundation.

Jensen, N. M., & Malesky, E. J. (2017). Nonstate Actors and Compliance with International Agreements: An Empirical Analysis of the OECD Anti-Bribery Convention. *International Organization*.

Kaufmann, D., & Vicente, P. (2005). *Legal Corruption*. World Bank.

Kaufmann, D., & Vicente, P. (2011). Legal Corruption (revised). *Economics and Politics*, 23.

Klitgaard, R. (1998). *Controlling Corruption*. University of California Press.

Klitgaard, R. E. (2000). *Corrupt cities: A practical guide to cure and prevention*. ICS Press.

Kruse. (2015). *One Nation Under God: How Corporate America Invented Christian America*. Academic Press.

Lambsdorff, J. (2006). *The New Institutional Economics of Corruption*. Routledge.

Lambsdorff, J. G. (2006). *Corruption Perceptions Index 2006*. Transparency International.

Legvold, R. (2009). Corruption, the Criminalized State, and Post-Soviet Transitions. In R. I. Rotberg (Ed.), *Corruption, global security, and world order*. Brookings Institution.

Lin, T. C. W. (2016). Financial Weapons of War. *Minnesota Law Review*.

Locatelli, G., Mariani, G., Sainati, T., & Greco, M. (2017). Corruption in public projects and megaprojects: There is an elephant in the room! *International Journal of Project Management*, 35(3), 252–268. doi:10.1016/j.ijproman.2016.09.010

Material on Grand Corruption. (2014). United Nations Office on Drugs and Crime.

Merle, J.-C. (Ed.). (2013). Global Challenges to Liberal Democracy. Spheres of Global Justice.

Mishler v. State Bd. of Med. Examiners. 2021. Justia Law.

Mo, P. H. (2001). Corruption and Economic Growth. *Journal of Comparative Economics*, 29(1), 66–79. doi:10.1006/jcec.2000.1703

Morris, S. D. (1991). *Corruption and Politics in Contemporary Mexico*. University of Alabama Press.

OECD. (2015). *Country monitoring of the OECD Anti-Bribery Convention*. oecd.org.

OECD Convention on Combating Bribery of Foreign Public Officials in International Bearer of Transactions. (2012). oecd.org.

Olken, B. A., & Pande, R. (2012). Corruption in Developing Countries. *Annual Review of Economics*, 4(1), 479–509. doi:10.1146/annurev-economics-080511-110917

Osipian, A. (2013). Recruitment and Admissions: Fostering Transparency on the Path to Higher Education. In *Transparency International: Global Corruption Report: Education*. Routledge.

Pahis, S. (2009). Corruption in Our Courts: What It Looks Like and Where It Is Hidden. *The Yale Law Journal*.

Pogge, T. (2015). *Severe Poverty as a Violation of Negative Duties*. thomaspogge.com.

Senior, I. (2006). *Corruption – The World's Big C*. Institute of Economic Affairs.

Stephan, C. (2012). *Industrial Health, Safety and Environmental Management* (3rd ed.). MV Wissenschaft.

Tacconi, L., & Williams, D. A. (2020). Corruption and Anti-Corruption in Environmental and Resource Management. *Annual Review of Environment and Resources*, *45*(1), 305–329. doi:10.1146/annurev-environ-012320-083949

The Ignored Pandemic. (2019). Transparency International Health Initiative.

Transparency International. (2011). *Transparency International – The Global Anti-Corruption Coalition*. www.transparency.org

United Nations Handbook on Practical Anti-Corruption Measures For Prosecutors and Investigators. (2012). United Nations Office on Drugs and Crime (UNODC).

Vian, T., & Norberg, C. (2008). *Corruption in the Health Sector. (U4 Issue 2008:10)*. Chr. Michelsen Institute.

Wang, P. (2013). The rise of the Red Mafia in China: A case study of organised crime and corruption in Chongqing. *Trends in Organized Crime*.

Znoj, H. (2009). Deep Corruption in Indonesia: Discourses, Practices, Histories. In *Corruption and the secret of law: A legal anthropological perspective*. Ashgate.

KEY TERMS AND DEFINITIONS

Corruption: A form of dishonesty or a criminal offense which is undertaken by a person or an organization which is entrusted with a position of authority, in order to acquire illicit benefits or abuse power for one's personal gain. Corruption may involve many activities which include bribery and embezzlement, and it may also involve practices which are legal in many countries.

Grand Corruption: Is defined as corruption occurring at the highest levels of government in a way that requires significant subversion of the political, legal, and economic systems. Such corruption is commonly found in countries with authoritarian or dictatorial governments but also in those without adequate policing of corruption. The government system in many countries is divided into the legislative, executive, and judicial branches in an attempt to provide independent services that are less subject to grand corruption due to their independence from one another.

Petty Corruption: Occurs at a smaller scale and takes place at the implementation end of public services when public officials meet the public. For example, in many small places such as registration offices, police stations, state licensing boards, and many other private and government sectors.

Systemic Corruption (or Endemic Corruption): Is corruption which is primarily due to the weaknesses of an organization or process. It can be contrasted with individual officials or agents who act corruptly within the system.

Chapter 7
Terrorist Psychology and Its Impact on International Security

Ketevan Chakhava
International Black Sea University, Georgia

ABSTRACT

Terrorism is a policy based on the systematic use of terror. Despite the legal force of the term "terrorism," its definition up to the present time remains ambiguous. But experts agree that the best definition of terrorism is the achievement of political, ideological, economic, and religious goals by violent means. Synonyms of the word "terror" are the words "violence" and "intimidation." This term became widespread in various countries after the "Age of Terror" during the Great French Revolution. During the discussion about terrorism, one of the main directions of this phenomenon represents terrorist psychology. Thus, in the chapter, the main attention is paid to the psychological aspects of terrorism, including the determination of the main types of terrorism and the psychological characteristics of the terrorists and terrorist groups.

INTRODUCTION

Currently, the study of the topic "Psychology of Terrorism" is especially relevant in connection with the increase in the number of terrorist attacks committed by various terrorist organizations around the world. The constant threat of terror leads to the destabilization of the political, economic, and social situation in the state. Lack of confidence in personal safety contributes to the growth of anxiety, fears, and mental stress, which negatively affects psychological health, leading to the development of various psychosomatic disorders among the population. The genesis of the concept of "terrorism", the history of terrorism, the psychology of the personality of terrorists and terrorist groups, the victimology of terrorism, methods of providing psychological first aid in terrorist attacks, methods of negotiating with terrorists, technologies for forming a model of safe behavior are the main issues that are disclosed in this chapter.

GENESIS OF THE CONCEPT OF "TERRORISM", CLASSIFICATION OF TYPES OF TERRORISM, AND METHODS OF COMBATING THEM

Actual Problems of the Psychology of Terrorism

Throughout the history of its existence, humanity has faced various forms and manifestations of terrorism. This phenomenon reached a special scope in the late XX - early XXI century. Terrorist acts and sabotage, cruel in their manifestation, receive a wide resonance throughout the world, causing not only just public outrage but also serious fears for peace and security on the planet.

Terrorism violates the system of human legal protection, causes enormous damage to the stability of the world community, state interests, and in particular the prestige of the law enforcement system. At present, the problem of terrorism has again acquired relevance in connection with the emergence of a new large-scale terrorist group "The Islamic State", which organized and carried out a whole series of terrorist acts around the world. Many Experts believe that terrorism is one of the key phenomena of the growing chaos and the end of history (in the sense of the end of the democratic system). Some Authors suggest that terrorism can be regarded as a form of economic, military, political, criminal, and other activities aimed at the implementation of certain tasks. From their point of view, terrorism has economic and religious roots. In addition to the forceful solution of issues related to terrorism, such sciences as psychology, philosophy, sociology, political science, and psychiatry are engaged in the study of this phenomenon. A terrorist act refers to "extreme", "crisis", "emergencies", which are the subject of study of a new branch of psychology - the psychology of extreme situations. An integrated approach to the phenomenon of terrorism (considering the historical, political-economic, socio-psychological, psychiatric, and informational aspects) is just being formed. Despite the special relevance and practical need for study, the main problems of the psychology of terrorism are not sufficiently developed. So, until now, a clear definition of terrorism, both from a legal and social point of view, has not been formulated. However, "even at the first consideration of this complex and multifaceted phenomenon, one can single out: - individual, organized terror and terror as a policy of the state; - terror as a political method of struggle in peacetime and wartime; - terror as a method of internal political struggle and terrorist acts of international terror ". The manifestations of terrorism entail massive human casualties, the destruction of spiritual, material, cultural values that cannot be recreated. Moreover, terrorism breeds hatred and mistrust between social and national groups.

Many researchers believe that the information and psychological component plays an important role in the problem of terrorism since its main goal is to create public panic or provoke mass irrational horror. However, the more urgent and obvious the problem is, the more myths and misunderstandings it is surrounded by. From the point of view of leading experts in terrorism, a terrorist act is one of the manifestations of an extreme situation arising because of "organized violence" committed by extremists, representatives of totalitarian regimes, adherents of various sects. This type of emergency also includes wars, genocide, armed clashes, persecution on political, religious, ethnic grounds, etc. harm and damage to the health of others.

Definition of the Concepts of "Terror", "Terrorism", Their Similarities, and Differences

To study the psychology of terrorism, it is first necessary to give clear definitions of the concepts of "terrorism" and "terror". Some researchers do not distinguish between them, they consider them identical, but many authors still distinguish between them. First, one should understand what violence is in general. Violence is the physical or mental impact of one person on another, which violates the citizens' right to security of person, guaranteed by the Constitution of many countries. Violence is a social relationship in the course of which some individuals (groups of people), with the help of external coercion, pose a threat to living up to its destruction, subjugate others, their abilities, productive forces, property, usurpation.

The term "terror" comes from the Latin "terror" - horror, fear; and in the most general sense denotes a method of solving political problems and contradictions with the help of violence. It can be said that Terror is the systematic use of extreme violence and the threat of violence to achieve public and political goals, but this understanding is too generalized. In a narrower sense, terror refers to the violence carried out by the state against its citizens and political opposition. For the first time, terror as a political method for resolving contradictions appeared during the Great French Revolution. Distinctive features of modern terrorism are a) the generation of universal danger; b) openly demonstrative character of achieving goals; c) the deliberate formation of a stressful environment at the social level (tension, fear, depression); d) impact on certain people to satisfy any claims. In this case, we are talking about strategy and method, but let's not forget about goal setting. Terrorism is always generated by the policy of the state, it does not arise out of thin air, it is based on disagreement with certain norms and attitudes, which is very often overlooked by researchers.

Typology of Terrorism

For a more complete understanding of terrorism as a social phenomenon, it is necessary to bring a typology of terrorism. The next typology is built on the principle of the nature of terrorist activities, to whom it is directed, that is, whether it is domestic, transnational, or international, which determines the level of legislative suppression of terrorist activity.

1. Internal: actions of citizens against their state on their territory.
2. Transnational: actions of citizens of one state against their compatriots on the territory of another state.
3. International: international, interethnic groups of terrorist acts against another or other states.

Terrorist groups can combine traits of all three types in their activities, or they can belong to only one type. Many researchers distinguish international terrorism as a separate phenomenon: "International terrorism is a phenomenon in world politics associated with the spread of violence in the form of terrorist acts that threaten the normal course of international relations" or "international terrorism is violent acts aimed at causing political change, which undermine the international community and which the international community regards as incompatible with the desired norms of behavior. " In principle, these definitions are not so far from the truth, but they consider only one aspect of the phenomenon under study.

International terrorism is not an independent phenomenon, and it must be considered in the light of a general study of the problems of terrorism. The second typology is built according to the criterion of the ideological substantiation of terrorist activity, that is, according to what motive drives the terrorists.

The following types of terrorism are distinguished:

- political terrorism.
- social terrorism.
- national terrorism.
- territorial separatist terrorism; - ideological terrorism.
- criminal terrorism.

Political terrorism in a broad sense encompasses all the above-mentioned types of terrorism aimed at changing the social system or any part of it. In a narrow sense, political terrorism means "a struggle aimed at preventing (or making) any decisions related to the state structure." Social terrorism is formed based on deep internal socio-political conflicts and manifests itself in two main forms: left and right terrorism. Left-wing terrorism is ideologically oriented towards various left-wing doctrines (Marxism, Leninism, Trotskyism, anarchism, Guevarism, Maoism, etc.) parties.

As a rule, leftist terrorism activates when internal crises escalate. The militant organizations of the leftist terrorists have been operating for a relatively short time. Right-wing terrorism is guided by political doctrines and values traditional for the nation, and historically by national leaders of the past. It is activated for a short time during periods of the greatest threat from the left forces. The target is leftist and liberal politicians and activists. National terrorism is carried out along ethnic lines and is divided into separatist, national liberation, and repressive national terrorism. Separatist terrorism is carried out by national-political minority groups fighting for sovereignty or expanding the autonomy of the historical territory of residence.

Depending on the political situation, traditions, and social structure, they are guided by left or right ideology. Organizations of this type are the most long-lived. The target is officials, businessmen, and policemen. National liberation terrorism is carried out by the peoples of occupied or colonized states against representatives of the aggressor country. The goal is to restore state sovereignty. Such groups adhere to moderately nationalist views, ideological orientation fades into the background. The target is representatives of a hostile nation, regardless of social and professional status. Repressive national terrorism develops during periods of national conflicts within a single state. Representatives of privileged national groups aim to suppress the demands of national minorities, strive to create ethnically homogeneous states. Territorial separatist terrorism is carried out within the borders of one state by representatives of any dominant nation, fighting for the provision of sovereignty, that is, the creation of a separate state on the territory of the country.

This type of terrorism is the least common. This type can include Israeli terrorists who advocate granting Palestine broad autonomy. Worldview terrorism is carried out based on fundamental disagreement with the prevailing norms and relations. This type includes religious, environmental, "smuggling", feminist terrorism. The most widespread is religious terrorism, which in turn is subdivided into fundamentalist and sectarian. It is characteristic of fundamentalist terrorism that religion serves as an ideological position that allows terrorists to formulate the concept of anti-government struggle. Islamic terrorism is the most widespread in the modern world. Fundamentalists are united by the desire to rebuild reality following the norms of religious life. Sectarian terrorism is carried out by various marginal sects of a totalitarian nature, who view violence as a condition for seizing power and building a more perfect society. Criminal terrorism emerges in moments of political instability and is often confused with organized crime as such or attributed to other types of terrorism characteristic of it. We can say that its main subjects are organized criminal groups, communities, and organizations, of a national or transnational nature.

They use intimidation and direct violence in various forms as the main means of influencing the government, its representatives, lobbyists, and their competitors in illegal and legal business to redistribute spheres of influence, property, financial flows, types of criminal and legal activities. The terrorist component of organized crime tends to a certain politicization to weaken the activities of law enforcement agencies, inhibit legislative initiatives that are disadvantageous to the criminal environment, demoralize the population, enter the legislative authorities or their accomplices and patrons, occupy important posts in the executive federal and regional authorities, obtaining immunity from legal prosecution for committing crimes.

The following trends in the development of terrorism in the 20th and 21st centuries can be distinguished: ultra-left, ultra-right, ethnic-nationalistic, and religious. Ultra-right terrorism is usually based on a complete denial of the democratic institutions of the rule of law, violent rejection of the ruling regime, racism, religious intolerance, belief in the existence of secret conspiracies (for example, a Jewish financial conspiracy, a worldwide Masonic conspiracy, etc.). Organizations of this kind mainly aim not to change the existing economic system, but to establish a different way of distributing resources, income, and values. The spread of disillusionment in the ruling political parties, the deteriorating financial situation, and a massive influx of emigrants create a favorable background for the development of right-wing extremism. Against the background of the global political crisis, representatives of ultra-right terrorism are gaining more and more followers in Western Europe. According to experts, ultra-right terrorist organizations are more active in the modern world than ultra-left ones. Ultra-left terrorism emerged in Western Europe in the mid-1960s. XX century, first in Germany, and then in France, Belgium, and Italy. Members of the ultra-left groups viewed themselves as the vanguard of the popular revolution (neo-Marxist, neo-Maoist, anarchist, etc.) and advocated the immediate destruction of the existing state system and the construction of a "fairer" society, the prelude to which was the destruction of the authorities and mass intimidation of the population. The social face of the ultra-left groups was determined mainly by students and the marginalized. They professed a special, original vulgarized Marxism, sharply different from the orthodox.

In 1968, in some circles of the left intelligentsia, the ideology of violence began to mature, and theoretical substantiation of its necessity and justification was carried out. Theorists of left-wing extremism created a generalized image of a repressive oppressor state and sought to destroy it. The pseudo-Marxist branch in left-wing extremism was intertwined with the anarchist one, which was characterized by total nihilism, destructive, anti-institutionalism, and the cult of spontaneity. The activity of the leftist terrorists was often intertwined with the activity of the ultra-right, which was exacerbated by the deliberate infiltration of the ultra-left groups carried out by the neo-fascists. Nevertheless, at that time, Western countries demonstrated a margin of safety for civil society institutions and power structures, having developed mechanisms for directing the situation into a constitutional channel. Potential supporters of extremist actions received a legal political outlet.

Ethno-nationalist terrorism has recently become one of the most widespread types of terrorism. This is since ethnic nationalism has tremendous power and unpredictability, and ethnic conflicts have become a real problem for many countries, regions, and the entire world community. These conflicts are based on the contradiction between the recognition of the natural right of peoples to self-determination and the principle of national unity and territorial integrity of the state. The goal of ethnic terrorism is to defend and expand the rights of an ethnic group in the political sphere. When terrorists, using violence to assert ethnicity, call upon themselves the fire of state structures, it draws attention to the group and allows them to appear in the eyes of the public as a victim, which further increases public resonance, as well as provides financial and political support.

Violence is the raison d'être of such groups. If people use this method of influence, the idea is alive, and the presence of ethnic differences cannot be denied. The main stake in their activities ethnic terrorists makes on the constant intimidation of the population. On the one hand, fear testifies to the illegitimacy of the central government in an ethnic enclave and sends a signal to other ethnic groups that their presence in this territory is undesirable. On the other hand, fear does not allow the ethnic community to develop a different attitude towards their self-determination. It is significant that in the case of this type of terrorism, the state is limited in countermeasures. Thus, it can get involved in a conflict and try to assert a competing ethnic identity; can use forceful methods, but this has its downside - it brings moderates to the terrorist camp. Another option is to try to establish cooperation with moderate nationalists, but they, as a rule, cannot control extremists. You can try to include terrorists (who in this case act as fighters for national liberation) into the legal political process, as was done in many Western European countries, but this is a very difficult way out, because to some extent it means the defeat of the state and, therefore, justifying political violence. Unlike ideological terrorism, ethnic terrorism has a ready audience. Ideological terrorists should focus on some segment of the political spectrum, religious terrorists should appeal to their co-religionists, and ethnic terrorists simply tell their followers that they are part of a single whole. During counter-terrorism operations, violence escalates, since it is a breeding ground for terrorists to succeed in their struggle and maintain the desire to defend their ethnicity; the threat of violence from the authorities must be preserved and exaggerated in every possible way. Ethnic terrorism, unlike other terrorist areas, has existed for a very long time. In a small ethnic group, it is easier to create and maintain infrastructure, it is easier to hide. The fewer ethnic terrorists are focused on other political issues (that is, apart from the state status of the ethnos and the political structure of the country), the stronger they are since a high level of cohesion is maintained in the ethnos. In the modern world, in most cases, mixed forms of terrorism are widespread. This refers to the "cooperation" of terrorist organizations of different orientations, their unification to achieve certain goals, the combination in many specific cases of the ideological, ethnic-nationalistic, and religious components. Ideological ethnonationalism appeals not so much to a rational worldview as to the irrational aesthetic experience of representatives of a given ethnos, to its symbols, experiences, traditions, archetypes, etc. That is why ethnonationalism has a much greater mobilization potential than any political and ideological doctrine because around his "totems" you can relatively quickly gather a mass of people and, by manipulating the image of the "common enemy", give it a certain political impulse, turn off the factor of individual responsibility, infect the mass with aggressive slogans and, thus, at the level of the collective unconscious, prepare the commission of collective crimes within the framework of large-scale acts of terror. Recently, ethnic-nationalist groupings of all kinds have been gaining more and more strength both on the territory of the European Union and in the "post-Soviet space". This is mainly because the involvement of nationalism as a powerful determinant of inciting a socio-political conflict makes it possible to increase its scale and geography dramatically and qualitatively, giving it even an international character by involving foreign national diasporas in various forms, which greatly facilitates the financial and public support. In recent decades, ethnic-nationalist nationalism has manifested itself in the Middle East.

Terrorist gangs operating in this region are actively using the experience accumulated by terrorist groups for over a century. Accordingly, Middle East terrorism is the most striking manifestation of ethnic-nationalist terrorism in the world. The Middle East is the cradle of three leading world religions (Christianity, Islam, Judaism) - one of those regions of the world where the most complex socio-economic, national-territorial, confessional, and geopolitical contradictions have developed over the centuries. Having laid the ground for irreconcilable religious fanaticism on each side, terrorism in the Middle East has historically become a familiar form of conflict expression. The modern borders of the Middle Eastern states and the nature of political regimes in many of them are a direct result of the colonial policy of European powers in the 19th century and the results of two world wars. Since the 1980s, Middle East terrorism has included several varieties: - suicide attacks and other operations against Israeli and Western forces in Lebanon; - hostilities of various armed formations in Lebanon; - State terrorism of Libya, Syria, Iraq, and Iran; - "independent" terrorism of various structures, a kind of "free terrorist flight"; - terrorist attacks in support of the Palestinian people; - anti-Israeli and anti-Western terrorist attacks in Europe; - Israeli raids to liquidate persons suspected of terrorism. Middle East terrorism is currently not only a socio-political, but also an economic phenomenon. It regulates energy prices, affects stock prices, makes profits, and ruins. To date, the most formidable terrorist group in the Middle East is the Islamic State terrorist organization, banned in many countries of the world, which united representatives of several terrorist groups in its ranks, seized a certain part of the territory of Syria, and held them with the help of an armed conflict. The adherents of this terrorist organization carry out large-scale terrorist attacks not only in the Middle East but also in Europe, America, and around the world. Religious terrorism. Within each cultural paradigm, there are religious fanatics who are ready to sacrifice their (and not only there) lives for the sake of a higher truth, extended to the secular social system. "Holy terror", firstly, carries in itself such an integral system, which is not present in "secular" terror. Ordinary terrorists want to win within the dominant political and cultural pattern and seek not only to destroy but also to create new social structures. Religious fanatics see the world as a battlefield between the forces of light and darkness. Their victory has no political conditions: the enemy must be destroyed. Second, murder is a sacred act for them, and not just a means to an end. At the same time, a complex system of theological evidence is being erected, which makes it possible to justify the murder of innocent people, women, old people, children, including the pious. Third, since religious terrorists act as if outside reality, they have no deterrent to the extent of the violence. For those who fulfill the higher will, identifying themselves with it, the life of mere mortals does not matter; when the ultimate authority is God, public appraisal plays no role either. Fourth, they believe that their struggles and deaths to achieve personal salvation have cosmic implications that will ultimately change the course of world history. Thus, we can draw the following conclusion that terror and terrorism are different concepts, the main difference is who is the subject and who is the object. For terror, the subject is the state, and the object is the citizens, vice versa for terrorism. We can say that terror is the policy of the strong against the weak (since the state is objectively stronger than its citizens), and terrorism is the policy of the weak against the strong. Terror is aimed at preserving the existing political situation, while terrorism aims at any change in the political situation.

International Terrorism

Terrorism has many faces. Terrorism is not only a cult and practice of violence, but it also seeks to substantiate its ideology. Criminal in nature, it can be domestic, and in this case, it is carried out not only by criminal groups but also by the totalitarian state apparatus of suppression, thus being state terrorism. International terrorism inflicts great damage to world law and order and international relations, to a large extent growing out of hatred of the world, internecine religious extremism, and chauvinism. The definition of such concepts as "terrorism" and "international terrorism" refers to those international problems, the solution of which is of exceptional practical importance. The international community, politicians, scientists, and, of course, employees of special services and law enforcement agencies of various states, regardless of their political, social, and economic structure, are sufficiently aware of this. The development of a generally accepted legal definition of terrorism is a difficult and still unresolved task, especially when it comes to international terrorism. Now, there is no universal definition of the concept of "terrorism" and its derivatives - national (domestic) and international, recognized by the world community. The difficulties in developing an internationally agreed definition of "international terrorism" are due to many reasons. Among them, there are many objective ones, due to the different understanding of national security by many states, the divergence of ideas about various forms of international terrorism (state, non-governmental, transnational, individual, etc.). The process of developing a unified definition of the term "terrorism" is also hampered by subjective factors: the reluctance of some states to bind themselves with a firm formula that can create obstacles for their connection with terrorist activities, hidden from the world and their people. Due to cultural, civilizational, religious differences, as well as related ethical norms, terrorist attacks can be perceived as heroic or criminal. This fact, among other reasons, makes it possible to understand why the world community has not yet developed a generally acceptable universal concept of "terrorism". However, the development and, more importantly, the consolidation of this concept in the norms of international law is necessary to clarify the real positions of the members of the world community on this issue and, therefore, to form a certain legal basis of international treaty obligations to combat this phenomenon.

TERRORIST PERSONALITY PSYCHOLOGY. PSYCHOLOGICAL PORTRAITS OF CONTEMPORARY TERRORISTS

Many scientists, studying the motivation of a person to join a terrorist organization, believe that poverty, lack of education, unemployment, lack of life prospects, etc. are not psychological, but rather sociopsychological factors. The listed factors are psychologized to the extent that they mediate other actualized needs (self-realization, self-respect, desire for power, etc.). Terrorist activity as a psychological technology makes it possible to find a special "roundabout" way: a person does not become richer, more educated, does not find a decent job, but gains power over richer, more educated, and successful people than he is. His actualized needs are realized in a special - "displaced", symbolic form. It is precisely in the phenomena of "displacement" and expansion of symbolization that attracts new members to it: the rejection of the "principle of reality" and the achievement of goals by means that at first glance are simpler and do not require long-term efforts. Technologies of terrorism, like peaceful modern technologies for satisfying needs, are characterized by signs of illusory simplicity, ease, quick achievement of results and benefits. The cognitive-behavioral concept of the activity initiated in this way is simple and primitive. It has an unreal, illusory-compensatory character. Technologically developed terrorist ideologies not only represent, but actively impose a methodological toolkit for objectifying need states, well developed at different levels, transforming them into a ready-made, strictly determined needs of different levels. It is this ability to successfully satisfy various multi-level human needs that transforms terrorism technologies into a unique way to achieve their goals, giving terrorism its subjective attractiveness, which is a very important direction in the psychological study of the phenomenon of terrorism.

The Identity of the Terrorist

To solve the problem of terrorism, to create a unified scientific and methodological basis for its research, one of the main goals is to study the psychology of the terrorist, his typological, emotional, and moral-moral characteristics. But this task turned out to be intractable. Terrorist organizations are recruited from all walks of life, professions, they are representatives of various cultures and nationalities, religions, and ideological beliefs. Extremists have been described as people with schizophrenia and utopians, as fanatics and aggressors, as traumatized, notorious, self-asserting, over-ambitious people, or as martyrs for their beliefs. Terrorist acts, as a rule, are committed under the slogan of certain ideologies: political, religious, and ethnic-nationalistic. The decision to commit a terrorist attack requires a person to resolve several issues: the purpose, object, methods, place, and time of the crime, consideration of additional circumstances that may help or hinder the fulfillment of the plan. From a certain number of behavioral variations, the terrorist must choose, in his opinion, the most appropriate behavior option for certain tasks. Such a choice is due to such personality traits as orientation, ideological attitudes, personal experience, moral and ethical and value orientations, norms of internal social control. The choice is also associated with an analysis of the external environment, the current situation, and forecasting the future situation in which a terrorist act is planned, with the expectation of a response from members of his group and society. In general, extremism relies on destructive instincts and aggressiveness inherent in humans, expressed in different people to varying degrees, controlled with varying effectiveness by moral and legal norms, education, and culture. Representatives of the psychological type, who have a low level of control of emotions and expressions of emotional reactions in behavior, a low level of tolerance, a narrow worldview, easily arise and become commonplace the idea of violence and forcible achievement of their goals. A violent way of achieving their goals is also characteristic of people with a high level of intelligence, but an overestimated self-esteem, an overestimated level of ambition, a desire for power, a low level of tolerance, with the idea of the exclusivity of their political, religious, or ethnic-nationalistic convictions. There are several psychological models of the terrorist's personality. 1. The psychopathic fanatic. He is guided by his convictions (religious, ideological, political) and sincerely believes that his actions, regardless of their specific results, are beneficial to society. This is a person whose sphere of consciousness is extremely narrow, capable of doing anything. 2. Frustrated person, based on the behaviorist theory of frustration-aggressiveness. The feeling of frustration, generated by the impossibility for a person for some reason to achieve vital goals for him, inevitably gives rise to his tendency to aggressive actions. Consciousness in this case can play the role of an instrument in the rationalization of these actions, that is, in the selection of certain reasons for their justification. 3. A person from a flawed family. Abuse of parents with a child, his social isolation, lack of good relations can lead to the formation of an angry personality with antisocial inclinations. Under certain conditions, people of such a psychological make-up can easily become instruments of a terrorist organization. In general, the basic psychological characteristics of terrorists have been sufficiently studied. They are the conditions for a person to join one or another terrorist group. Usually, they are reflected in the charter or set of rules of each terrorist organization (unless the given criminal community is not particularly conspiratorial or has no documentary support at all). In a generalized form, one main and two secondary qualities are distinguished. The main thing is dedication.

Devotion to the main goal, to your group, to your associates, and readiness for self-sacrifice. The secondary features are organization and conspiracy. Obedience and fellowship with comrades are also important requirements. Loyalty presupposes the absence of individuality, one's principles, and position, integral, complete obedience to the laws of the terrorist organization. When a person enters a terrorist group, he is required to be completely subordinate, to give up his own life for the sake of accomplishing the plans of the organization. But in this position of terrorist organizations, there is a huge contradiction, since, opposing themselves to the whole world, the state, in general to other people, declaring their peculiarity, difference from everyone, within the organization demand a refusal of self-identification, from their individuality, require merging with everyone, to act as a single organism. Although individuality is possible, it is only for a terrorist acting alone, which is almost impossible in the real world. Scientists who deal with the problem of studying the personality of a terrorist consider it possible to rely on the typology of temperaments described by G. Eysenck. According to this classification of types of temperament, there are choleric, sanguine, phlegmatic, and melancholic. In essence, they are presented by the main characteristics of the properties of the nervous system and the intensity of their manifestation according to the parameters ``extraversion - introversion" and "neuroticism - emotional stability". A severely neurotic and extrovert choleric person is the most typical psychological type of terrorist, according to the authors. About gender characteristics in the psychology of terrorism, it was traditionally believed that terrorists can be mainly men, but in practice, it turned out to be different. Although most terrorists are men, the role of women in terrorist groups is important. So, in Russia, in the 60s-70s of the XIX century, when there was a wave of terrorist attacks associated with social and political reforms, women played the role of not only the perpetrators of terrorist attacks but also its ideological leaders (Vera Zasulich, Sofya Perovskaya, etc.). Based on the social status of a woman in society, it is easier for her to hide, infiltrate and carry out a terrorist act than it is for a man. There are even terrorist groups where women make up at least half of the total number of members. Terrorist organizations such as the Irish Revolutionary Army, the Red Brigades, and Latin American groups actively use women for intelligence and military purposes. The age range of people involved in terrorism is, on average, 20–35 years old, that is, the most capable, mentally, and physically active individuals. If we talk about national characteristics, then it is quite difficult to make any emphasis. Under national terrorism, representatives of one nation work against another. If we consider religious terrorism, then, of course, the most active remain Muslim, Protestant, Catholic, and sectarian groups. Overt psychopathology among terrorists is a rare thing. At the same time, it is possible to single out several personal predispositions, which often become incentives for individuals to enter the path of terrorism: over-focus on protecting one's "I" by projection with constant aggressive-defensive readiness; insufficient personal identity, low self-esteem, elements of personality split; strong need to join a group, ie, group identification and/or belonging; experiencing a large degree of social injustice with a tendency to project onto society the reasons for their failures; - social isolation and alienation, the feeling of being on the sidelines of society and the loss of life prospects. For all the nuances, the behavior of a terrorist is usually some vivid and obvious kind of asocial, deviant behavior.

According to the general assessment, this behavior is to one degree or another abnormal and inevitably includes some pathological component. It is generally accepted that a terrorist is not that not entirely normal but accentuated. This means that a terrorist is a normal person, however, certain personality traits in him are expressed unusually strongly, vividly, deviating somewhat from the norm. Sometimes psychopathy in terrorists is found in combination with particular personality traits. Such people give the impression of eccentrics by the unpredictability of their actions, impulsiveness, and inconsistency. In normal activities and studies, their results are low, their adaptability is unstable, and their behavior is uneven. They are prone to vagrancy, to frequent communication with asocial elements. The crimes committed by such persons are usually inadequately harsh, often impulsive, not always planned, often taking wild, unusually violent forms. An analysis of scientific research on this issue allows us to reveal a common factor in the development of a terrorist's personality, which can be called psychological impairment, a kind of deficiency of something in his life, the roots of which can sometimes be traced from early childhood. Such a deficit in mental development leads to the need for hyper compensation of the deficit while growing up and reaching maturity. It is known from autobiographies and other descriptions that many terrorists had their parents and relatives killed in childhood. On the one hand, because of this, a desire for revenge arose, on the other, there was an atmosphere of emotional deficit in which the future terrorist grew up. The disadvantage is also generated by socio-economic factors: for example, the low standard of living of people and the associated desire to "take away and divide" both within the framework of one country (then we are dealing with revolutionary terrorism), and in the relationship between the "poor" (developing) and "rich" countries. Lack of education and information also gives rise to destructive, destructive attitudes towards other cultures, beliefs, and beliefs. It is possible to analyze for long-time various areas in which this or that deficit may arise, leading to this or that inferiority. These are personal, family, social, economic, and political types of inferiority.

Accordingly, they give rise to different psychological roots of terror. However, there is a major common factor that unites the different options into a single mechanism. This is an inner impossibility, an inability to overcome this inferiority. Deficiency itself is not terrible - it is overcome through various mechanisms, through the mechanism of adequate, positive, constructive super-compensation, in which the deficit is eliminated using funds from the same sphere in which it arose. For example, a person who suffered from polio in childhood can become an Olympic champion - for this you only need to continuously play sports; receive a small salary, start working more, find a second job, etc. But neither one nor the other grabbed a gun and set off explosions. They become terrorists when there is not enough strength to overcompensate for the deficit with adequate means. Then overcompensation becomes inadequate, negative, and destructive, and inferiority turns into terror.

On the other hand, it should be noted that despite the presence of some common psychological characteristics, we cannot single out a single personal terrorist complex. But at the same time, the author singles out psychological types that can be relatively often found among extremists. Representatives of the first type are characterized by a high level of intelligence an overestimated level of self-esteem and ambition, and a desire to achieve their goals in any way. Representatives of the second type have a low level of self-esteem, a low level of aspirations, "losers with a weak I". Both types are characterized by a high level of aggression, a low threshold for the emergence of aggressive actions, a desire for self-assertion, low tolerance, inattention to the feelings and needs of other people, and fanaticism. They see the source of their problems outside, in the current external situation and the society around them.

Suicide Bombers

Terrorism is a pre-planned attack or threat of attack on civilians or civilian objects to achieve political, ideological, or religious goals. Suicidal terrorism is a politically, religiously, and ideologically motivated attack carried out by one or more individuals who deliberately give up their lives to cause maximum damage to citizens and civilian objects. The military and political structures of the state are also targets of terrorist attacks. F. Moghaddam, studying the prerequisites for the emergence of Islamic terrorism as a geopolitical phenomenon from the standpoint of the socio-cultural approach, highlighted the levels of identification of people with terrorists. The basic level is the search for a new identity, caused by dissatisfaction with the existing socio-economic and political conditions of life, characterized by a lack of social mobility and life prospects. - The first level is the search for who is to blame and how to deal with him. - The second level is finding an external enemy as a substitute for aggression, controlled by the authorities, religious extremists, and fundamentalists. - The third level is the acceptance of the terrorist's motivation, the formation of terrorist groups, and their ideology. - The fourth level - the formation of the specific functions of terrorists, including suicide bombers - implementation, motivation. - The fifth level - the execution of acts of terrorist attacks - is the achievement of the set goal, which justifies all means, including suicidal terrorism. According to the authors, the traditional social-cultural conditions of the Islamic society do not allow the young generation of Muslims to satisfy their need for individual identity, and it is the search for a new identity that pushes them to join terrorist groups. F. Moghaddam sees the prospect of a long-term, but not military struggle against terrorism in changing the socio-cultural foundations of their lives, leading to a solution to the crisis of socio-cultural identity in the Islamic community. Suicidal terrorism in terrorist organizations is preferred over other forms of terrorism, since a suicide bomber, choosing the time and place of the crime, is not distracted by the thought of saving his life, which allows him to inflict the greatest damage on innocent victims and civilian objects. Suicidal terrorism demonstrates to society the powerlessness of the government in countering terrorism and pushes government structures to change their policies (Moghaddam F. M., 2006). Many assume that there are few people with special personality traits among suicide bombers. Analysis of court materials and rare interviews with terrorists shows that terrorists most often demonstrate externalization (they explain their behavior because of negative external circumstances and the "psychological splitting" of the personality (the simultaneous existence of contradictory, incompatible justifications for their behavior). It is the search for an external enemy as a source of their own. failure is the dominant mechanism in the psychology of the personality of a terrorist. Previously, there was an opinion that people from the poor, without education and profession, become suicide bombers, but numerous studies have revealed that among them there are many highly educated people with highly paid professions. The leaders of terrorist groups strongly support the heroic myths about self-sacrifice and various ceremonies for the transition of members of the group to suicide bombers. The potential victim will soon be destroyed, and they strive to contribute to the approach of a new "correct, just" world. Also, the reason for the transition to death row can be the desire to get rid of negative identity (loneliness, shame, humiliation). Suicidal terrorism is especially characteristic of women since they are closest to the ideology of martyrdom. The state of post-traumatic stress disorder, the impossibility of contact with the outside world make a person more vulnerable to the ideology of suicidal terrorism.

Terrorist Logic and Thinking

Terrorists' thinking is as contradictory as their personalities. On the one hand, it is monoidal (all thoughts, reasoning, plans are associated with the main activity), and on the other hand, it is excessively mercantile. He thinks of other people either as his associates or as potential victims; he thinks about objects, how they can be useful in the commission of a terrorist attack - as a weapon of attack or a weapon of defense. At the same time, he is always ready to talk about the ideas for which he is going to attack. Here are some examples. So, in the logic of a terrorist, it is paradoxical and seemingly completely illogical that opposite things are connected: freedom and violence. And then violent terror turns out to be the best means of achieving freedom: "The majority of the militant organization held the point of view that the only guarantee of the acquired freedoms lays in real strength. Such a force, in any case, could have been the active influence of terror. From this point of view, the terror not only should not have been stopped but, on the contrary, taking advantage of the favorable moment, it was necessary to strengthen it and put at the disposal of the military organization as many people and means as possible. The only guarantee of the won rights is the real power of the revolution, i.e. that is, the power of the organized masses and the power of terror. " The extremist's logic is either clever or very straightforward, but in either case, it is "crooked", most often generalized, symbolic. An example is a terrorist attack on September 11, 2001, by the terrorist organization Al Qaeda against the United States, which they declared to be a symbol of the end of American domination in the world. Thus, the researchers conclude that terrorism is not only an indicator of social inequality but also expresses people's discontent caused by the collapse of their hopes and plans; terrorism is a way of accomplishing certain plans and is aimed against the sources of their misery. One of the important missions of terrorist attacks is to symbolize their intentions. So, trying to kill the tsar, the Russian terrorists, as it were, symbolically destroyed the entire monarchy. In problems not directly related to the main craft, the logic and thinking of terrorists are shaped by the general level of development and culture. Understanding the logic and peculiarities of the terrorist's thinking is of serious practical importance. So, in particular, it is known you can only negotiate with someone who understands the language in which you negotiate with him. If you think and reason logically ("wait to kill me, give me time, I will find what you need and give it to you"), and your opponent does not understand the logic, but only experiences emotions ("I will kill you anyway, and right now! "), Such attempts do not make sense. Moreover, they are dangerous: after all, you think that you have agreed, and your opponent considers himself free from all agreements. Terrorists are a special type of people in whom rational components in behavior and character are almost absent, and emotional components prevail to such an extent that they become effective. It is difficult to talk to them: if something is wrong, then the eyes instantly fill with blood, and the fingers clenched into fists and reach for the gland. Such a person simply does not know the normative words like "can" and "not", "possible" or "impossible". Its vocabulary is very simple: "I want!", "Give!", "Mine!", And here and now, immediately. Unlike a normal person, who is equally capable of understanding "rationality" and experiencing "emotions" without going beyond the accepted framework, a terrorist is not capable of this. The psych type of these people is designed in such a way that it acts according to the "all or nothing" law. To a large extent, this is facilitated by the excessive simplicity of manners accepted among terrorists, their banal bad manners, and ignorance. It is these factors that are the main source of the emergence of more and more "waves" and even generations of terrorists.

Features of the Emotional Sphere of Terrorists

The emotional sphere of members of terrorist organizations is as contradictory and ambivalent as to their personality and thinking. There are two extreme options among terrorists. One, rarer, is devoid of emotionality. These are people with complete composure, completely immune to emotions, or capable of completely controlling them. The second, nevertheless much more common type among terrorists, is distinguished by its diametrical opposite. Such people have a very diverse inner emotional life. For all the external composure, rationality, severity, even asceticism, emotions rage inside the terrorist. And the stricter the restrictions imposed on a member of a terrorist organization, the stronger the inner, restrained emotions of the terrorist. His notorious restraint, "iron nerves" are the result of the influence of the rational components of the psyche, cruelly depressing emotions. Such containment cannot be permanent. But such violent emotional experiences do not affect the main activity. They are engaged in organizing and carrying out the terrorist act with cold calculation and intelligence. Although many researchers of the problems of terrorism agree that they have a low level of development of intelligence and thinking. The life of a terrorist goes on in constant emotional distress. He lives in the emotions of fear, fearing falling into the hands of opponents. At the same time, he lives in the emotions of anger and contempt for his opponents and inspiration from anticipating the harm that he is going to inflict on them. Naturally, such conflicting emotions often collide with each other, leading to internal emotional conflicts, which predetermine the severe state of chronic emotional stress inherent in a terrorist. Chronic stress is characterized by emotional lability, the ease of almost instantaneous transition from one emotional state to the exact opposite. Often a terrorist who is forced to harshly suppress his emotions in the framework of terrorist activities is emotionally licentious in other matters, for example, in everyday matters. Usually concentrated in their main occupations, Palestinians, for example, are characterized by complete emotional liberation in everyday life. One detail is striking: people, deprived of their state and fighting for its creation, always and everywhere feel "at home": after difficult many days of illegal travel, for example, they instantly find themselves in slippers and immediately extremely emotionally, without hesitation in expressing their feelings, start exploring the hotel. Except for deeply religious Islamic fundamentalists, all other terrorists have deeply emotional personal lives. As a rule, they are not very picky and restrained in sexual relations. An increased temperament leads not only to hypersexual activity but also simply to hyper emotionality. Although the overall emotional sphere is under control, the terrorist is ready to remove this control as soon as he considers it possible. Then feelings break free and manifest themselves violently. However, the most important and most common emotional state of a terrorist is his constant alertness. The phenomenon of alertness is manifested in constant readiness to repel the threat of an attack, an increased level of wakefulness and concentration of attention on the slightest changes in all, primarily physical, environmental parameters, pronounced hyperesthesia. Even outwardly noticeable constant suspicion of the terrorist is manifested in the continuous division of all those around him into "friends" and "aliens." Naturally, the "alien" is a priori identified with the disgusting and alien "image of the enemy" (the reaction of hostile distrust). It is curious that when confirming that the "stranger" is in fact "our own," the nature of the relationship changes dramatically to massive manifestations of trust and openness (sometimes excessive). This indicates a sharp polarization of emotions and emotional lability of the terrorist.

Moral Sphere

A blind fanatic who carries out a brutal terrorist act on a rational "autopilot" does not suffer from moral problems. It is a blind destruction machine that does not think about moral questions simply because such questions are foreign to such a machine. Moral problems arise only when there is a certain intellectual level. Illiterate, uneducated Islamists, acting on the principle of "inshallah" ("everything is in the power of Allah, by his grace"), do not suffer from moral doubts. However, relatively intellectually developed terrorists are constantly worried internally by the question of how right they are in their actions. In the descriptions of various specialists, for example, considerable attention is paid to this site. Every time they prepare for a terrorist act, terrorists seek a moral justification for it. Sometimes it comes to complete paradoxes when believing Christians resort to completely Jesuitical logic, believing that by killing someone's body, they thereby save the soul of their victim. However, such psychological paradoxes are still alive today: Islamic terrorists believe that their actions not only save their souls (a feat in the name of Allah) but also help the souls of their victims to quickly go to heaven. The militants of the Hamas movement know from a special memo for the militants of their organization: "Allah will forgive you if you fulfill your duty and kill the unbeliever; in paradise, Allah will take care of all your problems. "So this is precisely what some Islamic theologians explained the essence of the explosions of skyscrapers in New York, which entailed thousands of victims. The skyscrapers themselves were viewed as "sacrifices to Satan," and people who died under the rubble were declared "delivered from serving false gods." For a deeply religious terrorist fanatic, everything is simple - God himself relieves him of moral problems - but all the same, it turns out that he also needs some kind of moral self-justification. However, even such self-justification is not always sufficient, and moral suffering can continue even after a "victory", that is, a successfully committed terrorist act. Although even convinced of their moral right to violence, male terrorists usually have a hard time experiencing moral problems after the terrorist attacks. Even Palestinian terrorists often talked about "heaviness on the soul", although they explained their violent actions by external, forced circumstances. The terrorist's moral problems can become strange, even pretentious. The flip side of moral problems is the need for understanding expressed by almost all terrorists, the need to "speak out" in front of other people (usually in front of "their own", but sometimes in front of strangers, including investigators). In the absence of the possibility of oral communication with a suitable interlocutor, the epistolary genre is actively used.

Thus, we see that the main and characteristic feature of a terrorist's personality is extreme inconsistency. Maintaining internal contradiction and social isolation is the main condition for the psychodynamics of a terrorist's personality. The immanent prohibition on social forms of communication and activity is the result of the personality's contradictions. At the same time, certain types of terrorist activities are not interconnected with specific personality types of terrorists. The inconsistency in the personality of terrorists is also manifested in their thinking and emotional sphere. The main qualities of a terrorist's personality are 1) dedication to his cause (terror) and his organization; 2) readiness for self-sacrifice; 3) consistency, discipline; 4) "conspiracy"; 5) obedience; 6) collectivism - the ability to maintain good relations with all members of their combat group.

Within the framework of static analysis, the main property of a terrorist's personality is integrity, concentration on terrorist activities, and his group, organization. However, from a dynamic point of view, these properties turn out to be only "fixed moments" of the personality's continuous throwing along a special psychological sinusoid with the broadest range. The wider the range, the less adequate such a person can be considered. In the structure of a terrorist's personality, a psychopathological component is usually noticeably expressed, primarily of a psychopathic nature. It is associated with a feeling of real or imaginary damage suffered by the terrorist, the lack of something necessary, urgently needed for such a person. Typically, the logic and thinking of terrorists are confusing and contradictory. Emotionally, two extreme types of terrorists stand out: the extremely "cold", almost emotionless version, and the emotionally labile version, prone to strong manifestations of emotions in a sphere unrelated to terror, when usually tight control over emotions is removed during the preparation and implementation of terrorist acts. Emotions are associated with moral and ethical problems ("sinfulness complex"), sometimes painful for terrorists with a sufficiently high level of education and intellectual development.

PSYCHOLOGY AND ORGANIZATION OF A TERRORIST GROUP

The group Nature of Terrorist Activities

Terrorist activity is almost always of a group nature since the basis for the unification of extremist groups is a sense of social injustice. Social injustice is a type of unrighteousness that is interconnected with a person's group affiliation, that is, it is always unrighteousness in relationships between social groups. Thus, it is not an interpersonal problem, but an intergroup one. Studying the prerequisites for the emergence and formation of terrorist groups, K. Markoulli identifies three stages (or, as he calls them, "crisis") through which a terrorist act passes when a decision is made on its implementation. The first stage is the "secrecy crisis". A group of ordinary people or one person covertly express dissatisfaction with the existing system, disapprove of it, but accept its norms and rules and follow them. The main expression of activity during this period of crisis is the hidden search for like-minded people and their integration into the conspiratorial community. In the second stage - "the crisis of the collision of ideologies" - the disagreement between the ideology of the community and the existing system around it is expressed in an open form of polemics and protest. This stage lasts until such a community comes to a cardinal behavioral pattern to demonstrate its position to everyone. A similar behavioral pattern, as a rule, seeks commonality in other terrorist groups and then functions according to the principle "If it is permissible for terrorists, then it is possible for us." In this regard, the terrorist group enters the third stage - the "crisis of completeness." Open opposition to the existing system develops into aggressive actions. A community or a person transcends all moral and legal norms that previously restrained an open manifestation of aggression. Violence becomes an integral part of their existence and is declared as the only effective tool for opposing the system (McCauley C., 2001). Scientists who are studying the problem of studying terrorist groups agree that there are no and cannot be two identical extremist organizations.

It is very difficult to compare with other terrorist organizations that are only planning a crime and have already implemented a terrorist act. Very often, the model by which the main characteristics are studied is the terrorist groups that committed the act of terrorism, but the characteristics of the groups that have not yet committed it, but are probably no less dangerous, are not considered. Describing the features of terrorist organizations that have achieved success in their plans, L. Gozman writes: "These groups are closed, and entering them means recognizing the right of other people to total control over their lives, including personal, including intimate relationships. For an ordinary person, such total control would be a sacrifice that cannot be made, but for an outsider, for a person who never felt like his own, whom no one had ever accepted anywhere, all this turns out to be rather a plus than a minus. Participation in terrorist groups compensates for many of their failures. They have a meaning in life. The goal is the liberation of the Motherland or the triumph of one's religion or ideology. The attention of the whole world is riveted to them, they no longer have doubts about their significance. The boredom and routine of everyday life are replaced by balancing on the brink of life and death. There is a feeling of being chosen, belonging to fate "(L. Gozman 1996.).

There is another feature of the functioning of terrorist organizations - the cult of perished comrades-in-arms, expressed in the fact that each member of the group honors his comrades who have laid down their heads for a just cause. The group members have a sense of a whole community. But this is not the case for all terrorist groups. And yet, in the end, the members of the organization have a sense of community, and each member of this community knows that if he dies, then his name will be treated with the same respect. However, such cults do not exist in all terrorist organizations, some simply cannot afford any cults (Olshansky D.V., 2002). Researchers of terrorist groups note that all these reasons are insufficient to attract a mentally healthy, psychologically harmonious, successful person in their profession, and even more so they cannot lead him to abandon the principles of respect for human life learned in childhood. For a maladjusted, disharmonious personality with a pronounced intrapersonal conflict, a terrorist group can be a saving option. The psychological characteristics of the personality of individual members of terrorist groups also affect the activities of the entire organization. So, in social psychology, the phenomenon of "risk shift" is widely known, when a group decision is always riskier than the sum of individual decisions. The organization approves more and more risky plans, strives for more and more daring tasks. Terrorists are targeting ever more high-ranking officials and planning more widespread terrorist attacks, and eventually, the community ceases to exist in the face of professionally organized resistance from the state's law enforcement agencies. A terrorist organization, as a special kind of group, belongs to the "intermediate group" because it occupies a transitional position on the scale set by the two poles. "At one extreme point, we see a highly organized, cohesive, functioning collective of individuals as members of a social group. At the opposite extreme point, we have a bunch of individuals characterized by anonymity, erratic leadership, basing their actions on emotions, and in some cases representing a destructive element within the framework of the social system into which it belongs ... Those formations that do not represent close-knit, integrated groups, or disorderly, poorly functioning gatherings or crowds, correspond to the concept of "intermediate group" (Yablonsky L., 1966).

Specific features of terrorist groups

Researchers in the field of the psychology of terrorism has identified the following distinctive features of terrorist groups:

- First, it is a vague definition of the role played by members of the organization. Who are they? The problem of defining functions is always relevant and scrupulous for terrorists. On the one hand, they may identify themselves as "freedom fighters" or "sacred avengers". On the other hand, they fully understand the anti-legal and even criminal nature of their plans and actions. The definition of roles as "militants" and even "terrorists", "terrorists", characteristic of the Combat Organization of many groups, serves rather as a deviation from the rules.
- Secondly, the conditional cohesion of such a community. As a result, terrorist activity is a transient occupation, since a terrorist organization is formed for the implementation of one, less often several, actions. It cannot exist for a long time, and the riskiness of terrorist activities further shortens the period of its existence. All these factors do not contribute to the cohesion of the organization's members, despite the assurances of the members of the terrorist groups themselves of loyalty to their comrades-in-arms.
- Third, the variability of the structure. The structure of an organization that implements its ideas in extreme conditions is subject to change in one way or another.
- Fourth, the variability of the members of the group relates to the variability of the composition. This makes it impossible for the emergence of stable internal relationships between members of the organization. Although in such an organization there is always a stable structure of job responsibilities.
- Fifth, all these factors are due to the limited plans about the composition of the organization. The "personnel reserve" of each terrorist group is extremely narrow, and the members of the organization take this into account.

- Sixth, there is little compliance with the norms of behavior within the organization. The uniting factors of members of a terrorist group are most often strict coordination of official duties (separation of functions during the preparation and implementation of a terrorist act) and the presence of some common motivation, which is meaningful in terrorist activity. Moral norms, rules of communication, one's behavior, etc. are agreed at the lowest level.
- Seventh, relatively chaotic management. In such an organization, as a rule, there is no authoritarian leader or, moreover, no officially appointed leader. Such leaders are rare as leaders of terrorist organizations. Usually, the leaders are average, unremarkable members of the group who cannot exercise systematic total control. Scientists studying the socio-psychological structure of "intermediate groups" conditionally distinguish three levels in the organization of membership. At the center of the organization at the first level are the mentally least stable members of the organization - the leaders. These are the people who need the gang the most. This core is the main cementing force of such groups. They are the ones who hold or even cobble together the group and force it to act, constantly planning, plotting and organizing its actions.

They serve, if not strategic (this is the function of the leadership of the entire organization), then the tactical center of the intermediate group. At the second level of the intermediate group, people usually appear who declare their belonging to the group, but who actively participate in its activities only following their emotional needs at a given time. At the third level of the group, the structure is peripheral members who participate in its activities from time to time and rarely identify with the group. As a rule, these are "auxiliary personnel", "accomplices" of terrorists.

They can take part in a terrorist act mainly as a result of a coincidence, and neither they nor other members of the group consider them equal members. Often terrorist groups use such people "in the dark", not sharing with them all available information and easily "handing over" them to the authorities in case of danger to the main group. The size of a terrorist group is usually determined by the leadership of the entire organization if the group is part of it. Where autonomous terrorist groups are involved, the size depends on the mission of the organization and the emotional needs of the main members of the group. The socio-psychological functions of a terrorist group are related to the motivation for membership in it. As a rule, such a group functions as a convenient means for manifesting various individual needs and solving personal problems. To the leaders, such a group looks like a super-powerful organization through which, in their imagination, they subdue and control the lives of thousands of people. For group members unable to achieve anything in more demanding social organizations, the possibility of rapid and sudden violence serves as a means of social advancement and reputation gain. Sometimes the group can function as a convenient temporary escape from the boring and harsh claims of a difficult and demanding society. Of course, these are just some psychological functions that are not related to its direct purpose - the commission of a terrorist act. Thus, by its socio-psychological nature, the terrorist group belongs to a special type of "intermediate group". All relationships in it are subordinated to the main target function - the preparation and commission of a terrorist act. This gives rise to the specific characteristics of such groups.

CONCLUSION

The study of the Psychology of Terrorism is relevant and necessary in connection with the increase in the number of terrorist attacks that destroy the system of human legal protection, causing enormous damage to the stability of the world community, state interests, and the prestige of the law enforcement system and the education system. An integrated approach to the phenomenon of terrorism (considering the historical, political-economic, socio-psychological, psychopathological, and informational aspects) is only being formed. Despite the relevance and practical necessity, the main problems of the psychology of terrorism are not sufficiently developed. In the current geopolitical situation, the threat of terrorism has become every day for ordinary citizens and politicians in many countries. Various regions of the world, such as India, Turkey, Great Britain, Indonesia, Pakistan, Afghanistan, Iraq, Syria, Israel, Russia, USA, France, Germany, etc., are subject to terrorist attacks. In this regard, countering terrorism is becoming one of the main tasks of ensuring national security for the country and the world community. Modern terrorists are actively using the global world resources for the dissemination of information to realize their own goals and thus cause a systemic reaction that extends not only to the direct victims of the terrorist attack and their loved ones but also to the entire population. As a result, the mass consciousness of people changes, panic reactions, states of anxiety, and anxiety arise, which negatively affects the psychological health of citizens and their ability to work. Thus, there is an urgent need for the training of highly qualified psychologists who can realize professional competencies in providing psychological assistance to people who have suffered as a result of a terrorist act and their loved ones, to provide psychological support for employees of various structures performing anti-terrorist activities and participating in the elimination of the consequences of terrorist acts., to carry out preventive measures for psychological education of the population, prevention of deviations, and maintenance of mental and psychological health. Specialists of this profile are in demand in the following spheres of society: in the defense, security, and law enforcement structures of the state - the system of the Armed Forces, the system of the Ministry of Internal Affairs, the system of the FSB; in rapid response and control services, various emergency services (including the fire brigade, ambulance, etc.); in the penitentiary system; in the structures of the personnel service of transport companies, airlines; in social infrastructure (public administration, social protection of the population, etc.); in healthcare and medicine; in the system of upbringing and education; in the socio-ethnic, socio-political, socio-religious spheres (work on the prevention and resolution of various social conflicts, etc.).

REFERENCES

Bockstette, C. (2008). *Jihadist Terrorist Use of Strategic Communication Management Techniques.* George C. Marshall Center Occasional Paper Series (20).

Gozman, L. (1996). *Terrorism. Socio-Psychological Research.* Omsk State University.

Hoffman, B. (1998). *Inside Terrorism.* Columbia University Press.

Khan, A. (2006). A Theory of International Terrorism. *Connecticut Law Review.*

McCauley, C. (2001). *Group Identification under Conditions of Threat: College Students' Attachment to Country, Family, Ethnicity, Religion, and University Before and After September 11, 2001*. Wiley Online Library.

Moghaddam, F. M. (2006). *From the terrorists' point of view: What they experience and why they come to destroy*. Praeger Security International.

Olshansky, D. V. (2002). *Terrorism Psychology*. Piter.

Sageman, M. (2004). Understanding Terror Networks. *International Journal of Emergency Mental Health*, 7. PMID:15869076

Yablonsky, L. (1966). *Terrorism Psychology*. North-Caucasus State University.

KEY TERMS AND DEFINITIONS

Asymmetric Warfare: Armed conflict between belligerents of vastly unequal military strength, in which the weaker side is often a nonstate actor that relies on unconventional tactics.

Crimes Against Humanity: A category of activities, made illegal at the Nuremberg war crime trials, condemning states that abuse human rights.

Cyberspace: A metaphor used to describe the global electronic web of people, ideas, and interactions on the Internet, which is unencumbered by the borders of the geopolitical world.

Ethno-Nationalist Terrorism: One of the most widespread types of terrorism. This is since ethnic nationalism has tremendous power and unpredictability, and ethnic conflicts have become a real problem for many countries, regions, and the entire world community. These conflicts are based on the contradiction between the recognition of the natural right of peoples to self-determination and the principle of national unity and territorial integrity of the state. The goal of ethnic terrorism is to defend and expand the rights of an ethnic group in the political sphere. When terrorists, using violence to assert ethnicity, call upon themselves the fire of state structures, it draws attention to the group and allows them to appear in the eyes of the public as a victim, which further increases public resonance, as well as provides financial and political support.

Failed States: Countries whose governments have so mismanaged policy that their citizens in rebellion, threaten revolution to divide the country into separate independent states.

Info War-Tactics: Attacks on an adversary's telecommunications and computer networks to penetrate and degrade an enemy whose defense capabilities depend heavily on these technological systems.

Information Warfare: Attacks on an adversary's telecommunications and computer networks to degrade the technological systems vital to its defense and economic well-being.

International Terrorism: The threat or use of violence as a tactic of terrorism against targets in other countries.

Political Terrorism: In a narrow sense, political terrorism means "a struggle aimed at preventing (or making) any decisions related to the state structure." Social terrorism is formed based on deep internal socio-political conflicts and manifests itself in two main forms: left and right terrorism. Left-wing terrorism is ideologically oriented towards various left-wing doctrines (Marxism, Leninism, Trotskyism, anarchism, Guevarism, Maoism, etc.) parties.

Smart Bombs: Precision-guided military technology that enables a bomb to search for its target and detonate at the precise time it can do the most damage.

Terrorism: Premediated violence perpetrated against noncombat targets by subnational or transnational groups or clandestine agents usually intended to influence an audience.

Xenophobia: The suspicious dislike disrespect, and disregard for members of a foreign nationality ethnic or linguistic group.

Chapter 8
Main Characters of Globalization in the 21st Century

Irakli Kervalishvili
Georgian Technical University, Georgia

ABSTRACT

The aim of this chapter is analysis of the main aspects of globalization, which are interrelated to the political, economic, information, cultural, etc. aspects of the global processes, and discussion about main characters of globalization, main approaches to the globalization problems, manifestations of globalization, development of new technologies, leading factors of the globalization process, ambiguity and non-equality of the globalization processes, and in general, about the main positive and negative sides of globalization.

INTRODUCTION.

According to the Oxford English Dictionary, the word "globalization" was first employed in a publication entitled Towards New Education in 1952, to denote a holistic view of human experience in education (Chitadze, 2011). An early description of globalization was penned by the founder of the Bible Student movement Charles Taze Russell who coined the term 'corporate giants' in 1897, although it was not until the 1960s that the term began to be widely used by economists and other social scientists. The term has since then achieved widespread use in the mainstream press by the second half of the 1980s. Since its inception, the concept of globalization has inspired numerous competing definitions and interpretations, with antecedents dating back to the great movements of trade and empire across Asia and the Indian Ocean from the 15th century onwards.

The historical origins of globalization are the subject of ongoing debate. Though some scholars situate the origins of globalization in the modern era, others regard it as a phenomenon with a long history.

Thomas L. Friedman divides the history of globalization into three periods: Globalization 1 (1492-1800), Globalization 2 (1800–2000), and Globalization 3 (2000–present). He states that Globalization

DOI: 10.4018/978-1-7998-9586-2.ch008

Main Characters of Globalization in the 21st Century

1. involves the globalization of countries, Globalization 2. involved the globalization of companies, and Globalization 3. involves the globalization of individuals. Thomas Loren Friedman is an American journalist, columnist, and author. He writes a twice-weekly column for The New York Times. He has written extensively on foreign affairs including global trade, the Middle East, and environmental issues, and has won the Pulitzer Prize three times (Chitadze, 2011).

Perhaps the most extreme proponent of a deep historical origin for globalization was Andre Gunder Frank, an economist associated with dependency theory. Frank argued that a form of globalization has been in existence since the rise of trade links between Sumer and the Indus Valley Civilization in the third millennium B.C. Critics of this idea contend that it rests upon an over-broad definition of globalization.

Globalization refers to the worldwide phenomenon of technological, economic, political, and cultural exchanges, brought about by modern communication, transportation, and legal infrastructure as well as the political choice to consciously open cross-border links in international trade and finance. It is a term used to describe how human beings are becoming more intertwined with each other around the world economically, politically, and culturally.

The International Monetary Fund defines globalization as "the growing economic interdependence of countries worldwide.

Through increasing volume and variety of cross-border transactions in goods and services, freer international capital flows, and more rapid and widespread diffusion of technology". Meanwhile, The International Forum on Globalization defines it as "the present worldwide drive toward a globalized economic system dominated by supranational corporate trade and banking institutions that are not accountable to democratic processes or national governments." While notable critical theorists, such as Immanuel Wallerstein, emphasize that globalization cannot be understood separately from the historical development of the capitalist world-system the different definitions highlight the ensuing debate of the roles and relationships of government, corporations, and the individual in maximizing social welfare within the globalization paradigms. Nonetheless, globalization has economic, political, cultural, and technological aspects that may be closely intertwined. Given that these aspects are key to an individual's quality of life, the social benefits and costs brought upon them by globalization generate strong debate.

The economic aspects stressed in globalization are trade, investment, and migration. The globalization of trade entails that human beings have greater access to a plethora of goods and services never seen before in human history. From German cars to Colombian coffee, from Chinese clothing to Egyptian cotton, from American music to Indian software, human beings may be able to purchase a wide range of goods and services. The globalization of investment takes place through Foreign Direct Investment, where multinational companies directly invest assets in a foreign country, or by indirect investment where individuals and institutions purchase and sell financial assets of other countries. Free migration allows individuals to find employment in jurisdictions where there are labor shortages.

Critics of free trade also contend that it may lead to the destruction of a country's native industry, environment, or a loss of jobs. Critics of international investment contend that by accepting these financial schemes a country loses its economic sovereignty and may be forced to set policies that are contrary to its citizen's interests or desires. Moreover, multinational companies that invest in a country may also acquire too much political and economic power over their citizens. Finally, migration may lead to the exploitation of workers from a migrant country and the displacement of workers from a host country. Critics of globalization also contend that different economic systems that either augment or supplant globalization may maximize social welfare more efficiently and equitably.

Figure 1. Advantages of globalization for small businesses
Source: https://www.advergize.com/insights/advantages-of-globalization-for-small-businesses-things-you-need-to-know/

The political aspects of globalization are evidenced when governments create international rules and institutions to deal with issues such as trade, human rights, and the environment. Among the new institutions and rules that have come to fruition as a result of globalization are the World Trade Organization, the Euro currency, the North American Free Trade Agreement, to name a few. Whether a government is to consciously open itself to cross-border links, is the central question of this aspect.

Social activists and non-profit organizations are also becoming more global in scope. These include Amnesty International and Friends of the Earth to mention a couple. Some of these organizations take issue with the economic and political aspects of globalization as they fear that economic interests either subvert the nation-state in its ability to protect its citizens from economic exploitation, or support governments that violate the human rights of its citizens.

Cultural global ties also grow through globalization as news ideas and fashions through trade, travel, and media move around the globe at lightning speed. Global brands such as Coca-Cola, Puma & Sony serve as common references to consumers all over the World. An individual in China enjoys the same soft drink as an individual in Puerto Rico--at opposite ends of the globe. However, these ties may also cause strains: for example, Western Ideas of freedom expression may clash with Islamic views on religious tolerance. And if not strains, critics contend this is an imposition of cultural imperialism to preserve economic interests.

The other aspect of globalization is the revolutionary changes in technology, particularly in transport and communications, which ostensibly creates a global village. In 1850 it took nearly a year to sail around the World. Now you can fly around the world in a day, send an email anywhere almost instantly, or be part of the 1.5 billion viewers watching the final match of the World Cup. Transportation costs have come down as a result of technological advances that make foreign markets more accessible to trade. Globalization describes the process by which regional economies, societies, and cultures have become integrated through a global network of political ideas through communication, transportation, and trade. The term is most closely associated with the term economic globalization: the integration of national economies into the international economy through trade, foreign direct investment, capital flows, migration, the spread of technology, and military presence. However, globalization is usually recognized as being driven by a combination of economic, technological, socio-cultural, political, and biological factors. The term can also refer to the transnational circulation of ideas, languages, or popular culture through acculturation. An aspect of the world that has gone through the process can be said to be globalized. While suggestions have been made to distinguish between specific parts of globalization (like increased international trade) and parallel developments (like technological advances), others have pointed out that the separation of interconnected processes is not feasible.

MAIN APPROACHES TO THE GLOBALIZATION PROBLEMS

Globalization - is one of the most discussed phenomena in recent years phenomena in the contemporary development of the world and at the same time, perhaps, the least strictly defined. The term itself entered a broad scientific circulation in the 1990s, largely superseding the notion of "postmodernism," which was widely used to describe the complexity and diversity of the modern political world. At the same time, in the late 1980s, the word "globalization" has rarely met in the scientific vocabulary. American sociologist, R. Robertson was one of the first to address the study of globalization problems, using the word "global" in the title of his work "Interpreting Globality" (Robertson, 1983). At the same time, in the field of ecology and technological disciplines specialists began to talk about globalization earlier in the 1960s, although in other terms.

Today, for describing the processes, which are connected with globalization, not very seldom are used other meanings - *postindustrial epoch, the age of the information revolution, techno globalism*, etc. All of them reflect the most important changes that it consists of.

There are different points of view regarding the essence of globalization. One research is focused on its economic aspects, in others on the formation of a common information space, and thirdly on the development of common standards. The latter refers primarily to the organization of production, social life, and so on. In this regard, as a metaphor, the meaning *McDonaldization* of the world is used, which is understood as a certain standardization and "conveyance" of processes in the organization of economic and social life. From the universal blocks, such as from the cubes of the "Lego," various kinds of finite forms are formed, which have many variabilities. A vivid example of such "MacDonald" is the furniture, which is offered by the Swedish company "IKEA": From the standard blocks, there are virtually countless options for furnishing the apartment, depending on the area, tastes, and human needs (Lebedeva, 2007).

There are, although relatively few, skeptical assessments of the processes that have been called "globalization." Thus, M. Veseth considers that globalization is not at all a new phenomenon. The processes, which gained this name, are connected with the complexity of the world processes, which has always existed (Viseth, 2006). However, in his opinion, globalization attracts so much attention, because with its help experts try either to prove the existence of new threats, or, on the contrary, make a prognosis

Figure 2. The causes and effects of globalization
Source: https://www.slideshare.net/AislingMOConnor/the-causes-and-effects-of-globalisation

on the prosperity of mankind. A similar position is shared by the many researchers, who point out that globalization is a politically demanded concept.

The understanding of globalization differs depending on the theoretical positions of the authors. Realists, by recognizing the existence of significant changes in the world, consider globalization, rather, as the process of the evolutionary development of the world, and not as a qualitative leap in its transformation. The neo-Marxists see in modern processes an endeavoring stage in the development of capitalism, which generates an ever-greater polarization of the world according to the economic parameter, and as a consequence, political instability. For the majority of researchers who adhere to the neo-liberal tradition, globalization is a qualitatively new stage in the political structure and the world, and also in human civilization as a whole.

There is one more point of perception of the globalization process, connected with political practice and the estimated characterization of changes in the "good-bad" dichotomy. This is more relevant to political practice and generates, on the one hand, many movements conditionally united by the concept of "anti-globalists" (they often come from extremely radical positions against the development of globalization processes, as well as the institutions that are most closely associated with them, in particular, IMF, WTO). On the other hand, although in a less pronounced form, the movements of supporters of the globalization process, for example, Internet users, etc. Such a variety of opinions and views regarding globalization is due to the complexity, complexity of the processes, and the covering of the spheres of human activity and relations.

Returning to the scientific interpretation of such a phenomenon as globalization, let us dwell on its three dimensions, which the French researcher B. Badie singles out as:

- a constantly moving historical process;
- homogenization and universalization of the world;
- "blurring" of national borders (Badie, 2000).

If we take the first of these dimensions, we will see that the history of the development of mankind does indeed observe a tendency to expand the space where intensive interaction takes place: from individual villages, cities, principalities to states, regions, and finally, through the era of great geographical discoveries to the world in whole.

Nevertheless, the process of globalization is complex and ambiguous. In historical development, it went non-linearly and did not at all assume the accession of new peripheral territories to a certain invariable center. So, G. Modelski, using an example of the development of cities in the ancient world, shows the "pulsating" nature of this process (Modelski, 2000). He distinguishes two phases, each of which lasts for millennia: centralization, when the central zones of the world system are formed, and decentralization if the periphery becomes the main one, there is a change of place in the "center-periphery" system. In principle, close to the idea of the Concept of "pulsations" are also contained in the works of Paul Kennedy, when he speaks about the rise and fall of great powers (Kennedy, 1989).

If we extrapolate the results of G. Modelski to further historical development, we can assume that such a "pulse" takes place not only on a territorial basis, but which is especially important, and based on which substantial aspects are formed Center and periphery. In history, such a substantive foundation was, in particular, ideology, religion, economic development.

Much more controversial is the second dimension of the globalization process that Badie identifies: the universalization and homogenization of the world in its extreme form. Within the framework of this approach, various assumptions were made regarding the creation of a *global village* - a universal community of all people living on earth or a global government, which would regulate the whole complex of interrelations among the countries and people. In the other words, it was suggested the formation of some world confederation (Badie, 2000).

Those examples, ideas, and hypotheses are widely used in journalism, popular literature, reflecting the notion that all people inhabited on our planet are united by a single destiny, and it has become possible thanks to the dissemination of universal cultural patterns, the development of technologies - primarily transport, information and communication, world trade and financial system, that unite all people in an interconnected and interdependent community.

Universalization and homogenization of the world are sometimes considered as its *westernization*. In this case, it means that the values and norms of behavior characteristic of Western civilization are gaining increasing popularity. Indeed, many types of behavior, production, consumption, emerged in the West, and then became accustomed to other countries and cultures. Moreover, in these countries, they are often perceived as inherent to them. In this regard, an amusing example is given by the leading New York Times columnist Thomas Friedman in the book "The Lexus and the Olive Tree". The little Japanese woman who first visited the United States exclaimed: "Mom, look, they also have McDonald's" (Friedman, 2012).

There are many other examples in this regard. However, it is necessary to take into account that under external universalization, more complicated processes are hidden.

First, each culture perceives and assimilates the norms inherent in other cultures in its way. This is the focus of many researchers who are engaged in the analysis of the influence of cultures. Samples of the behavior of Western civilization in different regions of the world (including the sphere of consumption)

Figure 3. The world interacting together
Source: https://corporatefinanceinstitute.com/resources/knowledge/other/globalization/

are included in another cultural context, sometimes have a completely different meaning, sometimes the opposite one. In the case of the external identity of the Western types of behavior, completely different things may be hiding: for example, the intention to be "as everybody" in one country to be seen as the person with different views in other countries. In general, external forms always have their fillings in the cultures due to the very complex intertwining of what is imported from the outside, with the existing traditions and norms. Emphasizing the specificity of each culture, the French explorer Thierry de Montbrial believes that when speaking about globalization, "we do not mean the unification and standardization at all" (De Montbial, 2006). As an example, the constructors of automobiles are not intending to create the "world car", which should satisfy all standards. It is not real. For example, the production of the French company Danone is determined by the different approaches on the tastes of the inhabitants of Paris (for French), London (for the British), Beijing (for Chinese), etc. The difference in taste, as well as in mentality will never disappear". From the other side, for example, the modification of the car model, or for example any food product, which is oriented on the different consumers are "collected" from the unified structural components.

Secondly, Western civilization itself is not homogenous. In this sense, the universalization of the world like the type of melting pot, about which very much was talked related to the American culture is not going on. It can be mentioned that today in the US more and more is used the metaphor of "salad", thereby emphasizing the preservation of the identity of each nation. Thus, we cannot always mean under globalization the westernization of the world.

Third, it is necessary to take into account that not always the exact western cultural forms are spread. There is also a reverse process, which manifests itself in the interest of the west to the Eastern religions, African culture, etc. Therefore, it is hardly legitimate to speak about globalization as a Westernization of the world.

What has been said, however, does not exclude the processes, which are connected with the unification of mankind into a single whole, i.e., what can be somehow called *mega-community*. It should be pointed out that it is a question of creating a global community in which existing national-state entities act as more or less independent structural units. However, the differences between the parts of this new formation do not disappear. Moreover, by some parameters, differentiation can increase.

Finally, the last of the aspects (or measurements) of globalization having been mentioned by B. Badie, "blurring" of the state borders, perhaps most reflecting this process (Badie, 2000). It is manifested in the intensification and increase in the volumes of various kinds of exchanges and interaction beyond the state frontiers, in all areas. As a consequence, one of the most important results is the formation of the world market of goods and services, the financial system, and the global communication network. In this connection, sometimes the concepts of *cross-border interaction or trans boundary processes* are pointed out.

If we talk about the spheres of development of cross-border processes, in the beginning, the borders of national states turned out to be the most transparent in the field economy on the European continent, when the restoration of the economies of various states having been destroyed during the Second World War has required close cooperation. This process then shifted to social, political, cultural, and other relationships, as well as to other regions.

Questions: how transparent the borders are; first of all, which countries are included in this process; what are the consequences and the others topics remain controversial. Nevertheless, several researchers, in particular P. Katzenstein, R. Keohane, and St. Krasner see in the process of transparency of the borders the essence of globalization itself. This point of view is shared by many authors (Keohane, Nye, 1977).

Transparency of interstate borders made the world interconnected. It is for this reason that some scholars, especially those working within the framework of neoliberalism, link globalization to interdependence, which, by J. Nye, determine whether participants or events in the system's parts affect each other (Keohane, Nye, 1977). A close understanding is found in the works of A. Giddens, who speaks about the intensification of social relations linking the different points with each other in such a way that what is going on in one place, is determined by the processes in a quite different part of the planet and reverse. Somehow can be considered, that there is the expansion and deepening of social networks and institutions in space and time by such way, so that from one side, on the daily activities of the people more growing influence have such events, that occur in other parts of the Earth, and on the other hand, the actions of local communities can have important global consequences. Developing this point of view can be underlined, that concretely the interdependence of different societies, their increasing, and not the leveling of the world at all "stairs" of the public reality create the essence of globalization (Giddens, 1995).

Transparency of interstate borders, caused by globalization, "turned" the previous ideas about the security, conflicts, their settlement; diplomacy, and other basic problems into classical studies of international relations. But most important, everywhere it has erased the rigid barriers that existed earlier between foreign and domestic policy. So, in the area of security, the immediate threat of one or a group of states, in the relation of one or several other states, goes into the background and gives the place for consideration to the problems of terrorism, separatism, nationalism, etc. The same can be said about the conflicts that from one side transferred from internal to interstate, or on the contrary. New conflicts require different approaches to their analysis and regulation.

Having opened the interstate borders, globalization has simplified the activities of the new, non-state actors in the world arena: TNCs, regions, and municipalities of the concrete states, nongovernmental organizations, thereby stimulating their activity and quantitative growth. But there is a reverse influence: the non-state actors themselves stimulate the development of globalization and the transparency of the borders.

Globalization affects all spheres of life. Th. Friedman notes that the global international system as a whole form both as domestic policy, also international relations, covering the markets, national states, technologies on such a level, which has never existed before (Friedman, 1999). At the same time, globalization does not deny the existence of Nation-states. The same E. Giddens emphasizes that one of the dimensions of globalization is the system of national states.

MANIFESTATIONS OF GLOBALIZATION

In the human sciences, the first were economists, who started actively writing about globalization, they paid special attention to the fact of forming a factually unified world market. According to the International Monetary Fund, globalization is just an increasing integration of the goods and services market, as well as capital. The global economy, says M. Castells, a Professor at the American University of Berkeley, "is an economy in which national economies are dependent on the activities of the globalized core. The latter include financial markets, international trade, transnational production, to a certain extent science and technology, and related types of labor. In general, it is possible to define the global economy as an economy whose main components have the institutional, organizational and technological ability to act as integrity in real-time or in selected time on a planetary scale" (Castells, 1996).

American researcher T. McKeown notes that within the first 15-20 years after the Second World War, the main indicators of international trade were approximately the same as in the 1930s-1940s but did not reach the level of 1914. The situation changed dramatically in the early 1970s. If the import of the developed countries with the strong market economy in the period from 1880 to 1972 was from 10 to 16% of the GDP, then during 1973-1987 this index reached 22%. According to the different researcher's position, until 2025 the average annual rate of world exports would increase to 7%. Especially great is the role of export of direct investment, which, according to the position of the various scientific institutions, will increase by this time, approximately 3 times (Lebedeva, 2007). Within the first two decades of the XXI Century, import of the developed countries in the structure of GDP prevailed 30% (World Bank, 2020).

In 1996, world import was implemented at the sum of about 5,2 Trillion USD, which is more than 2 trillion in comparison to 1986 (Lebedeva, 2007) and within the second decade of the XXI volume of the world, import prevailed 10 trillion USD (UNCTAD, 2020).

About world merchandise exports, in 1983 it was 1 trillion 838 billion, in 1993 3 688 billion and 7 379 in 2003, 17 198 in 2019. Nominal trade values also rose in 2018 due to a combination of volume and price changes. World merchandise exports totaled US$ 19.48 trillion, up 10% from the previous year (WTO, 2019). In 2019 world trade in goods was valued at close to US$19 trillion, while trade in services accounted for about 6 trillion USD (UNCTAD, 2020).

Transnational corporations and banks are in many ways the founders of globalization. As early as 1878, an American firm "Zinger" – producer of the sewing machine had opened a branch plant in Scotland. Today, the Coca-Cola Corporation has production capacities in dozens of "international countries in all regions of the world." This is called a simple "internationalization" of production. But at the same time, it is growing a circle of companies of the global transnational "citizenship", capital of which is attracted from investors from different countries; Factories and plants are scattered across many states and often change their location depending on the world conjuncture; the sales network covers different continents, and the management network is essentially cosmopolitan. "Global factories" are producing an increasing number of "global goods" from computers to toothpaste, the nationality of which cannot be determined".

Globalization of the financial sector means a sharp increase in the role of centralization of financial markets by integrating cash flows. They easily move around the world with the help of computer networks. If in the first decade of XXI the daily volume of transactions was about a trillion Dollars, this number was significantly increased in the second decade of our century. For example, over-the-counter foreign exchange trading rose almost 30% to $6.6 trillion per day in April 2019, up from $5.1 trillion three years earlier (Forbes, 2019). In this connection, as R. O'Brien pointed out figuratively, for a financier, globalization means "the end of geography". A key role starts to play in such financial centers as London, New York, Tokyo. They promote centralization in the area of finance. At the same time, financial markets impose their own rules of conduct on both - states and individual politicians

How are all those processes in the field of finance explained? According to scientists Ch. Kegley and Eu. Wittkopf, three key factors contributing to the globalization of finance are identified: the first is tied with the 1973-1974 oil crises, followed by a sharp increase in financial flows, which stimulated significant growth in investments and the introduction of new managerial procedures into financial management. The second factor was the introduction in the minds and practice in the 1970s and 1980s of the ideas of the so-called "deregulation of the market", according to which its effectiveness increases if the government does not interfere with the functioning of the market. Finally, the third factor, which has influenced the globalization of Finance – the widespread introduction of computer technologies in such fields, which allowed increasing sharply financial interaction and contacts beyond the national borders (Kegley, Wittkopf. 2010-2011).

At the same time with the process of globalization of trade and finance, the labor market is also being globalized. Here again, a huge role is played by Transnational Corporations (TNC). TNC entirely provides about 50% of the world's industrial production. On TNC is coming more than 70% of the world trade. Within the period 1985-2015, according to the estimations of the World Bank, by transnational corporations more than 15 million jobs were created, among them about more than 10 million job places in developing countries (World Bank, 2016). The number of employees in the largest TNC`s consists of several hundreds of thousands – e.g., General Motors in 2015 employed 708 000 workers, Siemens 486 000, Ford Motor 464 000, etc. (Kordos, Vojtovic, 2016). At the same time, more and more, since the 1970s, there has been a tendency towards a division of labor on a worldwide scale. The well-known American economist L. Thurow in the journal "World Economy and International Relations" brings the characterized example of the existing global manufacturing networks. Particularly, he notes, that "the goods can be produced in any place of the World, depending on the fact, where production will be cheaper, and be on sale there, where it will be possible to sell them by the highest price. Production chains can acquire a global scale. For example, an accelerometer (a miniature semiconductor chip, which is used as a sensor for a Car safety pillow) can be worked out in Boston, produced and tested in the Philippines, packaged in Taiwan, and mounted in a BMW car in Germany with the purpose, that this machine to be successfully sold in Brazil " (Thurow, 1996).

The division of labor is accompanied by fierce competition, which forces manufacturers to constantly seek new reserves for the purpose, whose products would remain on the market. At the same time, the Migration of the labor force has considerably increased. Particularly, according to the estimations of the UN Department of Economic and Social Affairs, in 2017 the world counted 258 million international

Figure 4. The global network
Source: https://www.nationalgeographic.org/article/global-network/

migrants, which is about 3.4 percent of the global population (United Nations Department of Economic and Social Affairs, 2017). In this regard, together with some negative aspects of international migration, it is necessary to point out some positive tendencies of migration for developing countries. Particularly, according to the World Bank Group report for April 8, officially recorded annual remittance flows to low- and middle-income countries reached $529 billion in 2018, an increase of 9.6 percent over the previous record high of $483 billion in 2017. Global remittances, which include flows to high-income countries, reached $689 billion in 2018, up from $633 billion in 2017 (The World Bank, 2018).

The development of the media is also a manifestation of globalization. The events on which the accent is focused form the public opinion virtually in the whole world. This in turn leading to the fact that the National Governments and international organizations are forced to react to events in the media. This phenomenon has gained the name of the "CNN effect", due to the Broadcasting Company, which broadcasts news 24 hours a day in many countries of the world. To that news are relied on the national television companies of the various states. Thus, the military actions against Iraq in 1991, or Libya in 2010 the world watched "from the picture" of CNN.

Development of new Technologies – Leading Factor of the Globalization Process

The political development of the world, more or less, but always was connected with scientific-technical progress, which during history not only provided economic and social growth but factually formed the political system of the world. F. Fukuyama in his article "Second thoughts: The Last Man in a Battle", which was published in 1999, has written, that the industrial epoch – the epoch of locomotive, railways, factories - created possible Weber`s theory about the centralized state (Fukuyama, 1999).

The scientific-technical development of the last XX century and the beginning of the XXI century radically changed the face of the usual state-centric model of the world. On the substitute to the industrial epoch, with its factories, enterprises, locomotives, and orientation on the natural resources (gas, oil, corn, forest, etc.), came other epoch, where the dominant position has obtained, from one side, high technologies and connected with their information, communication branches; from the other side – biotechnologies; the central resources has become the knowledge. Lester Carl Thurow called all of this as a whole "man-made brainpower industry" and J. Rosenau, without pathos noticed, that the high technologies accelerated the globalization process.

As a result of such changes, in the countries of the Organization for Economic Cooperation and Development (OECD), more than 50% of GDP is produced in the High-Tech fields. In this regard, in the USA even has appeared the term – new economics, which determined the fields, which are oriented on scientific, high Technological spheres of industry.

Within the new technologies the following issues are considered:

- Information-communication technologies;
- Biotechnologies.

Information and communication technologies occupy the world with high speed. Thus, based on the dates of the US official sources, in 1998, the number of internet users was doubled every 100 days, as a result, 100 million people were connected to the internet, when only 3 million people were internet users in 1994. About the internet users in the XXI Century, according to statistics, as of March 31, 2017, there are 3,731,973,423 internet users in the World, 49.6% of the World population. At the same time, it should be pointed out that Internet users' growth within 2000-2017 was about 933,8% (Internet World Stats, 2018). For comparison: for radio, it was necessary 38 years to spread information to over 50 million people, and for television 13 years.

By the rapid way is developing an electronic trade. For example, the volume of the e-commerce market grew by 13% in 2017, and its turnover amounted to $ 29 trillion; the number of online shoppers increased by 12% (there were 1.3 billion people) (UNCTAD, 2019).

Information for Consideration

It seems that new technologies not only format the new world but also change ideas about our planet. Thus, if earlier the world was described by metaphors, which were taken from classical mechanics, physics, and chemistry, where the core and periphery were the main structural elements, then for its forming structure the samples from the sphere of already new technology are more similar - the world appears as complex Web network on the example of the Internet.

Question for Consideration

Compare metaphors about the structure of the world, for example, the theory of world systems, which was developed before the active introduction of new technologies, and ideas about the future structure of the world according to James Rosenau.

Figure 5. Digital globalization
Source: htttps://www.newamerica.org/oti/events/digital-globalization-the-new-era-of-global-flows-and-what-it-means-for-the-united-states/

It is no dough, that the development of electronic trade by the agency of the internet introduces serious and significant changes in the organization of trade of those firms, which produce the goods and services. The traditional management of expenses, which are based on the analysis of the used resources, more and more give way to the management of the relations with clients. Under those circumstances' entrepreneurs – suppliers of goods and services concentrate their efforts on keeping the trust from the client's side, by offering to them an additional service and at the same time are trying to be more adapted to the disappearance of borders.

It is becoming a usual event that the high technologies began to gain a legal form. For example, in several US states, it is introduced the concept of recognition as a juridical norm the electronic signature. Analogical questions and as a whole the general problems, which are connected with the legal aspects of the determined electronic trade, are considered in such international organizations, as World Trade Organization, Organization of Economic Cooperation and Development, United Nations Conference on Trade and Development, UNCTAD, International Chamber of Commerce, ICC, etc.

Information for Consideration

One of the leading American journalists, an observer of "New York Times" Thomas Friedman pays attention to the fact, that the symbols of the bipolar world were a wall, which was dividing the world, and also "hotline" between Moscow and Washington, which was allowing superpowers, at least to the determined time, to control the development of the "dividing" World. Symbol of the end of the XX Century, as he considers, become the internet, with the help of which, all participants of the international community "manage" the world and at the same time, nobody has general control over them. Due to it, if during the epoch of the cold war the traditional question was focused on the fact, how many and which nuclear warheads possessed this and another superpower, today the same question sounds by different way? How successful is your modem?

Friedman Th. L. The Lexus and the olive tree: Understanding Globalization, N.Y. 1999

Main Characters of Globalization in the 21st Century

Question for Consideration

What do you think, what can be the symbol of the future?

The influence of *biotechnology* on political processes is less noticeable. What is done in this field, first of all, today is expressed as a curiosity of the experiences of scientists, like the ship Dolli or in fighting against the production of genetically changed products.

However, biotechnologies promise to resolve many problems in the field of health care, open principally new opportunities to fight against hunger, create new types of production, increase the length of life, etc. But at the same time, they provoke new challenges, particularly, which are connected with fact, to determine how secured for the health are those products, which are received as a result of the using the biotechnologies; how are the moral and ethical aspects of the interference in biological development, will the humanity be faced before the problems of the using the biotechnologies; how will be reflected the economic production of genetically changed products on those people, who are oriented on the production and consumption of the natural products; will the discoveries in the field of biotechnology be used by the totalitarian states and criminal groups for the control of the people's behavior. The last problem is especially actual from a political point of view. The consequences of the development of biotechnology, its influence on the political structures of the world, can become more important than the consequences of using high technologies. About it, particularly has been written by F. Fukuyama in his article: "Second Thoughts: The Last Man in a Bottle".

The problem of new technologies, due to their significant importance for the political development of the world, attracts the leading political activists. For the first time, the problem of new technologies was in the center of attention during the meeting of Great 7 in 2000 at the Ireland Okinawa. At the 55th anniversary of the Foundation of UN ("Millennium Assembly") in the same 2000 year, Secretary-General Kofi Annan noticed that the consequences of the development of information technologies, the internet, electronic trade, will have the same significance, as a result of the industrial revolution.

AMBIGUITY AND NON-EQUALITY OF THE GLOBALIZATION PROCESSES

Globalization is a comparatively contradictory process, which has many different consequences. In the phenomena of modern globalization together with the positive moments, there are several negative ones. Former Secretary-General of the United Nations Coffee Annan paid attention to the fact that the "profits of globalization are clear: More rapid economic growth, higher standard of living, new opportunities. However, in the contemporary period the negative reaction, because those benefits are distributed in a non-equal way" (UN Social Summit, 2000).

Two parameters: nonequality of globalization and its bad management – causes the biggest agitation. First mostly is connected with the objective processes, which are going on in our world and at the determined stage of the world's socio-economic development. The second parameter is mostly determined by subjective factors. From this, how humanity will be able to take under its control the globalization processes, is dependent on its future development.

Globalization does not present itself equally in all countries and regions of the world and not by all the aspects at the same time. In one group of the countries globalization, first of all, covers the economic sphere; at the other by the more rapid way is going on the process of the introduction of new, modern technologies. Thus, in South Africa from the beginning, the wide distribution was gained through the system of the distribution of cash machines (ATM), and also cell phone networks. At the same time, the standard of living of the African population was still very low. The majority of the basic population did not use not only modern technologies but even the usual telephones.

In connection with the geographic inequality of the globalization process, the Swedish researcher A.E. Anderson suggested the idea of the "Globalization Gate". Its content is connected with the fact that the different regions and cities are ready and trying different ways to enter into the globalization process. Thus, Canadian Vancouver is the multifunctional center of the North American Region, which connects three continents, and Hong Kong – the regional strategic net of the transnational industrial companies (Davitashvili, 2020).

Many countries in the world, because of several reasons (for example political isolation and self-isolation, technological or economic opportunities, etc.), Are at the periphery of the global processes. Even more, as a result of the high speed of modern globalization, which is determined first of all by technological capabilities, the difference between countries and different regions, which have the leading positions in the process of modern globalization with the other parts of the world is becoming more and more significant. It is going on the division of the population on those people, who use the results of globalization and on those, for whom those results are not accessible. As a result, it is seen as the new type of the formation of polarization in the modern world. From one side, the new centers are created, where the new intellectual forces are concentrated, new "intellectual branches" are developing, to which the new financial capital is "attracted". On the other side – there are criminalized spheres with a low level of education and living standards, which are outside the processes of modern communication and globalization in general.

From the territorial point of view, those different "worlds" have some networks. On the global level, it is formed by the developed "North" and developing "South" (on this difference the world community especially actively pays attention to those scholars, who work in the world system paradigm). However, inside of the comparatively developed "North" are created their "elite traces" in face of mega policies (for example Silicon Valley), policy and even urban blocks. But at the same time, there are created "islands" of outcasts, which are formed mostly from immigrants, who travel in the economically developed states to find jobs. From its turn, developed countries try to secure themselves, by creating barriers on the way of inflow of population from the countries of the "third world". In this regard, the French author O. Dolfius writes, "globalization – it is not only the opening of borders but their closure because the whole misery of the world is not to be transferred to those countries, which consider themselves richer and more privileged" (Chitadze, 2011).

Polarization inside of the various countries, also on the line "North-South" is gradually strengthening. According to several experts, In the USA, the fifth of families concentrate 80% of the national wealth. But, more clearly polarization is seen in the developing countries. For example, the incomes of the 10% of the richest families in Nigeria for 80 times prevail the incomes of the 10% of the poorest families (Maksakovski, 2009). As a result, those countries are faced with instability, strengthening of the internal conflicts, bad management, and further back from the countries of the developed "North".

It is more clearly a picture of the differences in the living standards between developed countries of the "North" and poor countries of "South". At the same time, this gap is gradually increasing, especially during the last years, due to the development and introduction of new technologies, which brought to the digital divide. It is not by accident, that during the gradual introduction of the internet, former US President William Clinton at the economic forum in Davos (January 2000), paid attention to the fact and predicted, that those countries, which will use the internet technologies, will successfully enter to the XXI

Main Characters of Globalization in the 21st Century

Century (World Economic Forum, 2000). Those countries, who will ignore this success, unfortunately, will not be able to be developed. In recent years, the problem of the technological gap has attracted the big attention of different countries and organizations. On the global level, the resolving of this problem is intensively involved in the United Nations.

Non-equality of the globalization development by geographic parameters brings to the strengthening the positions of its opponents (anti-globalists). It is seen as an attempt to prevent themselves from the globalization processes by the way of finding the specifics of its region, its identity. As a result, it is going on the acceleration of the regional or local aspects, which gained the name "regionalization" or "localization" of the modern world. One author determines it as a tendency, which acts equally with the globalization process, others are declined to consider, that localization and regionalization of the world is also the example of globalization, but from those points of view the tendency of the increasing the differences does not take the humanity to the "automatic division of the whole".

The differentiation is going on by such parameters, as fields of economy. One sphere is comparatively easily adapted to the new conditions and accepts technological innovations. To those spheres belong first of all the banking system, which practically fully is computerized. At the same time, the list of the branches of the industry due to the various reasons are not able to be adapted to new technologies and due to it, are remaining as traditionally oriented fields of economy. Accordingly, the people, who are involved in those fields, who have no connections with computers, the internet, and other innovations during professional activities, in general, are less adapted to new technologies used in daily life.

Not very seldom, those people, who are outside of the globalized processes in both, developed and developing countries, resist those processes and by this way try to abolish the differences. It has appeared in various forms: on the mass level – in anti-globalist demonstrations and meetings, which often are going on in such economically developed states as the USA, Canada, Switzerland, etc.; and on the level of governments of particular countries – in the isolationist policy. In general, significant differences in the level of development of the concrete regions, countries, and groups of the population can become the sources of potential conflicts. The inequality of globalization by the various parameters gave the reason to American author M. Castells to speak about the "global asymmetry" of the modern world (Castels, 2009).

According to the point of view of U. Beck, in his research under the title: "What is it Globalization?", he mentions, that "national state did not become old, even more, it is impossible without it for the purpose to provide the internal policy and geopolitics, political sources of law, etc. The purpose of the national state is also to politically form the globalization process and regulate it transnationally" (Beck, 2001).

Question for the Consideration

How do you think, is it possible to manage globalization, is it necessary to do it – or is it the spontaneous process, which is not subject to regulation at all?

Their difficulties have emerged before those who are involved in the globalization process. High speed of activities, the huge volume of information, the increasing the "price of the mistake" (for example the mistake of an operator, avia operators mistake can cause the death of more than several hundred people) take the people to psychological overloading, depressions, growth of mental kind of illnesses. This factor especially sharply affects industrially developed countries of the "North".

Another group of problems is connected with the management of the globalization processes. As a result of the transparency of the borders under globalization conditions, governmental agencies are becoming more and more difficult to control political, economic, social, and other processes. The examples can serve the financial crisis in 1997-1998 in South – East Asia and Russia when the states were not able to resist the radical devaluation of the national currencies.

The management with those processes is turned out especially complex if we take into consideration that globalization promoted the appearance on the global level not only of concrete international governmental and nongovernmental or commercial organizations and physical persons but various terrorist and organized crime groups. They have an opportunity to use the results of globalization in their interests. Especially dangerous this factor is in the information sphere, where the danger of information terrorism exists. Talking about management, it is necessary to point out that the delivery of information with high speed and its distribution can create the problem of the possible "multiplication" of the mistakes, about the consequences of which is difficult to make any kind of prognosis.

Finally, the problem of management and control also has the opposite side. The modern sources of information and communication give an opportunity not only for the criminal groups but to the authorities to invade by the easy way in the personal, private life of citizens, by the agency to detect their movement, payments through the cell phones, plastic cards, emails and other sources of communication.

As a whole, the problem of the management of globalization processes in a wide scene is formulated as a regulation of contemporary international relations and world political processes. Here emerged, from one side the question about the coordination activities of the various actors, from another – about the foundation of the active supranational institutes and mechanisms for the management.

CONCLUSION

Thus, "Globalization" is a meaning that has offered a wide choice of response, several terms have been quite so much used or abused. The term has been presented in different ways as a period, process, a condition, and even as a force. The resulting attributions and acknowledgments are diverse and always invite confusion. For sure, there is one side who will willingly argue for globalization's advantages, setting it up as a solution to all the contemporary political, economic and social organization problems. And there is an opposite party, who would equally loudly and convincingly argue that globalization has negatively reflected on the development of international society, first of all by establishing inequalities among the different states.

REFERENCES

Badie, B. (2000). *The imported State*. Stanford University Press. doi:10.1515/9781503618480

Castells, M. (1996). *The Rise of the Network Society, The Information Age: Economy, Society, and Culture* (Vol. 1). Blackwell.

Chitadze, N. (2011). *Geopolitics*. Universal.

Forbes. (2019). *Foreign Exchange Transactions And Over-The-Counter Interest Rate Derivatives Hit Record Highs*. Retrieved from: https://www.forbes.com/sites/mayrarodriguezvalladares/2019/09/16/foreign-exchange-transactions-and-over-the-counter-interest-rate-derivatives-hit-record-highs/#3a54d6e23c34

Friedman, T. (1999). *Lexus and the Olive Tree: Understanding globalization* (2nd ed.). Picador Paper.

Friedman, T. (2012). *Lexus and the Olive Tree.* Picador Paper.

Giddens, A. (1995). Politics, Sociology, and Social Theory: Encounters with Classical and Contemporary Social Thought. Cambridge University Press.

Internet World Stats. (2018). *Internet users distribution in the World.* Retrieved from: https://www.internetworldstats.com/stats.htm

Kegley, C., & Wittkopf, C. (2010-2011). *World Politics. Trend and Transformation.* Wadsworth, Cengage Learning

Kennedy, P. (1989). *The Rise and Fall of the Great Powers: Economic Change and Military Conflict from 1500 to 2000.* Academic Press.

Keohane, R., & Nye, J. (1977). *Power and Interdependence: World Politics in Transition.* Little, Brown.

Lebedeva, M. (2007). *World Politics.* Aspect Press.

Maksakovsky, V. (2009). *World Social and Economic Geography.* Aspect Press.

Modelski, G. (2000). *World Cities.* FAROS.

Robertson, R. (1983). Interpreting Globality. In *World Realities and International Studies Today.* Pennsylvania Council on International Education.

The World Bank. (2018). *Record High Remittances Sent Globally in 2018.* Retrieved from: https://www.worldbank.org/en/news/press-release/2019/04/08/record-high-remittances-sent-globally-in-2018

Thierry de Montbrial. (2006). *Géographie politique, collection "Que Sais-je?".* PUF.

Thurow, L (1996). *The Future of Capitalism: How today's economic forces shape tomorrow's world.* Academic Press.

UNCTAD. (2019). *Global e-Commerce sales surged to $29 trillion.* Retrieved from: https://unctad.org/en/pages/PressRelease.aspx?OriginalVersionID=505

United Nations Department of Economic and Social Affairs. (2017). *The world counted 258 million international migrants in 2017, representing 3.4 percent of the global population.* Retrieved from: https://www.un.org/en/development/desa/population/publications/pdf/popfacts/PopFacts_2017-5.pdf

Veseth, M. (2006). *Globaloney: Unraveling the Myths of Globalization.* Rowman & Littlefield Publishers.

WTO. (2019). *Global trade growth loses momentum as trade tensions persist.* Retrieved from: https://www.wto.org/english/news_e/pres19_e/pr837_e.htm

KEY TERMS AND DEFINITIONS

Actor: An individual, group, state, or organization that plays a major role in world politics.

Alliances: Coalitions that form when two or more states combine their military capabilities and promise to coordinate their policies to increase mutual security.

Asian Tigers: The four Asian NICs that experienced far greater rates of economic growth during the 1980s than the more advanced industrial societies of the Global North.

Barter: The exchange of one good for another rather than the use of currency to buy and sell items.

Biodiversity: The variety of plant and animal species living in the Earth's diverse ecosystems.

Civil Society: A community that embraces shared norms and ethical standards to collectively manage problems without coercion and through peaceful and democratic procedures for decision-making aimed at improving human welfare.

Clash of Civilizations: Political scientist Samuel Huntington's controversial thesis that in the twenty-first century the globe's major civilizations will conflict with one another, leading to anarchy and warfare similar to that resulting from conflicts between states over the past five hundred years.

Collective Good: A public good, such as safe drinking water, from which everyone benefits.

Collective Security: A security regime agreed to by the great powers that set rules for keeping the peace, guided by the principle that an act of aggression by any state will be met by a collective response from the rest.

Complex Interdependence: A model of world politics based on the assumptions that states are not the only important actors, security is not the dominant national goal, and military force is not the only significant instrument of foreign policy. This theory stresses cross-cutting ways in which the growing ties among transnational actors make them vulnerable to each other's actions and sensitive to each other's needs.

Democratic Peace: the theory that although democratic states sometimes wage wars against non-democratic states, they do not fight one another.

Development: The processes, economic and political, through which a country develops to increase its capacity to meet its citizen's basic human needs and raise their standard of living.

Diplomacy: Communication and negotiation between global actors that is not dependent upon the use of force and seeks a cooperative solution.

End of History: Francis Fukuyama's thesis that the end-point in the ideological debate about the best form of government and economy had been reached, with liberal capitalism and democracy prevailing throughout the world without serious competition from advocates of either communism or autocracy.

Environmental Security: A concept recognizing that environmental threats to global life systems are as dangerous as the threats of armed conflicts.

European Union: A regional organization created by the merger of the European Coal and Steel Community, the European Atomic Energy Community, and the European Economic Community (called the European Community until 1993) that has since expanded geographically and in its authority.

Exchange Rates: The rate at which one state's currency is exchanged for another state's currency in the global marketplace.

Floating Exchange Rates: An unmanaged process in which governments neither establish an official rate for their currencies nor intervene to affect the values of their currencies and instead allow market forces and private investors to influence the relative rate of exchange for currencies between countries.

Foreign Direct Investment (FDI): A cross-border investment through which a person or corporation based in one country purchases or constructs an asset such as a factory or bank in another country so that a long–term relationship and control of an enterprise by nonresidents results.

Functionalism: The theory advanced by David Mitrany and others explaining how people can come to value transnational institutions (IGOs integrated or merged states) and the steps to giving those institutions authority to provide the public goods (for example, security) previously, but inadequately, supplied by their state.

General Agreement on Tariffs and Trade (GATT): An UN-affiliated IGO designed to promote international trade and tariff reductions, replaced by the World Trade Organization.

Global Commons: The physical and organic characteristics and resources of the entire planet- the air in the atmosphere in conditions on land and sea- on which is the common heritage of all humanity.

Global East: The rapidly growing economies of East and South Asia that have made those countries competitors with the traditionally dominant countries of the Global North.

Global Level of Analysis: Analysis that emphasizes the impact of worldwide conditions on foreign policy behavior and human welfare.

Global Migration Crisis: A severe problem stemming from the growing number of people moving from their home country to another country straining the ability of the host countries to absorb the foreign emigrants.

Global North: A term used to refer to the world`s wealthy, industrialized countries located primarily in the Northern hemisphere.

Global South: A term now often used instead of the Third World to designate the less developed countries located primarily in the Southern Hemisphere.

Global System: The predominant patterns of behaviors and beliefs that prevail internationally to define the major worldwide conditions that heavily influence human and national activities.

Global Village: A popular cosmopolitan perspective describing the growth of awareness that all people share a common fate because the world is becoming an integrated and independent whole.

Globalization: The integration of states through increasing contact, communication, and trade as well as increased global awareness of such integration.

Globalization of Finance: The increasing trans nationalization of national international markets through the worldwide integration of capital flows.

Globalization of Labor: Integration of labor markets, predicated by the global nature of production as well as the increased size and mobility of the global labor force.

Globalization of Production: Trans-nationalization of the productive process, in which finished goods rely on inputs from multiple countries outside of their final market.

Globally Integrated Enterprises: MNCs organized horizontally with management in production located in plants in numerous states for the same products they market.

Good Offices: The provision by a third party to offer a place for negotiation among disputants but does not serve as a mediator in the actual negotiations.

Greenhouse Effect: The phenomenon producing planetary warming when gases released by burning fossil fuels act as a blanket in the atmosphere thereby increasing temperatures.

Human Security: A measure popular in the liberal theory of the degree to which the welfare of individuals is protected and promoted in contrast to realist theory's emphasis on putting the interests of the state in the military and national security ahead of all other goals.

Information Age: The era in which the rapid creation and global transfer of information through mass communication contribute to the globalization of knowledge.

Information Technology (IT): The techniques for storing, retrieving, and disseminating through computerization of the internet recorded data and research knowledge.

Interdependence: A situation in which the behavior of international actors greatly affects others with whom they have contact, making all parties mutually sensitive and vulnerable to the actions of the other.

Intergovernmental Organizations (IGOs): Institutions created and joined by state governments that give them authority to make collective decisions to manage particular problems on the global agenda.

International Monetary Fund: A financial agency now affiliated with the UN established in 1944 to promote international monetary cooperation, free trade exchange rate stability, and democratic rule by providing financial assistance and loans to countries facing financial crises.

International Monetary System: The financial procedures used to calculate the value of currencies and credits when capital is transferred across borders through trade, investment, foreign aid, and loans.

International Political Economy: The study of the intersection of politics and economics that illuminates why changes occur in the distribution of states' wealth and power.

International Regime: Embodies the norms, principles, and rules. An institution around which global expectations unite regarding a specific international problem.

Liberal International Economic Order (LIEO): The set of regimes created after World War II designed to promote monetary stability and reduce barriers to the free flow of trade and capital.

Liberalism: A paradigm predicated on the hope that the application of reason and universal ethics international relations can lead to a more orderly, just and cooperative world. liberalism assumes that anarchy and war can be policed by institutional reforms that empower international organizations and law.

Modernization: A view of development popular in the Global North's liberal democracies that wealth is created through efficient production, free enterprise, and free trade and that countries relative wealth depends on technological innovation and education more than on natural endowments such as climate.

Multinational Corporations (MNCs): Business enterprises headquartered in one state that invest and operate extensively in many other states,

New International Economic Order (NIEO): The 1974 policy resolution in the UN that called for a North-South dialogue to open the way for the less-developed countries of the Global South to participate more fully in the making of international economic policy.

Nondiscrimination: GATT principle that goods produced by all member states should receive equal treatment as embodied in the ideas of most-favored nations and national treatment.

Nongovernmental Organizations: Transnational organizations of private citizens maintaining consultative status with the UN. They include professional associations, foundations, multinational corporations, or simply internationally active groups in different states joined together to work toward common interests.

Pacifism: The liberal idealist school of ethical thought that recognizes no conditions that justify the taking of another human's life even when authorized by a head of state.

Transnational Religious Movement: A set of beliefs practices, and ideas administered politically by religious organizations to promote the worship of their conception of a transcendent deity and its principles for conduct.

World-System Theory: A body of theory that treats the capitalistic world economy originating in the sixteenth century as an interconnected unit of analysis encompassing the entire globe.

Chapter 9
Psychological Factors During the Foreign Policy Decision-Making Process

Natalia Beruashvili
International Black Sea University, Georgia

ABSTRACT

The problem of foreign policy decision-making has attracted attention since the 1950s. The study of this problem begins within the modernist direction. This is the direction that sought to apply the theoretical and methodological approaches of the natural and social sciences to the analysis of international relations. Political psychology has a special place in the given sciences. Since politics, including foreign policy, is the work of human beings, it is very important to analyze the motives by which they are guided.

INTRODUCTION

The formation of internal and foreign policy is a difficult process. Its key elements consist of the formulation and adoption of foreign policy decisions, and their character depends upon many factors. These are the geographical position of the country, the existence of military and economic power, cultural, historical traditions, as well as the type of political system, the social structure of the society, and individual features of political leaders.

Making foreign policy decisions may affect not only the country that initiated the decision but the fate of humanity as a whole. It became more evident after the Cuban crisis in 1962 when in Cuba the Soviet strategic missiles were placed and the United States of America (USA) replied by blockading the island. These decisions whether of the USA or Soviet leaders about nuclear attack could lead to an irreparable consequence. After awareness of this process, foreign policy decisions making, especially in the situation of conflict and crisis, became one the most important topics of scientific research.

For the present time, several directions and schools have been created, which are working on the problems of decision-making and finding ways for process optimization. These kinds of schools and

DOI: 10.4018/978-1-7998-9586-2.ch009

directions are overlapping, thus, it is difficult to classify them one by one. In such a situation, integrated aspects should be considered, that would be more interesting for researchers.

SELECTED APPROACHES RELATED TO THE FOREIGN POLICY DECISION-MAKING PROCESS

In political psychology, several approaches related to the process of making foreign policy decisions have been formed. Historically, the first approach and ideas based on psychoanalysis were presented by S. Freud and his followers. One of the founders of American political psychology, Harold Dwight Lasswell, analyzing the personalities of various political leaders, tried to explain the root causes of their behavior and the decisions they made in foreign policy (Yale University Library, 2020).

As critics of this field note, the tendency to study the methodology of psychoanalysis about the political processes and events ignores non-psychological factors that influence decision-making in foreign policy. This is why the use of psychoanalysis in international politics has become increasingly rare over time. Representatives of other areas of American political psychology focused on the personal qualities of political leaders, primarily presidents, and on the conditions under which certain personal qualities affect the process of making foreign policy decisions. They believed that in the context of a certain international political situation, especially during a crisis, the personal qualities of state leaders are of particular importance.

Within the framework of the process of making foreign policy decisions, the concept of the "Operational Code" has gradually gained recognition and is widely used at the present stage. From a general point of view, it includes a system of basic principles that guide political leaders in determining their foreign policy strategy.

According to the well-known American experts in this field A. George and O. Holst, the code of conduct primarily establishes the rules that allow political leaders to overcome obstacles in making rational decisions. These restrictions include Incomplete information about the situation in which the decision is made, insufficient information about the ratio of goals and means, which, in turn, reduces the predictability of the outcome of the decision (Chitadze, 2016). Significant difficulties arise in determining the selection criterion among the alternative solutions presented. The operational code also includes an understanding of the policy and its goals, general views on political conflicts and ways to resolve them, an understanding of patterns in the development of international political processes, knowledge of political strategy and tactics, as well as recognition of potential political opponents and partners. The existence of the operating code also considers the personal qualities of political leaders, their psychological characteristics, such as willingness to take risks, a propensity for adventurism, or, conversely, increased caution and timidity.

Another direction of political psychology was associated with the use of the neo-behavioral methodology. Its purpose was to model the personalities of political decision-makers. An example of the use of the traditional behaviorist formula is the stimulus-response principle, the main purpose of which is to explain foreign policy decisions. In this regard, it is worth considering the views of such an authoritative scientist as James Rosenau in the field of the theory of international relations. In the field of foreign policy decisions, the scientist identifies three phases. The first stage is associated with the leader's reaction to challenges in the field of foreign policy and the presence of an incentive to influence the international situation. The second stage is decision-making. The third phase includes the reaction of objects that were affected by the previous phase. According to Rosenau, the third stage indicates the presence of mutual ties in the process of making and implementing foreign policy decisions.

"Game theory" can be named as one of the popular modernist theories studying foreign policy decision making. The goal of the theory is to develop a course of action based on simulated political or economic experience. According to this theory, formulated by J. von Neumann and Morgenstern in the book "Game Theory and Economic Behavior", it is emphasized that every state that takes or uses certain foreign policy actions intends to defeat another state ("zero-sum is equal to the defeat of the other side" or, conversely, the state seeks to cooperate with the other side ("zero-sum game" - no one wins and no one loses).

This strategy must, on the one hand, preserve the legacy, but, on the other hand, cannot be permanently anchored in all future situations.

OPINIONS ABOUT THE DECISION-MAKING PROCESS DURING A POLITICAL CRISIS

Some researchers focused their attention on the process of creating a typology of the personality of political leaders responsible for making decisions in the foreign policy sphere. An example of such research can be considered the work of Walker. He proposed his concept of political leaders who made decisions during a certain international crisis. This typology is based on the motives used by politicians: the power demand; the need to achieve the goal; the need to support activities of a specific politician. The ratio of such needs determines foreign policy positions, respectively, the options for political behavior in the context of a specific international crisis (Walker, 1990).

For political leaders who have a strong need to justify their actions, but at the same time have a weak need to strive for power and achieve goals, the following policy positions are typical: Conflict in international relations is a temporary phenomenon, the source of conflict is human nature itself.

For political leaders who have a high demand for power and achievement, and at the same time a low demand for justification for their actions, the following positions are typical: Conflict is a temporary phenomenon because peace must always be maintained between democracies, peace-loving states; At the same time, the main source of conflict is the aggressive policy of anti-democratic, dictatorial states, therefore the main prerequisite for peace is the influence on such states.

Conflict is a zero-sum game, while the role of conflict is somewhat functional. All great dangers are a war that begins as a result of a policy of balancing lost peaceful opportunities, mistakes made, or actions of a potential aggressor. During a crisis, it is typical for such political leaders to exert forceful pressure on other states, that is, to make their own choice to resolve the conflict by military means. It is easy to see that in recent years this approach has become a priority in Russian political circles when making foreign policy decisions and actions in the international arena.

With the knowledge and appropriate approaches in the motivation and decision-making process, it would have been much easier to avoid conflicts. Conflicts, in turn, are a zero-sum game, their role in the development of society as a whole is negative, so conflicts should be avoided whenever possible.

COGNITIVE FACTORS IN MAKING FOREIGN POLICY DECISIONS

When determining foreign policy decisions, political psychologists also study cognitive factors. On the one hand, the already mentioned method of cognitive planning is actively used, and on the other hand, cognitive decision-making strategies will be studied. American political psychologists A. Etzioni, E. Janice, and L. Mann distinguish five such strategies:

A "gratification strategy" is when the decision-maker usually settles on the very first option that he or she considers a good enough opportunity, although he or she does not resist seeking more information and considering alternatives. It is enough for him to correct the situation by any means. This strategy is based on a simple rule: "Do what you did in the past if you got a positive result, and act against the result if the result was negative."

"The strategy of excluding parameters", in turn, means excluding parameters when making decisions that initially do not suit the leader himself. The "growth strategy" is characterized by the absence of predetermined goals. The deterioration of the international situation is the main motivating factor for decision-making in the foreign policy sphere. As soon as the situation improves, the impetus for action disappears. An "optimized strategy" is characterized by an increase in the number of alternatives being considered, at the same time, following his views and position, the political leader seeks to change the international situation as much as possible.

Instead, the "mixed scan strategy", developed by the famous political scientist A. Janis and constructed by L. Mann related to the decision-making in foreign policy has been presented. This strategy has seven stages. In the first step, the decision-maker considers the possibility of all alternative actions; At the second stage, all the goals that need to be achieved are taken into account; In the third stage, he deeply weights the negative and positive consequences of any decision; At the fourth stage, for more complete and accurate assessment of possible initiatives, he/she is actively looking for new information; The fifth stage - includes this information in his own analysis, as well as the opinions of experts, including those who oppose methods of action that were previously considered the best and even applied in practice; At the sixth stage, the leader returns to the positive and negative consequences of alternative solutions, including, if necessary, to the consideration of solutions that are unacceptable at the first stage; Finally, at the seventh stage, all options for the implementation of the selected actions take place, and at the same time, in the event of a given situation, fallback options are provided. According to E. Janis and L. Mann, even skipping one of the stages can negatively affect the decision-making process (Janis, Mann, 1988).

PERCEPTION FACTORS

Specialists who study the process of making foreign policy decisions take into account not only cognitive but also perception factors. This is especially true about possible errors that may be caused by the distortion of the information presented. The American political psychologist R. Jervis in his process of making foreign policy decisions sought to identify the causes and consequences of inadequate agreements resulting from errors of a perceptual nature (Jervis, 2004).

Within the framework of the foreign policy process, in the formation of characteristics of all participants in the field of political convictions and "examples" of the outside world, as well as in the process of the formation of procedures by political leaders based on the available information. The researcher paid great attention to the formation of foreign policy changes when receiving new information.

American researcher L. Falkowski tried to predict the "flexible behavior" of presidents. By this behavior, he sought to understand what opportunities each president had to change his political behavior as a result of the influence of new information. He conducted a comparative analysis of the decision-making behavior of various US presidents in the context of international crises (Chitadze, 2016). A key indicator of each president's flexibility was their ability to respond to new information.

The unsuccessful development of the crisis for the United States indicated a sharp influx of negative information to the leadership of this country. Consequently, the response to this information depended on the "flexibility" of the leaders. If their behavior did not change, this would mean the existence of so-called perceptual filters, which carried only the information that supported already formed leadership position, and prevented the absorption of "unfavorable" information indicating a real situation.

H. Laswell indicated that the foreign policy decisions making the process takes place through several stages. During the first stage – information is obtained, then - the specific analysis and recommendations based on the information received are developed, at the third stage-specific recommendations are formulated, which come into force at the fourth stage.

At the fifth phase - the solution is implemented, evaluation of the results of the solutions is implemented in the sixth phase, the seventh phase - the final phase of the cycle when the results are summarized and can become a starting point for new solutions. and hence, the beginning of a new cycle (Laswell, 1965).

KEY ACTORS IN THE FOREIGN POLICY GROUP'S DECISION-MAKING PROCESS

As the final word and most of the respondents rely on the political leader, he/she should be able to independently read the entire volume of information, and especially deeply analyze this information and work out in detail possible options for decisions and actions. Thus, making foreign policy decisions is a collective process. Several people take part in it, up to a hundred and even a thousand people. It is often talked about a small group of people - which are considered the closest associates of political leaders, etc. Therefore, foreign policy specialists study the decision-making process in small groups.

An increase in the number of people involved in the decision-making process, on the one hand, has a positive effect, which serves to increase competence in the process of assessing and analyzing information, as well as developing various options for decisions, but on the other hand, decision-making within the group has its drawbacks. In this regard, American political psychologist Janice, in connection with the practice of making decisions in the field of US foreign policy, noted that the quality of intellectual activity is characterized by a decrease in group thinking. In her analysis of the failures of American foreign policy, Janice highlighted the main shortcomings that characterized the decisions made by affiliated groups in the state apparatus. In particular, among these shortcomings, he singled out: reduction in the number of possible alternatives; On the course supported by the majority of the group members - an uncritical attitude, ignoring the information of experts - when the information provided by them can rationally evaluate the positive and negative consequences of the policy decisions and actions; Spend time discussing issues on which a consensus was initially formed; Ignoring facts and opinions that contradict the positions of group members.

A. Janis noted that in the context of foreign policy group decisions, there is a collective non-assessment of real risks. Lack of vigilance and unprovoked willingness to take risks, in his opinion, is a kind of group psychological disorder, to which the group has no immunity. The scientist concluded that in a group there is always a danger that independent critical thinking will be replaced by group thinking, which can lead to mistakes and the risk of making irrational decisions and actions in foreign policy.

Taking into account the conclusion of the American psychologist Semele, he experimentally proved that groups tend to make more dangerous decisions based on their results than the individual decisions of the majority of group members (Chitadze, 2016). But to avoid such negative impact, it is necessary to achieve interaction of participants within the required organization and within a small group, as well as to develop optimal interaction procedures.

This aspect of the problem was discussed by another well-known political psychologist C. Herman. He proposed his typology of small groups making decisions in foreign policy. Based on this typology, the following criteria are considered: number of groups; Redistribution of power; The functional role of the group members. According to the internal structure, Herman identified the following possible types of small groups: a group led by a leader; A group with an autonomous leader; Group with a leader-delegate; Autonomous group; Group of delegates; Standalone assembly; Meeting of delegates; Autonomous Consultative Assembly; Consultative meeting of delegates. The term "delegate" refers to a member of the group who represents the interests of certain structures outside the group and therefore has limited ability to express his or her personal views. Autonomous group members are free to choose their position.

Ch. Herman notes that groups differ in the time it takes to decide, they also differ in the way they develop a common position, as well as in their willingness to be innovative or conservative.

In the United States, where the president plays a key role in making foreign policy decisions, the methods of interaction between the head of state and his advisers and assistants are of particular importance (Druzhinin, 2009).

Based on a comparative analysis of the activities of several presidential administrations in the framework of international politics, A. George identified several theoretical models of foreign policy decision-making regarding methods of interaction with the subordinates of the US presidents.

The "formal model", in turn, is a balanced method of implementing foreign policy with strictly defined procedures and a hierarchical communication system. Free expression of different opinions is not supported. This pattern was typical of Harry Truman, Dwight D. Eisenhower, and Richard Nixon. However, within the framework of the formal model, you can find some differences in the options for its implementation, which are typical for any administration. In the Truman administration, the president himself had direct contact with ministers and closest advisers based on the alternatives presented and, based on this, made independent decisions in favor of or against one or another alternative proposal. Other presidents have assigned the duties of the "chief of staff" to one of the inner circles, and he has been given broad powers in the field of foreign policy decision-making (George, 1986).

The expression of different opinions is supported within the framework of the "model of competitiveness", therefore free communication can be established both horizontally and vertically. This pattern was typical of Roosevelt. He especially encouraged competition between his assistants and was willing to establish direct contact with subordinates for interesting information and advice.

The "collegiate model" existed during the administration of John F. Kennedy when the US president was at the center of his own communications system, which consisted of direct aides and advisers to the president. Their task was not to filter the information received but to analyze different positions following the instructions of the President. The President expressed his readiness to interact with all participants in the process of making foreign policy decisions, taking into account the most non-standard approaches and expressions.

Psychology of the Individual: The Personal Factor in Foreign Policy

In the first case, we are talking about the influence on a foreign policy of ideas and characters of individual, but influential political figures. Striking examples, in this case, are Hitler and Napoleon, Bismarck, and Emperor Justinian. When assessing the importance of the influence of individual character traits of a leader on foreign policy, the question naturally arises of the extent to which a person who has achieved power (or a group of persons) is the bearer of the dominant ideological, political, and social trends of his society and era. Within the framework of Marxist historiography, it was assumed that this personal factor is negligible, and every political figure is, first of all, an exponent of the interests of certain social strata and their material interests. It was in this Marxist sociological and economically determined paradigm that J. Stalin considered his activity, answering E. Ludwig's question about the role of individuals in history and his destiny. It is difficult to say whether Stalin was cunning when he spoke about the insignificance of his role and destiny in the historical process, but historical experience shows that the role of personality in foreign policy can play an extremely important and decisive role.

The example of Bismarck is quite indicative in this regard. Historians of diplomacy know, and many contemporaries understood, how subtle the Chancellor was to genius. The sobriety of his mind, flexibility of thinking and cold-blooded calculation, and the ability not to lose his head from success were the keys to Germany's foreign policy victories. The chancellor himself compared himself to a rider holding back a zealous horse, ready at any moment to rush into a gallop and get out of control. This horse was the united, rapidly developing Germany, whose successes on all fronts pushed her towards war and aggressive expansion. It was extremely difficult to keep society and the state apparatus from a big war. During the Franco-Prussian War, it was very difficult for politicians to stop the military. For example, the Chancellor had to make incredible efforts to prohibit the generals from taking Paris, so as not to provoke a reaction from the rest of Europe. A key role in this success of Bismarck and Germany under his leadership was played by such character traits as endurance - the ability to put oneself in the shoes of other political players in critical circumstances and not succumb to both one's own emotions and impulses and emotional influences from outside.

The personality factor in history is especially critical when there is no stable system of social institutions capable of reproducing itself and ensuring the balanced development of the state organism. As Henry Kissinger quite rightly notes, a political system, the success of which depends on the coming to power of geniuses like Bismarck, is doomed to failure. This was felt by many after William II took the throne. Von Caprivi, who replaced Bismarck, also understood this.

The influence of individual psychological traits on foreign policy is largely determined by the circumstances. In stable and well-established political systems with a solid institutional foundation and rooted traditions, the individual psychological factor in foreign policy may not have any significance. Although even such stable systems give us examples of people endowed with extraordinary talents and psychological traits that come to power in extraordinary circumstances, which seem to significantly change the overall balance of the prevailing forces and moods, people who come to power in "normal" circumstances "put up a cross ", but which proved to be indispensable in the moment of the crisis. Such personalities, undoubtedly, included W. Churchill, whose iron will, perseverance, desire for victory, and whose grip played an invaluable role in the fact that Britain survived the Second World War.

The influence on foreign policy, exerted by psychological disorders, manias, and phobias of political leaders, can be attributed to a separate category. Without being distracted by the notorious modern examples, here, first, it is appropriate to recall Adolf Hitler - an example worthy of special attention.

Manic character traits in politics are especially dangerous because they are often revealed and become apparent at those stages of development of socio-political processes when it is extremely difficult or completely impossible to change something for the better. Moreover, the very specificity of the political struggle, its inherent element of demagogy, and the need to appeal to the masses do not make it possible to correctly assess the psychological health and real motives of a politician's behavior. In particular, due to the factors of the need to "work for the public", many representatives of conservative circles in Germany and big business explained their support for Hitler's coming to power: they believed that his aggressive rhetoric, the texts he wrote were demagogy aimed at winning the attention of the masses and did not believe that he would carry out what he said. Moreover, an excellent understanding of the mechanisms of influencing the masses also gave reason to believe that behind the guise of a fiery leader lies the cold calculation of a politician striving for power.

Few people from the entourage of the "master of Germany" - the capitalist Thyssen assumed that Hitler was completely sincere, believing in his mission, a maniac, and if they did, they did not think that he would have enough talent to stay in power at the initial stage of his foreign policy career at the expense of personal conviction and will to achieve such impressive victories, which suppressed the latent resistance in military circles. How could one resist the Fuehrer if he went from victory to victory, if France and Great Britain, who had won the last Great War, gave in to him?

A completely different example of the personal factor in the political process and the psychological aspects of a leader that influenced foreign policy is the example of Mussolini, a significant part of whose foreign policy steps were dictated by his weaknesses, a constant desire for the personal assertion, and not some big, albeit generated by mania, idea fix. Analysis of Mussolini's foreign policy leads to the idea that its conductor was a talented demagogue, whose activities were largely determined by issues of prestige, and not real national interest.

A completely different attitude to national interests and foreign policy was demonstrated by such an "ally" of Hitler and Mussolini in the "fascist international" like Francisco Franco, whose pragmatism and endurance were enough not to get involved in the Second World War on the side of the Axis countries.

PSYCHOLOGY OF THE MASSES AND THE COLLECTIVE DRIVING FORCES OF FOREIGN POLICY

The collective driving forces of the foreign policy include such phenomena of collective psychology as a post-imperial syndrome and victim syndrome, geopolitical identity, national myths and historical narratives accepted by society, foreign policy traditions based on habit and ideas developed over time. One of such manifestations can be messianism, which consists in the desire for ideological and cultural-political expansion in the form of familiarizing other societies with their values, considered as universal, or the vicissitudes of the formation and development of collective identity, when a society is forced to seek its place in the world, colliding with hostile ideologies and alien narratives. All these phenomena, taking possession of the mass consciousness, form the political culture of the ruling classes and public opinion, which puts pressure on the government, thereby setting a certain framework for foreign policy behavior.

Historical memory and traditions of comprehending foreign policy reality strongly influence the actions of states in the foreign policy arena. For example, it was in this plane that Bismarck considered the policy of Russia to liberate the Slavs. To him, Russia's foreign policy line, aimed at crushing the Ottoman Empire, seemed idealistic romanticism, rooted in the dreams of Catherine II and devoid of any real political content. With such an approach, Russia's entry into the First World War could be regarded as irrationality. However, without going into the understanding of whether Bismarck was right or not, we can state that political activity is determined not only by material calculations and "common sense", but by ideals and values, dreams and illusions that must be taken into account when pursuing a foreign policy course.

In the context of the analysis of the political manifestations of collective psychology, the personality structures such as archetypes and superego, according to the theories of S. Freud and C.G. Jung, that might influence foreign policy and political decision-makers acquire key importance.

Archetypes are models and motives of behavior that arise in the collective unconscious, which have a strong influence on human emotions and are manifested in a certain way of responding. In favorable conditions for the manifestation of archetypes, the archetype evokes associations, thoughts, and impulses that distort the true intentions of a person. According to C.G. Jung, an archetype is a mental prototype of the collective unconscious, inherited by a person, and not formed based on his individual experience. Archetypes as models of unconscious mental activity spontaneously determine human thinking and behavior.

The concept of archetypes as unconscious ideas inherited by society is quite harmoniously combined with the concept of the "Superego" proposed by S. Freud - the super-I, or the I-ideal. Super-Ego - moral representations of groups of people, a system of values that has received the approval of society. The superego is formed by the environment and embodies the social traditions and values that, according to most of the society, each individual should correspond.

Archetypes and superego shape the value attitudes and motives of the elites that shape foreign policy. The manifestations of collective psychology may include post-imperial syndrome, victim syndrome, messianic foreign policy aspirations, which are becoming an unconscious tradition of the current foreign policy course.

IDEOLOGICAL CLICHES AS A FACTOR OF THE COLLECTIVE UNCONSCIOUS, INFLUENCING THE ADOPTION OF FOREIGN POLICY DECISIONS

Taking into account the tendencies rooted in the mass unconscious towards a certain perception and relaying of information, it becomes clear that the influence on the adoption of foreign policy decisions is exerted by the narratives widespread in public opinion and the prevailing ideological framework for comprehending reality. Vivid examples of this process are the foreign policy courses of the Soviet Union and the United States during the Cold War when decisions in the field of international relations were often made not based on pragmatic national interests but following the logic of an ideologically colored perception of the world, which allowed the Third World countries to receive substantial material help from two warring superpowers.

At present, the ideologization of foreign policy is most noticeably manifested in the actions of the United States and the European Union. First, it is associated with adherence to liberal values and pursuing a policy of multiculturalism. The value concepts formed by Western societies over decades of unprecedented growth in prosperity, supported by the traditions of the internal political struggle of parties, in which the controversy was based on attempts to justify the fact that each party rushing to power would better than others help to protect and promote these values, as well as support the ideological attitudes of multiculturalism influential ethnic groups and the opportunistic use of human rights rhetoric in the information war against the Soviet Union and the Warsaw Pact countries made the complex of liberal representations of Western public opinion and ruling circles the most important thinking matrix for making both external and internal political decisions, as a result of which liberal thought patterns become filters through the prism of which any phenomena of real politics and national interests are considered.

POLITICAL CULTURE ASPECTS IN THE FRAMEWORK OF FOREIGN POLICY

A separate issue of understanding the psychological motives of the foreign policy aspirations of societies and states is the identification of objective mechanisms that form subjective reality, the identification of those factors on which the values of individuals and the masses depend, and the motivation of their individual and collective aspirations. In the Marxist tradition, these factors were identified through the application of the base and superstructure construction - the study of the influence of the means of production, productive forces, and production relations on the socio-political development of society. However, in addition to such an economically determined approach, there is a powerful body of research concerning the importance of cultural factors that determine foreign policy actions of both individual statesmen and different countries.

This includes research by representatives of the civilizational approach to history - N.Ya.Danilevsky, K.N. Leontiev, O. Spengler, A. Toynbee, F. Braudel, S. Huntington, and others. Culturological and art history works, among which one can name the works of I. Tena, E. Fuchs, P.A. Sorokin, J. Hazingy, research in the field of collective values of survival and self-expression of R. Inglehart and K. Welzel.

The motives for foreign policy actions and assessments can be messianic, ideologically determined, or based on a geopolitically determined real-political foundation of national interests, which consists of upholding the political and economic benefits of a certain state organism.

As an example of foreign policy actions, the motives of which lay in the plane of pragmatically understood national interests, one can cite the foreign policy pursued by Cardinal Richelieu, who was guided in his foreign policy analysis and planning by the geopolitical realities of the position of the French kingdom.

A pragmatic approach in foreign and domestic policy allowed the cardinal to fight the Protestants at home while concluding alliances with Protestant states in the foreign policy arena. The greatness of Louis XIII and the interests of France were for the cardinal the main motive and measure of the expediency of foreign policy actions, while for his comrade-in-arms, the "gray cardinal" Father Joseph, the main motive for political action was dreams of the messianic destiny of France, designed to achieve domination in Europe to spread the light of the Catholic faith to the rest of the world.

Having taken root, messianic or pragmatic tendencies of foreign policy motivation can acquire the characteristics features of the psychology of the managerial class, representatives of the ruling elite, and entire political institutions.

Sometimes the traditional ideology as an ideal beginning is closely intertwined with real-political, but not always perceived motives. For example, in the developed countries of the West, such as the development of events led to the fact that the democratic pressure of society and the high importance of the values of the highest levels of the pyramid of needs of A. Maslow led to a complete lack of public understanding of the real problems of the rest of the world, a significant part of which, due to its poverty and social contradictions, cannot accept "Western values". Moreover, representatives of the political class of Western countries are also incapable of perceiving objective reality based on a comprehensive analysis and understanding of global development trends outside the context of ideological ought settings and ideas about how "should be".

Henry Kissinger has dedicated a number of his works to understand the formation of foreign policy from the point of view of the historically established tradition of building diplomatic relations with the outside world of specific societies. He was able to convincingly substantiate the psychological features of the worldview of some non-Western societies, reflected in their diplomatic practice and assessments of the foreign policy situation. If earlier classical works devoted to diplomacy issues, as a rule, relied on the comprehension of Western European experience, today it is becoming increasingly important to model alternative possibilities for the development of the world order.

The geopolitical conditions for the development of each specific state organism and its institutions, as well as the historically formed national character, are critical starting points for the analysis of foreign policy aspirations and actions of actors in the foreign policy arena.

CONCLUSION

When predicting the adoption of foreign policy decisions by the political leadership of a country, it is necessary to take into account the entire complex of the considered factors that form the assessments and actions of foreign policy players, since psychological, subjective reasons largely lie at the basis of their assessments, motives, and actions.

The study of the psychological motives of the actions of political counterparts is necessary, first of all, to coordinate the foreign policy courses of states, to be able to cross-cultural analysis of the reasons for the actions of the players of world politics. This is important in order not to measure the state, society, and political regimes that are at other stages of socio-economic and socio-cultural development with their yardstick and value standards and concepts, thereby avoiding the mistakes that representatives of the Western world might be making, trying to conduct foreign policy, guided by their own historical experience of socio-cultural development and economic growth. Such a policy might not take into account the prevailing culture of other societies and the civilizational laws of their development and lead to directly opposite results. Meanwhile, the complexity of the current period of development of the global system of international relations lies in the coordination and harmonization of the worldview positions of foreign policy actors as spokesmen and carriers of value attitudes of certain cultures, civilizations, and ideological trends that are unlike each other.

Only an objective and careful study of the subjective factors of goal-setting of foreign policy players will make it possible to build a relatively stable world order acceptable to most states and based on common sense, a balanced choice of ways for further development in the specific conditions of a possible mutually beneficial future, and not in abstract categories of romanticized construction that are divorced from the real world.

Recently, more and more attention in economic science is acquiring a direction called "behavioral economics", whose tasks include identifying the patterns of the irrational principle in the financial and economic activities of a person, however, given the knowledge accumulated by mankind in the fields of sciences about society and man, it is natural to say that the time has come, in parallel with mass and political psychology, to actively develop a direction of knowledge called "behavioral political science".

REFERENCES

Chitadze. (2016). *Political science*. International Black Sea University.

Drujinin. (2009). *Psychology*. Edition Piter.

Etzioni, A. (1988). *The Moral Dimension: Toward a New Economics*. The Free Press.

Etzioni, A. (2012). *Hot Spots: American Foreign Policy in a Post-Human-Rights World*. Transaction Publishers.

Gleason, S. E., & Langer, W. (2013). *The Undeclared War, 1940–1941. The World Crisis and American Foreign Policy Paperback*. Literary Licensing.

Jervis, R. (2004). The Implications of Prospect Theory For Human Nature And Values. *Political Psychology, 25*(2), 163–176. doi:10.1111/j.1467-9221.2004.00367.x

Lasswell, H. D. (1984). *Manuscripts and Archives*. Yale University Library.

Laswell, H. (1950). *World Politics and Personal Insecurity*. The Free Press.

Miller, G. A., Galanter, E., & Pribram, K. (1986). *Plans and the Structure of Behavior*. Adams Bannister Cox Pubs.

Morgan, G. A. (1988). *Human Resource Management*. Academic Press.

Rosenau, J. (2007). *People Count! Networked Individuals in Global Politics (International Studies Intensives)*. Academic Press.

Walker, S. G. (1990). The Evolution of Operational Code Analysis. *Political Psychology, 11*(2), 403. doi:10.2307/3791696

Chapter 10
The Branding of Political Leaders:
Hamid Karzai as a Political Brand and His Matrix of Brand Awareness and Positive Image

Kakhaber Djakeli
International Black Sea University, Georgia

ABSTRACT

This chapter explores the success secrets of political figures, described by the matrix of brand awareness and a positive image. The leaders became famous in the political scene, geniuses, or felt the time and changed themselves according to the time. Can we explore their secrets of success? According to the hypothesis of the research, all is learnable, and the answer is, yes, we can. According to the theory of the matrix of brand awareness and a positive image, we can guess what should be done to become stronger politicians and when to start new performance in the market of politics.

INTRODUCTION

"Two fundamentally important questions marketers face are: What do different brands mean to consumers? And how does the brand knowledge of consumers affect their response to marketing activity? The basic premise of the CBBE model is that the power of a brand lies in what customers have learned, felt, seen, and heard about the brand, as a result of their experiences over time. In other words, the power of a brand lies in what resides in the minds of customers" (Keller, 2011).

From the view of the Customer-Based Brand Equity model, it is seen that brand knowledge is the key to creating brand equity; hence brand knowledge establishes the difference between products, services, ideas, persons. Brand Knowledge is standing on two main components: Brand Awareness and Brand Image. Brand awareness is "related to the strength of the brand node or trace in memory, which we can

DOI: 10.4018/978-1-7998-9586-2.ch010

measure as the consumer's ability to identify the brand under different conditions" (Rossiter and Percy, 1987).

Brand awareness of customers to political brands and their image, in relation to the time they spent in politics, is represented by the Matrix of Brand Awareness and Positive Image MBAPI (Djakeli, 2012).

Figure 1. Matrix of brand awareness and positive image (Djakeli, 2012)

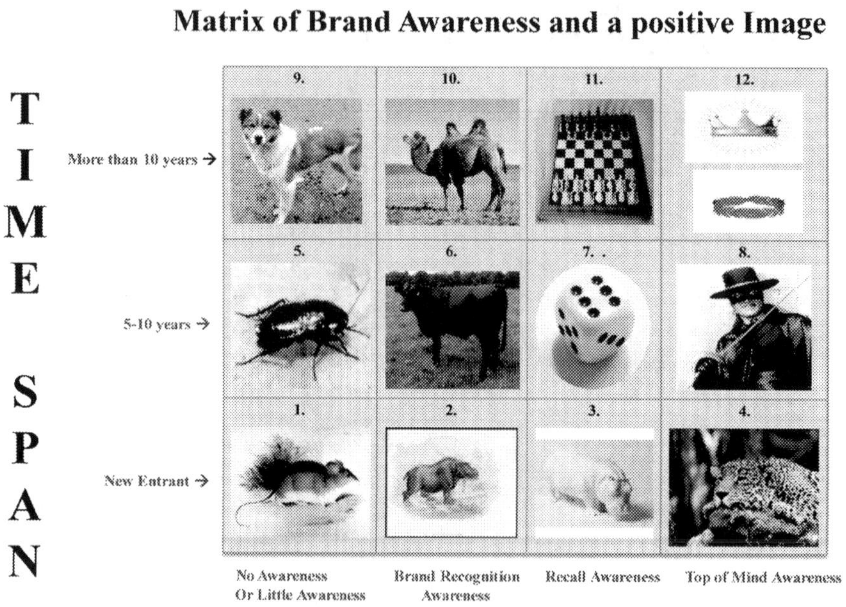

CONCEPT OF BRAND AWARENESS AND THE MATRIX OF BRAND AWARENESS AND A POSITIVE IMAGE (MBAPI)

The concept of Brand awareness is measuring consumers' knowledge of a brand's existence. Brand awareness is crucial to differentiating your product from other similar products and competitors. Brand awareness includes both brand recognition as well as brand recall. **Brand recognition** is the ability of the consumer to recognize prior knowledge of the brand when they are asked questions about that brand or when they are shown that specific brand, i.e., the consumers can differentiate the brand as having been earlier noticed or heard. While **the brand recall** is the potential of the customer to recover a brand from his memory when given the product class/category, needs satisfied by that category or buying scenario as a signal. We may ask ourselves, is brand awareness all that important? The answer is: There are few things more worthwhile than investing time in your brand's awareness. It can play a major role in purchasing decisions. The reality is, the more aware consumers are of your product and your brand, the more likely they are to buy from you **(Gustafson, et al, 2007).**

The important point about an image' (whether a company, brand, or anything else) is that it is the result of processing information (Percy, L. 2008). Having cleared that image itself is the result of good

and positive awareness; we use awareness as a ground on what success should be built. We found it important to distinguish the following types of awareness and a positive image:
  - Little awareness or no awareness to political figures.

- **Brand recognition awareness with positive image-** This means that on mentioning the category, the customers recognize some brands from the lists of brands shown.
- **Brand recall awareness with positive image–** meaning that people having category need, for example needing encouragement from political figure already recalling one or two political brands.
- **Top of mind awareness (Immediate brand recall) means top positive image too -** This means that on mentioning the category, the first brand that the customer recalls from his mind is the top brand with great political chances.

The Concept of Matrix of Brand Awareness and a Positive Image: the MBAPI aims to serve as an effective tool either for experienced or start-up politicians and their marketing teams to plan how to build their political brand development, to go through all the steps that will pull them to the political arena and help them to climb. The article aims to support political theorists and practitioners to bring new or encourage already existing political figures to the top political arena and make them, using this matrix, plan their future according to the type of awareness they already built and the time they spent in political markets or other markets influencing society and politics.

According to the time spent by political figures in politics or in other markets affecting political decisions and awareness they built to society, we divided them into 12 different types and titled them by different names.

- **Mouse** – A new entrant to politics. They need to have a great purpose and mission. They should create themselves with their method.
- **Black Hippopotamus** – This is a new figure in the political market, which already has brand recognition awareness.
- **White Hippopotamus** – Another political figure in our matrix is distinguished because of its success in its activities. The Society monitors (observes) them and they really can achieve great success if they set missions and purposes, and also the will to possess the whole political arena. Otherwise, they will remain as peaceful white hippopotamus.
- **Drowsy Tiger** –drowsy for power. Sometimes we call it a newly waking up tiger. In the current example, such a kind of personality can be a well-known businessman and public figure who achieved the greatest recognition because of his charitable activities.
- **Beetle** - Is a political figure with experience from 5 to 10 years. Despite its time spent in the political market, politicians under the image of "beetle" possess no awareness or little awareness. They are often associated with "beetle" because when this resident of the city appears, everyone is scared, but after the disappearance, everyone forgets about it. People carefully caulk cracks in the order it (beetle) not to appear anymore. We would like to advise beetles to take aggressive policy on the market to increase self-awareness and gain public sympathy for a certainty.
- **Cow** – Being in the political market for 5-10 years, this political figure possesses brand recognition. "Cow" has an opportunity to make its viewers surprise, on the one hand with its political experience and on the other hand with its feebleness. These political figures are not able to attract public attention and can't maintain this attention for a long period. All the time they are avoiding

shows, media, and the press. Often the public is unclear about what they are doing. We would like to advise these political figures to take into consideration and understand that the public has tired from waiting, and they must make at least one heroic and clever job.

- **Dice** – Possessing an excellent recall awareness, "dice" is in the political market for 5-10 years. When people need to get a category need, they remind about such kinds of political figures. The same happens when society needs a centrist politician with public administration and it immediately flares up their minds.
- **Zorro** – this noticeable political figure is in the political market for 5 to 10 years. Everyone thinks about him and hopes that he will save them; therefore, he has the image of Zorro and Robin Hood. Society expects a lot from him and over time he must show his goals to the public, identify his mission and objectives; the key is to find support, to act with maximum energy to achieve his goal, otherwise, on his next stage, competitors will make him the second-class brand.
- **Stray Dog** – Despite more than 10 years of political experience, its awareness is very low. Such a political figure feels that it has lost a lot of time, nothing was discovered and provided in the market by this figure, and accordingly, it is wandering like a stray dog. Their future is vague.
- **Camel** – political figures which are united under the image of "camel" are prominent only in case people find them with some formulated political leader or in a political group. They have great energy and political experience, but are not able and don't have the skills to use this experience wisely. That's why it is necessary to use them under strict supervision and management to strengthen a political team.
- **Chess-player** – chess-player in our matrix, is an experienced figure in the political market, possesses recall awareness, but doesn't have the carriage. Despite this chess player is distinguished with its clever ability to play chess. Political figures under the "chess-player" image are deep-minded and possess a variety of initiatives. In the free political market, this figure has less chance of becoming president but has an opportunity to become an influential expert on political issues.
- **CROWN**- at the Top of the Matrix is located Crown, which is submitted in two forms.
  1. **Laurel Crown**- a political figure who is united under the image of "laurel crown" is the most recognized politician in his political segment, among right-wing politicians, left-wing politicians, or among centrists. He can have a great influence on the country's social, economic, or political life. Laurel crown can turn into Golden Crown.
  2. **Golden Crown** – a political figure under the image of - Golden Crown – is the Top political governor of the country, the supreme leader.

As for advice to Golden Crown, it can be said, that such leaders should finish their work with dignity, to turn again into "laurel crown", and to become the most esteemed political figures.

As for Laurel Crown, the figure under this image, if it has not been a top leader yet, it must once again remind its voters, about its missions and goals, organize its supporters, start fundraising very strongly, to find the money, to develop a strategy using political marketing, and in case of compelling enough resources, it should have the desire to turn into a Golden Crown.

However, the current "Golden Crown" needs to take into consideration that the most important thing he should be able to do is to become the "Laurel Crown" - the most esteemed political figure in the political market.

The Branding of Political Leaders

Table 1. The MBAPI of Mr. Karzai and explanation of his political brand development (Source, the author)

	No or little awareness	Brand recognition awareness	Recall awareness	Top mind awareness
More than 10 years	Stray Dog	Camel	Chess Player	Golden or Laurel Crown
From 5 to 10 years	Beetle	Milky caw	dice	Zorro
New entrants	Mouse Motto: "To become a man like my father"	Black hippopotamus	White hippopotamus	Drowsy Tiger

THE RESEARCH AND THE RESULT - HAMID KARZAI AND HIS MATRIX OF BRAND AWARENESS AND POSITIVE IMAGE

Afghanistan is one of the most interesting countries for our study. Their leader Mr. Karzai has some unique art of leadership and his way of leading is challenging for political branding studies. What are the rules of success in the market of Afghanistan and countries like this? This question guided the research undertaken for this article to establish a special map of the Matrix of Brand awareness and positive image describing the way of Hamid Karzai to success. For the research, we used some books and special articles about Karzai and Afghanistan. Also, we undertake a literature review and desk study of the political brand development of this person, using public information.

On December 7, 2004, Mr. Hamid Karzai, was inaugurated as the President of Afghanistan. The long way he walked to this fantastic day. Let us start from his childhood. Mr. Karzai was born in a very rich, semi-royal family near Kandahar. Well known that his subtribe Popolzai had given the land to Shawn Duranni to build a City Kandahar, 200 years ago. The Karzai family, like a family of many leaders from Asia, had long been participated in the nation's politics. Karzai was even related to the Shah dynasty. Khair Mohamed, grandfather of Karzai was the deputy speaker of the Senate. The father was an active member of the Afghan resistance against Soviet Occupants and served as deputy of the parliament in 1960. Until his assassination in 1999 He was admired as chief of the famous and most relevant Popolzai Clan.

Hamid played golf, cricket, ride a horse, and had a very happy childhood. When his father become a member of parliament, the family moved from Kandahar to Kabul. This city is called one of the most beautiful cities of that time. Even mark and Spencer's opened their first branch there. Hamid was the fifth child of eight children of this family. When they moved to Kabul, this city already seemed like a very cosmopolitan one. The family respected education and young Hamid attended a very good school, even he was impressed by chemistry and wanted to continue his education this way. But as it is very common in Afghanistan, sons inherit families' interests in politics, Hamid followed the path of his ancestors. The troubles came from the conflict in Pakistan. The Prime minister of Afghanistan had been encouraging Pashtuns' rebellion against Pakistan and the propaganda was convincing the people that evil was coming from neighboring Pakistan. On 6th September of 1961 Afghanistan and Pakistan severed all relations and traffic between the two countries was halted making it unable for Afghanistan to ship goods to India, the traditional market of Afghan goods. The export fell and revenues fell dramatically. The country's economy deteriorated.

But Afghanistan had a king, who was entrenched in politics and fired the Prime minister who worsened the economic and political situation of the country. Soon King Zahir Shah encouraged the New Constitution of the country and the traditional representative board of all Ethnical Groups of Afghanistan Loya Jirga approved and signed the Constitution. In the New Constitution Islam was declared as Sacred. Royal Family members of a king, with exception of King himself, were bared to participate in Politics. Individual rights were championed and the term Afghan became a synonym of all people who lived in the country and not just the most powerful ethnos – Pashtuns. The parliament was bicameral. The low camera of Parliament, entitled as a Wolsei Jirga, gathering almost all political spectrum of the country tried to keep the balance between monarchy and a democracy. But soon in 1965 pro-Moscow oriented, Marxist Leninist political leaders Babrak Karmal and Nur Mohamed founded the People's Democratic Party of Afghanistan (PDPA). The 1969 Elections made conflicts between Religious and Leftist groups. The seasonal rains did not fall from 1969–to 1972. This caused widespread famine and an estimated 100,000 Afghan death. In 1973 when King was in Italy for health treatments, the ex-prime minister managed a coup in the capital and seized the country. Prisons began to be filled by Political Prisoners. The information about executions and torture shocked the country. In 1978 violent coup, that killed President and all his family members, started Afghanistan's bloody period, full of terrible events. The Communist Republic was born. Karzai,s father was imprisoned with other leaders. Amin seized political and military power. Almost 11000 leaders were killed by the government. Many fled from the country and some leaders from them: Burhanuddin Rabbani, Gulbuddin Hekmatyar, and Abdul Rabb Rasuul al-Sayyaf and their group members who wanted back the traditional Islam labeled the mujahideen, or "holy warriors." But in the country, a new leader tried to rule as an independent leader. Amin wanted good relations with Pakistan and China. He was too rigid to the Soviets. They were thinking about what to do to guarantee some stability in their southern border. But Soviets went to traditional dangerous way when they chose the violence to solve the problem and in December 1979 they invaded Afghanistan, historically one of the worst countries for occupants.

HAMID AS A MOUSE OF POLITICS

But our hero, Young Hamid Karzai in this period already is out of the country. In 1976 he left Afghanistan for India where he successfully continued his education, but there he started to know himself better. As he once said, he discovered that he was much reserved. Even he says very, very reserved. He studies how to be more open to others. In India young, Hamid learned the wisdom of Mahatma Gandhi, especially nonviolent ways to win the victory. He already knew from his father that guns and weapons were nothing in problem-solving. So he learns new ways.

In one of the interviews He says: "When I became an adult and began to know the world more, Gandhi was somebody that I admired very much and Mandela. He's still around, a magnificent man. Martin Luther King is somebody that came very often to mind and was discussed in some circles. But I'm most affected by Gandhi. The struggle for independence of his country, the way he did it through

The Branding of Political Leaders

non-violence, the tolerance he preached, the way he respected mankind as a whole, and his self-restraint. A wonderful human being".

But life has many checkpoints. Going to the university, suddenly Karzai is hearing about the Soviet invasion of his country. His immediate reaction was to take a bus as a student and to go something like 3,000 kilometers to the eastern border of Afghanistan to see the first refugees there. He had money and he wanted to help. He gave some money to young Afghans but met some pride. If you want to help me make me return – said to him some from refugees and these words forever left in his mind. Here starts his political life, but who is he if not a mouse of politics. Even though people recognized him as the son of their leader he was nobody, only a naïve student having no experience how to deal with risks of politics, war, refugees, and insurgents. As Karzai says in the interview to Mr. Kaplan in an interview for his book, Soldiers of God: With Islamic Warriors in Afghanistan and Pakistan, something occurred when he visited the refugee camp, located in Pakistan. The refugees thought that just because young Karzai was khan's son, he had the power to help them. But he felt ashamed because he knew he was someone who was spending his college years thinking only of himself and his ambition. He felt he was not a leader and the leader wanted. From these feelings and shame, he got a goal. "My goal from that moment on was to become the man that those refugees thought I was. **To become a man like my father** (Kaplan, 2000)."

HOW TO BE BLACK HIPPOPOTAMUS OF POLITICS

To fight for his country Karzai, already finished his university education, joined the Afghan Jihad wing of the Afghan National Liberation Front (ANLF). Like many groups fighting the Soviet occupation, this unit was based in Peshawar, to be in less than 100 kilometers (about 62 miles) from the Afghan/Pakistan border. But in differentiation from his peers, who wanted to fight to return to the old-style Afghanistan Monarchy, Karzai represents his different views for his country rejecting either the monarchy or Communism and supporting the idea of a new Islamic state. To be something like a differentiated figure you need an innovative vision and mission what Karzai elaborated.

HOW TO TURN INTO WHITE HIPPOPOTAMUS

Because he was from a rich family with all needed influences and followers and he was clever well educated and much familiar with people and languages he became a leader of planning and coordinating all efforts of Afghan fighters from Pakistan. He looked like an Eagle. As Kaplan described him "He was tall and clean-shaven, with a long nose and big black eyes. His thin bald head gave him the look of an eagle. Wearing a sparkling white shalwar kameez (the traditional male Afghan costume of baggy cotton pants and long shirt—although he often wore "Western" clothes like blazers and slacks), he affected the dignity, courtly manners, and high breeding for which the Popolzai are known (Kaplan,2000)."

ALREADY DROWSY TIGER

Even though he is an Asian leader, he learns many new skills that he did not have before. For example, in 1986 he visited France, Lille, to have journalism courses. Journalism and Public relation, content creation is something that is needed by all leaders. That's why coming back he is named deputy director of the political office of the National Rescue Front, also led by another political leader. In this New Role, he travels the world, meeting its great leaders, having speeches in relevant organizations, pleading for aid for the Afghan fighters. He was all times calm, much persuasive, and very diplomatic which helped him to attract people's hearts and provide fighters with needed assistance. He is drowsy to help his nation and hungry for more power.

BUT WHY DICE? WHY POLITICAL GAMBLER?

In 1989 Soviets forces left Afghanistan where they have lost from 30.000 to 50.000 soldiers. Even the country Soviet Union, demise and it was replaced by Russian Federation and some other independent countries. The Afghan government had been left by the Soviets was abolished and their leader executed. In the ruins of Soviet-Afghan and old Afghan Kingdoms, the new power was established with the very sacral name Taliban.

The beginning history of the Taliban is surprising and heroic. Some warlord had raped and killed three women. People for revenge visited their Mullah and asked him for help. The Mullah gathered students from madrasa and organized militia from them. These students and the mullah disbanded the warlord's unit and killed the warlord who raped and killed females, so the movement of Students of Madrasa began. Taliban was their fresh title, having some good ideas became the cruelest force in advance. But Hamid Karzai had contacts with them, he met also famous Mullah Omar and supported their activities. Was he a real politician at that moment?

Hamid Karzai explained his reasons in a 2002 interview: "When the country went to anarchy at the hands of various warlords and commanders, one of these people [Taliban] came to me and said, "Hamid, we were friends when we were fighting the Soviet Union in Afghanistan. Look at this country. What happened to this country? War everywhere, anarchy, looting, insults to women, insults to the sovereignty of this country. Can we do something about it?" I said, "Sure. But how?" He said, "Let's get together and get rid of these commanders and make the country all right." I said, "Fine." That is how the process of the Taliban began."

To be a political gambler is very risky in western politics, but either Asian or oriental leaders frequently play political dice, which makes them fail. Karzai changed his mind and went to more pragmatic actions in Afghan politics.

GREAT CHESS-PLAYER IS NEEDED

In 1996, Taliban forces took Kabul. They needed a representative to the United Nations. Without hesitation, they choose Mr. Karzai and asked him for new duties in a very respectful position. Suddenly, unexpectedly he refused. In this situation, Karzai shows his long-term vision and wisdom. He did not want to be blurred with bad people. For him, the Taliban already was some coalition of bad people making his country a Sanctuary of Terrorism.

In 1996 Karzai had a great visionary. It seemed that the Taliban will be hit by the modern world. Especially by Americans. Karzai is American. He appreciates Americanism. His brothers and cousins have many great businesses in America. The famous Restaurant "Helmand" belongs to the brothers of

The Branding of Political Leaders

Karzai. The American culture is the only culture where Afghan refugees flourish. Karzai was and remains a chess player, carefully assessing his political sympathies and empathies. He is an American guy.

Karzai never gave up. After refusing to be an ambassador of the Taliban to the UN he left the country for Pakistan and rejoined with his father. He traveled much to persuade people to help his country. Sometimes it was impossible but he overcome all obstacles. In 1999 his father is assassinated in Pakistan.

ZORRO - A BRAVE MAN IN BLACK AND HIS DOUBLE BRAVERY

Mr. Hamid Karzai seems to be the man of the word and sword. He proudly belonged to Popolzai Clan and he was trusted by Americans. The Popolzai subtribe was part of Pashtuns, divided into Durrani and Ghilzay.

Popolzai came from Duranni and contain the Saddozai clan. From this clan, many rulers of Afghanistan come. That year Afghanistan was ruled by the Taliban. They ruled the country by Sharia law. Already long period may be from 1841 when Afghans crushed the British rule, something like a Xenophobia (a fear or distrust of foreigners or strangers) had become an important part of the Afghan state of mind. But Karzai likes foreigners, especially Americans, Germans, French. He was waiting his time, but time wanted heroes and opportunities for double bravery and heroism challenging his manhood.

The first heroism and bravery closed to his tragedy. When his father was assassinated in Pakistan, he decided to bring his remains and bury him with high Royal respect to the family tomb. It was very risky at that time. Kandahar is one of the strongholds of Taliban warriors. Karzai was devastated at the loss of his beloved father.

If Karzai decided to bring his father's body out of Pakistan, home to Afghanistan, and bury him in the family burial ground, nobody could stop him. It was an extraordinary act of bravery and defiance. A procession of more than 100 cars left Pakistan for the Afghan city of Karz. Karz is near Kandahar, which remained the center of the Taliban. The Taliban, knowing the reputation of Hamid Karzai among Afghans were very afraid. They brought tanks in the city Karz, but did nothing, being influenced by the reputation of assassinated man and his son. The delegation with plenty of cars, went from Pakistan to Kandahar crossed the border. American friends were shocked but they felt the power of Karzai. Soon the fear of American friends changed with pride of appreciation. Karzai's bravery brought him new stature and prominence. Soon he was announced as a leader of Popolzai. The king gifted him, Sacred Koran, so he once again became the hero of his nation having all responsibilities and trust to rebuild the new Afghan Society.

The second heroism of Hamid starts after 2001, when he with his followers decided to march from Pakistan, through enemy terrain to come to his town and activate the second front against the Taliban. Karzai told his people that their chances were only 40% to win and 60% to die if they crossed the Afghanistan Pakistan border and try to move to their native place to gather more supporters. After you know the chances we have are you still following me – asked Hamid to supporters. All followers said yes and Mr. Karzai started his secret military march from Pakistan to his native town Kandahar. There he secretly met tribal leaders who asked Karzai to demand from Americans to bomb command centers of the Taliban. The worst enemy of Taliban traveled from village to village, urging people to fight against Taliban forces. After meetings with villagers Hamid took many of them to the mountains, but they lacked weapons and ammunition. So Karzai needed to call to Americans to demand their support. Soon Americans provided needed ammunition to Karzai through air transportation. Immediately when they received weapons from the air, they were attacked by strong Taliban forces. Karzai and his men had been rescued by American military jets that have been bombing Taliban forces. The recapturing of Kabul was near. On the 13th of November, they recaptured the capital, once the most beautiful but now ugly ruined city. Step by step most of Afghanistan was free from the Taliban, who escaped to the mountains.

NOW CROWN IS GAINED

After freeing Kabul, Americans organized a very needed conference in 2001, inviting all ethnic groups to build the government of Afghanistan. In December of 2001, after nine days' negotiations, all ethnic groups agreed to have a six-month interim government, headed by Hamid Karzai. But in the process of appointments as ahead of this government, misleading American missile, losing its course from military target hit the building where Karzai stationed. As a result, eight men were killed but Karzai was only injured.

Starting his office to govern the country Mr. Karzai traveled to find financial aid for Afghanistan. He invited investors to his country asked ethnic groups for support and innovations. In 2004 he encouraged his people and supporters to elect the nationwide President of the country. This was a great milestone in Afghan history.

On December 7, 2004, Mr. Hamid Karzai, was inaugurated as the President of Afghanistan. But as a first-ever elected president - Mr. Karzai received a very big responsibility to lead one of the most chaotic and poorest countries of the world.

- Laurel Crown- for Karzai is not even imagined. In 2020 he is a very active symbol of the nation, bearing plenty of terroristic attacks. It seems that Lord God supports the life of Afghan President
- Golden Crown – what Mr. Karzai bears today is strengthened by many of his advantages and some disadvantages.

ADVANTAGES AND SOME DISADVANTAGES OF MR. KARZAI

One of the most brilliant advantages of Mr. Karzai is his calm which is unchanged despite growing terrorism: "I've been through this before. I've been hit three times at summits. Did that stop us from fighting? My father was assassinated by terrorists. Did that stop him from fighting against them? I will not stop. I'll continue."-said Mr. President in one of the interviews.

But there are the following disadvantages:

1. His growing reliance on America made him look weaker and more dependent on America than ever before.
2. Taliban forces were not disarmed or eliminated as it was thought before. Even American President Donald Trump decided to have free negotiation with them about a ceasefire in 2020 March.
3. Big part of the country still is ruled by bad warlords. Taliban forces captured all of Afghanistan and its capital Kabul in 2021.
4. Illicit narcotic trade from this country is not stopped.
5. After the Taliban were defeated farmers of poppy products reverted their farms.

POLICY RECOMMENDATIONS FOR POLITICIANS AND THEIR MARKETING CONSULTANTS

Using a matrix of brand awareness and positive image, we analyzed one of the most complicated political market brands, Mr. President Hamid Karzai, whose political life is full of emotions hardship, bravery and kindness, tradition, and some non-discussable rules of the country. For example, Mr. President Karzai never appears with his wife because of Afghan tradition, which is refusing public leaders to show their consorts publicly.

To maintain his golden crown, such a great friend of American culture, who is Hamid Karzai, appears as a most traditional Afghan leader. Such things cannot be criticized by westerners, because only from marketing points of view, to support Karzai, we can find real ethnocentrism in the Afghan market of Politics. If Starbucks turned into China marketing to occupy the market segment of china, why Political Brands can be criticized for much ethnocentrism? Never. This seems to be a rule in marketing and many American and European Brands, behave following the rules of their cultures and communities. On other hand what is a Political Brand without its own national or community culture? Nothing is the answer.

Today brands are created not by manufacturers and plants but by cultures, and the same rule we can use to judge the development of Political brands, especially in Asian markets. Afghanistan's long period was and remained as a more closed culture that needs much knowledge and understanding from marketing scholars, trying to use inductive methods of case analysis. In this marketing study, we are using induction, trying to understand the Afghan market of Politics from the lives of leaders, like Karzai. For Marketing experiments and the future of marketing studies, it seems urgent to continue such analyzes in the future and assess the market. To use the historical analysis, it can be said that the political market of Afghanistan, being very normal before 1973, after the recession of economy, became abnormal. The next round and especially the coup in 1978 made the political market disappear from Afghanistan. Soviets threw the oil on the flame and the political market exiled from this country. But in exile, small political groups turned into islands of the political market and they promoted new political brands, one of them, the most brilliant and brave one we analyzed today.

REFERENCES

Abrams, D. (2007). *Hamid Karzai, Modern World Leaders*. Chelsea House Books.

Caplan, R. (2000). *Soldiers of God: With Islamic Warriors in Afghanistan and Pakistan*. Academic Press.

Gustafson, T., & Chabot, B. (2007). Brand Awareness. *Cornell Maple Bulletin, 105*. Available at: http://www.nnyagdev.org/maplefactsheets/CMB%20105%20Brand%20Awareness.pdf

Keller, K. L. (1987). Memory factors in advertising: The effect of advertising retrieval cues on brand evaluation. *The Journal of Consumer Research, 14*(3), 316–333. doi:10.1086/209116

Keller, K. L. (2001). Building customer – based brand equity. *Marketing Management, 10*(2), 14–19.

Kotler, P. (2006). *Marketing Management*. Elsevier Inc.

Percy, L. (2008). *Strategic Integrated Marketing Communication*. Elsevier Inc. doi:10.4324/9780080878294

KEY TERMS AND DEFINITIONS

Brand: Is a name, term, design, symbol or any other feature that identifies one seller's good or service as distinct from those of other sellers.

Branding Strategy: The long-term plan to achieve a series of long-term goals that ultimately result in the identification and preference of your brand by consumers. A successful branding strategy encompasses the brand's mission, its promises to its customers, and how these are communicated.

Political Leadership: A concept central to understanding political processes and outcomes, yet its definition is elusive. Many disciplines have contributed to the study of leadership, including political theory, history, psychology and management studies. Political Leadership reviews the contributions of these disciplines along with a discussion of the work of classic authors such as Niccolo Machiavelli, Max Weber and Robert Michels.

Political Marketing: A promotion process of political communication, where political candidates shares the ideas and promote themselves for voters. Political marketing is a strategic, technical, and crafted version of political communication in order to gain the public support.

Politician: A person active in party politics, or a person holding or seeking an elected seat in government. Politicians propose, support, reject, and create laws that govern the land and, by extension, its people. Broadly speaking, a "politician" can be anyone who seeks to achieve political power in the government.

Chapter 11
The Interplay Between Territorial Control and Violent Non-State Actors (VNSAs):
A Theoretical Perspective on the Middle East and Africa

Muhammed Karakuş
https://orcid.org/0000-0003-0078-8603
Adıyaman University, Turkey

ABSTRACT

The conundrum of the violent non-state actors (VNSAs) became the center of gravity in global politico-military settings especially after the disappearance of "patron-proxy" relationships. The threat to the authority of the central administration in internationally recognized boundaries by both deploying an assortment of tactics and more sophisticated structural stand points strengthened their competence. On the other side, social, economic, religious, environmental, and demographic conditions of the current century also contributed minacious divaricated frondeurs to sprout up. This chapter examines the interplay between territorial control and VNSA. There are empirical case studies related to the position of the VNSAs in the relevant literature, but little is known about the interplay between them that leads to governance functions and even foreign policy. The intention is to substantiate how these actors created legitimacy that ended up in almost all state activities although they are not recognized internationally.

INTRODUCTION

States and their relations with a broad diversity of Violent Non-State Actors[1] (henceforth VNSAs) in the framework of the international arena have taken attention especially at the turn of the 20th century and on the later period when significant chronicle regarding derivation and distribution of power of states and its exercise has been transformed through practices. The inversion mostly bred from the weakness

DOI: 10.4018/978-1-7998-9586-2.ch011

of the state that ultimately turns into failure. It is clear that there always had existed failed states (seen as lack of sovereignty) but characterizing the "failed state[2]" became prominent not only in academia but also within the international arena, especially after the 9/11 attacks. In those days, transnational terror organizations in the heaven of failed states (Rice, 2003) became perceived as the gravest degree of threat to global security rather than rival great powers.

The weakness of the state emanating from various conditions throughout the historical process, causes, objectives give rise to human rights abuses, migration, civil war, criminal networks and international terrorism. The recognition of the 'failing states' exposes the threat not only to its indigenous but also to the global security, commonly impaired by a serious intra-state conflict that conjointly also has a multiplier effect on destabilizing vicinal states (Cojanu, Valentin, Popescu, Alina Irina, 2007).

The state failure and the VNSAs such as frondeur groups, transnational terrorist groups, warlords, criminal networks and so on have been on the agenda regarding their integration and threat to the present world order. The turbulent environment resulting from weaknesses consequently have sucked international organizations and other actors into highly eclectic (due to ever-increasing interdependence) and anomic structural chaos. The Cold War period and its aftermath added a higher degree of state breakdown in return; it emaciated a 'social contract' between the ruling elites and the ruled crowds.

Although the crisis in statehood (more destructive than ever) is mostly perceived as an internal issue, its roots and ramifications have comprised the entire region even beyond. The layered correlation between VNSAs and territorial control is mostly embedded into the lack of factual capacity (an authority on the monopoly on violence that mostly results in civil violence and intra-state conflicts) of the state and reluctance to allow non-state actors to proliferate.

As in disruptive effects of state failure topic, the security environment has gone through fundamental changes over the years. Therefore, some other researchers have focused on the results of the failed state and claimed that the territories that are part of failed state turned into ungoverned spaces. These areas, as Cronin (2009) counsels, "exist not only in fragile, failing and failed states" but also in inaccessible border regions, isolated regions or inhospitable terrain. Indeed, they are not new, however; Hillary Clinton who pointed to the Afghanistan-Pakistan border region as a security matter popularized them. In these spaces, armed groups such as al-Qaeda, Boko Haram or PYD have carved out strongholds or provided the type of fertile ground to extend their regional and global impact.

The debate regarding these areas followed the concept of *'limited statehood'* that emphasizes the inability to govern and control the territory. Unlike the ungoverned spaces that are the result of a failed state, and the limited statehood resembles failed state (Nay, 2013; Robert, 1998; Schneckener, 2006) or quasi-state (Jackson, 1995; Malejacq, 2017; Stanislawski, 2008) it, indeed, is an orientation towards the Western model (Eurocentrism) and its benchmarks are the democratic, capitalist, and interventionist apparatus.

The literature on limited statehood criticizes the state failure concept and claims that most of the states can no longer be defined as *states* upon their failure at providing governance. Risse (2015) asserts that the state failure concept suffers from the understanding of statehood and it is not an ungoverned space where anarchy and chaos exist. Rather, it is a place where various actors provide social and political order. In these states where VNSAs engage in political and socio-economic governance, as well as their relations, became more complicated since most of the time they are interrelated with other states (Seeberg, 2016).

The civil war or intra-state war can illuminate significant characterizations and images of legitimacy crisis and governance models. The civil war normally evokes the chaos and perpetuated violence by armed groups. As recent studies unearth that most of the armed groups and civil wars form the various type of wartime social and political orders, as well as fulfil governance functions normally state have been used to function. In other words, they can be characterized as anything but chaotic.

This study regarding the 'state failure' or 'limited statehood' has anchored with the Weberian type of statehood, besides, it critically determined whether the states sufficiently meet these requirements or not. This paper will not demonstrate every single detail of the long-lasting conflicts in respective countries and their relations with VNSAs but will rather focus on the period related to the study, especially on ISWAP and YPG.

VNSAs feeding from global imbalances, power gaps and failed-state models having affiliates and organizations in different parts of the world shall be examined. Furthermore, how these violent coteries enervate the state and how a failed state creates a fertile environment for these organizations shall be indicated at the same time. Accordingly, the line of argument will be focused primarily on Syria and Nigeria besides other examples.

VIOLENT NON-STATE ACTORS

As the majority of the scholars acknowledge, insecurity generates power struggles (as realists claim) not only between major actors of the international arena but also inside the state. The 'security' issue becomes opening the Pandora's Box upon the proliferation of non-state groups, specifically the violent ones and their gaining status and influence especially in the Middle East and Africa

Contemporary studies divide VNSAs into several different categorizations. Some of them may include liberation movements, religious and ideological or jingoist organizations and paramilitary groups. There are also differences according to their size, their area of influence (circumscribed geographical area or a wider transnational scope), the way they finance themselves (through national, regional and global levels), their structure (hierarchical and centralized or hybrids of networks and hierarchies), what sort and degree of functional state weakness they have filled and the functions (unpredictable use of violent means and tactics) and goals (means to achieve their political aims). Still, one should keep in mind that they are not static but adapt in accordance to the change over time.

It is possible to see hundreds of different names and definitions used to define and categorize these actors however, this study puts those under five headlines:

1. *Warlords* are charismatic individuals mostly linked to their ethnic community and having a military background. They use the power not only against the state but also against their rivals (Rich, 1999). In this fertile environment, they participate in economic facilities even in the global economic system. These actors are more akin to pseudo-states than local militias by imposing taxes and seeking to exploit the resources of the territory they control (Malejacq, 2016).
2. *Militias* operate within the territory of failed states. They are composed of young males benefitting from money, resources, power and security through being a member. "Militias come into existence to provide security where… in the absence of effective security institutions that … challenges the legitimacy of the state (Jones, 2012).
3. *Paramilitary forces* or *auxiliary forces* are an extension of incumbent government forces are organized to support/replace the regular military and these forces have a clear vision and official alliance with the regime.

4. *The terrorist organizations* (anarchist, anti-colonial, leftwing and religious) as the sub-concept of VNSAs, use indiscriminate violence against civilian targets. They seek political change, degree of legitimacy and some territorial control through the use of violence.
5. Finally, *criminal organizations* (local and transnational in context) are prevalent secretively operating actors involving illicit activities and organized crime such as drug, weapon, organ and human trafficking.

Nevertheless, categorizing them does not mean they do not perform intersecting and overlapping activities. For example, although the VNSAs have been operating under different names, they may adopt methods and structures similar to those of states' armed forces such as governance policy. Upon the example, the question of 'states and how civilians respond to this situation' arises.

THE CRITERIA FOR STRONG AND FAILED/FRAGILE STATES

Before attempting to draw the framework of the term 'failed state', defining the approaches of the duties of a state is more useful. At the essential level, there are three types of definitions of statehood. The first one rests upon the agreement among its members and the authority of the state, known as a social contract. It emphasized the submission of the entire membership to the state and the duties of the state to deliver services such as social justice and security (Abramchayev, 2004).

The 1933 Montevideo Convention on the Rights and Duties of States, as the second approach, is based on the generally accepted benchmark in which a state must possess a defined territory, a fixed population, an effective government and competence to enter formal international relations. German sociologist Max Weber identifies the last approach. He uses some elements of the previous study but emphasizes the means of the state. According to his definition, a state must have; 'binding authority' over its citizens', 'monopoly over the legitimate use of violence', 'the capacity to provide public goods', 'generate revenue' and 'international recognition (Bellina, Darbon, Eriksen, & Sendig, 2009; Uphoff, 1989). Moreover, according to Robert (2003), a state should provide public goods, services, and security to its citizens against any types of political and criminal violence while ensuring civil liberties, economic opportunity and well-maintained infrastructure are the main characteristics of strong states.

For the case study region, neither the definition of statehood nor its applicability seems possible. The existence of the problem regarding the application of these criteria, since the state practice does not show a uniform and consistent pattern naturally obstructs the possibility of designing a common definition of the state failure. The reason for this might be because the structure of the international system has historically set very different rules for the interaction of the states. Although the perception of how the failed states are identified has changed over time, the most cited and by this way, mostly accepted definition is the one that maintains few or no functioning state institutions.

According to the Political Instability Task Force (PITF),[3] the 'state failure' is the state of chaos circled with revolutionary wars, ethnic clashes, adverse regime changes, and genocides from the time of central authority disappeared (Robert, 1998). Furthermore, The Center for Global Development defines failed state based on capacity," "legitimacy," and "security dimensions while Fragile States Strategy defines state fragility by focusing on administrative capacity by asking the questions of does the state still have legitimacy? can the state provide public services? Is there a state within the state and any intervention of other states? The other one is the Fund for Peace which is one of the most comprehensive studies that define the 'failed state' as a condition of the state that can no longer carry out basic governance functions such as loss of physical control of its domain, erosion of legitimate authority, inability to provide public services (Fragile State Index, 2017). The United Kingdom's Department for International Development (DFID) takes a different view to the concept of fragility. It analyses it by the will and capacity to deliver basic needs. In addition, the World Bank's Fragile and Conflict-Affected Countries Group analysis states from an economic and bureaucratic perspective. Lastly, the U.S. Agency for International Development (USAID) measures the level of fragility by looking at the state's economic, political, security, and social spheres.

Effectively an assessment of state weakness by addressing and defining their fragility is far from reality. Beyond the definition, state failure is not an ending process but a continuum of circumstances that afflict other states depending on where the state is located. The case countries Syria, Nigeria and other examples are clear examples of this fragility from the perspective of Weberian state analogy and terms of the Montevideo Convention. However, to analyse the interplay between the central authority power struggle and the VNSAs, the position of the latter is remarkable.

THE CONCEPT OF "FAILED STATE"

Sometimes states fail to do their duties. Concerning the global humanitarian crisis, the violent transnational terror organizations and the mass refugee movements dealing with these states are unavoidable. These countries are more likely to link with not only the situations above mentioned but also regional instability, environmental degradation, energy insecurity, arms trafficking and international crime. Instability in governance due to several domestic and extraneous factors generate one of the biggest threats, the "failed state" as President George W. Bush pointed out, "threatened less by conquering states than we are by failing ones (James, 2011)." This threat was not contained only to Afghanistan but many others (war-torn, poverty-stricken, and strategically marginal countries) which lost one of the most important state apparatus ' monopolies on violence' especially after the demise of the Cold War.

When the Middle East (West Asia) is examined, especially following the notorious 2010-Arab Uprisings era, the failed states and military intervention of foreign powers are common to see. The outcome has become apparent as states failed to provide a minimal level of functions to ensure the well-being of their respective populations within the legal state borders. Taking into account the number of states and their relative capabilities, desirable norms have become difficult to achieve for most of them. From this sentence, one can reach that state may be able to but unwilling to provide services.

With the increase in violence emanating from state failure to perform key functions many scholars, organizations and state institutions have attempted to frame the issue considering the implications on international politics. It is clear that there always had existed failed states (seen as lack of sovereignty) but characterizing the "failed state" became prominent not only in academia but also in a diplomatic arena in the aftermath of the September 11 attacks.

It is the reality that, depending on their ability, the states demonstrate various degrees of territorial control. Therefore, the reaches of state or institutions impact differ accordingly. In certain pockets, the state may impose full strength (border and internal control, security and trade) while less state control in the limited statehood or failed state areas.

Causes and Consequences of State Failure

Comparing the powerful states of Europe to the failed or collapsed states of West Asia and Africa, studies may end up with numerous factors such as colonial history, borders drawn without considering sectarian and ethnic/lingual differences and so on. 2010-Arab Uprisings era and its inspiration for change caused hammer effect on already impotent state effectiveness such as in Libya, Syria, Iraq, and Yemen and relatively in others; on the other hand, long felt state weakness and colonial past caused resulted in catastrophic effects in Africa.

The fact that the democratic discourses surrounded the years of uprising underpinned the continuity of the clashes in autocratic regimes. Foreign support and interventions mainly due to sectarian understanding and striving for superiority in the region to countries above enforced the emergence of the lack of sufficient legislative and executive governmental control and the monopoly on the use of force. The latter resulted in a vicious cycle for state failure in tandem with foreign intervention or vice versa (Coyne, 2006). To categorize the state failure, listing internal and external reasons is significant. The former category focuses on the relationship between the failed state and its population, state structure and governance while the latter concerns the relationship with the international community.

Internal Factors and Results

Failed States are frequently pictures of brutality and complete rebellion. There are no failed states that do not harbour types of intrastate wars. In the absence of peaceful outlets, frustrated groups are to adopt violence against repressive regimes and their internal and foreign collaborators, which at last results in the use of state violence on its citizens as it had taken place in many countries during the 2010-Arab Spring era.

Not only state violence directed at people but also the power of governance shifted from the state apparatus to other players at the local level. The internal conflict or its turns into civil war attract terrorist infiltration and operations in connection with the loss of control of contested state borders. As related to the classical Weberian state definition and Montevideo Convention, this chapter seeks to evaluate the governance dynamics and their failure prepares the ground for a more significant composite of conflict spiral, the emergence of non-state actors and their violent fashion.

Lack of Binding Authority and Civil War

From the Weberian perspective and within the Westphalian framework, one of the most important apparatus of the capacity of the state is the authority over the political space (Caporaso, 2000). According to Ruggie (1993), there should exist a legal reach of public authority over administrative tasks, tribes and believers. However, what most of the states confront in the MENA is the existence of diverse sub-national actors and identities (shaped around ethnic, sectarian, tribal, or local-regional loyalties) in respective countries, which is the basic reason it undermined the belonging of nation-state model in the region. In other words, states have failed to create a national identity that appealed to everyone.

Besides these factors causing erosion to the state authority, upheavals in the 2010-Arab Spring era had a direct challenge on the existed power of authority. Although many states could not handle the case and have turned into a victorious regime change for their citizens or have experienced transformation in their unique ways considering the conservative mentality of the Middle East, some others managed it with a mix of sticks and carrots.

Indeed, life deteriorates to a struggle for the most basic needs that those locals living under conflicts weaponized and create systems of governance to make their situation more predictable and livable (Khalaf, 2015). In this respect, VNSAs gets into the game by using potential recruits composed of insecure, rebellious, alienated and disloyal citizens.

Monopoly on the Legitimate Use of Force and Territorial Control

As a political science term, "the state monopoly on violence" points that the state has the right to use physical force against breach the law and only power for legitimizing actors in its use. It means that the state would not lose its capacity to enforce this monopoly in case it authorizes another actor the right to use violence. When states become weakened or failed, there exist some violent non-state actors that threaten this power of the state. In this state model, the army has a limited size and is generally undisciplined while police forces have been dissolved. Most of the time regimes in failed states may victim their people, which end up in escalating criminal violence within state borders (Rotberg, 2004). Here, when the monopoly of power of the state may be and most of the time is destroyed, the society reverts to the case of *Bellum omnium contra omnes* (the war of all against all).

An indicator of the state failure is the expanse of land the central government controls (Elden, 2009) or adversely the amount of territory violent non-state actors control presents the level of success they have acquired for their actions. In terms of the states in the Middle East continuing to possess legal sovereignty on paper; indeed, due to competing centres of power, they barely controlled only the capital city leaving large areas outside the boundaries of legality. Those areas became fertile grounds for various terrorist groups, insurgents or criminal networks (Yeşiltaş & Kardaş, 2017). These areas, in other words, more or less are under the control of the state monopoly, unlike the limited statehood where the central government cannot implement decisions and has a monopoly of the use of force (Esguerra, Helmerich, & Risse, 2017).

Capacity to Provide Public Goods and Economic Activities

The syntheses of economic, social and political underdevelopment engender structural instability where declining socioeconomic conditions (high crime rates) feed the political underdevelopment (corrupted bureaucracy, military interference in politics and so on) while decayed political institutions emasculate the socio-economic progress. It is what has brought about the failure of state institutions (religious and sociopolitical institutions, and economic health of the countries).

In other words, states are in turmoil or the civil war (mass dislocation, insecurity and massive sufferings) mostly unable to serve some basic sub-components of state to its denizens. In such areas, usually, new actors[4] offering essential social services have arisen. Nowadays, state authorities of Syria, Libya, Yemen and many other West Asia and African countries have not pressed their authority onto unregulated/limited areas due to both physical infrastructural networks have deteriorated (Rotberg, 2003) and the lack of capacity of the state economically and administratively. Rotberg (2004) claims that states can be ranked according to how many dimensions to deliver such as education, healthcare, economic profits, environmental surveillance, making the institutional framework, providing infrastructure.

LIMITED STATEHOOD

The reveal of the normative orientation of the Western model and the benchmark of the capitalist, consolidated and democratic state have created intense criticism since not all states are completely consolidated or failed one rather, they can be characterized as 'limited statehood.' Those who criticize the failed state concept, claims that statehood must be differentiated "as institutional structures of authority to govern and the state capacity to govern (Arda & Banerjee, 2021)." It is also argued by Esguerra, Helmerich, and Risse (2017) who puts forward that if statehood is defined as only providing public goods and services, it is no longer possible to distinguish state capacity and provision of services.

From this perspective, according to Stollenwerk (2018) "More than two-thirds of the world's countries display limited state capacity in some parts of their territory or several policy fields." In these areas, the incumbent government of the state does not simply disappear; rather its effects over the related territory have lost to a degree to implement the decision. These VNSAs, as rational actors, make strategic decisions in pursuit of their self-interests. Therefore, in these areas that are mostly engaged in civil (intrastate) war, they must decide how to interact with civilians. Some of them (different governance actors in these contexts) play an indispensable role and, as a central motivator, lean-to creates social trust or legitimacy (voluntary compliance), where the latter is both crucial start-up (to govern effectively they need a certain degree of legitimacy) and outcome (upon providing the essential needs of the individuals) of any type of governance.

In other words, whether it is failed state or limited statehood, VNSAs (domestic or transnational) usually establish a shadow of hierarchy or constellations of governance institutions within their jurisdictions. As a specific rebel-civilian socio-political interaction in which VNSAs participate in the administration process - historically present and common phenomenon- through dedicating a portion of their valuable and scanty resources. However, sometimes, the level of governance becomes much more sophisticated and complex than the incumbent government even with regard to the elections, diplomacy or providing essential needs (Esguerra et al., 2017). In this sense, the creation of predictability and order (the feeling of safety) by the establishment of authority -not like the stationary bandits who choose to protect civilians in exchange for their taxes- is one of the other parts of legitimacy.

The relevance of legitimacy and VNSAs is the undermining power of providing service provision by the latter- since people devote their will to other actors rather than the state at the time of the strenuous conditions of intrastate war limited statehood or failed state. The legitimacy of the population towards newly established governance system in these areas can be ensured by either setting incentives (through material such as money or security and non-material such as religious or nationalist motivations) or threatening sanctions (sanctions and credible threats or violence).

As numerous studies have made clear, whether it is minimal regulations to maintaining already established institutions, providing basic needs or inventing new facilities in accordance with the demands of civilians; the VNSA needs to complete three conditions to create rebel governance (Arjona, Kasfir, & Mampilly, 2015). These are firstly controlling of a territory, secondly, a civilian population residing in this territory and lastly the violence or the threat against civilians and other enemies. Upon the fact that rebel organizations mount a challenge to replace partial (increased self-determination) or full state (secession) practices depending on their aims such as religious armed groups aim to govern (i.e., ISIS) while organized crime groups do not. The following part will define how these actors implement governance functions.

GOVERNANCE BY VNSAS

The research about limited statehood (Risse, 2015) or frequently called failed states (Rotberg, 2004) that mentioned in the previous chapters and a variety of non-state forms of public authority have gained prominence in the last decades in the political and social sciences. Since the discourse of governance has been state-centric, its weakness of it has long been considered as a situation of Hobbesian anarchy (Furlan, 2020).

Since the demise of the Cold War (some types even became a critical part of the decolonization process), states have been under the threat of VNSAs than other nation-states. People become vulnerable to the stimulus of agitators and hatemongers when they encountered depredation and are denied access to essential services that the normal state should serve (Krasner, Stephen D., 2005). In other words, debility of the states to create, maintain and solidify the loyalty, offer public goods and security; substantial numbers of people who lack the means of making a living develop alternative patterns of affiliation (Williams, 2008) such as joining those violent organizations that usually offers functions mimicry of the state system.

Governance, as Risse (2011) identifies, refers to "various institutionalized (structural dimensions) modes of social coordination (process dimensions) to produce and implement collectively binding rules, or to provide collective goods." Yet, it is not a western hierarchical or top-down steering rather these modes of authority have the ability of non-hierarchical modes of social coordination that includes distinct local communities, indigenous stakeholders and sometimes-external participants.

The collective organization of civilians or armed groups within an area where the state's power is hard to reach or rebel-held territory for a public purpose (Kasfir, 2015), the rebel governance embraces governmental institutions but it also subsumes informal non-governmental mechanisms. This system of governance harbors inter-subjective meanings while ends up with not only the structures that provide certain public goods but also regulatory measures in the sphere of activities arenas. Armed groups like Al-Shabab and Boko Haram (both are adept at engaging with populations) have leveraged weak institutions in society. The prior, in Somalia, benefitted from the crannies of the traditional clan system together with discernible religious fissures, which pave the way to recruit, do radical preaching and expand its powerbase. By addressing the grievances and fluctuations, armed groups used it to win hearts and minds (Ali, 2017).

The rebel governance definition above is significant as it covers all types of non-state armed groups aiming to secede a piece of territory from the jurisdiction of a state (i.e. Kurdish armed groups), state capture (Hay'at Tahrir al-Sham or other rebellious groups in Syria), impose revolutionary ideology or just to survive; so that their organizational and operational besides political motivations change and evolve (Worrall, 2017). Armed groups having power over inhabitants in a defined region may play a different set of rules, unlike the formal governments at the time of intrastate war conditions. The legitimacy or the trust is established in traditional customs or moral codes rather than legal systems or formal coordination as in Nigeria and Senegal where patronage system or network is valid. Similar to this mentality, in Lebanon permission from Hezbollah is a must for including social services (Idler, 2019).

VNSAs engage in a wide range of governance activities, ranging from providing security against government forces and other rival armed groups (Bruderlein, 2000); providing shelter (Krause & Milliken, 2010), establishing trials (Mccartan & Jolliffe, 2016), meeting education (Bruderlein, 2000) and health needs (Heffes, 2019) including food production (Brück, 2016) and regulating trade and market transactions (Mansfield, 2018) and diplomacy. Moreover, VNSAs provides stability through institutions that are the formal and informal norms, patterns and rules organizing human daily interactions. Muslim Brotherhood in Egypt put into service a number of schools and hospitals (Brooke, 2015) while the Taliban, in Afghanistan, the operationalized justice system in their jurisdiction and The Liberation Tigers of Tamil Eelam (LTTE) in Sri Lanka provides police force for security and courts for justice.

In other words, the governance apparatus and the institutions eventually impress order and predictability together with regulating conflict and competing interests in human exchanges. Mimicking the government, the governance stands on at least four pillars (sometimes interrelated with each other) in the literature. The *first* one is the structure that signifies the architecture of formal and informal institutions, which compromises including systems of rules, regulatory institutions and administrative practices. The *second* one is the process that is about the dynamics and steering functions involved in lengthy neverending processes of policy-making. It aims the gather more dynamic aspects rather than stable. The *third* one is the mechanism that presents procedures of decision-making while *lastly,* the strategy asserts about design, creation, and adaptation of governance systems.

Although the governance seems systematic in its nature, it is not unified and most of the time not hierarchical besides it should not be understood as the prerogative of a formal government (Terpstra, 2020). It is an alternative to the government but not synonymous with it (Levi-Faur, 2012).

Why VNSAs Govern and in Different Ways

The question of why some VNSAs establish governance while others do not, took the attention of scholars. Following the collapse of traditional central authority across the Middle East and Africa created a power vacuum, VNSAs filled that power vacuum by taking control of large swaths of territories (Kaplan, 2017) and populations away from the state for extended periods. Then they face the same dilemma: from the rebel's point of view, should they initiate to control territory by establishing state-like structures (Weiss, Conor, & Coolidge, 2013) while the state in most of the cases confronts rivals for civilian loyalty. At this point, it is clear that *a state-centric analysis is no longer sufficient* to explicate ongoing developments related to politics, and security even goes beyond to redefine the concepts like statehood and anarchy.

The struggle to uphold a constructive role as "governance groups" what the traditional state actors used to offer becomes a political strategy. According to Nelson Kasfir, the term governance is "the range of possibilities for organization, authority, and responsiveness created between guerrillas and civilians" within a defined territory (Kasfir, 2002, p. 4). Providing governance, establishing rule-based administration and proposing guarantees to protect civilians opens facets in the study of civil war and comparative political analysis.

Over the years, VNSAs moved from an inept position to operate complex political and social entities by administering and delivering social benefits to the inhabitants once they began controlling the territory. Moreover, simultaneously, upon their degree of dispersion, influence, and effect on international politics, they establish more bureaucratized organizations and conduct advanced operations. In other words, they take the seat of states as an alternative governance against the traditional owner of "monopoly use of force", which at the end blurs the line between state and non-state much more than ever before, as another explanation of undermining the key source of legitimacy (Grynkewich, 2008).

The VNSAs are eager to follow effective governance engagements (Förster, 2015) despite how difficult (Menkhaus, 2006) it is to provide state-like practices such as the provision of security, the legal mechanism for resolving disputes and implementing social control (Ledwidge, 2017; Schwab, 2018b), police the population (Blomberg, Gaibulloev, & Sandler, 2011), providing education, health services and economic facilities (Bakonyi & Stuvøy, 2005) even trade (Raeymaekers, 2010) and banking (Hutt, 2004) –all are the key determinants to shift from a desultory insurgency to a stationary one to garner public support and to mobilize behind the cause.

The literature suggests that at the time of scarce resources relative to the state and deadly environment of intrastate wars, establishing highly expensive governance is a serious burden for them. In this environment, the VNSAs must decide how best to succeed their political, territorial, organizational and operational goals within this constraint. In a nut, they must be ready in strategic meaning in where, when and how they challenge the legitimacy of the state. Coordinating, monitoring, organizing, implementing and enforcing tasked with providing security by the police force, solving disputes by establishing a justice system (Schwab, 2018a), engaging in regularized extraction/ taxation (Florea, 2017), logistic and recruitment require valuable resources. Accordingly, the answer of the question -as the essential motivation of this study- of what drives VNSAs to provide services centres around the competition/ challenge/ operation between other VNSAs that provide the services such as Boko Haram against ISWAP or HTS in Syria where PYD (Democratic Union Party) and its armed-wing YPG (People's Protection Units) is active.

They (VNSAs to each other or VNSAs to the state) are a visible threat to each other in that harsh and competitive environment where each needs to maintain civilian support and legitimacy, which generates political concessions (Wagstaff & Jung, 2017). To this logic, according to Huang (Huang, 2016), roughly 43% of VNSAs established not more than three institutions while only 13% could create more than seven institutions. On the other hand, Stewart (2018) claims that only 29% of VNSAs provided essential services like education and health care yet most of them either provided no services or were restricted for only the use of their fighters and collaborators.

This study seeks to understand the reasons of rebel governance vary in character and digs into how civilians respond and shape this governance structure. Taking into account the position of civilians, how combatant interactions transmute from solely using violence to building a new order where civilians may take part and this structure contribute combatant's defence, respect, territorial control or its resilience. Research in this strand of literature highlights that according to the study Florea (2017) conducted, the governance activities are shaped by the threat environment, level of external military support, the organizational structure and resource endowments.

In part overlapping, the character and extent of VNSA order vary widely. Breslawski (2020) conceptualizes that armed groups create governance institutions either excluding civilians or including them similar to the other studies such as Arjona (2015), Mampilly (2017) and Stewart (2020) who focused on one dimension of civilian involvement, taxation regime or various mini authorities. For example, Arjona (2016) puts forward a distinction in the governance model as "idiocracy" and "rebelocracy." The prior refers to the armed group's engagement in security and taxation since civilians regard VNSA's institutions as legitimate while the latter is including other areas of service provisions to create this legitimacy. Furlan (2020) developed a seven-dimensional typology whose three is related to civilians, which are inclusiveness (taking part in governance), participants (regards civilians beyond subjects) and compliance (persuasion rather than using violence).

The VNSAs emphasized the legitimacy in a level that they become much more responsive to the civilian preferences in some places during the civil war. Baalen (2020) identifies two domains of governance. The first is responsive governance with civilian involvement in the decision on local governance, having security apparatus, taxation and service provision system. The other is the Unresponsive governance in which there is repressive security policy and unfair taxation but there is no sign of civilian involvement. During the civil war in Côte d'Ivoire in 2002, following the state fragile (Sany, 2010), the Forces Nouvelles

Table 1. Governance models

Arjona's Typology	Furlan's Typology	Baalen's Responsivness
• Aliocracy	• Inclusiveness	• Responsive governance
• Rebelocracy	• Participants	• Unresponsive governance
	• Compliance	

(FN) captured the Odienné that is close to Guinea and Mali. The life under the armed group permeated slowly that ended up even civilian representatives taking part in the decision-making procedure in local governance. The change from unresponsive governance to responsive one continued by the police force, education (Sany, 2010), rehabilitation of infrastructure and even public cleaning (Baalen, 2020).

There are many claims in regard to the potential governance facility of the VNSAs. First of all, as Loyle (2020) and Mampilly (2011) claims, the governance for VNSAs creates potential civilian compliance and cooperation. Non-violent tactics, according to Stephan and Chenoweth (2008), is one of the key weapons to be successful for achieving political objectives and attracting domestic supporters. In the same vein, many other scholars regard governance as a type of social contract especially during intrastate war conditions (Arjona et al., 2015) while others considered violence as a means of gathering legitimacy (Duyvesteyn, 2019). Under the umbrella of the social contract, the civilians turn into constituents who voluntarily support the VNSAs in exchange for service provision, financial benefits, personal security (Bruderlein, 2000), health care (Lillywhite, 2015) including justice. Whatever the constituents are opt for, the VNSAs may gather crucial information or intelligence, which assures violence that is more selective that prevents extra alienation. Secondly, the VNSAs may present governance provisions in order to cease or reduce the collaboration of civilians with the state (Grynkewich, 2008), which is in turn strength social contract with rebels. In some cases, civilians may exploit the opportunity in the territory where both the state and the VNSAs may provide benefits. It is also true that in some other cases both state and VNSAs may partake in the provision of governance. Lastly, VNSAs (especially those who are secessionist, irredentist, and ethno-nationalist) may use the provision of services to demonstrate they are viable or better off than the state not only to civilians but also to the international community.

Covering up all the information above, it is possible to categorize the literature about VNSA governance into three groups. The first group seeks to explain the variations in VNSA governance while taking into account the institutional differences, the impact of geography, the degree of constituents' participation and representation in the governance process (Pourmalek, 2021). The second group uses governance to explain the interplay between governance and military strength or between the use of violence and governance.

The last group focuses on the post-conflict process that includes state-building or peace negotiations. As in the scope of this study, it will first seek what sort of governance facilities do the case organizations provides so it will highlight the types of governance structure. Moreover, taking into account the case of armed groups, whether legitimacy (and the service provider role to gather legitimacy will be explained) is cemented or not will be discussed.

ISWAP and YPG persist to establish governance despite how difficult and costly it is. Using only coercion to have legitimacy, as they are aware, cannot take their relationship with civilians granted. Counting all the factors, legitimacy holds the central position, which is the existential element to cement the position, outbid their competitors and impose a new political, economic, or religious order (Huang

Table 2. VNSA governance policy

Empowers	Apparatus	Provides	Ends up
Territorial Control and Intelligence	• Security • Healthcare • Food and Services • Education • Marketing • Trade • Justice • Diplomacy	Legitimacy	Resilience

and Sullivan, 2020). Therefore, they involve in governance (if they do not have direct access to lootable resources or direct third-party assistance) since VNSAs are depended on civilians in terms of food (Brück, 2016), other supplies (Wood, 2003), extraction of natural resources (Ross, 2004), taxes (Piazza & Piazza, 2017), moral support (Malthaner & Waldmann, 2014), intelligence (Momodu, 2020) against state and other enemies, recruits (Eck, 2010) and sometimes cover (Oktav, Parlar Dal, & Kurşun, 2017) or sanctuary (Arjona et al., 2015; Z. C. Mampilly, 2017).

Even taking into account the well-supplied and organized armed groups, it is possible the witness civilian dependence on producing food for the very survival of the rebel group (Baalen, 2020). Civilians or recruits are usually needed for predatory armed group activities like natural resource exploitation, processed, and transportation. Civilian cooperation provides also a sanctuary, intelligence and coverage against state power especially in mountainous areas as in the case of PKK in Turkey.

ARMED ORGANIZATIONS

Non-state actors and VNSAs more specifically, in the last few decades, have evolved about political, social and military capabilities. For the last few years, the cycle of insecurity and instability has reached its zenith especially during the notorious Arab Spring where the states-system has not been successful to stabilize order. Hence, VNSAs have burgeoned in numbers. Over time, their capacity authority was buttressed by ominous, pernicious, and pervasive religious or political will. Thus, soon they started to play decisive roles, and have contributed to the rapid erosion in regional security affairs (Durac, 2015; Yeşiltaş & Kardaş, 2017).

Having the territorial and political imagination, after taking control of revenue-generating resources (smuggling, human trafficking, and oil), they have taken the steps of state-building. Both PYD and ISWAP benefitted from the insecurity and terrorism that empowered their position to construct governance factors to create legitimacy edifice. These are the provision of *territorial control, security, public services, and international and public diplomacy* (Khalaf, 2016), while its local legitimacy remains contested.

ISWAP

Nigeria gained its independence in 1960 and since then has continued to challenge by both local and external peculiar socio-economic and political strains besides one of the biggest outcomes of these

Figure 1. Nigeria

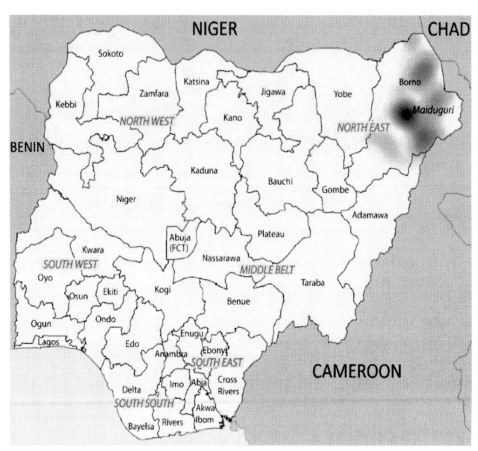

challenges, the Jama'atu Ahlis Sunnah lid-Da'wati wa'l-Jihad (JAS) or as mostly known Boko Haram (roughly translates to "Western culture is forbidden"). Because of this armed group and more others accelerated the challenges in the region it completely put the existing socio-economic difficulties into the second position in the contemporary period. The armed group, as a Salafist Sunni Muslim insurgency, started its resistance against the Nigerian state in 2009, caused the killings of tens of thousands of people, and triggered a massive and swayed humanitarian crisis beyond Nigeria to Cameroon, Chad and Niger.

Despite its various criminal and terror activities besides the enjoyment of a vast area, their action gained the world's attention in 2014 when they kidnapped 276 Chibok girls from the Government Secondary School in northeastern Nigeria. Following the support from the international arena, a Multinational Joint Task Force (MNJTF) that is comprised of bordering countries and Benin forces drove the Boko Haram to their roots, the Sambisa Forest. It followed to flare up the internal tensions especially after the Boko Haram's legitimacy weakened upon the continuous MNJTF pushbacks.

The year 2016 was the year of Boko Haram's split into two factions, Boko Haram led by Abubakar Shekau and the Islamic State's West Africa Province (IS-WA, aka ISIS-WA or ISWAP) led by Abu Musab al-Barnawi (Mohammed Yusuf's son, the founder of Boko Haram and previously served as the spokesman for Boko Haram under Shekau). The clashing personalities (Al-Barnawi and Mamman Nur vs Shekau) and religious ideologies (violent sect vs moderates) were resolved by the decision of Islamic

The Interplay Between Territorial Control and Violent Non-State Actors (VNSAs)

State (caliphate in Iraq and Syria, IS, ISIS or Daesh) leadership upon the letter sent by Shekau's dissidents to the IS leadership outlining the dispute. Abu Musab al-Barnawi, who questioned Shekau's leadership, pledged allegiance to the Islamic State despite all the refusal of Shekau to be under any other leader. Some other sources, on the other side, claims that in 2015, Shekau had already pledged loyalty to the IS and the group was rebranded as ISWAP however, the ongoing internal disturbances were resolved by the change of leadership (Zenn, 2021).

In contrast to all the violence and indiscriminate attacks of Boko Haram since this split, ISWAP presented and claimed to be more gentle and theologically more correct to civilians and even to the internal dissenter. In other words, as Foucher (2019) claims because Shekau treated Muslims and infidels as equally legitimate targets, Boko Haram continued to stage attacks on civilians, confiscated their properties, conducted mass killings, conducted suicide bombings in markets and mosques. On the other side, ISWAP, having realized how important to keep civilians on their side, make efforts to spare civilians and focus primarily on military targets, military camps, enforcement headquarters and civilians (officials, vigilantes or chiefs) working with the state.

ISWAP leadership have continued closely monitoring their members in terms of their relations towards civilians especially in those areas was once under the rule of the state or Boko Haram. The town of Baga can illuminate important dynamics of this policy. Foucher (2019) draws on the same logic that ISWAP highlighted to reflect much more tolerated behaviours in direct contact with unaffiliated Muslim civilians but people in uniforms, unlike Boko Haram that forayed into Chad (Awosusi, 2017). As a result of this policy, the civilian casualties dramatically decreased in North-Eastern Nigeria since 2016 (Campbell & Harwood, 2018). On the other side, ISWAP overrun state military points and killed hundreds of soldiers by 2018 (Onuoha, Nwangwu, & Ugwueze, 2020). The strategy of bonding with civilians allowed ISWAP to form its territorial base marshland around, islands of Lake Chad, Mandara hills on the Nigeria-Cameroon border, forests of Borno and Yobe states, helped them to cover from Nigerian and allied air power and sustain waging war across these areas. ISWAP overran a major military base in Baga in 2018 and on the day of Nigeria's general elections, in 2019, launched its first-ever attack on Maiduguri. The salient point is that their vision has ranged beyond the confines of their immediate beat. They have extended their sphere of influence beyond the borders of Cameroon and Niger.

Grazing lands, fertile land and fish played an underappreciated role for ISWAP to grow in power and progressively become able to provide the essential need of civilians at the time of Nigerian state is plagued with a high level of corruption, which ceased state's ability to offer public services and economic opportunities (Yagboyaju & Akinola, 2019). ISWAP, to concrete its position and consolidate its networks, exploited the power vacuum and started offering policies cattle rustling, provides a modicum of health care, justice, loans. Cunningham (2020) and Mampilly (2021) claims that sometimes the success of the armed group depends on the armed groups' ability to rule and be recognized as legitimate rulers in the areas it controls (Péclard & Mechoulan, 2015).

ISWAP provides healthcare to fighters and civilians by a number of medical specialists most of the time for free. The medicines and medical apparatus are procured at the time of the raid in neighbour states. The standard of health care dramatically increased. Moreover, ISWAP engaged in latrine construction program. Furthermore, unlike Boko Haram, ISWAP humanitarian workers to vaccinations (Foucher, 2019).

People living in intra-state war conditions are mostly eager to have justice, after having security, against including those who have committed crimes, murder or confiscation. ISWAP is also similar to other armed groups and can be categorized as Baalen's Responsive governance in which civilians living under ISWAP's governance demanded the establishment of a justice system (Ngari & Olojo, 2020). The armed group released the photos of a typical Sharia court where members dressed in 'uniforms' with a turbaned "*Qadhi*" (Sharia court judge) who stood behind the huge ISWAP flag. Under their control, these types of courts can be found in a remote village in Northern Nigeria. The other photo released showed the existence of "*Diwanil Qadha'a Was Shurta*" (Court of the Judiciary and Police) for the "terrorism" crimes committed by Shekau (Dahiru, 2021). As a strategic move, the ISWAP attempts to change its visibility. Distinguishing itself from its parent organization (Boko Haram) or other parallel organizations, which was never responsive, ISWAP has brought about a drop in crime as well as resolving disputes, adjudicating allegations through local chiefs (Foucher, 2019). The harsh conditions in the internally displaced people's camps that are under the control of the government and the absence of economic opportunities both increased the people's join to ISWAP and the increase in banditry, kidnapping for ransom outside of ISWAP's area of direct control.

By continuing Boko Haram's policy of micro-loans, ISWAP offered financial assistance for youth and farmers to enlarge their trade activities. Moreover, to increase agricultural production, ISWAP distributes seeds and fertilizers besides constructing wells for farmers (Carsten & Kingimi, 2018). According to Foucher (2019), ISWAP-controlled agricultural production has risen dramatically in recent years. However, the food crisis emanated from drought and the effects of Covid, ISWAP changed its pricing policy and banned the exit of locally produced foodstuff (Foucher, 2020).

Hellem (2021) highlights that locals have preferred ISWAP (now a quasi-state) governance position and taxation rules since civilians have regarded their system as more predictable and much less exploitative than Boko Haram and state officials. Armed groups finance themselves through an array of mechanisms including taxation, control of ports, illicit activities, a range of smuggling[5] and abduction (Pearson & Zenn, 2021), oil sale and as ISWAP does, through collecting zakat (religiously obligatory alms) during Ramadan as a different political tool (Thurston, 2021). Furthermore, to revive the trade, ISWAP encouraged locals to sell and buy at local markets (including charcoal, cattle, hides and fish) without capping the prices or creating an extended environment where they can do business (Fredrick, 2021). Even, ISWAP demands people return to the territories they had left due to attacks by Boko Haram (Felbab-Brown, 2020a) to compensate for the deficit of population. Therefore, ISWAP resorts propaganda videos to propagate how sustained and well-coordinated the life under their control (TribuneOnline, 2021).

Side by side with these politically expedient behaviours better than its parent organization, a process of filling gaps in governance and service delivery translated into greater military success for the ISWAP. According to Felbab-Brown (2020b) ISWAP become a particularly potent and effective armed group while the state army suffered from deep-seated problems. By waging guerrilla warfare and controlling the swath of areas, ISWAP both encouraged those who were hesitant to resist the government and intended to indicate to civilians that it is a reliable and capable actor to attack the state. In reports reminiscent of the mounting of Boko Haram, ISWAP's deepening roots in the civilian population, to a greater extent because of their much more moderate ideology and legitimacy generating activities, according to recent research (Felbab-Brown, 2020a; Manchin & Perkins, 2021) indicates that ISWAP recruited 4000-10000 members while Boko Haram could roughly recruit 2000-2500 members. The civilian-oriented approach ISWAP persists under al-Barnawi rule allowed recruit and launch much more attacks paved the way for a new leader to consolidate his position.

Similar to some secessionist-armed groups, ISWAP has maintained the policy to persuade subjects at home and abroad. The policy towards prior involves seeking public acknowledgement from the pillars of the society including religious leaders and strongmen. Simultaneously, armed groups seek to gain the legitimacy of the latter, international actors. In other words, any type of recognition from foreign powers especially for the post-civil war period. The clear examples are the Rwandan and Ugandan armed groups were in a position to negotiate with Western powers as their forces were still fighting.

This part includes the third party support or network channels of the armed groups. ISWAP received money flows and operational assistance (including improvised explosive and infantry tactics), from the Middle East, ISIS until 2017 as it went under severe pressure. The foreign fighters network (an unspecified number of Nigerian, Middle East Arabs and West African militants) worked for the recruitment procedure (ICG, 2019).

PYD/YPG or Syrian PKK

The heavily- felt results of Arab Spring, especially concerning the bloodshed in Syria, Yemen, Libya and others, changed every piece related to these territories and politics. In terms of the Syrian conflict and subsequent events transmuted all the pre-known facts, relations, power dynamics, territorial rules and facts as well as weak-armed groups, as the one known as PYD or PKK (Kurdistan Workers' Party). The answer to the question "who is the gainer of the Syrian war?" is without a doubt is PYD.

Kurdish youth, at the very beginning of the 2011 uprising, managed to organize (unifying smaller parties, women and youth groups, and their political demands by the indefatigable and incessant support of experienced, organized, and disciplined PKK. Moreover, PYD created the *Movement for a Democratic Society* (TEV-DEM)) to form local anti-government activities and protests across Kurdish populated cities and towns. To be able to organize around a policy, pragmatism and strategic clarity played a preponderant role in their swiftly taking over most towns in northern Syria following the withdrawal of Syrian troops to fight other armed rebel or secessionist groups (Kajjo, 2020). PKK provided weaponry and training to bolster YPG's regional influence. Following the control of large swaths of territories by the American assistance, Kurdish armed forces established a governance system under the "Constitution of the Rojava Canton" and the Tevgera Civaka Demokratîk or the TEV-DEM was assigned responsibility to governing all three cantons (Özçelik, 2019) that are Cezire (Jazira in Arabic), Efrin and Kobane (Ain al-Arab in Arabic). Each of the cantons has its legislative, judicial and executive councils. As a highly organized and decentralized system, they also have academies, committees, commissions and cooperatives operating within them. They are related to the diplomatic, social, political foundations, economic, legal and self-defence functions (Khalaf, 2016).

In terms of security, which is one of the crucial assets during the cruel days of the intrastate war, PYD having the support of the international arena, through imposing military conscription on the local Kurdish population and together with the foreign recruits, provided relatively secured areas (Kajjo, 2020). Kurdish struggle established a concrete legitimacy upon the pool of support from the USA that regards the YPG as the most effective fighting force against ISIS, Russian support upon the Turkish downing the Russian aircraft in late 2015 and lastly ISIS's defeat in Kobane. This level escalated to a level that many Arabs who suffered much from ISIS, although they are deeply fearful from PYD, appreciate the security environment (Khalaf, 2016).

The public services, as the second tool, are the essential factor to gain legitimacy under the establishment of the PYD-led Rojava project. It relates to the effective, sustainable and equitable service provision, which is modelled according to the teachings of PKK leader Abdullah Ocalan through the Autonomous Administration in northeast Syria (Kajjo, 2020). According to Khalaf (2016), the institutions -ostensibly managed in a decentralized manner- that PYD has run functions like the Syrian state in accordance with its ideology in Cezire, Efrin and Kobane (Ain al-Arab in Arabic). As perception

Figure 2. Syria

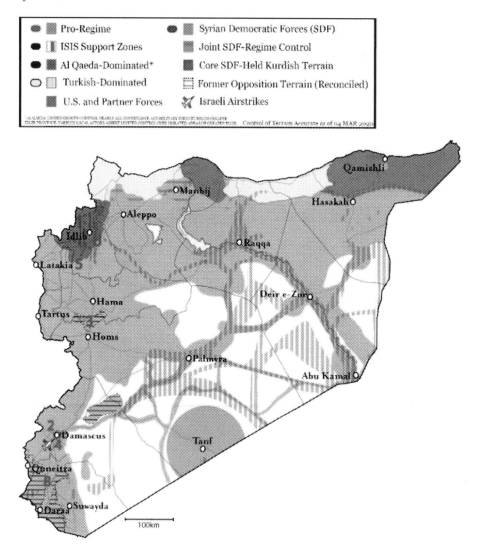

differs in security and governance in the cantons, service provision varies from one canton to another depending on the situation. The Kobane mostly destroyed during the conflict, received reconstruction services along with electricity, bakeries, housing, healthcare and education according to Khalaf (2016) while the international community have been providing water and sanitation. He claims that in Hassaka, the PYD and regime compete to coordinate the territory since the latter still controls part of the city and governmental institutions. PYD's social contract was propagated much more democratic, emphasising the participation of civilians from Arabs, Assyrians, Turcoman and minorities into councils as a pluralist policy while in reality both the Peoples' Protection Units (Yekîneyên Parastina Gel, YPG) and the Women's Defence Units (Yekîneyên Parastina Jin, YPJ), according to Özçelik (2019), have installed one-party rule and reported to commit human rights abuses against political opponents.

PYD created a parallel justice system and structure of that of the regime to fulfil civilian demands and establish its legitimacy through urging locals to register PYD-run system although regime institutions do not accredit PYD institutions (Khalaf, 2016).

VNSAs to strengthen their service-related legitimacy and compete with either state or other service providers need large financial resources. Khalaf (2016) puts forwards that PYD provides its public services for a fee and generates income from taxes, border trade, construction permits and agriculture. Yet, PYD has continued coercive strategies in part because it is not dependent on local populations thanks to the sales of oil from the fields it has conquered in northeastern Syria, financial support from the international coalition and illicit smuggling economy (Netjes & Van Veen, 2021).

In terms of education provision, despite the heavy criticism due to the politicized curriculum, civilians appreciate the Kurdish language education system (after a ban on speaking and studying in their mother tongue) that taking place since 2012. Syrian government's Directorate of Education offered the local government to set up an education system allowing five hours of Kurdish language at specific stages of school education but rejected by the Kurdish armed groups who had considered it as a form of submission to the central government. Kurdish authorities announced their formation of the education system in 2014 and trained two thousand six hundred teachers in 2016. In contrast to ongoing developments, there is no consensus within the Kurdish population. The Kurdish National Council (KNC) opposed the democratic self-rule and voiced their disapproval of the new Kurdish curriculum as similar to the Arabs who regard it as a move for secession (Drwish, 2017). The regime's opposition to the Kurdish curriculum led to a crisis. The crisis started from the suspension of regime curriculum in Kurdish areas finalized with a lawsuit against 18 institutes teaching the Arabic curriculum and arrested dozens of educators on charges of teaching the regime's curriculum in private institutes in the city of Qamishli, Hasakah and Deir ez-Zor (Hardan, 2021).

DISCUSSION

Since the Hobbesian era, the state has been perceived as a model for organizing and securing a public order (as a legitimate user of violence), binding authority over its citizens, which can provide public goods, extract resources, generate revenue and have international recognition. However, due to historical, geographical, ethnic, sectarian, economic and international challenges; most of the states are not capable of fulfilling these requirements. Moreover, the worst of them have been positioned in the Middle East and Africa.

The malfunctions, as identified in the previous part, have caused and are still causing central governments to lose their power base and confront a governing legitimacy crisis. It does not only pervert domestic order but also the failed state itself causes problems at the regional and global level. As VNSAs grow stronger, states have lost the influence in their legal territory even more. Furthermore, because of the state's debility over territorial integrity, it is not possible to mention control over population, resources and having complete security since VNSAs present aliened, disregarded and vulnerable civilians as a credible actor.

As explicated, neither in Syria since the devastating effects of Arab Spring nor in Nigeria, the central administration has been enjoying full territorial integrity, control over population and resources. Large parts of the northern (Idlib region) and eastern Syria are still dominated by opposition VNSAs. While the central government controls "Damascus, Aleppo, Homs, Hama, Latakia, Tartus, Deraa, and Deir

Table 3. Territorial Perspective

Central Government	Authority over		
	Territorial Integrity	Population Control	Control over Resource
Syria	Not Present	Weak	Weak
Nigeria	Not Present	Weak	Weak

Table 4. Weakness of the incumbent governments

Central Government	Authority over		
	Territorial Integrity	Population Control	Control over Resource
Libya	Not Present	Weak	Weak
Somalia	Not Present	Weak	Weak
Yemen	Not Present	Weak	Weak
Syria	Not Present	Weak	Weak

al-Zour" yet, it "controls only 15 per cent of the country's international land borders" (Balanche, 2021). On the other side, in Nigeria, Wilayat Gharb Afriqiyya (WGA) operates primarily in northeast Nigeria ISWAP (operates from Lake Chad) and factions of Boko Haram (operates mainly from Sambisa Forest in southern Borno state, the Mandara Mountains and the islands of Lake Chad) controls North-East states of Borno, Adamwa and Yobe.

The same conditions are valid for Libya, Yemen and Somalia. Even though they and their affiliates sprawl throughout the region and organize under different names, their sphere of influence does not appear to have any concern of official international border agreements such as Sykes-Picot.

The emergence of the VNSAs and their imitation of the governance roles indicate that Weberian ideal-type statehood is outdated. In this framework, VNSAs should not be simply regarded as a security threat and a challenge to the state's monopoly on the use of force. In reality, increasingly effective and capable VNSAs have been the designer of alternative systems of governance that are not only autonomous from the state (as ISIS did) but often challenging them.

Table 5. Capabilities of VNSAs

VNSAs in	VNSAs capable of		
	Territorial Control	Social and Economic Control	Security
Syria	Present	Weak/Medium	Present/ Weak
Nigeria	Present	Weak/Medium	Present/ Weak
Libya	Present	Weak/Medium	Present/Medium
Yemen	Present	Weak/Weak	Present/ Weak
Somalia	Present	Weak/Medium	Present/ Weak

Table 6. Political territoriality of the case actors

	The Design	ISWAP	PYD
Willingness to control	Rhetoric	Yes	Yes
	Attempt to Establish	Limited	Yes
	Local Judiciary	Yes	Yes
	Attempt to Control	Limited	Yes
	Finance (without looting)	Limited	Yes
Ability to Control	Population Density	Medium	High
	Economic Facilities	Low	Medium
	Security	Low	Low
	Governance	Medium	High
	Infrastructure	Low	High
	Diplomacy	Low	High

In cases, we easily observe territorial control; however, their level of social and economic control and security varies depending on numerous factors. It can be argued that the relationship between VNSAs and failed states or limited statehood is based on the principle of supply and demand. PYD in Syria seeks to preserve the gamut of gains achieved after a long struggle and is eager to maintain its governance model, called as "Autonomous Administration of North and East Syria (AANES)" (Frantzman, 2021) while neither the Syrian government nor Turkey officially recognizes the autonomous administration established in the provinces of Hasakah, Raqqa and Dayr az-Zawr. The groundbreaking fact of deteriorating economic and security conditions weakens the hand of Damascus and present PYD and other small armed groups to strengthen its established presence and legitimacy by using agricultural resources and including major oil fields like Qamishli and Hasakah at the time of catalyzing tendencies such as extremism, mass displacement and further regional instability. While PYD formed *Asayish* as a police force, the minority armed groups such as the Syriac Union Party formed Sutoro which collaborates with PYD or the Assyrian Democratic Party established its Sutoro that is tied to the National Coalition of Syrian Revolution and Opposition Forces (SNC) (Khalaf, 2016). According to the report of Tsurkov and El Gazi (2020), since 2019 more than 83 per cent of Syrians have already been living below the poverty line, which obliges civilians to submit their legitimacy to PYD or HTS in the north.

As modified in the table from the study of Doboš (2016), the rhetoric to establish an independent Kurdish state became the main motivator of PYD's attempt to establish institutions. Moreover, having oil revenues and international support as a financial source, ratchet up its control apparatus, which allowed PYD to have much more population density following the secure the internal order and borders. The intention was based on the requirement of legitimacy through governance policy as explained earlier. Furthermore, the desire to establish an autonomous state structure played a preponderant role in PYD to have infrastructure and diplomacy policy. Although relationships between PYD and international actors may vary diachronically between overlapping phases flowing the defeat of ISIS, the secular PYD for these actors are much more credible. The international support granted imprimatur of legitimacy for PYD, although its human rights abuses, human trafficking, and illicit smuggling are being mostly disregarded.

On the other side, ISWAP emerged as a moderate armed actor in Nigerian territories to establish an Islamic caliphate, unlike the secular PYD regime. The reports indicate that PYD's secular policies, similar to the Baath regime, have caused people to criticize the PYD's rule. At the same time, despite the limited economic resources that resulted in ISWAP not being able to fully establish governance and infrastructure, they still have the capacity to provide security for their members. Boko Haram's wanton practices and disregarding civilian needs pave the way for ISWAP to recruit and attract a population that fled from atrocities (Dailytrust, 2021). Taking into account Boko Haram's indiscriminative policies, ISWAP followed a much more human-focused policy. This adaptation has allowed it to foster ties with local communities that neither Boko Haram nor other armed groups enjoyed so far (Foucher, 2019). Having a population-centric strategy after the notorious Boko Haram example and significant freedom of movement to establish soft power policies in Borno's rural areas escalated the reputation of ISWAP.

CONCLUSION

The incompetence of the state has long created a political vacuum out which VNSAs can parcel this gap or force people -without access to basic services- to look for alternative structures to the state. For instance, the repressive and sectarian practices of the Syrian government along with the weakness of the state institutions in Nigeria Yemen and Libya have created fusion energy that prompted the VNSAs to become a considerably higher threat against the survival of the state after its failure. As the result of this incompetence, playing an active role in the Middle East and Africa, these armed groups -connected with the humanitarian efforts- turned into a major responsible for inflicting various forms of violence against civilians, causing displacement of millions and human and organ trafficking and drug smuggling.

In this regard, in these areas, where the capacities of states have been undermined by the amalgamation of colonial footprint, authoritarianism and policy of ostracism has gradually dissolved the social contract between the states and their citizens. In other words, instability caused by the operations carried out by VNSA's, economic losses, the collapse of the regional balances of power and the perception of a threat to both the regional and other countries had a huge impact on the rise of attention towards these countries.

As a form of rebelocracy or responsive governance model, these actors enhanced their visibility and legitimacy as like Hayat Tahrir al-Sham in Syria or Somalian Boko Haram, Al Shabaab. The case countries, having long-lasting internal problems, gave birth to armed organizations that have violated the Weberian mode of state and established a proto-state structure in limited statehood areas or failed-state. Mimicking the state legitimacy, these armed groups have sought internal and external legitimacy through playing the role of proxy warriors like PYD and or taking a more moderate political ideology like ISWAP. Özçelik (2019) emphasized that the secessionist or autonomist VNSAs who formed a governance model are generally motivated by ethnic-nationalist relations and focus more directly on external legitimacy rather than having the policy to comply with civilians under their sphere of influence. PYD maintains its territorial policy and receives external legitimacy while ISWAP is far from international help. The usage of child recruitment in the civil war, human rights abuses, and pressures from Damascus may lead PYD to have internal problems while ISWAP adopted IS' strategies to please its fighter and civilian to maintain their resilience.

Concerning the fluidity of the political and security situation in both countries, PYD has not been able to implement the demands from civilians due to the no need for civilian support thanks to the financial revenues that come from oil and external assistance. This policy may weaken the resilience of PYD's long-term policy while ISWAP's lack of international recognition, satisfying degree of revenues to supply expensive governance functions may become an obstacle to sustaining this legitimacy-gaining policy.

REFERENCES

Abramchayev, L. (2004). A social contract argument for the state's duty to protect from private violence. *St. John's Journal of Legal Commentary*, *18*(3), 849–874.

Ali, F. A. (2017). *Winning hearts and minds in ungoverned spaces*. Retrieved from https://www.undp.org/content/undp/en/home/blog/2017/winning-hearts-and-minds-in-ungoverned-spaces.html

Arda, L., & Banerjee, S. B. (2021). Governance in Areas of Limited Statehood: The NGOization of Palestine. *Business & Society*, *60*(7), 1675–1707. doi:10.1177/0007650319870825

Arjona, A. (2016). Creating Rebelocracy, Aliocracy, and Disorder. In *Rebelocracy* (pp. 159–211). Cambridge University Press. doi:10.1017/9781316421925.006

Arjona, A., Kasfir, N., & Mampilly, Z. (2015). Rebel governance in civil war. In *Rebel Governance in Civil War*. Cambridge University Press. doi:10.1017/CBO9781316182468.009

Awosusi, A. E. (2017). Aftermath of Boko Haram violence in the Lake Chad Basin: A neglected global health threat. *BMJ Global Health*, *2*(1), e000193. doi:10.1136/bmjgh-2016-000193 PMID:28589004

Baalen, V. S. (2020). *Guns and Governance Local Elites and Rebel Governance in Côte d'Ivoire*. Retrieved from http://urn.kb.se/resolve?urn=urn:nbn:se:uu:diva-425401

Bakonyi, J., & Stuvøy, K. (2005). Violence & social order beyond the state: Somalia & Angola. *Review of African Political Economy*, *32*(104–105), 359–382. doi:10.1080/03056240500329379

Balanche, F. (2021, February 10). *The Assad Regime Has Failed to Restore Full Sovereignty Over Syria*. Retrieved September 11, 2021, from https://www.washingtoninstitute.org/policy-analysis/assad-regime-has-failed-restore-full-sovereignty-over-syria

Bellina, S., Darbon, D., Eriksen, S. S., & Sendig, O. J. (2009). The Legitimacy of the State in Fragile Situations. *Norad*. Retrieved from https://www.norad.no/globalassets/import-2162015-80434-am/www.norad.no-ny/filarkiv/vedlegg-til-publikasjoner/the-legitimacy-of-the-state-in-fragile-situations.pdf

Blomberg, S. B., Gaibulloev, K., & Sandler, T. (2011). Terrorist group survival: Ideology, tactics, and base of operations. *Public Choice*, *149*(3), 441–463. doi:10.100711127-011-9837-4

Breslawski, J. (2020). The Social Terrain of Rebel Held Territory. *The Journal of Conflict Resolution*.

Brooke, S. (2015). The Muslim Brotherhood's social outreach after the Egyptian coup. Rethinking Political Islam.

Brück, T. (2016). *The Relationship between Food Security and Violent Conflict*. Retrieved from www.isd-center.org

Bruderlein, C. (2000). The role of non-state actors in Building Human Security: the Case of Armed Groups in Intra-State Wars. Centre for Humanitarian Dialogue.

Campbell, J., & Harwood, A. (2018, August 20). *Boko Haram's Deadly Impact*. Retrieved September 7, 2021, from https://www.cfr.org/article/boko-harams-deadly-impact

Caporaso, J. A. (2000). Changes in the Westphalian order: Territory, public authority, and sovereignty. *International Studies Review*, 2(2), 1–28. doi:10.1111/1521-9488.00203

Carsten, P., & Kingimi, A. (2018). *Islamic State ally stakes out territory around Lake Chad*. Retrieved September 7, 2021, from https://www.reuters.com/article/us-nigeria-security-idUSKBN1I0063

Cojanu, V., & Popescu, A. I. (2007). Analysis of Failed States: Some Problems of Definition and Measurement. *Romanian Economic Journal*, (25), 113–132.

Coyne, C. J. (2006). Reconstructing weak and failed states. *The Journal of Social, Political, and Economic Studies*, 31(2), 143–162.

Cronin, P. M. (2009). *Global strategic assessment 2009: America's security role in a changing world*. National Defense University Press.

Cunningham, K. G., & Loyle, C. E. (2020). Introduction to the Special Feature on Dynamic Processes of Rebel Governance. *The Journal of Conflict Resolution*, 65(1), 002200272093515.

Dahiru, A. (2021). *Soft-Jihad: How Terrorists Use Propaganda To Attract Local Support*. Retrieved September 14, 2021, from https://humanglemedia.com/soft-jihad-how-terrorists-use-propaganda-to-attract-local-support/

Dailytrust. (2021). *How ISWAP is wooing IDPs back to Borno villages*. Retrieved September 14, 2021, from https://dailytrust.com/how-iswap-fighters-wooed-idps-back-to-borno-villages

Doboš, B. (2016). Shapeshifter of Somalia: Evolution of the Political Territoriality of Al-Shabaab. *Small Wars & Insurgencies*, 27(5), 937–957. doi:10.1080/09592318.2016.1208282

Drwish, S. (2017). *The Kurdish School Curriculum in Syria: A Step Towards Self-Rule?* Retrieved September 14, 2021, from https://www.atlanticcouncil.org/blogs/syriasource/the-kurdish-school-curriculum-in-syria-a-step-towards-self-rule/

Durac, V. (2015). The Role of Non-State Actors in Arab Countries after the Arab Uprisings. *Crisis and New Agenda of the Arab States*, 37–41.

Duyvesteyn, I. (2019). *Rebels and Legitimacy: Processes and Practices*. Routledge.

Eck, K. (2010). *Raising Rebels: Participation and Recruitment in Civil War*. Department of Peace and Conflict Research.

Elden, S. (2009). *Terror and territory: The spatial extent of sovereignty*. University of Minnesota Press.

Esguerra, A., Helmerich, N., & Risse, T. (2017). *Sustainability politics and limited statehood : Contesting new modes of governance*. Palgrave Macmillan.

Felbab-Brown, V. (2020a). Militias (and Militancy) in Nigeria's North-East: Not Going Away. In A. Day (Ed.), *Hybrid Conflict, Hybrid Peace: How Militias and Paramilitary Groups Shape Post-conflict Transitions*. United Nations University.

Felbab-Brown, V. (2020b). *The problem with militias in Somalia: Almost everyone wants them despite their dangers*. Retrieved March 7, 2021, from https://www.brookings.edu/research/the-problem-with-militias-in-somalia-almost-everyone-wants-them-despite-their-dangers/

Florea, A. (2017). De Facto States: Survival and Disappearance (1945-2011). *International Studies Quarterly*, *61*(2), 337–351. doi:10.1093/isqqw049

Förster, T. (2015). Dialogue direct: Rebel governance and civil order in northern côte d'ivoire. In *Rebel Governance in Civil War* (pp. 203–225). Cambridge University Press. doi:10.1017/CBO9781316182468.010

Foucher, V. (2019). *Facing the Challenge of the Islamic State in West Africa Province*. Retrieved from https://www.crisisgroup.org/africa/west-africa/nigeria/273-facing-challenge-islamic-state-west-africa-province

Foucher, V. (2020). *The Jihadi Proto-State in the Lake Chad Basin*. Retrieved September 6, 2021, from https://www.ispionline.it/en/pubblicazione/jihadi-proto-state-lake-chad-basin-25441

Fragile State Index. (2017). *What Does State Fragility Mean?* Fragile States Index. Retrieved January 4, 2020, from https://fragilestatesindex.org/frequently-asked-questions/what-does-state-fragility-mean/

Frantzman, S. (2021, July 22). *The struggle to achieve recognition for Kurdish North and East Syria*. Retrieved September 12, 2021, from https://www.jpost.com/middle-east/the-struggle-to-achieve-recognition-for-kurdish-north-and-east-syria-674637

Fredrick, H. (2021). *ISWAP: Islamic State West Africa Province*. Retrieved September 14, 2021, from https://www.greydynamics.com/islamic-state-west-africa-province/

Furlan, M. (2020). Understanding Governance by Insurgent Non- State Actors : A Multi-Dimensional Typology Understanding Governance by Insurgent Non-State. *Civil Wars*, *00*(00), 1–34.

Grynkewich, A. (2008). Welfare as warfare: How violent non-state groups use social services to attack the state. *Studies in Conflict and Terrorism*, *31*(4), 350–370. doi:10.1080/10576100801931321

Hardan, M. (2021). *Authorities in northeast Syria struggle to impose Kurdish curriculum*. Retrieved September 14, 2021, from https://www.al-monitor.com/originals/2021/02/syria-kurdish-administration-education-arrest-teachers.html

Heffes, E. (2019). Armed Groups and the Protection of Health Care. *International Law Studies, 95*.

Hellem, F. (2021). *ISWAP: Islamic State West Africa Province*. Retrieved September 1, 2021, from https://www.greydynamics.com/islamic-state-west-africa-province/

Hofmann, C., & Schneckener, U. (2011). Engaging non-state armed actors in state-and peace-building: Options and strategies. *International Review of the Red Cross*, *93*(883), 603–621. doi:10.1017/S1816383112000148

Huang, R. (2016). The wartime origins of democratization: Civil war, rebel governance, and political regimes. In *The Wartime Origins of Democratization*. Civil War, Rebel Governance, and Political Regimes. doi:10.1017/CBO9781316711323

Hutt, M. (2004). *Himalayan People's War: Nepal's Maoist Rebellion*. Indiana University Press.

ICG. (2019). *Facing the Challenge of the Islamic State in West Africa Province*. ICG.

Idler, A. (2019). *Borderland Battles Violence, Crime, and Governance at the Edges of Colombia's War*. Oxford University Press. doi:10.1093/oso/9780190849146.001.0001

Jackson, R. H. (1995). Quasi-States: Sovereignty, International Relations and the Third World. *Verfassung und Recht in Übersee*, *28*(2), 256–258. Advance online publication. doi:10.5771/0506-7286-1995-2-256

James, T. (2011). *Think Again: Failed States – Foreign Policy*. Retrieved January 4, 2020, from https://foreignpolicy.com/2011/06/20/think-again-failed-states/

Jones, S. G. (2012). The Strategic Logic of Militia. Notes and Queries.

Kajjo, S. (2020). *Prospects For Syrian Kurdish Unity Assessing Local and Regional Dynamics*. Retrieved from https://www.washingtoninstitute.org/media/3879

Kaplan, S. D. (2017). *The Return of the "Old Normal": How the Rise of Non-State Actors Affects Fragile States*. Retrieved July 11, 2020, from https://fragilestates.org/2017/11/06/return-old-normal-rise-non-state-actors-affects-fragile-states/

Kasfir, N. (2002). *Dilemmas of popular support in guerrilla war: the National Resistance Army in Uganda, 1981–1986*. Paper Presented to the Laboratory in Comparative Ethnic Processes 6, UCLA.

Kasfir, N. (2015). Rebel governance – constructing a field of inquiry: Definitions, scope, patterns, order, causes. In *Rebel Governance in Civil War* (pp. 21–46). Cambridge University Press. doi:10.1017/CBO9781316182468.002

Khalaf, R. (2015). Governance Without Government in Syria: Civil Society and State Building During Conflict. *Syria Studies*, *7*(3), 37–72.

Khalaf, R. (2016). *Governing Rojava: Layers of Legitimacy in Syria*. Retrieved from https://issat.dcaf.ch/Learn/Resource-Library2/Policy-and-Research-Papers/Governing-Rojava-Layers-of-Legitimacy-in-Syria

Krasner, S. D. C. P. (2005). *Addressing State Failure*. Retrieved January 4, 2020, from https://www.foreignaffairs.com/articles/2005-07-01/addressing-state-failure

Krause, K., & Milliken, J. (2010). Introduction: The Challange of Non-State Armed Groups. In *Contemporary Security Policy* (p. 202). Routledge.

Ledwidge, F. (2017). *Rebel Law: Insurgents, Courts and Justice in Modern Conflict*. C Hurst & Co Publishers Ltd.

Levi-Faur, D. (2012). *From "Big Government" to "Big Governance"?* Online Pub. doi:10.1093/oxfordhb/9780199560530.013.0001

Lillywhite, L. (2015). *Non-State Armed Groups, Health and Healthcare*. Retrieved from https://www.chathamhouse.org/sites/default/files/events/special/NSAGs

Loyle, C. E. (2020). Rebel Justice during Armed Conflict. *The Journal of Conflict Resolution, 65*(1), 108–134. doi:10.1177/0022002720939299

Malejacq, R. (2016). Warlords, Intervention, and State Consolidation: A Typology of Political Orders in Weak and Failed States. *Security Studies, 25*(1), 85–110. doi:10.1080/09636412.2016.1134191

Malejacq, R. (2017). From Rebel to Quasi-State: Governance, Diplomacy and Legitimacy in the Midst of Afghanistan's Wars (1979–2001). *Small Wars & Insurgencies, 28*(4–5), 867–886. doi:10.1080/09592318.2017.1322332

Malthaner, S., & Waldmann, P. (2014). The radical milieu: Conceptualizing the supportive social environment of terrorist groups. *Studies in Conflict and Terrorism, 37*(12), 979–998. doi:10.1080/1057610X.2014.962441

Mampilly, Z., & Stewart, M. A. (2021). A Typology of Rebel Political Institutional Arrangements. *The Journal of Conflict Resolution, 65*(1), 15–45. doi:10.1177/0022002720935642

Mampilly, Z. C. (2011). *Rebel Rulers: Insurgent Governance and Civilian Life during War* (1st ed.). Cornell University Press.

Mampilly, Z. C. (2017). Rebel Rulers. In *Rebel Rulers*. Cornell University Press.

Manchin, G., & Perkins, T. (2021). *Factsheet: Violent Islamist Groups in Northern Nigeria*. Academic Press.

Mansfield, D. (2018). Turning deserts into flowers: Settlement and poppy cultivation in southwest Afghanistan. *Third World Quarterly, 39*(2), 331–349. doi:10.1080/01436597.2017.1396535

Mccartan, B., & Jolliffe, K. (2016). Ethnic Armed Actors and Justice Provision in Myanmar. Academic Press.

Menkhaus, K. (2006). Governance without government in Somalia: Spoilers, state building, and the politics of coping. *International Security, 31*(3), 74–106. doi:10.1162/isec.2007.31.3.74

Momodu, J. A. (2020). Non-State Security Groups and Their Role in Countering Boko Haram Terrorism in North East Region of Nigeria. *African Review (Dar Es Salaam, Tanzania), 47*(1), 67–96. doi:10.1163/1821889X-12340009

Nay, O. (2013). Fragile and failed states: Critical perspectives on conceptual hybrids. *International Political Science Review, 34*(3), 326–341. doi:10.1177/0192512113480054

Netjes, R., & Van Veen, E. (2021). *Henchman, Rebel, Democrat, Terrorist The YPG/ PYD during the Syrian conflict CRU Report*. Retrieved from www.clingendael.org/cru

Ngari, A., & Olojo, A. (2020). Besieged but not relenting Ensuring fair trials for Nigeria's terrorism suspects. West Africa Report.

Oktav, Ö. Z., Parlar Dal, E., & Kurşun, A. M. (2017). *Violent non-state actors and the Syrian Civil War: The ISIS and YPG cases*. Springer International Publishing.

Onuoha, F. C., Nwangwu, C., & Ugwueze, M. I. (2020). Counterinsurgency operations of the Nigerian military and Boko Haram insurgency: Expounding the viscid manacle. *Security Journal, 33*(3), 401–426. doi:10.105741284-020-00234-6

Özçelik, B. (2019). Explaining the Kurdish Democratic Union Party's Self-Governance Practices in Northern Syria, 2012–18. *Government and Opposition, 1*(21).

Pearson, E., & Zenn, J. (2021). *Boko Haram, the Islamic State, and the Surge in Female Abductions in Southeastern Niger*. Retrieved from https://icct.nl/app/uploads/2021/02/Pearson-And-Zenn-research-paper.pdf

Péclard, D., & Mechoulan, D. (2015). *Rebel Governance and the Politics of Civil War*. Retrieved from www.sagw.ch

Piazza, J. A., & Piazza, S. (2017). Crime Pays: Terrorist Group Engagement in Crime and Survival. *Terrorism and Political Violence, 32*(4), 701–723. doi:10.1080/09546553.2017.1397515

Pourmalek, P. (2021). *The Rebel Iron Fist: Reframing Violence as a Condition for Rebel Governance*. doi:10.14288/1.0398461

Raeymaekers, T. (2010). Protection For Sale? War and the transformation of regulation on the congo-ugandan border. *Development and Change, 41*(4), 563–587. doi:10.1111/j.1467-7660.2010.01655.x

Rice, S. E. (2003). The new national security strategy: focus on failed states. *The Brookings Institution, 2*(116), 1–8.

Rich, P. B. (1999). Warlords, state fragmentation and the dilemma of humanitarian intervention. *Small Wars & Insurgencies, 10*(1), 78–96. doi:10.1080/09592319908423230

Risse, T. (2011). Governance in Areas of Limited Statehood: Introduction and Overview. In Governance without a State? Policies and Politics in Areas of Limited Statehood. Academic Press.

Risse, T. (2015). Limited Statehood: A Critical Perspective. In The Oxford Handbook of Transformations of the State. Oxford University Press.

Risse, T., & Stollenwerk, E. (2018). Legitimacy in Areas of Limited Statehood. *Annual Review of Political Science, 21*(1), 403–418. doi:10.1146/annurev-polisci-041916-023610

Robert, G. T. (1998). *State Failure Project Report.pdf*. Retrieved from http://mstohl.faculty.comm.ucsb.edu/failed_states/1998/papers/gurr.html

Ross, M. L. (2004). What Do We Know about Natural Resources and Civil War? *Sage (Atlanta, Ga.), 41*(3), 337–356. doi:10.1177/0022343304043773

Rotberg, R. I. (2003). *State Failure and State Weakness in a Time of Terror*. World Peace Foundatiton Brookings Institution Press.

Rotberg, R. I. (2004). Failed States, Collapsed States, Weak States: Causes and Indicators. In *State Failure and State Weakness In a Time of Terror*. Princeton University Press.

Ruggie, J. G. (1993). International Organization Foundation Territoriality and Beyond : Problematizing Modernity in International Relations. *International Organization*, *47*(1), 139–174. doi:10.1017/S0020818300004732

Sany, J. (2010). Education and Conflict in Cote d'Ivoire. Special Report.

Schneckener, U. (2006). *Fragile Statehood, Armed Non-State Actors and Security Governance*. LIT.

Schwab, R. (2018). Insurgent courts in civil wars: The three pathways of (trans)formation in today's Syria (2012-2017). *Small Wars & Insurgencies*, *29*(4), 801–826. doi:10.1080/09592318.2018.1497290

Seeberg, P. (2016). Analysing security subcomplexes in a changing Middle East—The role of non-Arab State actors and non-state actors. *Palgrave Communications*, *2*(1), 2. doi:10.1057/palcomms.2016.87

Stanislawski, B. H. (2008). Para-States, Quasi-States, and Black Spots: Perhaps Not States, But Not "Ungoverned Territories," Either. *International Studies Review*, *10*(2), 366–396. doi:10.1111/j.1468-2486.2008.00795.x

Stephan, M. J., & Chenoweth, E. (2008). Why civil resistance works: The strategic logic of nonviolent conflict. *International Security*, *33*(1), 7–44. doi:10.1162/isec.2008.33.1.7

Stewart, M. A. (2018). Civil War as State-Making: Strategic Governance in Civil War. *International Organization*, *72*(1), 205–226. doi:10.1017/S0020818317000418

Stewart, M. A. (2020). Rebel governance: Military boon or military bust? (Isard Award Article). *Conflict Management and Peace Science*, *37*(1), 16–38. doi:10.1177/0738894219881422

Terpstra, N. (2020). Rebel governance, rebel legitimacy, and external intervention: Assessing three phases of Taliban rule in Afghanistan. *Small Wars & Insurgencies*, *31*(6), 1143–1173. doi:10.1080/09592318.2020.1757916

Thurston, A. (2021, July 12). *Why Jihadists Are Collecting "Zakat" in the Sahel*. Retrieved September 6, 2021, from https://politicalviolenceataglance.org/2021/07/12/why-jihadists-are-collecting-zakat-in-the-sahel/

Tribune Online. (2021). *Boko Haram/ISWAP terrorists now resort to video propaganda, says Army*. Retrieved September 12, 2021, from https://tribuneonlineng.com/boko-haram-iswap-terrorists-now-resort-to-video-propaganda-says-army/

Tsurkov, E., & El Gazi, S. (2020). *"People can't even afford to buy bulgur": Discontent is on the rise as Syria's economic crisis worsens*. Retrieved September 12, 2021, from https://www.mei.edu/publications/people-cant-even-afford-buy-bulgur-discontent-rise-syrias-economic-crisis-worsens

Uphoff, N. (1989). Distinguishing Power, Authority & Legitimacy: Taking Max Weber at His Word by Using Resources-Exchange Analysis. *Polity*, *22*(2), 295–322. doi:10.2307/3234836

Wagstaff, W. A., & Jung, D. F. (2017). *Terrorism and Political Violence Competing for Constituents: Trends in Terrorist Service Provision*. Academic Press.

Weiss, T. G., Conor, D., & Coolidge, K. (2013). *The Rise of Non-State Actors in Global Governance Opportunities and Limitations a One Earth Future Discussion Paper by.* Academic Press.

Williams, P. (2008). Violent non-state Actors And National and international security. *International Relations and Security Network*, 1–21.

Wood, E. J. (2003). Insurgent collective action and civil war in El Salvador. Insurgent Collective Action and Civil War in El Salvador. doi:10.1017/CBO9780511808685

Worrall, J. (2017). (Re-)Emergent Orders: Understanding the Negotiation(s) of Rebel Governance. *Small Wars & Insurgencies*, 28(4–5), 709–733. doi:10.1080/09592318.2017.1322336

Yagboyaju, D. A., & Akinola, A. O. (2019). Nigerian State and the Crisis of Governance: A Critical Exposition. *SAGE Open*, 9(3). Advance online publication. doi:10.1177/2158244019865810

Yeşiltaş, M., & Kardaş, T. (2017). Non-state armed actors in the middle east: Geopolitics, ideology, and strategy. In *Non-State Armed Actors in the Middle East*. Geopolitics, Ideology, and Strategy.

Zenn, J. (2021, June 4). *ISWAP Launches Hearts and Minds Strategy to Counter Nigerian Army Offensive.* Retrieved September 6, 2021, from https://jamestown.org/program/iswap-launches-hearts-and-minds-strategy-to-counter-nigerian-army-offensive/

ENDNOTES

[1] They are also known as Non-State Armed Actors or Armed Non-State Actors.

[2] The definitional and conceptual issues of "failed," "failing," "fragile," and the like have been utilized in extant literature. The clarification regarding the concept of state failure for the purposes of the analyses is out of the scope of this study. Most of the study do not regard totalitarian, dictatorial or rogue states as failed since they have working governmental machinery such as present-day North Korea. However, this argumentation is also out of scope of this study.

[3] The U.S. government-sponsored research project aims collecting database of political conflict. For detailed information, please visit https://globalpolicy.gmu.edu/political-instability-task-force/.

[4] They become the symbol of the state weakness. As the representative of distinct interests, the violent actors turns into industry of long-standing conflicts. Please follow the link for further information: Claudia Hofmann and Ulrich Schneckener, "Engaging Non-State Armed Actors in State-and Peace-Building: Options and Strategies," *International Review of the Red Cross*, 2011.

[5] To portray itself as an armed group do not victimize civilians, ISWAP claims that they do abducting women only if they collaborate with the state officials. Moreover, ISWAP do not regard them as civilians but apostates. Similar to Boko Haram's Chibok case, ISWAP abducted thirty-three women and six children in 2017 but received no international attention.

Chapter 12
Benefits and Risks of Digital Diplomacy:
Is Traditional Diplomacy in Decline?

Diana Khomeriki
International Black Sea University, Georgia

ABSTRACT

Diplomacy is a key tool for conducting foreign policy, and it has experienced changes throughout the past centuries. Information and communication technologies (ICTs) and social media platforms began playing a highly important role in achieving diplomatic objectives leading to the emergence of the term "digital diplomacy." Being one of the main trends in contemporary diplomatic communication, especially during the COVID-19 pandemic, taking a closer look at digital diplomacy is worthwhile. This chapter analyzes the main characteristics of digital diplomacy as well as its opportunities and challenges, compares digital and traditional diplomacy, and aims to determine whether traditional diplomacy is in decline. The author argues that traditional diplomacy is not antiquated; traditional and digital diplomacy complement each other. Diplomats will need to function in a hybrid regime, both in offline and online environments. Utilizing digital diplomacy will improve the effectiveness of traditional diplomacy contributing to more multifaceted, comprehensive, and results-oriented foreign policy.

INTRODUCTION

Technology has been developing at a rapid pace and has permeated all aspects of our lives. The increased use of digital communication technologies, such as the Internet and social media, has significantly influenced the way foreign policy is conducted and has become an indivisible part of diplomatic work. Diplomats use digital tools in their daily work, from negotiations and representation, to communication and policy analysis. Although the traditional form of conducting diplomacy - the interaction between different government representatives, remains crucial, individuals and non-governmental organizations started playing a significant role in international affairs.

DOI: 10.4018/978-1-7998-9586-2.ch012

Broadly defined, digital diplomacy is "the use of the Internet and new Information Communications Technologies to help carry out diplomatic objectives" (Hanson, 2012), while "the digitalization of diplomacy refers to the overall impact digital tools have had on diplomacy ranging from the creation of smartphone applications for delivering consular aid to the adoption of new norms and values such as practicing more transparent diplomacy" (Diplomat Magazine, 2017).

The use of the Internet, mainly social media has brought millions into open conversation spaces. With more than two billion people using Facebook, Twitter, Snapchat and other social media platforms daily, digital connectivity has made the world smaller and allowed for unlimited dialogue and information exchange between people from around the world. In countries like Egypt, Tunisia, and Yemen, in the period of the Arab Spring, rising action plans such as protests made up of thousands, have been organized through social media such as Facebook and Twitter (Kassim, 2012). In addition, social media platforms have been actively used to influence public opinion. Thus, digital diplomacy has significantly affected the practice of public diplomacy. While moving online is pivotal for contemporary diplomacy, it carries some challenges including increased risks of dis-information and mis-information that negatively influence its effectiveness.

Digital technologies gained even greater significance during the spread of the COVID-19 pandemic. "The pandemic has severely tested Ministry of Foreign Affairs' (MFA) capacity to offer timely and effective consular assistance, to protect the national image of their countries as the crisis escalated, and to counter the digital disinformation spread by an anxious public or by strategically minded actors" (Bjola & Manor, 2020). Moreover, the pandemic demonstrated the need for MFAs to adapt to a new environment, upgrade digital know-how and develop the ability to think digitally "outside the box."

Considering the significance of the digitalization trend in diplomacy and the fact that digitalization does not simply include the adoption of digital tools but also, influences norms and working procedure of diplomats and diplomatic institutions, it is essential to grasp the influence of technological advancements on diplomacy, understand what are major characteristics of digital diplomacy, and what challenges and opportunities digital diplomacy might bring. Moreover, it is crucial to analyze whether digital diplomacy might replace traditional diplomacy.

Despite the availability of some research in this field, analyzing the above-mentioned topics, reviewing existent works from a contemporary perspective considering the impact of COVID-19 on diplomacy, will provide interesting additional insights to the matter. Existent studies lack a comprehensive analysis of the benefits and the risks of digital diplomacy. This chapter will attempt to bring together the key advantages and disadvantages of utilizing digital tools in diplomatic practice. Moreover, exploring the interconnection between digital and traditional diplomacy will be an important added-value of this chapter. The chapter aims to contribute to the existing research on digital diplomacy by dealing with issues that have yet to be investigated by scholars as the process of digitalization of diplomacy is ongoing.

Chapter's hypothesis: Digital diplomacy does not intend to replace traditional face-to-face diplomacy. Traditional and digital diplomacy complement rather than compete with each other. Digital diplomacy provides significant opportunities to project foreign policy positions to domestic and foreign audiences more effectively. The benefits of digital diplomacy prevail over the risks. Diplomacy will operate in a hybrid regime in the years to come.

Qualitative interpretivist approach was applied in this chapter. Review and analysis of relevant literature including scientific journals and articles, as well as various sources from the Internet was conducted. Moreover, the chapter comprises the examples and experience of different countries using digital tools in their diplomatic practice. Lastly, the paper includes a comparative analysis of traditional and digital diplomacy.

BACKGROUND

Even though digital diplomacy is the dimension of diplomacy that is still in the process of development, it has already attracted the attention of various scholars and numerous works have already been dedicated to its study.

Firstly, it is worth noting that there is no single widely accepted definition of digital diplomacy. Segev and Manor define digital diplomacy as the use of social media by a state to achieve its foreign policy goals and manage its national image (Segey & Manor, 2015, pp.89-108). Bjola and Holmes define digital diplomacy as a tool for change management (Bjola & Halmes, 2015). Hanson describes digital diplomacy more generally as the use of the Internet and new ICTs to help carry out diplomatic objectives. Despite broad definition, he outlines eight policy goals for digital diplomacy that provide a holistic understanding of the term: knowledge management, public diplomacy, information management, consular communications and response, disaster response, internet freedom, external resources and policy planning (Hanson, 2012).

In 2016 Manor re-defined digital diplomacy and shared the understanding of Hanson by arguing that digital diplomacy can be defined as the overall impact ICTs have had on the conduct of diplomacy ranging from the email to smartphone applications (Manor, 2016). This chapter adopts the latter definition and outlines the importance of understanding digitalization as a process rather than a binary state. Manor highlights that "... the view of digitalization as a long term process whose influence far transcends the utilization of innovative technologies is better imbued by the term the 'digitalization of diplomacy'" as it captures the temporal and normative influences of digital technologies better (Manor, 2017).

The article of Kurbalija "The Impact of Internet and ICT on Contemporary Diplomacy" (2012) provides an excellent basis for understanding the technological evolution of diplomacy. He evaluates the very first shifts in traditional diplomacy including the invention of the telegram and its impact on international relations. According to him, the role of the Internet in diplomacy is very significant as it promotes more accessible informational flow and communication. He argues that the Internet has replaced traditional one-way public diplomacy with intense communication. As a result, interaction has become two-way and more inclusive and participatory.

Rashica's article "The Benefits and Risks of Digital Diplomacy" (2018) stands as a groundwork to analyze major risks and benefits of digital diplomacy. The author emphasizes that the reachability of various audiences, fast and effective communication and increased access to information essentially strengthen international relations while cyber risks stand as the biggest threat.

Adesina (2017) argues that "digital diplomacy has brought about a transformation of the conduct of traditional diplomacy" and concludes that more countries should embrace digital diplomacy as they can significantly benefit from these emerging diplomatic trends and more successfully project foreign policy positions to various audiences.

Duncombe's article "Twitter and the Challenges of Digital Diplomacy" (2018) together with Kajsa Hugher's article "Trump's Twiplomacy: A New Diplomatic Norm?" (2020) provides a comprehensive analysis of the use of Twitter by different leaders including Donald J. Trump. These authors evaluate "Twiplomacy" as a main tool for influencing the public by international actors.

Hocking and Melissen in their report (2015) have made a far-reaching conclusion that provided a vital contribution to this chapter: "No area of diplomacy will become redundant as a result of digitalization. Diplomatic functions will be re-defined to meet changing needs... Ironically, the enhanced information through social media platforms and big data gives added importance to the traditional diplomatic functions of information analysis and policy prediction" (Hocking & Melissen, 2015, p.55).

Hence, various authors have studied the influence of digital tools on diplomacy and provided different insights into the matter. However, existent works lack a comprehensive analysis of the benefits and risks of digital diplomacy. In addition, very few works include extensive analysis of the influence of the COVID-19 pandemic and upsurge in the use of online conferencing platforms on diplomatic practice. The chapter aims to contribute to the available literature by evaluating the benefits and pitfalls of digital diplomacy and comparing traditional and digital diplomacy.

THE INFLUENCE OF TECHNOLOGICAL ADVANCEMENTS ON DIPLOMACY

Jönsson (2016) has pointed out that "without communication, there is no diplomacy." Indeed, representing country's national interests without clear communication and the means to express them is absolutely impossible. Historically, technological developments and innovations have brought new elements and tools to diplomatic communication that started reshaping the way diplomats engage with each other and the public. This section focuses on particular technological innovations that made a special impact on diplomatic practice.

"My God, this is the end of diplomacy" - this was the reported reaction of Lord Palmerston, British Prime Minister, on receiving the first telegram in the 1860s. The invention of telegraph has provided new opportunities for communicating with the foreign public. It made communication quicker and more frequent. With the help of the telegraph several advancements became possible: the evolvement of global communication network, rapid and frequent messages, a more integrated world economy and telegraphic cables. Telegram had played a special role in the period between the Congress of Vienna (1815) and the First World War (1914) as fast communication was strategically important.

However, some diplomats expressed dissatisfaction with a new reality as they reported the loss of independence. Diplomats did not already have the freedom of independent on-the-spot decision-making as they needed the approval of the Minister of Foreign Affairs on almost every issue. For example, British ambassador to Vienna, Sir Horace Rumbold noted that there was a "telegraphic demoralization of those who formerly had to act for themselves and now had to be content at the end of the wire" (Phalen, 2014, p. 43). In addition, as sending a telegram was related to high costs, diplomats were urged to write concisely. One of the first telegrams cost $20.000 and was sent to France from the U.S Department of State. It should be noted that the invention of the telegraph led to the creation of the International Telegram Union, which later transformed into the International Telecommunication Union that still operates in the field of information and technology.

Despite the fact that leading countries of that period started actively using telegram in diplomatic activities, it did not result in the end of diplomacy but rather, created a basis for further improvements in the diplomatic field brought about by technological developments. Moreover, diplomacy has survived not only the invention of telegraph but, also, subsequent technological innovations, such as radio, telephone, TV and faxes.

Later, the Internet has changed both the environment in which diplomacy is conducted and the diplomatic agenda. The first massive use of computer technologies in diplomatic practice took place during the Rio de Janeiro Earth Summit in 1992, United Nations Conference on Environment and Development, where e-mails with updates from the conference were sent to interested people. Unlike traditional methods of diplomacy, already at that time diplomats had less monopoly over information that promoted a more transparent practice of diplomacy. Afterwards, this mailing technique was used during international conferences, including the World Conference on Human Rights (Vienna, 1993), the International Conference on Population and Development (Cairo, 1994), the United Nations Fourth World Conference on Women (Beijing, 1995) and the World Summit for Social Development (Copenhagen, 1995). During the World Summit on the International Society (2002) and Internet Governance Forum (2005) the Internet was firstly used in conference rooms by participants. And later, remote participation in conferences became possible which allowed participants to ask questions and contribute to discussions online.

The Internet has had a profound effect on two cornerstones of diplomacy - information and communication. According to Westcott (2008), the Internet has three fundamental impacts on international relations: firstly, it multiplies and amplifies the number of voices and interests involved in international policy-making, complicating international decision-making and reducing the exclusive control of states in the process; secondly, it accelerates and frees the dissemination of information, accurate or not, about any issue or event; and, thirdly, it enables traditional diplomatic services to be delivered faster and more cost-effectively, both to ones' own citizens and government, and to those of other countries. Therefore, the Internet has become the source of both challenges and opportunities. However, despite the availability of a new medium and new possibilities to exert influence on the public, face-to-face negotiations still remain a prerogative of diplomats and this function maintains its relevance.

The emergence of verbatim reporting was another technological advancement that made the word-for-word report of speeches possible. During various conferences, speeches were shown on the screen, which allowed diplomats to decrease any kind of ambiguity and increased transparency. Thus, information technologies opened up the diplomatic practice that was mostly conducted behind the closed doors to the global community and made instantaneous communication possible.

Therefore, technological innovations have revolutionized diplomatic practice and provided numerous opportunities to improve diplomatic performance. However, they did not reduce the need for diplomats and their substantial diplomatic skills of negotiation and communication.

Social Media and Other Online Platforms

In the 21st century, diplomacy has experienced even more significant changes as social media platforms such as Twitter, Facebook, Instagram, YouTube, Snapchat, Zoom and others have attracted millions of users while search engines like Google, Yahoo, and Ask.com made a considerable influence on information gathering process.

Social media revolutionized interaction among state officials, diplomats, and ordinary people. In addition, social media platforms are used to shape and build domestic support for a government's foreign policy. Among all social media platforms, Twitter is the most widely used service by diplomats and state officials. It is a micro-blogging service with a limited communication of short messages with no more than 140 characters. Majority of MFAs share messages in English. Countries engage with domestic and foreign audiences simultaneously. Increased use of Twitter resulted in coining a new term – "Twiplomacy." According to the BCW's Twiplomacy study 2020, the governments and leaders of 189 countries had an official presence on this social network, representing 98 percent of the 193 UN member states. Governments of only four countries do not have a Twitter presence, namely Laos, North Korea, Sao Tome and Principe, and Turkmenistan. The heads of state and government of 163 countries and 132 foreign ministers maintain personal accounts on Twitter. Based on 2020 data, Donald Trump remains the most followed world leader with more than 81 million followers and counting, and the most effective world leader on Twitter since his each tweet garners on average 24,000 retweets.

Trump's "Twiplomacy" has caused great interest among various scholars; his use of Twitter with harsh language received huge criticism as, generally, diplomatic language is known for its balanced nature and constructiveness. Commenting on Trump's "Twitter diplomacy," Dejevsky (2017) claims that Trump "has earned almost universal disapproval from the political and especially the diplomatic establishments, which regard such heedless commentary as, first, ill-advised in the extreme and, second, plain crass." However, Simunjak & Caliandro (2019) have found that despite the fact that Trump's diplomatic communication on Twitter disrupts traditional codes of diplomatic language, there is little evidence that new codes of diplomatic interactions on social media are being constructed, given that other diplomatic entities around the world mostly remain within the confines of traditional notions of diplomacy in (not) communicating with Trump on Twitter.

During 2020, from early March, Twitter was used by government officials to spread information and messages related to COVID-19. Twitter has become a messenger for diplomats; its logo - a light blue bird is a demonstration of a messenger getting to its digital destination.

Unlike Twitter, governments and government leaders use Facebook to share personal information and interact with various audiences. According to BCW's Facebook study 2020, the heads of state and government of 153 countries and 90 foreign ministers maintain personal pages on Facebook, and, in general, they are more popular than pages of their respective institutions.

Another social media platform used by governments and government leaders is Instagram – a video and photo sharing social networking. In comparison to Twitter and Facebook, Instagram is not as actively used for diplomatic purposes. However, it is used for sharing stories on ongoing official meetings, conferences, etc. Instagram promotes visualization of digital diplomacy. 81 percent of 193 UN member countries are active on Instagram (BCW, 2018). Leaders of all G7 and G20 countries have a personal account on Instagram except the President of the Russian Federation, Vladimir Putin and the President of the People's Republic of China, Xi Jinping.

Blogs have also played a pivotal role in terms of gathering information since 1990. For example, the U.S Department of State has opened the official blog "DipNote" that aims to offer first-person perspectives from U.S. government employees working to implement the mission of the U.S. Department of State. The blog makes a forum available for informal discussion among the public on foreign affairs and global issues. As blog-writing requires much time and creativity, a couple of diplomatic services hired experienced bloggers to influence the debate on certain topics in more effective way. For instance, the U.S Department of State established a Digital Outreach Team with bloggers fluent in Arabic and Farsi to follow relevant blogs and enter a debate as representatives of the U.S State Department.

Outbreak of the coronavirus has transformed intergovernmental cooperation and hastened the process of digitalization of diplomacy. Within days most diplomatic activities moved online, with leaders facing each other via their respective computer screens. Bilateral and multilateral meetings were held via telephone or videoconferencing apps such as Zoom and Webex. Despite the fact that online conferencing platforms have helped to bring a wider range of people together - people who would never otherwise have been at the same table, many diplomats outline that they have felt like fish out of water during implementing their mission online because "diplomacy is tactile and about relationships" (Wintour, 2020). Detailed analysis of "Zoom diplomacy" is provided below.

Overall, the use of social media and other online platforms has become an indivisible part of diplomatic practice and the global pandemic has strengthened this tendency even more. "Diplomacy has changed more than most professions during the pandemic" (The Economist, 2021). Leaders who only half-heartedly embraced digital platforms are now actively chatting via Google Meet, Skype and Zoom calls. However, despite a new reality, virtual diplomacy can hardly replace face-to-face communication.

BENEFITS AND RISKS OF DIGITAL DIPLOMACY

Benefits of Digital Diplomacy

Digitalization of diplomacy has become an inevitable long-term process that introduces new opportunities for diplomats and foreign ministries to efficiently implement foreign policy priorities. Considering the preponderance of this trend in international relations, knowledge about the major benefits of digital diplomacy is indispensable.

Firstly, digital diplomacy has provided for a significant increase of actors involved in international relations and politics, including states, ethno-nationalist groups, multinational corporations, intergovernmental organizations, non-governmental organizations, various transnational movements and networks, or even individuals (Mingst, 2008). For instance, a network of international organizations plays an important role in keeping the group of countries and the world united in adherence to international principles and norms. For example, the United Nations Security Council is often considered "the apex of global diplomacy" (Heath, 2020). Consequently, digital technologies can reduce political exclusion by allowing new routes for access and influence by offering chances to interest groups to place issues on the policy agenda and/or alter policy decisions (Hocking & Melissen, 2015, p. 18).

The first factor is closely connected to the second one - the availability of a huge amount of information online. Big data affects diplomacy in a number of ways reflecting developments in the changing relationship between government and society. In 2000, only 25% of the world's stored information was in digital form; by 2014 the figure had risen to around 98% (Hocking & Melissen, 2015, p.16). Thus, substantially increased access to information by a wide range of actors allows for the empowerment of people by boosting their ability to express views through new channels.

Availability of a large amount of information online is quite beneficial for diplomats themselves as they can observe events and international political developments, gather and process information and identify the key influencers easily.

Possibilities to engage in online debate is a third crucial benefit of digital diplomacy that results in more proximity of government officials and diplomats with various audiences around the world without the interposition of mass media. Diplomats might use new digital tools to reach vast audiences, be able to segment them and direct messages more precisely, thus, overcoming the limitations of traditional diplomacy. Moreover, diplomats can understand people and their needs better. Notably, two-way communicative nature of social media represents the fundamental difference between digital diplomacy and 20th century diplomacy practiced via radio or television (Hocking & Melissen, 2015). Digital tools substantially assist diplomats in establishing a united and strong diaspora closely linked to the homeland that can positively influence perceptions about the country abroad.

Digital tools have also proven themselves a powerful medium for nation branding. One interesting example is Finland's national emoji application available on the App Store. The application enables consumers to use a variety of emojis or images that represent Finland's culture and history. The project has attracted the attention of mass media and Finland managed to brand itself as a vibrant, technologically oriented and humorous nation (Manor, 2016).

According to the Twiplomacy study of 2016, Obama White House had the most popular government account. During Obama's presidency, federal agencies had increased their presence on social media platforms and, also launched blogs and websites in order to establish closer contacts with the audience (BCW, 2016). The White House was regularly broadcasting events from the Oval Office on Facebook while videos of town hall meetings were uploaded on YouTube (Kreisberg, 2019, p. 14). During Obama's presidency, the White House launched "We the People" platform where anybody could create a petition online and speak directly to the Administration.

Fourthly, access to information and the opportunity to engage in online debates influence governments in terms of more effective top-down delivery of services. Introduction of various digital tools is essential to improve public policy performance and build and maintain trust in government services.

Fifthly, digital technologies provide for fast communication in urgent situations that can be a significant advantage to protect national interests. In times of crisis, embassies can create groups in WhatsApp that include the ambassador, consular officer, press secretary, staff, diplomats from the headquarter, etc. to ensure timely information exchange. This group can function as a crisis management cell and enable the collection of real-time information, decision-making and dissemination of information (Raschica, 2018, p.81). In December 2014, as a result of a series of interviews with Geneva-based Ambassadors, Manor found that the Ambassadors were using WhatsApp groups to coordinate initiatives at UN forums, identify possible challenges and even collectively engage in coalition-building ahead of votes at the Human Rights Council (Manor, n.d.).

Furthermore, swift communication is of utmost importance for contemporary diplomacy as it should react to events as they unfold giving rise to what Philip Seib has dubbed "real-time diplomacy" (Seib, 2012). Indeed, due to the increased used of social networking platforms foreign ministries are required to expedite working routines in order to affect the coverage and framing of international political events and developments. For example, during 2017 London terror attacks, embassies found themselves curating online information and providing citizens with advice as events unfolded on their television screens (Manor, 2017).

Sixthly, due to availability of various online tools and platforms, people living under authoritarian regimes can maintain their ability to continue communicating internally and internationally about the situation in the country. Digital technologies might ensure freedom of expressing objections to certain issues (McGlinchey, 2017). In the contemporary world, media coverage is almost instantaneous. For instance, through social networks, Arab Spring activists have not only gained the power to overthrow powerful dictatorships but Arab civilians have become aware of the existent underground communities willing to listen to their stories. In countries like Egypt, Tunisia, and Yemen, protests made up of thousands were organized through social media such Facebook and Twitter (Kassim, 2012). However, it should be noted that despite active use of social media as a tool for communication, coordination and mobilization, it cannot be seen as a catalyst of any revolution by itself (Salanova, 2017, p.53).

Low cost is another crucial benefit of digital diplomacy. Accessiblity of the Internet brings millions of users online allowing them to stay tuned about all international, regional and local events and developments at any time. In addition to cheap access to the Internet for users, more cost-effective modes of

Benefits and Risks of Digital Diplomacy

diplomatic representation and experimentation with alternatives to the traditional embassy have also become more and more popular among governments. For instance, Israel launched its first virtual embassy in July 2013. It is located on twitter and aims to promote dialogue between Israel and the population of six gulf countries with which Israel does not have official diplomatic relations. Over the past year Israel's virtual embassy has tweeted some 400 tweets and attracted 1,797 followers (Manor, n.d.). The example of Israel's virtual embassy is just one step in the long evolution of virtual embassies.

Eightly, digital diplomacy is especially attractive for small states that often have fewer resources necessary for effective interaction with other states. Many of them might not have enough resources to project their positions, deploy alignments and circumstances supporting their priorities. Moreover, small states often find it difficult to be recognized by others. In such situation, social media is a great tool for realization (Goetschel, 1998, pp. 13-31). For example, Kosovo's Ministry of Foreign Affairs is proactively engaging in advancing Kosovo's digital diplomacy agenda, focusing on securing Kosovo's recognition by the global internet infrastructure. A strategy on digital diplomacy was adopted that encompasses various initiatives to strengthen Kosovo's overall online presence and quality multimedia content. Turkish magazine Yeni Diplomasi awarded the Kosovo Strategy for Digital Diplomacy the 4th best place in the world (Ministry of Foreign Affairs and Diaspora, n.d.).

Ninethly, digital diplomacy has become even more prevalent during the outbreak of a new coronavirus. Diplomacy has gained greater significance as during the pandemic its scope was extended; it has flexed its muscles on health, science and technology matters. Active action on health diplomacy was deployed by governments, international organizations and many other stakeholders with an interest and commitment in solving this world scourge, bilaterally and multilaterally, and digitalization proved to be a timely and available means to facilitate interaction (Bartolome, 2021).

Furthermore, as people moved to remote work after lockdowns were enforced to slow the spread of the coronavirus, the number of Zoom's daily participants jumped from 10 million in December 2019 to more than 200 million in three following months ("Zoom's daily participants," 2020). Digital platforms were used early on in the pandemic enabling diplomats to hold conferences and discussions from a distance. The possibility to continue activities uninterrupted is an important advantage provided by digital conferencing platforms. Online meetings also increase inclusion by making dialogue and negotiations more accessible as more participants can be allowed to get involved without any costs like travel and other expenses. In addition to reducing airfare costs, savings in carbon emissions are also vast. Moreover, technology helps to make activities more transparent and democratic as video conferences are published on different platforms including Facebook and Twitter (Abdeleli, 2021).

Therefore, digital diplomacy provides various valuable opportunities to improve efficiency of diplomatic work. Due to digital tools more actors might get involved in online debates and influence decision-making processes, communication has become more democratic, cost-effective, fast and timely, the voice of small countries can be heard easier, public diplomacy might be conducted more effectively as diplomats can reach larger audiences from all around the world, and, lastly, global pandemics do not necessarily lead to cancellation of all events and negotiations as they can move online. However, despite the fact that digital tools do have substantial benefits and are important elements for realizing contemporary foreign policy, "Zoom diplomacy" seems to be unable to replace face-to-face negotiations; the lack of physical contact reduces the efficiency of diplomatic activities. Disadvantages of digital tools and platforms for diplomatic work are provided in details below.

Risks of Digital Diplomacy

Changing foreign policy environment by the increased role of digital tools and capacity of non-state actors as well as changing power configurations create various risks for diplomacy.

Firstly, virtual diplomacy can be just another dividing line between the haves and have-nots: if a country lacks funds for elaborate system of embassies or diplomatic travel, it is likely to have subpar broadband and 5G connections too. For example, during one virtual meeting of the Warsaw International Mechanism - a U.N. climate initiative - a Sudanese representative was unable to participate because of low bandwidth (Heath, 2020).

Secondly, in the process of digitalization of diplomacy, it becomes more difficult to manage communication in a highly fragmented information environment. Public trust might be easily reduced, confidence and reputation can be manipulated and destroyed through effective campaigns conducted by civil society groups using a range of media formats.

The Internet and social media, in particular, might become a tool to spread terrorism, extremism and impose foreign ideologies. According to Weimann, 90% of organized terrorism on internet takes place on social media (Weimann, 2014, p. 12). Since August 2015 till December 2017, Twitter has blocked about 1.2 million accounts for terrorist content to prevent the promotion of terrorism (Twitter Public Policy, 2018). However, social networks like Twitter, Facebook and YouTube cannot fully control terrorist propaganda.

Thirdly, one of the main goals of a diplomat - obtaining information that traditionally takes place via embassies, permanent delegations and temporarily posted diplomats, can now be assisted by digital information sources, such as social networks, blogs and search engines. However, diplomats should be careful with huge amount of available information and should learn to discern reliable and accurate data from disinformation.

Fourthly, as various audiences with different opinions and interests are present online, verbal attacks and hate speech against diplomats have become an inseparable part of digital diplomacy. Fifthly, despite the fact that the Internet multiplies the number of voices involved in drafting international policies promoting more transparent and democratic approaches, it also significantly complicates international decision-making and reduces the country's exclusive control of the process.

Sixthly, digital diplomacy creates risks to successfully conducting public diplomacy. Social media is driving home the message that governmental control over the projection and perception of its image is becoming a delusion (Hocking & Melissen, 2015). Technical difficulties complicate the situation. For instance, by using bots, computer programs that are meant to imitate internet users and post certain comments and opinions, one nation can impact the social media discourse and people's perceptions of reality in another country. Moreover, social networking sites are all based on algorithms that tailor our online experience and might detect political affiliation, world view and even sexual orientation. Algorithms then expose us primarily to the content that confers with our opinions and beliefs limiting what we know about the world. This is a major challenge for MFAs and diplomats looking to alter the way their nation is perceived (Manor, 2016).

Seventhly, one of the biggest risks of digital diplomay is hacking. With rapid expansion of the Internet's use, cybersecurity has immediately attracted much attention. Diplomatic rivals, including both state and non-state actors might try to hack government systems and extract classified information for their own goals. Risks are increasingly sophisticated as cyberspace vulnerabilities have been already exploited not only by underground communities' hackers but also by global and well-organized criminal and terrorist groups, government security services and defence forces. The fact that most of the internet infrastructure and services are privately owned further complicates the situation. Therefore, state and non-state actors might employ digitalization towards undermining diplomatic processes via spreading fake videos, bots and fictitious news sites. Combating the emergence of digital disinformation has become one of the main tasks of modern diplomats.

Eighthly, digitalization of diplomacy implies the need for new skills and structures. In order to continue working successfully, diplomats need to adapt to new tools and learn how to use the Internet to meet the goals of diplomacy. However, the development of competencies in digital diplomacy requires time. To make matter worse, "it is easy to see that adaptation is not a matter of choice. A failure to adopt new technologies questions the standing of the MFA as a modern organization within the shifting structures of government and, in the final analysis, its continuing relevance" (Hocking & Melissen, 2015, p.44). For that reason, countries have developed comprehensive digital foreign policy strategies. For example, several countries adopted comprehensive digital foreign policy strategies (Australia, Denmark, France, and Switzerland), others just refer to digitalization in their foreign policy documents (Estonia, Canada, Bosnia and Herzegovina). Hence, countries have started paying more attention to digital aspects of contemporary foreign policy in order to formulate a holistic vision and approach to this issue.

Moreover, an additional challenge lies in MFAs' need to maintain their online diplomatic empires (Manor, 2016). MFAs should create attractive social media content, converse with online publics and respond to questions and comments. MFAs must regularly follow journalists and other diplomatic institutions to stay updated on ongoing events and political developments that might influence their countries. All these require substantial resources.

Ninthly, another challenge for e-diplomacy is the Internet "culture of anonymity" – anyone can adopt any persona, address or even attack anyone (Yakovenko, 2012). This can result in widespread disinformation that can hinder the ability of leaders to manage various situations. For example, in 2018 Facebook faced its biggest crisis ever - the "Cambridge Analytica Data Scandal." The firm that has worked with former US President Donald Trump's electoral team used data improperly obtained from Facebook to build voter profiles (Confessore, 2018). Cambridge Analytica had access to information of over 87 million Facebook users without their knowledge.

Tenthly, the global pandemic COVID-19 has shifted our day-to-day activities from offline to online. New conferencing platforms emerged while existing ones gained popularity. The world has been looking to diplomats to coordinate responses to a crippling pandemic. However, diplomats were deprived of the major tool at their disposal - personal contact - to successfully implement their mission. "Zoom diplomacy" gave rise to new concerns that diplomats and organizations should keep in mind while holding online meetings. The most recurring questions include how to choose the right video conferencing platform as well as how to tackle numerous security and privacy challenges. For example, "Zoom Bombing" that refers to uninvolved parties joining other people's meetings and sharing unwanted or offensive content, has become a significant security challenge related to online meetings. On the other hand, manifold leakages of meeting recordings, transcripts, and participants' data have come to public attention and led platform companies to tighten their security and privacy settings ("Future of Meetings," n.d.). Recently, Zoom agreed to pay $85 million and improve its security practices in order to settle a lawsuit that alleged that the platform violated the privacy of its users. The lawsuit was filed in March 2020. Plaintiffs claimed that Zoom shared personal data with third-party companies and that allowed hackers to interrupt online meetings through so-called "Zoom bombing" ("Zoom settles lawsuit," 2021).

Diplomats have also highlighted threats to confidentiality as one of the main pitfalls of "Zoom diplomacy." Hreinn Pálsson, the Deputy Chief at Iceland's UN mission, explained that "the trouble is everything is on the record… We do not write reports back home about the political situation in the US. What we do is provide the background, and you get the background from private conversation" (Wintour, 2020). In London a senior ambassador fulminated: "We cannot do our job. This cannot go on much longer. Diplomacy is all about confidentiality. We cannot trust Zoom and other technology. The assumption must be that the security is compromised" (Wintour, 2020). This "opening up of diplomacy" underscores the key problem of balancing the requirements of confidentiality in negotiations with the growing demands for transparency (Hocking & Melissen, 2015, p.24).

Lastly, moving diplomacy online directly affects diplomatic performance as without physical presence and personal contact including impromptu side meetings instead of formal exchanges, there is no real interaction creating difficulties with building trust and empathy, and it becomes harder to make important decisions and compromises. "Coalition-building at multilateral forums and establishing ties with diaspora leaders rest on diplomats' ability to establish a positive rapport with their counterparts. This can primarily be achieved through personal interactions" (Bjola & Manor, 2019, p.93). This is why, gradually, as epidemiological situation has improved, diplomacy has started "waking up." Thus, despite the fact that diplomacy has experienced many changes as the pandemic unfolded, it seems that it will not totally move online. However, hybrid diplomacy, a blend of physical and digital options will remain in place in the years to come.

To sum up, along with opportunities, utilizing digital tools in diplomatic work brings considerable risks that diplomats and government officials should keep in mind. Pitfalls of digital diplomacy include unequal distribution and availability of digital tools among nations, difficulties with managing communication, huge amount of unreliable and imprecise information and propaganda online, more complicated international decision-making process as more actors are involved, hacking and various threats to cybersecurity, the lack of skills and knowledge to successfully operate online, need for more resources to maintain diplomatic presence online, confidentiality and anonymity issues, lower level of diplomatic performance due to the lack of personal contact. Taking into account mentioned disadvantages, diplomacy is more likely to continue working in hybrid regime comprising both, online and on-site options of communication.

TRADITIONAL AND DIGITAL DIPLOMACY: COMPARATIVE ANALYSIS

This section aims to compare traditional and digital diplomacy and intends to determine whether traditional diplomacy remains relevant and, if so, in what way.

Main functions of diplomacy such as negotiation and representation as well as two main pillars of diplomacy, information and communication have not changed substantially over the centuries. However, technological innovations starting from telegraph and radio up to the Internet have significantly influenced the way diplomacy has been performed. The introduction of each new e-tool challenged conventional diplomatic practices and opened up new opportunities to improve diplomatic performance.

Conventional diplomacy was a profession reserved for aristocrats. Nevertheless, as a result of the professionalization of diplomacy, this field is no longer elitist aristocratic profession (Kurbalija, 2012, p. 153); diplomats' skills and intellectual abilities lie at the core of their success. Introduction of ICTs to diplomatic practices contributed considerably to this process.

Traditional diplomacy has been based on representation. An Ambassador Extraordinary and Plenipotentiary served as king's representative to the court of another king to negotiate and sign treaties. Yet in the age of ICTs, relevant leaders of the country whether presidents, ministers or prime ministers might gather by themselves to reach an agreement bypassing the ambassador. In addition, ICTs allow diplomats and foreign ministers to constantly exchange information and diplomats are regularly informed on new instructions and priorities. Thus, diplomats no longer have a monopoly in managing relations with foreign entities.

Digital tools have almost eliminated physical distance between diplomats and their respective governments. Constant and fast communication and coordination between MFAs and diplomats during negotiations/conferences has become feasible whereas traditionally, exchange of received and gathered information needed time to reach their respective ministries. As political situation is characterized by rapid and unexpected changes, a reply received by a diplomat from a sending state could be already irrelevant. ICTs and the possibility of instantaneous communication have totally overcome this difficulty.

Traditionally, diplomatic work included mostly government-to-government representation and communication without chances to converse with people. However, by utilizing digital tools diplomats have got actively involved in nation branding, in the process of shaping and promoting sending country's image abroad. Therefore, despite the fact that diplomatic relations might not be established between two countries, diplomats still have possibilities to reach the population and successfully conduct public policy. Thus, the lack of representation does not necessarily mean the lack of communication anymore.

Furthermore, diplomats might influence political attitudes not only in foreign countries but domestically as well. "Digitization further blurs the distinction between domestic and foreign, as citizens' migration to digital platforms creates new opportunities for diplomats to rally domestic public support for foreign policy achievements or sway public opinion in favor of a chosen policy" (Bjola & Manor, 2019, p.89). Hence, digital tools allow for active and intensive engagement with both domestic and foreign publics creating positive climate of accepting country's policies and approaches. Moreover, this can be achieved cost-effectively as social media is accessible for everyone for low cost.

As the former Ambassador of the Kingdom of the Netherlands to the USA, Rudolf Bekink noted: "the digital arena opens new possibilities, from one-on-one conversations to dialogues with communities." Traditional diplomacy is still relevant, he says, "but digital diplomacy adds enormously to the capabilities of every diplomat" (Colemen, 2014).

Previously, diplomatic negotiations and meetings were traditionally held behind the closed doors while digital tools allowed to ensure openness and transparency. Traditionally, only diplomats could take part in negotiations and international events. Digital tools made negotiations, international high-level conferences and other events more inclusive as they allowed for remote participation of various members of the society from all around the world. Secrecy has been one of the main aspects of diplomacy that to some extent will remain an indivisible part of diplomatic work. However, gradually the principle of openness has become a requirement of time. Already in 1918, U.S. President Woodrow Wilson formulated his well-known fourteen points the first of which stood for "open covenants of peace, openly arrived at, after which there shall be no private international understandings of any kind but diplomacy shall proceed always frankly and in the public view" ("Fourteen Points," n.d.). Introduction of ICTs fastened this process and created more challenges to the principle of secrecy. In modern diplomacy, secrecy concerns became closely linked with cybersecurity matters as governments started intensively working on diminishing the possibilities of information leakage.

Diplomats are no more facing the scarcity of information and resources, they do not have to rely only on MFAs and embassies for information as digital diplomacy exposes them to large amount of information, not only factual but also personal (through blogs and personal social media accounts) that might make their core function of information gathering faster and easier. However, it should be outlined that often diplomats still need to obtain information from official sources or check the available information online with MFAs as sometimes it becomes extremely difficult to distinguish reliable and accurate information from disinformation. "State has already begun conceptual work on the idea of 'networked diplomacy' – that is, moving beyond the traditional siloed approach to information gathering in capitals, where every embassy closely guards all its information, to a networked approach where information is easily shared between like-minded governments" (Hanson, 2012, p.5).

Digital platforms create new comfortable possibilities for storing information and documents. Diplomats and ministries do not have to keep all information and documents in paper versions as they can easily be preserved, managed and searched on various digital platforms.

COVID-19 has extensively affected the process of digitalization of diplomacy. Zoom has become one of the most widespread video conferencing platforms. Due to the pandemic, the G7, G20, International Monetary Fund and World Bank have all convened teleconferences in place of in-person gatherings. However, "Zoom diplomacy" has perfectly demonstrated limitations of virtual diplomacy. Hreinn Pálsson, the Deputy Chief at Iceland's UN mission, explained that "so many conversations on Zoom end with 'I will tell you the background to all this over a cup of coffee later.' That is the hindrance. You cannot get hints, nods and winks to guide you" (Wintour, 2020). In London a senior ambassador in the thick of a major crisis fulminates: "With Zoom, there is no real interaction, but compromise needs interaction and diplomacy feeds off compromise" (Wintour, 2020). Therefore, virtual negotiations can hardly substitute for the reality. Former UK Ambassador Charles Crawford noted that "You just can't generate any sense of urgency or importance via online events" ("Diplomacy in the Age of Zoom," 2021). All of the above complicate decision-making processes, likeliness of making compromises and building trust. In addition, no personal contact, informal meetings and chats, confidential talks become possible. Moreover, it becomes especially difficult to build strong networks online while diplomacy has been based on personal networks. Security and privacy issues also hinder safe communication. Consequently, personal interaction remains vital to achieve diplomatic objectives.

Despite the fact that diplomacy has historically experienced various changes related to the applied means of communication starting from messengers and/or merchant caravans to using cipher systems, telephones and finally, the Internet and various new mediums of communication, communication has remained at the heart of diplomacy. A wide array of actors involved in diplomacy and increased importance of multilateral diplomacy in more globalized and interdependent world boost the role of diplomacy in international relations. Kurbalia (2016) has correctly outlined that:

In the digitally-driven world, interdependence requires diplomatic solutions. They lie more in persuasion and engagement than in military might, as we can see from the latest diplomatic breakthroughs (Iran Nuke, Cuba, and Kosovo, to name a few). We need to negotiate more than ever before - be it in the family or in global politics (paragraph 8).

Therefore, diplomats should continue adapting to new available tools for effective communication in order to ensure proper implementation of foreign policy priorities of their respective countries. The

Benefits and Risks of Digital Diplomacy

need for and importance of skills and knowledge of diplomats did not wither away; rather, professional diplomats are needed as never before.

Digital diplomacy does not intend to replace traditional diplomacy; when used appropriately, digital diplomacy is a persuasive and timely supplement to conventional diplomacy that can help a country advance its foreign policy goals, extend international reach, and influence people who will never set foot in any of the world's embassies (Lowy Interpreter, 2015). Similarly, Permyakova (2012) argues:

...Digital diplomacy is mainly applicative in nature and is particularly useful in working with foreign audiences in matters of relaying the official position and building up the image of the state. It is important to understand that it is unlikely to ever replace diplomacy in its conventional sense. Closed talks will remain closed. However, digital diplomacy is capable of explaining why a certain decision was made, what results it will give, how it will influence the foreign policy process, i.e. of opening public access to the results of conventional diplomacy (paragraph 8).

All in all, digital diplomacy does not intend to replace traditional diplomacy. The former is a perfect supplement to the latter. Digital tools provide various opportunities to enhance the work of diplomats and assist them in implementing their mission more efficiently. Core aspects of diplomacy, information and communication as well as negotiation and representation remain relevant. While "Zoom diplomacy" is a fascinating platform to exchange information and discuss general issues, it does not provide for chances to build strong personal contacts and trust so that making compromises and ultimate political decisions become possible. Therefore, negotiations via online platforms cannot replace in-person gatherings. This is why, hybrid diplomacy combining online and on-site meetings is likely to dominate future diplomatic practice. This means that diplomats will need to continue constantly improving their digital skills so that they can use digital tools at their disposal in the best possible way for the benefit of countries they represent.

FUTURE RESEARCH DIRECTIONS

The chapter has outlined that digital technologies have created challenges to secrecy, one of the major features of traditional diplomacy. Despite the fact that backstage diplomacy is still crucial for diplomats to engage in personal and confidential conversations, digitalization of diplomacy has pushed for more transparency and openness of diplomatic activities. Future research should address the issue whether and how more open and transparent diplomacy affects diplomatic performance.

Besides, as the COVID-19 pandemic has begun, many countries closed their borders leaving thousands of people stranded in foreign countries. Offering comprehensive consular assistance and support to citizens abroad has become a top priority for governments. Future research may focus on the importance of digital tools for consular services in particular, and evaluate digital channels applied by consulates to offer timely advice to their nationals during the COVID-19 pandemic.

CONCLUSION

Digitalization of diplomacy has brought various benefits and risks to diplomatic practice. The chapter argues that by utilizing digital tools and platforms diplomats can implement their mission more efficiently. Participation of multiple actors in online debates and policy-making has made the conduct of diplomacy more democratic, inclusive and transparent; digital tools have also provided for more cost-effective, fast and timely communication with more chances for small countries to raise their voice; online platforms and search engines assist diplomats in information gathering process that has become easier with chances to find necessary information in a short period of time; digital diplomacy brings special advantages to conducting public diplomacy as diplomats can reach larger and more diverse audiences. As boundaries between foreign and domestic have started to blur, diplomats might use digital tools to influence both foreign and domestic publics. Thus, they can formulate a more results-oriented and successful nation branding strategy. Digital technologies allowed for continuation of the work online without interruptions in the period of the global pandemic.

However, despite substantial benefits of digital diplomacy, risks should also be kept in mind while applying digital tools to diplomats' everyday work. Digital tools are not equally available for all countries, managing knowledge and information has become more complicated as huge amount of unreliable and imprecise information and propaganda is available online; involvement of wide array of actors in international decision-making process has complicated negotiations as well as increased the risks of employing digitalization by state and non-state actors to undermine diplomatic processes via spreading fake videos, bots and fictitious news sites. Risks of hacking and information leakage have increased significantly making cybersecurity one of the top priorities of governments. Successful operation online might also be hindered by the lack of skills and knowledge of utilizing digital tools and platforms. Maintaining digital presence online is also related to additional resources within embassies and MFAs. Digital tools might constrain diplomats as online platforms provide for less confidentiality and anonymity. Moreover, diplomatic performance online seems to be diminishing as "Zoom diplomacy" is unable to replace face-to-face negotiations; the lack of physical and personal contact negatively affects the efficiency of diplomatic activities as only backstage diplomacy allows diplomats to foster personal ties and leverage them to achieve national goals.

Comparison of traditional and digital diplomacy paved the way for the conclusion of the chapter: traditional diplomacy is not antiquated but advanced by digital tools and platforms. Digital diplomacy does not intend to replace traditional face-to-face diplomacy. Traditional and digital diplomacy complement rather than compete with each other. Digital technologies provide exceptional benefits to public diplomacy as diplomats have many tools at their disposal to reach out and project foreign policy positions among large domestic and foreign audiences quickly, easily and efficiently. Moreover, diplomacy has transformed from monologue into dialogue with wide range of opportunities to openly communicate with the public. Hence, core aspects of diplomacy, information and communication as well as negotiation and representation remain relevant. Diplomats will still need to be effective and strong negotiators in order to demonstrate foreign policy positions and priorities of their sending state. Nevertheless, means of communication and information gathering and dissemination have changed for the better. Benefits of digital diplomacy prevail over the risks. As "Zoom diplomacy" can hardly be a good substitute for in-person diplomacy, diplomacy will operate in a hybrid regime comprising both, online and on-site options of communication in the years to come.

REFERENCES

Adesina, O. S. (2017). Foreign policy in an era of digital diplomacy. *Cogent Social Sciences*, *3*(1), 1297175. doi:10.1080/23311886.2017.1297175

Bartolome, G. D. (2021, July 6). The hybrid future of diplomacy. *The Washington Diplomat*. https://washdiplomat.com/the-hybrid-future-of-future-diplomacy/

BCW. (2016, May 31). *Twiplomacy Study 2016*. https://twiplomacy.com/blog/twiplomacy-study-2016/

BCW. (2018, December). *World Leaders on Instagram*. https://twiplomacy.com/blog/world-leaders-instagram-2018/

BCW. (2020, April 23). *World Leaders on Facebook*. https://twiplomacy.com/blog/world-leaders-on-facebook-2020/

BCW. (2020, July). *Twiplomacy Study 2020*. https://twiplomacy.com/blog/twiplomacy-study-2020/

Bjola, C., & Holmes, M. (2015). *Digital Diplomacy: Theory and Practice*. Routledge. doi:10.4324/9781315730844

Bjola, C., & Manor, I. (2020, March 31). *Digital Diplomacy in the Time of the Coronavirus Pandemic*. University of Southern California Center of Public Diplomacy. https://uscpublicdiplomacy.org/blog/digital-diplomacy-time-coronavirus-pandemic

Cave, D. (2015, April 17). Does Australia do digital diplomacy? *The Interpreter*. https://www.lowyinterpreter.org/post/2015/04/17/Does-Australia-do-digital-diplomacy.aspx

Coleman, L. D. (2014). *Diplomacy must embrace digiculture*. Diplomatic Courier.

Confessore, N. (2018, April). Cambridge Analytica and Facebook: The Scandal and the Fallout So Far. *New York Times*.

Dejevsky, M. (2017, February 5). In defence of Donald Trump's Twitter diplomacy. *The Guardian*.

Digwatch. (2021, August 6). *Zoom settles lawsuit over privacy issues*. https://dig.watch/updates/zoom-settles-lawsuit-over-privacy-issues

Diplo. (2013, June 21). *Wikipedia for Diplomats*. https://www.diplomacy.edu/calendar/webinar-wikipedia-diplomats

Diplo. (n.d.). *Future of Meetings*. https://www.diplomacy.edu/future-of-meetings

Diplomat. (2017, July 5). *Ambassadors in a Digital Age*. https://diplomatmagazine.com/ambassadors-in-digital-age/

Diplomat. (2021, July 7). *Diplomacy in the Age of Zoom*. https://diplomatmagazine.com/diplomacy-in-the-age-of-zoom/

Encyclopaedia Britannica. (n.d.). *Fourteen Points*. https://www.britannica.com/event/Fourteen-Points

Friedman, T. (2005). *The World is Flat: A Brief History of the Twenty-first Century* (1st ed.). Farrar, Straus and Giroux.

Goetschel, L. (1998). The Foreign and Security Policy Interests of Small States in Today's Europe. In L. Goetschel (Ed.), *Small States Inside and Outside of European Union* (pp. 13–31). Swiss Peace Foundation. doi:10.1007/978-1-4757-2832-3_2

Hanson, F. (2012). *Baked in and wired: eDiplomacy@State. Foreign Policy Paper Series no 30*. Brookings Institution.

Heath, R. (2020a, April 17). For global diplomats, Zoom is not like being in the room. *Politico*. https://www.politico.eu/article/coronavirus-global-diplomacy-on-zoom/

Heath, R. (2020b, April). For global diplomats, Zoom is not like being in the room. *Politico*. https://www.politico.com/news/2020/04/16/zoom-diplomacy-coronavirus-188811

Hocking, B. & Melissen, J. (2015). *Diplomacy in the digital age*. Netherlands Institute of International Relations.

Jönsson, C. (2016). Diplomacy, Communication and Signalling. In C. M. Constantinou, P. Kerr & P. Sharp (Eds.), The SAGE Handbook of Diplomacy (pp. 79-91). SAGE Publications Ltd.

Kassim, S. (2012, July 3). *Twitter Revolution: How the Arab Spring Was Helped by Social Media*. Mic. https://www.mic.com/articles/10642/twitter-revolution-how-the-arab-spring-was-helped-by-social-media

Kreisberg, A. A. (2019). Social media data archives in an API-driven world. *Arch Sci, 20,* 105–123. doi:10.1007/s10502-019-09325-9

Kurbalija, J. (2012). *Diplomacy in a Globalizing World Theories and Practicies*. Oxford University Press.

Kurbalija, J. (2016, May 17). *diplomacy – Diplomacy – DIPLOMACY*. Diplo. https://www.diplomacy.edu/blog/diplomacy-%25E2%2580%2593-diplomacy-%25E2%2580%2593-diplomacy

Manor, I. (2014, June 25). On Virtual Embassies in the Age of Digital Diplomacy. *Digdipblog*. https://digdipblog.com/2014/06/25/on-virtual-embassies-in-the-age-of-digital-diplomacy/

Manor, I, (2016, November). What is Digital Diplomacy, and how is it Practiced around the World? A brief introduction. *Diplomatist Magazine*.

Manor, I. (2016, February). Are We There Yet? Have MFAs Realized the Potential of Digital Diplomacy? *Brill Diplomacy and Foreign Policy*.

Manor, I. (2017, August 8). The Digitalization of Diplomacy: Toward Clarification of a Fractured Terminology. Working Paper. *Digdipblog*. https://digdipblog.com/2017/08/08/the-digitalization-of-diplomacy-toward-clarification-of-a-fractured-terminology/

Manor, I. (2017, March 23). How Embassies Managed the London Terror Attack. *Digdipblog*. https://digdipblog.com/2017/03/23/howembassies-managed-the-london-terrorattack/

Manor, I. (2018, February 20). The Evolution of WhatsApp as a Diplomatic Tool. *Digdipblog*. https://digdipblog.com/2018/02/20/the-evolution-of-whatsapp-as-a-diplomatic-tool/

Manor, I., & Segev, E. (2015). America's selfie: How the US portrays itself on its social media accounts. In C. Bjola & M. Holmes (Eds.), Digital Diplomacy: Theory and Practice (pp. 89-108). Routledge.

McGlinchey, S. (2017). *International Relations*. E-International Relations. Ministry of Foreign Affairs and Diaspora of the Republic of Kosovo. Digital Diplomacy. http://www.mfa-ks.net/en/politika/486/diplomacia-digjitale/486

Permyakova, L. (2012, September 28). *Digital diplomacy: areas of work, risks and tools*. Academic Press.

Phalen, W. (2015). *How the telegraph changed the world*. McFarland Company. https://russiancouncil.ru/en/analytics-and-comments/analytics/digital-diplomacy-areas-of-work-risks-and-tools/

Rashica, V. (2018). *The Benefits and Risks of Digital Diplomacy*. SEEU Review. doi:10.2478eeur-2018-0008

Reuters. (2020, April 2). *Zoom's daily participants jumped from 10 million to over 200 million in 3 months*. https://venturebeat.com/2020/04/02/zooms-daily-active-users-jumped-from-10-million-to-over-200-million-in-3-months/

Saeed, S. (2021, August 21). Taliban 2.0: Older, media-savvy and still duplicitous. *Politico*. https://www.politico.eu/article/taliban-afghanistan-rebrand-social-media-twitter-international-recognition/?utm_source=POLITICO.EU&utm_campaign=5637600182-EMAIL_CAMPAIGN_2021_08_20_04_59&utm_medium=email&utm_term=0_10959edeb5-5637600182-190784736

SalanovaR. (2012, December 1). *Social media and political change: the case of the 2011 revolutions in Tunisia and Egypt*. International Catalan Institute for Peace. Working Paper No. 2012/7. doi:10.2139/ssrn.2206293

Seib, P. (2012). Real-time diplomacy, politics and power in the social media era. Academic Press.

Šimunjak, M., & Caliandro, A. (2019, January). Twiplomacy in the age of Donald Trump: Is the diplomatic code changing? *The Information Society*, *35*(1), 13–25. doi:10.1080/01972243.2018.1542646

The Economist. (2021, May 1). *Diplomacy has changed more than most professions during the pandemic*. https://www.economist.com/international/2021/04/29/diplomacy-has-changed-more-than-most-professions-during-the-pandemic

Twitter Public Policy. (2018, April 5). *Expanding and building #TwitterTransparency*. https://blog.twitter.com/official/en_us/topics/company/2018/twitter-transparency-report-12.html

US Department of State. (n.d.). *DipNote*. https://www.state.gov/blogs

Weimann, G. (2014). *New terrorism and new media*. Woodrow Wilson International Center for Scholars. https://www.wilsoncenter.org/publication/new-terrorism-and-new-media

Westcott, N. (2008, July). *Digital diplomacy: The impact of the internet on international relations*. Oxford Internet Institute. https://www.oii.ox.ac.uk/archive/downloads/publications/RR16.pdf

Wintour, P. (2020). Bye bye bilaterals: UN general assembly to embrace Zoom diplomacy. *The Guardian*. https://www.theguardian.com/world/2020/sep/19/bye-bye-bilaterals-un-general-assembly-embrace-zoom-diplomacy

Yakovenko, A. (2012, September 7). Russian digital diplomacy: clicking through. *Russia Beyond*. http://rbth.com/articles/2012/09/06/russian_digital_diplomacy_clicking_through_18005.html

ADDITIONAL READING

Bjola, C., & Zaiotti, R. (2020). *Digital Diplomacy and International Organisations*. Routledge. doi:10.4324/9781003032724

Cassidy, J., & Manor, I. (2016). *Crafting strategic MFA communication policies during times of political crisis: a note to MFA policy makers*. Global Affairs., doi:10.1080/23340460.2016.1239377

Kantchev, G. (2015). Diplomats on Twitter: The good, the bad and the ugly. *Wall Street Journal*

Kurbalija, J. (2016, November 4). 25 Points for Digital Diplomacy. Diplo. https://www.diplomacy.edu/blog/25-points-digital-diplomacy

Manor, I. (2015). Digital Diplomacy 2.0? A cross-national comparison of public engagement in Facebook and Twitter. *The Hague Journal of Diplomacy*. Volume 10. Issue 4.

Manor, I. (2021). *Russia's Digital Diplomacy: The good, the bad and the satirical*. Russland-analysen.

Pamment, J. (2016). *British Public Diplomacy and Soft Power: Diplomatic Influence and the Digital Revolution*. Palgrave Macmillan. doi:10.1007/978-3-319-43240-3

Sandre, A. (2015). *Digital Diplomacy: Conversations on Innovation in Foreign Policy*. Rowman & Littlefield.

Zaharna, R. S., & Rugh, W. A. (2012). Issue Theme: The use of social media in U.S. public diplomacy. Global Media Journal-American Edition, 11(21), 1-8.

KEY TERMS AND DEFINITIONS

Chatbot: A form of artificial intelligence used in messaging applications. Chatbots are based on an automated program and communicate with people like a human being and are not limited by time and physical location.

Conventional/Traditional Diplomacy: The work conducted by diplomats who represent a sending state in another state. Conventional diplomacy implies conducting negotiations with representatives of a foreign country to help a sending government pursue its foreign policy objectives and protect its national interests. In a traditional sense, conventional diplomacy entails government-to-government communication.

Diaspora: People living abroad, far from their ancestral homelands but identify with a "homeland."

Digital Diplomacy: The use of the Internet and various social media tools to carry out diplomatic objectives. Digital diplomacy implies expanding diplomatic practice from government-to-government communication to public diplomacy that allows for reaching both domestic and foreign publics.

Digitalization of Diplomacy: A process of adopting digital tools in diplomatic practice and an overall impact digital tools have had on diplomacy.

Nation Branding: The process of building, managing, and promoting a particular self-image and a unique identity to improve international reputation of a country that will most effectively serve its national interests. Contemporary diplomats are actively involved in nation branding through working not only with foreign governments but with foreign audiences in general.

Public Diplomacy: Direct communication and engagement of governments with foreign public that aims to influence mass perceptions in the best interests of a government and country's foreign policy goals.

Virtual Embassy: Establishment of a virtual embassy implies using the Internet to establish a virtual presence in a particular part of the world. If a traditional embassy or consulate does not exist, a virtual embassy may provide e-services to people from sending and receiving states.

Zoom Bombing: Unwanted intrusion by uninvolved parties/uninvited attendees into other people's virtual meetings. Zoom bombing might include sharing negative, disturbing or offensive content to ruin a meeting.

Zoom Diplomacy: The use of Zoom, a video conferencing platform to conduct diplomacy. The global COVID-19 pandemic has transformed the ways governments work together; Zoom diplomacy has provided new opportunities to continue international and regional communication and cooperation uninterrupted.

Chapter 13
The Economic Component of World Politics and the Main Global Social and Economic Problems

Nika Chitadze
International Black Sea University, Georgia

ABSTRACT

The purpose of this research is consideration and analysis of the main social and economic problems of the world, which are connected with the existence of the gap between "Global North" and "Global South" and problems of the consumption of mineral resources, including energy and water resources, unemployment, illiteracy, health issues, food supply, demography, etc. We are watching the world become one. Countries and regions are interconnected by a thousand threads that make them interdependent. The world economy today is undergoing a process of globalization – the increasing interdependence of the economies of various countries of the world due to the growth in the movement of goods and services and the intensive exchange of goods, information, technologies, and labor migration.

INTRODUCTION

We are watching the world become one. Countries, regions are interconnected by a thousand threads that make them interdependent. The world economy today is undergoing a process of globalization - the increasing interdependence of the economies of various countries of the world due to the growth in the movement of goods and services, the intensive exchange of goods, information, technologies, and labor migration. This process began in the second half of the last century. In industry, the process of globalization is expressed in the deepening of the international division of labor and the strengthening of the internationalization of production. Transnational corporations (TNCs) have stretched out their tentacles around the world. The 5 largest TNCs control more than half of the world's production of cars, aircraft, computers, and other goods.

DOI: 10.4018/978-1-7998-9586-2.ch013

The commonality of the fate of mankind is most clearly manifested in its general, global problems.
Global problems of the economy are problems caused by the active economic activity of a person. The main problems of the economy are:

1. the economic backwardness of several countries;
2. ecological;
3. demographic;
4. food;
5. prevention of nuclear war.

The problem of the economic backwardness of the poorest countries in Asia and Africa and some other regions from the economically developed countries was called the "North-South" problem. The gap in the level of economic development also leads to a significant gap in the standard of living of the population. The gap between rich and poor countries is widening. It is in the countries of the South that most of the world's poor and ultra-poor people are concentrated. Poor people are those with an income of fewer than two dollars a day. There are two and a half to three billion of them on the planet. The super-poor is about one billion. These are the people whose daily income does not even reach one dollar. So, at the beginning of the twenty-first century, more than forty percent of the ultra-poor people lived in sub-Saharan Africa.

The demographic problem is the rapid population growth. In 2023, the world's population will exceed 8 billion (Wordometers, 2021). By the middle of the 21st century, it is projected to overcome the nine billion milestones (Wordometers, 2021). Moreover, the fastest growing population is in developing countries. The populations of the poorest countries are growing at a faster rate than the gross domestic product of those countries.

In the field of fertility and population growth in the modern world, two opposite trends have developed: population aging in developed countries; dramatic growth in developing countries.

The food problem is expressed primarily in the problem of hunger. Population growth is outstripping agricultural production, leading to food problems in many developing countries. According to international organizations, approximately six million children die from hunger or its consequences in the world every year. About sixteen thousand - a day, 11 children every minute (UN, 2021). In the future, hunger is not an inevitable problem due to the use of modern methods of intensifying agricultural production, modern biotechnologies, and other achievements of scientific and technological progress.

The environmental problem is one of the most pressing today. An increase in the scale of economic activity is fraught with global natural disasters. Non-renewable reserves of natural resources are nearing the end. The economic activity of people causes such damage to the natural environment that it has lost the ability to self-repair. Not all states can transfer their economic activities to waste-free technologies. The state of the natural environment largely determines the need for a transition from extensive to intensive farming methods based on resource provision with the use of environmental protection technologies. Scientific and technological progress occupies a special place in the aggravation of global problems. The scale of its impact on the environment has no similarity in the history of human development. The natural environment is saturated not only with production waste but also with completely new substances from production activities that do not decompose under the influence of natural processes. The problem of environmental pollution and waste disposal (especially radioactive) has acquired a planetary character.

Economic problems are the result of environmental pollution and environmental disasters. For a long time, leading economists have recognized the significant impact of environmental pollution problems on the level of economic development. It becomes obvious that one of the points of economic development should be the allocation of funds for environmental protection.

Economic problems are the result of environmental pollution and environmental disasters. For a long time, leading economists have recognized the significant impact of environmental pollution problems on the level of economic development. It becomes obvious that one of the points of economic development should be the allocation of funds for environmental protection.

The problem of the threat of a third world war is related to the economy since the arms race itself is ruinous for humanity. It wreaks havoc on the economy

Global problems are interconnected. So, the solution of environmental problems is impossible without solving economic issues, the economic lag of the third world countries is closely related to a sharp increase in population in them, it is no less obvious that the aggravation of environmental and economic problems was influenced by the arms race, etc.

All these problems are interconnected and, in one way or another, tied to the economy. The rapid population growth leads to an increase in the consumption of natural resources, increases the pressure on the environment, worsening the ecological situation. Huge military spending reduces investment in sectors of the economy that meet the needs of the people. The lack of opportunities for the majority of the population of poor countries to receive a normal education does not provide a sufficient number of qualified workers. This means that there is no need to talk about efficient production and the use of the latest technologies.

PART 1. THE PROBLEM OF NORTH-SOUTH RELATIONS

Parameters of Uneven Development in the Countries of the South and North

The concepts of "rich north-poor south" are widely used today to refer to the phenomenon, which consists in a significant polarization of the world along with the axis "North-south". As a result, in the countries located in the northern hemisphere (developed states), the overall socio-economic level of life is significantly higher than in the developing countries in the southern hemisphere. Sometimes, although recently much less frequently, the countries in the "South" are much more often called "countries of the third world". This term was originally disseminated in the framework of neo-Marxism in the years of the Cold War when the world was divided into capitalist, socialist, and "other" countries.

About 20% of the world's population lives in the prosperous countries of the northern hemisphere. According to data provided by the United Nations Development Program for the beginning of the second decade of the XXI Century, they consume about 90% of all goods produced on the Earth. They own approximately 85% of the entire park of cars. They account for almost 60% of the total generated energy. And the incomes of their citizens exceed those who live in developing countries by 60 times or more (Davitashvili, Elizbarashvili, 2012).

At the same time, the growth of the population is observed in developing countries (here lives 85% of those who were born in 1960 and later). According to the World Bank, in such regions as Africa and the Middle East, the annual population growth is about 3% (Chitadze, 2017). The high tempo of population growth proposes the solution of such problems, such as education, health, creation of new working places. However, instead of economic growth and improvement in the social sphere, there is a decline in these areas.

In developing countries, the number of AIDS patients is increasing: Currently, they account for almost 90% of all HIV-infected people. Concerning the World Bank, such data is often given. In Africa, in the sub-Saharan region, where the situation is most difficult, every 40th adult is HIV-infected. Along with the AIDS epidemic in developing countries, there is a high incidence of hepatitis (2 million deaths annually), tuberculosis (3 million, respectively), malaria (1 million deaths with 300 million diseases annually), and others, including tropical diseases. The Health system in this region is at a lower level in comparison to developed countries. According to the World Health Organization - WHO, 75% of the world's population, living in developing countries, account for 30% of doctors within the first decade of the XXI Century (Lebedeva, 2007). To this, it should be added that the incomes of adults in these countries do not allow them to spend significant sums on medicines and medical care. As a result, even sharp respiratory disease can lead to death.

Lack of drinking water, shelter, food, and other vital funds are also typical for these countries. In some countries, for example in India, Pakistan, Indonesia, Nigeria, Brazil, etc. part of the population, especially in rural areas, not only doesn't have water pipeline, but also has to daily overcome significant distances for drinking water, and this problem leads

to the spread of gastrointestinal diseases that lead among the causes of death (4 million deaths per year), as well as to the deterioration of the sanitary conditions of life in general.

At the beginning of the XXI Century, the World Bank cited figures that about 80% of all incidents in developing countries were related to the quality of consumed water. This results in the death of about 10 million people annually (Lebedeva, 2007).

The spread of diseases is facilitated by the low level of housing conditions. In one room there are large families and housing, for reasons of cost savings, is often built without taking into account seismic conditions, possible actions of monsoons, typhoons, etc. In developing countries, the percentage of homeless people is also significantly higher. The absence of a house is one of the most acute problems of the "global South".

Complicated sanitary and housing conditions are accompanied by a shortage of food supply. The percentage of people living in rural areas of developing countries is much higher than in developed countries. J. Goldstein cites data according to which in the developed countries about 70-80% of the population lives in the urban areas, while in Asia and Africa this indicator is not above 20%. Despite the involvement in the field of agriculture, approximately 800 million people in developing countries are chronically undernourished, as a result, they can't perform even the simplest work. However, among those who rose a little above the extreme poverty line, a large percentage of people don't get enough protein and vitamins. This is due to the need to allocate huge areas of agricultural lands under export crops: tea, coffee, cocoa. Even those cultures, which make good the deficiency of proteins (for example, soybeans) and could be used to fight hunger in their country, are used for export or for feeding the middle class (Goldstein, 2011).

Bad socio-economic conditions in developing countries lead to the fact that the average life expectancy in them is about 60 years (in the poor - 50, and some, due to the development of AIDS epidemic is much lower), while in developed countries length of life is approaching 80 years. At the same time, more than 17% of newborn babies in developing countries do not survive until the age of five (in developed countries, this figure averages just over 1.5%) (Maksakovsky, 2009).

Table 1. Comparison of socio-economic conditions in economically developed and developing countries on the example of Japan and Nigeria for the period of the crossing XX-XXI centuries

Comparison of the two countries: Developed (Japan) and developing (Nigeria) according to the most important indexes		
Indexes	Japan	Nigeria
Life expectancy	80	53
Infant mortality rate per 1000 newborns	4	80
GDP Per Capita	39640	250
Reproduction of the population within the 90-th of the XX Century	0,2	2,9
Adult Literacy, %	98	57
Number of doctors per 100 thousand people	164	2

Source: Rourke, Boyer, 2000.

The level of education in developed and developing countries is different. If in the "Global North" about 97% of the population are literate, in some regions of the "Global South" literacy may be less than 40%; people basically can't read and can't write the simplest sentences. Instead of school children of these countries are more often sent for earnings. Homelessness and child criminality is growing (Chitadze, 2017).

Low standard of living, education, and health, unemployment is often accompanied by conflicts, instability, and political coups. Especially alarming is the fact that for several indicators the gap between "North" and "South" continues to be increased. J. T. Rourke and M. A. Boyer cite the data according to which in 1990 the annual GDP per capita in the countries of "the Global North" was an average of 19 590 US dollars, and in "Global South" - 840, i.e., the difference in income is 18,750 dollars. At the beginning of the XXI Century, the difference was even greater - $ 24,260 with annual income per capita in developed countries $25 510 and in developing countries 1 250 (Rourke, Boyer, 2009).

The countries with the lowest per capita incomes are of particular concern. These states, according to the classification of the International Monetary Fund, are among the least developed among the developing countries – the least-developed of the less-countries, LLDCs. In those states, the average income per capita is about one dollar per day, and commodity-money relations are replaced by natural exchange, although the standard of living of a small percentage of persons belonging to the political and economic elite of these countries, can be quite high. In the least developed countries, according to various estimates, lives from 1.3 to 2 billion people. There are many such countries in Africa, to the south of the Sahara. There are some of the lowest indicators in per capita income and other socio-economic parameters. Moreover, in some countries in Africa since the late 1980s, there has been a decline of GDP, as well as production (till 80%) with the simultaneous growth of population (Maksakovsky, 2009).

To compare different countries in terms of development level, taking into account much of what has already been mentioned, various indicators have been worked out. One of the most widely used is the *Human Development Index*, which takes into account not only the GDP of the state but also social parameters such as lifespan, educational level, etc. According to an estimate of the United Nations Development Program - UNDP for 2021, the top five leading countries were included Norway, Switzerland,

Ireland, Hong Kong, Germany, and last places were taken by African countries - Burundi, South Sudan, Chad, Central African Republic, Niger (HDI, 2021).

Other indicators are taken into account when assessing the socio-economic development of the countries. Among them is the *Gender Development Index*, GDI, fixing the differences in socio-economic indicators of life between men and women. By this criterion, Canada had again leading positions within the first decade of XXI Century, it was followed by Norway, the United States, Australia, Sweden (in these countries, gender differences were very law), Guinea Bissau, Burundi, Burkina Faso, Ethiopia, Niger closed the list (Kereselidze, 2011).

Quite sharply there is a question - the indebtedness of the "South" to the "North" countries.

It was formed as a result of loans that developing countries received from the West. The situation began to deteriorate dramatically in connection with a jump in oil prices in the 1970s. Many developing countries, which did not extract oil, were forced to import "Black gold" by significantly higher prices, for which the money loans in Western banks were taken. However, among borrowers, there were also such countries that exported energy resources, in particular Mexico. Generally, the debt of developing countries in 1982 was 805 billion American Dollars and by 1996 reached 2 trillion 95 billion USD. In 1982, Mexico announced that it could not liquidate a foreign debt, and asked for 4 billion US dollars. Following Mexico for the help appealed to other countries too (Lebedeva, 2007). Within the second decade of the XXI century, the foreign debt of the developing countries prevailed at 5 trillion USD (World Bank, 2020).

The problem was that the growing debt of developing countries began to threaten both the states of the "South" and "North". The first simply could not pay off. As for the "North", the creditors lost huge sums of money. The default of developing countries could have the most direct impact on them. All this led to the need to address the foreign debt of developing countries and the crisis of debt as such. In 1989, the United States, as one of the leading creditors, proposed a plan under which part of the debt of developing countries was forgiven, while another concept was directed to decrease the interest rates; New loans were also guaranteed under the guarantee of the International Monetary Fund, the World Bank and the governments of creditor countries. This somehow has weakened the crisis. However, in general, the problem of foreign debt of developing countries has not yet been resolved.

Particularly alarming were the financial upheavals of the 1990s, in particular, problems with the Mexican currency in 1994; worsening economic situation in developing countries. They also again started to take significant credits. Complex internal socio-economic situations in developing countries also questioned the ability of their governments to cope with a budget deficit, which is necessary for the payment of a debt. The situation especially deteriorated as a result of the spreading COVID 19 pandemic in 2020. Many developing countries were forced to take new foreign debts for taking preventive measures against this disease.

This is the general picture of differences in the standard of living between developed and developing countries. This social and economic gap has been named the North-South gap. Immediately after the end of the Cold War, there were allegations; that in the modern world the confrontation along the line "East-West" was replaced by a confrontation along the axis "North-South ". In Reality, at first sight, there is quite significant polarization of the world by several indicators. However, this gap is not as unambiguous as it may seem.

First of all, the statistics require interpretation. Obviously, in the countries of the "Global South," the standard of living is lower than in the states of the "Global North". Statistics give an overall picture and individual statistical indicators need to be compared with each other. Thus, per capita income should be

Figure 1. World map showing a traditional definition of the North - South divide.
The north; Blue; High income economies + High Human Development Index states + G7 + Eastern Europe Developed World
Developing World
Source: North South divide. Svg

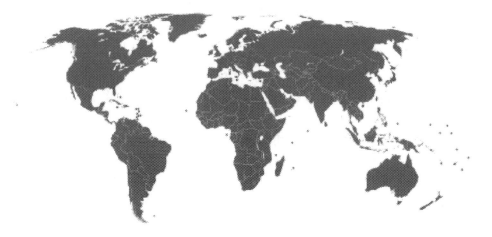

compared with prices for basic consumer goods – price index, access to health care, education, etc. For these purposes, the indicator is associated with purchase parity. By this standard, developing countries are not so strikingly different from developed ones, although, of course, they lag behind them, especially if we take into account the quality of the consumed goods.

Secondly, "South" is far from being uniform in terms of socio-economic criteria. Some countries of the "South" managed to overcome the backlog in socio-economic development. First, economic success was achieved by individual States in the Middle East, in particular member countries of OPEC, which is associated with the export of oil. For example, countries such as Kuwait, United Arab Emirates, Qatar, were able to reach the level of life, which by socio-economic indicators is comparable with developed states of the "North". Several other countries in the Middle East Region were included in the group with average development indicators.

Later arose the phenomenon of the so-called newly industrialized/industrializing countries - NICs, to which relates the countries of South-East Asia. Their success in socio-economic life is even more impressive than in the countries of the Middle East. In the 1980s, in a relatively short historical period, South Korea, Singapore, Taiwan, Hong Kong, which gained the name of the so-called "Asian tigers ", managed to become developed industrial countries. Their economic strategy was aimed at developing their industry and attracting investments. As a result, according to the International Monetary Fund, IMF by the beginning of XXI Century, the share of these countries was coming up to 10% of the total trade turnover and 3.4% of production (Chitadze, 2016).

In general, it can be assumed that at the base of the indisputable economic success of several developing countries lies a powerful leap of a limited number of states. Thus, during the past decades, over 4/5 of the GDP growth in the "third world" was provided by 26 countries, where about 28% of the whole population lived (Chitadze, 2016). The degree of differentiation level of the socio-economic development of the countries of the world "South" today is such, that it can be assumed about the stratification of them into three different groups, the gap between which grows.

Third, there is not only a gap between countries but also within individual countries by different indicators. For example, Kuwait, which in the mid-1990s, was one of the five countries with the highest per capita income, at the same time was also among those countries, where a large percentage of the adult population remained illiterate. A similar pattern is observed in some other countries of the The Middle East, which is engaged in oil exports. And from the other side here are some countries, former Soviet republics, which have a literacy approaching 100% among the adult population, which puts them on a par with the developed countries of the "North" (Chitadze, 2018). At the same time, they have low per capita incomes, which brings them closer to the states of the "South".

The "North" is also heterogeneous. There are some areas and population areas virtually with the same problems as in the "South". Although, of course, the number of such people is much less and the problems themselves usually do not have such acuity. In general, in some African countries the ratio between the income of the poorest and the richest diverges more than 50 times, while in North America and Western Europe, this gap is less than 10. According to the World Bank, at the beginning of the XXI Century, it was the largest between the richest and the poorest categories of the population, in Brazil (Maksakovsky, 2009).

Thus, the modern world is more a kind of "Mosaic" by the level of life and not divided in half the scope. However, the mosaic nature of the world does not, in general, eliminate the problem of uneven social and economic development of the "North" and "South".

The Reasons for the Differences between the "Global North" and "Global South" and Possible Ways to Overcome Them

How to explain the disproportion of socio-economic development between "Global North" and "Global South"? Many researchers tend to believe that the gap between developed and developing countries is conditioned by both internal factors of development, also by relations between the "South" and "North". In this case, different emphases are made on various factors, respectively, there are stand out different theoretical approaches.

The first approach to the problem of "rich North" - "poor South" comes from the *theory of classical economic development*. The main message in the framework of this approach is supported by the provision that the level of well-being is determined by the availability of efficient production, free

entrepreneurship, trade, technological innovation and not by climate and natural resources. This is based on the ideas of the modernization approach that arose shortly after World War II and proceeded from the fact that industrial development began in the "global North." Industrialization first came to Europe, and then to North America. This, on the one hand, has brought improved living conditions, on the other hand, led to the improvements of the armaments, which later were used for the colonial wars.

The theory of classical economic development is based on the fact, that the colonial heritage, of course, has become a kind of a brake on development (but at the same time several authors pay attention to the fact, that colonialism, despite its negative moments, has provided by technical and social innovations countries of the "South"), but the main obstacles in the modern development of the "global South" lie in itself of the countries from this geographic area. A great impact on the formation of this approach was provided by the American economist and political figure W. Rostow. In 1960 he published a book "The Stages of Economic Growth", later, in 1991 the third edition of the book was published. In his research, the author suggested that developing countries would pass the same stages in their development as the developed ones. Even though the "global North" continues to develop, the pace of development of the "global South" would be much higher, which will create the conditions to finally catch up with the countries of the "North". In addition, the "North" itself, according to this theory, will be interested in this development, since it is oriented by its nature on liberal values, the openness of the borders, and the creation of a single economic space (Rostow, 1991).

At the end of the 20th century, the theory of classical economic development experienced its revival and is called *neoclassical*. The incentive to address the ideals of market development has become largely the example of new industrial estates, which were directed at times for a general liberalization of the socio-economic life of society. This phenomenon has led to several studies in which analyzed the relationship between political freedoms and economic development. And anyway, the main problem in neoclassical theory has been attempts to find ways to overcome the significant differences between developed and developing countries.

Supporters of this approach in principle agree that the "North" is responsible for the backwardness of the "global South". Developing countries can't cope without outside aid with their problems, because, on the one hand, they lack the qualified personnel, due to the low level of education of the population as a whole; on the other hand – they are economically dependent on the former metropolis. According to this approach, the countries of the "South" should be assisted in economic development, as well as for their democratization. Both these spheres in neoclassical theory are closely related.

At the same time, supporters of this approach emphasize that the most important argument in favor of the need to develop relations with the "global South" is not so much the historical responsibility of the "North", but the orientation toward future relationships. Neoclassical theory is inclined to consider them between "North" and "South" as a game with a non-zero sum, when the winners maybe both - "North", and "South". In the other words, interaction can be beneficial for both parties. The advocates of this point of view emphasize the interdependence of the world, the need to integrate its parts into a single world system. To illustrate the liberal approach in the North-South relations J.T. Rourke and M.A. Boyer use the metaphor associated with the death of "Titanic" in 1912. The modern world is so interconnected, that it can either be proportionally developed and achieve a certain general "port of prosperity", or sink like this ship. In the last case, it is not significant the differences between passengers of expensive cabins and those who bought the cheapest tickets (Rourke, Boyer, 2009).

The greatest discussion of the problem of the socio-economic gap between the "rich North" and "poor South" started perhaps, in the framework of another approach - neo-Marxism. It underlines the structural stratification of the globe on the exploited ("global South") and the exploiters ("global North"). Hence, one more of its name - *a structural theory* that was quite popular in the 1970s-1980s years.

The stratification of the world is conditioned, according to this approach, by the imperialist policy of the developed countries, which could make it a result of the occupation and exploitation of colonies. Despite gaining independence in the second half of the 20th century, former colonies remained economically dependent from the former metropolitan countries or wider from the "global North". Moreover, this dependence on the "rich" is characteristic even for those countries that were not colonies.

In the economy of the developing countries, this or that branch of the economy prevails. Thus, the economic development of Ethiopia is largely oriented on the supply of coffee, Botswana-diamond mining, Zambia – production of copper, etc. In this economic dependence exists, according to neo-Marxism, not only the gap between the "North" and "South", but also its deepening. Neo-Marxism proceeds from the premise that the "Global North" is not interested in the dynamic development of the "South", because for the economically developed states the former colonies remain as suppliers of raw materials and cheap labor force.

In the framework of the neo-Marxism theory, two areas are distinguished: *the world-system approach* and direction, oriented to the *theory of dependence*. The world is a systemic understanding of the gap between the "North" (the core) and "South" (periphery) proceeds from the fact that the functioning of the economy of the core and periphery are specialized and simultaneously interdependent. In other words, they can't exist without each other. Prolonged historical cycles that consider this direction, provide the countries the opportunity to "move around" within the structure: the core, semi-periphery, and periphery. At the same time, this theory can hardly explain the rapid economic development of the new industrial countries.

The special attention to the gap between the "North" and "South" in the framework of neo-Marxism, pays the dependence theory. It proceeds from the fact that this gap is the key in modern political economy. Representatives of the dependence theory, including A. G. Frank and others, oppose the thesis on the stages of economic development (Frank, 1996), which was pursued in the framework of neoliberalism by William Rostow, according to which each state consistently passes one after another the same stages (Rostow, 1991). Objecting to this, the adherents of the theory of dependence say that for the developing states this is not a stage of development at all, but a result of the hierarchy of the world and the exploitation of the "South" by the "North". They emphasize that modern developed countries have never been in a situation of developing, compelled to catch up with more developed states. Therefore, economic development or backwardness is not "natural", but are caused by unequal relations between the countries of the "global North" and the "global South".

The argument, confirming the inequitable relationship between the "North" and "South", also serves for supporters of this theory *the phenomenon of a two-tiered economy*. The essence of it is that some industries – branches of economy of the developing countries are in the field of the interests of the "North" and turn out to be "tied up" on modern information and communication technologies (computers, telecommunications), while others remain at the "prehistoric" level.

In many respects responsible for the division of the world into the "rich North" and "poor South" representatives of the dependence theory consider Transnational Corporations - TNC. In their opinion, Transnational Corporations are instrumental in modern neo-colonialism. It is also stressed that the introduction of innovation, investment in developing countries - all this contributes to disproportional development of the "South" and in the end - strengthening the gap between "South" and the "North". In these positions, their theoretical orientations are based on many anti-globalization movements.

To overcome the differences between the "North" and "South", which, as neo-Marxists emphasize, are unfair, world production and trade must be radically rebuilt.

Finally, the third approach in "North-South" relations is oriented toward *neo-realism*. In the sphere of economic relations, it has received the name of *mercantilism*. This approach is based on the fact that the problem should be solved first of all by the developing countries themselves. Respectively, economically developed countries in their interaction with the countries of the "South" should focus on their interests, but not on patronage.

Supplying the states of the "global South" with food, medicines and other necessities leads to an increased birth rate, but not to the restructuring of the economic system, declare the supporters of neo-realism. This approach practically does not take into account the fact of interdependence in the modern world; therefore, it proceeds from the premise that the problems of developing countries should have less interest by developed countries. Moreover, some authors who are oriented on this approach, believe that the actions of developing countries are aimed at changing the "Rules of the Game" and obtaining

Figure 2. The future of north-south relations. conflicts or cooperation?
Source: hhttps://www.twn.my/title/futu-cn.htm

their advantages. In general, neo-realism to a lesser extent, compared to the other classical approaches, deals with the problem of socio-economic development between the "North" and "South".

Several authors draw attention to the fact, that if in the period of the "Cold War", the own development of the "South" countries was restrained by ideological considerations based on which, the main factor was the economic assistance, investment policy, etc. fort eh countries of "South", then after the end of the "Cold War" this factor ceased to function.

Nevertheless, in the practical aspect, today the problem of development of the "South" is quite difficult. Developing countries use different strategies for overcoming the economic gap. One of them is oriented toward the domestic production of products that were previously imported (import substitution policy). Its meaning is in the development of its industry. This strategy was used by many Latino American countries. However, in its extreme form, it can lead to the fact that the country will be outside of the global economic system and this will only aggravate its economic backwardness. In addition, restrictions on the use of import substitution policies related to the fact that their product is often not high quality, expensive and uncompetitive.

Nationalization is another strategy. Like the already discussed strategy, it has negative moments associated with a possible lowering of economic efficiency. The problem is in the choice of optimal means and methods of development in each specific case.

There are also undertaken collective efforts of the developing countries for overcoming the economic gap. So, in 1973, their leaders at the meeting in Algeria presented the initiative, which was named the New International World Order, NIEO. In 1974, within the General Assembly of the United Nations, it has proposed:

- To implement reform in the field of international trade, including Improvement and stabilization of the market in the field of raw materials;
- To reform the financial sector, thereby making it easier to access for developing countries to loans of the International Monetary Fund (IMF) and other international financial organizations; to stabilize inflation and exchange rates;
- to provide foreign assistance to developing countries in the amount of about 0,7% of their GDP; to develop a program of assistance in repaying the debt of developing countries; introduce international control for the activities of TNC, which has particularly negative consequences for developing countries;
- to assist developing countries in acquiring new technologies and conducting industrialization;
- to provide the countries of the South with rights and control functions about their resources (UN, 2005).

In the first stage, the reaction of developed countries was negative, but the dialogue of the "South" and "North" took place and continued. Currently, developing countries actively participate in various international organizations, including the UN. Thus, the United Nations Conference on Trade and Development (UNCTAD), which was established as a permanent body of the UN General Assembly in 1964, was focused on solving the economic problems of developing countries. It is a permanent international institute, which organizes meetings once approximately every four years. As of May 2018, 195 states were UNCTAD members (UNCTAD, 2018).

Assistance to developing countries goes also through other international organizations and specialized United Nations agencies, including through World Health Organization (WHO). As a result, in 1980 only 20% of children were vaccinated against the 6 most prevalent diseases, in 1991 this indicator reached 80%, first of at the expense of developing countries (UN, 2005). As of 2019, the Global vaccine coverage of children with only one-year-old in such diseases as Tuberculosis (BCG), Polio (Pol3), diphtheria/tetanus/pertussis (DTP3), Measles, first dose (MCV1), Hepatitis B (HepB3) was about 85% (Global vaccine coverage, 2019).

Much attention to the problems of developing countries, especially in the field of education, human development is paid by the Program - United Nations Development Program (UNDP). In general, there are many programs and areas for assistance to developing countries that are being implemented by intergovernmental organizations, individual states, and non-governmental associations. They are very diverse both by region and by focus (for example, aimed at improving health care, education, or categories of the population, etc.).

Finally, it is another approach that is proposed to overcome differences between the "South" and "North". Its essence boils down to the fact that in the era of globalization the confrontation of the "North-South" will disappear naturally, since the "development centers" will be formed according to different principles, for example, in the form of the creating small entities - located both in the "North" and on the "South", particularly territories-cities, which by communication, information

and other "nodes" will link the remaining territories to the global world. This view is supported, in particular, by the Swedish researcher O. E. Andersson, who believes that with the globalization of transport and communication networks "the leading" economy will not be concentrated in the West but will spread all over the globe (Lebedeva, 2007). Such countries and cities as South Korea, Japan, Taiwan, Hong Kong, Singapore, Australia, New Zealand represent the "North" in terms of per capita income, infrastructure, and access to important markets. Concretely in this sense that the "global economy" is formed anywhere in the world.

The Volume of Global Debt has Reached a Record High

According to the data of the first quarter of 2017, the volume of global debt reached its historical maximum and amounted to 327% of global GDP.

According to the information of the different International Finance Institutes, the amount of global debt has reached $ 217 trillion, which is by $ 500 billion more than in the previous year.

According to the International Institute of Finance, this volume of global debt and its growth of $500 billion has been caused not only by the state, but also by the debts of banks, corporations, and household debt.

The largest increase in debt was also shown by the US and China economies. Debts in both countries rose by $ 2 trillion. In particular, debt in China reached $ 32.7 trillion, while in the US it reached more than $ 63

According to the Food and Agriculture Organization of the United Nations, by the beginning of the 21st century, the daily norm for 30% of the world's population was less than 1,800 kcal. Another 20% were getting enough calories but were experiencing a protein deficiency. Thus, half of the world's population is malnourished, and their number, who are starving or on the verge of starvation, is estimated at 500-550 million people (Davitashvili, Elizbarashvili, 2012).

Food Problem and Developing Countries

The fact is that the food problem is mainly related to developing countries. At the same time, it should be noted the certain successes that the Third World states have achieved in the development of agriculture and food supply. As a result of the so-called "Green Revolution", many developing countries were able to fully or almost completely meet their own food needs, while the rate of annual growth of basic agricultural products was 4.5%. Accordingly, the daily rate of consumed calories has increased and on average, for the developing world, it amounted to 2500 kcal (Davitashvili, Elizbarashvili, 2012). However, it should be noted that these calories have a very small share of animal products, while plant foods are dominated by one or two products (for example, in South Asia, rice accounts for 70-80% of the food ration).

Despite some success, food security for the population remains one of the most acute global problems in developing countries (and the world as a whole).

Figure 3. A third of Haitians (the poorest country in the Western Hemisphere) do not receive the daily calories needed.
Source: https://en.public-welfare.com/3906676-ways-to-solve-the-food-problem-the-geography-of-hunger-un-food-program

The geography of hunger is generally presented as a fairly regular picture. The malnutrition "belt" covers a fairly wide range of developing countries, with two poles: tropical Africa and South Asia. In absolute numbers, South Asia, with an estimated 300 million malnourished people (more than 20% of the region's population). The share of the hungry is highest in tropical Africa, where it exceeds one-third of the total population. It is 14 percent in Latin America, 11 percent in the Middle East, and 10 percent in Southeast Asia (Chitadze, 2017).

Under such conditions, developing countries are forced to increase food imports. If by the end of the 50s of the 20th Century, grain imports to developing countries did not exceed 12 million tons, by 2010 it had reached almost 150 million.

The great importance is the food aid, which is provided to developing countries by developed countries. 40% of food products imported to the African countries are selfless aid. The main donors are the US (60% of all aid), Canada, Australia, and Western European countries (Chitadze, 2017).

Ways to Solve Global Food Problems

The food problem is a complex, global problem. Its complete solution requires fundamental socio-economic, political, and cultural-psychological transformations and is a rather distant prospect. However, of course, there is one necessary condition for solving the problem - to ensure constant growth of food production. There are two main ways to increase food production: extensive and intensive.

The extensive direction involves the development of new agricultural lands, an increase in the number of cattle, and the expansion of the farming area. Today, agricultural land occupies only one-third of the land resources.

According to various calculations, it is theoretically possible to additionally cultivate more than ten percent of the land. But the reserves of land, which can be developed at low cost, are practically exhausted. Bringing food products in extreme conditions is associated with huge costs and due to the current scientific and technical capabilities, it is still premature.

Figure 4. Food Security Risk Index S
Source: https://reliefweb.int/map/world/world-food-security-risk-index-2013

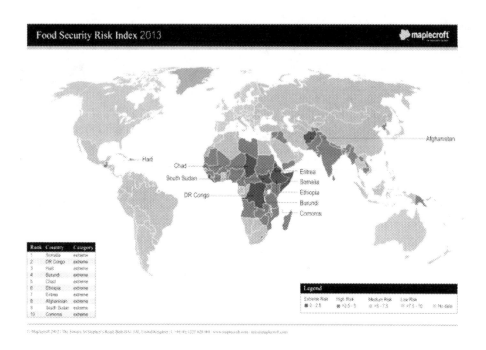

As for the geographical distribution of lands - promising for development, Latin America and Africa stand out in this respect. In Latin America, these are mostly lands in the humid tropics and subtropics. Most of them are located in Brazil, and according to Brazilian scientists, after the full development of these lands and some reclamation, Brazil will be able to feed on 900 million to 1 billion people (Chitadze, 2017). In Africa, the main reserves come to the savannah zone, where two-grain crops per year can be obtained. However, the risk of soil degradation is very high.

The intensive path involves the growth of agricultural production without increasing the area of cultivated hills or the number of cattle. In agriculture, it means getting more crops from the same area of land, which is achieved at the expense of mechanization, irrigation, and the introduction of high-yielding species. Inbreeding is related to breeding improvement.

Intense growth is mainly characteristic for the developed countries, but recently it has become a major means of food production growth in several developing countries as well. This is primarily due to the increase in the area of irrigated lands, which has allowed several countries to significantly increase yields. No less a contribution to the growth of food production in developing countries is the mechanization of agriculture, although the latter does not have a positive impact on the ecological quality of the product.

Taking all resources into account, if all the theoretically possible land were to be developed and the level of intensification maximized, the Earth would be able to feed some 33 billion people. However, according to researchers, the real number is much smaller and probably does not exceed 12-15 billion (Chitadze, 2017).

Figure 5. 10% of the world's population lives on less than $1.90 a day
Source: https://www.dosomething.org/us/facts/11-facts-about-global-poverty

PART 2. THE PROBLEM OF POVERTY AND UNEMPLOYMENT

The modern world is characterized by sharp inequalities in terms of material wealth and prosperity. Although in recent decades the material conditions of the population as a whole have been improved almost everywhere and the average per capita income is rising, poverty remains one of the most acute global problems. According to some scientists, the situation, on the contrary, has even worsened in some regions of the world.

Poverty is not only determined by the amount of financial income. It consists of many different parameters. Poverty is also determined by factors such as unemployment, housing conditions, the composition of the consumer basket, etc. It also should be remembered that poverty is a relative concept and that the same income and living conditions, if they indicate obvious poverty in one country, may in another country be considered quite sufficient for a normal life.

In total, according to the UN, at the beginning of the 21-st century, the average daily income of about 1.5 billion people in the world did not exceed $ 1, and for 2.5 billion people $ 2. That is, in total, the daily income of about 4 billion people did not exceed $ 2 (UN, 2005).

Subsistence and Consumer Basket

One of the indicators of poverty is the share of the population whose income is less than the subsistence level. The subsistence minimum is the minimal amount necessary for a person to exist, that is, not to starve and satisfy the essential needs of life. The subsistence level varies from country to country. If in North America and Western Europe this figure is quite high, in most developing countries, on the contrary, it is so small that living with this amount is completely unimaginable for a resident of the developed world. Although the subsistence level in Asia, Africa, and Latin America is much lower than in Europe and North America, the proportion of the population living below the subsistence level is much higher in the developing world than in the developed world.

Sometimes the share of the population whose average income does not exceed one dollar per day is used to determine the level of poverty. Such incomes are an indicator of extreme poverty and are particularly high in the tropical regions of Africa and South Asia.

Another indicator of living standard is the structure of the consumer basket, i.e., how a person distributes the received income. In developing countries, a large part of the population's income is spent on food: the lower the income, the higher is the food expenditure in the consumer basket, and the lower-income Funds are spent on meals. In contrast, food expenditures in developed countries at the beginning of the second decade of the XXI century was on average, less than 20% of the consumer basket (Davitashvili, Elizbarashvili, 2012).

Before the COVID 19 Spreading, the number of populations, who lived in extreme poverty has been reduced to the historical minimum

Together with the discussion about the problems related to poverty, it is necessary to point out, that is 2018, the percentage of the population, who lived in poverty has reached the historic minimum, and unfortunately, there was no appropriate reaction of the onternational community on this issue.

During the last 30 years, the number of people who lived in poverty decreased by 1 billion. However, in the contemporary period, more than 750 million people spent less than $1,90 daily, but their number in 1990 was reaching 1/3 of the world`s population (In both cases, income was calculated by PPP method, in constant prices for 2011.) China has made a huge contribution to the formatting of this common picture. The income per person in the whole world (in constant prices for 2010) within 1990-2017 has been increased by 48%, from $7170 to $10 635, in China income growth per capita within the same period reached 1000%, from $730 to $7300. In Comparison with China, comparatively modest, but anyway impressive growth for 300% took place in India, where the average income was increased for 4 times till $2000 (Interpressnews, 2018).

During the discussion of "Global Poverty", the main problematic region remains Africa. Asia is moving toward progress by the rapid steps, the progress is noticeable in Latino America too, but no radical economic growth has been fixed in Africa. From 1990-2015, the number of inhabitants in the African continent, who lived in extreme poverty, increased from 278 to 413 million. But this happened first of all because of population growth and not by the percentage indicator. By 2030, it is expected that from every ten African, who will live in extreme poverty, 9 will come on the share of Sub-Saharan Africa (Interpressnews, 2018).

The reduction of Global poverty does not mean that socio-economic conditions of all countries have been improved. Besides the fact that 750 million people remain in poverty, the situation within the last 5-10 years has become extremely worse in such states as Venezuela and Syria. The problems have increased in Egypt and Libya too. At the same time, the similar situation is often deteriorating in the separate one state too, when the gap related to the economic income between rich and poor parts of the population in one concrete country is increasing, but, together with the economic growth in a particular state, in the long term perspectives, those people (poor) also have the profit. Two centuries ago, at the beginning of the industrial revolution, in extreme poverty lived about 80% of the world population, many of them were spending their lives under slavery conditions (Chitadze, 2017). In the contemporary period, the situation has radically changed, and even in the rapidly developing country can be found people, whose conditions are bad. But, in the framework of long-term policy, all people can take benefits.

Thus, nowadays, the situation is radically different and even though the near future does not guarantee the full elimination of poverty, it makes possible the further prediction of its reduction.

The Economic Component of World Politics and the Main Global Social and Economic Problems

The majority of economists are agreed, that discussing sentimental statistics, according to which about 26-27 richest people on our planet have more property than more than 3 billion people together - is not significant and even unfair. Together with Bill Gates, who has spent his 30 billion USD for the saving millions of children's lives in Africa, Microsoft, Google, and other different giant companies create an opportunity for the delivering knowledge and establishment of communication, from where many poor people are finding their possibilities and, in many cases, manage to avoid the poverty (Chitadze, 2017). Neither Bill Gates nor Mark Zuckerberg or Elon Musk - none of them accumulated their property by colonization policy against African, Asian or Latino American people, they have created new wealth, which did not exist before and which has implemented the huge contribution in reducing the level of poverty in the different regions of the world.

A very important role in reducing poverty on the global level is the Sustainable Development Goals, which have been worked out by the leading representatives of the International democratic community. In general, The Sustainable Development Goals (SDGs), otherwise known as the Global Goals, are a universal call to action to end poverty, protect the planet and ensure that all people enjoy peace and prosperity.

These 17 Goals build on the successes of the Millennium Development Goals while including new areas such as climate change, economic inequality, innovation, sustainable consumption, peace, and justice, among other priorities. The goals are interconnected – often the key to success on one will involve tackling issues more commonly associated with another.

The SDGs came into effect in January 2016, and they will continue to guide UNDP (United Nations Development Program) policy and funding until 2030. As the lead UN development agency, UNDP is uniquely placed to help implement the Goals in some 170 countries and territories (Chitadze, 2019).

Unemployment

Unemployment is an extremely serious global problem that affects more or less every country. Unemployed is any person who does not have a paid job despite having the desire and ability to work. The category of unemployed is often attributed to the so-called category as semi-unemployed, i. e. the part of the labor force that has no source of income and their employment is temporary, seasonal, or occasional.

The problem of unemployment is acute in both developed and developing countries but manifests itself in different ways. Unemployment in developing countries is caused by common socio-economic and cultural backwardness. Added to this is the very rapid growth of the youth, which is growing the ranks of the unemployed every year. A significant part of the rural population has no land at all. The threat of famine forces them to leave the village and travel to the city, where there are already many unemployed. Due to the lack of professionalism, such a workforce is only involved in so-called "blackwork" (loader, unskilled worker, janitor, cleaner, washer, etc.) and can perform mostly physical operations. More than enough people are employed in these jobs. Part of the unemployed population, deprived of a livelihood, is trying to penetrate developed countries and seek salvation there, which further exacerbates the problem of illegal migration and xenophobia. For the significant part of the unemployed left on the ground, begging or being connected to the criminal world remains the only way to survive.

In the developed world, unemployment takes a different form. Finding an unskilled job is much easier here. On the contrary, the demand for such work is high and it becomes necessary to support workers, most of whom are from developing and former socialist countries (including illegal migrants). The local population is more worried about the so-called problem of functional unemployment - when a highly

Figure 6. Types of Unemployment
Source: https://pcsb.instructure.com/courses/5054/assignments/180184

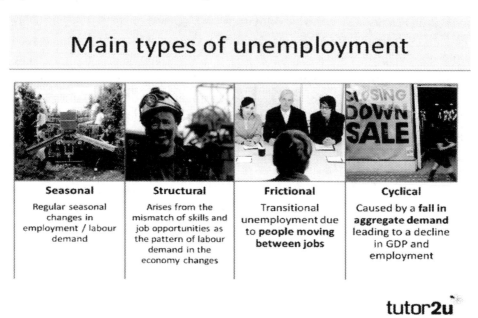

qualified specialist (engineer, doctor, economist, teacher, lawyer) cannot find a job according to his/her profession. In such a case, he/she refuses unskilled and non - prestigious activities and remains unemployed until he/she gets a suitable job. These expectations can last for years.

The unemployment rate is determined by the percentage of unemployed people in the economically active population but it is quite difficult to determine the number of unemployed. In most developed countries it is determined by the number of unemployed registered on the labor exchange, which of course does not match the actual number of unemployed, but neither does it differ much.

The situation is quite different in the developing world and in the post-Soviet republics, where only a small number of unemployed are registered on labor exchanges. This is because the population has less hope of being able to find employment through the labor exchange. Some countries' statistics deliberately hide the number of unemployed and publish reduced data. Because of this, the unemployment rate in the countries of the world is very high and often goes beyond the real picture.

It should also be noted that in the case of unemployment, citizens of developed countries usually receive monetary compensation from the state, which significantly exceeds the subsistence level. Consequently, the problem of unemployment here is not such a painful problem nor does it cause as severe consequences as in the developing world.

In general, as for 2019, according to statistical data from the International Labour Organization, there were about 188 million unemployed people worldwide. In the first quarter of 2020, the International Labour Organization (ILO) predicted that up to additional 25 million jobs would be lost worldwide as a result of COVID-19 (ILO, 2020).

Homelessness

Homelessness is a serious social problem. A person who does not have a permanent home is considered homeless. In a broad sense, the homeless can be considered the part of the world's population that lives a nomadic life (about 120 million people, or 2% of the world's population). Refugees and internally displaced persons are often classified in the same category, but more often the homelessness is used in the narrow sense of the word to refer not to the above groups but to those nationals and foreigners (mostly illegal immigrants) who are permanently homeless due to extreme hardship.

Homelessness is not uncommon in rural areas, but it is mainly a problem in big cities. Unemployed and landless peasants are facing the city and further aggravating the already dire situation. This layer of the population takes refuge in the basements of large houses, roofs, so-called huts built in the suburbs, or live directly on the streets. Their main activity is begging.

This form of homelessness has become a serious problem in the developed world as well. Up to 3 million are homeless only in EU countries. In the US their number exceeds 2 million, in Japan exceeds 200 thousand, and even in such high-welfare countries as Canada and Australia, respectively, 150 thousand and 100 thousand people have no homes (Chitadze, 2017). The increase in the number of homeless children is particularly noticeable, which is a cause for concern.

PART 3. EDUCATION PROBLEMS ON THE GLOBAL LEVEL

It can be assumed, that one of the reasons for the weakness of democratic institutions and the tendency to violence is the educational factor. Despite advances in education over the past few decades, more than 115 million children at the beginning of the 21st century - almost 56% of whom were girls in the developing countries - had no access to primary education, and many have been forced to drop out of poverty due to family or social pressures (UN, 2005). Despite international efforts to increase literacy, 862 million adults (two-thirds of whom were women) became illiterate at the beginning of the 21st century.

So, it is not accidental that one of the main indicators of the development of this or that country is the level of education of the population, along with such important components of the field as GDP per capita and average life expectancy, etc. Therefore, within the Human Development Index of the state, determining the level of education is one of the most important components.

In an era of scientific and technological revolution, when the process of globalization has swept the entire planet and humanity is a participant in the rapid development of information technology, without educated and highly qualified staff it is impossible to discuss any progress in a particular country. Due to this, many countries, especially the highly developed countries, allocate significant funds in the field of education. At the same time, most of the developing countries face other problems in the field of education: in many countries of the "Global South," the main problem is illiteracy and issues related to primary education.

Due to the above, in developed countries, secondary education is usually compulsory. In developing countries, secondary education is not available to a significant portion of the population. Consequently, in many developing countries, the proportion of people with secondary education in the total population is relatively low. It is noteworthy that, at the beginning of the second decade of the XXI Century, in Western Europe, as well as in North America and the countries of Central and Eastern Europe, which included the former communist camp, 350 to 600 people out of every 1,000 people had secondary education.

In developing countries, this figure was 150, while in the least developed countries of Asia and Africa this figure did not exceed 30 people per thousand population (Davitashvili, Z. Elizbarashvili, N. 2014).

As already mentioned, millions of children in developing countries are unable to attend school. Based on this factor, in tropical Africa and South Asia, the proportion of all children who do not even attend primary school varies from one-third to half of the whole amount of children in the concrete state. At the same time, in developed countries, all children receive their education at the first and second stages. Together with this, the problems of primary and secondary education are not limited to this fact (Chitadze, 2017).

The second problem is determining the quality of education, in particular, what is the teaching methodology in this or that educational institution and how useful knowledge is acquired by a particular young person in a complex and competitive environment. This problem is especially acute in the countries of the former communist regime, where a significant part of the population was unprepared to meet the new reality of the post-Cold War period. Especially in the post-Soviet space, an important part of the population is still unprepared for a market economy and democratic transformations. As a result, there is existed the term - Functional illiteracy, when a person has received some education in school and later even at the institute but is unable to use it in practical life. In this regard, in some countries, the education reform issues have been included in the agenda, which implies maximum integration of the education system of a particular country with the educational standards of the leading Western countries. All those factors do not mean that somebody should deny the national educational programs or weaken attention toward the native language and literature, history, or geography. It is just mentioned about the general principles and standards, with the purpose that gaining education in the native country should satisfy all those requests, which are necessary for the starting study at the universities of Europe and USA.

Geography of Illiteracy

As it was mentioned at the beginning of this chapter, despite the progress in the field of education in recent years, nevertheless, at the beginning of the XXI Century, more than 115 million children – nearly 56 percent of them girls in developing countries – had no access to primary education, and many who begin to study were forced to leave study process because of poverty, family and social pressures (UN, 2005). Thus, in the developing world, even in the modern period, illiteracy is one of the most serious problems, in some countries it is a real catastrophe. When it is mentioned about the level of illiteracy of the population, it is not only the part of the children (under 18 years), who cannot read and write. In this case, also discussion is going on as well as about adults (over 18 years old) who do have not enough education and do not have the opportunity to do it throughout their life.

Despite some progress made in recent decades on the way to overcoming the problems related to education, the issue of illiteracy is still considered a serious problem. According to the United Nations Education, Scientific and Cultural Organization`s (UNESCO) statistical information for 2019, about 773 million adults in the world were illiterate. Consequently, a very significant part of the world's population is not integrated into real modern life and lives in another - past epoch. It is also important to note the radical territorial disproportion observed in this area. It should be noted that 95,6% of illiterate people inhabit the developing world (UNESCO, 2019). A particularly large number of illiterates are observed in South Asia and tropical Africa, where more than half of the population is illiterate.

It is very interesting to point out that in 2012, according to official statistics of the US Central Intelligence Agency, there were 4 countries in the world at that time, where 100% of the population was literate. Those countries were Norway, Luxembourg, Finland, and Georgia (Davitashvili, Z. Elizbarashvili, N. 2012).

At the beginning of the second decade of the XXI Century, in more than 30 countries, literacy rates ranged from 99% to 100%. In about 85 states, the share of literacy was more than 90%. The lowest literacy rates (less than 20%) were in Bhutan, Afghanistan, Somalia, Burkina Faso, Chad, Mali, and Niger. India, Pakistan, Bangladesh, and China hold the leading positions in the total number of illiterate people. The high number of illiterates in China, which is on the path of economic prosperity, together with other reasons is explained by the complexity of Chinese hieroglyphs (Davitashvili, Elizbarashvili, 2012).

Most governments in developing countries are aware of the fact that education is a major driver of further development in the 21st century. Taking into account this factor, the goal of the developing states is to minimize the share of illiterate people in the total population of the country. For this reason, with the assistance of the developed countries and international donor organizations, significant financial resources for increasing literacy and level of education are allocated. However, achieving ultimate success in this area is a difficult task.

At the same time, it should be noted that the illiteracy rate is gradually declining worldwide, which is generally a result of global socio-economic and cultural development. In particular, all over the world, at the beginning of the twentieth century, the share of illiterate people in the elderly population exceeded 90%. A particularly high rate of literacy was observed among women. In the second half of the twentieth century, respectively after the Second World War, the situation was significantly improved, but in the 70s of the last century, 37% of the world's population was still illiterate, including 45% of women and 28% of men worldwide. In 2010, illiteracy rates halved worldwide - to 18% of the entire population of the planet. By the end of the first decade of the 21st century, the literacy rate for women was 23% and for men, it was 14%. Significant progress has been made in overcoming illiteracy since the late 1990s when the proportion of illiterates dropped from 25% to 18% over 10 years (Chitadze, 2017).

As it was pointed out, among the illiterate, 95.6% of people are from the developing world. By region, this level is particularly high in tropical Africa (52.7%) and South Asia (Chitadze, 2017).

PART 4. RAW MATERIAL PROBLEMS ON THE GLOBAL LEVEL

General Signs of Raw Material Problems

One of the serious problems of modernity is the maximum provision of humanity with raw materials. This problem has always existed, but it has acquired global significance in recent decades when unprecedented population growth and increasing production capacity have raised the raw material problem with all its severity.

Global raw material problems are associated with very rapid, often spontaneous growth in demand for raw materials (both energy and metallic and non-metallic minerals). Suffice it to say that in the last half-century the world has extracted and used more raw materials than in the entire history of mankind. At the same time, this process is irreversible, and the supply of raw materials is steadily declining, which will pose an unresolved dilemma in the future.

The raw material crisis in recent decades has shown everyone, that it is impossible to continue the growth of raw material consumption at such a pace and it is necessary to find a solution.

The raw material crisis is exacerbated by the fact that along with the reduction of raw material stocks, the mining-geological conditions of the deposits are deteriorating and, consequently, extraction is becoming more expensive.

In addition, the mining industry is associated with a whole range of environmental problems. Open-source mining reduces the cost but leads to land degradation and disruption. Pollution of the atmosphere, water, and soil is also an important problem. In recent years, the use of high-sulfur oil and coal has been increasingly avoided, and some countries (where the so-called acid rain is being actively fought) have banned the consumption of such raw materials altogether. All this creates new difficulties in providing raw materials.

Raw Material Problem: A Future Perspective

Given current consumption trends, which mean stabilizing or reducing demand for raw materials in developed countries and significant growth in the developing world, it is likely that the existing stock of some mineral wealth will already be depleted shortly. In particular, the depleted reserves of tin ore will be available to mankind only until 2002, by 2030 will run out of stocks of tungsten, silver, lead by 2040 - cobalt, molybdenum, copper, nickel, by 2060 - aluminum (bauxite), 20 and iron - Manganese stock. Reusable metal materials (scrap recycling) can indeed be used repeatedly, which significantly increases the service life of metal raw materials, but the final introduction of other, containing materials is inevitable.

The situation is relatively better in terms of the supply of chemical and other non-metallic minerals. The threat of depletion of stocks of phosphorites, apatites, potassium salts, sulfur, and building materials does not threaten us in the 21st century, but unlike metal, most of these raw materials are impossible to use. Thus, it is impossible to consume those materials eternally, accordingly, sooner or later this problem will arise.

The situation is especially difficult in terms of fuel and energy raw materials (oil, natural gas, coal). The rate of their consumption is rapidly increasing, and stocks, despite the discovery of new deposits, are depleted and can be disappeared within 60-80 years (except for coal, the extraction of which will be possible for more than two centuries). That is why the provision of fuel and energy resources is the main problem of mankind related to raw materials. Due to their special severity and importance, energy problems are often singled out and attributed to several major global problems (Davitashvili, Elizbarashvili, 2012).

Fuel-Energy Problems

Despite the rapid growth of energy consumption in the past, no serious problems were encountered until the 1970s. The increase in energy production was provided by the growth of cheap oil and natural gas, also with the extraction and development of new fields. Those products were quite cheap and easy for transportation as well. Because of all those factors, oil and gas have become the main source of energy. Their share in the world energy balance in the 70s of XX Century exceeded 70%, while in the 50s of the last century it was less than 40%. Accordingly, in the second half of the XX century, the role of other energy sources has consequently diminished and the economies of most states have become entirely dependent on oil and gas imports (Davitashvili, Elizbarashvili, 2012).

The unprecedented growth of demand on energy resources and the enormous scale of their use has made it clear, that humanity is facing before serious problems. It has become clear to everyone, that the supply of energy resources can not continue eternally and a lot of effort is needed to avoid the current situation.

The above does not mean that the situation is catastrophic. Mankind is not facing an energy famine yet, but the fact that the era of cheap energy sources (oil and natural gas) is finally over, is beyond doubt.

Fundamental changes in the world energy balance are inevitable within the next 60-80 years. Today, humanity has entered the so-called "transitional" period, which means the gradual movement from the consumption of energy resources to the consumption of alternative sources (solar, wind, tidal, geothermal, water) of energy. This is a very difficult and expensive task. There are incredible difficulties in replacing petroleum products with other energy sources in several industries (for example transport), that new energy sources should have the same power and effect as, for example, petrol or aviation kerosene. But sooner or later this must happen, because, in addition to the limited supply of organic fuel resources, the widespread use of this raw material has already brought severe environmental consequences.

The Problem of Renewable Energy Resources

Coal: The share of proven coal reserves in the entire geological reserves is quite small (about 7%, or 700 billion tons), but given the current level of consumption and future trends, these reserves alone will be available for mankind for more than 200 years.

The sharp rise in oil and gas prices in recent years has significantly increased the role and importance of coal. The volume of coal stockpiles has also increased. All this indicates that the share of coal in organic fuels and energy resources will increase significantly.

Oil: According to modern estimations, there are 1.65 trillion barrels of proven oil reserves in the world as of 2016 (About 170 billion tonnes) (Wordometers, 2016). About 40% of this amount belongs to the traditional oil category. Annual world oil production exceeds 35 billion Barrels (More than 5 billion tonnes) (Wordometers, 2016). Almost 2/3 of the stock comes to the Middle East region. The main consumers are the European states, North America and Japan, although the share of China, India and Southeast Asia is also rapidly growing.

It is expected that the rather high volume of oil production will be maintained until the 2040s. Then, a decrease in values is expected, on the one hand, due to the depletion of stocks and, consequently, a sharp rise in prices, and on the other hand, due to the development and introduction of alternative energy sources.

Natural Gas: Natural gas is one of the most convenient and high-calorie fuel-energy resources. Its special popularity and growing role are due to its high thermal capacity, as well as the relative easiness of extraction and transportation, as well as ecological cleanliness. It is therefore not surprising that the imbalance between liquid and gaseous fuels shifts in favor of the latter, especially when the world supply of natural gas to mankind will last for a longer time than oil supply. However, the share of oil is expected to increase again shortly, as the supply of oil that is technically feasible (but not yet in operation today) is significantly higher than the total supply of natural gas. In addition, transporting gas across the ocean (i.e. liquefying gas and converting it to a gaseous state on the ground) increases the cost several times and is highly unprofitable. As of January 1, 2020, there were an estimated 7,257 trillion cubic feet Tcf (more than 150 trillion Cubic meters) of total world-proved reserves of natural gas (US Energy Information Administration, 2021).

Nuclear Fuel: The main source of nuclear energy is natural uranium ore. However, it is important to consider the costs associated with its extraction and processing, as uranium mining is unprofitable due to the high cost. Many experts thought that nuclear power was the energy of the future and that its

Figure 7. World oil reserves by countries
Source: http://www.endofcrudeoil.com/2011/04/world-oil-reserves.html

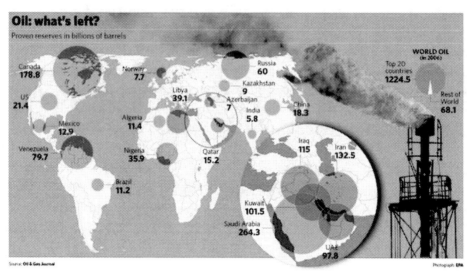

share would grow steadily, but this position has been changed after the 1986 Chernobyl disaster and the 2011 Fukushima earthquake in Japan, when many countries are intending to close the existed atomic power stations and accordingly are refusing the construction of new nuclear power stations. According to current trends, the share of nuclear energy will decrease in the future and the importance of non-traditional, renewable energy sources will increase at its expense. As of 2017, identified uranium reserves recoverable at US$130/kg were 6.14 million tons (compared to 5.72 million tons in 2015). At the rate of consumption in 2017, these reserves are sufficient for slightly over 130 years of supply (OECD, 2018).

Renewable Energy Resources: The high capital capacity is a limiting factor for the consumption of hydropower resources. Only very expensive large hydropower plants, with their large volume of dams (which in its turn cause flooding of huge areas and serious environmental problems), can produce the same amount of electricity, as large thermal or nuclear power plants. The construction of small capacity hydropower plants is less profitable. It should also be noted that most of such hydropower plants depend on the regime of the rivers and may stop altogether during a low level of water.

Some countries use geothermal resources as their energy source. In countries such as Iceland and New Zealand, where there is a high volume of geysers and groundwater, geothermal power plants may be able to satisfy the entire electricity demand. This direction is promising in several other regions, but overall, worldwide, geothermal resources are unlikely to play an important role in solving energy problems.

Some researchers were optimistic about the inexhaustible sources of energy (solar, wind, tidal energy) and considered them to be the future of world energy and the solution to energy problems. Clearly, with technical progress and scientific advances, the role of non-traditional energy sources will increase significantly and to some extent replace even traditional fuel and energy resources, but their consideration as a solution for mankind the energy problems are clearly exaggerated and far from reality.

Another possible resource for solving energy problems is considered biomass, having been obtained from the recycling of agricultural, industrial, and household organic waste, from which energy can be received in the form of biogas. However, this resource also only can be considered as an additional

Figure 8. Different types of renewable energy
Source: https://ohs9sciencestelr.weebly.com/renewable-energy-sources.html

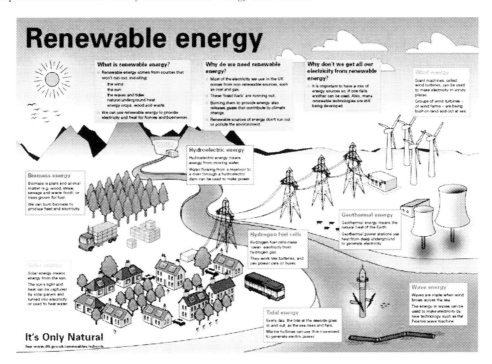

source. As for growing different crops as an energy source (e.g., extracting alcohol from sugar cane and using it as fuel), this is probably a less promising way, due to its yield and high cost.

All this shows that renewable and inexhaustible sources of energy can only play a supporting role in solving energy problems. So far they can not compete (except for hydro, and in some regions geothermal resources) with non-renewable fuel and energy resources. The latter will likely remain a major resource in the first half of the 21st century.

PART 5. THE PROBLEM OF WATER CONSUMPTION IN THE CONTEMPORARY WORLD POLITICS

At the end of XX and the beginning of the XXI century more and more attention is paid to the global problems of water resources. This global problem is interrelated with the other global issues – political, ecological, and demographic. From one side, pollution of the environment causes the fact, that the sources of the drinking water are becoming useless for the consumption. On the other side, population growth on our planet is the reason for the emergence and strengthening of its deficit.

The whole stock of the water of our planet is about 1,4 Billion km3 (Chitadze, 2017). But its biggest part is salted. Particularly, water occupies 70% of the surface of our planet, but almost the entire part is coming to the saltwater - 97.5%. In this case, the share of freshwater among the all-available water resources is 2,5% (Chitadze, 2017). It is concentrated mainly in the glaciers and therefore, it is predominantly inaccessible. Thus, only 1% of the available water resources of the planet are accessible for direct use by mankind (Chitadze, 2017).

At the same time, specialists consider possible the consumption of not only fresh but even salted marine water. And they solve this problem by transferring the marine water to freshwater, however, it is rather expensive and accessible only for the economically developed states.

In this case, for centuries, the volume of accessible (available) water resources in the world, practically has not been changed toward their increasing.

Main Reasons Causing the Deficit of the Water Resources

The basic reasons for strengthening the global scarcity of water are briefly examined below.

Population Growth. The yearly growth of the World population is 80 million people, which creates an additional demand for drinking water in the size of 64 billion m3 per year. Taking into account the fact, that 90% of the expected increase of the population by 2050 relates to the regions, which already have problems with freshwater, the situation can seriously be aggravated (Chitadze, 2017).

In the 20th Century, the population of the World was tripled from 1.6 to 6 billion people, in 2011, the number of the World population prevailed 7 billion people (Chitadze, 2017) and the area of watered agriculture increased from 50 to 267 million hectares, and the consumption of water within the XX century increased for the six times – annually from 500 to 3 500 km3 (Gleick, 2000). The real shortage of water provokes the increased demand, connected, according to the estimations of experts and international organizations, with the demographic boom, by a change in the food ratio by the large groups of the population, by the development of industry and power engineering, by urbanization, by the popularization of the biofuel. The factors, which reduce the volume of accessible water resources, include ineffective/rapacious water consumption, pollution of water, and climate changes.

Economic Growth: According to the World Bank prognosis, the global economy will grow by about 4% in 2021 and most probably within the third decade of the XXI century, though this growth will be different in different countries (World Bank, 2021).

Thus, together with the economic growth, it is increasing the consumption of water. For example, if within the ancient and middle centuries periods, during the 24 hours, one person consumed 12-18 liters, in XIX Century – 40-60 liters, in the economically developed countries daily consumption per person at the beginning of XXI Century was 300 liters, in the big cities 500 liters and more (Neidze, 2004).

Non-Equal Distribution of Water by the Regions of the World: Freshwater resources are distributed unequally between different regions and countries of the modern world. Moreover, where water sources are abundant - in Canada, the countries of the North Europe, Siberia, Alaska, most of South America - water demand is less than in regions where it is not enough, for example in North Africa, the Middle East, Central, and South Asia. By the beginning of the XXI century, 70% of the world's population lived in the countries, where the population experienced very severe water stress, i.e., an acute deficit of water resources. After a quarter-century, the proportion of people living in such conditions will amount to 80% (Maksakovsky, 2009).

Climate Change: Among all processes, which influence the availability of freshwater, this process is exogenous and for humanity has not been remained a different way, except adaptation. Climate change aggravates the situation both in the traditionally arid regions and in the developing countries of Asia. One of the reliable manifestations of a global climate change scientists call a change in the water cycle (United Nations Water Development Report, 2009). In the regions with the arid climate the amount of

Figure 9. Water for a sustainable development
Source: https://www.un.org/waterforlifedecade/water_and_sustainable_development.shtml

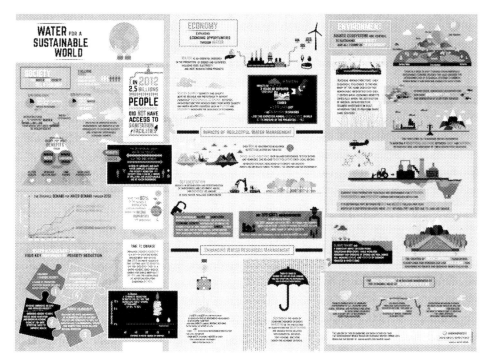

precipitation will be reduced and in the areas with the moist climate will be increased. The decrease of the area of glaciers moreover, directly affects the volume of accessible water resources.

But the most visual influence of climate change on the water cycle occurs through a radical increase in the number of natural disasters. Natural disasters have a direct and destructive effect on the situation with the water supply, they require additional investments into the steadier infrastructure. The creation of special dams for the restraining of floods and construction of reservoirs for the economy of water in the arid years becomes a vital need for the majority of the countries. From 1980 to 2004, a third of all-natural calamities were coming to floods (29%) and droughts (5%) (UNICEF, 2020).

Water as a Reason for Potential Conflicts

Water scarcity negatively affects the quality of life of ordinary people, interferes with the tasks of socio-economic development of many of the world's poorest countries. As practice shows, the not-abundance of freshwater can cause both internal, and international conflicts. For example, the disputes about using the water resources of the Jordan River, are an additional factor that complicates the procedure for resolving the Middle East conflict.

Both, Israel and neighboring Arab countries together with Palestine seek to secure a priority in using scarce of in the Middle East of water resources. In the countries of this region, as well as in many Asian and African states internal contradictions about the use of water resources often lead to fierce conflicts among interest groups, to the confrontation between population and official authorities.

Figure 10. Predictable water stress by country in 2040
Source: https://www.weforum.org/agenda/2019/10/water-inequality-developing-world-usa-west/

Internationalization of previously purely inland river basins may become a prerequisite for the emergence of new conflict zones in world politics.

Trans-Border Regulation: The Source of the problems of trans-border regulation is, in the essence, the imposition of the political map of the World on the map of the water basins. On the Earth are located 263 international basins (such basins include those, on whose territory are located two and more countries). In those basins is concentrated about 60% of the fresh water and by the territory, they occupy half of the earth's surface. International basins partially seize the territory of 145 countries and the territory of 21 states completely enters into the international ponds (Giordano, 2003).

In general, to solve the problems of water scarcity the international cooperation on the global level is required. Since March 22, 1992, it is celebrated as a World Day of water resources. In 1996, the World Water Council was established, headquartered in Marseille (France).

Once within three years, the World Water Forum, which is the next step in organizing cooperation on water issues is held. The goals of the Forum are not only in conducting discussions and developing provisions for solving water problems but also in creating political obligations and mechanisms for international cooperation. However, here, just as in solving other global problems, it is emerged a contradiction between universal interests and the economic-political, and political priorities of individual states.

PART 6. HEALTH PROTECTION PROBLEMS

The health problem is one of the oldest and global social problems. Low level of medical development, poor sanitary conditions, economic and socio-cultural backwardness were the reasons that determined the high mortality rate and the prevalence of diseases. In recent decades, the socio-economic situation and sanitary-hygienic conditions in the world as a whole have significantly improved, and great progress has been made in the development of medicine. Consequently, some successes will undoubtedly be observed. The mortality rate has decreased, the average life expectancy has increased, and the incidence of the number of diseases has been reduced to a minimum. Nevertheless, in many regions of the world, some significant progress in this direction has not yet been observed, while in other regions, where there has been apparent progress and many diseases have been virtually eliminated, there has been a growing trend towards other diseases. Thus, the health problem remains an extremely serious, global problem.

Average Mortality and Life Expectancy

The overall mortality rate (the number of deaths per 1000 inhabitants per year) is primarily a demographic indicator and gives us little idea of the overall state of health care. In developing countries, due to the high birth rate, the share of young age groups is usually very large, and therefore the overall mortality rate is relatively low. In developed countries, however, due to the excess of elderly people in the population, the mortality rate has increased significantly. Thus, the relatively high overall mortality rate in the developed world and the low rate in several developing countries are due to the age structure of the population and not to the health care situation. The picture will change significantly if we calculate the mortality rate, not for the whole population, but individual age groups. (The so-called standardized mortality rate), it turns out that the mortality rate in developing countries (especially in the so-called poorer countries) is several times higher than the similar rate in developed countries.

The standardized mortality rate is directly related to the level of social, economic, cultural development, health status and does not depend on the age structure of the population. In this sense, a completely regular general picture is drawn. Mortality rates are very high in most of tropical Africa, as well as in the developing countries of Asia and Latin America. For the best part of the world is characterized by an average mortality rate, while in developed countries the standardized mortality rate is very low.

The overall picture of health status is well illustrated by infant mortality rates. This is the number of stillbirths per 1,000 live births. Obviously, the higher this rate, the lower the level of health care and unsatisfactory medical care and sanitary-hygienic conditions. The situation is particularly dire in Angola, where 184 out of every 1000 infants do not reach one year of age, as well as in Sierra Leone (158), Afghanistan (157), Liberia (150), and Niger (126). While in Japan, Singapore, Hong Kong, Iceland, Norway, and Sweden the figure is less than 3 (Chitadze, 2017).

The average life expectancy is also clear in some countries. It varies greatly by region and country. The average life expectancy in the world as a whole is 65.8 years. Men - 63.7 years, women - 67.8). In Japan, the figure is more than 82 years (men - 83.7 years, women - 85.5), while in Andorra, San Marino, Singapore, Hong Kong, Sweden, Switzerland, Australia, France, Iceland, and Canada, it is more than 80 years, then When in Swaziland it is 32.2 years (men - 31.8, women - 32.6). The average life expectancy is less than 40 years in Angola, Lesotho, Zambia, Zimbabwe, Sierra Leone, and Liberia. The average life expectancy in Georgia is 76.3 years (men - 73.0, women - 80.1). And with this figure, it is ranked 65th among 221 countries in the world (Interpressnews, 2021).

In the picture of the average life expectancy in the modern world, we can have some idea of the differences that can exist between economically developed and developing countries in the field of health care. Let's look more specifically at the picture in healthcare. In particular, in determining the level of health of the population in this or that country, one of the main parameters can be considered the issue of access to health care for the population. Typically, in economically developed countries, health care accounts for more than 5% of the country's GDP, and in some countries, this figure exceeds 10%, while in the US it exceeds 14%. In developing countries this figure is less than 5%, in many extremely backward countries, it is less than 1% (United Nations Development Program. 2013).

As for the definition of health care expenditures per capita, worldwide, this figure is $ 630. Among the regions, North America spends $ 4,700 per capita, Europe - $ 1,500, South America - $ 550, Asia - $ 250, and Africa, for example, in the case of sub-Saharan Africa, it is released no more than 100 Dollars. According to individual countries, about $ 5,000 per capita on health care is spent in the United States and $ 3,500 in Switzerland. As for the "global South" countries, for example in the Democratic Republic of the Congo and Sierra Leone, health care costs are about $ 15 per capita (World Health Organization. Countries. 2014).

The level of medical care in the country is also determined by the number of doctors and hospital beds per 100,000 people. The comparison of these figures further reveals a huge gap between economically developed and developing countries. For example, the number of doctors per 100,000 inhabitants worldwide is estimated at an average of 150 doctors, in North America their number exceeds 500, and in Europe exceeds 350. At the same time, the number of physicians in South America is estimated by 200, in Asia by 70, and in sub-Saharan Africa up to 15 medical staff (Health Statistics. 2014).

Judging by individual countries, Italy leads by the number of doctors per 100 thousand population - 600 doctors, USA - 550, Russia - 480. At the same time, in sub-Saharan African countries, the number of doctors varies from 2 to 10 people. It turns out that in developed countries to one doctor for consultations applies from 200 to 350 patients, this is when one doctor serves every 50 thousand people in the case of Chad, Eritrea, Malawi!

In addition, according to the number of hospital beds per 100 thousand inhabitants, Japan is in the first place - 1500, followed by Russia and Belarus - 1100, while in Ethiopia, for example, the number of beds is only 25 (World Health Organization. Countries. 2014).

Several Opinions about the Main Reasons for the COVID 19 Emergence. Myths and Reality

As it is known, during the last period, there has been constant speculation about the source of coronavirus origin. Different countries blame each other for the virus spreading. In addition, there is a scandalous version that the virus was artificially created in the form of biological weapons in the laboratory of Wuhan in China.

It is important to note that the Wuhan Institute of Virology opened in 2015 (Cyranoski, 2017). The laboratory has been assigned the highest level of security or the fourth level. In this regard, it is important to point out, that the fourth level of laboratories in the world is represented by a very small number. According to various theories, experiments in this laboratory were carried out with the most dangerous microorganisms that could cause deadly diseases (Ebola and others).

According to media reports from several countries, during the conducting research at the Wuhan Institute in 2018, the heads of this institute proudly claimed, that they have investigated the immune mechanism of bats. Bats could have been carriers of the virus for a long time, and at that time they were not infected with the virus. Thus, the Wuhan Institute hoped that the virus-carrying bats would allow people to learn how to fight against viruses (Lolashvili, 2020).

The Economic Component of World Politics and the Main Global Social and Economic Problems

Figure 11. COVID-19 has severely impacted people and business all over the world
Source: https://www.iru.org/covid19

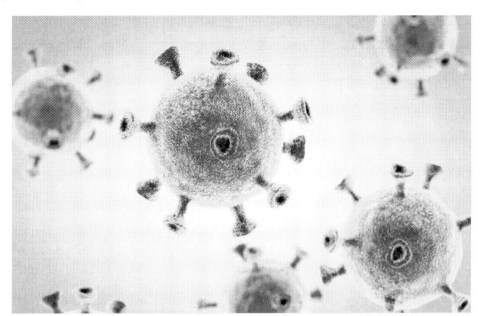

It should be pointed out, that the French virologist Luke Montagne, who was awarded the Nobel Prize in 2008 for his discovery of HIV, said that the new type of coronavirus had not had the natural origin of COVID-19 and has been created in a laboratory with added HIV particles.

The professor does not share the view that the virus emerged as a result of pollution in the Wuhan market. According to him, Wuhan's laboratory has been specializing in coronaviruses since 2000 and he has extensive experience in this field. In addition, the Nobel laureate said that he had analyzed the issue with his math colleague, Jean-Claude Perez.

"We have concluded that this virus has been manipulated. This is the work of molecular biologists," Montagne said in an interview with CNEws (Xinhuanet, 2020).

The Nobel Laureate says COVID-19 added HIV particles. "For what purpose? It's vague. My job is to present the facts and I don't blame anyone. I don't know who did it and why. Maybe they wanted to create a vaccine against AIDS," Montagne said.

Luke Montagne is a French virologist, a knight of the Legion of Honor, and a Nobel laureate. He received an award in medicine and physiology in 2008 and was awarded Harald Zur Hausen and Francoise Barre-Sinus. Together with Barre-Sinus, Montana discovered the human immunodeficiency virus in 1983 (Xinhuanet, 2020).

Earlier, Fox News reported that, according to Chinese authorities, the first patient who was diagnosed with a new type of coronavirus was not a market worker, but he worked in a laboratory at the Wuhan Institute of Virology.

Coronavirus and Information War Between the States

The debate about the possible artificial creation of coronaviruses is still ongoing. Several opinions were presented in March this year. In particular, a former senior Israeli military intelligence analyst, Dan Shohanma, in an interview with The Washington Times, said there was an attempt to produce biological weapons in a Wuhan laboratory, which in turn represents one of the leading research institutes. in the world (Washington Times, 2020).

Also noteworthy is the fact that back in 2019, the US State Department expressed doubts about the ongoing secret programs and experiments in this country related to the creation of biological weapons. China denies the allegations in an official statement that said: "Similar, unfounded allegations of China's foreign intelligence service have been made several times." At the same time, several experts conclude that the leak of the new virus from the Wuhan laboratory occurred during the corresponding experiments in this scientific center.

While China denied possessing any aggressive biological weapons, the U.S. Department of State report for 2019 was mentioned Washington's suspicions that China was conducting a hidden biological war (US State Department Report, 2020).

In response, China leaked through the Internet information that the virus is part of a US conspiracy to use biological weapons against China.

While the countries were involved in recriminations of each other, in early March of this year, the Chinese Ministry of Foreign Affairs accused the U.S. Army of the spreading of the epidemic on the territory of China. In particular, Zhao Lijian, Deputy Director-general of the Information Department of the Chinese Ministry of Foreign Affairs, wrote on his Twitter that the United States should present concrete explanations and transfer its data to be more transparent.

"When did the infection begin in the United States?" How many people are infected? What are the names of hospitals? The US Army may have introduced an epidemic in Wuhan. Be transparent, make your data publicly available, "wrote Zhao Lizziani (QUARTZ, 2020).

For other media outlets, such as Political Trends, China seeks to relieve itself of responsibility for the pandemic.

Another source of information, more precisely misinformation has been spread by the Russian media, according to which the Coronavirus is a special weapon created by the United States to destroy China and Russia.

Military expert Igor Nikulin calls the spread of the virus sabotage and develops several versions: Americans are trying to destroy the Chinese from within; Coronavirus may be artificially created; The proliferation of coronavirus is in the interest of American pharmaceutical companies; The spread of coronavirus is in America's interest, as American laboratories operate not only around Russia but also in Asian countries (For. Ge, 2020).

Interestingly, at the end of April, Russia, through the puppet regime in the Tskhinvali region (formerly the South Ossetian Autonomous Region), issued another disinformation regarding the US laboratory in Georgia.

In particular, the so-called South Ossetian Security Service Application calls that "the residents of the Republic of South Ossetia should not take into attention the Georgian side`s suggestions to participate at any type of medical research." The main reason is the "area of Lugar Laboratory biological activity, which creates the preconditions for the deliberate infection of the residents of South Ossetia by Coronavirus.

Figure 12. Some states not sharing all COVID – 19 Details
Source: https://www.youtube.com/watch?v=k2V7AAjL6L4

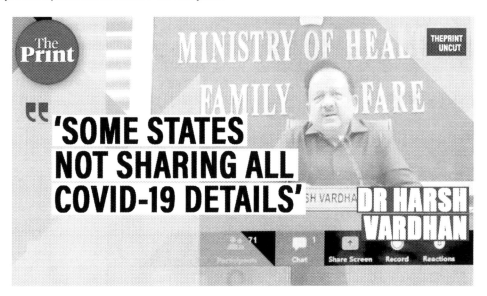

It further underscores the fact that, according to the State Security Service, American and Georgian specialists are working to create and modify the spread of dangerous diseases, including those for military purposes" (Sputnik, 2020).

Later, the Chinese media, in particular the Chinese Global Times, blamed Russia for the spread of COVID-2019on the territory of China. In particular, the Chinese edition noted that Russia became the main source of COVID-2019 entry into China when 309 Chinese citizens were diagnosed with the disease as soon as they returned from Russia.

Later, however, the media reported that Russia and China were working together to condemn "dangerous" American laboratories which are operating in the former Soviet republics.

China's Ministry of Foreign Affairs organized a regular press briefing, where the spokesman of the ministry said that Beijing is concerned with the functioning on the territories of the former Soviet republics American research laboratories and supports the allegations of the Russian Foreign Ministry spokesman, Maria Zakharova (TASS, 2020).

It is possible to assume that the statements made by Russia and China are related to the statements of US President Donald Trump and Secretary of State Mike Pompeo that it is necessary to study the activities of the Wuhan Institute of Virology, which may have been one of the sources of coronavirus (Chitadze, 2020).

How Credible is a Conspiracy Theory about COVID 19 Taking into Consideration the Foreign Policy and Foreign Economic Priorities of the Leading Countries of the World?

Against the backdrop of accusations leveled against each other by the world's leading states about Coronavirus, it is possible to analyze how much it is possible for this or another country in the world, including leading geopolitical players, to be interested in spreading the virus.

The epidemic spread would not have been interested China, from where the virus has been widespread, taking into consideration that within the last years the rapid development of China's economy was provided. Its GDP is 14 trillion USD and China is coming to the world stage with the strengthening its geopolitical position first of all by taking the appropriate economic measures. For example, this country is the first exporter in the world and in 2019 China exported to the international market the products for $ 2 trillion 494 million (12% of world exports), which is about 1.5 times higher than the export potential of its main competitor in the world economy - United States of America. However, due to Koronavirus - in the first quarter of 2020, the volume of the Chinese main economic lever - export, has decreased by 13.3% (Trading Economics, 2020). It will lead to economic stagnation in this country (as well as around the world). Therefore, it is impossible not to consider official Beijing would not take into account the consequences of the spread of the virus from this country to different regions of the world.

In addition, the spread of coronavirus has significantly shaken the international reputation of China as a country - that spreads coronavirus. It is known that several states are also demanding the imposition of economic sanctions against China. It is also important to note that many transnational companies are already trying to withdraw their capital from China, which will significantly reduce the volume of investment in the Chinese economy (previously annually about $ 40 billion were invested in the different sectors of the Chinese economy). All the above will lead to economic stagnation in this country (as well as around the world). Naturally, therefore, it is impossible not to consider that official Beijing could not predict the consequences of the spread of the virus from this country to different regions of the world.

As for the possible spread of Coronavirus by the United States and, first of all, its import into China, this position also excludes the real picture. In particular, despite the geopolitical and ideological rivalry and the problems in the trade-economic relations between the United States and China within the last two years, new agreements were signed in October-December 2019, according to which important steps were taken to remove the trade barriers. Trade turnover between the US and China in 2018 was estimated at $ 737 billion, while the volume of US direct investment in the Chinese economy ranged to about $100 billion (Office of the United States Trade Representative, 2019).

Of course, the relevant US state agencies would also be able to calculate the consequences of COVID 19 spreading taking into consideration the volume of the trade between the United States and China. Therefore, the US was aware of the fact that due to the spread of the virus in China, it would primarily affect the US, whereas of April 27, 2020, 987, 322 thousand people were infected with coronavirus and the total number of deaths was 55, 415 thousand people. As for jobs, the number of unemployed in the United States has risen by about 300,000 as a result of the virus (Wordometers, 2020). In addition, experts estimate that by 2020, the U.S. economy will shrink by about 3%. In addition, COVID 19 negatively reflected on the income of US Companies. For example, only in March 2020, Dow Jones Index fell by about 26% (Chitadze, 2020).

Justice requires to mention, that Russia also would not be interested in the spread of coronavirus. Of course, this country can be blamed for many issues, including how Russia occupied the territories of the neighboring countries, spreading various types of disinformation around the world, including the possibility of artificially spreading the Coronavirus by the west, which has already been mentioned before.

But about the artificially spreading of COVID 19 by Russia, there is a low probability that the Kremlin was interested in the Coronaviruses pandemic, first of all, because of the fact, that the Russian political elite understood, that a new pandemic could cause the new World Economic crisis, which from its turn could decrease the demand on the energy products, first of all, oil and gas. As it is known, Russia represents one of the main oil producers and exporters in the World. For example, about 35% of the income part of the Russian budget is dependent on the profit from the oil export.

In this regard, it is important to note that as a result of the coronavirus, oil prices per barrel within the first quarter of 2020 reduced by more than 60%, from $ 65 per barrel in 2019 to $ 20 in April 2020 (Marketwatch.2020). As to another lever of the Russian economy and political pressure - natural gas, it should be mentioned that as a result of COVID 19 spreading, the Russian energy giant Gazprom announced a decrease in the demand for natural gas and a sharp reduction in gas exports. The company estimates that the decline within 2020 will be about 16.4%. Alexander Ivannikov, director of Gazprom's finance and economic department, said.

He said natural gas prices from Russia to foreign consumers would be further reduced, from $ 210.6 per 1,000 cubic meters to $ 133, or by 37 percent (Lenta. Ru. 2020).

Furthermore, Russia has overtaken China in terms of the number of illnesses. In particular, as of May 4, the number of people infected with the virus in Russia was 145,268 (82880 in China), and the death number was 1,356 people (Wordometers, 2020).

At the same time, no other country can be interested in the spread of coronavirus and in the global economic crisis, given the fact that the according to the World Bank estimations, the world economy within 2020 will be reduced by about 3%, which will create a problem for each country in our planet (Chitadze, 2020).

Coronavirus and Existing Biological Laboratories in the World

Many analysts rule out any rumor about the artificial emergence of COVID 19, saying that various laboratories for biological or medical purposes operate in different parts of the world, and if we develop a conspiracy theory, then we can bring the example of Lugar's laboratory in Georgia. This case is given because, within the propaganda policy of Russia, the official Kremlin has often accused the United States, that after the opening of Lugar Laboratory in Georgia, with the support of the US government - different types of experiments on humans have been implemented.

The lab was named in honor of American Senator Richard Lugar. After the Kremlin's propaganda, it turned out that Lugar's laboratory was indispensable in conducting various scientific research. Even at this stage, Lugar's laboratory turned out to be the only surviving facility that promptly allowed Georgian doctors to prevent Coronavirus from developing an epidemiological psychosis. As a result, Lugar's lab is a real tool that has, to some extent, localized the pandemic virus.

In addition, many experts believe that it is the Wuhan laboratory mentioned above that has played an important role in stopping the virus in China and in general has prevented more serious negative consequences. At present, the problem of coronavirus in the Wuhan province has been localized. The scale of the virus spreading is declining, thus, talking about biological theories is not true. This is a classic information propaganda war waged primarily by the official Kremlin, claiming that the virus, and various diseases, are biological weapons of Washington.

World-Renowned Pandemics - Black Death, Plague, Swine Flu, AIDS, etc.

The natural and not artificial origin of Coronavirus can be confirmed by the fact that at different times in world history, the origin and spread of various epidemics or pandemics in different regions of the planet have occurred many times. However, among the diseases listed below, none of the artificial origins of those viruses have been confirmed.

Perhaps the most horrific epidemics in history, or rather pandemics that have caused great harm to the world's population, have been linked with the plague. Several pandemics of this terrible disease are known to us.

Noteworthy is the fact that information about various diseases can be found in ancient Egyptian manuscripts. However, the first pandemic in which relatively more specific clues have been found is known as the "Athens plague." According to various ancient Greek sources, the plague spread on the modern territory of Ethiopia and via Northern Africa, particularly Egypt has reached Greece. As a result, in 430, the plague killed about 25-30% of the Athenian population during the period, when this city-state was involved in the Peloponnesian Wars (Histoire Géo, 2020).

In 165 CE, on the territory of the Roman empire the new pandemic, with the name "Antonius' Illness" was emerged. According to various reports, the virus entered the Apennine Peninsula from Mesopotamia. The pandemic claimed the lives of about 5 million people, in a situation when the world's population at that time was just over 200 million (Histoire Géo, 2020).

Later, a new, so-called "plague of Justinian" appeared, which within the 40th of the VI century began to be spread in the different regions of the world from Central Asia (by other sources from Egypt) and in 541 reached the Byzantine capital of Constantinople. The plague was most likely spread from rats and micro-fleas. It has claimed the lives of about 30 million to 100 million people over two centuries. In other words, the cause of the epidemic was the plague, which later became known as the "Black Death" pandemic (Histoire Géo, 2020).

The second pandemic caused the deaths of millions of people in Europe during the 14th century. The disease spread from Asia and spread from rodents in all European port cities. In addition to the European Continent, the plague has inflicted huge losses to China, with up to 90 percent of its population lost in some provinces. Several factors contributed to the emergence and spread of the plague: the wars that engulfed Europe (the movement of large armies), the rapid development of trade, the general situation in sanitation, and the climatic factor. The problems with Global glaciation weakened the immunity of the population, especially in Europe.

Outbreaks appear to be exacerbated in Europe by the outbreak of chickenpox and pelagic fever. The place of origin of the "black death" was the Gobi Desert - animals (mostly rodents) that lived in this area, found to be closer to humans who were fleeing from hunger and drought. Traders who followed the Silk Road were transporting various goods to the Asian cities, which later led to the deaths of millions of people. There was no cure for the plague then. Infection with "black death" meant that a person would die in a few days. The symptoms were several: in the case of the bubonic plague, the disease-causing human body was exposed to a flea bite. Those fleas were located on the body of the rats.

As a result, If about 80 million people were living in Europe in the early fourteenth century, by 1360 there were about 50,000,000 left. Outbreaks appear to be exacerbated in Europe by 200-300 years after the outbreak of the epidemic.

The third plague began in China in the mid-nineteenth century. It has once again spread around the world by merchant ships, especially in port cities and coastal areas. It was at the end of the 19th century that scientists discovered the cause of the plague. More than 10,000,000 people only in Asia have died since the last pandemic.

Another disease that has caused the panic of all of humanity is known as the chickenpox pandemic. Infectious disease has killed tens of thousands of people in a year and a half. Only in 1980, the World

Figure 13. Plague is an infectious disease caused by the bacterium Yersinia pestis. Symptoms include fever, weakness and headache
Source: https://news.stanford.edu/2020/05/12/combating-black-plague-just-much-politics-science/

Health Organization declared that the disease could be eradicated worldwide with the help of vaccination. The average mortality rate was 40%. The chickenpox epidemic was registered in China in the 4th century, and a little later in the 7th century in India, Korea, and Japan. In the latter case, it destroyed a third of the country's population (Khutsishvili, 2020).

In the modern era, it is difficult to find a European, especially in large cities, who was not infected by chickenpox. In the 18th century, 1.5 million people died every year in Europe from this disease. Chickenpox is transmitted by airborne droplets. Cases of skin transmission have also been reported. The first symptoms are fever, muscle and limb pain, vomiting, headache, dizziness.

Cholera - Acute intestinal infection has long been spread in Asia, Africa, and South America, and it reached Europe in the 19th century. By the beginning of the last century, seven cholera pandemics had been recorded, most recently in 1961-1975. Cholera was mainly transmitted by water, and the water was contaminated with the feces of the infected people. Unsanitary conditions were a major cause of cholera. Rapid dehydration often led to death. Cholera has claimed the lives of tens of millions of people since the 1800s.

Typhoid becomes a real disaster during World War I Europe. There were several types of this disease: skin, abdominal, and reversible. It raged in the first quarter of the twentieth century. Known since the time of Hippocrates, this disease appeared mainly during the wars. Infections that transmit the disease can easily spread to the fighters. Typhoid killed 2 million people during the Civil War in Russia (Intermedia, 2020). The disease begins with itching, fever, backache, and headache. Slowly pink spots appear on the abdomen. People start dreaming, losing the sense of time and space. Half of the patients with typhoid died. There is currently an antidote to typhoid fever, so the probability of death is significantly lower, even in severe cases.

Malaria is another disease that has killed millions of people over the centuries. About 2-3 million people die from malaria each year. This disease, which is characteristic of tropical and subtropical regions, has historically been known in Europe. In the Roman Empire, it was called "Roman fever". The disease is transmitted by mosquitoes, but it is also possible to transmit by blood from person to person.

Influenza - The emergence of many mutations in this disease has sowed panic in recent decades. The reason for this panic exists. The Spanish flu ("Ispanka") struck millions of people between 1918 and 1919, infecting 550 million people and killing more than 25 million. The Spanish flu pandemic has been recorded as one of the greatest tragedies in human history. This time too, the war became the main cause of the spread of the disease, particularly the First World War and the series of military conflicts that followed. The name of the disease is related to the place from which the terrible disease began to go around the world. According to the second version, Spain was not the place where this virus was born, although it was the country that first experienced this catastrophe (Intermedia, 2020).

In the first six months, Ispanka has killed more than 10 million people worldwide. The technological development of vehicles has allowed the virus to reach all the settlements around the planet. The main symptoms of the disease are pneumonia, bloody cough, as well as the characteristic blue tint of the skin, cyanosis - an excessive accumulation of carbon dioxide, which in turn causes hypoxemia - lack of oxygen in the blood.

In the early 1980s, the world faced a new global problem. In 1981, a strange disease appeared, which caused a complete loss of immunity, and thus, any illness could become fatal for a sick person. The disease became known as AIDS (Acquired Immunodeficiency Syndrome). According to one version, monkeys - inhabited in tropical Africa were the main source of virus infection. Consequently, AIDS has spread as a result of the bites of monkeys, particularly chimpanzees. This hypothesis is supported by American researcher B. Corbett.

In 2006, the total number of AIDS deaths was 2.9 million, and by January 2007, the total number of AIDS carriers in the world was 39.6 million people (Davitashvili, Elizbarashvili, 2012).

The Influenza H1N1, which killed a million people in the first quarter of the 20th century, revived in a new form in 2009 and became known as the "swine flu." It was a subtype of the Spanish flu, and the source was an infected pig. This illness is characterized by the symptoms of the common flu - cough, fever, vomiting, diarrhea. Approximately 250,000 cases of the infection have been reported in 140 countries, killing up to 3,000 people. The mass-media means in the past, as well as today, began to escalate the situation, predicting what the second Spanish flu ("Ispanka") would emerge. Nevertheless, the standards of medicine and health are more or less different from those of the previous century, and the absence of global military conflicts has reduced the risks of high lethality and the spread of the disease to a minimum. It was later revealed that the governments of various states had squandered huge sums of money on the purchase of medicines and vaccines that had never been used for their intended purpose (Intermedia, 2020).

The same story was repeated in 2013, in the case of the H7N9 flu virus, better known as the "bird flu". The first case of human infection was reported in China. The main symptom, again and again, was pneumonia. 450 cases were registered, 175 of them lethal. Fortunately, the pandemic did not occur.

The last viral challenge of the century was the Ebola fever. It was first observed in South Sudan in 1976 but became widely known in 2014 when an epidemic crossed the boundaries of West Africa and invaded the United States and Europe. The virus is transmitted through the body fluids of an infected person or animal, such as blood (Chitadze, 2020).

The disease is characterized by a feeling of weakness, severe pain in the head and muscles, diarrhea. Later symptoms include coughing, nausea, and dehydration. Some patients develop a hemorrhagic rash. If treatment is not started in time, internal and external bleeding begins. Within the second week of illness, the patient dies. In 2015, Ebola-infected 30,000 people, nearly half of whom died. In this case, too, the media predicted the inevitability of the apocalypse of mankind, and again, their prophecy did not come true. Of course, the modern media industry makes money in similar panic news or stories. People are attracted to the excitement, and journalists very often love exaggeration.

Humanity is constantly threatened by many viral diseases, but some media means are not bothered by this. Maintaining a healthy lifestyle and taking sanitary measures is enough to protect yourself from the types of flu that spread to the Far East or the South. Otherwise, it seems, humanity will not get sick until some journalists or so-called experts find out about new flu mutations and start sowing panic, which, in itself, serves in no way to eliminate the causes of the problem.

The World Health Organization has Named the Probable Source of COVID 19

The official statement made by the World Health Organization (WHO) confirms the evidence of the natural origin of coronavirus. In particular, the official representative (spokesman) of the World Health Organization, Fadella Chaib, said at the briefing that the source of COVID-19 is still unknown, but it has likely been transmitted by the mediation of the bats.

"All available evidence suggests the virus has an animal origin and is not manipulated or constructed in a lab or somewhere else" mentioned WHO spokeswoman (Reuters, 2020).

Later she added: "most likely is that its ecological reservoir is bats. However, it is necessary to determine how the virus moved from bats to humans. It is obvious that there is a mediator that transmitted the disease to humans."

"At this moment we know nothing about the origin of the virus. We need to focus on facts and not on theories. The World Health Organization is a scientific organization and we suggest that the virus is of animal origin," said a World Health Organization`s spokesman.

Chaib noted that 70% of new viruses, including Ebola, plague, and coronavirus, are of animal origin (Reuters, 2020).

The statement was made in response to an earlier statement by French virologist Luke Montagne, a Nobel Prize-winning. His position has already been mentioned at the beginning of the article.

In an interview with the website of the California Institute of Technology, another Nobel laureate, David Baltimore, shared his opinion. The professor believes that biologically HIV and SARS-CoV-2 are completely different from each other and belong to different families of viruses.

The opinion of the World Health Organization is shared by Australian experts, who believe that the new type of coronavirus could not be created artificially.

"At the moment we know nothing about the origin of the virus. We need to focus on facts, not theories. The World Health Organization is a scientific organization and we suggest that the virus is of animal origin," said a World Health Organization spokesman.

Chaib noted that 70% of new viruses, including Ebola, plague, and coronavirus, are of animal origin.

The statement was made in response to an earlier statement that "there has been a backlash from French virologist Luke Montagne, a Nobel Prize-winning French virologist, about the fact that COVID-19 was created in the laboratory and added to it."

In an interview with the website of the California Institute of Technology, another Nobel laureate, David Baltimore, shared his opinion. The professor believes that biologically HIV and SARS-CoV-2 are completely different from each other and belong to different families of viruses (Interpressnews, 2020).

The opinion of the World Health Organization is shared by Australian experts, who believe that the new type of coronavirus could not be created artificially.

At the same time, scientists have discovered the first significant mutation in coronavirus. Anthony Fauch, head of the National Institute of Allergy and Infectious Diseases in the United States, later said the best evidence was that the coronavirus had not been created in a Chinese laboratory.

"If we look at the evolution of the virus in bats, the scientific evidence is very, very strong that it could not be artificially created or deliberately manipulated. If we observe the evolution of the virus within the concrete period, we will find the strong determinant that the virus has emerged naturally and then moved to other species, "Fauch said in a statement (Interpressnews, 2020).

Based on the above, based on the majority of specialists, the most solid theory at this stage is the fact that coronavirus is a virus transmitted from bats because as a result of deciphering the genetic sequence, this virus is closest to the virus found in bats, where the similarity is up to 99%. The coronavirus circulates us, meaning it is not a virus that is completely new.

In addition to that, it is very interesting to note the fact that there are certain old traditions in China, according to which a strange habit is spread among the poor population of China in the form of a kind of folk medicine. When a person is ill, has the flu, or has another illness, he or she is often offered to eat the meat of the snake. Most likely, it was this tradition and the consumption of bats that most probably led to the spread of the virus. That is, it can be said that a biological mutation has taken place. One of the sick people ate bat meat. It is quite real that the virus mutated in one human body and spread to other humans.

It is important to note that the international community is very often under the influence of some scientists or experts, also information propaganda of several states, especially the countries with authoritarian regimes. The main purpose of some specialists is - to make some scandal statements and by this way to attract the attention of the population of one concrete country or whole international community. The purpose of some states is to conduct the information policy with the purpose of discretization the international authority of its geopolitical or ideological rival etc.

Thus, it can be assumed, that the rumors about artificial spreading the COVID 19 represent false information.

PART 7. GLOBAL DEMOGRAPHIC PROBLEMS

International aspects of such problems, as the population growth, its aging in the economically and industrially developed countries, environmental pollution, are directly connected with the topics of globalization and interdependence of the modern world, and also with the economic activity of humanity, inequality of the distribution and limitation of the natural resources in our planet. From its turn, the topics on population growth and environment are interconnected with each other. Population growth influences the environment, at least by two means: First, increasing the number of inhabitants on our planet causes the consumption of more quantities of products, energy, and other resources. Second, it is an increase in economic activity, which is connected with environmental pollution due to the exhaust of gases, air pollution, water resources, etc.

The growth of the number of people on our planet, ecological problems affect the climate changing environment and influence not only on the separate countries or regions (even though some of them have the pressure of one or another problem) but on the whole of humanity in general. Due to this fact, they gained the name of global problems. In this regard, it should be underlined, that all of them:

- Have gained the planetary, universal character and concern the interests of the people from all states;
- Threaten to humanity by the serious regress in the further development of the productive forces, under the conditions of the life itself;
- There need urgent decisions and actions for the overcoming and prevention of the dangerous consequences and threats to the life support and security of the citizens;
- Require the collective efforts and actions from all the states, whole world community."
- At the same time, different countries and regions by different levels are under the influence of global problems and have various means for their resolution. Here are the different approaches to them.

What are the perspectives of the development of global problems, among them one of the leading places having the problems of demography and ecology? How do they threaten humanity? Will the demographic and ecological problems be the sources for new conflicts? Or, possible or not, that those threats are exaggerated?

The Population of the Planet

About two centuries ago, English researcher Thomas Malthus presented the theory, according to which the number of populations on the planet was growing more rapidly, than the possibilities of their providing food products (Malthus, 1798). In this process, he noticed the serious political consequences and offered to take some measures, for example, the limitation of birthrate, among them one of the main aspects could be the late marriage. Those ideas have caused the discussions, this theory had supporters and opponents, and the theory itself had a significant influence on the development of public opinion.

Then, for some period, Malthus' ideas faded into the background, but in the second half of the XX Century, due to the rapid population growth in the developing countries, it started again the discussion about possible catastrophe related to the overpopulation of the planet. It not only revived the interest in the positions of T. Malthus but introduced the idea for the development of a new direction in science, which gained the name *neo-Malthusianism*.

The topics of population growth have been dedicated to the reports of the Rome Club, which united the different researchers of the world for the resolution of the global problems. However, the worst fear did not come true; scientific-technical innovations give the opportunity, at least at this stage, to resolve this problem by more rational methods. Thus, the introduction of the new scientific developments in agriculture in the second half of the XX century increased the possibilities to sharply increase the grain harvest (production of grain started to outstrip the rate of the population growth) and cope with hunger. In the next period, this gained the name of *the Green Revolution*. More opportunities for the production

Table 2. World population growth between 1820-2021

Year	Population. Billion People	The time (space) of the increasing the number of populations above billion
1820	1	The whole previous history
1927	2	107
1960	3	33
1974	4	14
1987	5	13
1999	6	12
2011	7	12
2021	7.9	-

Source: https://www.worldometers.info/world-population/#:~:text=7.9%20Billion%20(2021),Nations%20estimates%20elaborated%20by%20Worldometer.

of food products promise biotechnologies. Indeed, there are some questions, and some concerns related to the fact, how this type of food products are harmless for the health of the people. But today, when about 1 billion people in the world suffer from hunger, the question related to using biotechnologies is resolved mostly in a positive way (UN, 2020).

Rapid Growth of the World Population

Each year, the number of people in the world is growing to 80-85 million people. The main reason for this is the fact that the birth rate is still high in developing countries. According to demographers, in the case of the continuation of this rate of population growth, in 2200 the number of the world population can reach 20 billion people. It is necessary to point out that, since 1987, for the world population growth of 1 billion people, it is necessary only 12 years. This table is a clear example of this date (Wordometer, 2021).

On the other hand, as of 2012, among the 156 million newborn babies, 125 million were born in the developing world. Accordingly, in the age structure of the countries from the global south the young people (Bliadze, M. Chanturia, G. Kereselidze, D. 2012).

In this regard it should be mentioned the following: There are two types of reproduction and age structure of the population. The first type of reproduction and age structure is characteristic the low fertility and relatively low mortality and very high average life expectancy. This type includes regions of Europe, North America, Australia, and Oceania. The most characteristic feature of the first type is lower than the worldwide proportion of young people of school and university ages and a higher proportion of the older people.

On average, people over the age of 60 years in the above–mentioned regions of the world account for 1/5 of the total population, including 3-4% of those over 80 years (Chitadze, 2017).

The second type is characteristic for the age structure of the second type of population reproduction, which is typical for their high fertility and greatly reduced mortality rates and high or very high natural increase. Admittedly, in this case, Africa, Latin America, and Asia are involved. Those regions are characterized by a high proportion of people with school and university ages and a low percentage

Table 3. Population by age groups in percentage by continents and sub-regions. Data: July, 2013

Continent region	% age 0-14	% age 15-44	% age 45-64	% age 65+	Total
World	26.1%	46.2%	19.7%	7.9%	100%
Africa	39.8%	45.2%	11.4%	3.6%	100%
Americas	24.1%	44.5%	21.5%	9.8%	100%
Asia	25.0%	47.9%	20.1%	7.1%	100%
Caribbean	25.6%	45.2%	20.4%	8.8%	100%
Central America	29.6%	47.4%	16.7%	6.3%	100%
Eastern Africa	42.6%	44.5%	9.7%	3.2%	100%
Eastern Asia	17.8%	46.3%	25.6%	10.3%	100%
Eastern Europe	15.3%	43.1%	27.5%	14.1%	100%
Europe	15.6%	40.3%	27.3%	16.8%	100%
Middle Africa	44.0%	43.4%	9.6%	2.9%	100%
Northern Africa	30.9%	48.2%	15.8%	5.1%	100%
Northern America	19.7%	39.9%	26.4%	14.0%	100%
Northern Europe	17.3%	39.5%	25.8%	17.4%	100%
Oceania	23.8%	43.0%	21.9%	11.3%	100%
South America	25.6%	47.3%	19.4%	7.6%	100%
South-Central Asia	29.9%	48.8%	16.3%	5.0%	100%
South-Eastern Asia	26.3%	48.8%	19.0%	5.9%	100%
Southern Africa	30.2%	49.5%	15.4%	4.9%	100%
Southern Europe	15.0%	39.5%	26.9%	18.7%	100%
Western Africa	42.7%	43.8%	10.3%	3.2%	100%
Western Asia	30.7%	48.9%	15.5%	4.8%	100%
Western Europe	15.6%	36.9%	28.3%	19.1%	100%

Source: UN Department of Economic and Social Affairs. 2013

of older ages. Averages for these three regions are children - 30%, the older people - 8% (CIA World Factbook. 2014).

It is no wonder that such an age structure also generates a big problem, but quite different from those in developed countries. First, it is the problem of "demographic burden", i.e., the ratio of young people to the labor force. Second, it is the problem of education, to provide for the younger generation the basic and secondary education under the conditions, when the rapid growth of population in the countries of global south significantly prevails over the increasing the number of the schools, colleges and other types of educational institutions. Thus, it creates a deficit of the schools and teachers (as it was mentioned above, it is the percentage of people with high education in developing countries).

At the same time, despite the opportunities, having been offered by scientific-technical progress, the problem of the population of the planet and using human resources remains one of the most important problems in the development of the world. As of May 2021, the population prevails 7 billion 900 million people, at the same time, if we take into consideration the history of humanity, this reproduction of the population within the different periods of world history was going on irregularly (Worldometers, 2021). The number of populations in 1 billion people was reached in the first quarter of the XIX Century, 2 billion in the middle of the XX c. As it was mentioned above, then, it is noticed the rapid leap since 1987, because from this period the world population has been increasing by 1 billion people every 12 years. By the UN estimations, by 2050, the world population can reach 9 billion 300 million people (Chitadze, 2017).

However, there is another prognosis too, the Australian demographers are more restrained during the estimation related to the population`s growth. According to their estimates, in 2070, it will be about 8,4 Billion, and after that will start to decrease and never will reach the number 9 billion people (Lebedeva, 2007). Other scientists also somehow support this point of view and consider that the number of populations will reach some maximal index, but later the stabilization will start.

It should be mentioned, that during the last years the prognosis related to the population's growth has become more restrained. Thus, in 1980th UN experts predicted world population growth by 2050 to 10 billion people (Kereselidze, 2012). The reasons for the corrections have become more strict methodological approaches to the estimations and more accurate relations with statistics. To those factors can be added other aspects too. For example, in many countries (first of all in Europe) the birth rate has fallen down and in the developing countries, the demographic growth was not so rapid, as it was expected. As a result of all those tendencies, some panic dispositions, which are connected with the neo-Malthusianism concerns related to the overpopulation of our planet, we're going down, but have not fully disappeared.

Today there is a discussion on three versions of the basic prognosis about changing the number of populations in the world: rapid, moderate, and negligible growth.

However, it is important not only the absolute index of the population of the planet, but its composition too (ethnic, gender, age groups, etc.), and also distribution of the reproduction and number of populations according to the different regions of the world. Population growth is mostly implemented as a result of the reproduction processes in the Global "South". Due to it, demographic problems are strongly connected with the relations "North-South". Thus, Iraq for example has one of the highest rates of reproduction of the population, about 3% per year and India has the leading positions by absolute indexes. By some estimates, by 2050 this country's population will increase by 600 million people and as a result will surpass the population of China (as it is known as the first country according to the number of population) in the middle of XXI century (Chitadze, 2019).

In the annual report of the United Nations for 2001 it was pointed out that by 2050, the population of the 48 poorest countries in the world would have increased three times, even though the AIDS epidemic will somehow restrain the population`s growth in Africa. From the UN materials from the previous years, it should be pointed out that if from 1950 to 1955 the developing countries were contributing 79% of the annual growth of population, within the second decade of the XXI century this index has prevailed 90% (Chitadze, 2017). For the prognosis in 2045-2050, the whole growth will come on the share of the countries from the global "South" (UN Population Fund, 2001). This inequality in the increasing number of populations between developing and developed countries has obtained the name of *the demographic divide* between the North and South Hemispheres.

For the developing countries, in several of them, the problem of population growth is especially acute, the high level of birthrate and many children in families represents the main demographic character for those states. But at the same time, in many countries, the mortality rate among children is also high. In the developed states, on the contrary, both indexes, birthrate and children`s mortality are law. On average, if in the developed countries there are 1,6 children per woman, in the developing countries – 3,4

(Davitashvili, 2012). During the last years, by the estimation of the demographic situation, more and more attention is paid to the problem of AIDS and other infectious diseases, which concerned, first of all, all countries of the "global south" and secondly, the young generation.

A high level of the birthrate in developing countries leads humanity to more misery because families need to feed the little children. Many experts consider that poor family is forced to spend much more percent of their budget on nourishment in comparison with those who have higher income. However, as the volume of GDP per capita is increasing, the living standards are improving. As a result, such states pass through so-called *demographic transit*. At the beginning of this process, the rates of birthrate and mortality are close to each other, then, as a result of the improvement of health care, providing the people with food and water, the rapid prevailing of birth rate over mortality takes place. After the ending of this transit, both curves are becoming closer again, but first of all because of the decreasing birth rate. Countries of Europe and the USA passed from the demographic transit within the period from the second half of XVIII c. till the first third of XX c. Majority of the states in the world are still in the demographic transit stage (Maksakovsky, 2009).

If we take in general the population of our planet, today two of those curves are in a rapprochement stage. This tendency gained the name of *stabilization rate* and is also considered as a base for the recognition of the groundlessness of the pessimistic positions related to the overpopulation of the planet.

During the period of demographic transit, other demographic indexes are also changed. For example, the educational level of the population is improved, the average life expectancy is increased. Characterized for developing countries, the prevailing position of the young population (where families have many children, but life expectancy is the law) is changed by the "leadership" of the elder age group. According to a UN expert's prognosis, the average age of the world population will be higher, because the average life expectancy will be increased. As a result, people with 60 years old will become more than three times, in comparison with the modern time, and the number of those people, whose age prev 80 years, will be increase five times. And this is despite the factor, that every 9 people among 10 will live in developing countries (Lebedeva, 2007). The consequences of this will be various economic problems, which will be connected with the social protection of the people with the pension age. For the resolving of this problem, several versions are being discussed, including increasing the pension age.

During the analysis of the demographic policy in the developing countries, several authors, for example, L. Brown, pay attention to the danger of falling into a "demographic trap", when the state is oriented on the birth rate growth for the purpose, to gain more labor force and do not pay attention to the high mortality rate and low living standards, which takes the society to the social tensions and conflicts (Brown, 1994).

For the developed states, who passed the demographic transit, in comparison to the developing ones, is characterized by the law of reproduction of the population, or even it's decreasing. Due to it, according to UN prognosis, by 2050 in the developed countries (the USA is an exception) the decreasing population will be fixed (Chitadze, 2017).

Inside of the different states, also exists the difference in the rate of reproduction of the population. Usually, it is higher in rural areas than in urban areas. With the social groups with high incomes, as a rule, the number of children in families is lower in comparison with those who have less income.

Differences in the living conditions of the different countries, conflicts, ecologic problems, lack of access to the resources, etc. cause such phenomena, as migration of the population. During the estimation of the migration waves, some difficulties have emerged: it is not always possible to get information about the exact number of populations, because a very important part of migrants crosses the borders illegally, thus, they live in the foreign country illegally. In addition, there is a huge number of refugees, who are forced to leave their native countries because of conflicts. With them and internally displaced persons/peoples – there are special difficulties. The last group is the people, who left the places of the previous residence due to the social, ecologic and political difficulties but who have not at the same time the status of refugee to another state due to the fact, they have moved from one to another region inside of one country.

A significant number of people left their country, for example in Afghanistan, which is determined by the political situation and instability in the native state, or in Ethiopia – due to the low level of living standards. Based on the indexes of the World Resources Institute, WRI, at the end of the 1990th, outside of their countries lived more than 140 million people (including illegal migrants and refugees) (World Resources Institute, 2001) and in 2017 number of migrants prevailed 255 million people (International Migration Agency, 2018).

Within the 1990th, the main part of emigrants was directed in the USA, Canada, Australia, and countries of the European Union. In Europe, within the 1990th, the biggest part of immigrants was coming on the share of Germany. They were about 7% of the inhabitants of this country. In general, in European states about 5% of European states had immigrants. And in the USA, at the end of 1990th, according to the dates, which presents B. Hughes, several thousand people were admitted to enter this country and about 250 thousand of them were illegal immigrants (Chitadze, 2016).

Usually, immigrants have less income than the basic population. But, at the same time, those people have more salaries in comparison to what they could earn in their native countries. The state's attitude toward immigrants is different. Deficit of the labor force in one or another field of the economy causes their admission to the internal market and offers them new job places. However, the existence of the important number of immigrants often causes social tensions (because they take job places from the local population) and the development of xenophobia (i.e., not tolerance toward the people with the other ethnic and racial groups); increasing the nationalistic dispositions and activation of the nationalistic parties; conflicts on the ethnical and racial base; deterioration the criminal situation in the country. At the same time, immigrants need legal and social protection (providing accommodation, pensions, education of children, health care, etc.), which only expands the circle of problems.

As it was mentioned, the migration of population is going on not only among the countries but inside of them. In the modern world, it is observed the clear tendency of the movement of the rural population to the urban areas, which gained the name of *urbanization*. Till 2030, for example, it is expected to double the number of urban inhabitants in comparison to the beginning of the XXI Century. At the same time, 4 billion people, as is expected, will live in the cities of the economically developing states. It will improve their chances for medical treatment, access to fresh water, and receiving education. However, at the same time, urbanization takes us to the increasing danger of epidemics (especially in the developing states); the number of terrorist acts, and the growth of technological catastrophes with a significant number of human victims. There are more and more cities with the number of inhabitants, prevailing 10 million people, which also create a list of problems – ecological, municipal management, etc. (Kereselidze, 2012)

The international community has been actively involved in the problems of population growth since the second half of the XX Century. In 1974, the first conference of the United Nations on population was held in Bucharest to fix the phenomena, which is the fact, that the economic development of the states causes the decrease of the birthrate (UN Department of Economic and Social Affairs, 2020). In connection with it, representatives of the "global south" appealed to the developed countries to implement economic aid for the developing states, which had to bring the improvement of the living standards and as a rule, the decreasing birth rate. However, during the second conference of the United Nations on population, which was held in Mexico in 1984, the issue about the necessity by the developing countries themselves to be involved in the control over the number of populations was discussed (UN Department of Economic and Social Affairs, 2020).

To conduct the policy in the field of the population is possible by the stimulation of the birthrate, releasing the additional allowances for the children, social protection of the large families with many children, etc. At the same time, to implement countermeasures: to limit the birth rate by economic means of legislative norms. India is one of the first countries, which at the beginning of the 50th adopted the program of family planning (Neidze, 2004). In the second half of the 1990th, this policy was conducted by 100 countries in the world (but not all of them were effective). It should be pointed out that in many developing countries, according to B. Hughes, such types of programs were not enough worked out, or they were absent (Chitadze, 2016).

In 1994, in Kairo, the third conference of the UN was held. This conference had a little bit of another name – the UN Conference on Population and Development (UN Department of Economic and Social Affairs, 2020). In the determination of the name itself, new approaches have found their reflection. The problems of population and development started to be considered in the close ties. It was declared, that for example, the question about stabilizing the speeds of the population`s growth of our planet could be resolved only in the context of the wider complex of the problems of the economic and social development. It was also underlined, that during the control over the number of populations, it is necessary to pay attention not only to the economy but also to humanitarian aspects, which are connected with education, opening the creative potential of the people, which come at the first stage at the beginning of the XXI Century.

PART 8. MIGRATION – ONE OF THE MOST IMPORTANT GLOBAL PROBLEMS

Migration is one of the most important global, and at the same time, complex problem, because it represents not only demographical but also serious social, economic, and political problems and creates many difficulties in many countries of the world. As it is known, there are two types of migration: Internal and external.

Despite the existence of the significant problems in the case of internal migration, it is anyway the problems of separate countries and their resolution should be regulated by the conducting the concrete policy of the presented state (adoption of the concrete legislation, etc.). Thus, there are much more problems during the external or international (especially illegal) migration, which has already gained global character and the fighting against illegal one requires international efforts.

In the contemporary period, there are three main centers of the international migrant's concentration: Western Europe, North America, and Arabic states of the Persian Gulf.

Number of International Migrants Globally and According to the Countries

Let`s consider the number of migrants according to the separate countries:

According to the estimates of the UN Department of Economic and Social Affairs, in 2017 the world counted 258 million international migrants, which is about 3.4 percent of the global population (United Nations, 2017).

According to the International Migration Report of the United Nation, in 2017 about 50 million migrants lived in the United States of America (International Migration Report, 2017). People are moving from all over the world towards the state between two Oceans, with the purpose that the "American Dream" will come true.

United States leadership in rankings is no surprise to anyone. As a rule, immigrants leave their homeland for economic hardship or for some reason they have been persecuted in their home countries. No one will go from one poor country to another poor country in the search of happiness. The US is the world's largest economy in the world, GDP of which as to the first quarter of 2019 prevails 21, 06 trillion USD and where **the Real gross domestic product** (GDP) increased at an annual rate of 3.2 percent within the same period – presented in the report of the U.S. Bureau of Economic Analysis (Bureau of Economic Analysis, 2019). Furthermore, if we take into consideration the political factors, the USA is the country, where people are not persecuted because of political views or religious beliefs. It was not a matter of many difficulties to enter into the states illegally until recently, but the initiative of building a wall on the Mexican border and determining the new standards for those people – particularly, more requirement in professionalism for those, who are trying to gain the "Green Card" - might change this condition radically.

There is no comprehensive answer to the question of whether migrants are good or bad for the recipient country? On the one hand, migrants are cheap labor, which reduces the cost of production and makes a country much more competitive on the world market. On the other hand, the criminal rate in migrants is significantly higher, and the directly affected portion of residents by the crime is added to the increased costs of police and penitentiary institutions.

Based on the Eurasia net report, about 12 million migrants live in Russia (Eurasianet, 2018). Most probably, this number of migrants might seem unbelievable in the country, which is authoritarian and where the standard of living is lower in comparison with the average income in Europe, but people from post-soviet countries are still intensively traveling to this country. In comparison with English, Russian does not represent a language barrier to the migrants in Russia from the former Soviet republics. While standards of living in Russia are lower than in the USA, Germany, Switzerland, or even in Estonia (as a former soviet republic), it is higher than in for example Uzbekistan, Moldova, Kyrgyzstan, Ukraine, and Tajikistan. At the same time, in comparison with US and European countries, Russia is not a safe country for migrants, many of them have even become victims of racial attack.

About the same number of migrants (12-12 million) are in Saudi Arabia and Germany, pointed out in the UN International Migration Report in 2017 (International Migration Report, 2017).

A high number of immigrants in Saudi Arabia is a result of the size of this country and income from the export of oil. Those factors are attracting millions of migrants from other Arab countries.

Regarding Germany, immigrants constitute, this country is fourth in the World and first in Europe by socio-economic development (according to the volume of GDP), Germany is attractive for Turks, Russians and people living in Eastern Europe.

At the same time, the percentage of migrants in each country varies considerably. As it is presented in the material of the International Organization for Migration, which is functioning in Slovakia, the countries with the highest percentage are the United Arab Emirates (88.4%), Kuwait (75.5%), Qatar

(65.2%), Liechtenstein (65%), Monaco (54.9%), Bahrain 46%) and Luxembourg (45.3%) (International Organization for Migration, 2019).

Thus, The United Arab Emirates occupies the absolute championship in terms of percentage data. Migrants in this country are mainly from India, Pakistan, Bangladesh, and the Philippines. Burj Khalifa, Palm Jumeirah, and other architectural marvels are built by migrant workers.

In general, it should be mentioned that there are many serious problems related to immigration practically in all those countries of the world, where the number of immigrants is more or less significant. In western Europe, immigrants are mostly from the Near East and Africa. Racial, cultural, and religious differences complicate their adaptation, and language barrier and in most cases, low level of education and qualification and different style of life emerges the new tensions.

It should be mentioned that the Population in the world is currently (2018-2019) growing at a rate of around **1.07%** per year (down from 1.09% in 2018, 1.12% in 2017, and 1.14% in 2016). The current average population increase is estimated at **82 million people per year, reports Wordometer (Wordometer, 2019). Thus, as** of January 1, 2019, the population is estimated at 7.67 billion people (Wordometer, 2019). From its turn, based on this statistical data, also on the fact, that the world population growth for 90% is coming on the share of the countries of the global South, it can be predicted, that the number of immigrants from the countries of the global South to the countries of the global North will gradually increase in the short-term and long-term perspectives.

At the same time, it is necessary to point out some positive tendencies of migration for developing countries. Particularly, according to the World Bank Group report for April 8, 2018, officially recorded annual remittance flows to low- and middle-income countries reached $529 billion in 2018, an increase of 9.6 percent over the previous record high of $483 billion in 2017. Global remittances, which include flows to high-income countries, reached $689 billion in 2018, up from $633 billion in 2017 (Interpressnews, 2018).

The basis for such record growth is the increase of the employment rate in the US, as well as the growth of the industry in the Persian Gulf countries and several EU member states. This factor somehow simplifies the economic conditions in the countries from the Global South and decreases such global problems, such as the existence of the North-South gap.

Modern Internal Migration Problems

Migration is one of the most important globals, and at the same time, complex problems, because it is not only a demographic but also a serious social, economic and political problem and creates many difficulties in many countries around the world.

Migration itself is a normal, common occurrence and has always played a major role throughout human history, in most cases it has contributed to progress and rapprochement of peoples, and in many cases, the states themselves have sought to facilitate and regulate this or that migration process. Migration has become a problem only when it is not managed and the processes are uncontrolled. This is what they mean when they talk about migration as a global problem.

The main reason for modern migration is socio-economic problems. This applies equally to both internal and external migrations.

The most common type of internal migration is "village-city" migration. In developed countries it has been going on for several centuries and, in practice, has already reached its maximum. In Western European countries, 80-90% of the population lives in cities, while agriculture accounts for only a small part of the rural population, and the majority work in cities (Chitadze, 2017). Here the opposite process has already begun: the migration of the population from the city to the village. Relatively secured strata prefer to avoid city dust and noise and settle in rural nature near the city. Thanks to the best roads and your car, it takes no more than 1-1.5 hours to get to work in the city.

The situation is completely different in the developing world, where migration from rural to urban areas has reached a particularly large scale. The main reasons for this situation are the very high natural increase of the population and the increase of the density of the rural population. Added to this are the land degradation, erosion, desertification, and other natural disasters, due to which the area of arable land per capita is steadily declining, while part of the population remains completely uninhabited. The threat of famine is becoming real and every year tens of millions of people are forced to flee the city and look for work there. This impoverished and unprepared mass fills the ranks of the city's unemployed and criminals and exacerbates the city's problems.

Modern Problems of International Migration

Despite their severity, internal migration is a problem for individual states, and it is more or less possible for the state to solve or regulate it by pursuing certain policies. A much bigger problem is external, i.e., international (especially illegal) migration, which has acquired truly global chaos, and the fight against it requires universal effort.

Currently, three main centers for attracting international migrants are identified: Western Europe, North America, and the Arab states of the Persian Gulf.

Immigrants pose a serious problem in virtually every country, where their numbers are more or less significant. Immigrants to Western Europe come mostly from the Middle East and Africa. Racial and cultural-religious differences already complicate adaptation, while the language barrier, low levels of education and qualifications, and different lifestyles exacerbate the situation. As a result, a confrontation arises between immigrants and the local population. Immigrants are sometimes seen as competitors in the labor market, more often than not they fill the ranks of vagrants and criminals. All this revived the almost forgotten ethnic nationalism of Western Europe and reinforced xenophobia.

The problem of immigration to the United States is no less acute, with the vast majority of migrants currently coming from Latin America illegally. Every day, at least 3,000 illegal migrants cross the U.S.-Mexico border, forcing the state to begin building costly barriers along the entire perimeter of the border. Currently, 20-25% of the population in the southern US states are Hispanic, and by the end of the 21st century, according to some estimates, 40-50% of the entire population of the country will be Hispanic. The United States, which painlessly managed to "deport" millions of migrants of different ethnicities to the United States, is now facing a very serious threat, and for the first time in its history, the problem of xenophobia has emerged (Interpressnews, 2018).

Immigration problems turned out to be less acute for the Arab countries of the Persian Gulf. The reason for this is that the vast majority of immigrants are from other Arab countries. Consequently, the problem of cultural adaptation and the language barrier has been removed.

Migration is a serious problem not only for migrant recipients but also for issuing countries. The countries of mass immigration leave the active, able-bodied, and intellectual part of the population, which has a severe impact on the social, economic, and demographic picture of the country.

Problems of Refugees and IDPs

A separate, very acute manifestation of migration problems is the problems of refugees and internally displaced persons (IDPs). A refugee is a person who is forced to leave his / her country and seek refuge in another state due to war, political repression, ethnic, racial, religious persecution, natural disasters, and any other extreme reasons. Persons who have left their homes for the same reasons but have remained in the country are referred to as IDPs.

The UN High Commissioner for refugees presented statistical data on refugees and IDPs. According to those dates, in 1995 there were 27, 4 million people, but in 1999 this number decreased to 21,5 million (Office of the UN High Commissioner for Refugees, 2001). The biggest part of refugees and Internally Displaced Persons (IDP) is a result of the existing armed conflicts. So, even before the starting of the antiterrorist operation in Afghanistan by US and British armed forces after the events of September 11, 2001, about 6 million people was forced to leave this country; Conflict in Rwanda in the middle of 1990th caused the fact, that homeless become more than 2 million people (Lebedeva, 2007). Those events represented the real catastrophe. As a result of the conflicts on the territory of former Yugoslavia, from the different republics number of emigrants consisted of more than 3 million people (NATO, 2006). It should be pointed out that Europe did not know such several refugees since the period of World War 2.

The number of refugees and IDPs has grown particularly rapidly at the beginning of the XXI Century, largely due to the "merit" of the conflicts in the former socialist and developing countries. By 2007, there were approximately 12.1 million refugees and 34 million refugees worldwide. This poses a very serious problem both for the countries where their significant concentration is observed and for the world as a whole. As for 2020, Among the forcibly displaced, there are 25.9 million refugees, 41.3 million people displaced in their own country, and 3.5 million asylum-seekers awaiting a determination on refugee status (UNHCR, 2020).

Most of the refugees are from countries where civil war and armed conflict have been going on for several years. Palestine, Afghanistan, Iraq, Myanmar, Syria, and Sudan stand out in this respect. The picture is roughly similar in terms of the number of internally displaced persons. The "champions" in this regard are Sudan (more than 5 million refugees), and Iraq (4.2 million people).

As for the countries receiving refugees, the United States (2.6 million refugees), Iran, Pakistan, Germany, France, the Netherlands, and some other European countries stand out with this figure.

The problem of refugees and internally displaced persons is very serious in the post-Soviet states, especially in the South Caucasus. There are more than 100,000 refugees in Armenia, the vast majority of whom are Armenians who previously lived in Azerbaijan and left Azerbaijan during the Nagorno-Karabakh conflict. Up to 100,000 refugees in Azerbaijan are Azerbaijanis from Armenia, far more refugees from Azerbaijan are in Russia, and almost a million people are internally displaced persons. The number of foreign refugees in Georgia is not large (10 thousand people), but officially 270 thousand IDPs from Abkhazia and Tskhinvali are mentioned. Up to 200,000 more refugees from Georgia's conflict regions are in other countries (Chitadze, 2017). This is a serious problem for the country.

Territorial Location of the Population and Accommodation Problems

Population Deployment Factors

Among the global demographic problems, the territorial distribution of the population is the most "geographical". The unequal distribution of the population, its high density in individual countries and regions, and vice versa, extremely sparsely populated or uninhabited large areas in other states is a serious problem with many accompanying complications.

The unequal distribution of the population is caused by many factors, which can be divided into 4 main groups: natural-geographical, historical, socio-economic, and demographic. Their role and significance were various in the different historical epochs and different regions.

The Problem of Population Density and Territorial Settlement

Clear evidence of the unequal distribution of population on Earth is provided by several figures: 80% of the Earth's population lives in the Eastern Hemisphere and 20% in the West. 90% of the world's population is concentrated in the Northern Hemisphere and only 10% in the Southern Hemisphere. Almost 60% of the earth's population lives up to 200 meters above sea level, up to 500 meters - 85%, while above 2000 m only 1.5% of the population is concentrated. More than half of the world's population is settled on the coast (no more than 200 kilometers away) and is characterized by a steady growth trend, with more than 7% of the world's land area is concentrating more than 70% of the world's population (Chitadze, 2017).

These data are indicative of the fact that on the world map there are several regions where a large population is observed and, consequently, the population density is very high. Three areas stand out in this respect - Europe (excluding Northern Europe), the US East Coast, East, South, and Southeast Asia. However, the high density of Western Europe and the eastern coast of the United States is due to the high share of the urban population. The rate of urbanization in the US and Europe is 70-90%, in the respective regions of Asia - where lives almost half of world population - high population density is due to the high share of the rural population (50-70%). Consequently, a large part of the Asian population is employed in agriculture. At the same time, the production of agricultural products under extensive agricultural conditions is often unprofitable and often fails to provide food for the population. In addition, as a result of rapid population growth and soil degradation, there is a steady decline in the average number of agricultural lands per capita. In Asia, for example, in 1985 the average area of the agricultural land per capita was 0.22 ha, and in 2005 it was 0.18 ha. Similar data were 0.4 and 0.3 ha for Africa. The situation is especially difficult in South Asia, the Indonesian island of Java, the Nile Delta, etc. (Chitadze, 2017).

The problem of area congestion and the status change is a serious global problem. The Population in overpopulated regions is forced to leave their place of residence and seek fortune in other regions, by this way creating serious problems in their immigration areas. In addition, relocation can pose a problem for food security and hunger. In some countries, there were attempts to carry out planned, organized migration of people from densely populated regions to less populated regions, but the effect was negligible. It seems that the only way to solve this problem is to limit the natural increase of the population and socio-economic progress.

Rural Housing and Rural Problems

For centuries, the rural settlement has been the main, and in some sense, the only form of territorial settlement of the population. It should be mentioned, that by the beginning of the 19th century, 97% of the world's population lived in rural areas. However, in recent centuries the role of cities has been growing rapidly and the city is gradually becoming (it has long been in Europe and North America) the main form of settlement. In the modern period, almost half of the world's population (more than 3,5 billion people) still lives in the countryside (Davitashvili, 2014). The share of the rural population was particularly large in the countries of Africa, East, and Southeast Asia. Rural problems are also fundamentally different in developing and developed countries.

Rural problems in developing countries are mainly manifested in relative displacement, area congestion, and socio-economic backwardness. In most countries in Asia, Africa, and Latin America, a significant portion of the countryside lacks electricity, gas, radio, television, and telephone connections. In many places, there are no schools, medical centers, cultural institutions. In addition, in many countries, people are engaged in agricultural activities using outdated technology. As a result, in the developing world, the countryside is "expelling" millions of people each year who seek refuge and employment in the cities. A huge mass of people deprived of education and qualifications fill the ranks of the unemployed and the homeless and mostly fill themselves with begging or criminal activities. This is the biggest problem not only for the developing world, but for the whole of humanity, and it belongs to several global problems.

In most of the highly developed countries, the village, as already mentioned, is a conditional concept and is a small settlement that does not have the status of a city. Such "villages" are formed mainly within the urban agglomeration and are inhabited by the most affluent strata of the population. This is a category that can have its villas and live in an isolated doorway hidden in green areas instead of city noise and dust. This part of the population, with few exceptions, has no connection with agriculture, they work in cities and daily move from the "green areas" to the cities. In southern Europe and the former communist countries, traditional villages are still preserved, the main problem of the countryside is population migration and demographic aging. The youth, in most of the cases, moves to the city and in the village, there are remained only elderly people. This leads to a shortage of labor resources. For this reason, seasonal work in rural areas is mainly implemented by foreign immigrants, some of whom are constantly staying and significantly changing the ethnic and religious image of the population. It creates a new base for xenophobia and ethnoreligious controversy.

Problems of Urbanization and Cities

Among the global problems, the problems of urbanization are becoming more and more urgent. In its content, this problem is complex and does not fit alone within the framework of demographic problems. It is often connected with social, economic, ethnocultural, and even political problems. At the same time, the problems of urbanization are global and are manifested in practically every country, although it is manifested differently depending on the level of socio-economic and historical-cultural development of a given state.

Types of Urbanization and Related Problems

Among the global problems, the problems of urbanization and cities are becoming more and more urgent. In its content, this problem is complex and does not fit alone within the framework of demographic problems. It is often connected with social, economic, ethnocultural, and even political problems. At the same time, the problems of urbanization and cities are a global problem and occur in virtually every country, although this is manifested differently depending on the level of socio-economic and historical-cultural development of a given state.

Urbanization manifests itself differently in developed and developing countries.

In most countries of Asia, Africa, and Latin America, both the absolute number and the share of the urban population are growing very fast. In Asia, for example, as of for second decade of the XXI century, the average annual population growth rate was 3.3%, in Africa - 4.9%, and in Latin America - 2.7%. At the same time, in Europe and North America, this index did not exceed 0.7%. In 1975, the urban population of developing countries exceeded that of the number in developed countries. By 2005, the difference was 2.5 times higher (1.0 billion people in developed countries and 2.5 billion in the developing world), but obviously, this does not mean that developing countries are more urbanized than developed ones (Davitashvili, 2014).

The growth of the urban population in the Third World is driven by mass migration from the countryside. Millions of people without livelihoods are forced to flee to the city and seek refuge there, but because of the weak economic potential, the developing country does not allow migrants to be employed and this mass of the people, mostly unemployed, fill the group of beggars and criminals. In addition, it is very difficult or not at all possible for the new arriving population to adapt to the urban environment. On the contrary, migrants bring their way of life, which was typical for the countryside and not suitable for urban conditions. In particular, in several cities in developing countries, it is common practice for residents to own cattle and has a small vegetable garden. And as the share of the rural population in the urban population grows steadily, such a lifestyle is becoming more and more prevalent in the urban areas. Thus, the so-called False urbanization emerges, when the share of the urban population in the structure of the total population increases, but it does not spread the urban lifestyle and increases the role of urban functions. On the contrary, it is going on devaluation of urban traditions and the establishment of a rural lifestyle in the cities.

The situation is completely different in most developed countries. The norms of urban life here have a long history and instead of any devaluation, on the contrary, they are becoming more and more widespread among the non-urban population. The growth of the urban population in developed countries is driven by the demand for labor. Thus, the cities gain additional new urban functions. Therefore, the population, who is migrating to the cities (including foreigners) is undergoing a rather severe adaptation and has an urban lifestyle. At the same time, there are some tendencies, according to which the share of the urban population in the number of developed countries does not increase and it even decreases as the affluent layers of the population leave the city and settle outside the urban area. Formally, they are considered rural residents but have nothing in common with agriculture. The village lives within the urban lifestyle and the vast majority of the rural population also works in the city. Thus, a process diametrically different from developing countries and develops - the universal spread of urban life, including among the rural population.

Problems of Large Cities and Urban Agglomerations

The vast majority of urban problems come from the big city. It is in the big cities that a large part of the urban population is concentrated, the main industrial enterprises and trade-financial, administrative, or cultural-educational institutions are located. Major areas of environmental pollution are also large cities.

Itself the fact, that millions of people live in a few square kilometers and the population density is estimated at tens of thousands per square kilometer is an extremely serious problem and creates many difficulties.

With such a concentration of population, traffic is extremely difficult, air pollution reaches a critical level, serious problems arise in water supply and other utilities, the housing problem is very acute (especially in the suburbs of large cities of the developing countries). Meanwhile, big cities have become centers of the criminal world and criminal problems are extremely troubling the population.

In many countries, the hypertrophic development of one city (usually the capital and main port) has created serious difficulties. From rural and small towns, massive population migration is taking place in the main city, the provinces are "empty" and a large part of the country's economic, labor, or intellectual potential is concentrated in one big city. This has a severe impact on the economic and demographic picture of the country and poses a serious threat to the preservation of the nation's ethnographic and cultural traditions, as, unlike the countryside, a large city is less interested in ethnic features.

Small Town Problems

The concept of a small city varies considerably from country to country. If in the case of China and Japan for the obtaining the status of the city, the number of inhabitants should exceed 30 000 people, 200 inhabitants for the gaining city status in Denmark and Iceland is sufficient (Davitashvili, 2014). But the problems of small towns are not so much related to the population as to its functions. In many cases, the loss or change of function fundamentally changes the development perspective of cities and creates serious problems.

In most developing countries, small towns are large villages, where a significant portion of the population is engaged in agriculture. Only some functions (administrative, commercial, etc.) distinguish such cities from villages. The style of urban housing is not felt here, and since the prospects for agricultural development are also limited, the problem of poverty and unemployment is even more acute in such cities than in rural areas. The population is constantly moving. Relatively "experienced" citizens move to big cities, and their place is taken by the population coming from the village. Due to severe economic and socio-cultural conditions, a large number of small towns in developing countries are experiencing a permanent crisis.

In developed countries, as a rule, small towns are considered to be the most prestigious and comfortable housing. Own houses and green backyards are the defining factors of such cities. The relatively clean ecological environment, tranquility, and safe criminal situation further increase the attractiveness of small towns. That is why in developed countries the proportion of people living in small towns is increasing and we are witnessing the birth of many new cities.

A special situation is created in the case of small towns that change their profile or lose their old function. This problem affects cities in both developed and developing countries. For example, a severe crisis was created in cities that were centers of the mining industry, and due to depletion of mineral resources or reduced demand for them, these functions were lost. The same can be said for the cities that had the function of a transportation center and found themselves in a traffic deadlock due to various circumstances (construction of a new highway, construction of a new port, etc.). The only solution in such a situation is to change the profile of the city and take on new functions, which are associated with high costs and require great efforts of the state.

CONCLUSION

As a result of the research, the following conclusions can be drawn:

First, in the world economy, the gap in the level of wealth between developed and developing countries is still increasing, and the concentration of world wealth in a few countries is increasing. The world community must guarantee developing countries equal participation in international trade, fair compensation for the costs of labor and natural resources that come from them at the disposal of developed participants in the world economy. Meanwhile, the current level of development of science and technology makes it possible to increase food production by at least 4 times. This is enough to meet the food needs of more people than what, according to modern ideas of demographers, will ever live on our planet at the same time.

Second, the growing lag of developing countries has become the most important global economic problem. If we conditionally divide all countries into three parts according to the average level of GDP per capita, then the upper, richest part will show a steady growth of this indicator over the past decades. Also, the demographic problem affects not only the position of individual countries of the world but also affects the development of the world economy and international relations, requiring serious attention, both scientists and governments of various states.

Thirdly, the food problem has long historical roots and, with its aggravation, inevitably posed on all continents a serious threat to the health and very existence of their inhabitants, as well as to the normal functioning of the economic mechanism. It has now acquired global significance for reasons of a humanistic nature and due to the integrity of the modern world, where hunger and malnutrition are still widespread, the fight against which is interconnected with the equally difficult and urgent task of overcoming the economic backwardness of the former colonies and dependent territories. Many international experts agree that food production in the world in the next 20 years will be able to generally meet the population's demand for food, even if the world's population grows by about 80 million people annually (Wordometers, 2021).

The global problems of mankind cannot be solved by the forces of one separate state. The entire world community is tasked with creating a single regulatory mechanism at the global level that meets all human needs. The United Nations must play a particularly important role in solving global problems. Modern international organizations of a governmental nature have become a suitable forum for cooperation: they mitigate emerging contradictions, resolve possible conflicts. Within these organizations, there is sometimes a struggle between different - sometimes contradictory - concepts; in a word, they form a modern, developed form of international cooperation.

International organizations play an important role in solving global problems and searching for joint actions to resolve them. The United Nations Development Program (UNDP), the World Health Organization, the United Nations Food and Agriculture Organization (FAO), the World Bank, and several others initially assumed that a sharp gap in the level of material well-being of the population in the world economy would adversely affect the development of all its participants. The first reaction was the official assistance programs within the UN system, through which funds were received in lagging economies to weaken or prevent mass hunger, epidemics, and millions of refugee movements.

The first and foremost condition is peace, peaceful development, and a sharp reduction in military spending. Another condition is all-around cooperation, mutual consideration of interests, the development of science, and its enrichment with the achievements of all states. All peoples today must go through difficult universities on global issues and rethink the practice of their lives, the policies of their states, and overestimate their development resources. It is necessary to significantly expand international cooperation at various levels - bilateral, multilateral, regional, and global, with the use of various international institutions and organizations, and, above all, the UN.

Cooperation of all states in solving global problems should serve not only to eliminate emerging threats in terms of protecting the natural environment, solving energy, raw materials, food, demographic, information problems, as well as problems of world debt, world use of space, and resources, seas and oceans, it should contribute to the creation of decent living conditions for all peoples.

REFERENCES

Bliadze, M., Chanturia, G., & Kereselidze, D. (2012). *Global Geography*. Tbilisi State University.

Bloomberg. (2021). *World's $281 Trillion Debt Pile Is Set to Rise Again in 2021*. https://www.bloomberg.com/news/articles/2021-02-17/global-debt-hits-all-time-high-as-pandemic-boosts-spending-need

Brown. (1994). *Demography versus habitat fragmentation as determinants of genetic variation in wild populations*. Retrieved from: https://www.sciencedirect.com/science/article/abs/pii/S0006320700002032

Chitadze, N. (2016). *Political Science*. International Black Sea University.

Chitadze, N. (2017). *World Geography. Political, Economic, and Demographic Dimensions*. Scholar`s Press.

Chitadze, N. (2019). *The number of populations, who lived in extreme poverty has been reduced to the historical minimum.* Blog of the Center for International Studies. Retrieved from: https://centerforis.blogspot.com/2019/05/the-number-of-populations-who-lived-in.html

Chitadze, N. (2020). *Several Opinions about the main reasons for the COVID 19 emergence*. Myths and Reality. The Center for International Studies of the International Black Sea University.

Chitadze, N. (2019). US-China Relations. The U.S.-China Relations and Their Possible Reflection on the World Economic Order. Journal in Humanities, 8(2).

CIA. (2014). *Literacy World Factbook*. CIA.

Covid 19. (2020). *Some states not sharing Covid-19 info, war has to be fought together: Harsh Vardhan*. Retrieved from: https://www.youtube.com/watch?v=k2V7AAjL6L4

Cyranoski, D. (2017, February 23). Inside the Chinese lab poised to study world's most dangerous pathogens. *Nature, 542*(7642), 399–400. doi:10.1038/nature.2017.21487 PMID:28230144

Davitashvili, Z., & Elizbarashvili, N. (2012). *Global Geography*. Meridiani.

Dosomething. (2021). *11 facts about global poverty. 10% of the world's population lives on less than $1.90 a day.* Retrieved from: https://www.dosomething.org/us/facts/11-facts-about-global-poverty

For.Ge. (2020). *Coronavirus-natural virus or biological weapon?!* Retrieved from: https://for.ge/view/182236/koronavirusi-bunebrivi-virusi-Tu-biologiuri-iaraRi.html

Frank, A. G., & Gills, B. (1996). *The World System: Five Hundred Years or Five Thousand?* Taylor & Francis.

Géo, H. (2020). *Histoire des grandes épidémies et pandémies.* Retrieved from: https://www.youtube.com/watch?v=UxvR95pegZ8

Giordano, M. (2003). *Sharing waters: Post-Rio international water management.* Blackwell Publishing Ltd.

Gleick, P. (2000). A look at twenty-first-century water resources development. *Water International, 25*(1).

Goldstein, J., & Pevehouse, J. (2011). *International Relations* (9th ed.). Better World Books Marketplace Inc.

HDI. (2021). *Human Development Index (HDI) by Country.* Retrieved from: https://worldpopulationreview.com/country-rankings/hdi-by-country

ILO. (2020). *Almost 25 million jobs could be lost worldwide as a result of COVID-19, says ILO.* Retrieved from: https://www.ilo.org/global/about-the-ilo/newsroom/news/WCMS_738742/lang--en/index.htm

Intermedia.ge. (2020). *Coronavirus: Is there a pandemic or an unfounded panic in Mass-media?* Interpressnews.

Interpressnews. (2020). *Anthony Fauch - Scientific evidence confirms that the coronavirus was not created in a Chinese laboratory.* Retrieved from: https://www.interpressnews.ge/ka/article/598143-entoni-pauchi-mecnieruli-mtkicebulebebi-adasturebs-rom-koronavirusi-chinetis-laboratoriashi-ar-shekmnila

IRU. (2020). *An industry distress call.* Retrieved from: https://www.iru.org/covid19

Kereselidze, D. (2011). *World Geography.* Tbilisi State University.

Lebedeva. (2007). *World Politics.* Aspect Press.

Lenta.Ru. (2020). *«Газпром» приготовился к обрушению спроса на газ.* https://lenta.ru/news/2020/04/30/gas_ne_nuzhen/?fbclid=IwAR3m2IXN31frc5Zm5ZVeoObtnHjyJTX2TWJ3fk5ko-sLtf8MdGPC6Z1710o

Liberty, R. (2017). *State Debt in the World and Georgia.* Retrieved from: https://www.radiotavisupleba.ge/a/sakhelmtsifo-valebi/28587576.html

Maksakovsky, V. (2009). World Social and Economic Geography. Academic Press.

Malthus. (1798). *An Essay on the Principle of Population.* Retrieved from: http://www.esp.org/books/malthus/population/malthus.pdf

Market Watch. (2020). *Crude Oil WTI (NYM $/bbl) Front Month.* Retrieved from: https://www.marketwatch.com/investing/future/crude%20oil%20-%20electronic

NATO Handbook, . (2006). *Berlin Plus agreement*. NATO Public Diplomacy Division.

Neidze, V. (2004). World Social and Economic Geography. Publishing House "Lega".

OECD. (2018). *Uranium 2020. Resources, Production, and Demand*. Retrieved from: https://www.oecd-nea.org/upload/docs/application/pdf/2020-12/7555_uranium_-_resources_production_and_demand_2020__web.pdf

Office of the United States Trade Representative. (2019). *The People's Republic of China*. https://ustr.gov/countries-regions/china-mongolia-taiwan/peoples-republic-china

Peak, O. (2011). *World Oil Reserves*. http://www.endofcrudeoil.com/2011/04/world-oil-reserves.html-http://www.endofcrudeoil.com/2011/04/world-oil-reserves.html

Public Welfare. (2021). *Ways to solve the food problem. The geography of hunger*. UN Food Program. Retrieved from: https://en.public-welfare.com/3906676-ways-to-solve-the-food-problem-the-geography-of-hunger-un-food-program

Quartz. (2020). *A conspiracy theory linking the US army to the coronavirus now has an official Chinese endorsement*. Retrieved from: https://qz.com/1817736/china-fuels-coronavirus-conspiracy-theory-blaming-us-army/

Reliefweb. (2013). *World: Food Security Risk Index 2013*. Retrieved from: https://reliefweb.int/map/world/world-food-security-risk-index-2013

Reuters. (2020). *Coronavirus very likely of animal origin, no sign of lab manipulation: WHO*. https://www.reuters.com/article/us-health-coronavirus-who-virus/coronavirus-very-likely-of-animal-origin-no-sign-of-lab-manipulation-who-idUSKCN223180

Rostow, W. (1991). *The Stages of Economic Growth: A Non-Communist Manifesto* (3rd ed.). Cambridge University Press. doi:10.1017/CBO9780511625824

Rourke, J., & Boyer, M. (2000). *International Politics on the World Stage, Brief* (8th ed.). Dushkin/McGraw-Hill.

Sputnik. (2020). *The special service called on the residents of the republic not to give in to the proposals of the Georgian side to participate in any medical research*. Retrieved from: https://sputnik-ossetia.ru/South_Ossetia/20200428/10494848/KGB-zayavil-ob-ugroze-prednamerennogo-zarazheniya-grazhdan-Yuzhnoy-Osetii-COVID-19-iz-Gruzii.html

Stanford News. (2020). *For Renaissance Italians, combating the black plague was as much about politics as it was science, according to a Stanford scholar*. Retrieved from: https://news.stanford.edu/2020/05/12/combating-black-plague-just-much-politics-science/

TASS. (2020). *Chinese Foreign Ministry pointed to the danger of US laboratories in the territory of the former USSR*. Retrieved from: https://tass.ru/mezhdunarodnaya-panorama/8361667

Trading Economics. (2020). *China, Trade*. Retrieved from: https://tradingeconomics.com/china/exports

TWN. (2021). *The Future of North-South Relations: Conflict or Cooperation?* Retrieved from: https://www.twn.my/title/futu-cn.htm

UN. (2005). *Basic Facts about the United Nations*. United National Office of Public Information.

UN. (2020). *Promoting Sustainable Development*. Retrieved from: https://www.un.org/ecosoc/en/content/promoting-sustainable-development

UNCTAD. (2018). *195 states were UNCTAD members*. Retrieved from: https://unctad.org/

UNDP. (2013). *Human Development Report*. Retrieved from: http://hdr.undp.org/en/media/HDR_2013_EN_TechNotes.pdf

UNESCO. (2019). *Literacy*. Retrieved from: https://en.unesco.org/themes/literacy

UNICEF. (2005). *Report Emergencies: Refugees, IDPs, and child soldiers. Natural disasters*. Retrieved from: https://www.unicef.org/eapro/05_Emergency.pdf

United Nations. (2021). *Losing 25,000 to Hunger Every Day*. Retrieved from: https://www.un.org/en/chronicle/article/losing-25000-hunger-every-day

USA State Department Report. (2020). Retrieved from: https://www.state.gov/reports-bureau-of-democracy-human-rights-and-labor/country-reports-on-human-rights-practices/

Washington Times. (2020). *Coronavirus may have originated in a lab linked to China's biowarfare program*. Retrieved from: https://www.washingtontimes.com/news/2020/jan/26/coronavirus-link-to-china-biowarfare-program-possi/

Wordometer. (2020). *COVID 19 Pandemic*. Retrieved from: https://www.worldometers.info/coronavirus/

Wordometers. (2016*). Oil Reserves*. Retrieved from: https://www.worldometers.info/oil/

Wordometers. (2021). *Current World Population*. Retrieved from: https://www.worldometers.info/world-population/#:~:text=7.9%20Billion%20(2021),Nations%20estimates%20elaborated%20by%20Worldometer

Wordometers. (2021). *World Population Projections*. Retrieved from: https://www.worldometers.info/world-population/world-population-projections/

World Bank. (2021). *International Debt Statistics*. Retrieved from: https://data.worldbank.org/products/ids

World Bank. (2020). *The global economy will expand by 4 percent in 2021*. Retrieved from: https://www.worldbank.org/en/news/press-release/2021/01/05/global-economy-to-expand-by-4-percent-in-2021-vaccine-deployment-and-investment-key-to-sustaining-the-recovery

World Bank. (2021). *Global Recovery is Strong but Uneven as Many Developing Countries Struggle with the Pandemic's Lasting Effects*. Retrieved from: https://www.worldbank.org/en/news/press-release/2021/06/08/world-bank-global-economic-prospects-2021

World Economic Forum. (2019). *Water inequality is a global issue - here's what we must do to solve it*. Retrieved from: https://www.weforum.org/agenda/2019/10/water-inequality-developing-world-usa-west/

World Health Organization. (2019). *Global vaccine coverage in 2019.* https://www.who.int/news-room/q-a-detail/vaccines-and-immunization-what-is-vaccination?adgroupsurvey=adgroupsurvey&gclid=Cj0K CQjwm9yJBhDTARIsABKIcGbuqgPPZKcyweOx2z7p-GYHl4s5Gy1VRpELfAbrtyuw9Iupc3m1VHI-aAnEjEALw_wcB

Worldometer. (2021). *Countries in the world by population.* Retrieved from: https://www.worldometers.info/world-population/population-by-country/

Xinhuanet. (2020). *Spotlight: COVID-19 virus not created in the lab, say French experts.* Retrieved from: http://www.xinhuanet.com/english/2020-04/21/c_138995413.htm

KEY TERMS AND DEFINITIONS

Absolute Advantage: The liberal economic concept that a state should specialize in the production of goods in which the costs of production are lowest compared with those of other countries.

Antidumping Duties: Taxed placed on another exporting state's alleged selling of a product at a price below the cost to produce it.

Arbitrage: The selling of one currency (or product) and purchase of another to make a profit on changing exchange rates.

Asian Tigers: The four Asian NICs that experienced far greater rates of economic growth during the 1980s than the more advanced industrial societies of the Global North.

Barter: The exchange of one good for another rather than the use of currency to buy and sell items.

Boycotts: Concerted efforts, often organized internationally, to prevent transactions such as trade with a targeted country to express disapproval or to coerce acceptance of certain conditions.

Bureaucracies: The agencies and departments that conduct the functions of a central government or a non-state transnational actor.

Cartel: A convergence of independent commercial enterprises or political groups that combine for collective action, such as limiting competition, setting prices for their services, or forming a coalition to advance their group's interests.

Civil Society: A community that embraces shared norms and ethical standards to collectively manage problems without coercion and through peaceful and democratic procedures for decision-making aimed at improving human welfare.

Classical Liberal Economic Theory: A body of thought based on Adam Smith's ideas about the forces of supply and demand in the marketplace, emphasizing the benefits of minimal government regulation of the economy and trade.

Collective Action Dilemma: Paradox regarding the provision of collective goods in which, though everyone can enjoy the benefits of the good, no one is accountable for praying for the cost.

Collective Good: A public good, such as safe drinking water, from which everyone benefits.

Commercial Liberalism: An economic theory advocating free markets and the removal of barriers to the flow of trade and capital as a locomotive for prosperity.

Communist Theory of Imperialism: The Marxist-Leninist economic interpretation of imperialist wars of conquest as driven by capitalism's need for foreign markets to generate capital.

Comparative Advantage: The concept in liberal economics that a state will benefit if it specializes in the production of those goods which it can produce at a lower opportunity cost.

Complex Interdependence: A model of world politics based on the assumptions that states are not the only important actors, security is not the dominant national goal, and military force is not the only significant instrument of foreign policy. This theory stresses cross-cutting ways in which the growing ties among transnational actors make them vulnerable to each other's actions and sensitive to each other's needs.

Cornucopias: Optimists who question limits-to-growth analyses and contend that markets effectively maintain a balance between population, resources, and the environment.

Cosmopolitan: An outlook that values viewing the cosmos or entire world as the best polity or unit for political governance and personal identity, as opposed to other policies such as one's local metropolis or city of residence (e.g., Indianapolis or Minneapolis).

Decolonization: The achievement of sovereign independence by countries that were once colonies of the great powers.

Demography: THE study of population changes, their sources, and their impact.

Dependency Theory: A theory hypothesizing that less developed countries are exploited because global capitalism makes them dependent on the rich countries that create exploitative rules for trade and production.

Dependent Development: The industrialization of peripheral areas within the confines of the dominance-dependence relationship between the Global South and the Global North, which enables the poor to become wealthier without ever catching up to the core Global North countries.

Developed Countries: A category used by the World Bank (WDI2009) to identify Global North countries, with a GNI per capita of $11,456 or more annually.

Developing Countries: A category used by the World Bank to identify low-income Global South countries with a 2009 GNI per capita below $935 and middle-income countries with a GNI per capita of more than $935 but less than $11,456.

Development: The processes, economic and political, through which a country develops to increase its capacity to meet its citizen's basic human needs and raise their standard of living.

Dollar Overhang: A condition that precipitated the end of the Bretton Woods era, in which total holdings of dollars outside of the U.S central bank exceeded the number of dollars backed by gold.

Domino Theory: A metaphor popular during the Cold War that predicted that if one state fell into communism, its neighbors would also fall in a chain reaction, like a row of falling dominoes.

Economic Sanctions: Punitive economic actions, such as the cessation of trade or financial ties, by one global actor against another to retaliate for objectionable behavior.

Ecopolitics: How political actors influence perceptions of, and policy responses to changing environmental conditions, such as the impact of carbon dioxide emissions on the temperature of the Earth.

Embedded Liberalism: Dominant economic approach during the Bretton Woods system, which combined open international markets with domestic state intervention to attain such goals as full employment and social welfare.

European Commission: The executive organ administratively responsible for the European Union.

European Union: A regional organization created by the merger of the European Coal and Steel Community, the European Atomic Energy Community, and the European Economic Community (called the European Community until 1993) that has since expanded geographically and in its authority.

Exchange Rates: The rate at which one state's currency is exchanged for another state's currency in the global marketplace.

Export Quotas: Barriers to free trade agreed to by two trading states to protect their domestic producers.

Export-Led Industrialization: A growth strategy that concentrates on developing domestic export industries capable of competing in overseas markets.

Fertility Rate: The average number of children born to a woman (or group of women) during her lifetime.

Fixed Exchange Rates: A system in which a government sets the value of its currency at a fixed rate for exchange about another country's currency so that the exchange value is not free to fluctuate in the global money market.

Floating Exchange Rates: An unmanaged process in which governments neither establish an official rate for their currencies nor intervene to affect the values of their currencies and instead allow market forces and private investors to influence the relative rate of exchange for currencies between countries.

Foreign Aid: Economic assistance in the form of loans and grants provided by a donor country to a recipient country for a variety of purposes.

Foreign Direct Investment (FDI): A cross-border investment through which a person or corporation based in one country purchases or constructs an asset such as a factory or bank in another country so that a long-term relationship and control of an enterprise by nonresidents results.

Functionalism: The theory advanced by David Mitrany and others explaining how people can come to value transnational institutions (IGOs integrated or merged states) and the steps to giving those institutions authority to provide the public goods (for example, security) previously, but inadequately, supplied by their state.

General Agreement on Tariffs and Trade (GATT): An UN-affiliated IGO designed to promote international trade and tariff reductions, replaced by the World Trade Organization.

Geo-Economics: The relationships between geography and the economic conditions in the behavior of states that define their levels of production, trade, and consumption of goods and services.

Global Commons: The physical and organic characteristics and resources of the entire planet- the air in the atmosphere in conditions on land and sea- on which is the common heritage of all humanity.

Global East: The rapidly growing economies of East and South Asia that have made those countries competitors with the traditionally dominant countries of the Global North.

Global Migration Crisis: A severe problem stemming from the growing number of people moving from their home country to another country straining the ability of the host countries to absorb the foreign emigrants.

Global North: A term used to refer to the world`s wealthy, industrialized countries located primarily in the Northern hemisphere.

Global South: A term now often used instead of the Third World to designate the less developed countries located primarily in the Southern Hemisphere.

Global Village: A popular cosmopolitan perspective describing the growth of awareness that all people share a common fate because the world is becoming an integrated and independent whole.

Globalization: The integration of states through increasing contact, communication, and trade as well as increased global awareness of such integration.

Globalization of Finance: The increasing trans nationalization of national international markets through the worldwide integration of capital flows.

Globalization of Labor: Integration of labor markets, predicated by the global nature of production as well as the increased size and mobility of the global labor force.

Globalization of Production: Trans nationalization of the productive process, in which finished goods rely on inputs from multiple countries outside of their final market.

Globally Integrated Enterprises: MNCs organized horizontally with management in production located in plants in numerous states for the same products they market.

Gross National Product (GNP): A measure of the production of goods and services within a given period that is used to delimit the geographic scope of production. GNI measures production by a state's citizens or companies regardless of where the production occurs.

Group of 77 (G-77): The coalition of Third World countries that sponsored the 1963 Joint Declaration of Developing Countries calling for reform to allow greater equality in North-South trade.

Heavily Indebted Poor Countries: The subset of countries identified by the World Banks Debtor Reporting System whose ratios of debt to the gross national product are so substantial they cannot meet their payment obligations without experiencing political instability and economic collapse.

Hegemon: A preponderant state capable of dominating the conduct of international political and economic relations.

Hegemonic Stability Theory: A body of theory that maintains that the establishment of hegemony for the global dominance by a single great power is a necessary condition for global order in commercial transactions and international military security.

Hegemony: The ability of one state to lead in world politics by promoting its worldview and ruling over arrangements governing international economics and politics.

Human Development Index (HDI): An index that uses life expectancy literacy, the average number of years of schooling, and income to assess a country's performance in providing for its people's welfare and security.

Human Needs: That basic physical, social, and political needs, such as food and freedom that are required for survival and security.

Imperial Overstretch: The historic tendency for past hegemons to sap their strength through costly imperial pursuits and military spending that weaken their economies about the economies of their rivals.

Imperialism: The policy of expanding state power through the conquest and or military domination of foreign territory.

Import: Substitution industrialization – a strategy for economic development that centers on providing investors at home incentives to produce goods so that previously imported products from abroad will decline.

Import Quotas: Numerical limit on the number of particular products that can be imported.

Infant Industry: Newly established industries (infants) that are not yet strong enough to compete against mature foreign producers in the global marketplace until in time they develop and can then compete.

Intellectual Property: Inventions created by the use of human intelligence in publications art and design by individuals that are often illegally used for commercial purposes without credits or royalties to their creators in violation of GAT's agreement.

Interdependence: A situation in which the behavior of international actors greatly affects others with whom they have contact, making all parties mutually sensitive and vulnerable to the actions of the other.

Intergovernmental Organizations (IGOs): Institutions created and joined by state governments that give them authority to make collective decisions to manage particular problems on the global agenda.

International Liquidity: Reserve assets used to settle international accounts.

International Monetary Fund: A financial agency now affiliated with the UN established in 1944 to promote international monetary cooperation, free trade exchange rate stability, and democratic rule by providing financial assistance and loans to countries facing financial crises.

International Monetary System: The financial procedures used to calculate the value of currencies and credits when capital is transferred across borders through trade, investment, foreign aid, and loans.

International Political Economy: The study of the intersection of politics and economics that illuminates why changes occur in the distribution of states' wealth and power.

International Regime: Embodies the norms, principles, and rules. An institution around which global expectations unite regarding a specific international problem.

Intra-Firm Trade: Cross-national trade of intermediate goods and services within the same firm.

Laissez-Faire Economics: The philosophical principle of free markets and free trade to give people free choices with little governmental regulation.

Least Developed of the Less Developed Countries (LLDCs): The most impoverished countries in the Global South.

Liberal International Economic Order (LIEO): The set of regimes created after World War II designed to promote monetary stability and reduce barriers to the free flow of trade and capital.

Liberalism: A paradigm predicated on the hope that the application of reason and universal ethics international relations can lead to a more orderly, just, and cooperative world. liberalism assumes that anarchy and war can be policed by institutional reforms that empower international organizations and law.

Linkage Strategy: A set of assertions claiming that leaders should take into account another country's overall behavior when deciding whether to reach an agreement on any one specific issue to link cooperation to rewards.

Long Cycle Theory: A theory that focuses on the rise and fall of the leading global power as the central political process of the modern world system.

Low Politics: The category of global issues related to the economy. Social, demographic, and environmental aspects of relations between governments and people.

Macroeconomics: The study of aggregate economic indicators such as GDP, the money supply, and the balance of trade that governments monitor to measure changes in national and global economies such as the rates of economic growth and inflation or the level of unemployment.

Marxist-Leninism: Communism theory as derived from the writings of Karl Marx, Vladimir Lenin, and their successors, which criticizes capitalism as a cause of the class struggle, the exploitation of workers, colonialism, and war.

Modernization: A view of development popular in the Global North's liberal democracies that wealth is created through efficient production, free enterprise, and free trade and that countries relative wealth depends on technological innovation and education more than on natural endowments such as climate.

Monetary Policy: The decisions made by state central banks to change the country's money supply to manage the national economy and control inflation using fiscal policies such as changing the money supply and interest rate.

Monetary System: The processes for determining the rate at which each state's currency is valued against every other state, so that purchasers and sellers can calculate the costs of financial transactions across borders such as foreign investments, trade, and cross-border travel.

Money Supply: The total amount of currency in circulation in a state calculated to include demand deposits such as checking accounts in commercial banks, and time deposits such as savings accounts and bonds in savings banks.

Most-Favored-Nation Principle (MFN): The central GATT principle of unconditional nondiscriminatory treatment in trade between contracting parties underscoring the WTO's rule requiring any advantage given by one WTO member to also extend it to all other WTO members.

Multinational Corporations (MNCs): Business enterprises headquartered in one state that invest and operate extensively in many other states.

Murky Protectionism: Nontariff barriers to trade that may be hidden from government policies not directly related to trading such as environmental initiatives and government spending.

Neo-Malthusians: Pessimists who warn of the global Eco political dangers of uncontrolled population growth.

Neocolonialism (Neo-Imperialism): The economic rather than military domination of foreign countries.

Neoliberalism: The new liberal theoretical perspective that accounts for the way international institutions promote global change, cooperation, peace, and prosperity through collective programs for reforms.

Neomercantilism: A contemporary version of classical mercantilism that advocates promoting domestic production and a balance of payment surplus by subsidizing exports and using tariffs and non-tariff barriers to reduce imports.

New International Economic Order (NIEO): The 1974 policy resolution in the UN that called for a North-South dialogue to open the way for the less-developed countries of the Global South to participate more fully in the making of international economic policy.

Newly Industrialized Countries (NICs): The most prosperous members of the global South which have become more important exporters of manufactured goods as well as important markets for the major industrialized countries that export capital goods.

Non-Aligned Movement (NAM): A group of more than one hundred newly independent mostly less developed states that joined together as a group of neutrals to avoid entanglement with the superpowers competing alliances in the Cold War and to advance the Global South primary interest in economic cooperation and growth.

Non-Aligned States: Countries that do not form alliances with opposed great powers and practice neutrality on issues that divide great powers.

Non-Tariff Barriers: Measures other than tariffs that discriminate against imports without direct tax levels and are beyond the scope of international regulations.

Nonalignment: A foreign policy posture that rejects participating in military alliances with the rival blocs for fear that formal alignment will entangle the state in an unnecessary involvement in the war.

Nondiscrimination: GATT principle that goods produced by all member states should receive equal treatment as embodied in the ideas of most-favored nations and national treatment.

Nongovernmental Organizations: Transnational organizations of private citizens maintaining consultative status with the UN. They include professional associations, foundations, multinational corporations, or simply internationally active groups in different states joined together to work toward common interests.

North American Free Trade Agreement (NAFTA): An agreement that brings Mexico into the free trade zone linking Canada and the US.

Official Development Assistance: Grants or loans to countries from donor countries are now usually channeled through such as the World Bank for the primary purpose of promoting economic development and welfare.

Opportunity Cost: The sacrifices that sometimes result when the decision to select one option means that the opportunity to realize gains from other options is lost.

Orderly Market Arrangements: Voluntary export restrictions through government-to-government agreements to follow specific trading rules.

Political Economy: A field of study that focuses on the intersection of politics and economics in international relations.

Purchasing Power Parity (PPP): An index that calculates the true rate of exchange among currencies when parity when what can be purchased is the same is achieved the index determines what can be thought of with a unit of each currency.

Retorsion: Retaliatory acts (such as economic sanctions) against a target's behavior that is regarded as objectionable but legal such as trade restrictions to punish the target with the measures that are legal under international law.

Sanctions: Punitive actions by one global actor against another to retaliate for its previous objectionable behavior.

Self-Help: The principle that because in international anarchy all global actors are independent, they must rely on themselves to provide for their security and well-being.

Semi Periphery: To world system theorists' countries midway between the rich core or center and the poor periphery in the global hierarchy at which foreign investments are targeted when labor wages and production costs become too high in the prosperous core regions.

Tariffs: Tax assessed on goods as they are imported into a country.

Third World: A Cold War term to describe the less-developed countries of Africa, Asia, The Caribbean, and Latin America.

Trade Integration: The difference between gross rates in trade and gross domestic product.

Transparency: About the GATT the principle that trade barriers must be visible and thus easy to target.

Virtual Corporations: Agreements between otherwise competitive MNCs are often temporary to join forces and skills to coproduce and export particular products in the borderless global marketplace.

Washington Consensus: The view that Global South countries can best achieve sustained economic growth through democratic governance fiscal discipline free markets a reliance on private enterprise, and trade liberalization.

World-System Theory: A body of theory that treats the capitalistic world economy originating in the sixteenth century as an interconnected unit of analysis encompassing the entire globe.

Chapter 14
Food and Nutrition Security:
A Global Perspective

Asim K. Karmakar
Netaji Subhas Open University, India

Sebak Kumar Jana
 https://orcid.org/0000-0002-3532-4350
Vidyasagar University, India

ABSTRACT

Food and proper nutrition are crucial inputs into performance and well-being. Many development programmes, projects, and policies therefore include food and nutrition security objectives. Food and nutrition are crucial inputs for the performance of the economy. But the irony is that the present food system is going to be captured by multinational actors with their shrewd politics so that the livelihoods of the most people of the globe are at stake. Amidst this, the rise of a few powerful titans, both economically and politically, is a fearful phenomenon. Such circumstances are not only dangerous for consumers everywhere but also disastrous for poor populations vulnerable to food price fluctuations. Annoyed with the world food system dominated by MNCs, the concept of food sovereignty like La Via Campesina's food sovereignty movement has come to the fore as a protest against the corporate control of the food system. The major objective of the study is to assess food and nutrition security and its link with food politics in a global perspective.

Let us all return to the soil

That lays the corners of its garments

And waits for us.

DOI: 10.4018/978-1-7998-9586-2.ch014

Food and Nutrition Security

Life rears itself from her breast,

Flowers blooms from her smiles

Her call is the sweetest music;

Her lap stretches from one corner to the other,

She controls the strings of life. Her warbling waters bring

The murmur of life from all eternity.

Rabindranath Tagore

The food is here but the main problem is distribution. Land is concentrated on very few hands. The big companies pay very little tax. Labour conditions on plantations are appalling. It's a very classic of how a very productive country with high rates of exclusion, especially among the indigenous population, cannot feed its own people.

------Aida Pesquera, Oxam Director of Guatemala

INTRODUCTION

There is no denying the fact that food and nutrition are crucial inputs for well performing of the economy. That is why many food and nutrition security objectives are the concerns of development projects and policies. The concept of food security embraces more than the current nutritional status. But the irony is that food system today is going to be captured by multinational actors with their shrewd politics so that the livelihoods of the most people are at stake. Amidst this, the rise of a few powerful Titans, both economically and politically is a fearful phenomenon. Such circumstances are dangerous for consumers everywhere but disastrous for poor populations vulnerable to food price fluctuations. Monitoring the activities of these corporations is vital for exposing some of the social and environmental impacts on global agriculture; opposition to their activities has fuelled some of the most effective transnational resistance movements contesting neoliberal capitalist globalization. Besides, the pandemic continues to expose weaknesses in the world food system, which threaten the food security and nutrition of millions of people around the world. The world has not been generally progressing either towards ensuring access to safe, nutritious and sufficient food for all people all year round (SDG Target 2.1), or to eradicating all forms of malnutrition (SDG Target 2.2). The COVID-19 pandemic has made the pathway towards SDG2 even steeper. It is estimated that between 720 and 811 million people in the world faced hunger in 2020. Beyond hunger, nearly one in three people in the world (2.37 billion) did not have access to adequate food in 2020 – that is, an increase of almost 320 million people in just one year (FAO, 2021). The number of undernourished people in the world is continuing to rise over the years, thus violating overall the very definition of food security, agreed upon at the 1996 World Food Summit during November,13-17: " a situation that exists when all people, at all times, have physical, social and economic access to sufficient,

Table 1. Four dimensions of food security

Physical AVAILABILITY of food	The timely availability and affordability of food critical for a country. Food availability addresses the "supply side "of the food security concept and is determined by the level of food production, stock levels and net trade or by emergency stocks of food that can offset shortfalls in production.
The Physical and Economic ACCESS to food	Hence, the second pillar of the food security concept is access that reflects the demand side of food security. It is defined in terms of entitlement to adequate food. Inter-and-inter household distributional questions also influence access.
Food UTILIZATION	Utilization reflects concerns about whether people have endowed with essential minerals such as iodine, iron organic, vitamins, in particular A and D.
STABILITY over time	This one matters for targeting of interventions and the very design of safety nets intended to safeguard food security for depressed persons. Some agencies, such as the United Nations' Food and Agriculture Organization (FAO), consider stability to be a fourth dimension of food security. Stability takes into account the susceptibility of individuals to food insecurity due to hindrances in access, availability or utilization. Adverse weather conditions, political instability or economic factor (unemployment, rising prices) may have an impact on one's food security status.

Source: *Food Security Information for Action Practical Guides(2008):1-3. & Authors' compilation*

safe, and nutritious food that meets their dietary needs and food preferences for an active and healthy life." Food insecurity exists when this condition is not met. When we explain the definition, what comes in is that we have failed miserably to deliver sufficient and safe food to millions of people worldwide.

From this definition also, four main multidimensional aspect of food security can be identified:

In policy circles, a distinction is made between transitory and chronic food insecurity. Transitory food security is associated with the risk-related to either access or the availability of food during off-season, drought or inflationary years and, that in most famines when people starve because of lack of entitlement to food. So the most serious episodes of transitory food insecurity are commonly labeled "famine." In contrast, the problem of chronic food insecurity is associated with poverty and arises due to continuous inadequate diet.

Of late, Global Food Security Index (GFSI), 2021 looks at four concerns of food security across 113 countries: (i) affordability, (ii) availability, (iii) quality and safety and (iv) natural resources and resilience. The GFSI ranks countries on a score of 0-100 based on the first three categories while natural resources and resilience is used as an adjustment factor. A rank of 100 is thought as most favorable. For example, India's overall Food Security Score is 50.1 out of 100 which ranks India 71 out of 113 countries. This reflects the need for India to further improve the management of food supply in various aspects. GFSI's major goal is to assess in a timely manner which countries are most and least vulnerable to food insecurity.

HISTORICAL AND POLITICAL OVERVIEW OF FOOD SECURITY

Human history directs us to the fact that lives are short and unhealthy due to insufficient nutrient intake. Full many a scholar argue that the escape to victory over the nutritional poverty trap has accelerated to the advancement of living standards over the past 300 years.(*Dasgupta 1995,1997, Fogel 2004*). At the time of World Food Conference of 1974, food security was widely viewed as a problem of insufficient and unstable production. But the disquieting fact is that with its heels comes also national level food consumption instability virtually in every country (*Diakosavvas, 1989*). The *second* generation of thinking on food security, focused more on the demand side and on issue of access by vulnerable people to food, stems directly from the path-breaking work of Sen (1981). Ironically, Sen explicitly eschewed the concept of food security, focusing instead on the "entitlements" of individual and households. Sen thus

Food and Nutrition Security

placed increased emphasis on the legal institutions of the states, as well as the moral and social norms of cultures. The entitlement approach has been critiqued by some as apolitical, ahistorical, and excessively legalistic and economistic (*de Waal 1990, Barro and Deubel 2006*). The emergent *third* generation view of food security builds on food availability and entitlement as a summary of food access and the complex health consequences of nutrient deficiencies. Food insecurity is thus closely related to poverty and to social, economic and political disenfranchisement (*Dreze& Sen, 1989*).

FAO (2018) estimates that the number of undernourished people in the world has been on the rise since 2015 and back to level seen in 2010-11. 821.6 million people were seriously under-nourhsised in 2018 (*FAO, 2019*). Meanwhile the World Bank estimates that 1.4 billion people lived on US $1/day or less in 2005 (*Chen and Ravallion, 2010*). Indeed, the two are directly coupled in the first MDG — to halve the proportion of people living in extreme poverty and hunger(*Barret and Lentz, 2010*), and the second for the fulfillment of the 2030 Agenda for Sustainable Development. Food insecurity remains widespread today in large measure because extreme poverty and hunger remains widespread and vice versa. In India, the capital of hunger, 214 million people are hungry (one in every four Indians goes hungry). In sub-Saharan Africa, 198 million people are hungry; in Asia/ Pacific. 156 million go hungry; in China, 135 million are hungry; and in South America, 56 million people are hungry (www.developmenteducation.ie), while 30 per cent, as FAO estimates, of global food supply is wasted, totaling $ 1 trillion of food waste every year. Data show that half of the industrialized world's food is wasted by retailers or consumers, while in the Global South there are growing losses after harvest.

Most food insecurity is chronic. Food security exists in the countries of the OECD. For example, in any given year, the US Department of Agriculture estimates that roughly 10 percent US household are food insecure.In China and Southeast Asia, rates of under-nutrition have fallen sharply. In other regions, including South Asia, east and southern Africa, under nutrition rates have fallen even while the number of people suffering under-nutrition has increased due to population growth. And in some regions (e.g., central Africa), both numbers and rates have increased. Nutrition security which exists when food security is combined with a sanitary environment, adequate health services and proper care and feeding practices to ensure a healthy life for all household members, is a crucial consideration in efforts to reduce malnutrition[7].

CHALLENGES TO FOOD AND NUTRITION SECURITY

Continued high rates of food insecurity and under-nutrition, for many countries, are resulting in a "double burden" of malnutrition. There is clear evidence that this burden is shifting rapidly to low-income groups. A solid understanding of the causes of food and nutrition insecurity is essential to generalized interventions and to long-term, aggregate improvement in food and nutrition security at the level of communities, countries, and regions. In 2007-08, increased food and bio-fuel demand, high fuel prices, US dollar depreciation, and adverse weather all fed rising international food prices. Additionally, precautionary stores by individuals, farmers, traders to protect against further prices rise and the speculative behavior of investors drove price increases even higher.

Creating an enabling environment to fight against hunger and malnutrition requires addressing a wide variety of constraints.

Socioeconomic and Health-Based Challenges: Gender-Inequality, HIV

Evidence based on household-level data shows that reducing gender inequality is an important part of the solution to global hunger. A series of studies have found clear association between female primary attendance and decreases in country-level poverty rates. Empowering women in terms of education, political participation, and control of assets and resources has great potential to improve purchasing power, the management of scare household resources, and self-respect as well as knowledge of good habits, regarding food consumption, which are all crucial to improved nutrition outcomes in the context different kinds of food insecurities faced by women, in particular, food insecurities based on: natality, basic facility, inequality in special facilitates, profession, ownership, household and seasonally –based food insecurities (*Mukherjee,2012*).

The continued high prevalence of HIV, especially in many countries in sub-Saharan Africa challenges food and nutrition security at multiple levels. At the household level, HIV can decrease purchasing power.

Demographic and Political Challenges: Population Growth, Political Instability and Conflict

Population growth affects food and nutrition security because it drives increased demand for food in terms of both domestic production and imports. Political instability is also a major challenge to food and nutrition security. It can also destabilize support systems, such as input distribution and subsidy programmes, and can destroy markets and other infrastructure. Dramatic political transition which is inversely related to sociopolitical instability leaves many people vulnerable, as has been true in recent year in country such as Afghanistan, Haiti and Zimbabwe. Such transitions often lead to devastating disruption of marketing channels, production systems, and traditional social security systems, particularly when accompanied by civil strife (Table 2).

Indeed, conflict displaces huge numbers of people and was a primary cause of famines in Africa. A conflict destroys not only lives and livelihoods, disrupt or prevents agricultural production, but also it disrupts markets, market access, production cycles, and humanitarian operations. It also creates large populations of refugees and internally displaced persons who actually make heavy demands on local and national food supplies. The resulting misery and desperation too often begets a vicious circle; chronic food insecurity is thus all too commonly the result of conflict.

Most of the countries in the Table 2 are crises ridden requiring external assistance; some have high levels of food insecurity.

Environmental Challenges: Climate Change and Demand for Biofuels

Climate change means a change of climate which is attributed directly or indirectly to human activity that alters the composition of the global atmosphere and which is in addition to natural climate variability observed over comparable time periods (Karmakar, 2012: 140). Climate change will exacerbate excising threats to food security. By 2050, the number of people suffering from hunger is projected to increase by 10-20 per cent (Parry et.al, 2009), and child mortality is anticipated to be 20 per cent higher compared to the scenario of no climate change. In addition, a UNEP report predicts that up to 25 per cent of world's food production is likely to be lost by 2050, as a result of "environmental breakdowns" (IFPRI, 2009).

Table 2. Effect of conflict and political instability on food supply

Nature of food insecurity	Main reasons
Exceptional shortfall in aggregate food production and /or supplies	
Kenya	Adverse weather, lingering effects of civil strife
Somalia	Conflict, economic crisis, adverse weather
Zimbabwe	Problems of economic transition
Wide spread lack of food access	
The Republic of Liberia	War-related damage
Mauritania	Several years of drought
Sierra Leone	War-related damage
Democratic Republic of Korea	Economic constraints
Several localized food insecurity	
Burundi	Internally displaced persons and returners
Congo	Internally displaced persons(not returners)
Ethiopia	Adverse weather, insecurity in part of the country
Guinea	Refugees, conflicts-related damage
Sudan	Civil strife , insecurity, localized crop failure
Uganda	Insecurity, localized crop failure
Afghanistan	Conflict and insecurity
Bangladesh	Cyclone
Myanmar	Past cyclone, political instabily, social unrest
Nepal	Poor market access, floods and /or landslides
Pakistan	Conflict. Internally displaced persons
Philippines	Tropical storm
Sri Lanka	Internally displaced persons. Post-conflict reconstruction
Yemen	Conflict , internally displaced persons

Source: FAO

Climate change can further negatively affect nutrition security through its effects on hygiene and sanitation, viz., increased incidence of diarrhea and other infectious diseases. Climate change is projected to increase the burden of diarrhoeal diseases in low income regions by approximately 2.5 per cent by 2021.

In summary, climate change will affect food and nutrition security through reduction of income from animal production, reduction of yields of food and cash crops, covered forest productivity, changes in aquatic populations and increased incidence of infectious diseases.In addition to climate change, the growing demand for *biofuel* poses a challenge to food and nutrition security.

Poverty, Malnutrition and Food Insecurity Traps

The various threats to food security we have identified point to four stylized groups that are extraordinarily food insecure (chronically or transitory). Besides, food insecurity, malnutrition and poverty are deeply interconnected because a lack of purchasing power forces millions of poor people to suffer from food insecurity and malnutrition, as shown in Figure 1.

Figure 1. Food insecurity, malnutrition and poverty are deeply interrelated phenomena
Source: Mark W. Rosegrant (2015). Food Security, Vol 1. Sage Reference. Los Angeles.

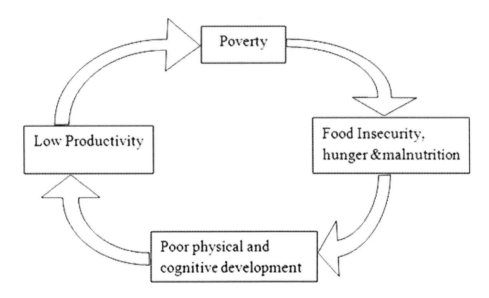

FOOD POLITICS

In the global food system, exploitation prevails. To redress it, there are anti-globalization, anti corporatist networks. Then, there are progressive political parties, numerous international and national NGOs and other transnational networks. Some of these are focused, such as anti- land-grab campaign. The nature of these various problems reflects the multifaceted character of the problems associated with food production and food security.

Radical Movements against the Food Politics

Via Campesina has become a major radical movement seeking to reduce global inequalities in the food system. The concept of food sovereignty is a core element of their perspectives.This transnational agrarian social movement is pressing UNs to implement international conventions on peasants' rights.This grassroots movement will promote food sovereignty and sustainable agriculture.Although originating in Latin America; it has now established links with small producers across the globe. They claim that peasant and small farmers hold the secret of a more ethical agricultural future.

The Declaration at Nyeleni in 2006 in Mali is a key document of the radical food movement. It is a call for the complete transformation of the food system and the power relations at the centre. Corporate control over food and its production is rejected in favour of the local control and demand. It is a green movement that rejects the chemical model of food production. It wants to reassert democratic control, rather than capitalists' control over the food systems, working towards the structural changes needed for sustainable, equitable and democratic food systems. as corporate actors have become so dominant at every stage of the food chains, from seed to plate and the corporate players are creating problems of hunger, malnutrition, food insecurity and environmental degradation.

MECHANISMS AND ACTIONS TO PROVIDE FOOD AND NUTRITION SECURITY

Single intervention to address the issue of food and nutrition insecurity is not at all enough as the nature and causes of both types of insecurity varies.

Individual Responses to Food Insecurity

To ensure the viability of the food insecure individuals' future livelihoods many choose food insecurity rather than sell productive assets. Food insecure individuals often choose less risky strategies, that keep them vulnerable. They never go on selling the productive assets, instead they accept food insecurity which causes physical damage, labour productivity losses or even mortality. These often lead to poverty traps: low level equilibria.

To be out from this quagmire, actions should be made to raise incomes, providing livelihood support, creating social safety nets and focusing on maternal and child health. Moreover, increasing dietary diversification through nutrition education and social marketing is essential to improving food and nutrition security. In order to decrease the double burden of malnutrition, educating consumers regarding the health risks of highly processed foods low in micronutrient content is highly important. Poverty reduction— at national, regional and international levels— is required.

Increasing Food Availability: Agriculture Acting as an Engine of Growth

Food availability is a necessary condition for food and nutrition security and remains distressingly limited in many countries. A common approach to improving availability is increasing agricultural productivity, which can improve food security for rural producers, landless labourers, and consumers.

Agriculture plays a central role in increasing food availability and income, supporting livelihoods and contributing to the overall economy (*World Bank, 2008*), and thus a key actor in effort to improve food and nutrition security. Sustainable agriculture is very important not only for ensuring the economic welfare of small holders and other vulnerable groups; it is also linked to improving dietary diversity and nutrition outcome.

Promoting Access: Economic Growth and Markets

Economic growth is associated with improved food security. Economic growth that is associated with improved food security, is clearly not a sinecure, though one can find that economic growth in tandem with food price stabilization policies leads to improved food security.

The 2007-08 rice price bubble was 'pricked" when Japan announced in June 2008 that it would sell surplus rice. By late August 2008, rice prices were half of what they had been in April of that same year.

Actions to Improve Food and Nutrition Security: Beyond Smallholders to Promote Access

The positive impact of social assistance measures increases when combined with livelihoods diversification initiatives. For example, Save the Children in the Amhara province of Ethiopia recorded significant progress in building livelihoods, assets and resilience after implementation of the government programmes. Save the Children documented improved dietary intake among some of the beneficiaries of the Amhara programme. Safety nets also directly improve nutritional status and maternal and child health. For example, conditional cash transfer programmes in Colombia, Mexico and Nicaragua decreased stunting rates.

So far so the picture is good. But there are some disquieting features in this respect. Perhaps the most important factor in determining the efficacy of food security interventions is the quality of targeting: do instruments reach intended beneficiaries? Good targeting is exceedingly difficult. Considering these complexities, some government interventions came into force in the following forms: China implements the minimum procurement price policies to maintain stability of grain market prices, protect farmers and control food supply, the government policy in Egypt is to encourage higher domestic wheat production through a guaranteed support price. In India, the FCI undertakes the procurement of food grains at MSP and provides it to the weaker sections of the society at subsidized prices through public distribution system (PDS). The government in Jordan purchases domestic wheat and barley at administered prices and sells them at subsidized prices. While addressing the issue of food security in Asia, Jana and Karmakar (2016) find that the progress in food and nutrition front in this region has been uneven, and the region remains home to over 60 per cent of undernourished people in the world. Their result reveals that there is no convergence in average food production in Asia and reveals also that there is significant relationship between food security and undernourishment. However, in order promote domestic maize production as well as to give incentives to farmers, the Government of Kenya provides price support to maize producers. The Grain marketing Board ensures national food security through procurement and management of strategic grain reserves in Zimbabwe, the Food Reserve Agency of Zambia ensures national food security and provides price support to maize producers (Sharma, 2016:12-13)

Right –based advocates, such as La Via Campesina's food sovereignty movement, India's Right to Food Campaign, and the FAO's Voluntary Guidelines to Support the Progressive Realization of the Right to Adequate Food in the context of National Food and Nutrition Security, are leading a resurgent interest in developing social protection programme to provide regular, continued support to those facing chronic food and nutrition insecurity. Very much being annoyed with the world food system dominated by MNCs, the concept of food sovereignty has come to the fore as a protest against the corporate control of the food system. As this is true is evident from the Speech delivered by the President of the General Assembly of the United Nations: condemning corporate profiteering:

The essential purpose of food, which is to nourish people, has been subordinated to the economic aims of a handful of multinational corporations that monopolize all aspects of food production, from seeds to major distribution chains, and they have been the prime beneficiaries of the world crisis. A look at the figure shows that corporations such as Monsanto and Cargill, which control the central market, saw their profits increase by 45 and 60 per cent, respectively.

(Source:www.Gmwatch.org/gm-firms-mobile/10595-monsanto-a-history.

Food and Nutrition Security

Accessed 11 October 2010)

Finding no other alternatives obviously, there sprang some protests: centred on claims for democracy and against social inequality, the Arab Spring(a term given to a series of revolutions, uprisings,mass mobilization, protests and riots in the Arab world that that began in December 2010) in the streets of Egypt protested against the rise in the price of breads (Fominaya (2014: 154); or in Syria, where the conflict started as dissent expressed by peasants seeking relief from crop failure due to an intense drought; or in Columbia where farmers to have seed sovereignty and seed freedom took to the streets to stop a seed law that would have made their seeds illegal or as the March Against Monsanto Movement, in which millions of people from across the globe and from all walks of life joined hands to protest the control of corporations over what we grow and eat. In India also, there sprang a protest from farmers against three farm bills. Protesting farmers dig in heels after talks with Centre fail to make headway. Some accused the government of betraying the farmers for benefitting their 'corporate friends.' There is widespread discontent everywhere because the industrialized and globalized food system, engineered and controlled by a handful of MNCs, is destroying the planet, farmers' livelihoods, people's health, democracy, and peace. While farmers breed for resilience, corporations breed for vulnerability. Farmers breed for taste, quality and nutrition, industries monitored by MNCs breed for industrial processing, and long distance transport in a globalized food system. Monocultures of industrial crops and monocultures of industrial junk food reinforce each other, wasting the land, wasting food, and wasting health as well (*Shiva,2017:84*). In the face of this, redesigning the food system in a prudent manner has become a survival imperative. That is why, several developing countries implement social protection programmes, such as the Productive Safety Net Programmes in Ethiopia, the Hunger Safety Net programme in Kenya, Bosla Familia in Brazil and PROGRESA/ Oportunidades in Mexico (*Jana & Karmakar 2015*). Even Russia banned the import of any GMO products, with commenting," If the Americans like to eat GMO products, let them eat it then. We don't need to do that; we have enough space and opportunities to produce organic food— chemical –free, pesticide-free, GMO-free farming.

Improving Utilization

Access to nutrition education may reduce vulnerability to hunger. Maternal nutrition education can influence child nutritional status but the effects differ by socioeconomic status. Good caring practices related to child feeding and the use of preventive health services can compensate for poverty and low material schooling.

Other interventions can support utilization and micronutrient delivery. Improving storage and post harvest handling can improve food safety and quality. Biofortification, the breeding of stable crops for higher nutritional content, is a potential longer-term, cost- effective solution to chronic micronutrient deficiencies. Improving access to sanitation and clear water, and providing health care are two common interventions that can improve utilization of food. In turn, good nutrition can decrease the risks of infections and illness. One research finding is that better nutrition improves the health status of individuals infected with HIV.

CONCLUSION

With hefty people worldwide suffering nowadays from shortfalls in their access-ability and refrain from sufficient, safe and nutritious food for an active and healthy life, due to endangering ill-treated political grab and other causes, food and nutrition insecurity remains a serious daunting global challenge. The heaviest challenge remains in the measurement of food insecurity and the identification and evaluation of which interventions work best and under what circumstances. Specific policies and targeted interventions for improving nutrition outcomes are urgently called for. For example, there are some meaningful sunlit pathways to follow food system transformation: integrating humanitarian development and peace-building policies in conflict-prone areas, scaling up climate resilience across food systems, intervening along the food supply chains to lower the cost of nutritious foods, tackling poverty and structural inequality that persist and strengthening food environments. Promotion of social protection, equitable land tenure regulations, national food fortification programmes, monitoring and evaluation of food and nutrition situations, and capacity-building measures are some of the most important aspects here. If we are to live in a world without hunger, food insecurity and malnutrition in any of its forms for attaining the 2030 Agenda for Sustainable Development, areas of focus should include also: (i) preservation of biodiversity, and conservation, sound management and sustainable use of natural resources preservation; (ii) incorporation of hunger reduction and nutrition objectives into climate change negotiations;(iii) promotion of pro-poor food and agricultural development policies that support low-income groups and are conducive to nutrition security and encourage positive spillovers; and (iv) promotion of fair and transparent global markets.

Government's food policy should examine domestic production possibilities, the importation of food items from the world market and strategies to improve the economic performance of the country and the income of its people. Typical objectives of a sound food policy include growth in the food and agricultural sectors emphasizing onmore ecologically and environmentally sustainable practices, with tremendous force on agro-ecological vibrancy focused on maintaining biodiversity and intercropping, improved income distribution, so that all segment of society can afford adequate food, satisfactory nutritional status for the entire population.

REFERENCES

Adams, M. (2014, Jan. 6). World Bank Warns of Food Riots as Rising Food Prices Push World Populations toward Revolt. *OpEd News*.

Baro, M., & Deubel, T. F. (2006). Persistent hunger: Perspectives on vulnerability, famine, and food security in sub-Saharan Africa. *Annual Review of Anthropology*, *35*(1), 521–538. doi:10.1146/annurev.anthro.35.081705.123224

Barrett & Lentz. (2010). Food insecurity. In The International Studies Encyclopedia.Wiley Blackwell.

Chen, S., & Ravallion, M. (2010). The developing world is poorer than we thought, but no less successful in the fight against poverty. *The Quarterly Journal of Economics*, *125*(4), 1577–1625. doi:10.1162/qjec.2010.125.4.1577

Dasgupta, P. (1995). *An inquiry into well-being and destitution*. Oxford University Press. doi:10.1093/0198288352.001.0001

Dasgupta, P. (1997). Nutritional status, the capacity for work, and poverty traps. *Journal of Econometrics*, *77*(1), 5–37. doi:10.1016/S0304-4076(96)01804-0

de Waal, A. (1990). A Re-assessment of Entitlement Theory in the Light of the Recent Famines in Africa. *Development and Change*, *21*(3), 469–490. doi:10.1111/j.1467-7660.1990.tb00384.x

Diakosavvas, D. (1989). On the Causes of Food Insecurity in Less Developed Countries: An Empirical Evaluation. *World Development*, *17*(2), 223–235. doi:10.1016/0305-750X(89)90247-7

Dreze, J., & Sen, A. (1989). *Hunger and Public Action*. Clarendon Press.

FAO. (2006). *Food Aid for Food Security?* Rome: FAO.

FAO. (2019). *The State of Food Security and Nutrition in the World 2019. In Safeguarding against economic slowdowns and downturns*. FAO.

FAO. (2021). *The State of Food Security and Nutrition in the World 2020*. FAO.

Fogel, R. W. (2004). *The escape from hunger and premature death, 1700-2100: Europe, America, and the Third World* (Vol. 38). Cambridge University Press. doi:10.1017/CBO9780511817649

Fominaya, C. F. (2014). *Social movements and globalization: How protests, occupations and uprisings are changing the world*. Macmillan International Higher Education. doi:10.1007/978-1-137-40216-5

Gráda, C. Ó. (2010). *Famine: a short history*. Princeton University Press. doi:10.1515/9781400829897

Hawkes, C. (2006). *Uneven dietary development: Linking the policies and processes of globalization with the nutritional transition, obesity and diet-related chronic diseases*. Globalization and Health. www.globalizationandhealth.com

IFPRI. (2009). *Climate change: impact on agriculture and costs of adaptation*. International Food Policy Research Institution.

Jana, S. K., & Karmakar, A. K. (2015). Globalization, Governance, and Food Security: The Case of BRICS. In R. C. Das (Ed.), *Handbook of Research on Globalization, Investment, and Growth- Implications of Confidence and Governance* (pp. 275–294). IGI Global. doi:10.4018/978-1-4666-8274-0.ch014

Jana, S. K., & Karmakar, A. K. (2016). Food Security in Asia: Is There Convergence? In R. C. Das (Ed.), Handbook of Research on Global Indicators of Economic and Political Convergence. IGI Global.

Karmakar, A. K. (2012). Achieving food and nutrition security in India. In B. Chatterjee & A. K. Karmakar (Eds.), *Food Security in India: A Comprehensive Plan for Sustainable Development*. Regal Publications.

Karmakar, A. K., & Mukhopadhyay, D. (2014). Towards a Prudent Policy for Food Security in India. *US-China. Law Review*, *11*, 221.

Mukherjee, A. (2012). *Food Security in Asia*. Sage Publications Pvt.Ltd.

Palutikof, J., Van der Linden, P., & Hanson, C. (Eds.). (n.d.). Climate change 2007--impacts, adaptation and vulnerability: Working group II contribution to the fourth assessment report of the IPCC (Vol. 4). Cambridge University Press.

Parry, M. (2009). *Climate change and risk of hunger: the scale of the challenge and required responses*. World Food Programme.

Robin, M. M. (2004). *Our daily poison: from pesticides to packaging, how chemicals have contaminated the food chain and are making us sick*. New Press.

Rosegrant, M. W. (2015). *Food security*. Sage Reference.

Sen, A. (1981). *Poverty and Famines Oxford*. Clarendon Press.

Sharma, S. K. (2016). *The WTO and Food Security: Implications for developing countries*. Springer. doi:10.1007/978-981-10-2179-4

Shiva, V. (2017). *Who really feeds the world*. New Delhi: Women Unlimited.

Tilly, C., & Wood, L. J. (2009). *Social movements, 1768-2008*. Paradigm Publishers.

World Bank. (2008). *World Development Report 2008: Agriculture for Development*. World Bank.

Young, E. M. (2012). *Food and Development*. Routledge.

KEY TERMS AND DEFINITIONS

Bolsa Familia Programme: The *Bolsa Familia*p rogramme in Brazil was created in October 2003 to improve the efficiency and coherence of the social safety. Main goals were to alleviate short-term poverty and the fight against inter-generational poverty traps. The World Bank articulates that *Bolsa Familia* programme is such an effective social protection programmes in the world, that it has been able to raise 20 million people out of poverty between 2003 and 2009 as well as reducing income inequality.

Famine: Every famine has its own character and an exact definition is impossible, but the following is a useful definition: Famine refers to a shortage of food or purchasing power that leads directly to excess mortality from starvation or hunger-induced diseases (O'Grada, 2010, p. 4). Simply, it is a widespread lack of access to food that occurs when drought, flood, or war disrupts the availability of food or income in a society of chronically undernourished people.

Food Insecurity: It exists when food people do not have adequate physical, social or economic access to food (FAO, 2009). A broader look at the extent of food insecurity, beyond hunger, shows, as FAO 2019 states that 17.2 percent of the world population, or 1.3 billion people, have experienced food insecurity.

Food Policy: The collective efforts of the governments to influence the decision- making environment of food producers, food consumers, and food marketing agents, in order to further social objectives. Food policy analysis poses question how individual nations or the world in general can assure that sufficient quantities of food are available to all people, regardless of their income level, and how food security can be established to avert the chance of famine if the production system is disrupted by a natural and man-made disaster. In posing this question, food policy analysis studies agriculture, food and nutrition and make decisions that affect linkages among these systems (Karmakar, & Mukhopadhyay, 2014).

Food and Nutrition Security

Food System: A set of processes that produce agricultural commodities on firms, transform these commodities into food in the marketing sector, and sell the food to consumers in order to satisfy nutrition needs. Today the world food system is dominated by a few major corporate players who enjoy immense power over producers, consumers, national policy-makers and international institutions of global governance and also over the World Bank, the IMF and the WTO. When governments are forced to take a backseat through policies enforced by the organizations such as the WTO, private companies step in and fill the gap. Trade liberalization forces poor countries to remove their import barriers, leaving them vulnerable to 'dumping': the process by which commodities that are subsidized in the Global North are off-loaded in large quantities into countries in the Global South, with the target to destroy local sources of food production and distribution, including farmers' livelihoods. It is not surprising that the last 20 years or more have shown NAFTA to be the key criminal in the systematic destruction of the Mexican people's all they belong: their standard of living, wealth, livelihoods and economies Following the implementation of a neoliberal doctrine, Indonesia in 1992 opened its doors to food imports, allowing cheap (in other words, heavily subsidized) American soya to flood their market. This destroyed national production of Soya-based tofu and tempeh— known there as 'meat of the poor', and today 60 per cent of the soya consumed in Indonesia is imported (Shiva, 2017, p. 97). In Mexico now some of the largest food corporations from the Unites States enjoy a significant presence. In large-and medium- sized cities, major supermarkets, discount and convenience stores capture over 55 per cent of the market. The story of Wal-Mart in Mexico is well known since their first venture in 1991 (www.Walmartstores.com). In rural places and smaller towns, the food manufacturers have marketed their products through the traditional road side outlets known as *"Tiendas"* (Hawkes, 2006, p. 4). As a result this planet is facing a deep and growing crisis. The planet's well being, people's health, and societies' stability are severely threatened by an industrial, globalized agriculture, primarily driven by profit making. Instead, an inefficient, wasteful and non-sustainable mode of food production is pushing the planet, its ecosystems, and its diverse species to the verge of destruction. Food, whose primary purpose is to provide nourishment, has emerged as the leading cause of some of the biggest health problems in the world today: nearly one billion people suffer from hunger and malnutrition, two billions suffer from diseases like obesity and diabetes, and countless suffer from terminal diseases, including cancer, caused by the poisons in our food (Robin, 2004).So instead of remaining a source of nourishment, food has been transformed into a commodity. Since 2007, we have before us 51 food riots in 37 countries including Tunisia, South Africa, Cameroon and India (Adams, 2014). Today, coming up with an alternative has become imperative for the survival of people like us. Food systems can provide affordable healthy diets that are sustainable and inclusive, and become a powerful driving force towards ending hunger, food insecurity and malnutrition in all its forms, for all.

Malnutrition: This concept means 'bad diet'. This is a broad term that refers to all forms of poor nutrition: a state of marked impairment of health caused by inadequate intake of proteins, calories, or specific vitamins or minerals. It is now true that more than half of the countries in the world have made progress on hunger, but the levels of malnutrition have not improved. The case of Peru appears to be an encouraging exception to the rule. With the support of CARE and other organizations from civil society and the donor community, the Peruvian government has generated political momentum to overcome obstacles and create national coordination structures and mechanisms, increase private and public spending on programmers to tackle mal-nutrition and align social programmes with the national nutrition strategy (known as CRECER).

Nutrition: The study of the components of food that provides necessary calorie and biochemical requirements in order to sustain life. Nutrition in the broader sense focuses on what type of food consumers need in order to remain healthy and what the determinants to food selections are, including consumer knowledge, home environment, health and incomes. Nutrition also examines the role of feeding programme in protecting the vulnerable groups until their income can be raised for them to purchase their own food.

Nutritional Status: The health of an individual, as measured by indicators directly related food consumption; in children, generally measured by weight for height and skinfold thickness. Nutritional status is generally a function of the ability of households to acquire food, household food acquisition behavior, and the intra-household allocation of food.

Under-Nourishment: This measures aspects of food security and exists when energy intake is below the minimum dietary energy requirement, which is the amount of energy needed for light activity and a minimum acceptable weight for attained height (FAO, 2009). It varies by country and from year to year, depending on the gender and age structure of the population.

Under-Nutrition: This occurs when an individual's diet is short of calories and/or protein necessary for normal activity. This type of hunger is most common among the poorest populations in the developing world but is not absent either in wealthier countries. Clear indications of under-nutrition are: low birth weights (one in seven live births, 20.5 million babies born globally) were characterized by low birth weight in 2015 (FAO, 2019), high infant mortality rates, low height for age, short for age, thin for height (wasted), and functionally deficient in vitamins and minerals (micronutrient malnutrition). The most extreme forms are exemplified by nutritional conditions known as 'kwashiorkor' and 'marasmus'. The word 'kwashiorkor' comes from Ghana and actually means 'the evil spirit that infects the first child when the second is born'. Marismas may occur in adults or children, but if it occurs within the two years of life, brain development is impaired (Young, 2012, p. 37).

Chapter 15
Information–Cyberspace Operations in Real-World Politics

Mari Malvenishvili

Cyber Security Studies and Education Center, Georgia

ABSTRACT

The chapter explores the concept of information and cyber operations. It identifies the role of cyberspace operations in modern military conflicts and addresses Western and Russian strategic approaches of using cyberspace as an emerging platform of modern warfighting. Since the end of the 19th century, the world entered the information age in which distribution of power is mostly dependent on the amount of information a state owns and knowledge of tools and tricks to use it. Information superiority is a power element and vulnerability at the same time. With the technological revolution, creation, distribution, and usage of information was simplified, but securing of created and distributed information became more difficult. Information itself can be used in different ways, starting from simple communication to military operations. Considering the fact that 'military power alone is insufficient to achieve sustainable political objectives', information operations and employment of information capabilities has been included at all stages of modern military operations.

INTRODUCTION

The social and economic well-being, health, and life of each citizen depend significantly on the security of information systems and electronic services. Cyber-attacks have a great impact on all sectors of the economy, hinder the proper functioning of the economic space, reduce public confidence in e-services and threaten the development of the economy through the use of information and communication technologies. Against the background of the existing global cyber threats, when cyber - attacks, cyber espionage, cyber terrorism, and disinformation are carried out daily, the development, introduction, and development of new defense mechanisms is an important issue. It is noteworthy that NATO plays an

DOI: 10.4018/978-1-7998-9586-2.ch015

important role in this direction and together with the EU is a kind of security umbrella for both member and partner countries.

Each century is accompanied by its problems. Cybercrime has become one of the most dangerous events in the 21st century, with many people, private companies, and government agencies being harmed daily. Billions of dollars are already being spent on defense.

All the concepts and doctrines of NATO and the world's democracies emphasize that, based on basic principles, no member state should be forced to rely solely on its strength. The strategy of democracies allows each member state to achieve its national security goals through collective means.

Every leading country in the world has a national cyber security strategy, which is a determining factor of state policy. The National Security Strategy aims to identify, prevent, reduce and eliminate existing threats.

CYBERWARFARE THEORY AND ITS PLACE IN MODERN WORLD POLITICS

Everything that exists has both theoretical and practical direction, when we talk about cyber warfare, we must first explain what event we are dealing with. It is the use of digital attacks by one country on another (computer viruses or hacker cyber attacks) to damage, liquidate, and destroy computer infrastructure.

There are differing opinions among experts regarding the term "cyber warfare". Some say that the term "cyber" is incorrect because to date no cyber-attack can be described as "war". The second part of the experts believes that this is an appropriate name because a cyberattack causes physical harm to people and objects in the real world.

Is cyber attack considered war production? It depends on many factors - what they do, how they do it, and what damage they do to the target object. The qualification of the attacks must be of considerable scale and severity. Attacks by an individual hacker, or group of hackers, are not considered cyber if the state does not assist or lead. Nevertheless, the virtual world is still vaguely represented in the direction of cyber-attacks. Some states support hackers in performing malicious actions, this is a dangerous but common trend.

For example, cybercriminals who destroy a bank's computer systems while stealing money are not considered cybercriminals, even if they are from another country, but state-backed hackers do the same thing to destabilize another country's economy.

There is also a difference between the target object and the scale: the destruction of an individual company website is not considered cyber, but the disruption of missile defense systems at the airbase is perceived as cyber. In this case, it is important what weapon the attacker uses. For example, launching a rocket for a data center would not be considered cyber, even if the data center contained secret government records. The use of hackers for espionage or data theft does not involve cyber warfare om and is defined by the qualifications of cyber espionage. There are many dark holes in cyber warfare, but it is impossible to consider all attacks as cyber (Ranger, 2020).

Although there are differing views on how to define "cyber warfare" as a term, many countries today, such as the United States, Russia, Britain, India, Pakistan, China, Israel, the Islamic Republic of Iran, and North Korea, are already They have cyber capabilities for both offensive and defensive operations.

Cyberwarfare is becoming an increasingly common and dangerous phenomenon in international conflicts. The fact that there are no clear cyber rules means that virtual space may become uncontrollable shortly. For the most part, cybercrime is not just about computer systems, it is about real-world infrastructure management, such as airports and power grids, since such infrastructure is important to all countries. Pressing a button with one finger can close airports, subway stations or cut off the electricity supply.

There are plenty of cyber scenarios. We live in an era where you might wake up one day and your bank accounts go down because someone hacker wanted it that way. Even in the case of mass attacks, it is possible to cause chaos in any country.

There are three main methods of cyberwarfare: sabotage, cyber espionage, or stealing information from computers through viruses and attacking power grids. The third is probably the most alarming, which implies a cyberattack on critical infrastructure (Lewis University, 2020).

Governments are becoming increasingly aware that modern society is highly dependent on computer systems - ranging from financial services to transportation networks. Therefore, by hackers using viruses or other means, stopping these systems can be just as effective and harmful as a traditional military campaign using armed forces, weapons, and missiles.

Unlike traditional military attacks, cyberattacks can be carried out from any distance. It is also possible that no trace is left and there is no evidence at all. Governments and intelligence agencies fear that digital attacks against critical infrastructure, banking systems, or power grids will allow attackers to evade the country's traditional defenses. That is why all countries are striving to improve computer security.

In 2012, hackers hired by the authorities of the Islamic Republic of Iran gained complete control over Bowman Avenue in New York. The most notorious example of a cyber-attack on critical infrastructure is the Stuxnet computer virus attack, which halted Iran's nuclear program, and the virus neutralized centrifuges used to extract nuclear material. The incident caused great concern because Stuxnet suspected that it might have been adapted to attack SCADA systems as well. SCADA systems are used by many critical infrastructures and manufacturing industries in Europe and the United States.

One such attack was reported in Germany in 2014, which caused extensive damage to a steel plant - a cyber - attack that caused the furnaces to shut down. The attackers used social engineering techniques (Allianz, 2020).

Historical aspects of cyber transformation: Spatial characteristics of military conflicts

The development of technology has not changed the priorities of state protection as in the Second World War - the main tactical strikes are aimed at energy facilities. Currently, most of the serious cyberattacks take place on fuel and energy complexes, followed by the financial sector. The digital world has given rise to new types of threats. As already mentioned, not all types of cyberattacks can be considered in cyberspace. Even though we have defined what cyberwarfare is and what a cyber-attack is, it is still difficult to qualify cyberwarfare because most of the facts around the world are based on assumptions. Traces often lead to any aggressor state, but often there is no evidence. We discuss cyber warfare or technical characteristics based on various studies, we do analysis - when it starts, how it was transformed, what role it plays in the production of conflicts, and so on. It is an important fact that many states not only carry out cyber espionage activities, intelligence and investigation, but also create their cyber capabilities. At the end of the 20th century, no one could have imagined that real war would become an adjunct to war created in a segregated dimension, or, conversely, surreal space would merge with real space. Perhaps no one could have imagined that a dimension would emerge that would be almost impossible to control and boundless, that humanity would face an invisible threat. When we try to explain the transformation of cyber warfare, we must highlight what changes all this. This is mostly related to the refinement of cyber-attack technologies and the creation of malicious hacking strategies, programs, or viruses. Therefore, we must distinguish the types of attack: there are passive and active cyberattacks, the passive attack involves the analysis of traffic and monitoring of vulnerable communications. During an active attack, a hacker attacks protected systems. It is mostly carried by viruses (DiGiacomo, 2017).

In Table 1, there are some of the most common types of cyber-attacks and malware attacks that hackers carry out:

Table 1. Types of cyber attacks

Denial-of-service (DoS)	During this attack, a large amount of unusable traffic is sent and the network goes down. Consumption is interrupted when the webserver is full and no longer meets legitimate requirements.
distributed denial-of-service (DDoS)	During an attack, several hackers or hacked systems make many requests to the webserver and block the service with useless traffic. A coordinated attack can do great damage.
Man-in-the-middle (MitM)	When someone interferes and controls your communication process, you think you are talking to a familiar person, or you have direct access to the server, but this time, all your personal information is seen by a hacker.
Phishing	An attacker creates a clone of a real website, sends a fake website link to the targeted user, if a user moves to that link and enters personal data, the hacker will gain access to that data.
War Drive	A method of obtaining access to wireless computer networks, such as a laptop, antennas, and a wireless network adapter for unauthorized access.
Password	Obtaining passwords is a common and effective method of attack. This can be done randomly or systematically.

MALWARE ATTACK - MALICIOUS CODE ATTACK

An unwanted program running on your system without your consent can add and multiply legitimate code. It can also be reproduced in different programs or interpreted on the Internet. Note that all viruses are Malware. Although not all Malware is a virus, it can be a program, application, and so on that allows a hacker to gain unauthorized access to personal data (Rapid7, 2020).

Some common types of malicious code attacks are demonstrated in Table 2:

Based on our research and the presented list, we distinguish three categories of the target group of cyber-attacks presented in Table 3:

As you can see, attackers have many options to try to gain unauthorized access to critical infrastructure and important data. States, therefore, create legal norms to ensure technological security. Cyberattacks have historically not been as devastating as they are today. There is a lot of statistical data based on facts that confirm our opinions.

Gartner, the world's leading research and consulting firm, publishes data on cybersecurity expenditures shown in Figure 1:

We see that in terms of cyber security, worldwide, very large sums of money are spent and growing every year. For example, spending in 2017 was $ 101.544 billion, increased to $ 114.152 billion in 2018, and reached $ 124.116 billion in 2019 (Gartner, 2018). According to Gartner, global cybersecurity spend-

Table 2. Types of malicious code attacks.

Ransomware	Encrypts files in the system and makes them temporarily inaccessible, in case of this attack hackers demand ransom in exchange for returning the information.
Logic bombs	It can be part of the software that turns into a malicious program after a certain date.
Trojan horse	Hidden in a useful program. It usually has a damaging function. A hacker can use the virus to intercept and carry out attacks.
Worm	An independent computer program that multiplies itself from one system to another on a network.

Table 3. Categories of cyber-attack target groups

Targeted attacks on equipment (Kinetic)	Targeted software attacks (hacked)	Targeted attacks on people (espionage)
Denial of Service (DoS), Distributed DoS	Ransomware, Logic Bombs, Trojan, Worm	Phishing, Trojan

Figure 1. 2017-2018-2019 data on cyber security expenditures by Gartner, the world's leading scientific consulting company (Gartner, 2019).
Source: *https://www.gartner.com/en/newsroom/press-releases/2018-08-15-gartner-forecasts-worldwide-information-security-spending-to-exceed-124-billion-in-2019*

Market Segment	2017	2018	2019
Application Security	2,434	2,742	3,003
Cloud Security	185	304	459
Data Security	2,563	3,063	3,524
Identity Access Management	8,823	9,768	10,578
Infrastructure Protection	12,583	14,106	15,337
Integrated Risk Management	3,949	4,347	4,712
Network Security Equipment	10,911	12,427	13,321
Other Information Security Software	1,832	2,079	2,285
Security Services	52,315	58,920	64,237
Consumer Security Software	5,948	6,395	6,661
Total	**101,544**	**114,152**	**124,116**

ing will reach $ 133.7 billion by 2022 (Varonis, 2020). While noteworthy is the fact that the damage to the world far exceeds the amount spent on security, a report by Cybersecurity Ventures estimates that by 2021 the damage from cyberattacks will be $ 6 trillion, up from $ 3 trillion in 2017 ($ 3 trillion in 2017).

This in turn means that the trend of cyber warfare and cyberattacks has recently taken on a larger scale and is undergoing a transformation. Russia has great potential in terms of cyber warfare, and numerous suspicions and events confirm this. Russia used cyberweapons against Georgia during the 2008 war, and in 2019 used the same method to launch cyber-attacks on Georgian government websites and television infrastructure. According to foreign media reports, at the closed session of the UN Security Council in 2020, the United States, Britain, and Estonia assessed this fact as a cyber-attack carried out by Russia. The same handwriting was observed during the attack on Ukraine in early 2014 (Georgian Public Broadcast, 2020).

THE CYBERWARFARE CONCEPT AND THE 21ST CENTURY INTERNATIONAL SECURITY SYSTEM

We see physical tools such as computers, cables, cell phones, and so on. Tools interact in the virtual and unreal spheres. It facilitates the production of war from one part of the earth to the other, and the identification of the culprit is not always possible. Cyberwarfare is often the conceptual framework behind traditional warfare - including demonstrations of force, physical harm, and violence. As time goes on, it becomes more and more important to specify what type of cyber-attack should be called cyber warfare. These types of definitions are important in resolving cyber-related issues, sometimes involving both kinetic and sometimes non-kinetic attacks. We have already discussed the difference between a cyberattack and a cyber - warfare, there have been many attempts around the world to pinpoint the essence of cyber cyberbullying at a conceptual level, such as the Tallinn Handbook under NATO's Cyber Defense Cooperation Skills Center. However, it is not a political, official document of NATO. The difficulty, in this case, is that nation-states and non-state actors do not always follow the laws. We think that some topics in the "Tallinn Handbook" are incompatible with general, superficial, and theoretical definitions of cyberspace and need to be refined. For example, in the Tallinn Handbook, cyberwarfare is equated with cyber-attack - it is said to be an offensive or defensive operation that can result in death, injury, or destruction of objects (Ranger, 2018).

In our opinion, this definition excludes psychological pressure during cyber operations or cyber intelligence. The main drawback of this definition is the discussion of cyber and cyber-attack as one term. Also, this definition excludes cyber operations, which may be aimed at destabilizing the financial system of states. In this case, the cyber - attack will not result in death or physical destruction.

When we talk about the cyber concept and the issue of security, we must consider it in the context of the North Atlantic Alliance - security and cyber defense are directly related to NATO. The need to strengthen defense against cyber-attacks was first discussed by NATO member states at a summit in Prague in 2002. Cyber security has since become an important component of NATO's agenda. The first cyber defense policy document was adopted in 2008. The process of integrating cyber security into the NATO defense system has been active since 2012. At the Wales Summit in 2014, the Allies made cyber defense a key part of collective defense, saying that a cyber-attack could lead to the application of Article 5 of the Collective Defense Treaty set out in the NATO Treaty. At the 2016 Warsaw Summit, Alliance member states recognized information and communication network security as one of their key defense areas and agreed that NATO should protect itself in cyberspace as effectively as on land, sea, and air. NATO's main partner in the field of cyber security is the European Union, with which the Alliance signed a technical agreement on mutual assistance and cooperation in February 2016 (RIAC, 2016).

The main issues discussed at the Warsaw Summit were how to allocate resources on cybersecurity to achieve the best effect - recognizing that large resources were needed to address this problem. Also, there were questions about how much money should be spent, what would be the minimum level of investment? For example, since 2014, the budget of Pacte Défense Cyber in France has included 1 billion euros for cyber defense. In 2016, the UK announced that it had allocated 9 1.9 billion to strengthen its cyber security program (Reuters, 2014).

At the 2018 Brussels Summit, the Allies agreed to set up a new cyberspace operations center. Given the common challenges, NATO and the EU are strengthening cooperation in the field of cyber defense, especially in the exchange of information. Joint training and research are conducted (NATO, 2018).

Of particular note is the merit of the United States, which spares no effort to develop new regulations on cybersecurity, and also spares no funds. Expenditures on cybersecurity in the U.S. budget increase every year, in 2015 the Barack Obama administration officially allocated $ 14 billion, and then there was information that much more would be spent (Cnet, 2015). Defense spending around the world is rising day by day, but U.S. finances are impressive. It is already known that by 2021 this sector will be funded with $ 18.8 billion (Homeland Security, 2020). As early as 2007, the United States Air Force established a cyber command, which lasted until the end of 2008, and then these functions were transferred to the Air Force Space Command (Council of Europe, 2020).

In May 2011, the United States unveiled its cybersecurity strategy, which is based on a model of cooperation with international partners and the private sector. The activities should be carried out in seven directions:

1. Economy - attracting international standards and innovations, open and liberal markets;
2. Protection of the national network - increasing security, reliability, and sustainability;
3. Legal side - expansion of cooperation and legal norms;
4. Military field - readiness for modern security challenges;
5. Government Internet Network - Expanding the efficiency and diversity of government structures;
6. International Development - Organizing security, developing international competencies and economic prosperity;
7. Freedom on the Internet - Supporting Citizens' Privacy and Freedom (The White House, 2011).

How many kinds of concepts can there be in the world today? In addition to the important concepts that the US, the EU, NATO, all countries have their national action plan, the most noteworthy is the new strategic concept approved at the Lisbon Summit in 2010 (NATO, 2011), according to which the United States established cyber-command. It was a response to Russia's actions. Whether or not Vladimir Putin came to power, he approved a new Information Security Doctrine (Information Security Doctrine of the Russian Federation, 2000), the strategy of which was to give the government the right to control information and media networks. Putin also signed a legislative change - giving the tax police, the Interior Ministry, the Kremlin's parliamentary and presidential security services, the border guard, and the customs service the same rights that only the Federal Security Service had.

On December 18, 2017, the first "National Security Strategy" (US National Security Strategy) (2017) was published by US President Donald Trump, which formed the basis of strategic documents such as the "National Defense Strategy" of the US Department of Defense. The strategy is based on four important national interests:

1. Protecting the American people and the American way of life;
2. Increasing America's prosperity;
3. Maintaining peace;
4. Increasing American influence.

It is Interesting is the document, entitled "Maintaining Peace through Force", which claims the two states - Russia and China:

"Russia is perceived as an existential threat to the United States. Russia is trying to restore the status of a great state and create its spheres of influence near the borders. Its goal is to weaken US influence, ally with allies and partners. The threat posed by China is seen as an increase in nuclear arsenals and military strength, as well as a desire to expel the United States from the Indian and Pacific regions, an attempt to bring order to the region and to establish desirable economic rules "(US Embassy in Georgia, 2017).

The handbook, Cyber Dragon - China's Information War and Cyber Operations, authored by researcher Dean Cheng, notes that over the centuries, Chinese leaders have analyzed the most important technological advances that are helping China improve its global position. They realized the importance of information control as one of the powerful elements in maintaining power. Cheng also focuses on the development of war species:

"The development of technology has affected the economy and society, as well as the nature of war. Historically, war has developed, with mankind developing swords, spears, and other "cold weapons," or replacing them with rifles, grenades, machine guns, and so on. Today, humanity has moved from "hot weapons" to "soft power" at the expense of technological development "(Cheng Dean, 2017).

That is why when we are talking on the New US Strategy explicitly states:

"Increasing American Influence," which focuses on America's role, influence, and active participation in international institutions. If existing institutions and regulations need to be modernized, the United States will lead the process, "the document states (US Embassy in Georgia, 2017).

When it comes to increasing US influence in Donald Trump's strategy, one can see how the White House is handling international relations, but it is difficult to say how real it will be when it comes to Russia, for which politics and ethics, fulfillment of promises and justice are far away.

TRANSFORMING CONFLICTS INTO A NEW GEOPOLITICAL ORDER

We discuss the topic based on the theory of political realism. Realism has long dominated the paradigm of international relations and is based on general assumptions about international politics. For example, the fact that states are the most important actors as independent entities in the international system has no centralized authority and have their interests to ensure power and security. The essence of this methodology is important in the field of cyber security.

The importance of the theory of political realism is great in international cyber politics. In this case, it is uniquely related to cyber security. Historically, the foundations of the theory of political realism can be found in Thucydides' description of the Peloponnesian War (5th century BC), where he emphasized the immoral nature of international politics and the importance of power for survival. The development of this theory in international relations may be mainly due to Hans Morgenthau (1948), who focuses on the struggle for power between independent states (Stanford Encyclopedia of Philosophy, 2010).

According to Paul D., Senezi - a follower of the theory of political realism and John A.Vasquez (Paul D. Senese and John A. Vasquez), some factors increase threats - e.g., military units, alliances, unions, alliances, are often unproductive and increase the likelihood of conflict (Paul, 2018).

Nevertheless, with a focus on security and conflict issues, realism seems to be a natural theory in addressing the acute issues of cybersecurity. In general, the study of the cyber conflict began when John Arquilla and David Ronfeldt developed the concepts of "cyber warfare" and "intom" and predicted the transformation of war into the rapid advancement of ICT (Arquilla, 2000).

Proponents of realism Brandon Valeriano and Ryan C. Maness view the issue in this way: This form of conflict takes place in cyberspace and involves "the use of computing technologies in cyberspace for evil and/or destructive purposes. For the purpose" (Brandon, 2015).

We focus on these politically motivated relationships because they have a direct impact on national security. Joint military units or the conclusion of treaties are often perceived as a threat by other states, which then take similar measures to enhance their security. This process is often referred to as the spiral model. The spiral model represents an escalation that causes a rapid shift in the balance of power, as well as an increase in international tensions and the risk of conflict. The cyber domain lacks effective global institutional governance.

Relevant organizations include the International Telecommunication Union (ITU) and the Internet Corporation for Assigned Names and Numbers (ICANN), but their functions and competencies do not extend to conflict management. The security dilemma is more acute when offensive and defensive capabilities do not differ from each other. In this case, the development of cyber security by states and increased funding for technology improvements are considered a potential threat. It is difficult to distinguish capabilities in cyberspace. Moreover, cyber-military organizations such as the US Cyber Command have both defensive and offensive roles, and if they say they are raising budgets or personnel, it is clear that this is both defensive and offensive reinforcements, which exacerbates uncertainty and competition between states.

VIRTUAL THREAT AND ASYMMETRIC MILITARY CHALLENGES

There are five war zones in the world - air, land, sea, space, and cyberspace. Our research topic is cyberspace. Virtual threats include not only cyber criminals, psychological terror, digital viruses, and hacker attacks, but also virtual information and disinformation manipulations, as well as the global Internet market known as the Black Market (Darknet). Let us first highlight information warfare, which involves the use of information technology and management to gain an advantage over an adversary. It can be used to gain tactical information, disseminate misinformation and propaganda to demoralize the public or the adversary. Can be used for manipulation as well as prevent the dissemination of real information.

The phenomenon of information-propaganda war is not new, it is as old a method as the most ancient craft. It was just changing and will probably change (progress) in the future with the development of technology. Propaganda - means the systematic use of any form of communication to influence people's minds, behaviors, and emotions. This means is considered by many to be the most effective and common means of persuading people to engage in political activity. Intelligence services have historically used propaganda for a long time. The full strength of the propaganda war was revealed during World War

II and is still relevant today. It is hard to believe, but it is a fact that when World War II ended, many in Germany said, "Yes, Adolf Hitler is guilty, he exaggerated a little, but he did a lot of good, restored dignity and built highways" (Deusche Welle, 2020). Moreover, the influence of Goebbels's ideology and propaganda was so strong in post-Hitler Germany that no witnesses appeared at the Nuremberg trials in 1948 (HistoryExtra, 2020).

Even three years after the end of the war, people believed (many feared) that the Nazis would return to power. Then there was no internet, there was no computer, but there was radio, there was ideology, there was agitation in the population, there were pressure underarms. In this regard, we can say that Russia has a long history of information, propaganda, and disinformation, but in the era of technological revolutions, this activity has become more effective. Russian propaganda is not truth-oriented, but that does not mean that everything is a lie. Here we have a mixed-method when mixed misinformation is spread in truth. There are cases when we are dealing with complete disinformation and "fake news". For example, a fake report on September 11, 2014, informed us that a chemical plant in Louisiana had exploded (Manufacturing, 2015). At the time this information seemed credible, it covered almost every social network. Generally, fake news spreads quickly and is easily believed. Especially when the information is spread by not one, but several media outlets. In this case, it is important to warn the public about impending misinformation. We are generally called upon to verify the facts, to look at several sources, but concerning the masses it is ineffective - verifying the facts requires time and knowledge when it is proved that the information was false, a story already told, self-justification or simply denial is relatively ineffective. However, there is no other way. The mainstay of Kremlin propaganda in Georgia is the media and social networks. At least one TV station, several Internet TV stations, a print edition, and a Web site feature anti-Western "message boxes" that rely heavily on Russian sources for information. The active use of social networks by Russian propagandists is also noticeable when viral dissemination of disinformation or anti-Western narrative material is viral. Numerous public opinion polls show that the main source of information in Georgia is television. According to a 2016 poll by the National Democratic Institute (NDI), 77% of the Georgian population names television as the primary source of information on politics and current events. Surveys also show that almost half of the Georgian TV viewers (47%) watch foreign channels in addition to Georgian ones. The most popular foreign channels are Russian (HTB, ORT, and RTR) (IDFI, 2016). It should be noted that there are countries where they actively control the Internet space and communication networks. For example, China, which also controls television and social media. It is known that the Chinese government has hired up to two million people, they write comments according to the instructions and influence, manage public opinion. A study by Carrie King, Margaret Roberts, and Jennifer Pan, based on leaked government emails on the Internet, has also been published. The study says the Chinese government fabricates 448 million comments a year. Employees in social networks often glorify China and the Chinese Communist Party, they try to divert people's attention to other, less important issues (Waddell, 2017).

What should we do to counter misinformation, fake news, false news, information warfare? Defining this is not so simple. In this case, it is important to attend, ie to disseminate real information. In case of delay, it is necessary to spread an alternative option. As mentioned above, the threats in cyberspace are multifaceted - one of which is the black market, which is not available to everyone on the Internet. In this case, we need to distinguish four areas of the Internet:

1. Surface Web - means a surface network. Also referred to as the Clear Web. This network is searched by standard web search systems. The network is indexed by search engines. This network includes Google, Facebook, Yahoo, Wikipedia, Instagram, etc.
2. Deep Web - Deep network, its content can be found directly in the URL or IP address. However, you may need to go through a password or other security mode to view websites. However, implies normal use. For example, when a user has limited access to various websites where they need to register to view content. On sites where you need to pay to download a magazine or newspaper. This space includes Pay pal, Facebook, Twitter, Whaps app, Gmail, etc.
3. Dark Web. This is a system that is not indexed by web search engines. You need a special program, configuration, or authorization to get here. It is possible to communicate anonymously, protect privacy, communicate privately, obtain illegal information, trade illegally, for example, in drugs, weapons, etc.
4. Darknet - Dark Network. Also known as a "hidden network". This is a system available using non-standard ports. Darknet differs from other networks in that file sharing is done anonymously, i.e. IP addresses are not publicly available. Communication in this space is uncontrolled and contains various dangers. We can draw a parallel between underground illegal activities that take place in real space and Darknet, which takes place in virtual space. Getting into this system is not easy, specific software and authorization are sacrificed. Darknet can also be considered as an alternative internet, or the dark side of the internet, it is a huge network that brings together thousands of unlicensed and illegal websites. There are lots of things available here - buying guns illegally, buying cloned cards, buying fake passports, subscribing to slaves, buying drugs, renting a killer, and so on. Darknet has lots of illegal forums, social networks, and non-standard websites. We do not consciously discuss the instructions for entering this system in the paper, it can be understood as an incentive.

In his book, Cybersecurity and Global Information Security - on Threat Analysis and Response Solutions, published by the US Air Force Academy in Colorado, Knauf Kenneth emphasizes that one of the major shortcomings of the software is the black market. In his view, the defenses of cyberspace users usually lag behind those of cyber-attackers. Kenneth also explains that the possible growth of black markets increases the chances of vulnerabilities in software. It is difficult to obtain statistics on black markets for vulnerable users and related transactions. Our observation is expressed as a dynamic model of the system. We conduct simulations to observe whether the number of users increases or decreases. From our observations, we can say that the rate is increasing. However, it is difficult to say what causes it. Kenneth writes that the simulation scenario of their operations causes the market to temporarily shrink:

"Security companies such as IBM ISS X-Force (2007), Panda Labs (2007), and Symantec (2008) report an increase in cyberattacks., Criminals and criminal organizations, trade in a variety of products. Their goal is ultimately to steal personal data. The Symantec report makes it clear that black markets pose a serious threat, both on a personal and global level. Using the black market poses a serious threat to the protection of personal information. Hackers also use cyber-attacks against specific users and specific sites to launch cyber-attacks on browsers and websites "(Kenneth, 2009).

THE IMPACT OF MODERN HIGH TECHNOLOGIES ON INTERNATIONAL SECURITY PROCESSES

The development of technology and cyberspace has changed the way countries make decisions, create policies, and interact with each other. The development of technology brings efficiency and success in almost every field. However, today it is unclear how much modern technology has changed the balance of global forces, or the balance of power in cyberspace. We have a slightly different picture in this regard.

Balance of forces is one of the oldest and most important issues in the theory of international relations. According to this concept, the main task of states is to fight for self-preservation and self-determination, they care about security and independence. Often states come together to confront a state, or group of states, that poses a threat. It turns out that the international system, let's say cooperation, is divided into several groups of states, which determines peace for them. The high possibility of asymmetric use of cyber opportunities in the modern era has made it possible for small countries to influence the ongoing proletarian processes in the world. Nevertheless, the general trend is to show that power is still in the hands of large and powerful countries. Since cyberwarfare has become the standard tool of international politics, we can say that modern technologies have somewhat changed the approaches to global security. In this regard, it is important to define the concept of balance of power and the conditions for strengthening cyber technologies, which implies the cyber capabilities, development, and balancing of states. This refers not only to the strengthening or dominance of one state in terms of cyber technologies but also to the various stages of cooperation.

The concept of balance of power implies: if one state is strengthened, it will take advantage of the weakness of other states, which will lead to the unification of weak states for defense. It is a chain reaction that has evolved against the background of the development of technology and has facilitated the production of cyber warfare. This has put the security of some countries in question. As mentioned in previous chapters, the United States continues to spend lame-doubled funding to enhance cyber capabilities. This is not surprising, since the United States created the Internet and introduced many new technologies in this country. In general, a wide range of cyber-instruments in politics also provide different options for strategic flexibility, which was previously almost unthinkable. The Russian factor is also noteworthy, which is also in the leading position in terms of cyber capabilities. What is Russian Cybercrime and what is its role in terms of the balance of power? Russia works innovatively in various conflicts. Due to the specific geopolitical environment, Russia has successfully adapted cyber-attacks to expand its interests. In the paper, we have discussed numerous examples of Russia. One of the 2007 cyber-attacks against Estonia. It was a simple DDoS attack that did not cause significant damage but had a positive impact on strengthening Estonia-NATO relations in terms of security. The same thing happened in 2008 during the Russian-Georgian war, which we have already mentioned many times. Also - about Ukraine, where the cyber-attacks turned out to be more "sophisticated" and damaging. We have many examples that point to Russia's enhanced cyber capabilities. Cyber-attacks carried out by Russia are mostly used in conditions of asymmetric conflict. Although hackers intervened in the 2016 US presidential election differently in the sense that Russia did not use cyber-attacks, it was not a punitive measure, it was intended to test cyber-capabilities to influence the election. Naturally, Russia's capabilities also have a limit. When carrying out a cyber-attack with a certain strategy, potential opponents have the opportunity to prepare in a defensive direction. Russia's cyberattacks on Georgia and Ukraine may be considered experiments, but it allows leading countries to fully explore the so-called Russian methods in technological terms. And then it becomes easier to improve defense mechanisms. For example, the interference of Russian hackers in the elections in France, Italy, the Netherlands, and Germany was not as effective as it may have been in previous cases. China's role in cybersecurity is also noteworthy. The intensive use of Chinese cyber-espionage has extremely irritated the White House administration. It was at the expense of these attacks that secret materials were leaked by Chinese intelligence. One of the most damaging was when the US Administration Office of Personnel Management system was attacked - the personal data of more than 20 million people were obtained (Cassella, 2015).

To this state is added the North Atlantic Alliance, which in terms of cyber security, plays an important role worldwide and cooperates with member or non-member countries. NATO, with the help of the European Union, is trying to deal with the threats posed in cyberspace, which further balances the situation, reduces risks and threats. It is clear that today, in terms of cyber technologies, the system is not single-pole. In this case, the number of potential allies is greater and it is easier to make policy. Today's international environment is multipolar in different dimensions. No one spends as much money as the United States, nor does anyone form a military alliance, not even China and Russia, but they still strengthen military cooperation and coordinate foreign policy. It should also be noted that the US has redoubled its efforts to counterbalance China around the world, especially in East Asia. Generally, China is considered the number one threat to the US. It is about American supremacy in global politics.

The review presented in the appropriate papers on this issue reveals how highly active different countries are in using cyber technologies in their international policy-making. The importance of the cyber element has a positive effect on maintaining the balance of power because there is no single dominant force here. Yet the ability of cyber technologies to be easily used for asymmetric attacks reveals what risks and challenges the world faces.

REFLECTING THE CYBERWARFARE PHENOMENON IN NATIONAL SECURITY STRATEGIES - MYTH AND REALITY

The National Security Strategy is the most important document for creating a safe environment for the state. Cyberwarfare plays an important role in the security strategies of the world's leading countries - for example, the United States, Great Britain, Russia, China, Iran, France, Spain, etc. This issue also occupies an important place in the national security strategy of Georgia. We must also focus on NATO-EU security strategies. However, it is important to consider the security strategy of the aggressor country. I wonder what the Russian government's vision is in terms of global threats. In the 2015 version of the Russian National Security Doctrine, the 16th and 17th paragraphs consider the US and NATO to be the main adversaries, while the 7th paragraph directly addresses the role of the Russian Federation in world order (Russian National Security Strategy, 2015).

The Russian Federation says it does not even pose a threat to other countries, but is itself a victim and has uplifting capabilities to deal with threats from the US and NATO. The real situation and the facts prove the opposite - for example, Russia, using the elements of the "hybrid war", was able to deal a serious blow to the United States, adding signs of political instability in the monolithic political system of this country during the presidential election. Even if the story of the hacker interference in the presidential election is a complete lie, at least Russia is benefiting, this fact shows that it is omnipotent, which is what causes the nihilism of the people of the United States. But why only the population of this country? When the whole of Europe, Asia, or Africa sees that even a superpower is vulnerable at certain moments, everyone gets a sense of frustration and helplessness. One example is the terrorist attacks of

September 11, 2001, in the United States. This is where not only "American nihilism" but "world nihilism" first appeared. It was during this period that the United States had the so-called Collaboration-Reset Policy - Secretary of State Hillary Clinton arrived in Moscow and presented a symbolic reset button to Russian Foreign Minister Sergei Lavrov, while in the current doctrine it was directly stated that constructive cooperation with Russia is necessary, so is NATO-Russia security. As we have seen later, such an approach did not work.

What exactly is written in the US National Security Strategy, published in December 2017? In the introduction to the strategy, it is stated that the well-being and security of the United States depend on how it responds to the capabilities and challenges of cyberspace. It also notes that critical infrastructure, national defense, and the daily lives of Americans rely on computer and information technology (National Security Strategy of the United States of America, 2017).

That is, on the very first page of the US National Security Document, we focus on the important factors of cyber technology, which means that threats from cyberspace affect all areas and damage both materially and intangibly. It is important to look at this issue in the context of a doctrine called "collective defense."

The "collective defense" model belongs to the American political scientist Richard Cohen, who developed the concept of "cooperative security", which is divided into four parts - individual security, collective security, collective defense, and maintaining stability. Individual security refers to the ability of a country to independently defend its territory, following Article 51 of the UN Charter, including through military means. Collective security means uniting countries against common types of military risks and challenges. Collective defense means uniting countries to defend themselves from other countries, which is the basis of NATO today - the principle of transatlantic solidarity. Achieving stability through joint efforts is, and is, an even more ideal option in a high-level global collective security scenario - for example, against the Islamic Caliphate (Cohen, 2001).

Reality shows that this concept is quite relevant even in the XI century. The development of cyber technologies has become more important. "Collective defense" is enshrined in the NATO Charter and obliges member states to protect each other. Collective defense means that an attack on one of the allies is considered an attack on all members of NATO - this principle is also enshrined in Article 5 of the Washington Treaty. NATO first enacted Article 5 after the September 11 terrorist attacks on the United States. The issue of the principle of collective defense also arose when Russia launched military aggression against Ukraine. On 1 April 2014, the NATO Secretary-General addressed the Alliance's military leadership to develop additional measures to strengthen the collective defense (NATO, 2019).

Under international law, states have the right to use force to defend themselves against an armed attack. The state affected by the cyber - attack has the right to respond to cyber-qualified attacks using military force. Although no such thing has happened yet, governments are still actively considering regulating such opportunities. For example, in 2014, NATO issued a declaration stating that the impact of cyberattacks could be as harmful to modern society as a conventional military attack. The same declaration states that a cyber-attack on a NATO member country could lead to the application of Article 5 of the North Atlantic Treaty Organization. The strategic concept of the Alliance pays great attention to the factor of partnership, cooperation, and dialogue. The Alliance strives for trust and transparency among the members of the Euro-Atlantic Partnership Council in all matters. This obliges non-EU or NATO countries to be actively involved in international security processes. In 2016, NATO member states recognized cyberspace as an area of hostilities (Brent, 2019).

Numerous international defense organizations have been established. One such center is CCDCOE - NATO's "Cooperative Cyber Defense Center", a multinational and interdisciplinary cyber defense organization. The director of the center, Colonel Jaak Tarien, explains that the operations center is not designed to conduct operations. According to him, their activities include research, training, and exercises:

"Our educational process includes 17 courses a year. The courses cover and teach, for example, critical infrastructure protection, international law, and cybersecurity planning "(Riazi, 2020).

Georgia, a country which was especially suffered from cyber-attacks from the Russian side and which is an integral part of the global political process, is an important object in the study of cyber themes. Therefore, it is important to discuss the national concept of Georgia and to evaluate and determine the cyber-technological security of the country. The concept of national security of Georgia is a document that the government should be guided not only in extreme situations but also to set priorities.

What are the country's priorities? Security, prosperity, peace. What are the national interests of Georgia? As stated in the concept, this includes ensuring sovereignty and territorial integrity, developing state institutions and strengthening democracy, developing an effective national security system, strengthening national unity and civic consent, European and Euro-Atlantic integration, sustainable economic growth, energy security, regional security, and regional security. and so on. The concept explains that the main threat is:

"Occupation of Georgian territories by the Russian Federation and terrorist acts organized by the Russian Federation from the occupied territories, the risk of new military aggression by the Russian Federation" (National Security Strategy of Georgia, 2018).

The concept repeatedly mentions the security of the country and cyber security. However, when describing Georgia's security environment, the focus is only on Russia and how the environment has deteriorated since 2008 when a northern neighbor showed unprecedented aggression. In the following chapters, where we talk about the challenges, threats, and risks, it is mentioned that Georgia is threatened not only by Russia. Other main threats are international terrorism, transnational organized crime, and the fact that terrorist threats from individual states and non-state actors have become a significant challenge to the security of the modern world. It is also noted that the existence of the occupied regions on the territory of Georgia creates a favorable environment for international terrorism and transnational organized crime. It is not specified what individual states and non-state entities mean. The concept of national security does not mention the word "media" at all, which represents the 4th power. There is also no mention of "social networks" and other Internet outlets.

CYBERWARFARE IN THE EU SPACE

Today, the whole of Europe is talking about the threats posed by Russia. That is why, based on the decision made in Warsaw, in early 2017, NATO deployed 4 battalion-type military units in the Baltic states (Lithuania, Latvia, Estonia) and Poland, acting in coordination with local military units. This decision was preceded by the approval of the RAP for the NATO Preparedness Action Plan for the 2014 Wales Summit, which was adopted mainly in response to the threats posed by Russia and their strategic impact. The Warsaw Summit Declaration also stated that the security of the Baltic Sea region has been threatened since 2014. In particular, Russia's intensified military activities and deployment of new military technologies were highlighted, which poses additional challenges to the security of the region. Of course, new military technologies in themselves imply both cyberspace control and cyber-attacks (GCSD, 2014).

The EU has also begun to step up its fight against fake news, and the European Commission has even presented an action plan against the spread of misinformation. The preamble to this plan states that we must maintain unity and unite our efforts to better protect our democracy from disinformation. We have seen numerous cases of interference in elections and referendums, and all the evidence indicates that Russia is to blame in most cases.

According to the action plan, the budget of the EU Foreign Ministry has already been increased - in particular, in the budget of 2019, 5 million euros will be spent on strategic communications. It is planned to increase the number of employees of the agency responsible for revealing misinformation within two years.

In March 2019, a rapid response system to disinformation campaigns was launched, allowing EU member states to receive information about the spread of false news easily and quickly.

The handbook, Cyber Security and Politics, Socially and Religiously Motivated Cyberattacks, published by the European Parliament in 2009, states that the first step in any cybersecurity analysis should be a cyber threat spectrum diagram of the challenges posed by ICT (Information) Through equipment. ICT is communication technology, it is the infrastructure and components that enable modern computing. There is no single universal definition of ICT, it is a generally accepted term and refers to all devices, network components, programs, and systems that combined allow people and organizations to interact with the digital world. For example - businesses, non-profit agencies, governments, and criminal enterprises.

"Communications have dramatically changed the equation of global cyber security. The ICT system can be used for evil activities as a tool in state-level aggression. It can also be done individually - for example, by hacking into a plan orchestrated by various groups, criminals, terrorists, governments "(Cornish, 2009).

When it comes to hybrid warfare, cyber-attacks, hacker attacks, spreading fake news, or fake news, why is Russia constantly pointing to Russia? For example, on January 17, 2019, hundreds of pages, groups, and accounts were deleted from the social networks "Facebook" and "Instagram". All these pages, groups, and reports were managed from Russia, acted in a coordinated manner, and disseminated information to the audiences of different countries. There were several of them, which targeted Georgian consumers. As explained in the administration of "Facebook", most of the accounts and pages belonged to the employees of the Russian news agency "Sputnik". This is not the first time that Georgia has fallen victim to false information and a coordinated information campaign coming from Russia. According to Vytautas Kersanskas, an employee of the European Center for Hybrid Threats in Helsinki, Russia's task is to provoke disagreements between different groups in society, escalating tensions between the public and the government, and confront allied countries. We must fight against misinformation and false news because it hurts the thinking of citizens. Moreover, there is an opportunity for citizens to take action at the behest of other states. For example, to vote for a candidate supported by a foreign country in an election or to take part in a protest rally that is in the interests of a foreign country (1tv, 2019).

A Record-breaking Cyber Attack

We can cite numerous examples of high-profile or not-so-large-scale cyberattacks. The largest attack on one of the most successful companies in the world - "Github". This company is an area of interest for developers. On the Github website, you can upload and manage your projects, create various applications. The company brings together more than 40 million developers. In 2018, DDos launched a record cyber-attack on Github, and in fact, the website withstood this cyber -attack.

Figure 2. Diagram - DDos record cyberattack on Github
Source: https://www.wired.com/story/github-ddos-memcached/

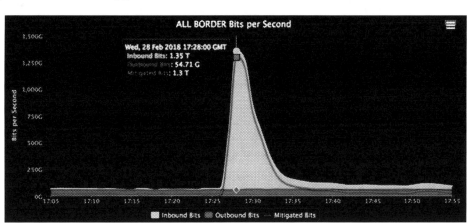

As we see from Figure 2, a 1.3 terabyte capacity attack was carried out but 1.35 terabytes was allocated for defense, during the cyber - attack, the site almost stopped for several hours, speed was down and projects were not seen, lots of projects were lost but all this was later restored. "Github" is protected by one of the most successful companies in the world in the field of cyber security - "Akamai". Within hours of the attack, Akamai Web site vice president Josh Schul said they had increased their capabilities fivefold, something no one had seen on the Internet. Schul noted that they can still handle the same power attack:

"We have increased our capabilities five times, it was a record cyber - attack. I'm sure you will handle the next attack as well if it does not exceed 1.3 Tbps. Self-confidence is one thing, but reality is another, we do not know how powerful the next attack will be "(the developer platform GitHub, 2018).

ANTIVIRUS AS ONE OF THE DEFENSE MECHANISMS

Against the background of viruses and cyber-attacks, their deterrent mechanisms are being actively invented, the first antivirus was created by Hopkins in 1984 (Leiden, 2012), and today there are many antivirus companies working on antivirus, -Antiviruses, which includes a complete package of antivirus. It is difficult to say which antivirus can be said to fully provide protection, as all antiviruses have some pluses and some minuses, but we can discuss the data on how they work. Kaspersky is one of the largest corporations in this regard.

Kaspersky is a Russian company that is officially used in various countries, including US government agencies. There is a suspicion that it is under the influence of the Russian government and that a hacking system may be added to the manufactured products to extract information. However, "Kaspersky" denies all the accusations or similar opinions. Read the statistics of Kaspersky Security Network, which is published electronically and obtained using KSN distributed antivirus networks that work with anti-malware protection components. Data were collected from KSN users who agreed to provide the information. Millions of Kaspersky Lab users participate in the global exchange of information about malicious activity. According to its security network: Kaspersky Lab solutions have blocked 989,432,403 attacks carried out from online resources in 203 countries around the world. 560 025 316 Unique URLs have been identified as anti-malicious components of the Website. Through a malware program designed to steal money by accessing bank accounts via the Internet, 197,559 users' computers were blocked. Kaspersky Anti-Virus handled ransomware attacks on 229,643 unique users' computers. This antivirus detected 230 051 054 unique malicious and potentially unwanted objects. Kaspersky Software has detected 870,617 malicious installation packages, 13,129 installation packages and mobile banking trojans to protect mobile devices. Also 13 179 installation packages for Mobile Ransomware Trojan.

According to statistics on the distribution of exploits used by cybercriminals, a large portion of the Microsoft Office suite is vulnerable (73%). The most common errors were in the last quarter (CVE-2017-11882, CVE-2018-0802) in the Equation Editor program, which was previously part of Microsoft Office. According to the latest data, CVE-2017-8570, CVE-2017-8759, CVE-2017-0199 are vulnerable in Microsoft Office.

The modern web browser is complex and voluminous in terms of code software, leading to the discovery of new vulnerabilities (13%). The most common target for cyber - attacks in the mass environment is the Microsoft Internet Explorer browser. For example, the Google Chrome browser, which received updated information on several critical vulnerabilities (CVE-2019-13685, CVE-2019-13686, CVE-2019-13687, CVE-2019-13688), was not without problems.

Most of the vulnerabilities to escalating privileges in the system come from individual operating system services and popular programs among users. Privileges of escalating privileges play a special role, as they often use malware to further fix the target system.

A Google researcher has released a tool to demonstrate this problem - CtfTool, which allows you to start processes with system privileges, as well as make changes to the memory of other processes and enter arbitrary code.

As we see from Figure 1, a 1.3 terabyte capacity attack was carried out but 1.35 terabytes were allocated for defense, during the cyber - attack, the site almost stopped for several hours, speed was down and projects were not seen, lots of projects were lost but all this was later restored. "Github" is protected by one of the most successful companies in the world in the field of cyber security - "Akamai". Within hours of the attack, Akamai Web site vice president Josh Schul said they had increased their capabilities fivefold, something no one had seen on the Internet. Schul noted that they can still handle the same power attack:

"We have increased our capabilities five times, it was a record cyber - attack. I'm sure you will handle the next attack as well if it does not exceed 1.3 Tbps. Self-confidence is one thing, but the reality is another, we do not know how powerful the next attack will be "(the developer platform GitHub, 2018).

ANTIVIRUS AS ONE OF THE DEFENSE MECHANISMS

Against the background of viruses and cyber-attacks, their deterrent mechanisms are being actively invented, the first antivirus was created by Hopkins in 1984 (Leiden, 2012), and today many antivirus companies are working on antivirus, -Antiviruses, which includes a complete package of antivirus. It is difficult to say which antivirus can be said to fully provide protection, as all antiviruses have some pluses and some minuses, but we can discuss the data on how they work. Kaspersky is one of the largest corporations in this regard.

Kaspersky is a Russian company that is officially used in various countries, including US government agencies. There is a suspicion that it is under the influence of the Russian government and that a hacking system may be added to the manufactured products to extract information. However, "Kaspersky" denies all the accusations or similar opinions. Read the statistics of Kaspersky Security Network, which is published electronically and obtained using KSN distributed antivirus networks that work with anti-malware protection components. Data were collected from KSN users who agreed to provide the information. Millions of Kaspersky Lab users participate in the global exchange of information about malicious activity. According to its security network: Kaspersky Lab solutions have blocked 989,432,403 attacks carried out from online resources in 203 countries around the world. 560 025 316 Unique URLs have been identified as anti-malicious components of the Website. Through a malware program designed to steal money by accessing bank accounts via the Internet, 197,559 users' computers were blocked. Kaspersky Anti-Virus handled ransomware attacks on 229,643 unique users' computers. This antivirus detected 230 051 054 unique malicious and potentially unwanted objects. Kaspersky Software has detected 870,617 malicious installation packages, 13,129 installation packages, and mobile banking trojans to protect mobile devices. Also 13 179 installation packages for Mobile Ransomware Trojan.

According to statistics on the distribution of exploits used by cybercriminals, a large portion of the Microsoft Office suite is vulnerable (73%). The most common errors were in the last quarter (CVE-2017-11882, CVE-2018-0802) in the Equation Editor program, which was previously part of Microsoft Office. According to the latest data, CVE-2017-8570, CVE-2017-8759, CVE-2017-0199 are vulnerable in Microsoft Office.

The modern web browser is complex and voluminous in terms of code software, leading to the discovery of new vulnerabilities (13%). The most common target for cyber-attacks in the mass environment is the Microsoft Internet Explorer browser. For example, the Google Chrome browser, which received updated information on several critical vulnerabilities (CVE-2019-13685, CVE-2019-13686, CVE-2019-13687, CVE-2019-13688), was not without problems.

Most of the vulnerabilities to escalate privileges in the system come from individual operating system services and popular programs among users. Privileges of escalating privileges play a special role, as they often use malware to further fix the target system.

A Google researcher has released a tool to demonstrate this problem - CtfTool, which allows you to start processes with system privileges, as well as make changes to the memory of other processes and enter arbitrary code.

Besides the list of vulnerable applications shown in Figure 3, Kaspersky Laboratory - also publishes data on the top ten web attacks of source countries. Kaspersky used the comparable real IP address of the domain name on which the domain is located to determine the geographical source of the cyber-attacks on the websites. Accordingly, the geographical location of this IP address (GEOIP) was determined.

As mentioned above, in the third quarter of 2019, Kaspersky Lab solutions repelled 989,432,403 attacks from Internet resources in 203 countries around the world. There are 560 025 316 unique URLs on which Web Antivirus has been installed. The list of top countries looks like this statistically:

Countries shown in Figure 4 are: USA (75.04%), Netherlands (14.77%), Germany (2.23%), France (1.75%), Russia (1.00%), Israel (0.84%), Ireland (0.51%), Luxembourg (0.49%), Great Britain (0.40%), Singapore (0.39%), and others (2.58%).

How to protect yourself from cyber-attacks on computer networks? Theoretical methods can be found in the textbook "Cyber Operations, Construction, Security and Attack, Modern Computer Networks" by Mike O'Leary. In his book, he discusses computer operations at the system level:

Figure 3. Diagram of vulnerable applications
Source: https://securelist.ru/it-threat-evolution-q3-2019-statistics/95163/

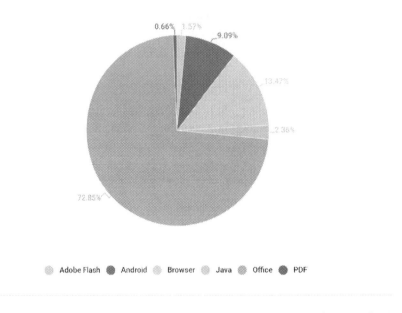

"Cyber defense, it can not be explained if we do not explain the whole working process of" windows "and Linux. Including Centos, Mint, OpenSuSE, and Ubuntu systems. These can be physical or virtual systems built with VMWARE Workstation or VirtualBox. In a cyber-attack, the attacker, who is in the system, wants to keep the so-called. Access, so he constantly carries out the attack. We can show the range of attacks used against internet Explorer, Firefox, Java, and Adobe Flash. Such cyberattacks leave a mark on the network, and if we have software-savvy protection, then we can see it "(O'Leary, 2015).

CONCLUSION

Ensuring cybersecurity is a relatively new field in the modern world. Globally, there is a problem of lack of legal framework and international standards in the world, which, given the globalization and the modern world order, complicates the process of developing a regional and national cyber security strategy. Nevertheless, cybersecurity mechanisms largely depend on the experience of a particular country.

The following answers are given to the research questions asked in the paper:

1. To what extent can cyberwarfare be perceived as a new reality of political conflicts?

Cyberwarfare is a new reality of political conflicts. This is also shown by the current political developments in the world - already interested states have interfered in the internal affairs of many states, mostly in the electoral process. By actively activating in cyberspace, Russia is trying to gain political

Figure 4. Company Kaspersky diagram showing the top ten countries for web attacks
Source: https://securelist.ru/it-threat-evolution-q3-2019-statistics/95163/

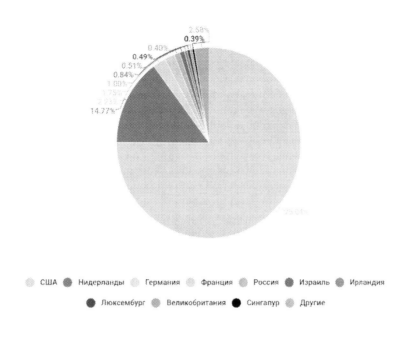

influence in both Eastern European countries and post-Soviet countries. Even the Islamic Caliphate of Iran, which is not a major political player in the world, is trying to interfere in the US presidential election. This has been repeatedly stated in the White House.

2. What impact can cyberwarfare have on the international community?

Cybercrime can have a devastating effect on the international community - do not rule out disrupting the normal functioning of states and societies. Cybercrime will be catastrophically affected from the unreal to the real space, business, economy, almost all leading industries will be affected, terrorist organizations will be activated, intelligence operations will be disrupted, the lives and health of many people will be endangered, financial security, private property rights.

3. What are the action plan and components of the military strategy in cyberspace?

In cyberspace, the action plan and components of the military strategy must be carried out following pre-arranged details. The implementation of the action plan is led by special agencies, in this case, the main agency is NATO at the international level, and the state security services across different countries and the relevant cyber security services under the relevant ministry.

REFERENCES

Allianz Global Corporate & Specialty. (2021). *Cyber attacks on critical infrastructure.* Retrieved from: https://www.agcs.allianz.com/news-and-insights/expert-risk-articles/cyber-attacks-on-critical-infrastructure.html#:~:text=Cyber%2Dattacks%20against%20critical%20infrastructure%20and%20key%20manufacturing%20industries%20have,against%20ICS%20and%20corporate%20networks

Arquilla, J., & Ronfeldt, D. (2000). *Swarming and the Future of Conflict.* RAND National Defense Research Institute. Retrieved from: http://www.analytictech.com/mb021/swarming%20db311.pdf

Brent, L. (2019). *NATO's role in cyberspace.* Retrieved from NATO: https://www.nato.int

Cheng, D. (2017). Cyber dragon, inside China's information warfare and cyber operations. In The Changing Face of War. Publishing House "Praeger".

CNet. (2015). *Obama asks for $14 billion to step up cybersecurity - The president urges Congress to pass legislation that would strengthen the country's hacking detection system and counterintelligence capabilities.* Retrieved from: https://www.cnet.com/news/obama-adds-14b-to-budget-for-stepped-up-cybersecurity/

Cohen, R., & Mihalka, M. (2001). *Cooperative Security: New Horizons for International Order.* European Center for Security Studies, The Marshall Center Papers, No. 3. Retrieved from: https://apps.dtic.mil/dtic/tr/fulltext/u2/a478928.pdf

DiGiacomo. (2017). *Active vs Passive Cyber Attacks Explained.* Retrieved from: https://revisionlegal.com/internet-law/cyber-security/active-passive-cyber-attacks-explained/

EU Staff Publishing Services. (2018). *Handbook of European Data Protection Law.* Retrieved from: https://op.europa.eu/en/publication-detail/-/publication/5b0cfa83-63f3-11e8-ab9c-01aa75ed71a1 https://rm.coe.int

Gartner. (2018). *Gartner Forecasts Worldwide Information Security Spending to Exceed $124 Billion in 2019.* Retrieved from Gartner Retrieved from: https://www.gartner.com

Georgian Center for Security and Development. (2014). *Brief overview of the NATO Warsaw Summit Declaration (impact on Georgia).* Retrieved from: http://gcsd.org.ge/storage/files/doc/NATO-Warsaw-Summit-FINAL.pdf

Georgian Center for Security and Development. (n.d.). *Brief overview of the NATO Warsaw Summit Declaration (impact on Georgia).* Retrieved from: http://gcsd.org.ge/storage/files/doc/NATO-Warsaw-Summit-FINAL.pdf

Georgian Public Broadcaster. (2020). *At a closed session of the UN Security Council, the United States, Britain and Estonia spoke about Russia's cyber attacks against Georgia.* Retrieved from: https://1tv.ge/news/gaero-s-ushishroebis-sabchos-dakhurul-skhdomaze-ashsh-ma-britanetma-da-estonetma-saqartvelos-winaaghmdeg-rusetis-kibertavdaskhmebze-isaubres/

Glaser, B. (2011). *Grounded Theory: The Philosophy, Method, and Work.* Universal Publishers.

Historyextra. (2021). *Forgotten trials: The other side of Nuremberg*. Retrieved from: https://www.historyextra.com/period/second-world-war/forgotten-trials-the-other-side-of-nuremberg/

Homeland Security. (2020). *Department of Homeland Security Statement on the President's Fiscal Year 2021 Budget*. Retrieved from: https://www.dhs.gov/news/2020/02/11/department-homeland-security-statement-president-s-fiscal-year-2021-budget

Institute for Development of Freedom of Information (IDFI). (2016). *Kremlin Information War against Georgia: The Necessity of State Policy in Combating Propaganda, Policy Paper*. Retrieved from idfi.ge: Retrieved from: https://idfi.ge/public/upload/Meri/Russian%20Propaganda%20in%20Georgia%20-%20Policy%20Paper.PDF

Kenneth, K. (2009). *Cyber Security and Global Information Assurance: Threat Analysis and Response Solutions*. U.S. Air Force Academy.

Lewis University. (2019). The history of cyber warfare - infographic. *The New Face of War: Attacks in Cyberspace*. Retrieved from: https://online.lewisu.edu/mscs/resources/the-history-of-cyber-warfare

Lindsay, J. (2014). *The Impact of China on Cybersecurity, Fiction and Friction*. Retrieved from: https://www.belfercenter.org/sites/default/files/legacy/files/IS3903_pp007-047.pdf

Lord Kristin, M., & Sharp, T. (2011). *America's Cyber Future: Security and Prosperity in the Information Age*. Center for a New American Security. Retrieved from: https://s3.us-east-1.amazonaws.com/files.cnas.org/documents/CNAS_Cyber_Volume-I_0.pdf?mtime=20160906081238&focal=none

Manufacturing. (2015). *Report: Russian 'Internet Trolls' Behind Louisiana Chemical Explosion Hoax*. Retrieved from: https://www.manufacturing.net/operations/news/13099148/report-russian-internet-trolls-behind-louisiana-chemical-explosion-hoax

Ministry of Foreign Affairs of Georgia. (2018). *National Security Concept of Georgia*. Retrieved from: https://mod.gov.ge/uploads/2018/pdf/NSC-GEO.pdf

Ministry of Justice. (2017). *Georgia ranks 8th in the Cyber Security Index*. Retrieved from: https://imedinews.ge/ge/politika/16724/kiberusaprtkhoebis-indeqsshi-saqartvelo-me8-adgilzea

Morgan, S. (Ed.). (2017). *Cybersecurity Ventures*. Cybercrime Report. Retrieved from: https://cybersecurityventures.com/2015-wp/wp-content/uploads/2017/10/2017-Cybercrime-Report.pdf

NATO. (2011). *NATO's new strategic concept: A comprehensive assessment*. DIIS. Retrieved from: https://www.econstor.eu/bitstream/10419/59845/1/656748095.pdf

NATO. (2018). *Brussels Summit Declaration - Issued by the Heads of State and Government participating in the meeting of the North Atlantic Council in Brussels 11-12 July 2018*. Retrieved from: https://www.nato.int/cps/en/natohq/official_texts_156624.htm

Nicu & Secrieru. (2018). *Hacks, leaks and disruptions Russian cyber strategies*. European Union Institute for Security Studies Paris, Chaillot Paper N° 148. Retrieved from: https://www.iss.europa.eu/sites/default/files/EUISSFiles/CP_148.pdf

North Atlantic Treaty Organization. (2019). *Collective defence - Article 5*. Retrieved from: https://www.nato.int/cps/en/natohq/topics_110496.htm

Rapid 7. (2020). *What is a malware attack?* Retrieved from: https://www.rapid7.com/fundamentals/malware-attacks/

Reuters. (2014). *France to invest 1 billion euros to update cyber defences*. Retrieved from: https://www.reuters.com/article/france-cyberdefence-idUSL5N0LC21G20140207

RIAC. (2016). *NATO's Cyber Defense Evolution - NATO's New Digital Wall*. Retrieved from: https://www.nato.int/docu/rdr-gde-prg/rdr-gde-prg-eng.pdf

Riazi, T. (2020). *Know The CCDCOE: Interview with Director Col. Jaak Tarie* (J. Tarien, Interviewer). Retrieved from http://natoassociation.ca

Rösch. (2011). *Hans J. Morgenthau, the "marginal man" in International Relations*. A "Weltanschauungsanalyse", Newcastle University School of Geography, Politics, and Sociology. Retrieved from: https://core.ac.uk/download/pdf/40019366.pdf

Russian Federation Presidential Edict. (2000). *Information security doctrine of the Russian Federation*. Retrieved from: https://www.itu.int/en/ITU-D/Cybersecurity/Documents/National_Strategies_Repository/Russia_2000.pdf

Russian Federation Presidential Edict. (2015). *Russian national Security Strategy, 2015*. Retrieved from: https://www.ieee.es/Galerias/fichero/OtrasPublicaciones/Internacional/2016/Russian-National-Security-Strategy-31Dec2015.pdf

Senese & Vasquez. (2018). The Steps to War: An Empirical Study. Princeton University Press.

Stanford Encyclopedia of Philosophy. (2017). *Political Realism in International Relations*. Retrieved from: https://plato.stanford.edu/entries/realism-intl-relations/

Steve, R. (2018). *What is cyberwar? Everything you need to know about the frightening future of digital conflict*. Retrieved from: https://www.zdnet.com/article/cyberwar-a-guide-to-the-frightening-future-of-online-conflict/

The White House. (2011). *International Strategy for Cyberspace, "Prosperity, Security, and Openness in a Networked World"*. Retrieved from: https://www.hsdl.org/?view&did=5665

The White House. (2017). *US National Security Strategy*. Retrieved from: https://www.whitehouse.gov/wp-content/uploads/2017/12/NSS-Final-12-18-2017-0905.pdf

US Embassy in Georgia. (2017). *National Strategy of the United States*. https://ge.usembassy.gov/ka/2017-national-security-strategy-united-states-america-president-ka/

Valeriano & Maness. (2015). Cyber War versus Cyber Realities. Oxford University Press. Retrieved from: https://global.oup.com/academic/product/cyber-war-versus-cyber-realities-9780190204792?cc=ge&lang=en&#

Varonis. (2020). *110 Must-Know Cybersecurity Statistics for 2020*. Retrieved from Varonis: Retrieved from: https://www.varonis.com

Welle, D. (2019). *The myth of Hitler's role in building the autobahn.* Retrieved from: https://www.dw.com/en/the-myth-of-hitlers-role-in-building-the-autobahn/a-16144981

Zengerle & Cassella. (2015). *Millions more Americans hit by government personnel data hack.* Retrieved from: https://uk.reuters.com/article/us-cybersecurity-usa/millions-more-americans-hit-by-government-personnel-data-hack-idUSKCN0PJ2M420150709

KEY TERMS AND DEFINITIONS

Cyber-Attack: An attempt to disable computers, steal data, or use a breached computer system to launch additional attacks. Cybercriminals use different methods to launch a cyber-attack that includes malware, phishing, ransomware, man-in-the-middle attack, or other methods.

Cyberspace: A metaphor used to describe the global electronic web of people, ideas, and interactions on the Internet, which is unencumbered by the borders of the geopolitical world.

Info War-Tactics: Attacks on an adversary's telecommunications and computer networks to penetrate and degrade an enemy whose defense capabilities depend heavily on these technological systems.

Information Warfare: Attacks on an adversary's telecommunications and computer networks to degrade the technological systems vital to its defense and economic well-being.

Compilation of References

Stergiou, C., Psannis, K. E., Kimb, B.-G., & Gupta, B. (2018). Secure integration of IoT and Cloud Computing. *Future Generation Computer Systems, 78*, 964–975. doi:10.1016/j.future.2016.11.031

Sudeendra, Sahoo, Mahapatra, Swain, & Mahapatra. (2017). Security Enhancements to System on Chip Devices for IoT Perception Layer. *IEEE International Symposium on Nanoelectronic and Information Systems*.

RF. (2021). *Political map of world with country flags*. Retrieved from: https://www.123rf.com/photo_23540827_political-map-of-world-with-country-flags.html

Al Hinai & Singh. (2017). *Internet of Things: Architecture, Security challenges and Solutions*. IEEE.

Banerjee, Lee, & Choo. (2018). Block chain future for internet of things security: A position paper. *Digital Communications and Networks, 4*, 149–160.

Saarikko, T., Westergren, U. H., & Blomquist, T. (2017). The Internet of Things: Are you ready for what's coming? *Business Horizons, 60*(5), 667–676. doi:10.1016/j.bushor.2017.05.010

Mahdavinejad, Rezvan, Barekatain, Adibi, Barnaghi, & Sheth. (2018). Machine learning for internet of things data analysis: A survey. *Digital Communications and Networks, 4*, 161–175.

Vermesan, O., & Friess, P. (Eds.). (2014). Internet of things-from research and innovation to market deployment (Vol. 29). River Publishers.

Minerva, R., Biru, A., & Rotondi, D. (2015). Towards a definition of the Internet of Things (IoT). *IEEE Internet Initiative, 1*, 1–86.

Evdokimov, S., Fabian, B., Günther, O., Ivantysynova, L., & Ziekow, H. (2011). RFID and the internet of things: Technology, applications, and security challenges. Foundations and Trends® in Technology. *Information and Operations Management, 4*(2), 105–185. doi:10.1561/0200000020

Yazdanifard, R., & Al-Huda Edres, N. (2011). Security and privacy issues as a potential risk for further ecommerce development. *Proc. International Conference on Information Communication and Management, 16*.

States.com. (2021). *Map of the United States of America*. https://www.50states.com/us.htm

Barskar, R., & Deen, A. J. (2010). The algorithm analysis of e-commerce security issues for online payment transaction system in banking technology. IJCSIS, 8(1).

Moftah, A. A. A. (2012). Challenges of security, protection and trust on e-commerce: A case of online purchasing in Libya. Academic Press.

Rane, P. B., & Meshram, B. B. (2012). *Transaction security for ecommerce application*. IJECSE.

Compilation of References

Ladan, M. (2010). E-commerce technologies and challenges. Journal of Communication and Computer, 7.

Yoon, S., Park, H., & Yoo, H. S. (2015). *Security issues on smarthome in iot environment. In Computer Science and its Applications*. Springer.

A Train Education. (2021). *What Terrorism Is, and Is Not*. https://www.atrainceu.com/content/1-what-terrorism-and-not https://www.atrainceu.com/content/1-what-terrorism-and-not

Abramchayev, L. (2004). A social contract argument for the state's duty to protect from private violence. *St. John's Journal of Legal Commentary, 18*(3), 849–874.

Abrams, D. (2007). *Hamid Karzai, Modern World Leaders*. Chelsea House Books.

Adams, M. (2014, Jan. 6). World Bank Warns of Food Riots as Rising Food Prices Push World Populations toward Revolt. *OpEd News*.

Adesina, O. S. (2017). Foreign policy in an era of digital diplomacy. *Cogent Social Sciences, 3*(1), 1297175. doi:10.1080/23311886.2017.1297175

Albright, J. (2017). *Welcome to the Era of Fake News*. Columbia University Press. doi:10.17645/mac.v5i2.977

Alcazar & Raul. (2001). *Diagnosis corruption*. Academic Press.

Aleksidze, L. (2004). *Dictionary of International Law*. Tbilisi State University.

Aleksidze, L. (2012b). *UN 1984. State-sponsored terrorism*. Logo Press.

Ali, F. A. (2017). *Winning hearts and minds in ungoverned spaces*. Retrieved from https://www.undp.org/content/undp/en/home/blog/2017/winning-hearts-and-minds-in-ungoverned-spaces.html

Allianz Global Corporate & Specialty. (2021). *Cyber attacks on critical infrastructure*. Retrieved from: https://www.agcs.allianz.com/news-and-insights/expert-risk-articles/cyber-attacks-on-critical-infrastructure.html#:~:text=Cyber%2Dattacks%20against%20critical%20infrastructure%20and%20key%20manufacturing%20industries%20have,against%20ICS%20and%20corporate%20networks

Alt, J. (2015). *Political and Judicial Checks on Corruption: Evidence from American State Governments*. Projects at Harvard.

Angolagate: les principaux acteurs de l'affaire. (2007). *Le Figaro*.

Antiwar. (2012). *Israeli Policies Making Two-State Solution Impossible, Says Palestinian Leader*. Retrieved from: https://news.antiwar.com/2012/04/23/israeli-policies-making-two-state-solution-impossible-says-palestinian-leader/

Antsupov, A. S. (2008). *Conflict studies* (3rd ed.). Aspect Press.

Arda, L., & Banerjee, S. B. (2021). Governance in Areas of Limited Statehood: The NGOization of Palestine. *Business & Society, 60*(7), 1675–1707. doi:10.1177/0007650319870825

Arjona, A. (2016). Creating Rebelocracy, Aliocracy, and Disorder. In *Rebelocracy* (pp. 159–211). Cambridge University Press. doi:10.1017/9781316421925.006

Arjona, A., Kasfir, N., & Mampilly, Z. (2015). Rebel governance in civil war. In *Rebel Governance in Civil War*. Cambridge University Press. doi:10.1017/CBO9781316182468.009

Arms Control Association. (2021a). *African Nuclear-Weapons-Free Zone Treaty*. Retrieved from: https://www.armscontrol.org/treaties/african-nuclear-weapons-free-zone-treaty

Arms Control Association. (2021b). *Treaties and agreement*. Retrieved from: https://www.armscontrol.org/treaties

Arquilla, J., & Ronfeldt, D. (2000). *Swarming and the Future of Conflict*. RAND National Defense Research Institute. Retrieved from: http://www.analytictech.com/mb021/swarming%20db311.pdf

Art, R., & Jervis, R. (2005). *International Politics*. Pearson.

Awosusi, A. E. (2017). Aftermath of Boko Haram violence in the Lake Chad Basin: A neglected global health threat. *BMJ Global Health*, 2(1), e000193. doi:10.1136/bmjgh-2016-000193 PMID:28589004

Baalen, V. S. (2020). *Guns and Governance Local Elites and Rebel Governance in Côte d'Ivoire*. Retrieved from http://urn.kb.se/resolve?urn=urn:nbn:se:uu:diva-425401

Badie, B. (2000). *The imported State*. Stanford University Press. doi:10.1515/9781503618480

Bakonyi, J., & Stuvøy, K. (2005). Violence & social order beyond the state: Somalia & Angola. *Review of African Political Economy*, 32(104–105), 359–382. doi:10.1080/03056240500329379

Balanche, F. (2021, February 10). *The Assad Regime Has Failed to Restore Full Sovereignty Over Syria*. Retrieved September 11, 2021, from https://www.washingtoninstitute.org/policy-analysis/assad-regime-has-failed-restore-full-sovereignty-over-syria

Banerjee, Ferg, & Choi. (2012). *Fake news Syntactic Stylometry for Deception Detection*. Retrieved from: https://www.researchgate.net/publication/233844582_Syntactic_Stylometry_for_Deception_Detection

Barenboim, P. (2009). *Defining the rules. Issue 90*. The European Lawyer.

Baro, M., & Deubel, T. F. (2006). Persistent hunger: Perspectives on vulnerability, famine, and food security in sub-Saharan Africa. *Annual Review of Anthropology*, 35(1), 521–538. doi:10.1146/annurev.anthro.35.081705.123224

Barrett & Lentz. (2010). Food insecurity. In The International Studies Encyclopedia. Wiley Blackwell.

Bar-Siman. (2004). *From Conflict Resolution to Reconciliation*. Oxford University Press.

Bartolome, G. D. (2021, July 6). The hybrid future of diplomacy. *The Washington Diplomat*. https://washdiplomat.com/the-hybrid-future-of-future-diplomacy/

Basic Facts about the United Nations. (2005). UN Department of Public Affairs.

Basic facts about the United Nations. (2005). UN Department of Public Information.

Basic Facts about the United Nations. (2005). UN Department of Public Information.

BCW. (2016, May 31). *Twiplomacy Study 2016*. https://twiplomacy.com/blog/twiplomacy-study-2016/

BCW. (2018, December). *World Leaders on Instagram*. https://twiplomacy.com/blog/world-leaders-instagram-2018/

BCW. (2020, April 23). *World Leaders on Facebook*. https://twiplomacy.com/blog/world-leaders-on-facebook-2020/

BCW. (2020, July). *Twiplomacy Study 2020*. https://twiplomacy.com/blog/twiplomacy-study-2020/

Beck, U. (1998). *World Risk Society*. Polity Press.

Beitz. (2009). *Human Rights*. Author.

Compilation of References

Bellina, S., Darbon, D., Eriksen, S. S., & Sendig, O. J. (2009). The Legitimacy of the State in Fragile Situations. *Norad*. Retrieved from https://www.norad.no/globalassets/import-2162015-80434-am/www.norad.no-ny/filarkiv/vedlegg-til-publikasjoner/the-legitimacy-of-the-state-in-fragile-situations.pdf

Bilefsky, D. (2013). On the Crony Safari, a Tour of a City's Corruption. *The New York Times*.

Bjola, C., & Manor, I. (2020, March 31). *Digital Diplomacy in the Time of the Coronavirus Pandemic*. University of Southern California Center of Public Diplomacy. https://uscpublicdiplomacy.org/blog/digital-diplomacy-time-coronavirus-pandemic

Bjola, C., & Holmes, M. (2015). *Digital Diplomacy: Theory and Practice*. Routledge. doi:10.4324/9781315730844

Björnsdóttir, A. L. (2013). *The UN Security Council and Climate Change: Rising Seas Levels, Shrinking Resources, and the 'Green Helmets'* (Master's thesis).

Blavatskyy, P. (2020). Obesity of politicians and corruption in post-Soviet countries. *Economics of Transition and Institutional Change*.

Blomberg, S. B., Gaibulloev, K., & Sandler, T. (2011). Terrorist group survival: Ideology, tactics, and base of operations. *Public Choice*, *149*(3), 441–463. doi:10.100711127-011-9837-4

Bloomberg. (2021). *World's $281 Trillion Debt Pile Is Set to Rise Again in 2021*. https://www.bloomberg.com/news/articles/2021-02-17/global-debt-hits-all-time-high-as-pandemic-boosts-spending-need

Blum, W. (2006). *Rogue state: A guide to the world's only superpower*. Zed Books.

Bockstette, C. (2008). *Jihadist Terrorist Use of Strategic Communication Management Techniques*. George C. Marshall Center Occasional Paper Series (20).

Brent, L. (2019). *NATO's role in cyberspace*. Retrieved from NATO: https://www.nato.int

Breslawski, J. (2020). The Social Terrain of Rebel Held Territory. *The Journal of Conflict Resolution*.

Brooke, S. (2015). The Muslim Brotherhood's social outreach after the Egyptian coup. Rethinking Political Islam.

Brown. (1994). *Demography versus habitat fragmentation as determinants of genetic variation in wild populations*. Retrieved from: https://www.sciencedirect.com/science/article/abs/pii/S0006320700002032

Brück, T. (2016). *The Relationship between Food Security and Violent Conflict*. Retrieved from www.isd-center.org

Bruderlein, C. (2000). The role of non-state actors in Building Human Security: the Case of Armed Groups in Intra-State Wars. Centre for Humanitarian Dialogue.

Bull, H. (1979). *Theory of International Politics*. Cambridge University Press.

Buzan, B. (1991). People, States & Fear: The National Security Problem in International Relations. Academic Press.

Cameron, R. (2014, June 2). *Corruption redefined as tourism in Czech Republic*. BBC News.

Campbell, J., & Harwood, A. (2018, August 20). *Boko Haram's Deadly Impact*. Retrieved September 7, 2021, from https://www.cfr.org/article/boko-harams-deadly-impact

Canetti, D., Gross, M., Waismel-Manor, I., Levanon, A., & Cohen, H. (2017). How Cyberattacks Terrorize: Cortisol and Personal Insecurity Jump in the Wake of Cyberattacks. *Cyberpsychology, Behavior, and Social Networking*, *20*(2), 72–77. doi:10.1089/cyber.2016.0338

Caplan, R. (2000). *Soldiers of God: With Islamic Warriors in Afghanistan and Pakistan*. Academic Press.

Caporaso, J. A. (2000). Changes in the Westphalian order: Territory, public authority, and sovereignty. *International Studies Review*, 2(2), 1–28. doi:10.1111/1521-9488.00203

Carney, G. F. A. S. (2016). Czech Republic Has Its Answer to the Beverly Hills Star Tour. *Wall Street Journal*.

Carsten, P., & Kingimi, A. (2018). *Islamic State ally stakes out territory around Lake Chad*. Retrieved September 7, 2021, from https://www.reuters.com/article/us-nigeria-security-idUSKBN1I0063

Castells, M. (1996). *The Rise of the Network Society, The Information Age: Economy, Society, and Culture* (Vol. 1). Blackwell.

Cave, D. (2015, April 17). Does Australia do digital diplomacy? *The Interpreter*. https://www.lowyinterpreter.org/post/2015/04/17/Does-Australia-do-digital-diplomacy.aspx

CGTN. (2021). *World's Worst Conflict Zones*. Retrieved from: https://newseu.cgtn.com/news/2021-08-24/War-and-want-How-conflict-drives-poverty-12ZzEMTXETS/index.html

Cheng, D. (2017). Cyber dragon, inside China s information warfare and cyber operations. In The Changing Face of War. Publishing House "Praeger".

Chen, S., & Ravallion, M. (2010). The developing world is poorer than we thought, but no less successful in the fight against poverty. *The Quarterly Journal of Economics*, 125(4), 1577–1625. doi:10.1162/qjec.2010.125.4.1577

Chipkin, I., & Swilling, M. (2018). Shadow State: The Politics of State Capture. Wits University Press.

Chitadze, N. (2019). *The number of populations, who lived in extreme poverty has been reduced to the historical minimum*. Blog of the Center for International Studies. Retrieved from: https://centerforis.blogspot.com/2019/05/the-number-of-populations-who-lived-in.html

Chitadze, N. (2019). US-China Relations. The U.S.-China Relations and Their Possible Reflection on the World Economic Order. Journal in Humanities, 8(2).

Chitadze. (2016). *Political science*. International Black Sea University.

Chitadze. (2016). *Political Sciences*. International Black Sea University.

Chitadze, N. (2011). *Geopolitics*. Universal.

Chitadze, N. (2015). *Global Dimensions of the organized Crime and Ways of the Preventing Threats at the International Level. Connections. The Quarterly Journal Connections. Partnership for Peace Consortium of Defense Academics and Security Studies Institutes*.

Chitadze, N. (2017). *World Geography. Political, economic and demographic dimensions*. Scholar Press.

Chitadze, N. (2017). *World Geography. Political, Economic, and Demographic Dimensions*. Scholar`s Press.

Chitadze, N. (2019). *Is New Cold War Started? Possible Military Confrontation between USA and Russia on the Examples of Comparing the Military Potentials of Two Powers and Withdrawal from Intermediate-Range Nuclear Forces Treaty by Both Countries*. Journal in Humanities, 8(1).

Chitadze, N. (2020). *Several Opinions about the main reasons for the COVID 19 emergence*. Myths and Reality. The Center for International Studies of the International Black Sea University.

Chochua, D. (2015). *Caliphate reloaded: Why the isil is not unique.* Retrieved from: https://www.gfsis.org/files/library/opinion-papers/38-expert-opinion-eng.pdf

Chomsky, N. (2002). What Anthropologists Should Know about the Concept of Terrorism. *Anthropology Today, 18*(2).

Christiano, T. (2006). A Democratic Theory of Territory and Some Puzzles about Global Democracy. *Journal of Social Philosophy, 37.*

CIA. (2014). *Literacy World Factbook.* CIA.

Club of Rome. (2021). *History.* https://www.clubofrome.org/about-us/history/

CNet. (2015). *Obama asks for $14 billion to step up cybersecurity - The president urges Congress to pass legislation that would strengthen the country's hacking detection system and counterintelligence capabilities.* Retrieved from: https://www.cnet.com/news/obama-adds-14b-to-budget-for-stepped-up-cybersecurity/

Cohen, R., & Mihalka, M. (2001). *Cooperative Security: New Horizons for International Order.* European Center for Security Studies, The Marshall Center Papers, No. 3. Retrieved from: https://apps.dtic.mil/dtic/tr/fulltext/u2/a478928.pdf

Cojanu, V., & Popescu, A. I. (2007). Analysis of Failed States: Some Problems of Definition and Measurement. *Romanian Economic Journal,* (25), 113–132.

Coleman, L. D. (2014). *Diplomacy must embrace digiculture.* Diplomatic Courier.

Commonwealth Network. (2008). *Commonwealth Secretariat.* Retrieved from: https://www.commonwealthofnations.org/commonwealth/commonwealth-secretariat/

Conca, K., Thwaites, J., & Lee, G. (2016). Bully Pulpit or Bull in a China Shop? Climate change and the UN Security Council. *Annu. Meet. Acad. Counc. United Nations Syst, 1.*

Conca, K., Thwaites, J., & Lee, G. (2017). Climate change and the UN Security Council: Bully pulpit or bull in a china shop? *Global Environmental Politics, 17*(2), 1–20. doi:10.1162/GLEP_a_00398

Confessore, N. (2018, April). Cambridge Analytica and Facebook: The Scandal and the Fallout So Far. *New York Times.*

Conroy, Rubin, & Chen. (2015). *Deception detection for news: Three types of fakes.* Retrieved from: https://asistdl.onlinelibrary.wiley.com/doi/full/10.1002/pra2.2015.145052010083

Conway, D. (2010). The United Nations Security Council and climate change: Challenges and opportunities. *Climate Law, 1*(3), 375–407. doi:10.1163/CL-2010-018

Coser. (1957). Social Conflict and the Theory of Social Change. *The British Journal of Sociology, 8*(3).

Countries of the world ordered by land area. (2021). Retrieved from: https://www.listofcountriesoftheworld.com/area-land.html

Covid 19. (2020). *Some states not sharing Covid-19 info, war has to be fought together: Harsh Vardhan.* Retrieved from: https://www.youtube.com/watch?v=k2V7AAjL6L4

Coyne, C. J. (2006). Reconstructing weak and failed states. *The Journal of Social, Political, and Economic Studies, 31*(2), 143–162.

Crime Museum. (2021). *Typical Activities of Organized Crime.* Retrieved from: https://www.crimemuseum.org/crime-library/organized-crime/typical-activities-of-organized-crime/

Cronin, P. M. (2009). *Global strategic assessment 2009: America's security role in a changing world.* National Defense University Press.

Cunnigham, W., & Greene, S. (2010). Distortion as a Validation Criterion in the Identification of Suspicious Reviews. *Conference: 1st Workshop on Social Media Analytics.*

Cunningham, K. G., & Loyle, C. E. (2020). Introduction to the Special Feature on Dynamic Processes of Rebel Governance. *The Journal of Conflict Resolution, 65*(1), 002200272093515.

Cyranoski, D. (2017, February 23). Inside the Chinese lab poised to study world's most dangerous pathogens. *Nature, 542*(7642), 399–400. doi:10.1038/nature.2017.21487 PMID:28230144

Dahiru, A. (2021). *Soft-Jihad: How Terrorists Use Propaganda To Attract Local Support.* Retrieved September 14, 2021, from https://humanglemedia.com/soft-jihad-how-terrorists-use-propaganda-to-attract-local-support/

Dailytrust. (2021). *How ISWAP is wooing IDPs back to Borno villages.* Retrieved September 14, 2021, from https://dailytrust.com/how-iswap-fighters-wooed-idps-back-to-borno-villages

Dasgupta, P. (1995). *An inquiry into well-being and destitution.* Oxford University Press. doi:10.1093/0198288352.001.0001

Dasgupta, P. (1997). Nutritional status, the capacity for work, and poverty traps. *Journal of Econometrics, 77*(1), 5–37. doi:10.1016/S0304-4076(96)01804-0

Davitashvili, Z., & Elizbarashvili, N. (2012). *Global Geography.* Tbilisi State University.

de Waal, A. (1990). A Re-assessment of Entitlement Theory in the Light of the Recent Famines in Africa. *Development and Change, 21*(3), 469–490. doi:10.1111/j.1467-7660.1990.tb00384.x

Deep, A. (2015). Hybrid War: Old Concept, New Techniques. *Small War Journal.*

Defining Terrorism. One Size Fits All? (2017). *Cambridge University Press.* Retrieved from: https://www.cambridge.org/core/journals/international-and-comparative-law-quarterly/article/defining-terrorism-one-size-fits-all/0E707CD33E7F656573C777BE23C27168

Dejevsky, M. (2017, February 5). In defence of Donald Trump's Twitter diplomacy. *The Guardian.*

Der Spiegel. (2008). *Spiegel interview with Strobe Talbott.* Author.

Diakosavvas, D. (1989). On the Causes of Food Insecurity in Less Developed Countries: An Empirical Evaluation. *World Development, 17*(2), 223–235. doi:10.1016/0305-750X(89)90247-7

Dieckhoff, A., & Jaffrelot, C. (2006). *Revisiting nationalism: Theories and processes.* Palgrave Macmillan.

DiGiacomo. (2017). *Active vs Passive Cyber Attacks Explained.* Retrieved from: https://revisionlegal.com/internet-law/cyber-security/active-passive-cyber-attacks-explained/

Digwatch. (2021, August 6). *Zoom settles lawsuit over privacy issues.* https://dig.watch/updates/zoom-settles-lawsuit-over-privacy-issues

Dimant, E., & Tosato, G. (2017). Causes and Effects of Corruption: What Has Past Decade's Empirical Research Taught Us? A Survey. *Journal of Economic Surveys.*

Diplo. (2013, June 21). *Wikipedia for Diplomats.* https://www.diplomacy.edu/calendar/webinar-wikipedia-diplomats

Diplo. (n.d.). *Future of Meetings.* https://www.diplomacy.edu/future-of-meetings

Diplomat. (2017, July 5). *Ambassadors in a Digital Age.* https://diplomatmagazine.com/ambassadors-in-digital-age/

Diplomat. (2021, July 7). *Diplomacy in the Age of Zoom.* https://diplomatmagazine.com/diplomacy-in-the-age-of-zoom/

Doboš, B. (2016). Shapeshifter of Somalia: Evolution of the Political Territoriality of Al-Shabaab. *Small Wars & Insurgencies, 27*(5), 937–957. doi:10.1080/09592318.2016.1208282

Dobos, N. (2015). Networking, Corruption, and Subversion. *Journal of Business Ethics.*

Dodds, F., & Sherman, R. (2009). *Climate Change and Energy Insecurity: The Challenge for Peace, Security and Development.* Routledge. doi:10.4324/9781849774406

Dolgovaya, A. (2005). Criminology (3rd ed.). Norma.

Dosomething. (2021). *11 facts about global poverty. 10% of the world's population lives on less than $1.90 a day.* Retrieved from: https://www.dosomething.org/us/facts/11-facts-about-global-poverty

Doss, E. (2020). *Sustainable Development Goal 16.* United Nations and the Rule of Law.

Doyle, M. (1983). *Kant, Liberal Legacies, and Foreign Affairs. In Immanuel Kant.* Routledge.

Dreze, J., & Sen, A. (1989). *Hunger and Public Action.* Clarendon Press.

Drujinin. (2009). *Psychology.* Edition Piter.

Drwish, S. (2017). *The Kurdish School Curriculum in Syria: A Step Towards Self-Rule?* Retrieved September 14, 2021, from https://www.atlanticcouncil.org/blogs/syriasource/the-kurdish-school-curriculum-in-syria-a-step-towards-self-rule/

Dubai's Role in Facilitating Corruption and Global Illicit Financial Flows. (2020). Carnegie Endowment for International Peace.

Durac, V. (2015). The Role of Non-State Actors in Arab Countries after the Arab Uprisings. *Crisis and New Agenda of the Arab States*, 37–41.

Duyvesteyn, I. (2019). *Rebels and Legitimacy: Processes and Practices.* Routledge.

Eck, K. (2010). *Raising Rebels: Participation and Recruitment in Civil War.* Department of Peace and Conflict Research.

Economia UOL. (2017). *Commercial dollar: quotation and charts.* Author.

Eddiegilman. (2016). Petrobras. *Fortune.*

Edenhofer, O., Pichs-Madruga, R., Sokona, Y., Seyboth, K., Kadner, S., Zwickel, T., & Matschoss, P. (Eds.). (2011). *Renewable energy sources and climate change mitigation: Special report of the intergovernmental panel on climate change.* Cambridge University Press. doi:10.1017/CBO9781139151153

Elden, S. (2009). *Terror and territory: The spatial extent of sovereignty.* University of Minnesota Press.

Elgan, M. (2020). *Only AI can save us from a world of fakes (a world AI is also creating).* Retrieved from: https://www.idginsiderpro.com/article/3528792/only-ai-can-us-from-a-world-of-fakes-a-world-ai-is-also-creating.html

Elliott, K. A. (1997). *Corruption as an international policy problem: overview and recommendations.* Institute for International Economics.

Encyclopaedia Britannica. (n.d.). *Fourteen Points.* https://www.britannica.com/event/Fourteen-Points

Esguerra, A., Helmerich, N., & Risse, T. (2017). *Sustainability politics and limited statehood : Contesting new modes of governance*. Palgrave Macmillan.

Etzioni, A. (1988). *The Moral Dimension: Toward a New Economics*. The Free Press.

Etzioni, A. (2012). *Hot Spots: American Foreign Policy in a Post-Human-Rights World*. Transaction Publishers.

EU Staff Publishing Services. (2018). *Handbook of European Data Protection Law*. Retrieved from: https://op.europa.eu/en/publication-detail/-/publication/5b0cfa83-63f3-11e8-ab9c-01aa75ed71a1 https://rm.coe.int

FAO. (2006). *Food Aid for Food Security?* Rome: FAO.

FAO. (2019). *The State of Food Security and Nutrition in the World 2019. In Safeguarding against economic slowdowns and downturns*. FAO.

FAO. (2021). *The State of Food Security and Nutrition in the World 2020*. FAO.

Fassihi, F. (2002, Oct. 27). In Iran, grim reminders of Saddam's arsenal. *New Jersey Star-Ledger*.

FBA. (2021). *Transnational Organized Crime*. Retrieved from: https://www.fbi.gov/investigate/organized-crime

Felbab-Brown, V. (2020b). *The problem with militias in Somalia: Almost everyone wants them despite their dangers*. Retrieved March 7, 2021, from https://www.brookings.edu/research/the-problem-with-militias-in-somalia-almost-everyone-wants-them-despite-their-dangers/

Felbab-Brown, V. (2020a). Militias (and Militancy) in Nigeria's North-East: Not Going Away. In A. Day (Ed.), *Hybrid Conflict, Hybrid Peace: How Militias and Paramilitary Groups Shape Post-conflict Transitions*. United Nations University.

Ferguson, Y., & Mansbach, R. (2007). *A World of Polities Essays on Global Politics*. Routledge.

Fitzgerald, G. (2008). *Chemical Warfare and Medical Response During World War I*. Retrieved from: https://www.ncbi.nlm.nih.gov/pmc/articles/PMC2376985/

Fitz-Gibbon, A. (2000). *In the World but Not of the World: Christian Social Thinking at the End of the Twentieth Century*. Academic Press.

Fleiner, T. (2009). *Current Situation with Federalism*. Dialnet.

Florea, A. (2017). De Facto States: Survival and Disappearance (1945-2011). *International Studies Quarterly*, 61(2), 337–351. doi:10.1093/isqqw049

Fogel, R. W. (2004). *The escape from hunger and premature death, 1700-2100: Europe, America, and the Third World* (Vol. 38). Cambridge University Press. doi:10.1017/CBO9780511817649

Fominaya, C. F. (2014). *Social movements and globalization: How protests, occupations and uprisings are changing the world*. Macmillan International Higher Education. doi:10.1007/978-1-137-40216-5

Fonseca, P. (2016). *Former Odebrecht CEO sentenced in Brazil kickback case*. Reuters.

For.Ge. (2020). *Coronavirus-natural virus or biological weapon?!* Retrieved from: https://for.ge/view/182236/koronavirusi-bunebrivi-virusi-Tu-biologiuri-iaraRi.html

Forbes. (2019). *Foreign Exchange Transactions And Over-The-Counter Interest Rate Derivatives Hit Record Highs*. Retrieved from: https://www.forbes.com/sites/mayrarodriguezvalladares/2019/09/16/foreign-exchange-transactions-and-over-the-counter-interest-rate-derivatives-hit-record-highs/#3a54d6e23c34

Compilation of References

Forgues-Puccio, G.F. (2013). *Existing practices on anti-corruption, Economic and private sector professional evidence and applied knowledge services helpdesk request*. Academic Press.

Förster, T. (2015). Dialogue direct: Rebel governance and civil order in northern côte d'ivoire. In *Rebel Governance in Civil War* (pp. 203–225). Cambridge University Press. doi:10.1017/CBO9781316182468.010

Foucher, V. (2019). *Facing the Challenge of the Islamic State in West Africa Province*. Retrieved from https://www.crisisgroup.org/africa/west-africa/nigeria/273-facing-challenge-islamic-state-west-africa-province

Foucher, V. (2020). *The Jihadi Proto-State in the Lake Chad Basin*. Retrieved September 6, 2021, from https://www.ispionline.it/en/pubblicazione/jihadi-proto-state-lake-chad-basin-25441

Fragile State Index. (2017). *What Does State Fragility Mean?* Fragile States Index. Retrieved January 4, 2020, from https://fragilestatesindex.org/frequently-asked-questions/what-does-state-fragility-mean/

Frank, A. G., & Gills, B. (1996). *The World System: Five Hundred Years or Five Thousand?* Taylor & Francis.

Frantzman, S. (2021, July 22). *The struggle to achieve recognition for Kurdish North and East Syria*. Retrieved September 12, 2021, from https://www.jpost.com/middle-east/the-struggle-to-achieve-recognition-for-kurdish-north-and-east-syria-674637

Fredrick, H. (2021). *ISWAP: Islamic State West Africa Province*. Retrieved September 14, 2021, from https://www.greydynamics.com/islamic-state-west-africa-province/

Freedom House. (2020). *Freedom House in the World 2019*. https://freedomhouse.org/report/freedom-world/2019/scores

Freedom House. (2020). *Freedom in the World*. Retrieved from: https://freedomhouse.org/report/freedom-world

Friedman, T. (1999). *Lexus and the Olive Tree: Understanding globalization* (2nd ed.). Picador Paper.

Friedman, T. (2005). *The World is Flat: A Brief History of the Twenty-first Century* (1st ed.). Farrar, Straus and Giroux.

Friedman, T. (2012). *Lexus and the Olive Tree*. Picador Paper.

Fukuyama. (1989). End of the History? *The National Interest*.

Fukuyama. (1989). The end of the history? *National Interests*.

Furlan, M. (2020). Understanding Governance by Insurgent Non-State Actors: A Multi-Dimensional Typology Understanding Governance by Insurgent Non-State. *Civil Wars*, *00*(00), 1–34.

Gachechiladze, R. (2008). *Near East*. Tbilisi State University.

García, P. J. (2019). Corruption in global health: The open secret. *Lancet*, *394*(10214), 2119–2124. doi:10.1016/S0140-6736(19)32527-9 PMID:31785827

Garthoff, R. (1994). The Great Transition: American-Soviet Relations and the End of the Cold War. Brookings Institution Press.

Gartner. (2018). *Gartner Forecasts Worldwide Information Security Spending to Exceed $124 Billion in 2019*. Retrieved from Gartner Retrieved from: https://www.gartner.com

Géo, H. (2020). *Histoire des grandes épidémies et pandémies*. Retrieved from: https://www.youtube.com/watch?v=UxvR95pegZ8

Georgian Center for Security and Development. (2014). *Brief overview of the NATO Warsaw Summit Declaration (impact on Georgia).* Retrieved from: http://gcsd.org.ge/storage/files/doc/NATO-Warsaw-Summit-FINAL.pdf

Georgian Center for Security and Development. (n.d.). *Brief overview of the NATO Warsaw Summit Declaration (impact on Georgia).* Retrieved from: http://gcsd.org.ge/storage/files/doc/NATO-Warsaw-Summit-FINAL.pdf

Georgian Public Broadcaster. (2020). *At a closed session of the UN Security Council, the United States, Britain and Estonia spoke about Russia's cyber attacks against Georgia.* Retrieved from: https://1tv.ge/news/gaero-s-ushishroebis-sabchos-da-khurul-skhdomaze-ashsh-ma-britanetma-da-estonetma-saqartvelos-winaaghmdeg-rusetis-kibertavdaskhmebze-isaubres/

Giddens, A. (1995). *Politics, Sociology, and Social Theory: Encounters with Classical and Contemporary Social Thought.* Cambridge University Press.

Giordano, M. (2003). *Sharing waters: Post-Rio international water management.* Blackwell Publishing Ltd.

Glaser, B. (2011). *Grounded Theory: The Philosophy, Method, and Work.* Universal Publishers.

Gleason, S. E., & Langer, W. (2013). *The Undeclared War, 1940–1941. The World Crisis and American Foreign Policy Paperback.* Literary Licensing.

Gleick, P. (2000). A look at twenty-first-century water resources development. *Water International, 25*(1).

Global Financial Integrity. (2017). *Transnational Crime and the Developing World.* Retrieved from: https://www.gfintegrity.org/wp-content/uploads/2017/03/Transnational_Crime-final.pdf

Goetschel, L. (1998). The Foreign and Security Policy Interests of Small States in Today's Europe. In L. Goetschel (Ed.), *Small States Inside and Outside of European Union* (pp. 13–31). Swiss Peace Foundation. doi:10.1007/978-1-4757-2832-3_2

Goldstein, J., & Pavehouse, J. (n.d.). *International Relations: 2010-2011.* Longman Publishing Group.

Goldstein, J., & Pevehouse, C. (2007). *International relations. International Relations. Update* (8th ed.). Pearson Longman.

Goldstein, J., & Pevehouse, C. (2011). *International relations. International Relations: 2010-2011 Update* (9th ed.). Pearson Longman.

Goldstein, J., & Pevehouse, J. (2011). *International Relations* (9th ed.). Better World Books Marketplace Inc.

Gooding, R. (2006). *What's wrong with terrorism?* SAGE Journals.

Gozman, L. (1996). *Terrorism. Socio-Psychological Research.* Omsk State University.

Gráda, C. Ó. (2010). *Famine: a short history.* Princeton University Press. doi:10.1515/9781400829897

Graeff, P., Sattler, S., Mehlkop, G., & Sauer, C. (2014). Incentives and Inhibitors of Abusing Academic Positions: Analysing University Students' Decisions about Bribing Academic Staff. *European Sociological Review, 30*(2), 230–241. doi:10.1093/esr/jct036

Grynkewich, A. (2008). Welfare as warfare: How violent non-state groups use social services to attack the state. *Studies in Conflict and Terrorism, 31*(4), 350–370. doi:10.1080/10576100801931321

Gupta, S. (2009). Environmental law and policy: Climate change as a threat to international peace and security. *Perspectives on Global Issues, 4*(1), 7–17.

Gustafson, T., & Chabot, B. (2007). Brand Awareness. *Cornell Maple Bulletin, 105.* Available at: http://www.nnyagdev.org/maplefactsheets/CMB%20105%20Brand%20Awareness.pdf

Compilation of References

Hagen, J. J. (2016). Queering women, peace and security. *International Affairs*, 92(2), 313–332. doi:10.1111/1468-2346.12551

Hamilton, A., & Hudson. (2014). *Bribery and Identity: Evidence from Sudan*. Bath Economic Research Papers, No 21/14.

Hamilton, A. (2013). *Small is beautiful, at least in high-income democracies: the distribution of policy-making responsibility, electoral accountability, and incentives for rent extraction*. World Bank. doi:10.1596/1813-9450-6305

Hancock, Woodworth, & Porter. (2011). *Hungry like the wolf: A word-pattern analysis of the language of psychopaths*. ResearchGate.net.

Hanson, F. (2012). *Baked in and wired: eDiplomacy@State. Foreign Policy Paper Series no 30*. Brookings Institution.

Hardan, M. (2021). *Authorities in northeast Syria struggle to impose Kurdish curriculum*. Retrieved September 14, 2021, from https://www.al-monitor.com/originals/2021/02/syria-kurdish-administration-education-arrest-teachers.html

Hawkes, C. (2006). *Uneven dietary development: Linking the policies and processes of globalization with the nutritional transition, obesity and diet-related chronic diseases*. Globalization and Health. www.globalizationandhealth.com

HDI. (2021). *Human Development Index (HDI) by Country*. Retrieved from: https://worldpopulationreview.com/country-rankings/hdi-by-country

Heath, R. (2020a, April 17). For global diplomats, Zoom is not like being in the room. *Politico*. https://www.politico.eu/article/coronavirus-global-diplomacy-on-zoom/

Heath, R. (2020b, April). For global diplomats, Zoom is not like being in the room. *Politico*. https://www.politico.com/news/2020/04/16/zoom-diplomacy-coronavirus-188811

Heffes, E. (2019). Armed Groups and the Protection of Health Care. *International Law Studies, 95*.

Heidelberg Institute for International Conflict Research. (2014). *Conflict Barometer 2013*. Retrieved from: https://hiik.de/de/downloads/data/downloads_2013/ConflictBarometer2013

Heidelberg Institute for International Conflict Research. (2021). *Conflict Barometer 2020*. Retrieved from: https://hiik.de/?lang=en

Hellem, F. (2021). *ISWAP: Islamic State West Africa Province*. Retrieved September 1, 2021, from https://www.grey-dynamics.com/islamic-state-west-africa-province/

Heyneman, S. P., Anderson, K. H., & Nuraliyeva, N. (2008). The cost of corruption in higher education. *Comparative Education Review*, 52(1), 1–25. doi:10.1086/524367

Heywood, A. (1998). *Political Ideologies*. Macmillan. doi:10.1007/978-1-349-26409-4

Heywood, A. (2007). *Politics*. Palgrave Foundations.

Historyextra. (2021). *Forgotten trials: The other side of Nuremberg*. Retrieved from: https://www.historyextra.com/period/second-world-war/forgotten-trials-the-other-side-of-nuremberg/

Hocking, B. & Melissen, J. (2015). *Diplomacy in the digital age*. Netherlands Institute of International Relations.

Hoffman, B. (1988). *Inside Terrorism*. Columbia University Press.

Hofmann, C., & Schneckener, U. (2011). Engaging non-state armed actors in state-and peace-building: Options and strategies. *International Review of the Red Cross*, 93(883), 603–621. doi:10.1017/S1816383112000148

Homeland Security. (2020). *Department of Homeland Security Statement on the President's Fiscal Year 2021 Budget*. Retrieved from: https://www.dhs.gov/news/2020/02/11/department-homeland-security-statement-president-s-fiscal-year-2021-budget

Hor, M. Y. M. (2005). *Global anti-terrorism law and policy*. Cambridge University Press.

Howell, L. (1998). *International Business in the 21st Century* (Vol. 3). Praeger Perspectives.

Huang, R. (2016). The wartime origins of democratization: Civil war, rebel governance, and political regimes. In *The Wartime Origins of Democratization. Civil War, Rebel Governance, and Political Regimes*. doi:10.1017/CBO9781316711323

Huntington. (1993). The Third Wave: Democratization in the Late of Twentieth Century. *Journal of Democracy*.

Huntington, S. (1993). Clashes of Civilizations. *Foreign Affairs*, 72(3), 22. doi:10.2307/20045621

Hutt, M. (2004). *Himalayan People's War: Nepal's Maoist Rebellion*. Indiana University Press.

Hyland, J. (1995). *Democratic Theory: The Philosophical Foundations*. Manchester University Press.

ICAN. (2019). *Nuclear-armed states set record $73bn spending on nukes as pandemic spreads: New report*. Retrieved from: https://www.icanw.org/ican_releases_2019_nuclear_weapons_spending_research

ICG. (2019). *Facing the Challenge of the Islamic State in West Africa Province*. ICG.

Idler, A. (2019). *Borderland Battles Violence, Crime, and Governance at the Edges of Colombia's War*. Oxford University Press. doi:10.1093/oso/9780190849146.001.0001

IFPRI. (2009). *Climate change: impact on agriculture and costs of adaptation*. International Food Policy Research Institution

ILO. (2020). *Almost 25 million jobs could be lost worldwide as a result of COVID-19, says ILO*. Retrieved from: https.//www.ilo.org/global/about-the-ilo/newsroom/news/WCMS_738742/lang--en/index.htm

Index of Economic Freedom. (2008). The Heritage Foundation.

Info Migrants. (2021). *UNHCR: Numbers of displaced people in world passes 80 million*. Retrieved from: https://www.infomigrants.net/en/post/29030/unhcr-numbers-of-displaced-people-in-world-passes-80-million

Institute for Development of Freedom of Information (IDFI). (2016). *Kremlin Information War against Georgia: The Necessity of State Policy in Combating Propaganda, Policy Paper*. Retrieved from idfi.ge: Retrieved from: https://idfi.ge/public/upload/Meri/Russian%20Propaganda%20in%20Georgia%20-%20Policy%20Paper.PDF

Intermedia.ge. (2020). *Coronavirus: Is there a pandemic or an unfounded panic in Mass-media?* Interpressnews.

Internet World Stats. (2018). *Internet users distribution in the World*. Retrieved from: https://www.internetworldstats.com/stats.htm

Interpressnews. (2020). *Anthony Fauch - Scientific evidence confirms that the coronavirus was not created in a Chinese laboratory*. Retrieved from: https://www.interpressnews.ge/ka/article/598143-entoni-pauchi-mecnieruli-mtkicebulebebi-adasturebs-rom-koronavirusi-chinetis-laboratoriashi-ar-shekmnila

IRU. (2020). *An industry distress call*. Retrieved from: https://www.iru.org/covid19

Jackson, R. H. (1995). Quasi-States: Sovereignty, International Relations and the Third World. *Verfassung und Recht in Übersee*, 28(2), 256–258. Advance online publication. doi:10.5771/0506-7286-1995-2-256

James, T. (2011). *Think Again: Failed States – Foreign Policy*. Retrieved January 4, 2020, from https://foreignpolicy.com/2011/06/20/think-again-failed-states/

James, P., & Friedman, J. (2006). *Globalizing War and Intervention* (Vol. 3). Sage Publications.

Jana, S. K., & Karmakar, A. K. (2016). Food Security in Asia: Is There Convergence? In R. C. Das (Ed.), Handbook of Research on Global Indicators of Economic and Political Convergence. IGI Global.

Jana, S. K., & Karmakar, A. K. (2015). Globalization, Governance, and Food Security: The Case of BRICS. In R. C. Das (Ed.), *Handbook of Research on Globalization, Investment, and Growth- Implications of Confidence and Governance* (pp. 275–294). IGI Global. doi:10.4018/978-1-4666-8274-0.ch014

Jensen, N. M., & Malesky, E. J. (2017). Nonstate Actors and Compliance with International Agreements: An Empirical Analysis of the OECD Anti-Bribery Convention. *International Organization*.

Jervis, R. (2004). The Implications of Prospect Theory For Human Nature And Values. *Political Psychology*, 25(2), 163–176. doi:10.1111/j.1467-9221.2004.00367.x

Jones, S. G. (2012). The Strategic Logic of Militia. Notes and Queries.

Jönsson, C. (2016). Diplomacy, Communication and Signalling. In C. M. Constantinou, P. Kerr & P. Sharp (Eds.), The SAGE Handbook of Diplomacy (pp. 79-91). SAGE Publications Ltd.

Kajjo, S. (2020). *Prospects For Syrian Kurdish Unity Assessing Local and Regional Dynamics*. Retrieved from https://www.washingtoninstitute.org/media/3879

Kalsnes, B. (2018). *Fake news*. Retrieved from: https://oxfordre.com/communication/view/10.1093/acrefore/9780190228613.001.0001/acrefore-9780190228613-e-809

Kant. (1995). *Perpetual Peace: A Philosophical Sketch*. Retrieved from: https://www.mtholyoke.edu/acad/intrel/kant/kant1.htm

Kaplan, S. D. (2017). *The Return of the "Old Normal": How the Rise of Non-State Actors Affects Fragile States*. Retrieved July 11, 2020, from https://fragilestates.org/2017/11/06/return-old-normal-rise-non-state-actors-affects-fragile-states/

Karmakar, A. K. (2012). Achieving food and nutrition security in India. In B. Chatterjee & A. K. Karmakar (Eds.), *Food Security in India: A Comprehensive Plan for Sustainable Development*. Regal Publications.

Karmakar, A. K., & Mukhopadhyay, D. (2014). Towards a Prudent Policy for Food Security in India. *US-China. Law Review*, *11*, 221.

Kasfir, N. (2002). *Dilemmas of popular support in guerrilla war: the National Resistance Army in Uganda, 1981–1986*. Paper Presented to the Laboratory in Comparative Ethnic Processes 6, UCLA.

Kasfir, N. (2015). Rebel governance – constructing a field of inquiry: Definitions, scope, patterns, order, causes. In *Rebel Governance in Civil War* (pp. 21–46). Cambridge University Press. doi:10.1017/CBO9781316182468.002

Kassim, S. (2012, July 3). *Twitter Revolution: How the Arab Spring Was Helped by Social Media*. Mic. https://www.mic.com/articles/10642/twitter-revolution-how-the-arab-spring-was-helped-by-social-media

Kaufmann, D., & Vicente, P. (2005). *Legal Corruption*. World Bank.

Kaufmann, D., & Vicente, P. (2011). Legal Corruption (revised). *Economics and Politics*, 23.

Kegley, B. (2010-2011). *Trend and Transformation*. Academic Press.

Kegley, C., & Wittkopf, C. (2010-2011). *World Politics. Trend and Transformation.* Wadsworth, Cengage Learning

Kegley, C., & Wittkopf, E. (2011). *World Politics: Trend and Transformation* (8th ed.). Wadsworth Publishing.

Keller, K. L. (1987). Memory factors in advertising: The effect of advertising retrieval cues on brand evaluation. *The Journal of Consumer Research, 14*(3), 316–333. doi:10.1086/209116

Keller, K. L. (2001). Building customer – based brand equity. *Marketing Management, 10*(2), 14–19.

Kelsen, H. (2000). *The law of the United Nations: a critical analysis of its fundamental problems: with supplement* (Vol. 11). The Lawbook Exchange, Ltd.

Kendall, R. (2012). Climate change as a security threat to the Pacific Islands. *New Zealand Journal of Environmental Law, 16*, 83–116.

Kennedy, P. (1989). *The Rise and Fall of the Great Powers: Economic Change and Military Conflict from 1500 to 2000.* Academic Press.

Kenneth, K. (2009). *Cyber Security and Global Information Assurance: Threat Analysis and Response Solutions.* U.S. Air Force Academy.

Keohane, R., & Nye, J. (1977). *Power and Interdependence: World Politics in Transition.* Little, Brown.

Kereselidze, D. (2011). *World Geography.* Tbilisi State University.

Khalaf, R. (2016). *Governing Rojava: Layers of Legitimacy in Syria.* Retrieved from https://issat.dcaf.ch/Learn/Resource-Library2/Policy-and-Research-Papers/Governing-Rojava-Layers-of-Legitimacy-in-Syria

Khalaf, R. (2015) Governance Without Government in Syria: Civil Society and State Building During Conflict. *Syria Studies, 7*(3), 37–72.

Khan, A. (2006). A Theory of International Terrorism. *Connecticut Law Review.*

Klitgaard, R. (1998). *Controlling Corruption.* University of California Press.

Klitgaard, R. E. (2000). *Corrupt cities: A practical guide to cure and prevention.* ICS Press.

Kofman, M. (2016). *Russian Hybrid Warfare and other dark arts.* Retrieved from: https://warontherocks.com/2016/03/russian-hybrid-warfare-and-other-dark-arts/

Kotler, P. (2006). *Marketing Management.* Elsevier Inc.

Kramer, A., & Specia, M. (2019). What Is the I.N.F. Treaty and Why Does It Matter? *The New York Times.*

Krasner, S. D. C. P. (2005). *Addressing State Failure.* Retrieved January 4, 2020, from https://www.foreignaffairs.com/articles/2005-07-01/addressing-state-failure

Krasner. (2009). Power, the State, and Sovereignty. In *Essays on International Relations.* Routledge.

Krause, K., & Milliken, J. (2010). Introduction: The Challange of Non-State Armed Groups. In *Contemporary Security Policy* (p. 202). Routledge.

Kreisberg, A. A. (2019). Social media data archives in an API-driven world. *Arch Sci, 20,* 105–123. doi:10.1007/s10502-019-09325-9

Kruse. (2015). *One Nation Under God: How Corporate America Invented Christian America.* Academic Press.

Compilation of References

Kurbalija, J. (2016, May 17). *diplomacy – Diplomacy – DIPLOMACY*. Diplo. https://www.diplomacy.edu/blog/diplomacy-%25E2%2580%2593-diplomacy-%25E2%2580%2593-diplomacy

Kurbalija, J. (2012). *Diplomacy in a Globalizing World Theories and Practicies*. Oxford University Press.

Lambsdorff, J. (2006). *The New Institutional Economics of Corruption*. Routledge.

Lambsdorff, J. G. (2006). *Corruption Perceptions Index 2006*. Transparency International.

Laqueur, W. (2007). *History of Terrorism*. Transaction Publishers, Emerald Group Publishing Limited.

Lasswell, H. D. (1984). *Manuscripts and Archives*. Yale University Library.

Laswell, H. (1950). *World Politics and Personal Insecurity*. The Free Press.

Lebedeva. (2007). *World Politics*. Aspect Press.

Lebedeva. (2007). *World Politics*. Aspects Press.

Lebedeva, M. (2007). *World Politics*. Aspect Press.

Ledwidge, F. (2017). *Rebel Law: Insurgents, Courts and Justice in Modern Conflict*. C Hurst & Co Publishers Ltd.

Legvold, R. (2009). Corruption, the Criminalized State, and Post-Soviet Transitions. In R. I. Rotberg (Ed.), *Corruption, global security, and world order*. Brookings Institution.

Lenta.Ru. (2020). *«Газпром» приготовился к обрушению спроса на газ*. https://lenta.ru/news/2020/04/30/gas_ne_nuzhen/?fbclid=IwAR3m2IXN31frc5Zm5ZVeoObtnHjyJTX2TWJ3fk5ko-sLtf8MdGPC6Z1710o

Levi-Faur, D. (2012). *From "Big Government" to "Big Governance"?* Online Pub. doi:10.1093/oxfordhb/9780199560530.013.0001

Lewis University. (2019). The history of cyber warfare - infographic. *The New Face of War: Attacks in Cyberspace*. Retrieved from: https://online.lewisu.edu/mscs/resources/the-history-of-cyber-warfare

Liberty, R. (2017). *State Debt in the World and Georgia*. Retrieved from: https://www.radiotavisupleba.ge/a/sakhelmtsifovalebi/28587576.html

Lillywhite, L. (2015). *Non-State Armed Groups, Health and Healthcare*. Retrieved from https://www.chathamhouse.org/sites/default/files/events/special/NSAGs

Lindsay, J. (2014). *The Impact of China on Cybersecurity, Fiction and Friction*. Retrieved from: https://www.belfercenter.org/sites/default/files/legacy/files/IS3903_pp007-047.pdf

Lin, T. C. W. (2016). Financial Weapons of War. *Minnesota Law Review*.

Locatelli, G., Mariani, G., Sainati, T., & Greco, M. (2017). Corruption in public projects and megaprojects: There is an elephant in the room! *International Journal of Project Management*, *35*(3), 252–268. doi:10.1016/j.ijproman.2016.09.010

Lord Kristin, M., & Sharp, T. (2011). *America's Cyber Future: Security and Prosperity in the Information Age*. Center for a New American Security. Retrieved from: https://s3.us-east-1.amazonaws.com/files.cnas.org/documents/CNAS_Cyber_Volume-I_0.pdf?mtime=20160906081238&focal=none

Loyle, C. E. (2020). Rebel Justice during Armed Conflict. *The Journal of Conflict Resolution*, *65*(1), 108–134. doi:10.1177/0022002720939299

Maksakovski, V. (2009). *World Social and Economic Geography*. Aspect Press.

Maksakovsky, V. (2005). *World Social and Economic Geography*. Academic Press.

Maksakovsky, V. (2009). World Social and Economic Geography. Academic Press.

Malejacq, R. (2016). Warlords, Intervention, and State Consolidation: A Typology of Political Orders in Weak and Failed States. *Security Studies*, *25*(1), 85–110. doi:10.1080/09636412.2016.1134191

Malejacq, R. (2017). From Rebel to Quasi-State: Governance, Diplomacy and Legitimacy in the Midst of Afghanistan's Wars (1979–2001). *Small Wars & Insurgencies*, *28*(4–5), 867–886. doi:10.1080/09592318.2017.1322332

Malthaner, S., & Waldmann, P. (2014). The radical milieu: Conceptualizing the supportive social environment of terrorist groups. *Studies in Conflict and Terrorism*, *37*(12), 979–998. doi:10.1080/1057610X.2014.962441

Malthus. (1798). *An Essay on the Principle of Population*. Retrieved from: http://www.esp.org/books/malthus/population/malthus.pdf

Mampilly, Z. C. (2011). *Rebel Rulers: Insurgent Governance and Civilian Life during War* (1st ed.). Cornell University Press.

Mampilly, Z. C. (2017). Rebel Rulers. In *Rebel Rulers*. Cornell University Press.

Mampilly, Z., & Stewart, M. A. (2021). A Typology of Rebel Political Institutional Arrangements. *The Journal of Conflict Resolution*, *65*(1), 15–45. doi:10.1177/0022002720935642

Manchin, G., & Perkins, T. (2021). *Factsheet: Violent Islamist Groups in Northern Nigeria*. Academic Press.

Manor, I, (2016, November). What is Digital Diplomacy, and how is it Practiced around the World? A brief introduction. *Diplomatist Magazine*.

Manor, I. (2014, June 25). On Virtual Embassies in the Age of Digital Diplomacy. *Digdipblog*. https://digdipblog.com/2014/06/25/on-virtual-embassies-in-the-age-of-digital-diplomacy/

Manor, I. (2016, February). Are We There Yet? Have MFAs Realized the Potential of Digital Diplomacy? *Brill Diplomacy and Foreign Policy*.

Manor, I. (2017, August 8). The Digitalization of Diplomacy: Toward Clarification of a Fractured Terminology. Working Paper. *Digdipblog*. https://digdipblog.com/2017/08/08/the-digitalization-of-diplomacy-toward-clarification-of-a-fractured-terminology/

Manor, I. (2017, March 23). How Embassies Managed the London Terror Attack. *Digdipblog*. https://digdipblog.com/2017/03/23/howembassies-managed-the-london-terrorattack/

Manor, I. (2018, February 20). The Evolution of WhatsApp as a Diplomatic Tool. *Digdipblog*. https://digdipblog.com/2018/02/20/the-evolution-of-whatsapp-as-a-diplomatic-tool/

Manor, I., & Segev, E. (2015). America's selfie: How the US portrays itself on its social media accounts. In C. Bjola & M. Holmes (Eds.), Digital Diplomacy: Theory and Practice (pp. 89-108). Routledge.

Mansfield, D. (2018). Turning deserts into flowers: Settlement and poppy cultivation in southwest Afghanistan. *Third World Quarterly*, *39*(2), 331–349. doi:10.1080/01436597.2017.1396535

Mansfield, H. (2001). *Those Hell-Hounds Called Terrorists*. The Claremont Institute.

Manufacturing. (2015). *Report: Russian 'Internet Trolls' Behind Louisiana Chemical Explosion Hoax*. Retrieved from: https://www.manufacturing.net/operations/news/13099148/report-russian-internet-trolls-behind-louisiana-chemical-explosion-hoax

Compilation of References

Market Watch. (2020). *Crude Oil WTI (NYM $/bbl) Front Month*. Retrieved from: https://www.marketwatch.com/investing/future/crude%20oil%20-%20electronic

Material on Grand Corruption. (2014). United Nations Office on Drugs and Crime.

Mccartan, B., & Jolliffe, K. (2016). Ethnic Armed Actors and Justice Provision in Myanmar. Academic Press.

McCauley, C. (2001). *Group Identification under Conditions of Threat: College Students' Attachment to Country, Family, Ethnicity, Religion, and University Before and After September 11, 2001*. Wiley Online Library.

McGlinchey, S. (2017). *International Relations*. E-International Relations. Ministry of Foreign Affairs and Diaspora of the Republic of Kosovo. Digital Diplomacy. http://www.mfa-ks.net/en/politika/486/diplomacia-digjitale/486

Menkhaus, K. (2006). Governance without government in Somalia: Spoilers, state building, and the politics of coping. *International Security*, *31*(3), 74–106. doi:10.1162/isec.2007.31.3.74

Merle, J.-C. (Ed.). (2013). Global Challenges to Liberal Democracy. Spheres of Global Justice.

Miller, G. A., Galanter, E., & Pribram, K. (1986). *Plans and the Structure of Behavior*. Adams Bannister Cox Pubs.

Ministry of Foreign Affairs of Georgia. (2018). *National Security Concept of Georgia*. Retrieved from: https://mod.gov.ge/uploads/2018/pdf/NSC-GEO.pdf

Ministry of Justice. (2017). *Georgia ranks 8th in the Cyber Security Index*. Retrieved from: https://imedinews.ge/ge/politika/16724/kiberusaprtkhoebis-indeqsshi-saqartvelo-me8-adgilzea

Mishler v. State Bd. of Med. Examiners. 2021. Justia Law.

Mkurnalidze, K. (2000). *Political Science*. Georgian Technical University.

Modebadze. (2016). *Two Wars in Chechnya*. Universal Press.

Modelski, G. (2000). *World Cities*. FAROS.

Moghaddam, F. M. (2006). *From the terrorists' point of view: What they experience and why they come to destroy*. Praeger Security International.

Momodu, J. A. (2020). Non-State Security Groups and Their Role in Countering Boko Haram Terrorism in North East Region of Nigeria. *African Review (Dar Es Salaam, Tanzania)*, *47*(1), 67–96. doi:10.1163/1821889X-12340009

Mo, P. H. (2001). Corruption and Economic Growth. *Journal of Comparative Economics*, *29*(1), 66–79. doi:10.1006/jcec.2000.1703

Morgan, S. (Ed.). (2017). *Cybersecurity Ventures*. Cybercrime Report. Retrieved from: https://cybersecurityventures.com/2015-wp/wp-content/uploads/2017/10/2017-Cybercrime-Report.pdf

Morgan, G. A. (1988). *Human Resource Management*. Academic Press.

Morris, S. D. (1991). *Corruption and Politics in Contemporary Mexico*. University of Alabama Press.

Mukherjee, A. (2012). *Food Security in Asia*. Sage Publications Pvt.Ltd.

Nairn, T., & James, P. (2005). *Global Matrix: Nationalism, Globalism and State-Terrorism*. Pluto Press.

National Institute of Justice. (2011). *The Evolution of Transnational Organized Crime*. Retrieved from: https://nij.ojp.gov/topics/articles/evolution-transnational-organized-crime

NATO Handbook, . (2006). *Berlin Plus agreement*. NATO Public Diplomacy Division.

NATO Handbook, . (2007). *NATO Public Diplomacy Division*.

NATO. (2011). *NATO's new strategic concept: A comprehensive assessment*. DIIS. Retrieved from: https://www.econstor.eu/bitstream/10419/59845/1/656748095.pdf

NATO. (2018). *Brussels Summit Declaration - Issued by the Heads of State and Government participating in the meeting of the North Atlantic Council in Brussels 11-12 July 2018*. Retrieved from: https://www.nato.int/cps/en/natohq/official_texts_156624.htm

Nay, O. (2013). Fragile and failed states: Critical perspectives on conceptual hybrids. *International Political Science Review*, *34*(3), 326–341. doi:10.1177/0192512113480054

Neidze, V. (2004). World Social and Economic Geography. Publishing House "Lega".

Netjes, R., & Van Veen, E. (2021). *Henchman, Rebel, Democrat, Terrorist The YPG/ PYD during the Syrian conflict CRU Report*. Retrieved from www.clingendael.org/cru

Ngari, A., & Olojo, A. (2020). Besieged but not relenting Ensuring fair trials for Nigeria's terrorism suspects. West Africa Report.

Nicu & Secrieru. (2018). *Hacks, leaks and disruptions Russian cyber strategies*. European Union Institute for Security Studies Paris, Chaillot Paper N° 148. Retrieved from: https://www.iss.europa.eu/sites/default/files/EUISSFiles/CP_148.pdf

Norouzi, N., & Movahedian, H. (2021). Right to Education in Mother Language: In the Light of Judicial and Legal Structures. In Handbook of Research on Novel Practices and Current Successes in Achieving the Sustainable Development Goals (pp. 223-241). IGI Global.

Norouzi, N. (2021). Post-COVID-19 and globalization of oil and natural gas trade: Challenges, opportunities, lessons, regulations, and strategies. *International Journal of Energy Research*, *45*(10), 14338–14356. doi:10.1002/er.6762 PMID:34219899

Norouzi, N., & Ataei, E. (2021). Covid-19 Crisis and Environmental law: Opportunities and challenges. *Hasanuddin Law Review*, *7*(1), 46–60. doi:10.20956/halrev.v7i1.2772

Norouzi, N., Khanmohammadi, H. U., & Ataei, E. (2021). The Law in the Face of the COVID-19 Pandemic: Early Lessons from Uruguay. *Hasanuddin Law Review*, *7*(2), 75–88. doi:10.20956/halrev.v7i2.2827

North Atlantic Treaty Organization. (2019). *Collective defence - Article 5*. Retrieved from: https://www.nato.int/cps/en/natohq/topics_110496.htm

Number of Federal Countries in the World. (2021). Retrieved from: https://www.answers.com/Q/List_of_federal_countries_in_the_world

Nye, J. (2007). *Public Diplomacy and Soft Power*. JSTOR Collection.

Occupation zones in Kosovo. (2000). Retrieved from: https://mapsontheweb.zoom-maps.com/post/114574543300/kfor-occupation-zones-via-reddit

OECD Convention on Combating Bribery of Foreign Public Officials in International Bearer of Transactions. (2012). oecd.org.

OECD. (2014). *OECD tax database for 2013*. Retrieved from: https://www.oecd.org/ctp/tax-policy/tax-database/

OECD. (2015). *Country monitoring of the OECD Anti-Bribery Convention*. oecd.org.

Compilation of References

OECD. (2018). *Uranium 2020. Resources, Production, and Demand*. Retrieved from: https://www.oecd-nea.org/upload/docs/application/pdf/2020-12/7555_uranium_-_resources_production_and_demand_2020__web.pdf

Office of the United States Trade Representative. (2019). *The People's Republic of China*. https://ustr.gov/countries-regions/china-mongolia-taiwan/peoples-republic-china

Oktav, Ö. Z., Parlar Dal, E., & Kurşun, A. M. (2017). *Violent non-state actors and the Syrian Civil War: The ISIS and YPG cases*. Springer International Publishing.

Olken, B. A., & Pande, R. (2012). Corruption in Developing Countries. *Annual Review of Economics*, *4*(1), 479–509. doi:10.1146/annurev-economics-080511-110917

Olshansky, D. V. (2002). *Terrorism Psychology*. Piter.

Onuoha, F. C., Nwangwu, C., & Ugwueze, M. I. (2020). Counterinsurgency operations of the Nigerian military and Boko Haram insurgency: Expounding the viscid manacle. *Security Journal*, *33*(3), 401–426. doi:10.105741284-020-00234-6

OPCV. (2021). *Chemical Weapon Convention*. Retrieved from: https://www.opcw.org/chemical-weapons-convention

Orwell, G. (1949). *Nineteen Eighty-Four*. Secker & Warburg.

Osipian, A. (2013). Recruitment and Admissions: Fostering Transparency on the Path to Higher Education. In *Transparency International: Global Corruption Report: Education*. Routledge.

Oyster Bay Conferences. (1966). *Definitions of Organized Crime*. Retrieved from: http://www.organized-crime.de/OCDEF1.htm

Özçelik, B. (2019). Explaining the Kurdish Democratic Union Party's Self-Governance Practices in Northern Syria, 2012–18. *Government and Opposition*, *1*(21).

Pachauri, R. K., Allen, M. R., Barros, V. R., Broome, J., Cramer, W., Christ, R., & van Ypserle, J. P. (2014). *Climate change 2014: synthesis report. Contribution of Working Groups I, II and III to the fifth assessment report of the Intergovernmental Panel on Climate Change*. IPCC.

Pahis, S. (2009). Corruption in Our Courts: What It Looks Like and Where It Is Hidden. *The Yale Law Journal*.

Palmer, R. (2014). The French Directory Between Extremes. In *The Age of the Democratic Revolution: A Political History of Europe and America, 1760–1800*. Princeton University Press.

Palutikof, J., Van der Linden, P., & Hanson, C. (Eds.). (n.d.). Climate change 2007--impacts, adaptation and vulnerability: Working group II contribution to the fourth assessment report of the IPCC (Vol. 4). Cambridge University Press.

Parry, M. (2009). *Climate change and risk of hunger: the scale of the challenge and required responses*. World Food Programme.

Peak, O. (2011). *World Oil Reserves*. http://www.endofcrudeoil.com/2011/04/world-oil-reserves.htmlhttp://www.endofcrudeoil.com/2011/04/world-oil-reserves.html

Pearson, E., & Zenn, J. (2021). *Boko Haram, the Islamic State, and the Surge in Female Abductions in Southeastern Niger*. Retrieved from https://icct.nl/app/uploads/2021/02/Pearson-And-Zenn-research-paper.pdf

Péclard, D., & Mechoulan, D. (2015). *Rebel Governance and the Politics of Civil War*. Retrieved from www.sagw.ch

Percy, L. (2008). *Strategic Integrated Marketing Communication*. Elsevier Inc. doi:10.4324/9780080878294

Permyakova, L. (2012, September 28). *Digital diplomacy: areas of work, risks and tools*. Academic Press.

Phalen, W. (2015). *How the telegraph changed the world.* McFarland Company. https://russiancouncil.ru/en/analytics-and-comments/analytics/digital-diplomacy-areas-of-work-risks-and-tools/

Piazza, J. A., & Piazza, S. (2017). Crime Pays: Terrorist Group Engagement in Crime and Survival. *Terrorism and Political Violence, 32*(4), 701–723. doi:10.1080/09546553.2017.1397515

Pogge, T. (2015). *Severe Poverty as a Violation of Negative Duties.* thomaspogge.com.

Political Map of Africa. (2013). Retrieved from: https://www.pinterest.com/pin/96757091973420425/

Pourmalek, P. (2021). *The Rebel Iron Fist: Reframing Violence as a Condition for Rebel Governance.* doi:10.14288/1.0398461

Pressreader. (2019). *Public libraries have an important role in sustaining democracy.* Retrieved from: https://blog.pressreader.com/public-libraries-have-an-important-role-in-sustaining-democracy

Primoratz, I. (2007). *Terrorism.* Stanford Encyclopedia of Philosophy.

Pruitt, G., & Rubin, Z. (1986). *Summary of "Social Conflict: Escalation, Stalemate and Settlement".* Retrieved from https://www.beyondintractability.org/bksum/pruitt-social

Public Welfare. (2021). *Ways to solve the food problem. The geography of hunger.* UN Food Program. Retrieved from: https://en.public-welfare.com/3906676-ways-to-solve-the-food-problem-the-geography-of-hunger-un-food-program

Purkitt, H. (1984). *Dealing with Terrorism.* Conflict in World Society.

Quartz. (2020). *A conspiracy theory linking the US army to the coronavirus now has an official Chinese endorsement.* Retrieved from: https://qz.com/1817736/china-fuels-coronavirus-conspiracy-theory-blaming-us-army/

Raeymaekers, T. (2010). Protection For Sale? War and the transformation of regulation on the congo-ugandan border. *Development and Change, 41*(4), 563–587. doi:10.1111/j.1467-7660.2010.01655.x

Ranker. (2021). *Around the World.* Retrieved from: http://m.ranker.com/list/countries-ruled-by-monarchy/reference

Rapid 7. (2020). *What is a malware attack?* Retrieved from: https://www.rapid7.com/fundamentals/malware-attacks/

Rashica, V. (2018). *The Benefits and Risks of Digital Diplomacy.* SEEU Review. doi:10.2478eeur-2018-0008

Reliefweb. (2013). *World: Food Security Risk Index 2013.* Retrieved from: https://reliefweb.int/map/world/world-food-security-risk-index-2013

Reuters. (2014). *France to invest 1 billion euros to update cyber defences.* Retrieved from: https://www.reuters.com/article/france-cyberdefence-idUSL5N0LC21G20140207

Reuters. (2020). *Coronavirus very likely of animal origin, no sign of lab manipulation: WHO.* https://www.reuters.com/article/us-health-coronavirus-who-virus/coronavirus-very-likely-of-animal-origin-no-sign-of-lab-manipulation-who-idUSKCN223180

Reuters. (2020, April 2). *Zoom's daily participants jumped from 10 million to over 200 million in 3 months.* https://venturebeat.com/2020/04/02/zooms-daily-active-users-jumped-from-10-million-to-over-200-million-in-3-months/

RIAC. (2016). *NATO's Cyber Defense Evolution - NATO's New Digital Wall.* Retrieved from: https://www.nato.int/docu/rdr-gde-prg/rdr-gde-prg-eng.pdf

Riazi, T. (2020). *Know The CCDCOE: Interview with Director Col. Jaak Tarie* (J. Tarien, Interviewer). Retrieved from http://natoassociation.ca

Compilation of References

Rice, S. E. (2003). The new national security strategy: focus on failed states. *The Brookings Institution, 2*(116), 1–8.

Rich, P. B. (1999). Warlords, state fragmentation and the dilemma of humanitarian intervention. *Small Wars & Insurgencies, 10*(1), 78–96. doi:10.1080/09592319908423230

Risse, T. (2011). Governance in Areas of Limited Statehood: Introduction and Overview. In Governance without a State? Policies and Politics in Areas of Limited Statehood. Academic Press.

Risse, T. (2015). Limited Statehood: A Critical Perspective. In The Oxford Handbook of Transformations of the State. Oxford University Press.

Risse, T., & Stollenwerk, E. (2018). Legitimacy in Areas of Limited Statehood. *Annual Review of Political Science, 21*(1), 403–418. doi:10.1146/annurev-polisci-041916-023610

Robert, G. T. (1998). *State Failure Project Report.pdf*. Retrieved from http://mstohl.faculty.comm.ucsb.edu/failed_states/1998/papers/gurr.html

Robertson, R. (1983). Interpreting Globality. In *World Realities and International Studies Today*. Pennsylvania Council on International Education.

Robin, M. M. (2004). *Our daily poison: from pesticides to packaging, how chemicals have contaminated the food chain and are making us sick*. New Press.

Rondeli, A. (2003). *International Relations*. Edition House "Neckeri".

Rondeli. (2003). *International Relations*. Neckeri.

Rösch. (2011). *Hans J. Morgenthau, the "marginal man" in International Relations*. A "Weltanschauungsanalyse", Newcastle University School of Geography, Politics, and Sociology. Retrieved from: https://core.ac.uk/download/pdf/40019366.pdf

Rosegrant, M. W. (2015). *Food security*. Sage Reference.

Rosenau, J. (2007). *People Count! Networked Individuals in Global Politics (International Studies Intensives)*. Academic Press.

Ross, M. L. (2004). What Do We Know about Natural Resources and Civil War? *Sage (Atlanta, Ga.), 41*(3), 337–356. doi:10.1177/0022343304043773

Rostow, W. (1991). *The Stages of Economic Growth: A Non-Communist Manifesto* (3rd ed.). Cambridge University Press. doi:10.1017/CBO9780511625824

Rotberg, R. I. (2003). *State Failure and State Weakness in a Time of Terror*. World Peace Foundatiton Brookings Institution Press.

Rotberg, R. I. (2004). Failed States, Collapsed States, Weak States: Causes and Indicators. In *State Failure and State Weakness In a Time of Terror*. Princeton University Press.

Rourke, J., & Boyer, M. (2000). *International Politics on the World Stage, Brief* (8th ed.). Dushkin/McGraw-Hill.

Ruggie, J. G. (1993). International Organization Foundation Territoriality and Beyond: Problematizing Modernity in International Relations. *International Organization, 47*(1), 139–174. doi:10.1017/S0020818300004732

Russian Federation Presidential Edict. (2000). *Information security doctrine of the Russian Federation*. Retrieved from: https://www.itu.int/en/ITU-D/Cybersecurity/Documents/National_Strategies_Repository/Russia_2000.pdf

Russian Federation Presidential Edict. (2015). *Russian national Security Strategy, 2015*. Retrieved from: https://www.ieee.es/Galerias/fichero/OtrasPublicaciones/Internacional/2016/Russian-National-Security-Strategy-31Dec2015.pdf

Saeed, S. (2021, August 21). Taliban 2.0: Older, media-savvy and still duplicitous. *Politico*. https://www.politico.eu/article/taliban-afghanistan-rebrand-social-media-twitter-international-recognition/?utm_source=POLITICO.EU&utm_campaign=5637600182-EMAIL_CAMPAIGN_2021_08_20_04_59&utm_medium=email&utm_term=0_10959ed eb5-5637600182-190784736

Sageman, M. (2004). Understanding Terror Networks. *International Journal of Emergency Mental Health*, 7. PMID:15869076

SalanovaR. (2012, December 1). *Social media and political change: the case of the 2011 revolutions in Tunisia and Egypt*. International Catalan Institute for Peace. Working Paper No. 2012/7. doi:10.2139/ssrn.2206293

Sany, J. (2010). Education and Conflict in Cote d'Ivoire. Special Report.

Saul, B. (2009). Climate Change, Conflict and Security: International Law Challenges. *NZ Armed FL Rev.*, *9*, 1.

Schachter, O. (1951). *The Law of the United Nations*. Academic Press.

Schmid, J. (2019). *The Hybrid Face of Warfare in the 21st Century*. Retrieved from: https://www.maanpuolustus-lehti.fi/the-hybrid-face-of-warfare-in-the-21st-century/

Schmid, A. (2011). *Routledge Handbook of Terrorism Research*. Routledge. doi:10.4324/9780203828731

Schneckener, U. (2006). *Fragile Statehood, Armed Non-State Actors and Security Governance*. LIT.

Schwab, R. (2018). Insurgent courts in civil wars: The three pathways of (trans)formation in today's Syria (2012-2017). *Small Wars & Insurgencies*, *29*(4), 801 826. doi:10.1080/09592318.2018.1497290

Secretariat of the Antarctic Treaty. (1959). Retrieved from: https://www.ats.aq/e/antarctictreaty.html#:~:text=The%20 Antarctic-,Treaty,to%20by%20many%20other%20nations

Seeberg, P. (2016). Analysing security subcomplexes in a changing Middle East—The role of non-Arab State actors and non-state actors. *Palgrave Communications*, *2*(1), 2. doi:10.1057/palcomms.2016.87

Seib, P. (2012). Real-time diplomacy, politics and power in the social media era. Academic Press.

Sen, A. (1981). *Poverty and Famines Oxford*. Clarendon Press.

Senese & Vasquez. (2018). The Steps to War: An Empirical Study. Princeton University Press.

Senior, I. (2006). *Corruption – The World's Big C*. Institute of Economic Affairs.

Sharma, S. K. (2016). *The WTO and Food Security: Implications for developing countries*. Springer. doi:10.1007/978-981-10-2179-4

Shiva, V. (2017). *Who really feeds the world*. New Delhi: Women Unlimited.

Sicurelli, D. (2016). *The European Union's Africa policies: norms, interests and impact*. Routledge. doi:10.4324/9781315239828

Šimunjak, M., & Caliandro, A. (2019, January). Twiplomacy in the age of Donald Trump: Is the diplomatic code changing? *The Information Society*, *35*(1), 13–25. doi:10.1080/01972243.2018.1542646

Sindico, F. (2007). Climate change: A security (council) issue. *Carbon & Climate L. Rev.*, 29.

Compilation of References

SIPRI. (2016). *Conflict, peace and security.* https://www.sipri.org/research/conflict-peace-and-security

SIPRI. (2019a). *Trends in World Military Expenditure, 2019.* Retrieved from: https://www.sipri.org/publications/2020/sipri-fact-sheets/trends-world-military-expenditure-2019

SIPRI. (2019b). *World Nuclear Forces.* Retrieved from: https://www.sipri.org/yearbook/2019/06#:~:text=At%20the%20start%20of%202019,were%20deployed%20with%20operational%20forces

Soll. (2016). Fake News. *Politico Magazine.* Retrieved from: https://www.politico.com/magazine/story/2016/12/fake-news-history-long-violent-214535/

Sputnik. (2020). *The special service called on the residents of the republic not to give in to the proposals of the Georgian side to participate in any medical research.* Retrieved from: https://sputnik-ossetia.ru/South_Ossetia/20200428/10494848/KGB-zayavil-ob-ugroze-prednamerennogo-zarazheniya-grazhdan-Yuzhnoy-Osetii-COVID-19-iz-Gruzii.html

Stanford Encyclopedia of Philosophy. (2017). *Political Realism in International Relations.* Retrieved from: https://plato.stanford.edu/entries/realism-intl-relations/

Stanford News. (2020). *For Renaissance Italians, combating the black plague was as much about politics as it was science, according to a Stanford scholar.* Retrieved from: https://news.stanford.edu/2020/05/12/combating-black-plague-just-much-politics-science/

Stanislawski, B. H. (2008). Para-States, Quasi-States, and Black Spots: Perhaps Not States, But Not "Ungoverned Territories," Either. *International Studies Review, 10*(2), 366–396. doi:10.1111/j.1468-2486.2008.00795.x

Stephan, C. (2012). *Industrial Health, Safety and Environmental Management* (3rd ed.). MV Wissenschaft.

Stephan, M. J., & Chenoweth, E. (2008). Why civil resistance works: The strategic logic of nonviolent conflict. *International Security, 33*(1), 7–44. doi:10.1162/isec.2008.33.1.7

Steve, R. (2018). *What is cyberwar? Everything you need to know about the frightening future of digital conflict.* Retrieved from: https://www.zdnet.com/article/cyberwar-a-guide-to-the-frightening-future-of-online-conflict/

Stewart, M. A. (2018). Civil War as State-Making: Strategic Governance in Civil War. *International Organization, 72*(1), 205–226. doi:10.1017/S0020818317000418

Stewart, M. A. (2020). Rebel governance: Military boon or military bust? (Isard Award Article). *Conflict Management and Peace Science, 37*(1), 16–38. doi:10.1177/0738894219881422

Stewart, P. (2007). 'Failed' States and Global Security: Empirical Questions and Policy Dilemmas. *International Studies Review.*

Stockholm International Peace Research Institute. (2007). *SIPRI Yearbook 2007: Armaments, Disarmament, and International Security.* Oxford University Press.

Stohl, M. (1984). *The Superpowers and International Terror.* Paper presented at the Annual Meeting of the International Studies Association, Atlanta, GA.

Stohl, M. (1988). *National Interests and State Terrorism, The Politics of Terrorism.* Marcel Dekker.

Strange, S. (1991). *Big Business and the State1.* Department of Political Science at the European University Institute in Florence. doi:10.1177/03058298910200021501

Sullivan, A., & Sheffrin, M. S. (2003). *Economics: Principles in Action.* Pearson Prentice Hall.

Tacconi, L., & Williams, D. A. (2020). Corruption and Anti-Corruption in Environmental and Resource Management. *Annual Review of Environment and Resources, 45*(1), 305–329. doi:10.1146/annurev-environ-012320-083949

TASS. (2020). *Chinese Foreign Ministry pointed to the danger of US laboratories in the territory of the former USSR*. Retrieved from: https://tass.ru/mezhdunarodnaya-panorama/8361667

Tayebi, S., & Zarabi, M. (2018). Environmental Diplomacy and Climate Change; Constructive strategic approach to reducer. *Human & Environment, 16*(4), 159–170.

Terpstra, N. (2020). Rebel governance, rebel legitimacy, and external intervention: Assessing three phases of Taliban rule in Afghanistan. *Small Wars & Insurgencies, 31*(6), 1143–1173. doi:10.1080/09592318.2020.1757916

The Economist. (2021, May 1). *Diplomacy has changed more than most professions during the pandemic*. https://www.economist.com/international/2021/04/29/diplomacy-has-changed-more-than-most-professions-during-the-pandemic

The Ignored Pandemic. (2019). Transparency International Health Initiative.

The Nobel Prize. (1997). *The Nobel Peace Prize, 1997*. Retrieved from: https://www.nobelprize.org/prizes/peace/1997/summary/

The White House. (2011). *International Strategy for Cyberspace, "Prosperity, Security, and Openness in a Networked World"*. Retrieved from: https://www.hsdl.org/?view&did=5665

The White House. (2017). *US National Security Strategy*. Retrieved from: https://www.whitehouse.gov/wp-content/uploads/2017/12/NSS-Final-12-18-2017-0905.pdf

The World Bank. (2018). *Record High Remittances Sent Globally in 2018*. Retrieved from: https://www.worldbank.org/en/news/press-release/2019/04/08/record-high-remittances-sent-globally-in-2018

Thierry de Montbrial. (2006). *Géographie politique, collection "Que Sais-je?"*. PUF.

Thurow, L (1996). *The Future of Capitalism: How today's economic forces shape tomorrow's world*. Academic Press.

Thurston, A. (2021, July 12). *Why Jihadists Are Collecting "Zakat" in the Sahel*. Retrieved September 6, 2021, from https://politicalviolenceataglance.org/2021/07/12/why-jihadists-are-collecting-zakat-in-the-sahel/

Tilly, C., & Wood, L. J. (2009). *Social movements, 1768-2008*. Paradigm Publishers.

Tome, L. (2015). *The "Islamic state": trajectory and reach a year after its self-proclamation as a "caliphate"*. Retrieved from: https://www.redalyc.org/pdf/4135/413541154008.pdf

Trading Economics. (2020). *China, Trade*. Retrieved from: https://tradingeconomics.com/china/exports

Transparency International. (2011). *Transparency International – The Global Anti-Corruption Coalition*. www.transparency.org

Tribune Online. (2021). *Boko Haram/ISWAP terrorists now resort to video propaganda, says Army*. Retrieved September 12, 2021, from https://tribuneonlineng.com/boko-haram-iswap-terrorists-now-resort-to-video-propaganda-says-army/

Tsurkov, E., & El Gazi, S. (2020). *"People can't even afford to buy bulgur": Discontent is on the rise as Syria's economic crisis worsens*. Retrieved September 12, 2021, from https://www.mei.edu/publications/people-cant-even-afford-buy-bulgur-discontent-rise-syrias-economic-crisis-worsens

Twitter Public Policy. (2018, April 5). *Expanding and building #TwitterTransparency*. https://blog.twitter.com/official/en_us/topics/company/2018/twitter-transparency-report-12.html

Compilation of References

TWN. (2021). *The Future of North-South Relations: Conflict or Cooperation?* Retrieved from: https://www.twn.my/title/futu-cn.htm

U.S. arms exports in 2020, by country (in TIV expressed in million constant 1990 U.S. dollars). (n.d.). https://www.statista.com/statistics/248552/us-arms-exports-by-country/

Ullman, R. (1983). *Redefining Security. International Security.* The MIT Press. Retrieved from: https://muse.jhu.edu/article/446023/summary

UN Reform, . (2005). *United Nations. March 21, 2005. Freedom from Fear backs the definition of terrorism–an issue so divisive agreement on it has long eluded the world community – as any action.* United Nations.

UN Security Council. (2000). *UN 51/45 about declaration the southern hemisphere as a zone – free from the nuclear weapon.* UN Security Council Report.

UN. (2005). *Basic Facts about the United Nations.* United National Office of Public Information.

UN. (2020). *Promoting Sustainable Development.* Retrieved from: https://www.un.org/ecosoc/en/content/promoting-sustainable-development

UNCTAD. (2018). *195 states were UNCTAD members.* Retrieved from: https://unctad.org/

UNCTAD. (2019). *Global e-Commerce sales surged to $29 trillion.* Retrieved from: https://unctad.org/en/pages/PressRelease.aspx?OriginalVersionID=505

UNDP. (2013). *Human Development Report.* Retrieved from: http://hdr.undp.org/en/media/HDR_2013_EN_TechNotes.pdf

UNDP. (2015). *Human Development Report 2014.* Retrieved from: http://hdr.undp.org/en/content/human-development-report-2014?utm_source=EN&utm_medium=GSR&utm_content=US_UNDP_PaidSearch_Brand_English&utm_campaign=CENTRAL&c_src=CENTRAL&c_src2=GSR&gclid=Cj0KCQjw4eaJBhDMARIsANhrQACsgGtmnDMR7DRy6qsvCHvDt8pnOHJFySJDMEWK_zaIGKbW9LrUosQaAto-EALw_wcB

UNESCO. (2019). *Literacy.* Retrieved from: https://en.unesco.org/themes/literacy

UNICEF. (2005). *Report Emergencies: Refugees, IDPs, and child soldiers. Natural disasters.* Retrieved from: https://www.unicef.org/eapro/05_Emergency.pdf

United National Office for Disarmament Affairs. (2021). *1925 Geneva Protocol. Protocol for the Prohibition of the Use in War of Asphyxiating, Poisonous or Other Gases, and of Bacteriological Methods of Warfare.* Retrieved from: https://www.un.org/disarmament/wmd/bio/1925-geneva-protocol/

United Nations Department of Economic and Social Affairs. (2013). *Report on World Social Situation 2013: Inequality Matters.* Retrieved from: https://www.un.org/en/development/desa/publications/world-social-situation-2013.html

United Nations Department of Economic and Social Affairs. (2017). *The world counted 258 million international migrants in 2017, representing 3.4 percent of the global population.* Retrieved from: https://www.un.org/en/development/desa/population/publications/pdf/popfacts/PopFacts_2017-5.pdf

United Nations Handbook on Practical Anti-Corruption Measures For Prosecutors and Investigators. (2012). United Nations Office on Drugs and Crime (UNODC).

United Nations. (1960). *General Assembly, 15th session: 885th plenary meeting, Tuesday, 4 October 1960, New York.* Retrieved from: https://digitallibrary.un.org/record/740836?ln=en

United Nations. (2021). *About Us.* Retrieved from: https://www.un.org/en/about-us

United Nations. (2021). *Losing 25,000 to Hunger Every Day*. Retrieved from: https://www.un.org/en/chronicle/article/losing-25000-hunger-every-day

UNODA. (2021). *Biological Weapons Convention*. United Nations Office for Disarmament Affairs.

Uphoff, N. (1989). Distinguishing Power, Authority & Legitimacy: Taking Max Weber at His Word by Using Resources-Exchange Analysis. *Polity, 22*(2), 295–322. doi:10.2307/3234836

US Department of State. (1992). *Treaty on Conventional Armed Forces in Europe (CFE)*. https://2001-2009.state.gov/t/vci/cca/cfe/index.htm

US Department of State. (2007). *Office of Coordinator for Counterterrorism*. Retrieved from: https://2001-2009.state.gov/s/ct/info/c16718.htm

US Department of State. (2018). *Remembering the 1998 Embassy Bombings*. Retrieved from: https://www.state.gov/remembering-the-1998-embassy-bombings-2/

US Department of State. (n.d.). *DipNote*. https://www.state.gov/blogs

US Embassy in Georgia. (2017). *National Strategy of the United States*. https://ge.usembassy.gov/ka/2017-national-security-strategy-united-states-america-president-ka/

US National Intelligence Council. (2015). *Global Trends 2015. Dialogue about future with non-governmental experts*. Author.

US National library of Medicine. (2021). *Chemical Warfare and Medical Response During World War I*. National Institutes of Health.

USA State Department Report. (2020). Retrieved from: https://www.state.gov/reports-bureau-of-democracy-human-rights-and-labor/country-reports-on-human-rights-practices/

Valeriano & Maness. (2015). Cyber War versus Cyber Realities. Oxford University Press. Retrieved from: https://global.oup.com/academic/product/cyber-war-versus-cyber-realities-9780190204792?cc=ge&lang=en&#

Varonis. (2020). *110 Must-Know Cybersecurity Statistics for 2020*. Retrieved from Varonis: Retrieved from: https://www.varonis.com

Veseth, M. (2006). *Globaloney: Unraveling the Myths of Globalization*. Rowman & Littlefield Publishers.

Vian, T., & Norberg, C. (2008). *Corruption in the Health Sector. (U4 Issue 2008:10)*. Chr. Michelsen Institute.

Wagstaff, W. A., & Jung, D. F. (2017). *Terrorism and Political Violence Competing for Constituents: Trends in Terrorist Service Provision*. Academic Press.

Walker, S. G. (1990). The Evolution of Operational Code Analysis. *Political Psychology, 11*(2), 403. doi:10.2307/3791696

Wallerstein, I. (2001). Democracy, Capitalism, and Transformation. Oxford University Press.

Wang, P. (2013). The rise of the Red Mafia in China: A case study of organised crime and corruption in Chongqing. *Trends in Organized Crime*.

Warwick & Lewis. (2017). *Media Manipulation and Disinformation Online*. https://datasociety.net/library/media-manipulation-and-disinfo-online/

Washington Times. (2020). *Coronavirus may have originated in a lab linked to China's biowarfare program*. Retrieved from: https://www.washingtontimes.com/news/2020/jan/26/coronavirus-link-to-china-biowarfare-program-possi/

Weedon, Nuland, & Stamos. (2017). *Information Operations and Facebook.* Retrieved from: https://i2.res.24o.it/pdf2010/Editrice/ILSOLE24ORE/ILSOLE24ORE/Online/_Oggetti_Embedded/Documenti/2017/04/28/facebook-and-information-operations-v1.pdf

Weimann, G. (2014). *New terrorism and new media.* Woodrow Wilson International Center for Scholars. https://www.wilsoncenter.org/publication/new-terrorism-and-new-media

Weiss, F. C. (1997). The United Nations and Changing World Politics. Westview Press.

Weiss, T. G., Conor, D., & Coolidge, K. (2013). *The Rise of Non-State Actors in Global Governance Opportunities and Limitations a One Earth Future Discussion Paper by.* Academic Press.

Welle, D. (2019). *The myth of Hitler's role in building the autobahn.* Retrieved from: https://www.dw.com/en/the-myth-of-hitlers-role-in-building-the-autobahn/a-16144981

Wells, M. (2017). *The mixed record of UN peacekeeping in South Sudan.* Retrieved from: https://odihpn.org/magazine/the-mixed-record-of-un-peacekeeping-in-south-sudan/

Westcott, N. (2008, July). *Digital diplomacy: The impact of the internet on international relations.* Oxford Internet Institute. https://www.oii.ox.ac.uk/archive/downloads/publications/RR16.pdf

Williams, P. (2008). Violent non-state Actors And National and international security. *International Relations and Security Network*, 1–21.

Williamson, M. (2009). *Terrorism, war and international law: the legality of the use of force against Afghanistan in 2001.* Ashgate Publishing.

Wintour, P. (2020). Bye bye bilaterals: UN general assembly to embrace Zoom diplomacy. *The Guardian*. https://www.theguardian.com/world/2020/sep/19/bye-bye-bilaterals-un-general-assembly-embrace-zoom-diplomacy

Wood, E. J. (2003). Insurgent collective action and civil war in El Salvador. Insurgent Collective Action and Civil War in El Salvador. doi:10.1017/CBO9780511808685

Wordometer. (2020). *COVID 19 Pandemic.* Retrieved from: https://www.worldometers.info/coronavirus/

Wordometers. (2016). *Oil Reserves.* Retrieved from: https://www.worldometers.info/oil/

Wordometers. (2021). *Current World Population.* Retrieved from: https://www.worldometers.info/world-population/#:~:text=7.9%20Billion%20(2021),Nations%20estimates%20elaborated%20by%20Worldometer

Wordometers. (2021). *World Population by Country.* Retrieved from: https://www.worldometers.info/world-population/population-by-country/

Wordometers. (2021). *World Population Projections.* Retrieved from: https://www.worldometers.info/world-population/world-population-projections/

World Bank. (2008). *World Development Report 2008: Agriculture for Development.* World Bank.

World Bank. (2020). *The global economy will expand by 4 percent in 2021.* Retrieved from: https://www.worldbank.org/en/news/press-release/2021/01/05/global-economy-to-expand-by-4-percent-in-2021-vaccine-deployment-and-investment-key-to-sustaining-the-recovery

World Bank. (2021). *Global Recovery is Strong but Uneven as Many Developing Countries Struggle with the Pandemic's Lasting Effects.* Retrieved from: https://www.worldbank.org/en/news/press-release/2021/06/08/world-bank-global-economic-prospects-2021

World Bank. (2021). *International Debt Statistics*. Retrieved from: https://data.worldbank.org/products/ids

World Economic Forum. (2019). *Water inequality is a global issue - here's what we must do to solve it*. Retrieved from: https://www.weforum.org/agenda/2019/10/water-inequality-developing-world-usa-west/

World Health Organization. (2019). *Global vaccine coverage in 2019*. https://www.who.int/news-room/q-a-detail/vaccines-and-immunization-what-is-vaccination?adgroupsurvey=adgroupsurvey&gclid=Cj0KCQjwm9yJBhDTARIsABKIcGbuqgPPZKcyweOx2z7p-GYHl4s5Gy1VRpELfAbrtyuw9Iupc3m1VHIaAnEjEALw_wcB

World Maps Online. (2021). *Classic Colors World Political Map Wall Mural - Peel & Stick Removable Wallpaper*. Retrieved from: http://www.worldmapsonline.com/classic_colors_world_political_map_wall_mural.htm

Worldometer. (2021). *Countries in the world by population*. Retrieved from: https://www.worldometers.info/world-population/population-by-country/

Worldometer. (2021). *World Population*. Retrieved from: https://www.worldometers.info/world-population/#:~:text=7.9%20Billion%20(2021),Nations%20estimates%20elaborated%20by%20Worldometer

Worrall, J. (2017). (Re-)Emergent Orders: Understanding the Negotiation(s) of Rebel Governance. *Small Wars & Insurgencies, 28*(4–5), 709–733. doi:10.1080/09592318.2017.1322336

WTO. (2019). *Global trade growth loses momentum as trade tensions persist*. Retrieved from: https://www.wto.org/english/news_e/pres19_e/pr837_e.htm

Xinhuanet. (2020). *Spotlight: COVID-19 virus not created in the lab, say French experts*. Retrieved from: http://www.xinhuanet.com/english/2020-04/21/c_138995413.htm

Yagboyaju, D. A., & Akinola, A. O. (2019). Nigerian State and the Crisis of Governance: A Critical Exposition. *SAGE Open, 9*(3). Advance online publication. doi:10.1177/2158244019865810

Yakovenko, A. (2012, September 7). Russian digital diplomacy: clicking through. *Russia Beyond*. http://rbth.com/articles/2012/09/06/russian_digital_diplomacy_clicking_through_18005.html

Yeşiltaş, M., & Kardaş, T. (2017). Non-state armed actors in the middle east: Geopolitics, ideology, and strategy. In *Non-State Armed Actors in the Middle East*. Geopolitics, Ideology, and Strategy.

Young, E. M. (2012). *Food and Development*. Routledge.

Zakaria, F. (2015). *Is Democracy Safe in the World?* https://www.youtube.com/watch?v=eIeRJmNS3rkForeignpolicy

Zengerle & Cassella. (2015). *Millions more Americans hit by government personnel data hack*. Retrieved from: https://uk.reuters.com/article/us-cybersecurity-usa/millions-more-americans-hit-by-government-personnel-data-hack-idUSKCN0PJ2M420150709

Zenn, J. (2021, June 4). *ISWAP Launches Hearts and Minds Strategy to Counter Nigerian Army Offensive*. Retrieved September 6, 2021, from https://jamestown.org/program/iswap-launches-hearts-and-minds-strategy-to-counter-nigerian-army-offensive/

Znoj, H. (2009). Deep Corruption in Indonesia: Discourses, Practices, Histories. In *Corruption and the secret of law: A legal anthropological perspective*. Ashgate.

About the Contributors

Sebak Kumar Jana is currently Professor of Economics in the Department of Economics, Vidyasagar University, West Bengal, India. Dr. Jana was graduated from Presidency College, Kolkata in 1989 and did his post graduation in Economics from University of Calcutta in 1991. He obtained M.Phil. and Ph.D. degree in Economics from Jadavpur University, Kolkata. His major area of academic interest includes environmental and resource economics, rural development and economics of education. He has about eighty publications in Journals and in edited books. He has published six books as author or editor including Tank Irrigation in the Dry Zones in India, Education in West Bengal – Looking Beyond Schools, Development in Development in Developing Economies (Edited). He, as Principal Investigator, has completed a few research projects funded by ICSSR, UGC and NABARD, IWMI, and IFPRI.

Muhammed Karakuş, PhD candidate, is a specialist in Middle East and Africa geopolitics, security and strategic affairs. His studies mainly focused on Violent Non-State Armed Actors and their governance and resilience capacities. He is currently instructor in Adiyaman University, Turkey. He has several book translations (best known with Arab Uprising: The Story of Arab National Movement- George Antonius) and several researches.

Asim K. Karmakar, PhD, is an Assistant Professor, Department of Economics, School of Professional Studies, Netaji Subhas Open University, Kolkata, India. Having diversified research interest, he has published more than 100 papers at home and abroad, and has written and edited books of high repute. He has more than 16 years of teaching and research experience. He is also editor of many books including Springer. Currently, he is the Managing Editor of Artha Beekshan, a peer reviewed journal. He is the recipient of two national and four international awards.

Diana Khomeriki is a Chief Specialist at the Cabinet of the Speaker of the Parliament of Georgia. She is specialized in the field of foreign affairs. She is also the Invited Lecturer at the International Black Sea University (Georgia). Previously, Diana Khomeriki worked at the Ministry of Foreign Affairs of Georgia and Georgian Chamber of Commerce and Industry. Diana has BA and MA degrees in International Relations.

Shanmuganantham M. is Lecturer (S.G) and Vice Principal of Electrical and Electronics Engineering, Tamilnadu Government Polytechnic College, Madurai. He obtained his B.E in EEE from Thiagarajar College of Engineering with I Class, Madurai in 1989. He has more than Twenty seven years (27) of teaching and research. His areas of interest are Circuit Theory, Digital Electronics, and Electrical machine design. He is a Member of ISTE.

R. Nagarajan received his B.E. in Electrical and Electronics Engineering from Madurai Kamarajar University, Madurai, India, in 1997. He received his M.E. in Power Electronics and Drives from Anna University, Chennai, India, in 2008. He received his Ph.D in Electrical Engineering from Anna University, Chennai, India, in 2014. He has worked in the industry as an Electrical Engineer. He is currently working as Professor of Electrical and Electronics Engineering at Gnanamani College of Technology, Namakkal, Tamilnadu, India. He has published more than 70 papers in International Journals and Conferences. His research interest includes Power Electronics, Power System, Communication Engineering, Network Security, Soft Computing Techniques, Cloud Computing, Big Data Analysis and Renewable Energy Sources.

Kannadhasan S. is working as an Assistant Professor in the department of Electronics and Communication Engineering in Cheran College of Engineering, karur, Tamilnadu, India. He is currently doing research in the field of Smart Antenna for Anna University. He is ten years of teaching and research experience. He obtained his B.E in ECE from Sethu Institute of Technology, Kariapatti in 2009 and M.E in Communication Systems from Velammal College of Engineering and Technology, Madurai in 2013. He obtained his M.B.A in Human Resources Management from Tamilnadu Open University, Chennai. He obtained his PGVLSI in Post Graduate diploma in VLSI design from Annamalai University, Chidambaram in 2011 and PGDCA in Post Graduate diploma in Computer Applications from Tamil University in 2014. He obtained his PGDRD in Post Graduate diploma in Rural Development from Indira Gandhi National Open University in 2016. He has published around 10 papers in the reputed indexed international journals and more than 85 papers presented/published in national, international journal and conferences. Besides he has contributed a book chapter also. He also serves as a board member, reviewer, speaker, advisory and technical committee of various colleges and conferences. He is also to attend the various workshop, seminar, conferences, faculty development programme, STTP and Online courses. His areas of interest are Smart Antennas, Digital Signal Processing, Wireless Communication, Wireless Networks, Embedded System, Network Security, Optical Communication, Microwave Antennas, Electromagnetic Compatibility and Interference, Antenna Wave Propagation and Soft Computing techniques. He is Member of IEEE, ISTE, IEI, IETE, CSI, and EAI Community.

Index

A

Absolute Advantage 343
actor 1, 6, 64, 79, 90, 95, 184, 203, 237, 246, 249, 252, 343-344, 349, 357
administrative division 1
Africa 6-8, 10-16, 18, 23, 34-36, 57, 67, 73, 95, 109, 111, 113-116, 118-121, 128, 135, 143-144, 199, 231, 233, 236, 240, 244, 249, 252, 255-257, 283-286, 295-299, 302-303, 308, 311-312, 318-320, 324, 326, 331-332, 334-336, 349, 353-354, 360-361, 363, 377
Agency 32, 35-36, 90, 133, 136, 142, 198, 202, 206, 235, 299, 302, 328, 347, 358, 380, 385
alliances 23, 47, 90, 94, 109, 128, 130, 204, 216, 348, 373
anarchy 90, 95, 131, 204, 206, 226, 232, 239-240, 347, 349
Antidumping Duties 343
Antipersonnel Landmines (APLs) 90
Arbitrage 343
armament 24, 38-39
Armed Aggression 23, 90, 128
Armed Conflict control 132
Arms Control 23-24, 27, 31-38, 85, 90, 128
arms race 24, 27, 84, 90, 128, 284
Asian Tigers 204, 288, 343
Asymmetric Warfare 90, 184

B

balance of power 23, 90, 373, 376-377
Bandwagoning 90, 128
Barter 204, 343
behavior 21, 57, 61, 67, 69, 83, 85, 95, 106, 112-113, 124-125, 151-152, 154, 156, 165, 167, 173-174, 176-177, 182, 191-192, 199, 205-209, 211, 214-215, 218, 344-347, 349, 353, 364
Bilateral 23, 90, 128, 266, 339
bilateral agreements 23, 90, 128
biodiversity 134-135, 204, 360
Bolsa Familia programme 362
Boycotts 343
brand 22, 219-223, 229-230, 268
Brand Awareness 219-221, 223, 229
brand recall 219-221
brand recognition 219-221
branding strategy 230, 276
Bureaucracies 343
Bush Doctrine 90

C

cartel 41, 45, 343
Chatbot 280
civil society 11, 84, 156, 160, 169, 204, 256, 270, 343, 363
civil wars 85, 90, 117-118, 128, 135, 232, 255, 259
Clash of Civilizations 90, 110, 204
Classical Liberal Economic Theory 343
climate change 25, 132-144, 299, 308-309, 354-355, 360-362
Coercive Diplomacy 91
Cold War 2, 13, 23, 27, 30-34, 37-40, 55, 72-73, 75, 84, 86-87, 91, 94-95, 109-111, 114, 128, 198, 215, 232, 235, 239, 284, 287, 292, 344, 348-349
Collective Action Dilemma 343
Collective Good 204, 343
Collective Security 18, 23, 91, 204, 378
combating 46-47, 52, 62, 137, 156, 162, 165-166, 271, 341, 387
Commercial Liberalism 343
Communist Theory of Imperialism 343
Comparative Advantage 344
Complex Interdependence 204, 344
Conciliation 91, 121, 129
conflict 3, 5, 18, 31, 37, 40, 52, 54-55, 65, 68, 70, 76-80, 88, 90-91, 93-94, 100, 108-119, 121-133, 138-

139, 141-143, 153, 170-171, 181, 184, 203-204, 207, 209, 223, 232, 236, 240, 247-248, 253-257, 259-260, 309-310, 333, 341, 354-355, 359, 365, 373, 376, 386, 388
conflicts 3, 5, 25, 36-37, 40-41, 48, 55, 67, 70, 75, 78-79, 83-85, 90, 93, 97, 108-122, 124-127, 132, 135, 139-141, 168-169, 178, 183-184, 193, 200-201, 204, 208-209, 224, 232-233, 237, 260, 286, 292, 309, 320, 323, 327-328, 333, 338, 365-367, 372, 376, 384
confrontation 13, 25, 31, 57, 59, 67, 79, 86, 108-111, 113-114, 118-119, 123, 138, 287, 294, 309, 332
Consequentialism 91
conventional 24, 35-38, 75-79, 83, 85, 89, 99, 153, 261, 272, 275, 280, 378
conventional diplomacy 261, 272, 275, 280
Cornucopias 344
corruption 4, 42-44, 46, 49, 51, 59, 84, 145-164, 245
cosmopolitan 5, 195, 205, 223, 344-345
Coup d'etat 91, 129
Covert Operations 129
COVID-19 143, 261-262, 264, 266, 271, 274-275, 281, 300, 313, 321-322, 339-340, 343, 351
Crimes Against Humanity 91, 129, 184
crisis 15, 30-31, 45, 64, 91, 94, 129, 138, 140, 143, 166, 169, 176, 180, 202, 205, 207-209, 211, 213, 218, 232, 235, 244, 246, 249, 254, 259-260, 262, 268, 271, 274, 280, 287, 303-304, 316-317, 337, 345, 358, 363
Cyber Attack 365, 380
cyber security 96, 99, 365-366, 368-373, 377, 379-382, 384-385, 387
Cyber Security and Global Security 96
cyber-attack 366-367, 369-370, 376, 378, 380, 384, 389
cyberspace 91, 100, 184, 270, 365, 367, 370-371, 373-379, 384-389

D

decision-making 67, 69-70, 73, 77, 127, 155, 204, 207-212, 240, 242, 264-265, 268-270, 272, 274, 276, 343
Decolonization 129, 239, 344
democracy 13, 16, 24, 66-68, 70-74, 80, 83, 86-88, 90, 94, 128, 131, 137, 148, 160, 162, 204, 224, 359, 379-380
Democratic Peace 23, 69, 91, 204
demography 282, 323, 339, 344
Dependency Theory 187, 344
Dependent Development 344
Détente 91, 129

developed countries 9-12, 92, 133, 135, 151, 156, 194, 200-201, 205, 216, 283, 285-286, 289-291, 293, 295-296, 298-304, 308, 311-312, 322, 325-328, 331, 335-337, 344-345, 347, 361
developing countries 9-12, 23, 36, 39, 92, 110, 114, 119, 135, 139-140, 151, 157, 162, 195-196, 200-201, 283-299, 301-303, 308, 311-312, 323-327, 329, 331, 333, 335-338, 342, 344, 346, 359, 362
development 1, 3-5, 8-12, 18, 20, 22, 25-26, 29, 31-32, 34-35, 40, 42-43, 49-50, 55-56, 59, 63, 65-67, 72-73, 75, 84, 97-99, 102, 107-114, 122, 124, 126-127, 136-137, 139-143, 146, 156, 158, 160-161, 165, 169, 172, 175, 177-179, 186-187, 189-191, 193-194, 196-204, 206, 208-209, 211, 213-214, 216-217, 221, 223, 229, 234-235, 258, 263, 265, 271, 283-296, 299, 301, 303-305, 308-312, 316, 318, 320, 323, 325, 328-330, 335-340, 342, 344, 346-348, 350-351, 353, 360-362, 364-365, 367, 371-373, 376, 378, 386-387
Diaspora 267, 269, 272, 279-280
DIFFERENT TYPES OF CORRUPTION 145, 148
digital diplomacy 261-264, 266-280
digitalization of diplomacy 262-263, 266-267, 270-271, 274-276, 278, 280
diplomacy 88, 91, 94-95, 122, 125-126, 128, 139, 143-144, 193, 204, 207, 213, 217, 238-239, 243, 251, 257, 261-281, 341
disarmament 27, 30-32, 36-38, 40, 88-89, 91, 129
Diversionary Theory of War 91, 129
doctrines 26, 91, 168, 184, 366
Dollar Overhang 344
Domino Theory 344

E

e-commerce 96-100, 103, 106, 197, 203
economic sanctions 95, 316, 344, 349
economy 1, 4, 10-11, 26, 43-45, 48, 73, 80, 95-98, 114, 133, 136-137, 160, 189, 193-195, 201-202, 204, 206, 224, 229, 249, 253, 264, 282-284, 290-291, 294, 302, 308-309, 316-317, 328-330, 338, 342-343, 347, 349-351, 357, 365-366, 371-372, 385
Ecopolitics 344
education 4, 12, 26, 52, 73, 80, 83-85, 97, 99, 143, 149, 152, 162-163, 172-173, 175-176, 179, 183, 186, 200, 203, 206, 223-225, 237, 239-242, 248-249, 259, 282, 284, 286, 288, 290, 293, 301-303, 325, 328-329, 331-332, 335, 347, 354, 357, 359, 361, 365
Embedded Liberalism 344
end of history 67, 109, 166, 204

Index

Environmental law 132, 142-144
Environmental Security 133, 204
Ethnic Cleansing 62, 91, 125, 129
ethnic groups 3, 23, 46, 48, 55, 75, 91, 121, 129, 170, 215, 228
ethnic nationalism 3, 23, 91, 129, 169, 184, 332
ethnicity 23, 55, 93, 129-130, 151, 170, 184
Ethno-Nationalist Terrorism 169, 184
European Commission 344, 380
European Union 10, 45, 47, 72, 117, 140, 143-144, 160, 170, 204, 215, 278, 328, 344, 371, 377, 387
Exchange Rates 204, 293, 343, 345
Export Quotas 345
Export-Led Industrialization 345
extremism 113, 165, 169, 172-173, 251, 270

F

failed state 231-236, 238, 249
failed states 3, 23-24, 91, 129, 184, 232-237, 239, 251, 254, 256-259
famine 131, 224, 299, 305, 332, 352, 360-362
Fascism 66, 91
Fertility Rate 345
Fixed Exchange Rates 345
Floating Exchange Rates 204, 345
food insecurity 352-357, 360-363
food policy 360-362
Food Politics 350, 356
food security 253, 294, 296, 334, 341, 350-358, 360-362, 364
food sovereignty 350, 356, 358
food system 350-351, 356, 358-360, 363
foreign aid 154, 206, 345, 347
Foreign Direct Investment (FDI) 204, 345
foreign policy 1, 18, 20-21, 49, 68-69, 73, 78, 94-95, 127, 137, 204-205, 207-218, 231, 256, 261-263, 265, 267, 269-271, 273-278, 280-281, 315, 344, 348, 377
Functionalism 205, 345

G

General Agreement on Tariffs and Trade (GATT) 205, 345
genocide 13, 71, 91-92, 121, 126, 129, 166
Geo-Economics 345
Geopolitics 91, 201-202, 260
Georgia 1, 5, 12, 24, 32-33, 62, 108, 113, 117, 121, 145, 165, 186, 207, 219, 261, 282, 303, 311, 314, 317, 333, 340, 365, 370, 372, 374, 376-377, 379-380, 386-388
Global Commons 205, 345
Global East 205, 345
Global Level of Analysis 205
Global Migration Crisis 205, 345
Global North 92, 204-206, 282, 286-287, 289-291, 331, 343-345, 347, 363
Global South 23, 92, 94, 205-206, 282, 285-287, 289-291, 301, 312, 324-325, 327-328, 331, 344-345, 347-349, 353, 363
global system 23, 90, 92, 94-95, 205, 217
Global Village 186, 188, 191, 205, 345
globalization 40, 42, 50, 67, 100-101, 111, 113, 132, 137, 143, 186-203, 205, 282, 294, 301, 322, 345-346, 350-351, 361, 384
Globalization of Finance 195, 205, 345
Globalization of Labor 205, 346
Globalization of Production 205, 346
Globally Integrated Enterprises 205, 346
Good Offices 92, 205
governance 1, 12-13, 61, 72, 156, 158, 231-243, 245-248, 250-260, 265, 344, 349, 361, 363, 373
government 2-4, 12, 14-16, 29, 44, 49, 51-54, 56-58, 61, 64-65, 69, 71, 75, 79-80, 90-91, 93, 96, 110-111, 119, 121, 128-130, 140, 145-147, 149, 151, 153-154, 156, 158, 160, 163-164, 169-170, 176, 186-188, 191, 195, 204, 214, 224, 226, 228, 230, 233-234, 237-240, 244, 246, 249, 251-252, 256-258, 261, 265-268, 270-272, 280-281, 317, 343, 345, 348, 358-360, 363, 366, 370-371, 374, 377, 379-381, 383, 387, 389
grand corruption 145, 162-163
Great corruption 145-146
great powers 23, 91-95, 129-130, 191, 203-204, 232, 344, 348
Greenhouse Effect 134, 205
Gross National Product (GNP) 10, 346
Group of 77 (G-77) 23, 92, 346

H

Hard Power 25, 76, 92, 129
Heavily Indebted Poor Countries 346
hegemon 23, 90, 92, 95, 346
Hegemonic Stability Theory 92, 346
Hegemony 92, 346
High Politics 92
Horizontal Nuclear Proliferation 92
Human Development Index (HDI) 12, 340, 346
human needs 172, 189, 204, 338, 344, 346
Human Security 83, 205, 254

Humanitarian Intervention 92, 129, 258
hybrid regime 261-262, 272, 276

I

Imperial Overstretch 346
Imperialism 92, 129-130, 188, 343, 346
import 84, 194, 287, 292-293, 316, 346, 359, 363
Import Quotas 346
In the Judicial System 150
Infant Industry 346
Info War-Tactics 92, 184, 389
Information Age 202, 205, 365, 387
information revolution 186, 189
Information Security 365, 371, 375, 386, 388
Information Technology (IT) 205
Information Warfare 92, 184, 373-374, 386, 389
Inside the Political System 145, 149
integration 67, 97, 106, 141, 180, 186, 189, 194, 205, 232, 302, 345-346, 349, 379
Intellectual Property 43, 346
interdependence 25, 111, 187, 193, 203-204, 206, 232, 274, 282, 290-291, 322, 344, 346
Intergovernmental Organizations (IGOs) 92, 206, 346
Intermediate-Range Nuclear Forces (INF) Treaty 92
International Aggression 92, 129
International Court of Justice (ICJ) 92, 129
International Criminal Court (ICC) 92, 129
International Criminal Tribunals 92, 129
international law 1, 5, 21, 36, 70, 85, 90, 95, 132, 138, 141, 143-144, 153, 172, 255, 349, 378-379
International Liquidity 346
International Monetary Fund 9-10, 72, 187, 194, 206, 274, 286-288, 293, 347
International Monetary System 206, 347
international peace 31, 84, 88, 110, 121, 132-133, 135, 137-139, 141-143, 150, 161
International Political Economy 206, 347
International Regime 206, 347
international security 25-27, 49, 88-89, 92, 108-109, 114-115, 132, 137-139, 141, 165, 257, 259-260, 370, 376, 378
international terrorism 24-25, 50-52, 63, 84, 92, 167-168, 171-172, 183-184, 232, 379
Intra-Firm Trade 347
Intraspecific Aggression 129
Irredentism 93, 130

J

Jus ad Bellum 93

Jus in Bello 93, 130
Just War Doctrine 93, 130
Just War Theory 93, 130

K

Kellogg-Briand Pact 93

L

Laissez-Faire Economics 347
Least Developed of the Less Developed Countries (LLDCs) 347
Liberal International Economic Order (LIEO) 206, 347
Liberalism 206, 343-344, 347
limited statehood 231-233, 235, 237-239, 251-254, 258
Linkage Strategy 347
location 1-2, 6, 35, 57, 70, 102, 195, 280, 334, 383
Long Cycle Theory 93, 347
Long Peace 23, 93
Low Politics 347

M

Macroeconomics 347
malnutrition 295, 338, 351, 353, 355-357, 360, 363-364
Marxist-Leninism 347
Massive Retaliation 93
mediation 84, 93-94, 121-125, 130-131, 321
Middle East 13, 39, 53, 111, 115-116, 154, 170-171, 187, 231, 233, 235, 237, 240, 247, 249, 252, 259-260, 284, 288-289, 295, 305, 308-309, 332
Militant Religious Movements 93
military intervention 5, 93, 130, 235
Military Necessity 93
Military-Industrial Complex 38, 40, 93, 130
Modernization 57, 206, 289, 347
Monetary Policy 347
Monetary System 206, 347
money supply 347
Most-Favored-Nation Principle (MFN) 348
Multilateral Agreements 93
Multilateralism 93
Multinational Corporations (MNCs) 206, 348
Murky Protectionism 348

N

nation 5, 16, 23, 55, 57, 60, 62-63, 70, 93, 130, 132, 162, 168, 174, 192, 223, 226-228, 268, 270, 273, 276, 281, 330, 337

nation branding 268, 273, 276, 281
national character 5, 130, 217
national interest 23, 73, 87, 93, 95, 130-131, 214
national security 1, 4, 23, 25-26, 46, 85, 93, 101, 130, 133, 137, 172, 183, 205, 258, 366, 371, 373, 377-379, 387-388
nationalism 3, 21, 23, 55, 57, 88, 91, 111, 118-119, 129-130, 169-170, 184, 193, 332
natural resources 25, 135, 144, 197, 243, 258, 282-284, 289, 322, 338, 352, 360
negotiation 91-94, 114, 121, 123, 129-131, 204-205, 228, 260, 265, 272, 275-276
Neocolonialism (Neo-Imperialism) 93, 348
neoliberalism 193, 291, 348
Neo-Malthusians 348
Neomercantilism 348
neutrality 20, 23, 93-94, 126, 130, 348
New International Economic Order (NIEO) 206, 348
Newly Industrialized Countries (NICs) 348
Non-Aligned Movement (NAM) 23, 94, 348
Non-Aligned States 23, 94, 130, 348
Nonalignment 94, 348
Noncombatant Immunity 94
Nondiscrimination 206, 348
Nongovernmental Organizations 125, 193, 206, 348
Nonlethal Weapons 94, 130
Nonproliferation Regime 94, 130
Non-Tariff Barriers 348
North American Free Trade Agreement (NAFTA) 348
North Atlantic Treaty Organization 18, 37, 94, 378, 388
nuclear weapons 24, 27-32, 34-36, 92-93, 95
nutrition 350-351, 353-355, 357-364
nutrition security 350-351, 353-355, 357-358, 360-361
nutritional status 351, 358-361, 364

O

Official Development Assistance 348
Opportunity Cost 344, 348
Orderly Market Arrangements 349
organized crime 24-25, 40-48, 84, 86, 88, 137, 145-146, 150, 163, 169, 202, 234, 238, 379

P

Pacifism 94, 130, 206
Peace Building 130
peace enforcement 94, 116, 124, 130
Peace Operations 94, 130
peacebuilding 27, 94, 108, 122, 124
Peaceful Coexistence 94, 131

peacekeeping 27, 84, 92, 94, 108, 116-117, 119, 121-124, 128-130
Peacemaking 27, 94, 117, 122-124, 131
Petty Corruption 145-146, 164
Polarity 94
polarization 94, 178, 190, 200, 284, 287
policy agenda 94, 267
Policy Networks 94
Political Economy 206, 253, 291, 347, 349
Political Leadership 217, 219, 230
political market 219, 221-222, 229
Political marketing 222, 230
political terrorism 55, 59, 168, 184
politician 65, 112, 149-150, 160, 209, 214, 222, 226, 230
politics 1, 4, 6, 10, 21-22, 24, 26, 31, 63, 66, 69, 74-75, 85, 87-92, 94-95, 110, 113, 127, 131, 142, 146, 153, 161-162, 167, 203-204, 206-208, 212, 214, 216-221, 223-226, 229-230, 235, 237, 240, 247, 254, 257-258, 267, 274, 279, 282, 307, 310, 340-341, 344, 346-347, 349-351, 356, 365-366, 372, 374, 376-377, 380, 388
polluter pays principle 144
population 1, 3, 6-8, 10-12, 14, 18, 20, 22, 25, 27, 34-35, 42, 48-49, 52-53, 56, 61-62, 68, 72-74, 78, 90, 111, 119, 121, 124-125, 135, 137, 165, 169-170, 183, 196-197, 200-201, 203, 234, 236, 238, 240, 246-247, 249, 251-252, 265, 269, 273, 283-286, 288-290, 293-295, 297-303, 307-309, 311-312, 318-319, 322-332, 334-338, 340, 342-344, 348, 351, 353-354, 360, 362, 364, 374, 377
postindustrial epoch 186, 189
poverty 135, 137, 139, 148-149, 160, 163, 172, 216, 251, 282, 285, 297-299, 301-302, 337, 339-340, 352-357, 359-362
power 2-4, 11, 14-16, 18, 21, 23, 25-28, 34, 49, 51-52, 54, 56-57, 61-62, 68, 71-72, 75-76, 78-79, 90-95, 102, 109-110, 124, 128-129, 131, 139-140, 145-146, 149-151, 155, 160, 163, 169, 172-173, 177-178, 184, 187, 203, 206-207, 209, 212-215, 219, 221, 224-227, 230-231, 233, 235-240, 243, 245, 247, 249, 252, 259, 268, 270, 279-280, 305-306, 308, 346-347, 349, 354, 356, 362-363, 365, 367, 371-374, 376-377, 379, 381-382
precautionary principle 144
Preemptive War 94, 131
prevention 25, 32, 47-48, 71, 84, 99, 101, 104, 108, 116, 121-122, 124, 139-140, 142, 144, 155, 162, 183, 283, 323
Preventive diplomacy 94, 122, 139
proliferation 24, 31, 78, 92, 95, 111, 137, 233, 314
psychology 126, 165-167, 172-174, 176, 180-181,

425

183-184, 207-208, 213-218, 230
public diplomacy 88, 128, 243, 261-263, 269-270, 276-277, 280-281, 341
public sector 145, 149
Purchasing Power Parity (PPP) 11, 349

R

rapprochement 95, 327, 331
Realism 95, 131, 372-373, 388
Realpolitik 95
refugees 53, 71, 110-111, 113, 125, 131, 135, 225, 227, 301, 328, 333, 342, 354
resolution 24, 36, 48-49, 51, 70, 108, 114, 121-127, 183, 206, 253-254, 257, 323, 329, 348
Retorsion 95, 349
Russian Federation 28-29, 33, 114, 226, 266, 365, 371, 377, 379, 388

S

sanctions 5, 29, 67, 94-95, 130, 152, 238, 316, 344, 349
Second-Strike Capability 95
security 1, 3-4, 18-19, 22-28, 32-33, 35-36, 40, 46, 49, 51, 60, 76, 79-81, 83-86, 88-93, 95-109, 112, 114-115, 117, 121-122, 128, 130, 132-133, 135-143, 162, 165-167, 172, 183-184, 193, 204-205, 232-235, 238-243, 245, 247-254, 256-260, 267, 271-272, 274, 278, 294, 296, 312, 314-315, 323, 334, 341, 344-346, 349-358, 360-362, 364-373, 375-388
security regime 23, 91, 95, 204
Self-Help 95, 349
Semi Periphery 349
Small Powers 23, 95
Smart Bombs 95, 185
social media 65, 81, 83, 86, 100, 261-271, 273-274, 278-280, 374
states 1-14, 16-24, 26-29, 31-40, 42, 46-47, 49-56, 58-62, 65-70, 72-74, 77, 79-80, 85, 87, 90-95, 108-109, 111-113, 117-119, 121-122, 124-125, 127-131, 133, 135-137, 144-145, 147, 151-152, 155-157, 160, 167-168, 171-172, 177, 183-184, 186, 191, 193-196, 198-202, 204-207, 209, 211-212, 214-217, 231-240, 245, 249-252, 254-260, 265-267, 269, 278, 281, 283-284, 286-291, 293-294, 298, 303-305, 308-310, 312, 314-317, 320-323, 326-334, 338-339, 341-342, 344-348, 353, 362-363, 366-368, 370-373, 376-380, 384-386, 388
systemic corruption 145-147, 154, 157, 164

Systemic Corruption (or Endemic Corruption) 146, 164

T

Tariffs 205, 345, 348-349
terrorism 3-4, 6, 24-25, 46-56, 58-64, 72, 84-90, 92, 95, 101, 117, 138, 165-178, 180-181, 183-185, 193, 202, 226, 228, 232, 243, 246, 255, 257-259, 270, 279, 365, 379
the Internet 74, 81, 91, 97-104, 106, 139, 184, 197-201, 205, 261-263, 265, 268, 270-272, 274, 279-281, 314, 368, 371, 373-376, 381-383, 389
Third World 9, 23, 25, 92, 95, 200, 205, 215, 256-257, 284, 288, 294, 336, 345-346, 349, 361
Trade Integration 349
transboundary responsibility 144
Transnational Religious Movement 206
Transparency 81, 147-148, 151, 153, 155-157, 160, 162-163, 193-194, 201, 265, 272-273, 275, 349, 378

U

Under-Nourishment 364
under-nutrition 353, 364
Unilateralism 95
Uni-Multipolar 95
Unipolarity 95
United Nations 2, 7-8, 21-22, 27, 34-36, 46-47, 49, 70, 85, 89, 92, 110, 116, 121, 127, 129, 132-137, 139, 141-143, 146, 161-163, 196, 198-199, 201, 203, 226, 255, 265, 267, 284, 286, 293-294, 299, 302, 308, 312, 326, 328-330, 338, 342, 358
United States of America 22, 27, 33, 207, 316, 330, 378
urbanization 111, 282, 308, 328, 334-336

V

Vertical Nuclear Proliferation 95
violent non-state actors 60, 231, 233, 237, 258, 260
Virtual Corporations 349
virtual embassy 269, 281

W

Washington Consensus 349
World Government 186
world politics 1, 6, 10, 21-22, 24, 26, 31, 63, 66, 69, 74-75, 87-88, 90, 92, 95, 110, 131, 167, 203-204, 217-218, 282, 307, 310, 340, 344, 346, 366
World-System Theory 95, 206, 349

Index

X

xenophobia 5, 95, 131, 185, 227, 299, 328, 332, 335

Y

Yalta Conference 95

Z

zero-sum 95, 131, 209
Zoom bombing 271, 281
Zoom diplomacy 261, 267, 269, 271-272, 274-276, 279, 281

Recommended Reference Books

IGI Global's reference books are available in three unique pricing formats:
Print Only, E-Book Only, or Print + E-Book.

Shipping fees may apply.

www.igi-global.com

ISBN: 978-1-5225-9866-4
EISBN: 978-1-5225-9867-1
© 2020; 1,805 pp.
List Price: US$ 2,350

ISBN: 978-1-5225-8876-4
EISBN: 978-1-5225-8877-1
© 2019; 141 pp.
List Price: US$ 135

ISBN: 978-1-5225-7847-5
EISBN: 978-1-5225-7848-2
© 2019; 306 pp.
List Price: US$ 195

ISBN: 978-1-5225-6313-6
EISBN: 978-1-5225-6314-3
© 2019; 349 pp.
List Price: US$ 215

ISBN: 978-1-5225-1941-6
EISBN: 978-1-5225-1942-3
© 2017; 408 pp.
List Price: US$ 195

ISBN: 978-1-5225-0808-3
EISBN: 978-1-5225-0809-0
© 2017; 442 pp.
List Price: US$ 345

Do you want to stay current on the latest research trends, product announcements, news, and special offers?
Join IGI Global's mailing list to receive customized recommendations, exclusive discounts, and more.
Sign up at: **www.igi-global.com/newsletters**.

Publisher of Peer-Reviewed, Timely, and Innovative Academic Research

www.igi-global.com   Sign up at www.igi-global.com/newsletters   facebook.com/igiglobal   twitter.com/igiglobal   linkedin.com/igiglobal

Ensure Quality Research is Introduced to the Academic Community

Become an Evaluator for IGI Global Authored Book Projects

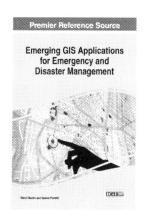   

The overall success of an authored book project is dependent on quality and timely manuscript evaluations.

Applications and Inquiries may be sent to:
development@igi-global.com

Applicants must have a doctorate (or equivalent degree) as well as publishing, research, and reviewing experience. Authored Book Evaluators are appointed for one-year terms and are expected to complete at least three evaluations per term. Upon successful completion of this term, evaluators can be considered for an additional term.

If you have a colleague that may be interested in this opportunity, we encourage you to share this information with them.

IGI Global Author Services

Providing a high-quality, affordable, and expeditious service, IGI Global's Author Services enable authors to streamline their publishing process, increase chance of acceptance, and adhere to IGI Global's publication standards.

Benefits of Author Services:

- **Professional Service:** All our editors, designers, and translators are experts in their field with years of experience and professional certifications.
- **Quality Guarantee & Certificate:** Each order is returned with a quality guarantee and certificate of professional completion.
- **Timeliness:** All editorial orders have a guaranteed return timeframe of 3-5 business days and translation orders are guaranteed in 7-10 business days.
- **Affordable Pricing:** IGI Global Author Services are competitively priced compared to other industry service providers.
- **APC Reimbursement:** IGI Global authors publishing Open Access (OA) will be able to deduct the cost of editing and other IGI Global author services from their OA APC publishing fee.

Author Services Offered:

English Language Copy Editing
Professional, native English language copy editors improve your manuscript's grammar, spelling, punctuation, terminology, semantics, consistency, flow, formatting, and more.

Scientific & Scholarly Editing
A Ph.D. level review for qualities such as originality and significance, interest to researchers, level of methodology and analysis, coverage of literature, organization, quality of writing, and strengths and weaknesses.

Figure, Table, Chart & Equation Conversions
Work with IGI Global's graphic designers before submission to enhance and design all figures and charts to IGI Global's specific standards for clarity.

Translation
Providing 70 language options, including Simplified and Traditional Chinese, Spanish, Arabic, German, French, and more.

Hear What the Experts Are Saying About IGI Global's Author Services

"Publishing with IGI Global has been *an amazing experience* for me for sharing my research. The *strong academic production* support ensures quality and timely completion." – **Prof. Margaret Niess, Oregon State University, USA**

"The service was *very fast, very thorough, and very helpful* in ensuring our chapter meets the criteria and requirements of the book's editors. I was *quite impressed and happy* with your service." – **Prof. Tom Brinthaupt, Middle Tennessee State University, USA**

Learn More or Get Started Here: For Questions, Contact IGI Global's Customer Service Team at cust@igi-global.com or 717-533-8845

www.igi-global.com

Celebrating Over 30 Years of Scholarly Knowledge Creation & Dissemination

InfoSci®-Books

A Database of Nearly 6,000 Reference Books Containing Over 105,000+ Chapters Focusing on Emerging Research

GAIN ACCESS TO THOUSANDS OF REFERENCE BOOKS AT A FRACTION OF THEIR INDIVIDUAL LIST PRICE.

InfoSci®-Books Database

The **InfoSci®-Books** is a database of nearly 6,000 IGI Global single and multi-volume reference books, handbooks of research, and encyclopedias, encompassing groundbreaking research from prominent experts worldwide that spans over 350+ topics in 11 core subject areas including business, computer science, education, science and engineering, social sciences, and more.

Open Access Fee Waiver (Read & Publish) Initiative

For any library that invests in IGI Global's InfoSci-Books and/or InfoSci-Journals (175+ scholarly journals) databases, IGI Global will match the library's investment with a fund of equal value to go toward **subsidizing the OA article processing charges (APCs) for their students, faculty, and staff** at that institution when their work is submitted and accepted under OA into an IGI Global journal.*

INFOSCI® PLATFORM FEATURES

- Unlimited Simultaneous Access
- No DRM
- No Set-Up or Maintenance Fees
- A Guarantee of No More Than a 5% Annual Increase for Subscriptions
- Full-Text HTML and PDF Viewing Options
- Downloadable MARC Records
- COUNTER 5 Compliant Reports
- Formatted Citations With Ability to Export to RefWorks and EasyBib
- No Embargo of Content (Research is Available Months in Advance of the Print Release)

*The fund will be offered on an annual basis and expire at the end of the subscription period. The fund would renew as the subscription is renewed for each year thereafter. The open access fees will be waived after the student, faculty, or staff's paper has been vetted and accepted into an IGI Global journal and the fund can only be used toward publishing OA in an IGI Global journal. Libraries in developing countries will have the match on their investment doubled.

To Recommend or Request a Free Trial:
www.igi-global.com/infosci-books

eresources@igi-global.com • Toll Free: 1-866-342-6657 ext. 100 • Phone: 717-533-8845 x100

www.igi-global.com

Publisher of Peer-Reviewed, Timely, and Innovative Academic Research Since 1988

www.igi-global.com

IGI Global's Transformative Open Access (OA) Model:
How to Turn Your University Library's Database Acquisitions Into a Source of OA Funding

Well in advance of Plan S, IGI Global unveiled their OA Fee Waiver (Read & Publish) Initiative. Under this initiative, librarians who invest in IGI Global's InfoSci-Books and/or InfoSci-Journals databases will be able to subsidize their patrons' OA article processing charges (APCs) when their work is submitted and accepted (after the peer review process) into an IGI Global journal.

How Does it Work?

Step 1: Library Invests in the InfoSci-Databases: A library perpetually purchases or subscribes to the InfoSci-Books, InfoSci-Journals, or discipline/subject databases.

Step 2: IGI Global Matches the Library Investment with OA Subsidies Fund: IGI Global provides a fund to go towards subsidizing the OA APCs for the library's patrons.

Step 3: Patron of the Library is Accepted into IGI Global Journal (After Peer Review): When a patron's paper is accepted into an IGI Global journal, they option to have their paper published under a traditional publishing model or as OA.

Step 4: IGI Global Will Deduct APC Cost from OA Subsidies Fund: If the author decides to publish under OA, the OA APC fee will be deducted from the OA subsidies fund.

Step 5: Author's Work Becomes Freely Available: The patron's work will be freely available under CC BY copyright license, enabling them to share it freely with the academic community.

Note: This fund will be offered on an annual basis and will renew as the subscription is renewed for each year thereafter. IGI Global will manage the fund and award the APC waivers unless the librarian has a preference as to how the funds should be managed.

Hear From the Experts on This Initiative:

"I'm very happy to have been able to make one of my recent research contributions *freely available* along with having access to the *valuable resources* found within IGI Global's InfoSci-Journals database."

— **Prof. Stuart Palmer,**
Deakin University, Australia

"Receiving the support from IGI Global's OA Fee Waiver Initiative *encourages me to continue my research work without any hesitation*."

— **Prof. Wenlong Liu**, College of Economics and Management at Nanjing University of Aeronautics & Astronautics, China

For More Information, Scan the QR Code or Contact:
IGI Global's Digital Resources Team at eresources@igi-global.com.

Are You Ready to Publish Your Research?

IGI Global offers book authorship and editorship opportunities across 11 subject areas, including business, computer science, education, science and engineering, social sciences, and more!

Benefits of Publishing with IGI Global:

- Free one-on-one editorial and promotional support.
- Expedited publishing timelines that can take your book from start to finish in less than one (1) year.
- Choose from a variety of formats, including: Edited and Authored References, Handbooks of Research, Encyclopedias, and Research Insights.
- Utilize IGI Global's eEditorial Discovery® submission system in support of conducting the submission and double-blind peer review process.
- IGI Global maintains a strict adherence to ethical practices due in part to our full membership with the Committee on Publication Ethics (COPE).
- Indexing potential in prestigious indices such as Scopus®, Web of Science™, PsycINFO®, and ERIC – Education Resources Information Center.
- Ability to connect your ORCID iD to your IGI Global publications.
- Earn honorariums and royalties on your full book publications as well as complimentary copies and exclusive discounts.

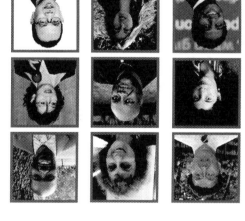

Join Your Colleagues from Prestigious Institutions, Including:
Australian National University
Massachusetts Institute of Technology
Johns Hopkins University
Harvard University
Tsinghua University
Columbia University in the City of New York

Learn More at: www.igi-global.com/publish
or Contact IGI Global's Aquisitions Team at: acquisition@igi-global.com